"[The Berkeley Guides are] brimming with useful information for the low-budget traveler — material delivered in a fresh, funny, and often irreverent way." **—The Philadelphia Inquirer**

"...hip, blunt and lively...these Cal students boogie down and tell you where to sleep in a cowboy bunkhouse, get a tattoo and eat cheap meals cooked by aspiring chefs." **—Atlanta Journal Constitution**

"...Harvard hasn't yet met 'On the Loose's' pledge to plant two trees in Costa Rica for every one felled to print its books — a promise that, given the true grit of these guides, might well mean a big new forest in Central America." **—Newsweek**

"[The Berkeley Guides] offer straight dirt on everything from hostels to look for and beaches to avoid to museums least likely to attract your parents...they're fresher than Harvard's 'Let's Go' series." **—Seventeen**

"The books are full of often-amusing tips written in a youth-tinged conversational style." **—The Orlando Sentinel**

"So well-organized and well-written that I'm almost willing to forgive the recycled paper and soy-based ink." **—P.J. O'Rourke**

"These guys go to great lengths to point out safe attractions and routes for women traveling alone, minorities and gays. If only this kind of caution weren't necessary. But I'm glad someone finally thought of it."

—Sassy

"The very-hip Berkeley Guides look like a sure-fire hit for students and adventurous travelers of all ages. This is real budget travel stuff, with the emphasis on meeting new places head on, up close and personal....this series is going to go places." **—The Hartford Courant**

"The guides make for fun and enlightening reading."

—The Los Angeles Times

"The new On the Loose guides are more comprehensive, informative and witty than 'Let's Go'." **—Glamour**

the BERKELEY guides

THE BUDGET TRAVELER'S HANDBOOK

CENTRAL AMERICA

FIRST EDITION

ON THE LOOSE

WRITTEN BY BERKELEY STUDENTS IN COOPERATION WITH THE
ASSOCIATED STUDENTS OF THE UNIVERSITY OF CALIFORNIA

THE BERKELEY GUIDE TO
CENTRAL AMERICA

Editor: Caitlin Ramey
Assistant Editors: Julie Ross, AnneLise Sorensen
Project Manager: David DeGusta
Production Editor: Caroline Liou
Map Editors: Bob Blake, Marcy Pritchard
Executive Editor: Andrew Barbour
Creative Director: Fabrizio LaRocca
Cartographers: David Lindroth; Eureka Cartography
Text Design: Tigist Getachew
Cover Design and Illustration: Rico Lins Studio (Rico Lins, Mauricio Nacif)

SPECIAL SALES

Contents

What the Berkeley Guides Are All About

Last year, a motley collection of Berkeley students launched the Berkeley Guides, a new series of budget guidebooks. We wrote the books because, like thousands of travelers, we had grown tired of the outdated information served up unblinkingly each year in other budget guides. We began by covering Eastern Europe, Mexico, California, and the Pacific Northwest and Alaska. In researching the guides, our writers slept in whorehouses in Mexican border towns, landed bush planes above the Arctic Circle, and milked cows in Romania in exchange for precious food. This year was no different. While working on our new guides, gutsy student writers weathered guerrilla attacks in the Guatemalan Highlands, police shake-downs in Britain, and racist skinheads in Germany. The result is five new guidebooks, covering Central America, France, Germany, San Francisco, and Great Britain and Ireland, as well as complete updates of the first guides. And in each book, we're brutally honest about what we found; if a place sucks, we say so and recommend somewhere else.

But most of all, these guides are for travelers who want to see more than just the main sights. We find out what the locals do for fun, where they go to eat, play, or just hang out. Most guidebooks lead you down the tourist trail, ignoring important local issues, events, and culture. In the Berkeley Guides we give you the information you need to understand what's going on around you, whether it's the crushing effects of the civil wars in El Salvador and Nicaragua or the environmental programs underway in Costa Rica.

It's one of life's weird truisms that the more cheaply you travel, the more you usually experience. You're bound to experience a lot with the Berkeley Guides, because we believe in stretching a dollar a long, long way. You won't find much in our guides about the style of curtains in a hotel room or how a restaurant prepares its duck à l'orange; instead, we tell you if a place is cheap, clean (no bugs), and worth your money.

Many of us are Californians, so it's not surprising that we emphasize the outdoors in these guides, including lots of info about hiking and tips on protecting the environment. To further minimize our impact on the environment, we print our books on recycled paper using soybased inks, and we plant two trees for every one we use. Coming from a community as diverse as Berkeley, we also wanted our books to be useful to *everyone,* so we tell you if a place is wheelchair-accessible; provide resources for gay and lesbian travelers; and recognize the needs of women travelers.

We've done our best to make sure the information in the Berkeley Guides is accurate, but the world changes: Prices go up, places go out of business, and museums close for renovation. Call ahead when it's really important. These books are new, and we'd really appreciate some feedback. Tell us about your latest find, a new scam, whatever—we want to hear about it. Write to the editors at 505 Eshleman Hall, University of California, Berkeley, CA 94720.

Thanks to You

As they say in Belize, lots of love and super-dynamic kisses to...

Belize: Ian Anderson, the August family, Winnil Grant-Borg, the duPlooy family, Rachel Emmer, Gamusa and Tina, the people of Hopkins, Cheryl Hubert, JB's Restaurant, Jennifer and Thelma, Bob Jones, Emory King, the villagers of Laguna, Mike, Quentin Scarborough, William Schmidt, Toni and Thomas.

Guatemala: Ashley Acuña, Van & Hope Alston, Tim Boucher, Natalie Boulens, Carol Devine, Sharron Cooper, James T. Duffy, Erick & Bryson & Pamela, Carlos Figueroa, Julie Garcia, Burl Ginther, Pierre and Debra Hawkins, Pat and Alan Heller, Peter Inzenhofer, Carlos Jimenez, German Javier Magallón Juarez, M. Elaine Kellogg, Neria Virginia Herrera Piuelo, Mary Reshidian, Jonathan Rossouw, Norman B. Schwartz, Tomás Suazo, Marco Antonio Urizar, Laurent & Catrin & Alexandra & Sebastian Vidal.

Honduras: Enrique Campo, Arnulfo Centeno, Susan Evans, Ignacio Martinez, Nelly Martinez, Juan Alvares Melendez, Vince Murphy, Jesuit Superior Antonio Ocaña, and all the volunteers in the Peace Corps.

El Salvador: Alba Elizabeth Bonilla de López and Wiliam Adonay Chávez, Carlos Alberto Rodriguez and Maurice Portillo, Doris Celia Sanchéz Díz, Fernando Soch Hurtado, Jorge Alberto Escobar Mejilla, Herminio Jovel Guevara, Mónica Marlene García.

Nicaragua: Sr. Castillo, Dr. Tomás Castillo, Nick Cooke, Susan Hawley, Joan Hegelund and her two girls, Marazul Tours, Gonzague Masquelier, The Norwegians, Trish O'Kane, the Santos family, Herman and Misha Wolsgaard-Iversen, Camilla Ziirsen.

Costa Rica: Leslie Abad, Raul Aguilar, Marielos Acevedo Alvarez, Sara Applebaum and family, Juan Bautista, Christian Brannstrom, Yesenia Calderón, Valerie Colacurcio, Sandra Campos, Miguel Vargas Comptes, Nicole Canon, Dhamuza Condir, Fernando Cortés, Victor Mara Coto, Daniel Chavarría, Eduardo Chavarría, Christian and Virginia Dahmen, Tom Dillon, Eney Fernández Elizondo and family, Rafael Elizondo, Germán Huy Forbes, Dr. Roberto Garfias, Leonel Maroto González, Philip Graham, Diego Guillúe, Mariechen Guevara, Walter Hedet, Alex Jimenez, Eduardo Jimenez, Miriam Jimenez, Ursina Jörimann, Lori Ksander, Ivan Lieben, Elsa Martinez, Michelle McClintock, Luís Arturo Mejías, Mari Metcalf, Tony Mora and Rodolfo, Ingrid Oehl, Juan Antonio Salas Picado, Rocíop Portocamero, Carolina Rizo, José Antonio Rodríguez, Eduardo Rodríguez, María Rosario Murillo Rodríguez, Alvaro Solis, John Jake Victor Veysey, Ronald, Costa Rica Expeditions.

Panamá: Nícolas Adams, Alcides Alvarado, Hernán Araúz, Amabel Boyos, Cabroli family, Richard Cahill, Manuel Castillo, Inga Collins, Oscar Contreras, Fanny Cruz, Chicho, Sarita de la Guardia, Luís de la Torre, Sara de Vergara, Marco Delgado, Cesar Diaz, José Danderis, Juan Franco, Alexander Gomez, Analio Gonzalez, Grimaldo, Silvano Ibarra, Irena Krajina, Oscar Lopez, Manual Mora, Nao, Alfredo Nieto, Norie Niki, Ligia Paget, Ruben Paz, Xenia Peck, Daniel Perez, Polo, Carlos Rodaniche, Mariafeliza Sarria, Michael Shaw, Stephen and the boat people, Tamara, Tenorio family, Michel Van de Pol, Enrique Villegas, Mr. Wenzel, Richard Zaleshi.

Berkeley Bios

The Writers

After four years (and an economics degree) at Berkeley, **Laurence Colman** had been lulled into the false belief that the strength of his character, not the length of his hair, would determine the world's reception of him. Panamá quickly disproved that one, as his blond mop elicited disbelieving stares wherever he went—the men got all excited until they realized it was not a California *girl* they were whistling at. Basically, nothing got him down: Not the career drunkards, many of whom, in their dull, slurry speech, tried to convey how much they wanted to have gringo friends; not the crackheads, one of whom went as far as to describe the kind of gun he would use to shoot Laurence if he couldn't spare some change; not the distinct lack of zealous, anti-imperialist revolutionaries ("Go to Nicaragua," he was told); not even a visit by George Bush. When ol' George stopped by, protests forced Laurence to hole up in his Panamá City hotel room for three days, eat a lot of delivered pizza, and watch Spanish-dubbed reruns of "CHiPS." The rest of Panamá, untamed jungles or no untamed jungles, was no problem after that.

Courtney Heller went hurtling through countless villages in the Guatemalan Highlands, stopping often to pray to the wildly popular, cigar-toting effigy of San Simón—who grants wishes to those who leave him a shot of booze or a smoke. She also took her pen to the Pacific coast, braving the sweltering black-sand beaches. The color, the beauty, and the way of life in Guatemala held her mesmerized, even when it seemed San Simón had abandoned her. Less than two weeks into her journey, while she was cruising around the Western Highlands by motorcycle, a Guatemalan mutt leaped out of nowhere and took a nice chunk out of her lower left calf. While nursing her leg she met two Peace Corps workers, who were in the area to vaccinate animals against rabies. They took one long stare at Courtney's swelling leg, frightened the hell out of her, and immediately sent her off to Guatemala City for rabies shots. Her next run-in was with the EGP, a guerrilla faction in the Ixil Triangle, which detained her bus for nearly four hours—being the only *gringa* aboard, Courtney stood out like the ugly duckling in her 501's and a baseball cap. The next time she encountered the EGP, she almost ran off to write their story—on the Berkeley Guides tab of course.

Tim Kessler spent most of his youth in Southern California's suburban Simi Valley (now of Rodney King fame). After getting his undergraduate degree, he ended up in western Guatemala through a sequence of events he still doesn't quite remember. He taught English and got to know his first Spanish teacher, Silvia, in a completely nongrammatical way—they were married a year after they met. While writing the El Salvador chapter, he quickly got sick of soldiers stopping him and asking, "*Qué es su misión aquí* (What is your mission here)?" He had to bite his tongue to keep from responding, "I'm a spy for the People's Republic of Berkeley. My mission is to colonize El Salvador. The army will have to wear Birkenstocks and all citizens must learn to meditate, love granola, and have sex in hot tubs." Tim, savvy as he is, controlled his mouth and came home without a bruise, scratch, or busted lip. He's an avid Central American travel connoisseur, but is now stateside for a while, living happily ever after with his lovely *esposa* and trying to weasel a Ph.D. out of U.C. Berkeley's Political Science Department.

While researching and writing the Costa Rica chapter's sections on San José, the Meseta Central, and the Caribbean coast, **Deborah Meacham** ate her first breadfruit, became a yucca devotee, and learned to cook with *manteca* (lard)—and like it! When she wasn't busy losing umbrellas (5) or evading marriage proposals (2), Deb crawled through mud to remote youth hostels, schmoozed with taxi drivers, and tried new and unusual bug repellent (coconut oil or citronella and rosemary oil). A student of Latin American literature and popular culture, Deborah studied for a year at the Universidad de Costa Rica in San Pedro before returning to Berkeley to complete her B.A. in Latin American Studies. Currently, the naturally curly blonde is off to Brazil on a Fulbright while she continues her research on the *canto novo* (new song).

Ian Signer's first experience in Central America was in 1987, when he spent a summer digging wells and latrines in Costa Rica. Living in a one-room hut with 17 people, he learned how to be close and friendly the Central American way. Assigned to write the "boring half" of Guatemala (the eastern regions that see relatively few tourists), he begs to differ with the description. From tracking radio-tagged birds with biologists in the jungles of Tikal to a voodoo ceremony on the Caribbean coast; from a flashing gay club in Guatemala City to the incense-filled *cofradía* of San Sebastian in San Pedro Carchá, Ian saw some incredible and diverse beauty. He experienced his share of ugliness, too, witnessing a murder (appropriately outside the ruins of Kaminal Juyu, or The Valley of Death) the first week he was there. His most soul-wrenching experience, though, was a cave odyssey that sent him alone to get lost in the depths of the earth in search of Mayan paintings. Three terrified hours of scrambling, jumping, climbing, and crawling through thousands of bats (and their guano) later, he emerged—to surprise a clean-cut U.S. tour group in a set of tourist caves five mountains to the east. Later, he found out that three Swiss explorers died last year in these same caverns. Now, armed with a B.A. in entomology (and a merit badge in spelunking) Ian's moving on to join the Peace Corps in West Africa.

Gregory Smith graduated from U. C. Berkeley with a degree in law and Latin American studies, before realizing that he would hang himself if he had to be a lawyer. Fleeing his suicidal urges, he skipped out on his bar exam to write the Nicaragua chapter. After a few weeks of fighting chronic diarrhea, belligerent drunks, cold shoulders, and post-apocalyptic disorganization, the bar exam started to sound like a lot of fun. By the end, though, he had decided that the ordeal was worth the effort, even if he did have to bribe his way out of the country (something about an overstayed visa). He came back from Nicaragua with a respect for the people of that complex and tortured land—a respect far more genuine than what he gained while working for Central American solidarity organizations before law school.

Trisha Smith had her first taste of Belize in 1990, when she spent six weeks backpacking in Central America. Even then, she knew that eventually she'd find her way back. While writing and traveling, she hooked up with a crazed Indiana Jones wannabe and found herself hurtling through jungle trails in a burly Ford Bronco. She also got to skin a stingray, punta dance in a Garífuna drumming circle, skinny-dip underneath thundering waterfalls, eat greasy-greasy for eight weeks without ever knowing exactly what it was, and get chased by a vicious moray eel on the barrier reef. She needed to come back to the rat race like she needed a hole in the head, and she's currently fishing for a cheap ticket to a far-away place.

Jeffrey Tyler, our man in Honduras, enjoys the accelerated pace of traveling. "It's like life in hyper-speed," he wrote us from the road. "You fall in love, make durable friendships, have crises, get sick, have revelations, and become complacent all within a few days. Then you're somewhere else and the world is fresh again." Though the constantly changing stimulus is a rush, music is Jeffrey's real high. Having collected traditional musical instruments during his travels in Africa and the Middle East, he became mesmerized by the haunting rhythms of the Garífuna people on Honduras' north coast. If it weren't for the checks that motivated him to run frantically around the country, he would have settled down in a seaside village to join the Garífuna and dance his soul into bliss. Since he couldn't stay, he took it with him, bartering his wristwatch for the lead drum in a Garífuna ensemble. That drum would become the instrument of his percussion debut several weeks later, when he sat in with a trio of mad rastafarian musicians before a drunken undiscriminating audience. Jeffrey is now editing the 1994 edition of the Berkeley Guide to Mexico.

By the time **Shirley Zahavi** returned from Costa Rica, she had gone skinny-dipping twice, had her tarot cards read for the first time, taught two locals to merengue, and learned to deal with her almost-pathological aversion to beans. Though she had never been to the country before, she soon learned to brave the wilds of the virgin jungle, and halt slimy, lecherous men with a string of the most disgusting Spanish curse words ever to come out of the mouth of a lady. She told us, "Costa Ricans are the nicest people—if you're their friend for a minute, you're friends forever, and you can always stay at their house." She wasn't kidding. While she was there, she flopped on the floor of a three-room house owned by a 10-member rural family; stayed at the quasi-mansion of a presidential representative in Liberia; and, when she stayed with a coffee-growing family, woke up to the most righteous cup of joe of her life.

The Editors

To avoid catching cabin fever while earning her B.A. in international relations, editor **Caitlin Ramey** was compelled to leave the country at least once a year. The best travel tip she ever received was from her father, also an avid internationalist, before her three-month bike tour of Western Europe: To *caer bien* (get along) with the new people, food, geography, timetables, telephones, et cetera that you'll encounter along the way, REMAIN FLEXIBLE!! After editing the forthcoming Berkeley Guide to Italy, she'll head to the London School of Economics for a masters in economic history and will subsequently luck right into an illustrious career in international journalism (knock on wood).

"Bring me back kitschy Central American souvenirs!" was the command Assistant Editor **Julie Ross** issued to her writers. Among the mementos she received from her dutiful employees: a Costa Rican perfume called "Cocaine"; a Spanish bubble-gum cartoon featuring Juanito Bazooka; and a poster of Panamá's favorite TV family, "Los Simpsons." But her personal favorite was a whip fashioned from the dried penis of a bull, which she brandished menacingly at the very mention of writer's block. To experience firsthand the trials and tribulations of being a writer, Julie will cover Venice and the Dolomites for the upcoming Berkeley Guide to Italy. She's currently looking for an apartment in San Francisco that accepts pet-owning, vegetarian smokers with poor credit. If you hear of anything, please call her.

Assistant Editor **AnneLise Sorensen** is a seasoned traveler who traversed most of the Asian and European continents before donning a training bra. A feminist and free thinker, AnneLise found her niche at the Berkeley Guides, where she and a coven of similar-minded editors found creative ways to deal with the stress of editing (i.e., office slumber parties, ritualized wine-drinking, and summoning ancient Mayan spirits with a ouija board made from an old pizza box). AnneLise is currently an editor for the upcoming Berkeley Guide to Europe. Much empowered by her experiences at the Berkeley Guides and armed with a B.A. in English from Berkeley, AnneLise plans to write a novel, syndicate her own television talk show, start a wildly popular magazine, and eventually overcome the limitations of the space-time continuum.

Central America

MEXICO

BIOSPHERE
RESERVE

Tikal

Río Hondo

Río Belize

Corozal

Altun Ha

Belize City

Turneffe
Islands

Belmopan

BELIZE

Dangriga

Golfo de
Honduras

Islas de la Bahía

GUATEMALA

Puerto
Barrios

Lago de
Izabal

Puerto
Cortés

La
Ceiba

Pal

Huehuetenango

Motagua

San Pedro Sula

El Progreso

HONDURAS

Totonicapán

Chimaltenango

Antigua

Guatemala
City

Comayagua

Tegucigalpa

Coco

Santa Ana

EL SALVADOR

San
Salvador

San
Miguel

Choluteca

Grande

Golfo
de
Fonseca

NICAR

Lago de
Managua

Managua

Masaya

Granada

Lago
de
Nicaragua

INTERAMERICAN HWY

Liberia

PACIFIC
OCEAN

Puntarenas

Península
de Nicoya

Golfo
Nico

CO

INTERAMERICAN HWY

N

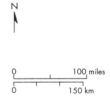

0 —————— 100 miles
0 —————— 150 km

Central America

JAMAICA

Caribbean
Sea

Puerto
Lempira

Coco

Puerto
Cabezas

aiogalpa

UA

Bluefields

*Bahía
Punta Gorda*

OSTA
RICA   Tortuguero

la Heredia   Puerto
San   Cartago   Limón
osé

Bocas   Colón   El Porvenir
de Toro   *Panama*
                Canal   Ciudad de   *Lago*
Golfo de los   Panama   *Bayano*
Mosquitos

*Bahía de
Panamá*

PANAMA

*Bahía de
Coronado*

VADO N. P.   David

*Península
de Osa*   *Isla del
            Santiago   Chitré   Golfo de Rey*
Golfo de   *Panamá*
Chiriqui   Las Tablas

*Isla de
Coiba*

Introduction

By Michael Johns

LANDSCAPES

Central America suggests a Salvador Dalí painting: stark and bright, yet eerie and warped; melting away, while holding its form; beautiful, but violently so. Central America also hints at the airy, almost farcical aura captured in the novels of magic realism, a school best known for Garcia Marquez's *One Hundred Years of Solitude*. Like magic realism, Central America is light and enchanted; like Dalí, heavy and hallucinatory.

Professor Michael Johns specializes in economic geography of Mezoamerica in the Geography Department at U.C. Berkeley. He's a frequent visitor to Central America for both research and pleasure.

The landscape itself is surreal. The long, flat west coast has two versions of heat: the dry, choking variety of winter, and the humid, enervating sort in summer. Whatever season, the sun beats down with ferocity. A novel set in the city of León, Nicaragua, depicts heat surges actually propelling people along pulsating sidewalks. This steamy, wavy heat makes you think you are dreaming, even if you aren't. There is no escape to the surrounding countryside, where long rows of white cotton, fields of swaying sugar cane, and herds of long-eared cattle stretch your hot dream into the distance. As you move inland from the Pacific coast, the mountains of the central interior gather strength on the eastern horizon. Volcanic, and prone to eruptions and earthquakes, these mountains harbor most of Central America's history and produce most of its wealth. The highlands were home to Central America's pre-Hispanic population; today they house the peasantry, still the mainstay of highland culture and economy. Heavily indigenous in Guatemala, and generally *mestizo*—the offspring of Spanish and indigenous people—in the rest of Central America, the peasants lead lives that seem to change little from year to year, despite sporadic rebellions. Corn, beans, and squash, the dietary triad of Central American life, prosper in these highlands, which are sunny, cool, and dry from October to March, and wet and warm from April to September. Coffee plantations are the highland's economic backbone. These plantations, generally located between 1,500 and 4,000 feet, are surrounded by peasant villages that furnish labor to pick the ripening coffee beans in December and January.

The east coast might as well be on another continent. Here live the mixed offspring of indigenous peoples, Spanish, and those of African descent. English is commonly spoken in Bluefields, Nicaragua, a legacy of the British timber and mining companies that had earlier worked the coastal area. And the small and sparsely populated Belize, where they still speak pidgin English, was until 1981 a British colony. The diet here consists less of corn and beans than of root crops like yucca and the catch from the sea. Most indigenous people along the Honduran, Nicaraguan, and Costa Rican east coast identify themselves first as members of certain tribal "kingdoms" and only secondarily, if at all, as citizens of their countries. If the arresting blue-green of the Caribbean, the sweltering heat, and the excessive rain issued from lowering skies are not enough, the foreign banana companies that swagger in big-boss style among native workers assure a sense of unreality. Few commodities have incited as much intrigue as the lowly and comic banana, which grows abundantly in plantations along the Caribbean coast, especially in Guatemala, Honduras, and Costa Rica.

The cities of Central America simply arise, unexpectedly, out of the countryside. They give little impression of power and domination, of security and self-possession, though they do house the elite, the government, the banks, and the military. They control the countryside, but parasitically; rather than manufacture food or clothing, they simply take the countryside's goods, sell them on the world market, and pocket the profits. Those doing the pocketing—generally the landed and financial elites, influential politicians, and upper-echelon professionals—live well. They have suburban homes, new cars, nice clothes, and the money to mimic the lifestyles of America's upper-middle classes. But most of the urban population live in crude conditions, many in shantytowns; they work odd, usually service-sector jobs, and have no economic security. The cornstalks in the backyard, the horse-drawn carts on the streets, the slow pace of urban life: These are "cities of peasants." As the rural population grows, and as agricultural jobs dry up and get replaced by mechanical planters and harvesters, more and more peasants jam into the cities. Many city dwellers keep their ties to the countryside, where they look for seasonal labor cutting sugar cane, harvesting coffee, or picking cotton. And many rural households have family members working in a city: A daughter lives and works as a domestic servant in an upper-class home; a son labors intermittently on construction crews; the mother travels daily by bus to sell homemade food items in an urban market. Walk through a shantytown in Managua, Tegucigalpa, or San Salvador on a weekend. You may very well see a cockfight stirring up a backyard or bloodying a dusty street. You might see a man shucking corn he grew in an outlying field. Central America's cities belie the rigid distinction between urban and rural, between modern and backward; mere extensions of the countryside, their culture is more bucolic than urbane, more provincial than cosmopolitan.

The cultural landscape is saturated with religion, which in Central America means Catholicism: Many people wear a crucifix around their neck; most cross themselves as they pass a house of God; and an imposing church dominates each highland village. Catholicism has always had to make deals with its Central American constituents, especially the peasants, to lure them into the fold. The church temple compels supreme acknowledgment of its deity, but lets local folks adore some idolatrous icons and worship some pagan spirits. Every rural village has a patron saint. In the indigenous towns of Guatemala (and other places), that saint inspires a yearly celebration, where the guest of honor, it seems, is Bacchus. Horse races, betting, firecrackers, dances, and booze liven up the town for a day or two, deplete its resources, depress the priest, and leave the men with pounding headaches.

Catholicism's long monopoly of the Central American soul is under challenge. Evangelical Protestants have begun to win over many *indígenas* (indigenous people). Religious sects among mestizo peasant communities in northern Costa Rica teach people to handle snakes and speak in tongues. Protestants of various stripes are also making headway in the shantytowns of Managua and San Salvador, where they preach abstinence from the salacious ways of city life. On the east coast, the old, German-descended Moravian church still holds sway in some areas.

The landscape of Central America is a bizarre mixture of diverse and often contrasting beliefs, technologies, peoples, and terrains. Place the region into the unstable arena of international geopolitics, and into the precarious quagmire of underdevelopment, and that apparently harmless mixture can turn explosive.

POLITICS AND POVERTY

Central America has been built on pillage. The Spanish, beginning in the early 1500s, sacked the place for three centuries. They took silver out of Honduras, indigo out of El Salvador, *cochineal* (a dye made from crushed bugs) out of Guatemala, and slaves from Nicaragua, whom they transferred by ship to the great Potosí mines of Bolivia. The dense and sedentary indigenous population of Guatemala, which was forced to provide labor for and pay tribute to local representatives of the Spanish Crown, made it Central America's most powerful colonial economy. Most of today's indigenous villages, which many visitors mistake for "authentic" communities, were set up by the Spanish. Government officials and private citizens, often with the aid of clergymen, used force and cajolery to resettle and concentrate natives in towns, where they could be more easily controlled. The churches, constructed by the indigenous people themselves, were the first things built in the new communities. Race was used by the Spanish to rank people in sophisticated blood hierarchies, and it still plays a heavy role in denoting one's social standing.

The colonial experience surely left its mark on the region. But the class divisions, the styles of governance, the military systems, and the economic structures that characterize today's Central America were established in the late 19th century. The typical pattern was as follows: The old colonial elite, along with some Europeans who migrated to Central America after the independence movements of the early 19th century, recognized the opportunities for producing exports (most notably coffee) for the booming economies of Europe and the United States. These elites used violence and legal chicanery to usurp the best lands from mestizo and indigenous peasants. With capital from Europe, they set up railroads, ports, power stations, and banks. The export of coffee generated lots of wealth, and certainly modernized the region's governments and economies. The problem was that these countries were run by small cabals of urban-based elites who owned most of the land, monopolized the government, and controlled the military. This system, which was in place by 1900, continued unabated for the next several decades.

A pot-bellied colonel glowers at a suspect peasant through mirrored aviator glasses; young rebels kidnap a President's daughter for ransom; the CIA illegally organizes a hapless group of mercenaries; Guatemalan guerrillas kill the town's mayor with a bazooka. These almost laughable images should be reserved for Rambo movies. But they are real enough in Central America. They are what makes the beauty of the place so haunting and surreal.

The 1960s brought significant political and economic changes. Exporting coffee and bananas no longer provided the wealth required to satisfy a growing and increasingly urban population, so each Central American country produced new export commodities. The most important were sugar, cotton, and cattle. The prevalence of these crops increased rapidly along the west coast, and cattle roamed into the tropical central highlands of Nicaragua and Costa Rica—recently deforested for just that purpose. Some peasants were pushed off their land, and many lost their jobs to the tractors and chemicals that now did much of the planting, weeding, and harvesting. Most headed for the cities. The explosive urban growth that began in the 1960s was tied directly to changes in the countryside. Despite the emergence of some light industry, most notably in Guatemala City and San Salvador, the cities of Central America have been unable to employ adequately the rapidly growing urban populations. The growing cities and rising expectations on one hand, and the persistent conditions of political and economic underdevelopment on the other, were fertile grounds for discontent and resentment. Reformers within the elite and the military questioned the continued monopoly of government by small cliques of privileged landowners and officers. A vocal if still modest middle class began to demand access to government. Significant numbers of young people from the middle and upper classes, driven largely by an immature idealism inspired by the Cuban revolution, took seriously the idea of armed revolt. The great majority of the population—peasants, the urban working class, the lumpenproletariat—had always had plenty of grievances. By the late 1970s and throughout the '80s, the situation was dangerous in Nicaragua, El Salvador, and Guatemala; uncertain in Honduras and Panamá; and firmly under control in Costa Rica, where an accessible government and equitable economy had allowed the nation to dismantle its army in 1948.

Few things tell you more about a society than its sexuality. The roles, identities, and attitudes of Central America's men and women are extremely polarized. The first thing you do to a baby girl is stick a pink earring in her lobe. More than identify the sex of a little female, it prevents the mistaking of infant boys for girls. In a society that equates manhood with *machísmo,* keeping the sexes straight is important. The sharp divide between male and female also asserts itself among homosexuals. A male who has sexual relations with another male, but who plays the role of the man (i.e., the penetrator), is not considered homosexual. Only the penetrated, the submissive, the passive among male lovers is the homosexual—that is, the "female."

Men are very proprietary about *their* women. The quickest way to incite an emotional outburst and possibly a fight is to insult a man's wife, his daughter, or his mother—especially his mother. There is a fabulous painting that keenly depicts Latino sexuality. A man is wearing a V-necked, sleeveless shirt. He also wears three tattoos. On his left arm, close to his heart, is a tattoo of a handsome but prim woman: his wife. He has sex with her, but dutifully, without passion, and for procreation. On his chest, closest to his heart and soul, is an older, matronly women with a faint halo: his mother. The mother is a sort of cult figure—half saint, half virgin. She is venerated because she gave birth to the *macho,* and because she ideally embodies the good female qualities—humility, duty, travail. On his right arm, farthest from his heart, is a nude, lascivious woman: his lover, perhaps a prostitute. She is the bad woman, but the one who excites him sexually.

Central American women can be very flirtatious. They flash their eyes, they attract stares and whistles, they smile easily. But only rarely does a girl or a woman initiate contact with a boy or man she does not know. It is the male's job to act upon her enticements. Sexual activity often begins at an early age. For women it has high costs. One is the burden of Catholic guilt; the other is the hardship of being a single teenage parent. Almost half of all births in Nicaragua and El Salvador are "illegitimate." Birth control is rarely used, owing to ignorance, poverty, religious belief, resignation, and the fact that many men want nothing more than to father plenty of children with

Blinded by the Fright in Guatemala

Guatemala has been a particularly sad and tragic place for over a decade. The 1980s saw a brutal and racist confrontation that pitted a ruthless military against armed revolutionaries camped in the mountains. The military, tightly linked to the elite, was able to use scorched-earth tactics to put down the armed struggle. Death, migration to Mexico and the U.S., and terror have been the results. In the early 1980s I was in a small indigenous town nestled among misty hills. The colorful patterns of the clothing resembled the patchwork of corn, bean, and wheat fields that embroidered the hillsides. Armed members of a revolutionary group came into town. They read a statement, probably looking for recruits or at least sympathy. Several hours later a government helicopter flew in. Soldiers got out. Several young men from the village were lined up and shot. The helicopter flew off. That was the lesson for consorting with the enemy. These tactics spread terror among the population. Once, I was in a bus that passed several dead bodies in the street. I was the only one who hadn't learned not to stare out the window. Perpetual fear causes blindness.

numerous women. Unfortunately, the patriarchal notions of providing, and of responsibility, are weak in these macho societies that demand little of men on these scores.

The visitor to Central America will immediately recognize the influence of the United States. Everyone is wearing a shirt that features a photo of an American sports figure, the name of an American rock band, or the logo of an American company. The movies people watch, the toys children enjoy, the basic commodities in homes: They are "Made in U.S.A." or produced by U.S. companies. The power of the United States inspires awe and respect as well as resentment and disdain. Some passionately adore it, some absolutely abhor it, most love *and* hate it, but everyone feels strongly.

Central Americans are very aware of their proximity to the world's great superpower, which has utterly dominated them—with its military force, diplomatic muscle, and economic might—for over a century.

The pervasive presence of the United States has not given Central Americans a very balanced view of it. Their images of the northern colossus are gleaned from magazines, second-hand stories, movies, and television. U.S. women, many think, sleep with anyone, at every opportunity, because their men do not exercise adequate control over them. Another common belief is that everyone in the United States is rich and lives comfortably. In comparative and general terms this may be true. But few Central Americans will believe that you don't have a car or own a home. Ask any adult which U.S. president they admire most. They will say, almost unanimously, John Kennedy. His Catholicism, his grace, his wife's elegance, and his role in the Alliance for Progress make him a favorite among Central Americans, even though Kennedy did little for them in real terms.

It's hard to plan, predict, and get things done in Central America. The crowded and belching buses are usually late, if they are running at all; store shelves are often bare; the universities are understaffed and underfunded; water and electricity are available only half the day, or every other day. These problems are especially common in Nicaragua, El Salvador, and Guatemala. For the average person it is no easy task to secure his daily subsistence, find or keep a job, get across town, or deal quickly with the inefficient and labyrinthine bureaucracy. The result is frustration, resignation, and a general want of ambition. Lacking control over fundamental aspects of their lives, many simply accept that someone or something else is controlling their destiny. What should be done today can thus wait until tomorrow. Making plans, whether for a career, university studies, or your children's future, only results in disappointment. The Catholic church's general counsel to accept one's lot in life does little to shake the pervasive fatalism.

The ways of Central American life are best witnessed in the household. There is nothing like being invited to spend a day or two with a family, whether in a peasant's country shack or in a tidy, middle-class home in the city. It's not an uncommon occurrence. Central Americans, especially those of modest origin, are curious about foreigners and are quick to show hospitality. They will do their best to make you comfortable. I was once invited, after sitting with a man for an hour on a train, to spend several days with his family in their small home. He and his wife gave me their bed. He slept on the floor, she in the bed of the two youngest of their six children. His pride, surely a bit misplaced, would not even let me chip in for some of the daily groceries. The household is where the relations between the sexes, the role of religion in daily life, the patterns of work and pleasure, and the intense importance that Central Americans attach to their families can best be observed.

In the homes or on the street, you'll see the cautious hopes of people trying to recover after a particularly intense, decade-long bout with violence and brutality. Travelers may never see a peaceful Central America, but experiencing the natural rhythms of daily life mixed with the backbeat of violence is a powerful rush.

BASICS

1

If you've ever traveled with anyone before, you know the two types of people in the world: the planners and the nonplanners. You also know that travel brings out the very worst in both groups: Left to their own devices, the planners will have you goose-stepping from attraction to attraction on a cultural blitzkrieg, while the nonplanners will invariably miss the flight, the bus, and the point. One way or the other, you're going to end up wanting to bury a hatchet in the back of your companion's head. And that just won't do. We offer you a middle ground, giving you enough information to help you plan your trip without saddling you with an itinerary. From the minute you decide to take a trip, you're confronted with a seemingly endless series of choices: how to get there, where to stay, where to buy M&Ms. We don't want to make the choices for you, but we provide you with the resources to help you make those all-important decisions yourself. If all else fails, we tell you where to buy the hatchet. Keep in mind that companies go out of business, prices inevitably go up, and, hey, we're only too human; as a Reagan official so eloquently said, "Mistakes have been made."

For important country-specific information, read the Basics sections in the individual country chapters.

Planning Your Trip

USEFUL ORGANIZATIONS

The **North America Coordinating Center for Responsible Tourism** (2 Kensington Rd., San Anselmo, CA 94960–2905, tel. 415/258–6594) will tell you how to travel in the Third World without having a negative impact on the economy or society of the host country. They publish a quarterly newsletter called *Responsible Traveling*, which states their goals and gives info on workshops around the United States.

The **South American Explorers Club** (126 Indian Creek Rd., Ithaca, NY 14850, tel. 607/277–0488) provides a ton of info about all of Latin America, and quite a bit on Central America. Among other things, membership gets you the quarterly *South American Explorer* magazine that covers all sorts of off-the-beaten-track activities; access to "trip reports" submitted by club members after their travels; discounts when buying books, maps, etc. from their comprehensive catalogue; and use of their clubhouses if you make it as far as Lima, Peru or Quito, Ecuador. Annual membership costs $30.

The **Center for Global Education** at Augsburg College (731 21st Ave. S, Minneapolis, MN 55454, tel. 612/330–1159) "operates in the belief that firsthand knowledge of other societies and cultures builds international awareness, informs debate on foreign policy, and contributes to a more just and peaceful world." They organize Central American trips that include talks with people from all walks of life—from career diplomats to teenage guerrillas to indigenous farmers—in order to foster understanding and action. Focus topics include ecology, women in the region, and the relation between the environment and economics. Programs are usually a week long and cost $1,500–$2,000 including airfare, meals, lodging, and a slew of things to do while you're there. They occasionally offer jobs in Central America; call for a copy of their newsletter, *Global Perspectives,* for up-to-date info.

BUDGET TRAVEL ORGANIZATIONS Council on International Educational Exchange **(CIEE)** (205 E. 42nd St., New York, NY 10017, tel. 212/661–1414) is a nonprofit organization dedicated to the pursuit of work, study, and travel abroad. Through its two subsidiaries, Council Travel and Council Charter, CIEE offers budget-travel services, including discounted airfares, rail passes, accommodations, and guidebooks. **Council Travel** is an international network of travel agencies that specializes in the diverse needs of students, youths, teachers, and indigent travelers. They also issue the **ISIC** (International Student Identity Card), the **IYC** (International Youth Card), the **ITC** (International Teacher Card), and **Youth Hostel** cards (*see* Student ID Cards, *below*). At least 36 Council Travel offices serve the budget traveler in the United States (*see*

Council Travel Offices

Arizona: Tempe, tel. 602/966–3544. California: Berkeley, tel. 510/848–8604; Davis, tel. 916/752–2285; La Jolla, tel. 619/452–0630; Long Beach, tel. 310/598–3338 or 714/527–7950; Los Angeles, tel. 310/208–3551; Palo Alto, tel. 415/325–3888; San Diego, tel. 619/270–6401; San Francisco, tel. 415/421–3473 or 415/566–6222; Sherman Oaks, tel. 818/905–5777. Colorado: Boulder, tel. 303/447–8101. Connecticut: New Haven, tel. 203/562–5335. District of Columbia: Washington, tel. 202/337–6464. Florida: Miami, tel. 305/670–9261. Georgia: Atlanta, tel. 404/377–9997. Illinois: Chicago, tel. 312/951–0585; Evanston, tel. 708/475–5070. Indiana: Bloomington, tel. 812/330–1600. Louisiana: New Orleans, tel. 504/866–1767. Massachusetts: Amherst, tel. 413/256–1261; Boston, tel. 617/266–1926 or 617/424–6665; Cambridge, tel. 617/497–1497 or 617/225–2555. Michigan: Ann Arbor, tel. 313/998–0200. Minnesota: Minneapolis, tel. 612/379–2323. New York: New York City, tel. 212/661–1450, 212/666–4177, or 212/254–2525. North Carolina: Durham, tel. 919/286–4664. Ohio: Columbus, tel. 614/294–8696. Oregon: Portland, tel. 503/228–1900. Pennsylvania: Philadelphia, tel. 215/382–0343; Pittsburgh, tel. 412/683–1881. Rhode Island: Providence, tel. 401/331–5810. Texas: Austin, tel. 512/472-4931; Dallas, tel. 214/363–9941. Utah: Salt Lake City, tel. 801/582–5840. Washington: Seattle, tel. 206/632–2448 or 206/329–4567. Wisconsin: Milwaukee, tel. 414/332–4740. United Kingdom: London, tel. 071/437–7767.

box), and there are about a dozen overseas in Britain, France, Germany, and Japan. The **Council Charter** division (tel. 212/661–0311 or 800/800–8222) buys blocks of seats on commercial flights and sells them at a discount. Departure dates, rates, destinations, and seat availability change seasonally.

International Youth Hostel Federation (IYHF) (733 15th St. NW, Washington, DC 20005, tel. 202/783–6161) is the grandmammy of hostel associations, with more than 6,500 locations in 70 countries around the world. Membership in any national Youth Hostel Association allows you to stay in any IYHF-affiliated hostel at member rates. A one-year membership is available to travelers of all ages and runs about $25 for adults (renewal $20) and $10 for those under 18; those over 55 pay $15 a year. Don't blow your money on a membership unless you're planning to spend time in Costa Rica—at the moment, it's the only Central American country with an IYHF network.

Student Travel Australia (STA) has 120 offices worldwide and offers students low-price airfares to destinations around the globe. STA offers the **ISIC** and their own **STA Travel Card** (about $5) for recent graduates, which gets you some travel discounts. Write or call one of the offices listed below for a slew of free pamphlets on services and rates. **U.S.:** 82 Shattuck Square, No. 4, Berkeley, CA, tel. 510/841–1037; 273 Newbury St., Boston, MA 02116, tel. 617/266–6014; 1208 Massachusetts Ave., Suite 5, Cambridge, MA 02138, tel. 617/576–4623; 7202 Melrose Ave., Los Angeles, CA 90046, tel. 213/934–8722; 914 Westwood Blvd., Los Angeles, CA 90024, tel. 213/824–1574; 17 E. 45th St., Suite 805, New York, NY 10017, tel. 212/986–9470; 48 E. 11th St., New York, NY 10003, tel. 212/986–9470; 6447 El Cajon Blvd., San Diego, CA 92115, tel. 619/286–1322; and 166 Geary St., Suite 702, San Francisco, CA 94108, tel. 415/391–8407. **U.K.:** 74 Old Brompton Rd., London SW7; 75 Deansgate, Manchester; 25 Queens Rd., Bristol; 19 High St., Oxford; and 38 Sydney St., Cambridge. **Australia:** 222 Faraday St., Carlton 3053, Melbourne, tel. 03/347–6911; 1A Lee St., Railway Sq., Sydney 2000, tel. 02/212–1255. **New Zealand:** 10 Hight St., Auckland, tel. 09/399–995; and 207 Cuba St., Wellington, tel. 04/850–561.

Canadian Universities Travel Service, Ltd. (Travel CUTS) (187 College St., Toronto, Ont. M5T 1P7, tel. 416/979–2406) is a full-service travel agency that sells discount airline tickets to Canadian students and issues the ISIC, IYC, and IYH cards. Their 25 offices are on or near college campuses. Call weekdays 9–5 for information and reservations.

WHEN TO GO

CLIMATE Central Americans divide their year into two seasons: *invierno* (hot and rainy) and *verano* (hot and dry). Invierno (literally, "winter") takes place in the months most of us would consider to include summer, generally April through November. If you crave natural beauty, the vegetation is at its most splendiferous during this period. Keep in mind, however, that a few places may be inaccessible, and more than a few roads will be washed out—don't expect to drive on any nonasphalt surface. You will also get rained on every day. Verano, the dry "summer" season (November– April), is more popular for travelers, with correspondingly higher airfares and hotel prices. Cities of the highlands and central plateaus are mild year-round; some, like Tegucigalpa in Honduras and San José in Costa Rica, are known as cities of eternal spring. Towns at higher altitudes are cooler during the day and can be downright chilly at night. Temperatures vary radically within short distances, too: One minute you sweat so much that your thighs and the vinyl bus seat become one; next, you turn a corner, head up the mountain, and make a mad scramble for that pullover.

PUBLIC HOLIDAYS If you need to do official business anywhere on the following days, expect to be out of luck: **January 1,** New Year's Day; Thursday and Friday of Holy Week (the week before Easter) and Easter itself; **May 1,** Labor Day; **October 12,**

Columbus Day (or Indigenous People's Day, or both); **November 1**, All Saints' Day; **November 2**, All Souls' Day; **December 24–25**, Christmas Eve and Christmas. *See* individual country Basics for their particulars (independence days, army appreciation days, etc.).

FESTIVALS Most communities have annual **patron saint festivals**, replete with parades, food, drink, and dance (*see* individual towns for more info). **Semana Santa** (Holy Week, the week before Easter) is a serious subject to Central Americans: It's one big party, and whole families join in. Beaches, islands, and hotels are packed, restaurants are usually closed Thursday and Friday of that week, and prices skyrocket. It's a lot of fun provided you don't mind getting plastered and dancing in the streets. Check out Semana Santa in Antigua, Guatemala—travelers from all over the world come for it. **Carnaval** usually refers to the Tuesday before Lent, a.k.a. "Mardi Gras" in other parts of the world. Bizarre costumes, booze, decadent food, and general hedonism are the order of the day. Las Tablas, Panamá and La Ceiba, Honduras are reputed to host the most excellent Carnavals in Central America, but you'll find some rockin' good times in other places, too.

PASSPORTS AND VISAS

Hang onto your passport for dear life—in some countries you can't do anything (check into accommodations, change money, etc.) without it, let alone cross a border. In case of mishap, report lost or stolen passports immediately to your nearest home embassy or consulate and to local police authorities. If you have a record of your passport info, the consular officer may hem and haw, but, after considerable red tape, will most likely issue you a new one. It's a good idea to make two photocopies of the passport ID page, one to leave with someone back home and the other to carry separate from your passport. In the United States, report a loss or theft to Passport Services, Dept. of State, 1425 K Street NW, Washington, DC 20522.

Clothes may not make the person, but how you look will often determine how you're treated in both personal and official situations. Most Central Americans know what a "hippy" is, and don't look approvingly at those with such a "laid-back" appearance.

OBTAINING A PASSPORT

➤ **U.S. CITIZENS** • First-time applicants should apply at least five weeks before their departure to one of the 13 U.S. Passport Agency offices. Also, local county courthouses, many state and probate courts, and some post offices accept passport applications. Necessary documents include: (1) a completed passport application (Form DSP-11); (2) proof of citizenship (certified birth certificate or naturalization papers); (3) proof of identity (valid driver's license, or state, military, or student ID card with your photograph and signature); (4) two recent, identical, two-inch-square photographs (black-and-white or color head shot); (5) $55 application fee for a 10-year passport (those under 18 pay $30 for a five-year passport). First-time applicants are also hit with a $10 surcharge. For more information or an application, contact the Department of State Office of Passport Services (tel. 202/647–0518) and dial your way through their message maze. You may renew in person or by mail: Send a completed Form DSP-82; two recent, identical passport photos; a current passport (less than 12 years old); and a check or money order for $55 ($30 for applicants under 18) to the nearest Passport Agency. Renewals take three to four weeks.

➤ **CANADIAN CITIZENS** • Canadians should send a completed passport application (available at any post office or passport office) to the Bureau of Passports (Suite 215, West Tower, Guy Favreau Complex, 200 Boulevard René Lévesque Ouest, Montréal, Québec H2Z 1X4, tel. 514/283–2152). Include C$35; two recent, identical passport photographs; a guarantor (as specified on the application); and proof of Canadian citizenship. You can also apply in person at regional passport offices in

Edmonton, Halifax, Montréal, Calgary, St. John's (Newfoundland), Victoria, Toronto, Vancouver, or Winnipeg. Passports have a shelf life of five years and are not renewable.

➤ **U.K. CITIZENS** • Passport applications are available from most travel agents and major post offices, or through the six regional passport offices (in London, Liverpool, Peterborough, Belfast, Glasgow, and Newport). The application must be countersigned by your bank manager or by a solicitor, barrister, doctor, clergyman, or justice of the peace who knows you personally. Send or drop off the completed form; two recent, identical passport photos; and a £15 fee to a regional passport office (address is on the form). Passports are valid for 10 years (five years for those under 18) and take about four weeks to process.

➤ **AUSTRALIAN CITIZENS** • Australians must visit a post office or passport office to complete the passport-application process. A 10-year passport for those over 18 costs AUS$76, although the under-18 crowd has to settle for a five-year passport for AUS$37. For more information, call toll-free in Australia 008/02–60–22 weekdays during regular working hours.

➤ **NEW ZEALAND CITIZENS** • You can pick up passport applications at any post office or consulate. Completed applications must be accompanied by proof of citizenship and cost NZ$50 for a 10-year passport. Processing takes about three weeks.

VISAS If you go to **El Salvador,** you absolutely have to get a visa—period. To enter **Guatemala,** citizens of the United States or Canada need only a tourist card. In **Belize,** no visas are required for U.S., Canadian, or U.K. citizens. To enter **Honduras,** you need a visa if you're from the United States, Canada, Australia, or New Zealand. In **Nicaragua,** you only need a visa if you're from the United Kingdom or its territories. Citizens of the United States, the United Kingdom, and Canada can stay 90 days in **Costa Rica** without a visa; Australians and New Zealanders are limited to 30 days. If you're from the United Kingdom, all you need is a valid passport to go to **Panamá;** everyone else needs a tourist card and an onward or return ticket.

STUDENT I.D. CARDS

The popular **International Student Identity Card (ISIC)** entitles students 12 years and older to special fares on local transportation as well as discounts at museums, theaters, sporting events, and many other attractions. If you purchase the card in the United States, the $15 cost also buys you $3,000 in emergency medical coverage; limited hospital coverage; and access to a 24-hour international, toll-free hotline for assistance in medical, legal, and financial emergencies. Student travel agencies in Guatemala, Costa Rica, and Panamá may sell the ISIC card for less, but you'll save only a few dollars and miss out on discounts on transportation into Central America, as well as access to the toll-free hotline. Also remember that the card carries insurance coverage only if purchased in the United States. For more info about the ISIC and where it's issued, call 800/GET–AN–ID. International Youth and teacher I.D. cards are also available. In the United States, apply to CIEE, a Council Travel office, or STA; in Canada the ISIC is available for C$12 from Travel CUTS (*see* Budget Travel Organizations, *above*). In the United Kingdom, students with valid university I.D.s can purchase the ISIC at any student union or student-travel company. Applicants must submit a photo as well as proof of current full-time student status, age, and nationality.

The **International Youth Card** is issued to travelers (students and nonstudents) under age 26. It provides services and benefits similar to those given by the ISIC card. The card is available from CIEE, Council Travel offices nationwide, and ISE (Europa House, 802 W. Oregon St., Urbana, IL 61801, tel. 217/344–5863). In Canada, contact Travel CUTS (*see* Budget Travel Organizations, *above*) or the Canadian Hostelling

Association (CHA, 1600 James Naismith Dr., Suite 608, Gloucester, Ont. K1B 5N4, tel. 613/748–5638).

MONEY

If your last voyage was to someplace like Europe, you're going to wet your pants with joy when you travel through Central America. You can seriously live on a third of a Euro-budget—less if you rough it some and eat modest meals. Though lodging and food are cheap across the board, there are degrees of cheapness. What you'll actually dish out depends on which country you're in: In Guatemala you can live it up for $15 a day, while in Belize you're rockin' if you can do it for under $35. Everywhere else falls somewhere in between; Panamá and Costa Rica are relatively expensive, El Salvador and Honduras less so. Outside Managua, food and lodging in Nicaragua are fairly cheap, but a day in the capital will drain $40 from your pocket. Islands and remote places are pricey; you'll pay anywhere from $10 to $100 for transportation, and food and incidentals cost more since they have to be shipped in. Be warned: Inflation is endemic in the region, and costs are perennially on the rise. Prices may be 30%–50% higher than those quoted in this book. We suggest that you use the listed prices only as ballpark figures, so don't cuss us out when they're wrong.

CURRENCY Each country in Central America circulates its own currency, with the exception of Panamá, which for some obscure reason just recycles the U.S. paper dollar, rechristened a "balboa." If you're the proud owner of U.S. greenbacks, you'll find it easy to get around Central America; dollars are happily accepted in many locales and are easily exchanged in others. Exchange rates in some countries are as predictable as carbon 14, while in others they're about as stable as plutonium.

All prices quoted in this book are in U.S. dollars unless otherwise noted.

TRAVELING WITH MONEY Cash never goes out of style, but traveler's checks and a major credit card are usually the safest and most convenient way to pay for goods and services on the road. Unfortunately, credit cards aren't widely accepted in budget establishments. Depending on the length of your trip, strike a balance among the various forms of dough, and protect yourself by carrying it in a money belt or "necklace" pouch (available at luggage and camping stores) or front pocket; keeping accurate records of traveler's checks' serial numbers; and recording credit-card numbers and an emergency number for reporting the cards' loss or theft. Carrying at least some cash (hard currency) is wise; many establishments (almost all in Nicaragua) prefer or even demand cash, and changing traveler's checks outside urban areas is practically impossible.

TRAVELER'S CHECKS Traveler's checks may look like play money, but they work much better. They can be used for purchases in the same way as a personal check— though usually just in the capitals or really gringoed-out places—and can almost always be exchanged for cash at banks, American Express offices, and *casas de cambio* (exchange offices). The most widely recognized traveler's checks are American Express, Visa, and MasterCard. Some banks and credit unions issue the checks free to established customers, but most charge a 1%–2% commission. Members of the American Automobile Association (AAA) can purchase American Express traveler's checks from AAA commission-free. Buy the bulk of your checks in small denominations (a pack of five $20 checks is the smallest); most establishments won't accept large bills, and, even when they do, breaking large checks for small purchases leaves you carrying too much cash. Call any of the toll-free or collect telephone numbers listed below for more information about where to purchase checks and how widely they are accepted in your destination.

American Express (in U.S. and Canada, tel. 800/221–7282) card members can order traveler's checks in U.S. dollars by phone, free of charge (with a gold card) or for a 1% commission (with your basic green card). In three to five business days you'll receive your checks: Up to $1,000 can be ordered in a seven-day period. Whether you have an American Express card or not, you can buy checks at most banks and credit unions. If your checks get lost or ripped off, American Express has the resources to provide you with a speedy refund (however, "speedy" in Central America may mean "sometime before you die"). At their Travel Services offices, you can do some or all of the following: buy and cash traveler's checks, write a personal check in exchange for traveler's checks (cardholders only), report lost or stolen checks, exchange foreign currency, and pick up mail. American Express now issues **Traveler's Cheques for Two,** checks that can be signed and used by either you or your traveling companion. Ask for the **"American Express Traveler's Companion,"** a handy little directory of their offices, to find out more about particular services at different locations. There is at least one office in each country except Nicaragua.

MasterCard International (in the U.S., tel. 800/223–7373; or call 609/987–7300 collect from anywhere outside the U.S.) traveler's checks, issued in U.S. dollars only, are offered through banks, credit unions, and foreign-exchange booths. Call for information about how widely their checks are accepted at your travel destination and for the local number to call in case of loss or theft.

Thomas Cook, a brand of MasterCard traveler's checks, is available in U.S. dollars and foreign currencies. If purchased through a Thomas Cook Foreign Exchange office, there is no commission. For more information, contact MasterCard (*see above*).

Visa (in the U.S. and Canada, tel. 800/227–6811; tel. 415/574–7111 collect outside the U.S.), as a sponsor of the '92 Olympics, boosted its name recognition and acceptance of their checks worldwide.

➤ **LOST OR STOLEN CHECKS** • Unlike cash, once lost or stolen, traveler's checks can be replaced or refunded if you keep the purchase agreement and a record of the checks' serial numbers and of those checks you've cashed. One modern translation of "don't keep all of your eggs in one basket" is "keep the purchase agreement in a separate place from the checks." Cautious travelers will even give a copy of the purchase agreement and checks' serial numbers to someone back home. Most companies that issue traveler's checks promise to refund or replace lost or stolen checks in 24 hours, but you can practically see them crossing their fingers behind their backs; expect the process to take a lot longer. In a safe place—or several safe places—write down the toll-free or collect telephone number to call for refunds.

EXCHANGING MONEY Hunting down the best exchange rate can be time-consuming and, in the end, not all that profitable—hotels, banks, and other establishments in Central America often offer the same rate. Generally, official rates differ minimally, if at all, from **black-market** rates. Avoid "banking black" unless you're in a bind: Though it's widely practiced, it's illegal in most places and cons aren't unheard of (bogus bills are a favorite trick).

OBTAINING MONEY FROM HOME Provided there is money at home to be obtained, here are a few ways to get it:

1) If you're an **American Express cardholder,** you can sometimes cash a personal check at an American Express office for up to $1,000 every 21 days, usually given in traveler's checks rather than cash. Likewise, an **American Express Moneygram** can be a dream come true if you can convince someone back home to go to an American Express Moneygram agent (in American Express offices, bus stations, airports, convenience stores), fill out the necessary form, and transfer cash to replenish your empty wallet. Transactions must be in increments of $50 and must be paid for with cash, MasterCard, Visa, or an Optima. Fees vary according to the amount of money sent but average 8%–10%. Currently, Moneygram transfers are accepted in several cities in each country, including Managua. You'll need to show I.D. when picking up the money, and you'll need to know the transaction reference number. Word is money will be available within a day, but don't bet on it. For the nearest Moneygram-agent loca-

tion and the addresses of receiving offices overseas, call 800/543–4080 in the United States; overseas, call 303/980–3340 collect.

2) Have funds sent through **Western Union** (tel. 800/325–6000). Fees vary with the amount of money sent, but for $1,000 the fee for sending funds to Central America is about $50. If your financial situation plummets from bad to worse, beg someone back home to take cash, a certified cashier's check, or a healthy MasterCard or Visa to a Western Union office. The money will reach the requested destination in two business days but may not be available for several more hours or days, depending on the whim of the local authorities. Western Union transfers are available only in the local currency, and the locations where they're accepted in each country are subject to change without notice, so call first. Western Union transfers money mainly through the following companies: In Guatemala, Honduras, El Salvador, Panamá, and Costa Rica, through **Air Pak**; in Belize, through **Barclay's Bank**; in Nicaragua, through **Banco Nacional.** Look in the phone book in the capital cities for numbers.

3) You can get someone to send you a money order through a courier service or registered mail, but it'll take about a week and you need to make sure the money order is cashable in the area it's sent to. **Urgente Express** (tel. 800/262–1389 in the U.S.; in Canada, tel. 514/341–2807) sends money orders from North America to El Salvador, Guatemala, and Honduras *only*.

4) In **extreme emergencies** (arrest, hospitalization, or something worse) there is one more way American citizens can receive money in Central America: Contact the Citizens' Emergency Center of the Department of State (tel. 202/647–5225). They can arrange for funds to be available, in the local currency, at the U.S. embassy or consulate nearest you, within 24 hours.

CREDIT CARDS Credit cards can be lifesavers for rental-car deposits, reserving a flight, or keeping a roof over your head when your pockets are empty. In Central America, cards are unevenly accepted. If you're on the tourist trail, you'll be fine; otherwise, use your plastic in the capital to get cash or as a supplement, and make sure you have local currency if you're going off the beaten track. Visa and MasterCard are more widely accepted than American Express. American Express is usually accepted by U.S. rental car and airline companies.

If You're Broke, You Can Take Some of the Credit

Even if you have no job, no credit, no cards, no little plastic thing to put them in—in short, absolutely nothing—you can still tap into fabulous services offered by the Visa Assistance Center if one of your parents has a Visa Gold or Business Card and you're a dependent of 22 years or younger who is at least 160 kilometers (100 miles) from home. Just memorize the card number (or write it down in a safe, memorable place), and call the Center for emergency cash service, emergency ticket replacement, lost-luggage assistance, medical and legal assistance, and an emergency message service. Helpful personnel await your call 24 hours a day, seven days a week (in U.S., tel. 800/759–6262; overseas, call collect 919/370–3203).

LUGGAGE

Don't bring too much luggage unless you want to depend on the kindness of strangers your whole trip. Backpacks are the most manageable way to lug belongings, but they instantly brand you a foreign tourist. Also, outside pockets on backpacks are especially vulnerable to pickpockets, so don't store any valuables there. If you want to blend in more with the local tourist population, bring a duffel or large shoulder bag. Like new shoes, luggage should be broken in: If you can't comfortably tote your fully packed bag all the way around the block at home, it's going to be worse than a ball and chain in Central America. Leaving some room for gifts and souvenirs is also wise. Lockers and baggage-check rooms (*bodegas*) are only sporadically available. Ask desk clerks at less-seedy hotels if they've got a place to hold your stuff; they'll either have a set charge for the service, or you can offer a small tip. You'll save time and money if you can easily carry your belongings with you.

BACKPACKS Packs are the best luggage for travelers who plan to walk a lot or do any hiking or camping. By distributing the weight of your luggage across shoulders and hips, backpacks ease the burden of traveling. You can choose among four types of packs: day packs (best for short excursions), external-frame packs (for longer travels and use on groomed trails), internal-frame packs (for longer travels across rougher terrain), and travel packs (hybrid packs that fit under an airline seat and travel well in cities or the backcountry). Although external frames achieve the best weight distribution and allow airspace between you and your goodies, they're more awkward and less flexible than packs with an internal frame. Be sure to have your pack fitted correctly when you buy it; there shouldn't be any gaps along your back, it should not drag down on your hips, nor should the frame stick up too high above your head. Height specifications are useful, but your torso length is the real deciding factor, so try a fully loaded pack on before investing in it (external-frame packs run $100–$225; about $50 higher for an internal frame). Check to see that it's waterproof, or bring an extra waterproof poncho to throw over it in downpours. An inside pocket is great for dirty laundry or food storage, and straps for a sleeping mat or hammock are handy. In cities, especially on public transportation, you may have a hard time negotiating yourself and your pack through doorways or down crowded aisles. Someone behind you could also be merrily stealing your passport and all your traveler's checks unless you pack them *inside* the pack.

SHOULDER BAGS AND SUITCASES Bags with a long strap can be worn across your body to distribute weight and minimize the chance that someone will rip it off, but this method will still result in aching shoulders if the bag is too heavy. Duffels and shoulder bags are less conspicuous than backpacks and suitcases, so, if you're the self-conscious or wanna-be-native type, they may be the best choice for you. They are

You Can Put AmEx on Your Mailing List

Travelers have another choice for receiving mail in Central America besides the potentially iffy lista de correos (poste restante) system. If you can get an American Express Card membership, have your mail sent to their regional offices and they'll hold it for you safely and usually for free. They have offices in every capital city except Managua, and in Honduras there's a second office in San Pedro Sula. See the Basics section in each capital for the mailing address, or call an American Express Travel Services office for an updated list. See individual country Basics for details about receiving mail at regular post offices.

not ideal if you plan to walk a lot, camp, or hike, or if you need instant accessibility to your stuff. Straps, zippers, and seams are the most vulnerable points on a bag; check that straps are wide, adjustable, and offer some padding; check the stitching on zippers and seams; and look for a wide zipper that can be locked.

Basically, suitcases are for those staying in resorts, traveling exclusively by car, or for those who would actually be seen using one of those carts with wheels.

WHAT TO PACK

As little as possible. What this actually means to you we can't say. If you think you might be miserable without such and such, you're probably right. Be realistic about how often you'll actually *use* the things you bring, and if they're truly worth their weight. Of course, you can't predict everything—there'll always be a time when you smack yourself in the forehead and say something like, "Oh, *why* didn't I bring my wire clippers!"

PACKING LIST

➢ **BEDDING** • Unless you're going to be camping in high elevations (where it does get cold, even in the tropics), you don't need a sleeping bag. If you're going to rough it a lot, consider getting a sleeping mat that can be rolled tightly and strapped onto the bottom of your pack; these make train- and bus-station floors a tad more comfy. Your best bet, though, is a hammock and mosquito net, which can be set up almost anywhere. For more info on what to bring for camping, *see below*.

➢ **CLOTHING** • Smart—and not terribly fashion-conscious—travelers will bring two outfits and learn to wash clothes by hand regularly. At the very least, bring comfortable, easy-to-clean clothes. Black hides dirt but absorbs heat, so pack a couple of light-colored T-shirts. Light cotton sweaters, long-sleeved shirts, and pants dry more quickly than jeans and sweatshirts; they also keep you cool and help prevent sunburn, bug bites, etc. If you sunburn easily—and you're going to burn more easily than you think near the equator—definitely bring or buy a large-brimmed hat to keep sun off your face and ears (baseball caps don't work). Shorts are customarily only acceptable at the beach, though you probably won't get drummed out of town if you wear 'em. You should also pack one pair of heavier pants and a sweater or heavy sweatshirt for colder nights, especially if you're traveling in the mountains. Pack a raincoat and/or umbrella for the inevitable (in the rainy months, continuous) rainstorms. Socks and undies don't take up too much room, so throw in a couple of extra pairs.

The Four Rules of Luggage

- *You must be able to carry it at least 2 miles.*
- *You must be able to fit it in a conventional storage locker and on an overhead rack in a train.*
- *Keep anything you cherish in the middle of your bag. Pack your heaviest belongings in the middle of a pack and whatever you need quick access to (maps, guidebooks, address book) in an outer pocket. Keep money and travel documents on your body.*
- *Attach a clearly marked luggage tag to your bag, and put an ID tag or label inside as well.*

Shoes can be your best friend or worst foe: Having a sturdy pair of *broken-in* walking shoes or hiking boots and some sandals allows you to switch off and give your tootsies a rest. Plastic sandals or thongs protect feet on hostile shower floors (which are often rough, wet, and/or skanky), and they're also useful when camping and beach-hopping.

➤ **TOILETRIES** • When packing health and beauty supplies, use a separate, waterproof bag and small containers that seal tightly; the pressure on airplanes can cause lids to pop off and create instant moisturizer-slicks inside your luggage. If you wear contact lenses, you may want to stock up on solution before you leave and when in major cities. Otherwise, consider reverting to plain old glasses for the duration of the trip; you can't find *solución para lentes de contacto* in most smaller towns. However, simple saline solution (*agua asalinada*), is available at practically any pharmacy.

Dr. Bronner's Magic Soap is safe both for clothes and your bod, and the label is cool reading material on bus rides.

➤ **LAUNDRY** • Laundry facilities—where you wash your clothes yourself or pay someone else to wash them—do exist throughout Central America. They're fairly cheap and very efficient in most places, but are a pain in the ass to find. The most common option is to wash your clothes yourself, by hand, if the hotel has a *pila* (washing sink). Many hotels have restrictions about drying clothes in your room, and will post notices to that effect. In some places, it's cool to wash your clothes in the pila and leave them to dry on the communal line; elsewhere, you shouldn't hang your stuff out unless you plan to stay and watch it. It's wise to bring your own laundry service: a plastic bottle of liquid detergent (Woolite's good), about six feet of clothesline, and some plastic clips (bobby pins or paper clips can substitute). Bring an extra plastic bag or two for still-damp laundry and dirty clothes.

➤ **CAMERAS AND FILM** • While traveling, keep your film as cool and dry as possible, away from direct sunlight and humid heat. Obviously, this is just a little difficult to accomplish in Central America. Mildew will creep into your camera equipment if you're not very, very careful—and it's truly impossible to remove. To prevent humongous fungus, pick up little bags of silica gel (the stuff that says "do not eat") at an electronics store and keep them with your camera equipment at all times. You may even have to dry the gel in an oven if it gets too humid. The smaller and lighter the camera the better, unless you're a photo artiste. If something goes wrong on the road, try large hotels—some stock camera equipment.

If, during your travels, you see a sign with a camera crossed by a big red line, this is a hint: Taking photographs here is forbidden (usually military or industrial sites and border crossings). Also, be aware of the cultural effrontery involved in barging into someone's neighborhood and snapping away. According to some belief systems, to take a picture of someone is to capture her/his soul. In some places, especially the more "picturesque" ones with "quaint natives," you'll be expected to pay the subject of a photo (usually 25¢–$1).

➤ **MISCELLANEOUS** • Stuff you might not think to take but may be damn glad to have: (1) extra day pack for valuables and short jaunts, (2) flashlight (good in electricity failures, caves, and for night trips), (3) Walkman, (4) pocketknife (multiple uses include cutting fruit, removing splinters, and opening bottles), (5) water bottle, (6) sunglasses, (7) several large zip-type plastic bags (useful for wet clothes, towels, leaky bottles, and stinky socks), (8) travel alarm clock, (9) needle and thread, (10) vitamins (meat is fatty, salads scarce), (11) journal/scrapbook/address book/whatever, (12) batteries, (13) Spanish/English dictionary (difficult to find there—same goes for English-language books in general), (14) photos of family and friends to show your new friends, (15) a couple days' supply of tissue/toilet paper.

CAMPING GEAR Before packing up loads of camping gear, seriously consider how much camping you will actually do versus how much trouble it will be to haul around a tent, sleeping bag, stove, and accoutrements in the heat. Central Americans don't usually go camping themselves, so facilities are either scarce or touristy and expensive. In the national parks (of which there are several kajillion, especially in Costa Rica and Honduras), camping is pretty easy; also, you can always ask a private landowner if you can set up camp. Rough it on open-looking land or beaches at your own discretion.

Sleeping bags have limited appeal: They're heavy and hot. A much better idea is to bring, buy, or rent a hammock. They're lightweight and easy to drape a mosquito net around. (They also happen to be a lot more comfortable than sleeping in mud.) Most people in Central America are more amenable to the idea of a traveler crashing while suspended between two trees than falling asleep on the side of the road somewhere. Hammocks do take a little getting used to, though—you might discover a whole new meaning for the word "crash" the first couple of times you try to sleep in one. Supposedly the best way to maintain equilibrium is to sleep diagonally across the thing. Bonus: Hammocks made in Central America are usually well constructed, fairly cheap, and really beautiful.

Tents come in cotton and synthetic-canvas breeds. The synthetic variety is more water-resistant and shelters you against wind. A 7- or 8-pound tent is probably the heaviest tent comfortable to carry. For camping in damp areas, make sure the tent has edges that can be turned up off the ground to prevent water from seeping in, or bring a plastic tarpaulin. Check the tent's windows and front flaps for mosquito-proof netting, and make sure the front flap can be zipped completely shut during rain. In general, the lighter the tent of a given size, the more expensive, but the expense may be worth it, especially if you're going to travel by bike or do a lot of backpacking. Expect to pay $150–$200 for an average two-person tent.

Camping stoves are no longer the bulky green numbers once lugged on family camping trips. You can buy a white-gas-burning ministove that provides one amazingly powerful flame and folds up into a little bag, all for about $35. A kerosene-burning lantern costs about $40. Other necessary odds and ends include matches in a waterproof container, a Swiss Army knife, mosquito repellent, a mess kit ($15), a water purifier ($35), and water-purification tablets or iodine crystals ($8). If you feel you'll need a shower, try a solar shower (about $10–$15), a bag that can be filled with water and set out in the sun for a quick, hot shower. Last but not least, bring zip-type plastic bags for garbage and recyclable items.

PROTECTING YOUR VALUABLES

Money belts may be slightly dorky and annoying, but wouldn't you rather be embarrassed than broke? You'd be wise to carry all cash, traveler's checks, credit cards, and your passport on your body, under your clothes. Neck pouches and money belts are sold in luggage and camping-supply stores. Fanny packs (those zippered bags strapped around the waist/hip region) are safe if you keep the pack part in front of your body, safer still if your shirt hangs over the pack.

Back pockets are fine for maps, but don't keep a wallet there; your butt might get the wrong kind of admiring attention.

When is it safe to take your valuables off your body? In public, almost never. As for leaving your traveler's checks or passport in your hotel room, each place and circumstance is different. It's your call—use your gray matter. Some hotels allow you to check valuables in at the front desk; this is usually safe if the establishment is licensed and wants to keep it that way. *Never* leave your pack unguarded or with a total stranger in bus stations or any other public places, even if you're only planning to be gone for a minute—it's not worth the risk. If you're carrying a smaller bag with a strap (or a camera), sling it crosswise over your body and try to keep your arm down over the bag.

CUSTOMS AND DUTIES

See individual country Basics for specific customs regulations.

U.S. CUSTOMS You won't have to pay duty unless you come home with more than $400 worth of foreign goods, including items bought in duty-free stores; 10% duty is charged after that point up to $1,000. Each member of the same family is entitled to the exemption, regardless of age, and exemptions may be pooled. Duty-free allowances include one liter of alcohol (for travelers 21 or older) and 200 cigarettes. Anything above these limits will be taxed at the port of entry and may also be taxed in the traveler's home state. Also, it's illegal to bring in any agricultural items—period. For more info, ask for "Know Before You Go" and "GSP and the Traveler," both available free from the U.S. Customs Service (1301 Constitution Ave., Washington, DC 20029, tel. 202/927-6724).

CANADIAN CUSTOMS Exemptions range from C$20 to C$300, depending on how long you've been away: for two days out, you're allowed C$100 worth of goods; for a week out, you're allowed C$300 worth. Above these limits, you'll be taxed 20%. You're allowed only one $300 exemption per year. Duty-free limits are 50 cigars, 200 cigarettes, 2.2 pounds of tobacco, and 40 ounces of liquor—all must be declared in writing upon arrival at customs and must be with you or in your checked baggage. For more scintillating details, request the Canadian Customs brochure "I Declare/Je Déclare" from Revenue Canada Customs and Excise Department (Connaught Building, MacKenzie Ave., Ottawa, Ont. K1A 0L5, tel. 613/957-0275).

U.K. CUSTOMS Travelers age 17 or over may bring back the following duty-free goods: 200 cigarettes; one liter of alcohol over 22% by volume or two liters of alcohol under 22% by volume, plus two liters of still table wine; and other goods worth up to £32.

AUSTRALIAN CUSTOMS Australian travelers 18 or over may bring back, duty-free: one liter of alcohol; 250 grams of tobacco products (equivalent to 250 cigarettes or cigars); and other articles worth up to AUS$400. If under 18, your duty-free allowance is AUS$200. To avoid paying duty on goods mailed back to Australia, mark the package "Australian goods returned." For more rules and regulations, request the pamphlet "Customs Information for Travellers" from a local Collector of Customs (Collector of Customs, GPO Box 8, Sydney, NSW 2001, tel. 02/2265997).

NEW ZEALAND CUSTOMS Travelers over 17 are allowed the following items duty-free: 200 cigarettes or a combo of tobacco products up to 250 grams; 4.5 liters of wine or beer and one 1,125-ml bottle of spirits; and goods with a combined value of up to NZ$700. If you want more details, ask for the pamphlet "Customs Guide for Travellers" from a New Zealand consulate.

STAYING HEALTHY

BEFORE YOU GO An estimated 80% of adults in the western hemisphere have not maintained their childhood immunizations. Use your upcoming trip as an excuse to update routine immunizations. These include tetanus-diphtheria, polio, measles, mumps, and rubella. Schedule vaccinations well in advance of departure because some require several doses, and others may cause uncomfortable side effects. Vaccinations are not required to enter Central America but, especially if you're going to be traveling in rural areas, it's important that you check into the gamut of shots you might need. Hepatitis is endemic in the region and you can be protected with a relatively painless dose of gamma globulin. It's recommended that you get cholera and typhoid vaccinations; however, opinions about the shots' nasty side effects versus their effectiveness in preventing disease vary widely. Talk to your physician and other travelers who've dealt with these shots and decide for yourself. If you are going to be in Panamá east of the Canal Zone, you should get vaccinated against yellow fever.

Malaria is transmitted by mosquitos and concentrated in coastal and jungle zones. You can take pills to prevent the disease; chloroquine is still good for most of Central America, but malaria strains in Panamá are becoming chloroquine-resistant, so Fansidar may be prescribed for that country. The medicine should be taken before, during, and usually up to six weeks after the end of the trip. Malaria won't strike if you don't get bitten, so use all the bug-repelling strategies you know of: long-sleeved shirts and long pants, insect repellent, and mosquito nets.

➤ **RESOURCES** • For up-to-the-minute information about health risks and disease precautions in all parts of the world, call the **U.S. Center for Disease Control's International Travelers' Hotline** (tel. 404/332–4559). A comprehensive pamphlet, *Health Information for International Travel,* can be purchased for $5 by sending a request to the **Superintendent of Documents** (U.S. Government Printing Office, Washington, DC 20402). The **Department of State's Citizens Emergency Center** (Bureau of Consular Affairs, Room 4811, N.S., U.S. Dept. of State, Washington, DC 20520, tel. 202/647–5225) provides written and recorded travel advisories. They'll tell you about ongoing dangers—like some contagious disease running rampant, a guerrilla uprising, or a government crackdown—rather than a single terrorist attack or if a country's food is just plain bad.

➤ **HEALTH AND ACCIDENT INSURANCE** • Some general health-insurance plans cover health expenses incurred while traveling, so review your existing health policies before leaving home. Most university health-insurance plans stop and start with the school year, so don't count on school spirit to pull you through. Canadian travelers should check with their provincial ministry of health to see if their resident health-insurance plan covers them on the road. Budget- and student-travel organizations, such as STA and CIEE (*see* Budget Travel Organizations, *above*), and credit-card conglomerates include health-and-accident coverage with the purchase of an I.D. or credit card. Otherwise, several private companies offer coverage designed to supplement existing health insurance for travelers; travel agents often provide travel-insurance information and sell policies.

Carefree Travel Insurance (Box 310, 120 Mineola Blvd., Mineola, NY 11501, tel. 516/294–0220 or 800/323–3149) is, in fact, pretty serious about providing coverage for emergency medical evacuation and accidental death or dismemberment. It also offers 24-hour medical phone advice.

International SOS Assistance (Box 11568, Philadelphia, PA 19116, tel. 215/244–1500 or 800/523–8930) provides emergency evacuation services, worldwide medical referrals, and optional medical insurance.

Travel Guard (1145 Clark St., Stevens Point, WI 54481, tel. 715/345–0505 or 800/782–5151), endorsed by the American Society of Travel Agents, is an insurance package that includes coverage for sickness, injury (or untimely death), lost baggage, and trip cancellation. You can choose from an advance-purchase ($19), super advance-purchase ($39), or a megaplan for trips of up to 180 days (8% of your travel costs).

➤ **PRESCRIPTIONS** • If you have a medical condition requiring prescription drugs, consult your doctor before leaving, and ask him or her to type the prescription and include the following information: dosage, the generic name (often Latin), and the manufacturer's name. To avoid problems clearing customs, bring a copy of the prescription along with the drug; diabetic travelers carrying needles and syringes should keep handy a letter from their physician confirming their need for insulin injections. A lot of drugs sold only by prescription in the United States are sold over-the-counter in Central America, but don't get any wacky ideas.

➤ **FIRST-AID KIT** • Packing a few first-aid items could save you physical and financial pain during your travels, when Pepto-Bismol—much less anything fancier—may not be readily available. Think about including bandages, waterproof surgical tape and gauze pads, antiseptic, cortisone cream, tweezers, a thermometer in a sturdy case, an antacid such as Alka-Seltzer, something for diarrhea, and aspirin. Depending on the health conditions in your destination, you might also ask a doctor for a general antibiotic. If you're prone to motion sickness and plan to use any rough modes of transportation during your travels (like the local bus), take along some Dramamine.

WHILE YOU'RE THERE

➤ **INTERNAL MALADIES** • You might as well face facts: No matter how hard you try, you'll probably get diarrhea. You can minimize your chances of spending your vacation on the toilet—and contracting more serious diseases—by taking the following precautions. Drink only bottled water or sodas (ask for a sealed bottle to be sure); avoid ice altogether; don't eat uncooked fish or vegetables; always peel your fruit yourself; and stay away from food that is exposed to flies (hopefully this won't be much of a sacrifice). Sterilize water yourself by boiling it for 15 minutes or using purification tablets or water filters. Fresh, unpasteurized milk may sound tempting, but it's also on the no-no list. Some travelers suggest that if you're going to spend a lot of time in the region, it might be worth it to experiment with dubious culinary items: Build up those antibodies and pray you don't get something horrendous. It's a personal decision; you know your physical constitution better than anyone.

As the U.S. Centers for Disease Control advise, "Boil it, cook it, peel it, or forget it."

➤ **EXTERNAL MALADIES** • Tropical insects will greet you by trying to drain a pint of your blood. *Bring the strongest insect repellent you can find and use it.* You'll still get nailed, but why surrender to the critters without a fight? The region has a number of poisonous snakes, spiders, and scorpions, especially in bushy areas. If you'll be heading off the beaten track a lot, bring a snake-bite kit and read up on the subject so you can recognize some of the most prevalent offenders. Many dogs in the region are homeless, wild, and rabid; if you are bitten, try to track down the owner of the dog, or the dog itself, to check if it's potentially rabid. When in doubt, a hellish series of rabies shots is probably in order (our Guatemala writer had to do it while she was on assignment there). Contact the nearest health authorities for more info. The tropical sun is very potent, and sunburn is a problem for travelers even with darker complexions. *Bring the strongest sunscreen you can find and use it.*

Beat the Biting Buggers

Mosquitoes are the scourge of travelers in Central America, and they can carry malaria. Thanks to modern science, we know mosquitoes don't like the taste of vitamin B. By megadosing (using 2–4 times the recommended daily allowance)  **on B-complex vitamins daily for at least a month before your trip, you'll put enough of the stuff in your blood to make you a less delectable dish than your friends. It won't completely solve the problem, but most people who try notice the difference. Be warned, though, that taking large doses of vitamin B (or any other vitamin) can have side effects and may not be good for you in the long run. Your pee will be bright orange, too. Another option is to apply Avon Skin-So-Soft Moisturizer, which bugs can't stand. The Marines have been using the stuff for years.**

➤ **DOCTORS** • Almost every town has at least one doctor, but finding one who speaks English will mean going to larger towns and cities (except in Belize). If you're spending time camping or traversing remote regions (like the Mosquito Coast or the Darién), schlepp a good first-aid kit and cross your fingers. If you have stomach problems, you can avoid a doctor altogether by going to a medical lab for blood and stool tests and asking the local pharmacist for medicine to treat your condition.

British travelers can join **Europe Assistance Ltd.** (252 High St., Croyden, Surrey CRO 1NF, tel. 01/680–1234) to gain access to a 24-hour, 365-day-a-year telephone hotline that can help in a medical emergency. The U.S. branch of this organization is **Travel Assistance International** (1133 15th St. NW, Washington, DC 20005, tel. 800/821–2828). Membership in the nonprofit **International Association for Medical Assistance to Travelers (IAMAT)** (417 Center St., Lewiston, NY 14092, tel. 716/754–4883; 40 Regal Rd., Guelph, Ont. N1K 1B5, Canada, tel. 519/836–0102; Box 5049, Christchurch 5, New Zealand) is free (donations are requested to keep it afloat) and entitles you to a worldwide directory of qualified English-speaking physicians who are on 24-hour call and who have agreed to a fixed-fee schedule. Also helpful are IAMAT's health pamphlets, such as the frequently updated *World Malaria Risk Chart* and *World Immunization Chart.*

As Billy Bragg says, "Safe sex doesn't mean no sex; it just means use your imagination."

➤ **SAFE SEX** • AIDS and other STDs (sexually transmitted diseases) do not respect national boundaries. Protection when you travel takes the same form as it does when at home. If contemplating activities that would involve an exchange of bodily fluids, condoms and dental dams (oral condoms) are the best forms of protection. Carry these with you rather than assuming you can purchase them on the road, and remember to cushion them in a pouch or case where they won't get too hot or damaged. Prophylactics are generally available at pharmacies in bigger cities.

RESOURCES FOR WOMEN

Woodswomen (25 W. Diamond Lake Rd., Minneapolis, MN 55419, tel. 612/822–3809 or 800/279–0555) specializes in adventure travel for women of all ages. This nonprofit organization, which claims to be the largest and most extensive women's travel outfit in the world, organizes safe, educational, and environmental excursions for their members; however, the only Central American country it visits is Costa Rica. If you're heading to other parts of Latin America, they also go to Mexico, Ecuador, and the Galapagos Islands. Yearly membership donations start at $20.

Women's groups within the region are about as hard to come by as profeminist men. There's one in Nicaragua (*see* Nicaragua Basics), but other than that, nothing organized exists. If you're a woman, especially if you're traveling alone and come even close to blonde, expect a lot of attention. Machismo usually takes the form of verbal rather than physical harassment, so pretend you don't hear and, with luck, the oaf will stop hissing, whistling, or barking. Exercise the same caution you would traveling anywhere—be alert, be cautious about who you are alone with, appear confident—and you should minimize problems. Needless to say, you'll attract less attention if less of your skin is showing. And a woman is definitely considered "loose" (as opposed to "on the loose," which is a good thing) if she doesn't wear a bra. The "good girl/bad girl, Madonna/whore" dichotomies still have a secure place in the regional consciousness; know this and do what you will with your libido.

RESOURCES FOR GAYS/LESBIANS

In this seething sea of machismo, gays and lesbians keep a low profile. Support groups are likely to be underground; check the gay clubs in the capital cities for tips. Since the Nicaraguan government's attempt to criminalize even the mention of non-heterosexuality, the gay voice has grown in strength, so organizations may come out soon.

ORGANIZATIONS The nonprofit **International Gay Travel Association (IGTA)** (Box 4974, Key West, FL 33041, tel. 800/448–8550) has 387 members worldwide and can provide travelers with listings of member agencies. The **International Lesbian and Gay Association (ILGA)** (81 Rue Marche au Charbon, 1000 Brussels 1, Belgium, tel. 32/2–502–2471) offers extensive information about conditions, specific resources, and hot spots (good and bad types) in any given country.

TRAVELERS WITH SPECIAL NEEDS

Diabetic travelers can find out about available resources before they go or while they're traveling by subscribing to *The Diabetic Traveler* (Box 8223 RW, Stamford, CT 06905, tel. 203/327–5832). It's published four times a year; subscriptions cost $18. Your country's diabetes association may have information as well.

Major airlines may offer a discounted "companion fare" if a passenger with disabilities needs medical attention. **American Airlines** offers a TDD line for the hearing impaired (tel. 800/543–1586), as does **TWA** (tel. 800/421–8480). Both provide flight information and reservations. *Access to the World: A Travel Guide for the Handicapped,* by Louise Weiss, is highly recommended for its worldwide coverage of travel boons and busts for disabled travelers. It's available from Henry Holt and Company (tel. 800/247–3912) for $13; the order number is 0805001417.

Once you get to Central America, you're pretty much on your own. Hotels are sometimes wheelchair accessible in the capitals; it's sketchier in the rest of the region (we note accessible places in our hotel reviews). Most other places are "accessible" only with the help of a strong pair of arms. Generally, sidewalks and curbs aren't conducive to a smooth wheelchair ride.

ORGANIZATIONS For more info, contact the following organizations. The **American Foundation for the Blind** (15 W. 16th St., New York, NY 10011, tel. 212/620–2147 or 800/232–5463) provides information on discounts and $6 I.D.s for legally blind persons. The **Information Center for Individuals with Disabilities** (Fort Point Pl., 1st Floor, 27–43 Wormwood St., Boston, MA 02210, tel. 617/727–5540, TDD 617/727–5236) offers useful problem-solving assistance, including lists of travel agents who specialize in tours for disabled travelers. **Travel Industry and Disabled Exchange (TIDE)** (5435 Donna Ave., Tarzana, CA 91356, tel. 818/343–3786) publishes a quarterly newsletter and a directory of travel agencies and tours catering to disabled persons. **Mobility International USA** (Box 3551, Eugene, OR 97403, tel. 503/343–1284, for voice and TDD) is an internationally affiliated organization that coordinates exchange programs for disabled people around the world and offers information on accommodations and organized study programs. There's a $20 annual fee for use of their services. The **Society for the Advancement of Travel for the Handicapped** (347 5th Ave., Suite 610, New York, NY 10016, tel. 212/447–7284, fax 212/725–8253) provides access information and lists of tour operators specializing in travel for disabled people. Annual membership is $45, $25 for students and senior citizens. Send $2 and a stamped, self-addressed envelope for information about a specific destination. **Travel Helpers Limited** (156 Duncan Mill Rd., Suite 5, Don Mills, Ont. M3B 3N2, tel. 416/443–0583, fax 416/443–0586) arranges travel and accommodations worldwide.

WORKING ABROAD

In order for you to work legally in most countries, your would-be employer must certify that no Central American is qualified to fill the post. In a region rife with unemployment, this is no easy task unless your employer is foreign or you're well connected (though working without documentation is not unheard of). Unless you have some highly sought skill (like advanced computer knowledge), finding a job is difficult. The most likely avenue is teaching English at one of the many private language schools, but don't expect to make much *dinero.* The classified section in daily newspapers often carries ads for English teachers. **CIEE** (*see* Budget Travel Organizations, *above*) sponsors a work program in Costa Rica *only;* $90 gets you a legit work permit for 3–6 months, but they don't actually arrange the work. CIEE also produces several books of interest to prospective worker/student travelers—*see* Studying Abroad, *below.* In Canada, **Travel CUTS** (187 College St., Toronto, Ont. M5T 1P7, tel. 416/979–2406) provides information on working abroad for Canadian students.

VOLUNTEER WORK Volunteer programs typically offer room and board in exchange for labor and can be a financial boon for cost-conscious travelers. Plan ahead: The best projects fill up fast. Agencies can help find programs and arrange placement, but some charge application fees. The **Archaeological Institute of America** (675 Commonwealth Ave., Boston, MA 02215, tel. 617/353–9361) annually publishes *Archaeological Fieldwork Opportunities,* a listing of field projects around the world.

STUDYING ABROAD

Studying in another country is the perfect way to scope out a foreign culture, meet locals, and learn or improve language skills. The main types of programs are: those affiliated with a university in your home country, those where you apply directly to a school in the host country, and language programs run by private folks. Do your homework—study programs vary greatly in expense, academic quality, exposure to language and culture, amount of contact with local students, and living conditions. Tap into the resources below, and write to foreign embassies for information on their university systems. Visit the study-abroad office of the university closest to you. To receive college credit for your studies abroad, you'll either have to enroll through a U.S. university or arrange credit with your university and a university abroad in advance. Antigua, Guatemala, is world-famous for its language schools, and biology students hang at the University of Costa Rica, but many universities (those without enough room for their own students) won't let you in.

The **Experiment in International Living/School for International Training (EIL)** offers the Semester Abroad Program (Kipling Rd., Box 676, Brattleboro, VT 05302, tel. 802/257–7751 or 800/451–4465). The **Council on International Educational Exchange** (University Programs Department, 205 E. 42nd St., New York, NY 10017, tel. 212/661–1414) publishes *Work, Study, Travel Abroad: The Whole World Handbook* ($13), which includes over 1,000 study programs as well as info on working abroad for students and nonstudents. CIEE also puts out *Volunteer! The Comprehensive Guide to Voluntary Service in the U.S. and Abroad* ($10); and *Going Places: The High School Student's Guide to Travel, Study, and Adventure Abroad* ($15). The **Institute of International Education (IIE)** (809 U.N. Plaza, New York, NY 10017, tel. 212/883–8200) publishes two comprehensive guides: *Academic Year Abroad* ($35) and *Vacation Study Abroad* ($30). The Information Center at IIE (tel. 212/984–5413) has reference books, foreign-university catalogs, study-abroad brochures, and other materials that may be consulted free. The **National Registration Center for Study Abroad** (823 N. 2nd St., Milwaukee, WI 53203, tel. 800/558–9988; c/o Doreen Desmarais, 341 Main St., Ottawa, Ont. K1V 8Y6) is a consortium of 88 schools that provides information on schools abroad and study programs, as well as preregistration.

Coming and Going

To find out how to get to Central America by bus from Mexico, *see* Coming and Going in Belize or Guatemala. There are few direct flights to Central America from the United Kingdom, Australia, or New Zealand; check with Council Travel or STA (*see* Budget

Travel Organizations, *above*) for the latest info and possible deals. You'll probably end up flying to Los Angeles or Miami and taking a connecting flight from there.

BY PLANE FROM THE U.S.

Flying is the quickest, but not the cheapest, means of travel. Although airline tickets will undoubtedly be your biggest expense, heavy (and early) research can scare up a reasonably good deal. Flexibility is the key to hefty savings. If you can play around with simple matters such as departure date, destination, amount of luggage carried, and return date, you'll save money. Also, being a student with the I.D. to prove it can save a buck or two from time to time. The rock-bottom, absolute cheapest round-trip price can be a jaw-dropping $300, but $500–$700 is a more realistic fare.

BUYING A TICKET The major airlines offer a range of tickets with wildly varying prices, depending on the day of purchase. As a rule, the further in advance you buy the ticket, the less expensive it is, but the greater the penalty (up to 100%) for canceling. **Advanced Purchase Excursion (APEX)** fares are the cheapest official fares the airlines advertise and offer directly to travelers. It's essentially a fancy name for buying a ticket early from the airline. Disadvantages are that reservations must be made 21 days in advance (30 for the even cheaper Super APEX); the length of your trip is often limited; and changing anything about your ticket usually costs $50–$100 if it's even possible.

When your travel plans are still in the fantasy stage, start studying the travel sections of major Sunday papers, where cut-rate travel agencies and fare brokers often advertise incredibly cheap flights. Don't believe everything you read, but most of the deals are legit. Many of these travel agencies are small, bustling operations; they're tapped into computer networks that allow them to hustle the lowest fares from the airlines, and they're also willing to forgo huge commissions in favor of keeping a steady flow of budget travelers coming through their door. Also, try travel agencies on or near college campuses for cheap fares.

Hot tips when making reservations: Call every toll-free number you can find—it's free and can't hurt. Don't be shy about asking for the cheapest flight possible. If the reservation clerk tells you the least-expensive seats are no longer available on a certain flight, ask to be put on a waiting list. If the airline doesn't offer waiting lists for the lowest fares, call on subsequent mornings and ask about cancellations and last-minute adjustments by airlines trying to fill their planes, which often mean additional cut-rate tickets. When setting travel dates, remember that off-season fares can be as much as 30% lower, and there'll be fewer people vying for the inexpensive seats at those times. Ask which days of the week are the cheapest to fly on—weekdays are often most expensive, as airlines can charge exorbitant rates to business travelers who just flash their company credit card without even asking the fare. Taking a roundabout route can sometimes be less expensive—you might try booking a flight to a travel hub (such as Guatemala City or San José) and then shop around for a cheap flight or bus from there.

Most travelers are unaware that unsold vacation packages that depart on a weekend go on sale on Monday, so this may be the best time to call for a cheap, last-minute flight.

If the end result of the search is biting the bullet and paying more than you'd budgeted, keep scanning the ads in newspaper travel sections for last-minute ticket deals and lower airfares offered by desperate airlines. Some airlines will refund the difference in ticket price when they lower fares and a passenger calls them on it. You can also call the airlines and ask about late-saver fares, which usually must be purchased one to three days before the flight. These tickets are a risk but offer big savings. Once you have your ticket in hand, do not—repeat—do not lose it (don't you love advice like that?) or let some flight junkie steal it, as you may not be able to get a refund or another ticket. Make a photocopy to expedite getting a replacement in the event of such a calamity.

➤ **CONSOLIDATORS AND BUCKET SHOPS** • Consolidator companies (bucket shops) buy blocks of tickets at wholesale prices from airlines trying to fill flights. Drawbacks: Consolidator tickets are often not refundable and may feature indirect routes, long layovers, and undesirable seating assignments. If the flight is delayed or canceled, you'll also have a tough time switching airlines. As with charter flights, you risk taking a huge loss or paying a stiff fine if you change your travel plans. Once your reservation is made, call and confirm it with the airline a few days later. Check again a day or two before departure. You may also want to check the consolidator's reputation with the Better Business Bureau. Most are perfectly reliable, but it's better to be safe than sorry. If you can deal with the restrictions and minor risks, consolidators might offer the cheap flight of your dreams. Try to pay with a credit card, so that if your dream goes up in smoke and the ticket never arrives, you won't have to pay. Bucket shops generally advertise in newspapers—be sure to check restrictions, refund possibilities, and payment conditions.

Among the best-known consolidators are **UniTravel** (1177 N. Warson Rd., Box 12485, St. Louis, MO 63132, tel. 314/569–2501 or 800/325–2222) and **Up & Away Travel** (141 E. 44th St., Suite 403, New York, NY 10017, tel. 212/972–2345).

➤ **STANDBY AND THREE-DAY-ADVANCE-PURCHASE FARES** • Flying standby is almost a thing of the past. The idea is to purchase an open ticket and wait for the next available seat on the next available flight to your chosen destination, but many airlines have dumped standby policies in favor of three-day-advance-purchase youth fares, which are open only to the under-25 market and only within three days of departure. Return flights must also be booked no earlier than three days prior to departure. Three-day-advance works best in the off-season, when flights aren't usually as jam-packed, and the savings are substantial.

A number of brokers specialize in discount and last-minute sales, offering savings on unsold seats on commercial carriers and charter flights, as well as tour packages. You can try **Last Minute Travel Club** (tel. 617/267–9800) or **Interworld Travel, Inc.** (tel. 305/443–4929); neither charges an annual membership fee.

➤ **CHARTER FLIGHTS** • "Charter flights" can have vastly different characteristics, depending on the company you're dealing with. Generally speaking, a charter company either buys a block of tickets on a regularly scheduled commercial flight (just like a consolidator) and sells them at a discount (this is the most prevalent form in the U.S.), or they may lease the whole plane and then offer relatively cheap fares to the public (most common in the U.K.). Despite a few potential drawbacks (infrequent flights, restrictive return-date requirements, lickety-split payment demands, etc.), a charter company may offer the cheapest ticket at the time you want to travel, especially during high season, when APEX fares are at their most expensive. Make sure you find out a company's policy on refunds should a flight be canceled by either yourself or the airline. Summer charter flights fill up fast and should be booked a couple of months in advance.

You're in much better shape when the company is offering tickets on a regular, commercial flight. After you've bought the ticket from the charter folks, you generally deal with the airline directly; essentially, you're treated like a normal, fare-paying customer. When a charter company has chartered the whole plane, things get a little sketchier: Bankrupt operators, long delays at check-in, overcrowding, and flight cancellation are fairly common. You can minimize risks by checking the company's reputation with the Better Business Bureau or a travel agency, and taking out enough trip-cancelation insurance to cover the operator's potential failure.

The following list of companies isn't exhaustive, so check the travel sections of major newspapers: **Council Charter** (tel. 212/661–0311 or 800/800–8222), **DER Tours** (Box 1606, Des Plains, IL 60017, tel. 800/782–2424), **TRAVAC** (tel. 212/563–3303 or 800/872–8800), **Travel Charter** (1120 E. Long Lake Rd., Troy, MI 48098, tel. 313/528–3570 or 800/521–5267), and **Travel CUTS** (187 College St., Toronto, Ont. M5T 1P7, tel. 416/979–2406).

➤ **COURIER FLIGHTS** • Restrictions and inconveniences are the price you'll pay for the colossal savings on airfare offered to air couriers, travelers who accompany shipments between designated points. Restrictions include luggage limitations (check-in luggage space is used for the freight you're transporting, so often you can only take carry-ons), limited stays of a week to a month, and usually only one courier is permitted on any given flight.

Check newspaper travel sections and want ads for courier companies, or mail away for a telephone directory that lists companies by the cities to which they fly. Send a self-addressed, stamped envelope to **Pacific Data Sales Publishing,** 2554 Lincoln Blvd., Suite 275-I, Marina Del Rey, CA 90291. A former *Berkeley Guides* writer, Michael McColl, has produced an informative guide to courier travel, *The Worldwide Guide to Cheap Airfares.* Send $9.95 plus $2.50 for shipping, to **Insider Publications,** 2124 Kittredge St., Third Floor, Berkeley, CA 94704.

Staying in Central America

GETTING AROUND

BY TRAIN Few train lines in Central America work, and those that do make you feel like you're hurtling to a violent death. Furthermore, most places served by trains are served more frequently and efficiently by bus.

BY BUS Bus travel in Central America is the functional equivalent of trains in Europe and private cars in the United States. Comfort is rather minimal, though; roads tend to be bumpy, seats lumpy, and on the longer trips, people grumpy. It's a bit of a gamble; seats on buses can be scarce during prime traveling hours, and drivers don't always stop where they should, although most leave promptly (usually when you're still waiting in line for a ticket). In most places, you can flag down a bus on the road; if there's room, the driver will let you on and might even give you a prorated fare. ("Room" in Central America often means an empty 2 foot x 2 foot standing space in the aisle, by the way.)

BY CAR If you have special considerations, such as a wheelchair, a surfboard, or that Costa Rican ox cart you just had to buy, a vehicle may be essential. If you've got the means and want to venture off the beaten track, a 4x4 is especially helpful for mountain or jungle travel. During the rainy season, don't expect a car to take you anywhere but on paved roads. If you're traveling with a number of *amigos,* renting a vehicle can sometimes turn out to be cost-effective. **Avis** (tel. 914/355–AVIS) has a **"Know Before You Go"** database that anyone—not just Avis renters—can use to find out about distances between foreign cities, buying gas and insurance, currency-exchange rates, and other useful stuff in various countries. This database now includes information on Central America, and the cost is the price of the phone call. For rental information only, contact a travel agent or call 800/331–1084.

BY MOTORBIKE If you think you can cruise through the entire region on a motorcycle or moped without massive problems, you're high. In the rainy season you'll definitely get stranded in mud, and some places are impassable even in the dry season. If you can fix your own bike, have spares and tools, and a direct line to God, your chances of a successful trip are slightly improved. In the capitals and more touristy towns, you can rent a moped and zip around looking cool for a pretty reasonable rate.

BY BIKE Cycling has the twin merits of being cheap and health-conscious. The mountainous regions will give all but hard-core cyclists pause, so plan routes with an eye to altitude. Riding in the jungles is virtually out of the question; even if you've done lots of "off-roading" before, an overgrown rainforest will humble you in seconds. During the rainy season, your bike will inadvertently be converted to the stationary kind.

HITCHHIKING Play it safe. Know where you're headed, don't flash cash, and try to offer gas money before getting in; stalling gives you time to check out the driver for psycho signals, as well as to prevent a nasty argument later (in many places, it's the norm to pay the driver). On many roads in Central America, you could spend a long stretch o' time without any cars passing. Usually, hitching is more accepted in places where the bus doesn't go, especially beachy areas. Drivers generally do stop for innocuous-looking hitchers; pickup trucks are most likely to do so. Head to the edge of town (on the road to your hoped-for destination) and stick out that thumb. Obviously, it's always safer to travel with a friend. Needless to say, women don't have the same freedom as men to take advantage of this cheap means of getting around. We hate to say it, sisters, but if you're traveling alone, *don't hitch*. It's not safe.

BY PLANE The only time you should even consider taking a domestic or intra-regional flight is when there's absolutely no other way, like when you're headed for an island or a park in the middle of nowhere, or when the bus ride is atrociously long. Domestic flights are expensive—usually at least 10 times the bus price.

WHERE TO SLEEP

HOTELS Lodgings go by a number of names—*posada, hotel, pensión, hospedaje, casa de huespedes*—but this means nothing in terms of quality or amenities. Accommodations run anywhere from $1 for a nasty sty in a whoretel to about $30 for a goody-filled room in a nice hotel. Expect to pay between $5 and $15 a night for something tolerable. Price ranges vary from country to country—see the country's Basics for more exact figures. If possible, get a room with a fan unless you enjoy sweltering in misery all night. No matter how nice a place is, you'll emerge from bed in the morning with mysterious bites, and *cucarachas* (roaches) make cameo appearances at even the best hotels.

CAMPING Definitely one of the cheapest options (ranging from free at freelance sites to a few dollars in organized campgrounds), camping also gets you out of crowded urban centers and into the more pastoral or mountainous outdoors (which is most of Central America anyway). Campgrounds are not all that common even in national parks, but usually you can set up on beaches and in the wilderness with little hassle. If you're camping off-road near a house or lodging, ask first.

ROUGHING IT Crashing on public beaches or on the side of the road is just deglorified camping—it's usually totally legal. Sleeping on park benches is dangerous in the larger cities and will attract undue attention in smaller towns; the same goes for bus stations (where they even exist). The police might give you a hard time if they catch you sleeping in parks.

SERVAS Servas, an organization begun in the aftermath of World War II, is dedicated to promoting peace and understanding around the globe. Membership enables you to arrange a stay with host families. Servas is not for tourists or weekend travelers; peace-minded individuals looking for more than just a free bed can write or call for an application and interview. Being a member entitles you to host directories for each of the seven countries. Membership is $55 per year, and a one-time deposit of $25 is required to help defray the cost of producing the host listings. They have at least one host address in each country in Central America. *11 John St., New York, NY 10038, tel. 212/267–0252; 229 Hilcrest Ave., Willowdale, Ont. M2N 3P3, tel. 416/221–6434; 83 Gore Rd., London, England E97HW; 16 Cavill Ct., Vermont*

South, 3133 Victoria, Australia, tel. 803–5004; 15 Harley Rd., Takapuna, Auckland, New Zealand, tel. 594–442.

BASICS

CRIME AND PUNISHMENT

PERSONAL SECURITY You always need to watch yourself and your stuff. Capitals and cities near borders, where a lot of smuggling goes on, are usually more dangerous. Don't wear conspicuous jewelry unless you want it ripped off your body, and keep all but a day's worth of cash stashed away under your clothes. If you're going to a country where guerrillas lurk, get your embassy's hot-spot update before you set off. Try to time your bus rides to arrive before nightfall. Respect customs and be humble—many people here resent gringos enough as it is, and your mere presence may be enough to enrage the more bellicose (or resentful, or hungry). Projecting a humble yet confident attitude is the key to avoiding many confrontations.

DRUGS AND ALCOHOL Getting busted with drugs will definitely ruin your trip and may ruin your life in the process. Unless you've got serious connections or the cash of a Pablo Escobar, the authorities will throw the book at you. Prison sentences of 20 years for cocaine possession are not unheard of, and Central American prisons match anything seen in *Midnight Express*. Also, don't expect your embassy to get you out of hot water: They can't.

Appearance has a lot to do with how the authorities treat you. If you look scruffy and act at all disoriented, they may suspect you're carrying drugs—and there have even been reports of officials planting drugs on people. Even rolling your own cigarettes may be viewed as suspect, so leave the rolling papers at home. Border towns are often sites of drug smuggling, so pull yourself together and play it cool in these areas. The capital cities (especially Belize City), some parts of the Caribbean, and Colón in Panamá are also pretty druggy. Public drunkenness, on the other hand, is common and results in no official harassment. Drinking in public is also legal in most places.

Two-Minute Toilet-Training— Using the W. C. in C. A.

Call it baño, servicio, or sanitario, you'll have to use it at one time or another and you can make the experience much pleasanter for yourself and those that follow if you adhere to one simple rule: Never throw paper in the toilet. Clean,

serviceable flush toilets are a scarce commodity in Central America, the few you find stay that way only if the user follows the no-paper policy. Most sewage systems in Central America are not designed to take paper, and few things here are worse than a clogged toilet—especially if you've been getting friendly with the germies from comedores. Toss your used t.p. (always bring your own) into the wastebasket next to the john. Like it says in the Pensión Mesa in Guatemala City, "Please do not toss your cigarette butts into the toilet as it makes them soggy and difficult to relight." (Of course in latrinas and pit toilets, feel free to throw the paper in because there are no pipes to be clogged—though usually you'll see a wastebasket for those who are in the habit.)

FURTHER READING

GENERAL *Turning the Tide: U.S. Intervention in Central America and the Struggle for Peace,* by Noam Chomsky (South End Press, 1985). *The Central America Fact Book,* by Tom Barry and Deb Preusch (Grove Press, 1986). *Inside Central America,* by Clifford Krauss. *The Inevitable Revolution: The United States in Central America,* by Walter LaFeber (Norton, 1983). *And We Sold the Rain...Contemporary Fiction From Central America,* ed. Rosario Santos (Ryan Publishing, 1989).

MAYAN HISTORY *Time Among the Maya,* by Ronald Wright (Henry Holt and Company, 1991). *The Modern Maya,* by Macduff Everton (University of New Mexico Press, 1991). *The Popol Vuh* (ancient Mayan text, Simon & Schuster, 1985). *The World of the Ancient Maya,* by John S. Henderson (Cornell University Press, 1981). *Scribes, Warriors, and Kings: The City of Copán and the Ancient Maya* by William L. Fash (Thames and Hudson Ltd., 1991).

COUNTRY-SPECIFIC READING *A Country Guide* (one book for each country), by the Inter-Hemispheric Education Resource Center, 1990.

➤ **BELIZE** • *The Formation of a Colonial Society: Belize From Conquest to Crown Colony,* by Nigel Bolland (Johns Hopkins). *Spirit Possession in the Garifuna Community of Belize,* by Byron Foster (Cubola Productions).

➤ **GUATEMALA** • *A Cry From the Heart,* by V. David Schwantes (Health Institutes Press, 1990). *Refreshing Pauses: Coca-Cola and Human Rights in Guatemala,* by Henry J. Frundt (Praeger). *Guatemala: Eternal Spring, Eternal Tyranny,* by Jean-Marie Simon (Norton, 1987). *Forest Society: A Social History of Petén, Guatemala,* by Norman B. Schwartz (University of Pennsylvania Press, 1990).

➤ **HONDURAS** • *Honduras: The Making of a Banana Republic,* by Alison Acker (South End Press, 1988). *Points of Light: Honduran Short Stories,* by Guillermo Yuscarán, 1990. *Honduras: Portrait of a Captive Nation,* edited by Nanvy Peckeuhan. *The Garifuna Story* by Guillermo Yuscarán (Nuevo Sol Publicaciones, 1983).

➤ **EL SALVADOR** • *El Salvador in Crisis,* by Philip Russell (Colorado River, 1984). *El Salvador: A Revolution Confronts the Unites States,* by Cynthia Arnson (Institute for Policy Studies, 1982). *Reform and Repression: U.S. Policy in El Salvador 1950 through 1981,* by Robert Armstrong and Philip Wheaton (Solidarity, 1982). *Salvador,* by Joan Didion (Washington Square Press, 1983).

➤ **NICARAGUA** • *Nicaraguan Sketches,* by Julio Cortázar (Norton, 1989). *The Jaguar Smile,* by Salman Rushdie (Penguin, 1987). *Fire From the Mountain: The Making of a Sandinista,* by Omar Cabezas (Crown, 1985).

➤ **COSTA RICA** • *The Costa Rica Reader,* by Marc Edelman and Joanne Kenen (Grove Weidenfeld, 1989). *The Costa Ricans,* by Richard, Karen, and Mavis Biesanz (Prentice Hall, 1987). *Life Above the Jungle Floor,* by Donald Perry (Simon & Schuster, 1986). *What Happened: A Folk History of Costa Rica's Talamanca Coast* (Ecodesarollo, San José, 1977) and *Wa'apin Man* (Editorial Costa Rica, 1986), both by Paula Palmer.

➤ **PANAMÁ** • *Panamá: A Country Study,* by Richard R. Nyrop (American University, 1981). *The Path Between the Seas: The Creation of the Panamá Canal, 1870–1914,* by David McCullough (Simon and Schuster, 1977).

BELIZE

2

By Trisha Smith

Belize is tiny, sparsely populated, green with jungles, English-speaking, sports the Caribbean Sea as a groovy backyard, and, for those hankering to meet the outdoors in all forms, pretty damn close to heaven. Jutting out from the eastern end of Guatemala on the southern coast of the Yucatán peninsula, Belize is physically isolated from its Latin neighbors by an ominous and rugged mountain range to the west and a spectacular barrier reef along the coast. This forbidding geography has helped protect Belize from a variety of hostile intruders throughout its history and contributes to its cultural and political isolation. More Caribbean than Latin, Belize is blessed with one of the most peaceful and stable political climates in the entire region. This unruffled little sliver of land, about the size of Massachusetts, doesn't usually make headlines; as stories of blood and war seep out of Guatemala, Belize goes blissfully unnoticed by most of the world.

This same forbidding geography has preserved Belize's beauty and drawn ecoconscious tourists, a more welcome and money-generating sort of intruder. The most well-known and popular feature of Belize is the barrier reef, which lies off the coast in the warm waters of the Caribbean. Ever since Jacques Cousteau came here in the '70s and showcased Belize's 280-kilometer- (175-mile-) long reef (the largest in the Western Hemisphere), divers, sun worshippers, tourist operators, and travelers of all sorts have descended upon the country in hordes. The Cayes (pronounced *keys*), small islands strewn along the reef, sport pristine waterfront property and idyllic towns. Nature buffs can indulge in anything from sea kayaking to snorkeling to spelunking to bird watching. Most travelers show up in Belize only to make a beeline for sand 'n' sea, but the stunning diversity of Belize's interior shouldn't be missed. In the south, you'll find vast tracts of untouched forest, churning rivers, and immense limestone cave networks. This is the least-touristed region in the country, and it's custom-made for the intrepid traveler yearning to blaze a trail and go where no one has gone before. In the west, the masses flock to the jungle and exquisite pine forests of the Maya Mountains; plenty of cool ranches and hotels also spot the western towns. The north is hardly as spectacular as the rest of Belize, but this flat countryside, saturated with mangrove swamps and sugar cane, is the abode of important wildlife reserves and Mayan sites.

The Prime Minister of Belize holds office hours every day. Anyone can come to visit, ask for help with a problem, or just say hi.

Belize

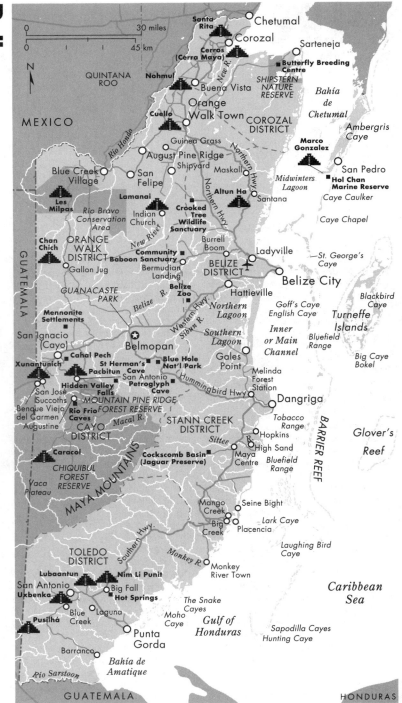

Chetumal

Santa Rita

Corozal

Sarteneja

Cerros (Cerra Maya)

Butterfly Breeding Centre

QUINTANA ROO

Nohmul

Buena Vista

SHIPSTERN NATURE RESERVE

Bahía de Chetumal

Orange Walk Town

COROZAL DISTRICT

Cuello

Ambergris Caye

MEXICO

Marco Gonzalez

Guinea Grass

August Pine Ridge

Shipyard

Maskall

San Pedro

Blue Creek Village

San Felipe

Midwinters Lagoon

Hol Chan Marine Reserve

Les Milpas

Rio Hondo

Lamanai

Altun Ha

Caye Caulker

Rio Bravo Conservation Area

Indian Church

Crooked Tree Wildlife Sanctuary

Santana

Caye Chapel

Chan Chich

ORANGE WALK DISTRICT

New River

Community Baboon Sanctuary

Burrell Boom

Ladyville

St. George's Caye

Gallon Jug

Bermudian Landing

BELIZE DISTRICT

Belize City

GUATEMALA

GUANACASTE PARK

Belize Zoo

Belize R.

Hattieville

Blackbird Caye

Mennonite Settlements

Northern Lagoon

Goff's Caye

English Caye

Turneffe Islands

San Ignacio (Cayo)

Western Hwy.

Sibun R.

Southern Lagoon

Inner or Main Channel

Bluefield Range

Big Caye Bokel

Belmopan

Cahal Pech

St Herman's Cave

Blue Hole Nat'l Park

Gales Point

Xunantunich

Pacbitun

San Antonio Petroglyph Cave

Melinda Forest Station

San José

Hidden Valley Falls

Hummingbird Hwy

Dangriga

Succoths

Rio Frio Caves

MOUNTAIN PINE RIDGE FOREST RESERVE

Tobacco Range

Glover's Reef

Benque Viejo del Carmen

Augustine

Macal R.

CAYO DISTRICT

STANN CREEK DISTRICT

Sittee R.

Hopkins

High Sand

BARRIER REEF

Caracol

Cockscomb Basin (Jaguar Preserve)

Maya Centre

Bluefield Range

CHIQUIBUL FOREST RESERVE

Yaca Plateau

MAYA MOUNTAINS

Mango Creek

Seine Bight

Lark Caye

Big Creek

Placencia

Laughing Bird Caye

TOLEDO DISTRICT

Southern Hwy.

Monkey R.

Monkey River Town

Caribbean Sea

Lubaantun

Nim Li Punit

San Antonio

Uxbenka

Big Fall

Hot Springs

The Snake Cayes

Moho Caye

Gulf of Honduras

Sapodilla Cayes

Hunting Caye

Pusilhá

Blue Creek

Laguna

Punta Gorda

Barranco

Bahía de Amatique

Río Sarstoon

GUATEMALA

HONDURAS

0   30 miles

0   45 km

N

The magic of Belize has as much to do with the people who live here as it does with its sensational countryside. Belize's society is mighty diverse, with a variety of ethnic groups coexisting peacefully. Although the British controlled Belize until 1981, the majority of the population is far from British—and far from white. Most Belizeans are English-speaking Creoles, descendants of African slaves (brought to the Mosquito Coast by British settlers) and colonial outlaws. Belize is also home to a small population of Mayans, as well as a good number of mestizos from Guatemala and Mexico. The Creoles share cultural ties with their brothers and sisters in Jamaica and the Caribbean much more than with their Latin American neighbors. The soft, lilting Creole English blends elements from English, Spanish, French, and indigenous languages into a multi-ethnic medley. Belize's polyglottal population also includes the Black Caribs or Garifuna, Chinese, Middle Easterners, and a small community of Mennonites, mostly of German descent.

With a chuckle and a grin, the Creole people often toss out philosophical tidbits that explain Belize in just a few words: "If you drink de Belize watta, you mus com bak" (one visit to Belize is not enough) or "Cow no bidness eena hoss glop" (a cow has no business in a horse race). The latter proverb aptly sums up Belize's graceful bowing out of the industrial world's manic pace. Trying to maintain a laid-back philosophy in a country that in the last 15 years has had to cater to gobs of travelers, Belize is a land of contradictions: It has one of the best telecommunications systems in Central America, yet can't maintain an agricultural base to feed its sparse population. Although over 50% of the population owns land and can afford to visit the United States on a regular basis, the country itself is poor. Walk into any remote village in the southern Toledo district and you'll find someone with a store selling Coke and Cheetos for less than a buck, but it'll cost you your first-born for imported produce that could easily be grown at home. Sometimes even Belize City runs out of gas for days at a time, yet you can always find a can of Spaghetti-O's on the shelves at Brodie's Supermarket. Prices can soar when a town is singled out as the new hotspot, and drop dramatically when the visitors don't show up.

The cost of living in Belize has always been much higher than in the rest of Central America—so the dirt-cheap prices which are the norm in Guatemala are basically nonexistent in Belize. But if you curb your splurging and explore less touristy regions, you'll easily be able to play within a budget.

Some parts of Belize are throwbacks to a different decade. Not long ago, electricity was a major issue in local politics. Electricity poles were erected to back up false campaign promises, only to be removed once votes were cast. This ongoing bullshit frustrated rural Belizeans for years, and only recently has the government made good on some of its promises. On a June night in 1992, the Mayan village of San Antonio, which had existed for years without electric light, refrigeration, or running water, suddenly found itself all lit up like a birthday cake. Other infrastructural things take much longer to change. Getting around Belize can sometimes be such a royal bitch that many tour buses don't budge any further than the Mexican border. Only two paved roads snake through Belize, and dirt tracks (referred to as highways) are often impassable in the rainy season. Potholes on the blacktop of the Hummingbird Highway, a principal road, are hellish: Their sharp edges puncture tires, and deeper craters challenge even the most rugged suspensions.

In Belize, the word "community" really has tangible implications. Try listening to the national radio station, Friends FM 88.9. If you're radioless, don't worry—everybody blasts them loud enough so that neighbors, people in the street, and birds overhead can hear. You'll hear announcements like "Marco Gonzalez, please come home, your mother is looking for you." And just about everyone in the country gets a birthday greeting and song dedication, always with the stock phrase, "with lots of love and super-dynamic kisses." You have to smile when the DJ starts in about *the* traffic light; Belize City has only recently installed the very first one in the entire country. The problem isn't the light itself but the lack of any sort of law prohibiting the running of red lights. Periodically, the DJs implore drivers at the intersection of North Front Street and Hydes Lane to please acknowledge the light and make life easier on everyone.

Belize lies along *La Ruta Maya* (The Mayan Route), and estimates put the ancient Mayan population here at close to two million—compare that to the 200,000 that live in Belize today. Long thought to be merely satellite settlements of the major centers in Guatemala and Honduras, some of the multitudinous sites in Belize are now seen as crucial to piecing together the Mayan mystery. Newly discovered evidence at the Cuello site, dating well before the Classic period (AD 250–900) and possibly as early as 2500 bc, puts Belize at the cutting edge of Mayan studies. Evidence also suggests that Caracol, in western Belize, may have been the largest ceremonial center in Latin America. Since the discovery of Tikal in Guatemala, no other Mayan center has been uncovered to rival its size and scale of achievement; yet deciphered hieroglyphs at Caracol tell stories of military victories over Tikal, thus bringing into question Tikal's big-bully-on-the-block reputation.

When the 16th-century Spanish conquistadors ravaged Central and South America in search of gold and silver, Belize was spared due to its lack of natural minerals. This left the coast open to colonization by the equally imperial British, though with a different bent. Piracy and the logwood industry dominated the early history of colonial Belize. British settlers (called Baymen) built a viable economy, based on timber and logwood, which continued to thrive until the mid-19th century. British lumber barons were joined by pirate–sailor types, who recognized an ideal opportunity to amass an illicit fortune carrying out raids against homeward-bound Spanish fleets full of Central American booty. The barrier reef offered protection for outlaws who snuck up in their shallow boats and attacked the heavy galleons laden with gold and silver.

Great Britain encouraged piracy in an effort to break the Spanish monopoly on trade in the New World. In the 17th and early 18th centuries, every renegade adventurer in Britain, hungry for a taste of easy fortune, flocked to the Caribbean to exploit everything from the people to the land. Throughout the 18th century, Spain harassed the British settlers, trying to make them get the hell out; a slew of government-to-government treaties consistently failed. Finally, on September 10, 1798, England defeated Spain for the final time at St. George's Cay in a battle that lasted only 2½ hours. This date is now a raging national holiday, and from this point on, Britain officially laid claim to Belize by right of conquest.

"The military presence, so pervasive in most of Central America, is all but invisible in Belize."

The combination of cultural diversity, an English-speaking majority, and political stability makes Belize an anomaly in Central America. Previously known as British Honduras, Belize became self-governing in 1964, was renamed Belize in 1973, and achieved independence from Britain on September 21, 1981. Modern Belize boasts one of the only true democracies in Latin America, based on the British parliamentary system. It's a two-party system, with the UDP (United Democratic Party) and the PUP (Peoples United Party), both centrist, constantly battling for power. The PUP and Prime Minister George Price have been in power almost continuously since independence. The military presence, so pervasive in most of Central America, is all but invisible in Belize. Since the Belizean Defense Force (BDF) numbers a mere 720 soldiers, the government has used British troops as protection, mainly against the "Guatemalan threat." Guatemala only recently recognized Belize as a nation, previously claiming it part of their own country; Guatemalan maps didn't even have lines or boundaries drawn between the two. In 1991, Guatemalan President Serano announced his intentions to begin diplomatic relations with the nation of Belize, thus removing the only real threat to Belizean national security. The British still hang around as a safety precaution, but you're more likely to find the soldiers helping build a bridge or wreaking havoc in local bars.

As a developing nation, Belize is taking an impressive risk by attempting an environmental and economic experiment designed to preserve the diverse natural terrain that covers most of the country. Belize boasts 80% of its forests still intact; compare that to El Salvador, which has little more than 2% of its pristine forest remaining. This unassuming little nation is the embodiment of the new environmental buzzword—ecotourism. Belizeans have developed a program of conservation and protection almost unheard-of in the Third World, or anywhere else for that matter. Flourishing jungle, rugged pine forest, lush swampland, and the colorful barrier reef are the habitats for thousands of species of wildlife. With locally based projects like the Community Baboon Sanctuary and Crooked Tree Wildlife Reserve in the north, Belize is working to put tourist dollars back into the effort to preserve fragile ecosystems. The barrier reef was also recently declared a World Heritage Site, "a place of such significance that its deterioration or disappearance would constitute a harmful impoverishment of the heritage of all nations of the world," according to the World Heritage Organization.

Unfortunately, the government's commitment to the environment is sometimes empty rhetoric. Much of the acreage in the undeveloped southern region is being turned over to the increasingly powerful citrus industry. Land that's thick forest one week is cleared for citrus the next, often displacing the supposedly valuable wildlife. Sustainable agriculture is a priority to many Belizeans, yet slash-and-burn farming is still rampant. With tourism growing in leaps and bounds, the balancing act of developing enough resources for visitors while maintaining the integrity of the countryside is a delicate issue. All in all, plenty of positive things are fueling Belizeans' hopes. The government recently expanded the acreage of the Cockscomb Basin Jaguar Preserve from 3,600 acres to a whopping 102,000 with a snap of its fingers. If positive conservation measures prove economically successful, irreplaceable tropical forests may have a chance for survival; Belize, and all its inhabitants (human and otherwise), will be a lot happier.

BASICS

VISITOR INFORMATION **Belize Tourist Board.** *415 7th Ave., New York, NY 10001, tel. 800/624–0686, 212/268–8798.*

Belize Tourism Industry Association. *99 Albert St., Belize City, tel. 02/75–717.*

➤ **TRAVEL AGENCIES** • A growing number of operators offer a wide array of tours into Belize. Some are geared to adventure travel and off-the-beaten-track itineraries. Try **Best of Belize** (Box 1266, Point Reyes, CA 94956, tel. 415/663–8028), which specializes in diving and jungle ranch tours. **Green Tortoise Adventure Travel** (Box 24459, San Francisco, CA 94124, tel. 415/821–0803) will tour you around on comfy converted buses with some camping thrown in. **Tropical Travel** (720 Worthshire, Houston, TX 77008, tel. 800/451–8017) specializes in diving trips.

➤ **WORK AND STUDY ABROAD** • Several conservation organizations and nature preserves welcome volunteers and research assistants. There aren't any organized study programs with these groups, so you need to make your own contacts and set it up yourself: **The Belize Audubon Society** (27/29 Regent St., Belize City, tel. 08/77–369), **The Belize Zoo** (c/o Sharon Matola, Box 474, Belize City), and **The Programme for Belize** (1 King St., Belize City, tel. 02/75–616). **The Belize Center for Environmental Studies** (Box 666, 55 Eve St., Belize City, tel. 02/45–545) also publishes a bi-monthly newsletter and the *Center Environmental Quarterly.*

In the United States, contact **The World Wide Fund for Nature** (1250 24th St. NW, Washington, DC 20037, tel. 202/293–4800), which supports a number of projects in Belize. **The Hol Chan Marine Reserve** (San Pedro, Ambergris Cay, tel. 02/2247) is a good contact for reef ecology work, and you might check with the **Smithsonian** in Washington, DC, which has a research station on Carrie Bow Cay.

Many universities have teams excavating ruins here in the summer, so check with the archaeology department at your university for possible connections. **Trent University** runs a summer research program. For more info contact Trent University, Dept. of Anthropology, Peterborough, ONT K9J 7B8, Canada, Attn: Jaime Awe. The program lasts for six weeks in the summer. You can also try **Southwest Texas State** at San Marcos, Attention: Jim Garber, Department of Anthropology.

WHEN TO GO Punta Gorda, in the south, is one of the wettest spots on earth, with an average rainfall of 160–190 inches per year. If you plan to visit near the end of the rainy season, in October–November, you may have difficulty reaching the southern part of the country when the dirt roads wash out and the bridges flood. Belize City has also been known to flood around October. Otherwise, as with the rest of Central America, the best time to visit is at the tail end of the rainy season (November–December), when the country is still green but you won't get deluged.

➤ **HOLIDAYS AND FESTIVALS** • Belizeans don't need much of an excuse to party and, when they do, you'll find food, drink, and Caribbean music with the obligatory Bob (Marley, of course, mon), reggae, punta rock, soca, calypso, and other rhythmic/raucous sounds. National holidays are punctuated by street parades, block parties, and jump-ups (huge street dances). Beware of Sundays, when the entire country virtually shuts down for the day. The main national celebrations are: March 9, Baron Bliss Day; May 24, Commonwealth Day; September 10, National Day or St. George's Cay Day; September 21, Independence Day; November 19, Garifuna Settlement Day.

Cool regional festivals are St. Joseph Day on March 19 and Holy Cross Day on May 3 in the village of San José Succotz, near San Ignacio. San Antonio, in the Toledo district, has a festival on January 17. San Antonio also recently revived a colorful traditional Mayan celebration that begins in late August and culminates in the feast of St. Luis around September 25. San Pedro Columbia has its festival at the end of June.

MAIL The Belize postal service is one of the quickest and most expensive in Central America. A postcard to the U.S. costs about 20¢, and a letter costs about 35¢. You can receive mail at the main post office in Belize City. Address it to Poste Restante, Belize City, Belize, C.A. They'll hold mail for three months, after which it's returned to sender. You can also receive mail at the American Express office in Belize City if you're a cardholder.

MONEY First things first: Compared to other Central American countries, Belize is *not* cheap. It has a good network of budget accommodations and restaurants, and public transportation won't cost you much, but many of the most spectacular sights and exciting adventures have high price tags. It's best to carry U.S. dollars in Belize; most other currencies will be changed first to U.S. dollars and then to Belize dollars, so you lose twice on the exchange. The Belize dollar is tied to the U.S. dollar at a fixed BZ $2 to U.S. $1 rate, and all banks charge a 2% commission on transactions. Many establishments will change U.S. traveler's checks, and almost anyone will take U.S. cash (some even prefer it). Traveler's checks are the best way to carry money. **Belize Bank** will cash AmEx traveler's checks at a BZ 1.98 rate. When prices are quoted in "dollars," make sure you are clear whether it's Belize or U.S. dollars. All prices in this book are in U.S. dollars. Due to inflation, real-life prices may be substantially higher than prices quoted in this book.

Visa cash advances are available at most banks; some charge up to $7.50 and some don't—it all depends on the bank's mood. Plastic is accepted in big resorts but is virtually useless in the budget market. The exception is the American Express card (office in Belize Global Travel, 41 Albert Street, Belize City, tel. 02/77–363), which gives you access to an incredible range of services.

PHONES BTL (Belize Telecommunications Limited) has offices in almost every village around the country where you can make direct or collect international calls. You can access a USA Direct operator from most phones in the country by dialing 555. The BTL office in Belize City has a USA Direct line as well as fax service. BTL offices are generally open daily 8–noon and 1–4. Dial 115 from any private phone to reach an international operator; some pay phones can also access the operator. The first two or three digits of phone numbers in this chapter are the district code, which you don't have to dial when you're calling within the district.

VISAS AND PASSPORTS All visitors to Belize must have a valid passport. No visas are required for citizens of the United States, Canada, and the United Kingdom. Citizens of Australia and New Zealand do need to get a visa. Nationals of certain other countries (check with an embassy for an up-to-date list), as well as those with one-way tickets, must obtain visitor's permits in advance. Maximum stay is 30 days, although it's fairly easy to extend your stay up to six months. Two immigration departments can help you out. One is in Belize City (115 Barrack Rd., tel. 02/77–237) and the other is in Belmopan (Half Moon Ave., tel. 08/22–423). The charge is $12.50 for each additional month.

Visitors rarely need to show proof of return tickets or sufficient funds, although those with a more alternative or scuzzy appearance may be harassed, as officialdom is impressed by a neat appearance. Technically, you need a return ticket and about $50 per day.

COMING AND GOING

➤ **BY PLANE** • Service has improved tremendously in the past few years, but flying directly into Belize City isn't necessarily the cheapest or easiest way to get there. Fares usually start at around $300 round-trip from U.S. hub cities for a 30-day return and go up from there, depending on your departure city. Those people lucky enough to live in or near the airline hubs of Miami, Houston, and New Orleans can get inexpensive and direct flights to Belize City. Airlines serving Belize are **American** (tel. 800/433–7300), **Continental** (tel. 800/525–0280), **Tan Sansa** (tel. 800/327–1225), and **Taca** (tel. 800/535–8780), Taca being the only carrier offering direct service from the west coast. Generally, fares from the United States to Belize City don't fluctuate much seasonally. The catch is that domestic fares within the United States and international fares from Europe, Australia, and Canada *can* be seasonal, so if you have to change planes, your ticket price might change. A practical option is to fly into Cancún, Mexico, and then bus it into Belize (*see below*) or connect with another flight into Belize City. **Tropic Air** (tel. 800/422–3435) has regular service from Cancún to Belize City for about $100. Travel agents also offer hundreds of charter flights and package deals into Cancún that can cut your costs immeasurably.

No direct flights leave from Canada, Europe, or Australia into Belize. From Europe, an option is **Iberia Airlines** (tel. 800/772–4642), which has a new hub in Miami where you can connect with certain major North and Central American carriers. Flights start at around $900 round-trip from Madrid to Miami. Iberia also has direct service from Madrid to Guatemala City for about $1,400 round-trip. **KLM** flies into Guatemala for about $1,600 round-trip. From Guatemala City, you can hook up with **Aerovias** (tel. 305/885–1775) to Belize City for about $125. (Call to make sure they're still flying.) Tropic Air and Taca fly from Guatemala City to Belize City for about $115. From Australia your best bet is to fly to Los Angeles and then into Central America from there. And, if you're thinking of doing one of those round-the-world fares, many carriers have stops in Mexico City or Guatemala City. Mexico City is another major hub city for connecting flights into Central America.

➤ **BY BUS** • Traveling by bus through Mexico into Belize is cheap but long and exhausting, and worth it only if you're really into checking out all of Mexico. It takes about two days from the Mexican border to Mexico City, another two days to the Belizean border, and then about four hours to Belize City. If you decide to reach

Belize through Cancún or are simply going through the Yucatán, you'll enter through the border town of Chetumal, Mexico. The trip from Cancún to Chetumal is about $15. **Batty Brothers Bus Service** (02/72–025) and **Venus Bus Lines** (02/77–3390) offer service from Chetumal into northern Belize and Belize City for $5. If you're entering Belize on its western border, **Pinitas** buses depart from Santa Elena (at the Hotel San Juan) in northern Guatemala to Belize City daily at 5 AM. The bus connects with a Novelo bus at the border. The whole trip costs about $10 and takes seven hours. Buses also depart from the market in Benque Viejo del Carmen (the Belize border town) for other parts of Belize including San Ignacio and Belmopan.

➢ **BY BOAT** • You can travel between Belize and Guatemala by ferry along the Caribbean coast. Ferries run between the southern town of Punta Gorda and Livingston and Puerto Barrios in Guatemala on Tuesdays and Fridays at 2 PM. The trip costs about $6 and takes 2½ hours. See Punta Gorda, *below*, for info on buying tickets.

➢ **BY CAR** • If you're interested in driving to Belize, check out **Crystal Car Rental** (1½ mile Northern Highway, Belize City, tel. 02/52–321) for their Houston to Belize City driveaway deal. They sometimes need people to drive the cars they buy in Houston down to Belize. Crystal delivers the car to you in Houston and you're given two weeks to get through Mexico. If you're thinking of driving your own car, make sure that you (and the car) can take a beating—some roads are unpaved horrors and you'll run into the gnarly tangle of bureaucracy often. Most U.S. car rental companies won't let you drive their cars past the Mexican border. To rent a car in Mexico, you need to have a credit card and deal with all sorts of restrictions. You also have to get separate car insurance for Mexico (that's sold at the border) and for Belize. **Belinsco** (21 Regent St., Belize City, tel. 02/77–025) provides car insurance in Belize. Customs in Belize will make you prove you're not importing the car you're driving. Depending on how suspicious they are, they might ask for a return ticket or other proof that you're not going to stay long. The best patch of road is from Cancún to Chetumal; it's flat and fast.

GETTING AROUND

➢ **BY BUS** • The bus system is efficient and cheap. All bus companies are privately owned and run their own specific routes (*see* Belize City, *below*). The comfort factor can run the gamut from plush old touring types in the north to burly, skanky schoolbuses in the south. You have access to all the big cities and even some of the national reserves by bus, but more remote jungles and forests might present a problem.

➢ **BY BIKE** • Much of the country is fairly flat, and the coastal roads all the way from Corozal in the north to Punta Gorda in the south have very few hills. A touring bike can easily haul you around the north and west, but if you want to head off the main highways or travel south of Belize City inland, you'll need a mountain bike to handle the rough dirt roads. You can rent bikes in San Ignacio, Punta Gorda, or the Cayes. **Red Rooster** (tel. 092/30–16), in San Ignacio, rents mountain bikes to explore the surrounding nature. Most bike rental places only allow you to ride their bikes in the immediate area. If you're interested in touring all of Belize by bike, bring your own, buy one, or ask the bike rental owners if you can work out a deal.

➢ **HITCHING** • Hitching in Belize is often a crapshoot, but sometimes it's the only option. In a country with a population of about 200,000, the traffic often trickles down to barely one car an hour. In the south, where bus service is sparse, hitching is common and most anyone who passes will give you a ride. Ask the driver if you owe any money, because more often than not the vehicle that picks you up is some sort of bus. As always, women alone should use their heads and avoid rides with carloads of men or anyone scary-looking.

➢ **BY CAR** • Cars are great for getting around the difficult parts of Belize, but renting one can ruin your budget. Many roads are unpaved, so try to rent a four-wheeldrive and be prepared to thrash it—they don't last long here. Expect to pay about $60 per day for a little Suzuki to $120 per day for a Ford Bronco. Belize City is the best place to rent a car; several car rental agencies are at the Goldson Airport. **Hertz** (2.5 Mile Western Highway, Belize City, tel. 02/32–981) has the best deal on Broncos at $70 per day.

WHERE TO SLEEP A large network of budget lodging runs throughout the country, but budget in Belize is not the same as budget in other parts of Central America. Basic rooms are about $5, and can be $10–$15. You'll usually average about $7.50 per night in clapboard or thatched lodging with shared baths. Most hotels add an extra 5% government tax on room rates. Bathrooms in Belize are all fitted with standard Motel 6-style toilets, unless you're out in the boonies. Even the cheapest dumps supply you with toilet paper, clean sheets, a fan, and sometimes a towel and soap.

Camping in Belize is sometimes heavily restricted, but when possible it's a great way to beat hotel prices. Many reserves have camping facilities, and people will often let you camp on their land if you ask nicely. Especially in the rainy season, mosquitos and other biting insects can land a huge bummer on your camping expedition.

FOOD Belize has never been lauded as a culinary paradise, but it's possible to get a damn good meal here if you're adventurous. The staple diet consists of beans and rice either stewed, fried, white, yellow, plain, or cooked in coconut milk. Chicken, beef, and fish make up the remaining staples. Vegetables are consistently at the bottom of the list. Grouper, snapper, barracuda, and lots of other creatures are served at cheap prices. Conch fritters and conch soup are specialties, and when lobster season (July 15–March 15) rolls around, everyone goes nuts.

You can pick mangoes up off the ground or buy bunches of bananas for 50¢. Papaya, pineapple, and watermelon are in good supply, and if you get a chance to try soursap, jump on it. Along the coast, you could eat for days just by climbing coconut trees. Coconut milk is often used in cooking, and the meat will put to shame anything you could buy at Safeway. Fruit-o-Plenty, a health-food store in the Cayo district, is now producing its own yogurt and granola, which is becoming widely available all over the country.

Chinese restaurants are scattered all over Belize and *comedores* (snack shops) are good places to get cheap eats. The local beer is called Belikin, and it's actually quite savory and cheap (a buck a beer). Rum is served up with a plethora of mixers: Coke, coconut juice, condensed milk, and even seaweed and sugar. Several brands of rum are available, from the cheap "Cane Juice" to the smooth "Caribbean."

All regional capitals now have water-treatment plants, making tap water in almost all of Belize drinkable. Most restaurants are fairly responsible about water purification. If you're nervous about getting sick, bring purification tablets because it's almost impossible to buy bottled water—and if you ask for it, you'll be served tap water in a bottle anyway. The exception is in Placencia and the Cayes, where rainwater is used as drinking water and tap water is unsafe. Here, bottled water is readily available.

➤ **TIPPING** • Belize is very laid-back about the whole tipping thing, so it really depends on your particular experience in a restaurant. If you want to be generous, leave as much money as you want; there are no percentages to follow. Some establishments may get offended if you don't tip, but it's hard to tell. If you're unsure, check out the other patrons and follow their example. Don't tip cabs.

OUTDOOR ACTIVITIES Belize *is* outdoor activities. From diving and snorkeling on the barrier reef to canoeing and tubing down inland rivers to trekking in the jungle, outdoor activities will dominate your stay in Belize. Anyone with a boat or car offers tours into the jungle or out to the reef, so no matter where you base yourself, you'll have a whole slew of trips to choose from. (Check around before forking over money.) One reason for high-priced outdoor trips are the incredibly expensive gas prices. One U.S. gallon costs $2.50, and often the heavy vehicles needed to navigate the crappy roads get very bad mileage. **Ian Anderson's Adventurous Belize** (c/o Glenthorne Manor,

27 Barrack Rd., Belize City, tel. 02/44–212) offers a wide array of jungle adventures, from soft-core day hikes to hard-core jungle treks in the Maya Mountains. Ian will tailor your trip to your specific interests, budget, time limitations, and skill level. **Caye Caulker** is the best and cheapest spot in the country to snorkel. For as little as $8 per day, you can snorkel the stunning reef, taking your pick between a huge number of experienced boat operators. *See* Caye Caulker, *below,* for all the details. **Ambergris Caye** is the prime spot to go diving, with dive shops and dive operators literally everywhere. Certification courses cost around $300, and the average two-tank dive and one day on the reef costs about $40. *See* Ambergris Caye, *below,* for recommended operators.

Belize City

Most descriptions of Belize City reflect a "love it or hate it" attitude. Aldous Huxley was not impressed, saying "If the world had any ends, then British Honduras would surely be one of them." Take this with a grain of salt, just as you would the quote by 19th-century Brit Richard Davies, who said Belize City "was one of the prettiest ports at which we touched." Today, struggling to maintain its colorful heritage while coping with the rapid advance of urban decay and strife, Belize City is a thriving, pulsating Caribbean capital. The streets bustle and rock with the sounds of soca and reggae while Belizeans go about their business, shuffling through the narrow, dusty maze of congested corridors. Dilapidated wooden homes on stilts hug the curb, and the canals have become a dumping ground for all kinds of human refuse. Rumor has it that Belize City, once a huge swamp, is built on a foundation of wood chips, loose coral, and rum bottles that were used to fill in the muck. Street vendors hawk their wares along the busy thoroughfare, while in other sections of the city, the sea laps the shoreline near peaceful tree-lined avenues. Everyone in the country comes to Belize City at some point, whether for mechanical parts, beauty supplies, or government business. As the most populated spot in Belize, you're guaranteed to meet all kinds of locals, travelers, adventurers, expatriate gringos, and the stray outlaw or two if you stick around for a while. Belize has a long history of piracy and debauchery, attracting rugged individualists, unorthodox entrepreneurs, and the disenfranchised.

British lumberjacks (Baymen) settled with their slaves in Belize City during the 17th and 18th centuries. They hung out on the breezy coast at the mouth of the Belize river so they could float logs, cut from the interior, down to town. Belize was generally seen as a rowdy and chaotic party place, and England didn't take much notice of what its settlers did, treating them like bastard children. Basically, anything went, and Brits who were averse to laws or government control came here to start a new life. Many of the expatriates in Belize today came because they were fed up with the inane bureaucracy in their homelands and were thirsty for freedom.

Belize grew as people migrated from the West Indies and the Mexican Yucatán Peninsula. It began to pull away from British rule in the early 20th century, and in 1981 it broke away completely, joining the British Commonwealth as a sovereign state. Belize City was all but destroyed in 1961, when Hurricane Hattie wreaked her terrible wrath and killed almost 300 people. (Hattieville, on the Western Highway, was constructed as a refuge settlement after the hurricane.) Anxious statesmen quickly made Belmopan the official capital, but Belize City remains the unofficial center of activity.

Belize City—like almost any urban area—has problems with poverty, drugs, and crime. Recently, Belize has been dealing with an abrupt rise in gang-related crime due to the advent of crack cocaine and Belize's "ideal" location as a stopover on the Colombia–United States drug run. A quick glance around town reveals clothing and paraphernalia identifying L.A.-based gangs like the Crips and the Bloods. Gang violence usually confines itself to internal quarrels and vendettas, and unless you get caught in the middle, gangs will remain peripheral to your Belize City experience.

Belize City

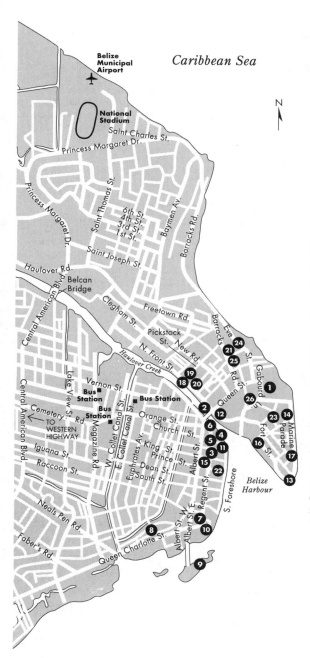

Caribbean Sea

Belize Harbour

BASICS

AMERICAN EXPRESS Belize Global Travel is the place to receive mail and cash AmEx traveler's checks. You can also book international and local flights here. *41 Albert St., tel. 02/77–363. Open weekdays 8–noon and 1–5.*

CHANGING MONEY Belize Bank, Barclay's, and **Bank of Nova Scotia** are all on Albert Street within two blocks of each other; they're open weekdays 8–1 and Fridays 3–6. The banks all give a rate of BZ $1.98 to U.S. $1. Cash advances from your credit card are available at all the banks, and they usually charge around $7. Barclay's generally doesn't charge for a cash advance, but you can never be sure. The black market gives you the full 2:1 rate, but the risk of having your money stolen in the process isn't worth the few extra cents.

CONSULATES The British High Commission and the Consulates of Costa Rica and Panamá have all moved to Belmopan. As of now, the rest are braving it out in Belize City. All are open weekday mornings.

Canada. *83 N. Front St., tel. 02/31–060. Open weekdays 9–1.*

United States. *29 Gabourel Lane, tel. 02/77–161. Open weekdays 8–noon and 1–4.*

Guatemala. This is the first Guatemalan consulate to open its doors in Belize. It's now possible to get visas here. *Mile 6.5 Northern Highway, Ladyville, tel. 02/52–612. Right before Raul's Rose Garden (the only brothel in the city) on the highway.*

Honduras. *91 N. Front St., tel. 02/45–889. Open weekdays 9–12.*

El Salvador. *120 New Rd., tel. 02/44–318. Open weekdays 9–12.*

Mexico. *20 North Park, tel. 02/30–193 or 02/30–194. Open weekdays 9–12:30.*

Attitude Is, By Far, Your Best Protection

If you believed every tale of murder, mayhem, and violent crime about Belize City, you'd never set a foot in town. Rumors about the city being hellishly dangerous are partly true, but no more or less so than any other metropolis keeping up with the times. Petty crimes like mugging and pickpocketing are your main worry. These days, hustlers aren't the brilliant manipulators that the buccaneers and pirates once were, but merely pathetic irritants—kind of like mosquitoes. You can have an awesome time with no hassles at all as long as you use common-sense precautions. If it looks like you're loaded with goodies that others want, you may be mugged. Leave all the glittering jewels at home, keep expensive camera equipment way out of sight, and carry your moolah underneath your clothes. Large purses or money belts can be snatched, sliced off, or pickpocketed. At night, it's safer to party it up in the main touristed areas; catch a cab home if you're roaming the skanky parts or if it gets really late. Attitude is, by far, your best protection. Obvious fear and naiveté are magnets for trouble. Be friendly, act streetwise, and keep your cool when hassled or approached. Street people may try to sell you drugs; be careful because tourists get suckered all the time. Also, if you're caught with one joint, the fine is $500.

IMMIGRATION The immigration office will extend visas in monthly increments for $12.50 per month. If you have time to cross the border and come back, you can avoid the charge—entering the country is free. *115 Barrack Rd., above the hardware store, tel. 02/77–273. Open weekdays 8:30–11:30 and 1–3:30.*

EMERGENCIES Dial 90 for **fire** and **ambulance,** 02/44–646 for **Crimestoppers,** and 02/72–222 for **police.** The **Belize City Hospital** (Eve St. at Craig St., tel. 02/77–251) has a fairly comprehensive treatment center. Many Belizeans, however, go to Mexico and the United States for treatment of serious problems.

MAIL The **main post office** (in the Paslow Building, on the corner of Queen and North Front streets) is open Monday–Thursday 8–5, and Friday 8–4:30. Poste restante is on the first floor. The **parcel post office,** for mailing packages, is right next door. **DHL** courier service (38 New Road) is open weekdays 8–noon.

PHONES Make long-distance and local calls, send a fax, or use the AT&T USA Direct lines at **BTL.** Dial 115 at any of the several BTL pay phones around town to try to access the international operator. *1 Church St., tel. 02/77–085. Open daily 8 AM– 9 PM.*

VISITOR INFORMATION Belize Tourist Board has all sorts of useful info like bus timetables, hotel guides, and city maps. *83 N. Front St., Box 325, tel. 02/77–213. Open weekdays 8–noon and 1–5.*

Belize Tourism Industry Association is the place to go for info on accommodations around the country. *99 Albert St., tel. 02/75–117. Open weekdays 8–noon and 1–5.*

Visit the **Belize Audubon Society** to book accommodations in the national park cooperatives. You can also get tons of info on all the national parks. *29 Regent St., tel. 02/77–369. Open weekdays 8–noon and 1–5.*

COMING AND GOING

BY PLANE The **Municipal Airport** handles domestic flights. **Phillip S.W. Goldson International** is actually in Ladyville, about 15 minutes away. The Goldson airport is quite pleasant, with a new terminal and a cute bar with a veranda, so you can get tipsy and watch the planes soar into the sky. Inside, you'll also find a **Belize Bank,** open daily 8–11 and noon–4. When leaving the country, be prepared to pay a $10 departure tax. For a complete schedule of domestic flights, contact the individual national airlines. **Maya Airways** (6 Fort St., tel. 02/72–312) has the most comprehensive flight schedule for the entire country. **Tropic Air** (tel. 02/45–671) mainly serves the Cayes, but it also has limited service inland. **Cari-Bee** (tel. 02/44–253), **Island Air** (tel. 02/31–140), **Javier's Flying Service** (tel. 02/45–332), and **Su-Bec Air** (tel. 02/44–027) serve the Cayes.

➤ **AIRPORT TRANSPORT** • It's fairly easy to get into the city from the international airport on the $1 shuttle (hourly service 6:10–6:10). From the airport, the shuttle will drop you at the Belcan Bridge (west of the Swing Bridge), where you can hop on a taxi. This works out much cheaper than a taxi from the airport, which will set you back $15. Shuttles also run from Belize City to the airport; the first leaves from the Belcan Bridge at 5:30 AM and the last at 5:30 PM. If you fly into the Municipal Airport, your only transport option into town is a $2.50 taxi.

BY CAR Hertz (2.5 Mile Western Highway, tel. 02/32–981) has the best deal on Broncos at $70 per day. **Crystal Auto Rental** (1.5 Mile Northern Highway., tel. 02/31–600) is the rent-a-wreck of Belize, where you can get 4x4s for $75 per day. The Goldson Airport has several car rental offices, including **Avis, National,** and **Budget,** which all charge about $60 per day.

BY BUS All four bus companies below have terminals in the same general area (called Mesopotamia) around the Collet Canal on the south side. This is a dicey part of town at night, so keep on your toes. You can get comprehensive bus schedules at the Belize Tourist Board (*see* Visitor Information, *above*). Depending on the route, especially on the infrequent ones going south, buses fill up fast. Seats are assigned; buy tickets in advance at the station.

Batty Brothers (15 Mosul St., tel. 02/72–025) serves the north to Chetumal and the west to Benque Viejo. Buses head north to Orange Walk (2 hours, $2.50), Corozal (3 hours, $4), Burrell Boom (1 hour, 75¢), and other towns nine times daily 4 AM–11 AM. Buses head west to Belmopan (1 hour, $1.50), San Ignacio (3½ hours, $2), Benque Viejo del Carmen (4 hours, $2), and other towns six times daily 6 AM–10:15 AM. Buses to Melchor de Mencos (Guatemala), just across the border from Benque Viejo del Carmen, leave at 6 AM, 6:45 AM, and 10:15 AM ($2.50).

Novelo's (West Collet Canal St., tel. 02/77–372) serves the west. Buses head to the Belize Zoo (1 hour, $1), Belmopan (1½ hours, $1.50), San Ignacio (3½ hours, $2), and Benque Viejo del Carmen (3½ hours, $2), Monday–Saturday 11–7.

Venus (Magazine Rd., tel. 02/77–390) serves the north. Buses leave 11:30–5:30 for Chetumal (4 hours, $5), Corozal (3 hours, $4), Orange Walk (2 hours, $2.50), Burrell Boom (1 hour, $1), and Sarteneja (4½ hours, $5).

Z-Line (Magazine Rd., tel. 02/73–937) serves the south. Buses head to Dangriga (4 hours, $5), Punta Gorda (11 hours, $10), Independence (6 hours, $8.50), and other towns, Monday–Saturday, five times a day, 8–4.

BY BOAT Boats leave daily for the Cayes from the dock at the Bellevue Hotel, from the dock south of the Swing Bridge, and from the A&R Texaco station, west of the Swing Bridge. (For times and rates, *see* The Cayes, *below*.)

HITCHING To hitch west, get a bit out of town (at least past the cemetery) on the Western Highway; if you're hitching north, head to the Northern Highway. If you're thumbing it to the south, it's easiest to take a bus to Belmopan and then head south on the Hummingbird Highway, since traffic on the coastal road is pretty scarce.

GETTING AROUND

Belize City is basically cut in half by **Haulover Creek**. The **Swing Bridge** across the creek marks the center of town. The **south side** (along Regent and Albert streets) is the commercial center, with all the banks, supermarkets, and stores within easy walking distance. On the **north side** (along Queen Street) you'll find the post office, the police station, and several stores that sell useful doohickies like auto parts. The north side, toward the coast, is also the exclusive side of town, with expensive hotels and surviving colonial buildings. The narrow streets throughout town are sans sidewalks, chaotic, and always jammed with kazillions of cars. Pedestrians beware: Drivers rarely use their horns so you'll need to rely on other warning signs to stay alive. Squealing tires are always a hint.

Belize City has no urban buses, but it's small enough to walk everywhere. In fact, the safe part of the city is very much like a small town—on the south side, east of West Canal Street, you're secure most of the time. The spots to really watch out for are on the north side in the alleys behind the Majestic Theater, as well as along North Front Street. The further west you go, especially on the south side, the more dodgy and derelict it gets. **Taxis** are a good option if you want to get around the outer parts of the city and to the bus terminals. Prices are fixed around town at $1.50 per ride plus $1 for each extra person. If you want to go further, make sure to agree on a price beforehand. You can find taxis at the two airports, the bus terminals, Central Park, and the Cinderella Taxi Park on Freetown Road. Taxis are recognizable by their green license plates.

WHERE TO SLEEP

Your experience in this city depends heavily on where you stay. If you decide to cheap out on a room that isn't secure, you may wind up losing much of what you've got anyway. The few accommodations surrounding the bus stations are not recommended as the neighborhood is skanky and dangerous. In general, though rates are higher here than in other parts of the country, Belize City does offer some good values—and you'll be much safer and happier if you take a room on the east side of the city. Some of the expensive chain hotels (The Radisson Fort George and The Holiday Inn Villa) are up near the point on the north side. With Belize turning into *the* tourist destination for the moneyed crowd, the Biltmore and Ramada Inn have recently opened overpriced monstrosities on opposite ends of town. The only thing about them that matters to you, dear backpacker, is the hotels' bars and happy hours, where you can get average-priced drinks and cheap snacks.

In the under $15 price range, the listed hotels are either okay but in a questionable neighborhood or run-down and in a better neighborhood. The under $20 range will get you the best value for your money with clean, safe accommodations, some of which are even charming. Although North Front Street isn't safe, west of the gas station on North Front Street is a budget-hotel ghetto popular with backpackers. **Dims Mira Río** (59 N. Front St., tel. 02/44–970) is right on the river with doubles for $12.50; the **Bon Aventure** (122 N. Front St., tel. 02/44–134) is across the street with $15 doubles. The Big Apple disco, next to these hotels, can get way out of hand on weekends.

➤ **UNDER $15 • Marin's Travelodge.** This run-down lodge used to be popular when the rooms were upstairs. It's still one of the cheapest places in town ($8 doubles), and it's in a fairly decent neighborhood, but the downstairs setup is dark 'n' dingy like a dungeon. *6 Craig St., tel. 02/45–166. 7 rooms, none with bath.*

North Front Street Guest House. This is the most popular of the North Front Street gang. It's a magnet for backpackers, and it fills up quickly. Rooms are clean, and the shared bath is average. Doubles are $12.50. You can unwind and schmooze with other travelers in the small sitting room. The street is a little dodgy, but since the building is secure, you should escape unscathed. *124 N. Front St., tel. 02/77–595. 8 rooms, none with bath.*

➤ **UNDER $20 • Eyre Street Guest House.** This restored colonial mansion sits in a quiet residential neighborhood. The rooms themselves are budget-style, but the sitting room and veranda have colonial character and warmth that make this place feel like, yes, home. Doubles go for $18. And, for all you stargazers, go touch the door on room 11—it comes from the old Mona Lisa Hotel, where the crew of the film *The Mosquito Coast* stayed when they were in Belize. Rumor has it that Harrison Ford was seen leaning against number 11 (oooh, ahhh). *7 Eyre St., tel. 02/77–724. On the north side, off N. Front St. toward the coast. 6 rooms, some with bath. Luggage storage.*

Freddie's Guest House. Freddie's only has three rooms, but every last one of them is immaculate. The surrounding residential neighborhood is quiet and super-safe. Doubles go for $19. Mrs. Griffith, the proprietor, is the closest thing to a mother away from home; this keeps her loyal guests flocking back. It's often full, so ring ahead. *36 Eve St., on the north side past the hospital, tel. 02/44–396. Luggage storage.*

Seaside Guest House. The Seaside is, hands down, the most popular budget spot in Belize City. True to its name, you can actually see the sea, and the rooms are clean, safe, and comfortable. The management is friendly and makes a valiant effort to keep abreast of the budget travel situation all over the country. Phillip, the owner, runs the Gales Point Project (*see* Near Belize City, *below*) so you can pick his brain for all you need to know. It's no surprise that Seaside is often full, so call ahead. Doubles are $18, but a space in the seven-bed dormitory is only $8. *3 Prince St., on the south side, near the sea, tel. 02/78–339.*

➢ **UNDER $40** • **Glenthorne Manor.** For a touch of luxury and a Caribbean ambience, the Glenthorne is it. Each of the eight rooms has its own unique look, replete with billowing mosquito nets. A $35 double includes one of the tastiest authentic Belizean breakfasts anywhere, starring freshly brewed coffee (you'll understand the importance of this after a few weeks of Nescafe). The spacious sitting room has a TV and a piano, and the veranda is a romantic spot for afternoon tea. Winnil Grant Borg, the gentle and helpful proprietor, looks after her place with care. The upstairs lounge has a kitchen for guest use. *27 Barrack Rd., tel. 02/44–212. Laundry, luggage storage.*

Mom's Triangle Inn. Mom's has been a U.S. family favorite for years. Rooms are spacious and some even have air-conditioning. The lively sitting room has games, toys, animals, and a TV. Doubles are $30. If you're dying to do some business while in Belize, they have a computer and typewriter for guest use. The restaurant downstairs, at one time a big expatriate hangout, serves Belizean food. *11 Handyside St., tel. 02/45–523. Laundry.*

FOOD

The seafood here is all fresh and mostly excellent—Belizean conch soup and conch fritters are a delicacy when prepared right. To get your taste buds hopping, feast on popular snacks such as *garnaches* (corn tortillas covered with beans, cheese, salsa, onions, and lettuce) and *panades* (the same, only deep-fried). They go for about 20¢ each, and can easily fill your belly for less than a buck. Lots of little stands also sell a greasy meal called "dollar chicken"—you get what you pay for.

Belize City (all of Belize for that matter) has been inundated with Chinese restaurants. Most are quite good, with large menus consisting of fried rice, egg fu yung, chop suey, chow mein, and various special dishes. Belize is also one of the few places left in the entire world where you can't find one single U.S. chain restaurant (even McDonald's has yet to rear its ugly head). Belize City does, however, have its own answer to burgers made quick. **HL's Burgers,** which are everywhere (one's on Albert Street next to Belize Global Travel), serves up a mean, spicy burger for about $1.

For cheap burgers, sandwiches, and snacks, try **Bluebirds** (35 Albert St., tel. 02/73–918). **Scoops Ice Cream** (on the corner of Eve St. and Gaol Lane, tel. 02/44–699) serves up homemade ice cream. **Kee's Bakery** (53 Queen St.) is where the masses go to get excellent French and whole-wheat bread. **Albert Street** is a snack mecca—peanuts, corn, and banana vendors line the sidewalk, **Brodies** and **Ro-Mac's** (the local supermarkets) have the standards, and the **market** at the Swing Bridge has a wide selection of fruits.

➢ **UNDER $5** • **Chon Sans II.** Once you get past the sleazy exterior littered with loitering crackheads and ram your way through the roughish bar, you'll find one of the best Chinese restaurants in town. The "special" soup ($3.50) has all sorts of special ingredients, or go for a lineup of rice, chop suey, egg rolls, and various meat dishes ($4.50). The chicken is the best around, and you get a quarter of a chicken with fries for $2. If the neighborhood really bothers you, grab some take-out. The original Chon Sans Palace is on Kelly Street near the Cinderella Taxi Park; it's more expensive but not as scummy as Chon Sans II. *184 N. Front St., tel. 02/30–709. Open daily 11–11.*

Dits Saloon. This consistently good Creole restaurant is often filled with locals—always the sign of a worthy eatery and watering hole. Chicken, beans, and rice are $2.50, and other meat dishes with beans and rice go for $3.50. The garnaches and panades are excellent and cheap (20¢). Dits also specializes in sinfully delicious cakes and pies for about 75¢ a slice. *50 King St., tel. 02/73–330.*

G G's Cafe. Local businesspeople and gringos flock here at lunchtime. The upscale atmosphere and cheerful patio make it hard to resist splurging. Delicious Belizean fare is $4–$5, and burgers and fries go for $3–$5. The seafood specials are excellent, but they can run up to $10. *2-B King St., tel. 02/74-378. Open Mon.-Sat. 11:30-2 and 5:30-9, Fri. and Sat. open until 10 PM.*

Goofy's. Goofy's serves Jamaican food, which is similar to Creole food (consisting mostly of chicken, fish, beans, and rice), but the spices are uniquely different. You'll get huge servings of pretty much everything for $3.50 a plate (try the jerk chicken or akee saltfish). Shrimp dishes are $4.50. *6 Douglas Jones St., tel. 02/32-480. Open daily 9:30-9.*

Macy's Restaurant. This spot is an old favorite with budget travelers. You can chow down on typical Creole fare for under $5. The chicken is juicy and fresh, but the fish can be skimpy. *18 Bishop St., tel. 02/73-419. Open Mon.-Sat. 11:30-10.*

➤ **UNDER $10 • The Grill.** The Grill's attempt at elegance flails, but the food is superb and worth the price. You can get a mean spinach fettucine Alfredo for $6, and the Creole shrimp is excellent at $9. Succulent meat and fish dishes ($5–$15) are prepared in a variety of local and international styles. Top the whole thing off with a slice of banana cheesecake ($2). *164 Newtown Barracks Rd., across from the Ramada, tel. 02/45-020.*

➤ **UNDER $15 • Four Fort Street.** If you have the dough and want to spend it on a gourmet meal, come here. This quaint old colonial mansion/restaurant (which also houses the way expensive Fort Street Guest House) just oozes ambience. Lanterns cast a romantic light, and fresh flowers grace every table. The menu is different every night, with various scrumptious dishes prepared international-style. From your first nibble on the delicious bread, you'll be bombarded by a slew of taste sensations. The meal itself will set you back $12–$15, but the drinks ($3–$6) are where you'll get killed if you're not careful. *4 Fort St., tel. 02/32-890. Open Mon.-Sat. 7 AM-2 PM and 6:30-10.*

WORTH SEEING

Belize City streets are filled with stunning examples of colonial architecture. Unfortunately, most old buildings don't have a chance unless someone intervenes and converts the space into a hotel or restaurant. Many buildings are run-down and dilapidated, but their beauty still shines through; stroll down any street and you'll get an eyeful. Other than the Swing Bridge, Belize City has no dominating sights, but it's speckled with little spots of interest. **Lords Ridge Cemetery** is the most spectacular cemetery in Belize. Straddling the Western Highway, with several majestic crosses smack in the center of the road, it's tough to miss on your way west.

THE SWING BRIDGE As with many Belizean names, the translation is literal: The Swing Bridge swings. Every day at 5:30 AM and 5:30 PM, four men hand-winch the bridge ¼ revolution so the bevy of waiting seacraft can enter Haulover Creek and head upstream to the Belize River. It's amusing to watch the police trying their best to stop traffic as intrepid pedestrians and bicyclists try to be the last one over. As traffic snarls up for blocks, people run and jump the ropes in last-ditch efforts to make it across. The bridge, made in Liverpool, England, opened in 1923; it's the only manually operated swing bridge left in the world. Before the Swing Bridge arrived, cattle were "hauled over" Haulover creek—get it?

SOUTH SIDE On the south side, **Regent Street** has the best surviving examples of colonial architecture. The **courthouse** is a cement reconstruction of the original wood structure which burned down in 1926. Next to the courthouse is the **Mona Lisa Hotel,** which was used as a set in Peter Weir's film *The Mosquito Coast* in 1985. The old **covered market** had survived storms, decay, and rot since 1820; in 1992, they demolished the decrepit, funky building and replaced it with a modern bummer. Check it out anyway, because markets are always the thriving center of a community. Further down Regent Street at Albert Street is **Saint John's Cathedral,** the oldest Anglican church in Central America (built in 1812). The kings of the Mosquito Coast were crowned in this red brick cathedral from 1815 to 1845. West of the Cathedral is the pathetic **Yarborough Cemetery.** Rumor has it that the stones are etched with exciting stories of derring-do, murder, and deceit, but you'd be hard-pressed to find any. Don't follow the cemetery too far west, because this is an especially dangerous part of town. At the end of Albert Street is **Bird's Isle,** a scuzzy little island with an open-air sports venue and dance hall. It's an okay place to party, but kind of depressing if you're looking for calm refuge from the hustle of the city. As you head around to Southern Foreshore, you'll pass the beautiful **government house,** where the governor lived when Belize was a British colony.

BLISS INSTITUTE All the way past the Bellevue Hotel sits the Bliss Institute, the cultural center of Belize. The center's namesake is the eccentric Baron Bliss, the country's greatest benefactor. The Baron was an avid fisherman who fell in love with Belize and the abundant sealife offshore without ever setting foot on the mainland. When he died, he left most of his estate to the people of Belize. The money has been used on tons of important projects such as roads, markets, and cultural centers. March 9, the day Baron Bliss bit the dust, is a national holiday. The institute houses the National Arts Council and hosts all sorts of plays, performances, concerts, and exhibits. On display in the entranceway are a few Mayan artifacts from Caracol. *2 Southern Foreshore, tel. 02/72–110. Open weekdays 8:30–noon and 2–8, Sat. 8:30–noon.*

NORTH SIDE The most important structure on this side of the bridge is the **Paslow Building** (built in 1842), where the post office lives. Up North Front Street and around the point is the **Fort George Lighthouse** and the **Baron Bliss Tomb,** an apt spot for the Baron's eternal rest, with a view of the sea and a peaceful breeze. As you head around the seafront on Marine Parade, you'll pass the hideous Radisson Fort George; right next door is the **Chateau Caribbean,** a beautiful colonial mansion which was once Belize's only private hospital. Many exquisite mansions (embassies and the like) dot the area. One of the most impressive is the **American Embassy** on Gabourel Lane.

CHEAP THRILLS

The unassuming colonial building on Regent Street (which houses **Burnaby's Coffeehouse and Gift Shop**) is the headquarters of the illustrious **Emory King** (*see* Hail the King, *below*). This local magnate has been in Belize forever (it seems), and he has a list of stories a mile long. Stop in at the gift shop to check out his books and travel guides on Belize. The Chamber of Commerce's **National Handicrafts Center** (on Fort St.) is fast becoming a clearinghouse for Belizean artists and craftspeople. You'll find Mayan slate carvings, baskets, jewelry, paintings, herbal medicine, and all sorts of knickknacks. It's open weekdays 8–noon and 1:30–5. The most awesome view of the city (all the way out to the Cayes) is from the roof of the **Radisson Fort George Hotel** (2 Marine Parade). Head to the park next to the Chateau Caribbean on Marine Parade if you want to mellow out.

AFTER DARK

Nightlife in Belize City is a blast. Plenty of dive bars give you the opportunity to meet hard-drinking Belizeans and share excellent local Belikin beer. **Guinness** has a brewery here, so their beer is cheap everywhere. The big hotels sport expensive air-conditioned bars and discos: **The Villa** has a cool view, and the **Biltmore** has karaoke Thursday–Sunday. Belize has a thriving music scene, where soca, reggae, and punta rock rule. Check out Santino's Messengers, a favorite local band and one of the best—look for flyers, because they often play at outdoor parties, festivals, and clubs. Also keep your eyes peeled for The Earthquake Band, Gilharry Seven, and Sounds Inc., which all have growing international reputations.

BARS **Four Fort Street.** If you're in the mood for a romantic rendezvous, head here. Hang out on the picturesque veranda and sip piña coladas ($6) and other mixed specialties. *4 Fort St. (duh).*

Lindbergh's Landing. This bar looks like it's not quite sure if this is Belize or Polynesia, but it's a favorite with Brits and gringos and often has an excellent sax player working the dance floor. *162A Newtown Barracks, across from the Ramada, tel. 02/30–890.*

CLUBS **Bellevue Hotel.** When the weekend bands start rocking, join in for some sweaty, exhilarating dancing from punta to disco. *5 Southern Foreshore, tel. 02/77–051.*

The Hard Rock Cafe. Unaffiliated with its international namesake, this is the spot where people flock to dance to recorded music in air-conditioned comfort. Weekends get jumping after 11 PM, when locals, soldiers, and tourists pack the place. Cool off with a beer ($1.25) on the third-floor roof. *35 Queen St. at Handyside St., tel. 02/32–041.*

Lumbayaad. Sip drinks on the river and play pool at this thatched-roof club that sits right on the water. Saturday afternoons are a great time to stop by; it gets rowdy at night on weekends. *On the way out of town on the Northern Highway; it's actually in a lumberyard.*

Hail the King

Reclining at an oak desk in the middle of his cluttered office, Emory King puffs on a stogie and recites his most recent quote: "Culture is what the poor people do. When they get money they quit doing it and sit around and grumble about **losing their culture." Mr. King is a literal gold mine of information, wry anecdotes, and witty conversation on every aspect of Belize. A local businessman, volunteer, author, and general guy-about-town, he came to Belize 40 years ago on a wing and a prayer. A budding journalist in Florida at the age of 22, he chucked it all for the life of a sailor and spent four years at sea before landing permanently in Belize.**

He's written several books on Belize, including travel guides, a collection of local stories, and his most recent history project: Belize 1798: The Road to Glory. He was even featured in the TV show "60 Minutes" as the local know-it-all in a story about Belize; he was quoted as saying "we're not fighters, we're lovers." With his big straw hat and easy grin, he's a beloved character, benefactor, and friend to many Belizeans. He helped the Mennonites establish their residence in Belize and brought the film crews of both The Mosquito Coast and the Dogs of War here. Of course, he was an extra in both films—standing at the bar with a shot of whiskey and a cigar. When I asked him about the possibility of meeting a local pirate or outlaw, he said, "My dear, you already have."

You can sometimes find Mr. King at Burnaby's Coffee House and Gift Shop (9 Regent St.). Or, for a pretty penny (about $50), you can arrange to have dinner at his charming country home. Call 02/77–453 for info.

Near Belize City

GALES POINT The tranquil fishing village of Gales Point stretches down a narrow, sandy peninsula which juts into the Southern Lagoon; it's accessible by bus on the coastal road from Belize City. Come here if all you want to do is schmooze with locals and hit the sack early. The lagoons and swamps surrounding the sleepy village have been targeted as a wildlife protection area, home to the largest manatee population in Central America and the main breeding ground for the extremely endangered hawkesbill turtle. Villagers have set up a cooperative as well as a private guest house. Gentle's Cool Spot has three simple, clean rooms ($10 double) right on the beach (it's impossible *not* to be on the beach here). Gales Point, in association with the Seaside Guest House in Belize City, has also set up a host-family network to keep tourism manageable. You can stay with a family in their home or at a cabana on the beach—either way, you'll eat and hang out with the family. Cost per night is about $5; make advance arrangements with the Seaside before arriving (tel. 02/78–339). The cooperative experience also includes boat tours of the surrounding lagoons and nearby inland caves. Cost is extra. Buses serve Gales Point on a Belize City–Dangriga loop on Monday, Wednesday, Friday, and Saturday. A bus leaves Belize City at 6 AM from the Poundyard Bridge, arriving in Gales Point at 8 am. It continues on to Dangriga, arriving at 10 am, returns at 2 pm, and hits Gales point at 4 pm, finally returning to Belize City at 6 pm. You can also reach Gales Point by boat through the lagoon for $13 per person.

THE BELIZE ZOO AND TROPICAL EDUCATION CENTER Most zoos, prisons that they are, are kind of depressing. The Belize Zoo, however, is a tiger of a different stripe. It came about after the shooting of a wildlife film, *Path of the Rain Gods,* left one Sharon Matola with a pack of semi-tame animals. They wouldn't have survived in the wild, so Sharon started this ambitious zoo. The land hasn't been truly cleared (they erected some fences and cut a few paths), so the animals are basically living in their natural habitats. All the animals are Belizean natives, and many are endangered species. You'll see the Baird's tapir, Belize's national animal (locally known as a "mountain cow"), the keel-billed toucan (the national bird), and peccaries (foul-smelling pig-like animals). The cats are all here: jaguar, ocelot, puma, red tiger, and jaguarundi. A whole mess of birds peacefully cohabitat with the felines; they include the scarlet macaw, the spectacled owl, and vultures.

The zoo has moved about a mile west of its old location, to Mile 30 on the Western Highway. Take any bus going west and ask the driver to drop you off. An education center and gift shop are at the entrance, but no water or any kind of drink is available. Bring water—you'll get hot and thirsty trudging around. Admission is $5. About a mile from the zoo on the Western Highway are **Monkey Bay** and **Parrot Hill Farm,** two privately owned enterprises hoping to join forces with the zoo to form an eco-educational triumvirate. The zoo houses the animals, Monkey Bay maintains the animals' habitats, and Parrot Hill explores organic farming techniques. You can take tours of Parrot Hill's innovative soil regeneration experiments and stay overnight at their new guesthouse. You can also hike the extensive trail system at Monkey Bay, where there is overnight camping. If you're not into the delicious organic food served at both these places or really need a beer, **JB's Restaurant and Bar** is right on the Western Highway next to Monkey Bay. This infamous British military hangout can get damn rowdy when rival battalions get loaded.

The Cayes

From the moment your boat speeds away from Belize City and out to sea, the air begins to change—and the attitude of the people with it. Belize is generally laid-back, but the slow and easy life on the Cayes is definitely an art form. And the water—how do you describe 10 different colors of turquoise and the subtle shades of indigo? How do you estimate depth when visibility can exceed 100 feet? Scattered along the reef and protected inside its wall are sand and mangrove islands called the Cayes. Sometimes merely a swath of sand with a few shady palms, the Cayes sport that perfect desert-isle ambience that people pay big bucks to experience. Dazzling arrays of colorful fish and tropical plants hang out among the coral drift, and the interdependent community along the reef and among the mangroves makes up one of the richest marine ecosystems on earth. Literally hundreds of these outcroppings lie scattered inside the reef, with only a small percentage of them inhabited. Not surprisingly, the reef and the Cayes are Belize's number-one tourist attraction.

This second-longest reef in the world was instrumental in shaping Belize's colonial history. The original Baymen loggers were joined in the 17th and 18th centuries by a motley assortment of Caribbean pirates—this was the age that Disneyland and Hollywood romanticized in tales of daring adventure on the mighty seas. The notorious Edward "Blackbeard" Treach, with his greasy black hair and deformed face, embodied the stereotype of the classic pirate. Blackbeard worked the Mosquito Coast, flying the dreaded Jolly Roger flag and striking fear into every orifice of even the surliest buccaneer. St. George's Cay became home base for many a "self-made man," developing a well-deserved reputation for decadence and debauchery. Spain and England had their big ol' battle for control of Belize right on this caye; today, it no longer bears any resemblance to the den of sin it once was. Now, it's a private residential caye with an expensive diving resort right over the water.

As your boat skims and bangs across the warm Caribbean waters, you can taste the salt on your lips and feel the heat beating mercilessly on your back.

A whole bunch of activities will keep you happy and out in the sun. Take your pick of swimming, diving, snorkeling, fishing, kayaking, windsurfing, sailing, and canoeing. Or just sit back, drink in hand, and do absolutely nothing while you bask in the glow of the tropical sun. Either way, time sort of ceases to exist, and you might find yourself sinking slowly into the mellow sand of island life.

Ambergris Caye

The general consensus among budget travelers is that Ambergris Caye is best avoided. In backpacker circles, it's often referred to as the Cancún of Belize. San Pedro, the "capital" city on the island, is the single most expensive spot in the country, where you'll pay double for almost everything. For diving, however, San Pedro is king; diving services and experienced guides abound. (Snorkelers will be much happier on Cay Caulker, where prices are lower and snorkeling better.)

San Pedro, an ex-fishing village, lies 59 kilometers (37 miles) northeast of Belize City, at the tip of a sandy peninsula separated from Mexico by a long trench dug by the Mayans. Only three streets wide and less than 1 kilometer long, it still retains a certain allure sadly lacking in most touristy resorts. It's so easy-going and friendly that shoes aren't a standard item around town, and many bars and restaurants have cool, sandy floors that are great for your tootsies. San Pedro is also blessed with wide beaches, where you can take a dip in the warm Caribbean or bake your hide in the fiery sun. This is the San Pedro that Madonna sang about. Remember?—"I fell in love with San Pedro . . . La Isla Bonita." San Pedroites practically treat it as their national

Coral Reef and Cayes

COROZAL
DISTRICT

Deer Caye

Ambergris
Caye

Bahía de Chetumal

Northern Hwy

Santana

San Pedro

HOL CHAN
MARINE RESERVE

**Marco
Gonzales**

Altun Ha

Cangrejo
Caye

Caye Caulker

Caribbean Sea

Hick's
Cayes

Caye Chapel

BELIZE

Ladyville

Montego Caye

St. George's
Caye

Crawl Caye

Three Corner Caye

Belize
City

Drowned Cayes

Belize
Harbour

Northern Caye

Water Caye

Goff's Caye

Douglas
Caye

Blackbird Caye

Lighthouse
Reef

Northern
Lagoon

Inner
or Main
Channel

Middle
Long
Caye

English
Caye

Turneffe
Islands

Calabash Caye

■ **Blue
Hole**

Southern
Lagoon

Bluefield Range

Alligator Caye

Deadman's
Cayes

Long Caye

Gales
Point

South Water Caye

Big Caye Bokel

HALF MOON
CAYE NATURE
RESERVE

Mullins
River

Colson Cayes

BARRIER REEF

Southern Long Caye

Mosquito Caye

Sandfly Cayes

Columbus Caye

Fly Range

Dangriga

Cross Caye

Silk Grass

Coco Plum
Caye

Man-of-War Caye

Hopkins

Sittee Point

Twin Cayes

Glover's
Reef

All Pines

Northeast Caye

Bread &
Butter Caye

Wee Wee Caye

Norval Caye

Southwest Caye

0 ____ 10 miles

0 ____ 15 km

N

song, and you'll often find yourself humming the damn ditty as you stroll down the street.

The area around San Pedro was used by the Mayans as a trading center. Lobster fishing was still the main industry 10 years ago, when commerical tourism slowly filtered in and took over the economic burden. So much of the island is owned by and operated for North Americans that Ambergris Caye hardly seems Belizean. To escape things gringo, go north of San Pedro's center or head to the lagoon at the western edge of town. San Pedro's popularity with foreigners makes it the best spot in all of the Cayes to party. People rage all night along the beach and in the bars to the jumping sounds of punta rock, soca, and reggae. On Ambergris Caye, fun in the sun is the focus, with culture often left in the dust. For all intents and purposes, San Pedro is the only real town on the caye; to get out of town, ask around or hop on a bike or horse (*see* Outdoor Activities, *below*).

BASICS San Pedro has two banks. **Belize Bank** (open weekdays 8–1, also Fri. 3–6) and **The Atlantic** (open Mon., Tues., and Thurs. 8–noon and 1–3, Fri. 8–3, Sat. 8:30–noon) are both on Barrier Reef Drive in the center. You won't have any trouble cashing traveler's checks at most local establishments. **BTL** (open weekdays 8–noon and 1–4, Sat. 8–noon) is on Pescador Drive, at the far north end of town past the electricity plant. The **post office** (open weekdays 8–5) is on Buccaneer Street, around the corner from Belize Bank.

COMING AND GOING Until recently, the three streets in San Pedro were called simply Front, Middle, and Back streets. Then town officials decided to get fancy and name the streets. Front is now Barrier Reef Drive, Middle is Pescador, and Back is Angel Coral Street. Keep both names in your memory bank, because locals often use the simple obvious names. San Pedro itself is small, and all the budget hotels, restaurants, services, and even the airstrip are within easy walking distance. North and south of town, the luxury resorts and hotels stretch along the sandy coast.

➤ **BY BOAT** • From Belize City you have your choice of two regular boat services. *The Andrea* (tel. 026/62–578) costs $10 and leaves the dock at the Bellevue Hotel (5 Southern Foreshore) weekdays at 4 PM and Saturday at 1 PM. It returns Monday–Saturday from San Pedro at 7 AM. *The Thunderbolt Express* (tel. 026/62–217) leaves daily from the dock on the south side of the Swing Bridge around 10:30 AM, returning at 7 AM. The trip takes about 1½ hours.

➤ **BY PLANE** • Flights head for San Pedro from both the Phillip Goldson International Airport and the Municipal Airport in Belize City from 7 AM to about 4:30 PM. Flights on **Tropic Air** run about $20 one-way. **Maya** and **Island Air** both have services from Belize City for about the same price and from Cay Caulker for about $17. Maya also flies from San Pedro into Corozal on a semi-regular basis.

WHERE TO SLEEP As is often the case, the priceyness of a town is painfully reflected in the lodging. Some doubles in town go for $10, but the cheapo digs are often full (even in the low season), so resign yourself to spending more money than you want to. You can easily walk to all the inexpensive pads from the airstrip and docks.

➤ **UNDER $10** • **Vasquez Family Rooms.** This is more of a boardinghouse than a hotel, but if you're alone it's the best deal in town. The Vasquez family rents four single rooms for about $5 per night or $33 per week. Most of the patrons are extended-stay tourists. *Pescador Dr., center of town, tel. 026/23–05. Look for the ROOM FOR RENT sign across from the Sea Turtle Gift Shop.*

➤ **UNDER $15** • **Casa Blanca Hotel.** This family-run establishment on Pescador Street is a fantastic find. Expensive rooms are in the front, but four basic back rooms with shared bath go for the damn good price of $10 a double. All rooms are immaculate, and guests have access to the sitting room, refrigerator, laundry service, and fabulous hot water in the shower. The windows don't look out onto anything spectacular, but whaddaya want fer nothin? *North side of Pescador Dr., tel. 026/20–77. 7 rooms, some with bath. Laundry.*

Milos Hotel. This is *the* budget hotel in town, so it's often chock-full. All nine rooms are basic and clean with ceiling fans, and the shared bath has hot water. The balcony overlooks Barrier Reef Drive, so you can sit and harass British soldiers if you're feeling rambunctious—or just watch the parade of neon-clad Americans strolling through town. Doubles are $10. *Barrier Reef Dr., far north end, tel. 026/20–33. 9 rooms, none with bath.*

Rubis Hotel. The friendly, homey Rubis Hotel is an excellent deal if you manage to snag one of the four budget rooms with shared bath for $13. This is probably the only chance a budget traveler has to stay right on the beach in San Pedro. Rubis also has its own dock and you can book tours to the reef or even take live-aboard (sleep on the boat) trips. If you miss out on the budget rooms, the others are a step up in quality as well as cost. Doubles with private bath will set you back $26. *Barrier Reef Dr., far south end, tel. 026/20–63. 17 rooms, some with bath.*

FOOD Eating in San Pedro can suck big-time. Even the bad food is more expensive than good food anywhere else in the country. Sure, you can chow down on some excellent meals at the resorts, but only if you're willing to fork over bucks. Otherwise, you'll have to settle for mediocre food at high prices. Supermarkets are stocked with expensive imported cheese and canned goods, so a picnic is not the way to save. **Rocks** (Pescador Dr., middle of town) is the largest supermarket; several fruit stands also line Pescador. Locals recommend **Leny's** (near the airstrip) and **The Coffee Shop** (further south on the strip) for tasty, affordable meals. Weekend **barbecues** on Barrier Reef Drive at dusk are often the best way to fill up. For $3, you can get ¼ chicken, rice, beans, cole slaw, and a tortilla. For pricey but mouth-watering pizza ($5–$10) head to **Fido's Pizza,** on the beach on the north end of Barrier Reef Drive.

Ambergris Delight. This is (pretty much) the only place in San Pedro with typical Creole food at average prices. It's nothing to write home about, but considering what ambergris really means (whale bile), it's not as bad as it could be. Chicken, rice, and beans go for $3, fish is about $4, and salads are $3. The atmosphere here is less "here we are in paradise" and more down-to-earth. *North end of Pescador Dr. Open daily 11–2 and 6–10.*

Elvi's Kitchen. With cutesy island decor, a sandy floor, a live tree as the dining-room centerpiece, and speedy service, Elvi's is popular with the resort crowd. The food is excellent; if you stick to chicken with rice and beans or a burger and fries, you can keep the price under $5. If the seafood's too hard to resist, know that your check will soar to over $10. Try a Mexican *licuado* (blended fresh fruit drink) for $2, or just come in for dessert. The *most* excellent cherry cheesecake in the world goes for $3. *Pescador Dr., in the center of town. Open daily 11–2 and 5:30–10.*

Emerald Restaurant. Snork down on heaping lunch specials of fried rice, chop suey, egg rolls, and your choice of a main dish for about $3. Like every good Chinese restaurant, the Emerald always has takeout. *Barrier Reef Dr. Open daily 11–3 and 5:30–11. Takeout only 11–midnight.*

CHEAP THRILLS It's not for the squeamish or the vegetarian crowd, but the Wednesday night **chicken drop** is extremely popular with locals and tourists alike. It's a bizarre gambling game in which you put your money on circled numbers spread out on a piece of cardboard. As the game begins, a chicken is held over the board and an audience member is asked to blow on its butt. When the chicken eventually takes a dump on the board, the lucky number wins the pot (the winner is also responsible for clean-up duty). Monday is another special game night, featuring the **crab race.** Put down $5, pick a crab, and win $100 if it scuttles to the finish line first. The little crabs can actually haul ass—you'd be surprised. Both these happening games go on at the Pier Lounge in the Spindrift Hotel, in the middle of town on Barrier Reef Drive.

AFTER DARK San Pedro is the place to go if you're looking for a party. Unfortunately, the party often includes a whole lot of annoying tourists, as well as a healthy dose of extremely young, drunk, and out-of-control British soldiers. Live bands often play in many of the bars. Try the **Barrier Reef** (north end of Barrier Reef Dr.) for good reggae and punta rock; admission is $2.50 on live-music nights. **Big Daddy's** (on the beach behind the basketball court) is the only disco in town with special promotions like "Macho Night" and "Ladies Night." **Sandals** (far north end of Barrier Reef Dr., off in a corner near Paradise Village) has drinks at reasonable prices. This is a friendly dive where locals, soldiers, and even the occasional tourist come to drink and play a little pool. The bar in the **Spindrift** is a popular watering hole, and the **Purple Parrot** at Fido's dock is always bustling in the evenings. The **Tackle Box Bar** (end of the pier, past the Spindrift) is one of the most popular bars in town and often has free live music on the weekends. Unfortunately, the decor is incredibly creepy, with polished turtle shells, jaguar skins, and photos of buxom blondes littering the walls. The pool full of fish and turtles is popular with visitors but not so to animal lovers.

OUTDOOR ACTIVITIES

➤ **DIVING** • Diving on the reef could be one of the most spectacular experiences of your life. Dive shops in San Pedro are as plentiful as mosquitoes in a mangrove swamp. Most offer the basic package: two-tank dives for $35, not including equipment. Many also offer night diving and almost all have day and overnight trips to various reef spots, cayes, and the outer atolls. If you're interested in certification, you can get a full four-day PADI course starting at around $300. Referral courses (where you do the first half of a diving course at home in a pool and the second, open-water half here) start at $125 and resort courses (where you don't get certified and you can only dive with the person who instructs you) run $85–$125. Try **Coral Beach Dive Shop** (tel. 026/20–01) for an excellent deal—$300 for a certification course, $125 for a referral, and $85 for a resort course. Linda Carter (not Wonder Woman) at the **Tortuga Dive Shop** (tel. 026/28–04) comes highly recommended as a good instructor. Her four-day, open-water course goes for $350.

For experienced divers, live-aboard dive trips to the outer atolls are the way to go. This is where you'll get unspoiled and pristine conditions which are often sorely missed on the main reef, where much of the coral has been destroyed through years of use by inept snorkelers and irresponsible guides. Try the **Bottom Time Diveshop** (tel. 026/23–48) for info on the *Reef Roamer I & II* trips. **Coral Beach** also does live-aboard trips. Many locals offer dive trips that can be cheaper.

One More Reason You Paid $16 For This Book

The guys on the **Manta IV&V** *(tel. 026/21–30) want to offer travelers reading this book a special deal on dive trips and courses because they know what it's like to be a backpacker on a budget. They'll give you a 20% discount on instruction courses and 10% off regular trips—just tell 'em you read it here. They also offer readers a great deal on day trips and multi-day overnighters to Turneffe, Lighthouse, and the Blue Hole. A day trip to Turneffe will run $100 with the Berkeley Guides discount, and an overnighter to all three places will cost a little under $200. The Manta office is in the A-frame house behind Ramon's Village on the south side of San Pedro.*

➢ **HORSEBACK RIDING** • Horses are a cool way to get out of town and explore other parts of Ambergris Cay. **Isla Equestrian** (at the airstrip, tel. 026/28–95) will take you on beach rides, nature rides, sunset rides, and picnic packages. The going rate is $20 per hour or $65 for a ½-day trip.

➢ **SNORKELING** • Most snorkeling trips from San Pedro are a big fat ripoff, since Caulker does it for so much less. If you want to do it here, your first lesson is to stay far away from travel agencies and organized packages. The best option is seeking out local guys who have glass-bottom boats. They usually take people out for two to three hours at $8 per person. If you want to go further than the off-shore reef, it can go up to $13 per person. Unfortunately, much of the reef near San Pedro is extremely eroded—huge chunks have turned white (i.e. dead), and you may want to snorkel farther out to get an authentic feel for the sea. Check out **Badillos** (in the blue house next to Milo's on Barrier Reef Dr., tel. 026/22–64), where you can get a great captain and trip for $6. You can also rent equipment from the various resorts, snorkel right off their piers, and see a few fish skirt about.

Everywhere in Belize is laid-back, but the Cayes are laaaiiiid baaaaaack, mon.

➢ **SWIMMING** • Swimming is something you can do for absolutely free, and the added bonus is that San Pedro has wonderful, sandy beaches. The best beaches are at the south and north ends of town at the expensive resorts. Ramon's Village in the south and the Paradise Hotel in the north also have long docks with swimming enclosures and a spot to sunbathe. Ramon's even has a thatched roof over the deck in case you overdid it in the sun.

➢ **BIKES, SCOOTERS, AND GOLF CARTS** • For a change from water sports, jump on a mini-vehicle and zoom north or south to explore the wildlife, white-sand beaches, sea turtle nesting colony, and expensive resorts that line the coast. **Amigo Travel** (Barrier Reef Dr., tel. 026/21–80) rents bicycles for $3 per hour and $9 for the whole day. Scooters go for $8 per hour and $25 a day. Golf carts and ATVs are the preferred mode of transportation around town, and if you want to join in the fun, **Universal Travel** (Barrier Reef Dr., tel. 026/21–37) rents them for $13 per hour or $30 a day.

Caye Caulker

Signs dotting the sandy island streets on Cay Caulker reiterate the obvious—you'll find little else to do but Go SLOW and STOP. It's difficult to figure out exactly whom the signs are directed at, since the few motor vehicles in sight are golf carts. Cay Caulker has a more alternative atmosphere than San Pedro, and it has attempted to maintain some of its heritage as a Creole fishing village. Lobster fishing has always been the main source of income for most islanders, but dwindling lobster populations and rising tourist populations have prompted many a fisherman to moonlight in the travel trade. The island is full of affordable lodging, food, and budget tour operators. If you're a nondiver who would like to experience the reef's underwater wonderland, Cay Caulker is the spot. Almost everyone on the island has a boat for hire, and you can arrange inexpensive trips up and down the reef for snorkeling, camping, and general exploration of outlying cayes.

BASICS **Belize Bank** (open weekdays 8–noon and 1–2) has a branch on Back Street across from Center's Grocery. No sign marks the place; just look for the only building with air-conditioning. **BTL** (Front St., next to Emy's Grocery, tel. 022/21–68) is open weekdays 8–noon and 1–4, Saturday 8–noon. The **post office** (open daily 8–noon and 3–8) is on the south side in Celi's Supermarket. You can **wash your grungies** at the red house on the south side of Front Street; look for the laundry sign. They charge 20¢ apiece for underwear, 35¢ for shirts, et cetera. Important tidbit: It's almost impossible to get laundry done in San Pedro, so do it here if you're heading to Ambergris Caye.

COMING AND GOING Caye Caulker itself is almost 7 kilometers (4 miles) long, but the inhabited portion extends only a kilometer up the southern portion of the island to the cut (or the split), a channel formed when Hurricane Hattie sliced the island in half. Two main streets run through the island: Front Street and Back Street. No addresses exist, but everything is fairly obvious and easy to spot.

➤ **BY BOAT** • Boats leave regularly for Caye Caulker from the A&R Texaco station (North Front St., just west of the Swing Bridge in Belize City). Several boats do this run, and the cost hovers around $8 (don't fork over the cash until you actually land on the island). Most boats leave Belize City daily between 10 AM and noon, but you'll usually find someone who'll take you to Caye Caulker until 4 PM. Boats leave Caye Caulker around 6:30 AM. Many hotels on the island will book a trip back to Belize City for $5. If you want to get to San Pedro from Caye Caulker, you can catch either the *Andrea* (tel. 026/25–78) or *Thunderbolt Express* (tel. 026/22–17) on their way from Belize City. Call them to let them know you need a pick-up. The *Andrea* leaves Belize City at 4 PM, and the *Thunderbolt* leaves at 10:30 AM. Both stop at the dock on the back side of Caye Caulker.

➤ **BY PLANE** • The airfield, which was hotly contested (for potentially bringing in hordes of screaming tourists on screaming planes), has finally become a reality on Caye Caulker. The island is still sharply divided on the merits of this new construction. One thing is sure—noise never used to exist in these proportions. **Skybird** is a local operation that flies from Belize City for $25 from the international airport or $17 from the municipal airport. They'll fly you to San Pedro for $17. **Maya** and **Island Air** also have flights to Cay Caulker.

WHERE TO SLEEP Compared to San Pedro, Caye Caulker has no shortage of affordable rooms—at least 15 budget hotels dot the island. Keep in mind that prices fluctuate seasonally from as low as $1 to as high as $10. The cheapest digs on the island are mostly in the center of town, a bit off the beach. **Rivas** (tel. 022/21–27) is above the Aberdeen on Front Street, and **Mira Mar** (tel. 022/21–10) is right next to Rivas. Both have clean, basic rooms with shared bath and cold water for about $8 a double. If you're planning on sticking around for a while, you can rent houses that sleep up to four for about $300 per month. Try **M&N's Cabins** (near the soccer field, tel. 022/22–29) for a tidy place with hot water and fridge for $250–$300 per month. **Heredias House Rentals** (tel. 022/21–32) rents a variety of places on the beach and around town.

➤ **UNDER $10** • **Ignacios Huts.** This place is a great deal for two or more people. For $15, you score a hut on the beach at the south end of town. It's a little pseudo-resort. Of course, the rooms are simple, but all are right on the water, with private baths and a shady palm tree. *Walk south down the beach; it's the second-to-last place, tel. 022/22–12. 9 huts, all with bath.*

Sandy Lane Hotel. For only $8 a double, Sandy Lane offers clean, basic rooms where you can catch a glimpse of the sea from the balcony. Bathrooms (cold water only) are outside. The hotel is a little off Front Street, which keeps it quieter than comparable hotels right on the street. *In the center of town on the south side of the soccer field, tel. 022/21–17. 6 rooms, none with bath.*

Tom's Hotel. A backpacker favorite, this big white building, with a porch and veranda overlooking the water, offers basic rooms for $10–$13 a double. Sunbathe and swim off the dock or relax on the veranda and schmooze with fellow travelers. Guests also have access to the washer and dryer for $5 per load (there's a reason why it's called "dirt-cheap travel"). Charles Young operates highly recommended trips on his boat *Nikita*, which heads out from Tom's. *On the south end of town, on the beach past Celi's Supermarket, tel. 022/21–02. 23 rooms, some with bath.*

➤ **UNDER $25** • **Jimenez Huts.** The lush garden setting and bamboo huts give the Jimenez place a jungle feel. The adorable huts all have private baths with hot water. The only catch is that it's on the back (western) side of the island; when the wind dies down, the mosquitoes get awfully thick out here. Doubles go for $18–$20. *On the south back side past Edith's, tel. 02/22–175. 5 huts, all with bath.*

Marin's. Often full, the family-run Marin's is a favorite with travelers. Rooms encircle a colorful garden with shady palm trees, where you can hang a hammock for luxurious afternoon siestas. Doubles with shared bath go for $10–$13, or $20–$25 for doubles with a private bath, with hot water in both. Marin's also arranges snorkeling trips to the reef. *On the south side between Front and Back streets, tel. 02/22–110. 9 rooms, some with bath. Laundry.*

The Split Village. As the name implies, the Split Village is located at the far north end of the island at—you got it—the split. It's the best swimming spot on the island, which guarantees daytime parties all week long. The cabins themselves are a notch above basic, with private baths and hot water for $21 a double. *At the split, tel. 022/21–27. 8 rooms, all with bath.*

➤ **CAMPING** • **Vega's Far Inn.** The Vegas are extremely enthusiastic and their interest in their guests borders on doting, which is good since they have the only space for campers on the island. Pitch your tent for a whopping $6 per person. Their beachfront property is well-maintained, with plenty of shade and tight security. Doubles with shared bath in their tidy-but-pricey hotel are $21. *On the beach at the south side of town, tel. 022/21–42. 9 rooms, none with bath.*

FOOD Eating on Caye Caulker is a magnificent experience, especially if you've just come from Belize City. The seafood is some of the best in the country, and a lobster dinner that would cost you $14 in San Pedro is only about $9 on Caye Caulker. For some reason, food just seems to taste better out here—the fruit is juicier, the seafood more succulent, and even the rice and beans seem to be cooked with tastier spices. Many restaurants serve an excellent burrito with beans, salsa, vegetables, and your choice of chicken or lobster wrapped in a thick flour tortilla. You can fill up on these babies for $1–$2. Caye Caulker has tons of little pastry and ice cream shops filled with sumptuous goodies, and kids walk up and down the street selling tasty coconut bread.

➤ **UNDER $5** • **Glenda's.** Open only for breakfast and lunch, Glenda's serves up some of the best pastries on the island. Tostadas and burritos ($1–$2) are first-rate, as are the fresh orange, pineapple, and mango juices. *On the back side past Back St.; follow the signs. Open daily 7–10 and noon–3.*

I&I Cafe. Salvador Marin has opened up the closest thing to a vegetarian restaurant in Belize—try a yogurt, granola, and fruit plate for $3 with, yes, *brewed* coffee. Nachos (starting at $2) or Creole dinners and seafood (about $4) are also good. The I&I has a multi-level outdoor garden with trippy lights and cool swings in the main bar. *On the south side between Front and Back streets, across from the Tropical Paradise, tel. 022/22–06. Open daily 7–1 and 5:30–11.*

Marin's Restaurant. A cheap restaurant with super-duper food, Marin's even has a classy dining room and garden patio for that extra touch of elegance. Lobster dinners start at $7, and a lobster breakfast is a mere $3. Excellent seafood soups are around $3. *South side on Back St. across from Edith's, tel. 022/21–04. Open daily 8–2 and 5:30–10.*

Pinx Restaurant and Bar. Pinx is the only place on Cay Caulker with an open bar right on the beach. It's a treat to watch the full moon rising over the water while you eat dinner outside. When the wind picks up, however, your own hair will become an integral part of your meal. Try a plate of breakfast waffles for $3 or a veggie lunch plate with garnaches, panades, rice, beans, and slaw for only $2. Their seafood specialties are delicious and served in garlic, curry, or hot cajun spices for $8. *Front St., center of town on the beach. Open daily 7:30–midnight.*

➤ **UNDER $10 • The Sandbox.** This is one of those gringo-run, health-food kind of places that you begin to dream about after a month of rice and beans. Shrimp lasagna dripping with cheese and stuffed with spinach, along with garlic bread and salad topped with homemade dressing, goes for $7. Fresh juice and homemade banana cake with chocolate sauce and scoops of ice cream round out this dreamy menu. *Front St., on the north side on the way to the split, tel. 022/22–00. Open daily noon–10, closed 3–5 in the off season.*

AFTER DARK Nightlife on Caye Caulker is in a state of limbo at this point. The only disco on the island has been converted into a grocery store, and the traditional hang-out bar, The Reef, has been closed indefinitely. Many locals would prefer that Caulker return to its tranquil days as a fishing village, and shutting down bars seems to be their way of driving riff-raff off the caye. Suffice it to say that if you want to rage all night, you should head to San Pedro. If, however, a mellow evening on the beach with a cold beer and warm friends sounds good, then Caulker is the place to be. Right now, Pinx is where people come to enjoy music, conversation, and drinks. The I&I Cafe is also open late for drinks.

WORTH SEEING Gallery Hicaco. Stop in here to look at Belizean handicrafts and have a chat about reef conservation with the knowledgeable Ellen McRae. The gallery offers a variety of ecoconscious tours, slide shows, and lectures. Besides reef ecology tours, you can also go on a three-hour bird walk through mangrove and forest habitats for $8. Slide shows are $5 per person, and while you're there, take a look at Ellen's nature photography. *On the south side of Front St., tel. 022/21–78. Open daily 9–4.*

Sea-ing is Belizing. Check out nature photos by Jim Beveridge and slide shows on conservation and natural habitats. Admission is $4 per person for a good-sized group. *Behind the soccer field, tel. 022/21–89. Open daily 9–5.*

OUTDOOR ACTIVITIES No question about it, outdoor activities are the raison d'être in the Cayes. Slather on the sunblock so you don't get shade-bound by painful blisters, and you're ready to go. With the ozone the way it is (or is not), the sun is always stronger than you think, so a #6 sun block is about as useful as baby oil. Since Caye Caulker is geared toward the money-conscious traveler, most activities cost about half of what they would in San Pedro. **Kayaking** and **windsurfing** are slowly catching on; if you want to join in the fun, contact Gallery Hicaco, where windsurfing boards and double kayaks go for around $10 each per hour. To bike around the caye, try **Island Sun Gift Shop** (Back St., tel. 022/22–15), where you can rent a bike for $2 per hour or $8 for the day. It's open daily 9–noon and 1–6.

➤ **DIVING •** To arrange a trip on a live-aboard dive boat, contact **Dolphin Bay Travel** (Front St., tel. 022/22–14); it's open weekdays 8–noon and 1:30–5, weekends 8:30–noon. Caye Caulker has one of the largest underwater caverns in Belize, right underneath the caye itself. If you're interested in exploring this groovy submarine world, contact **Belize Diving Services** (behind the soccer field, tel. 022/21–43), where a two-tank dive will run $40 and a one-tank night dive is $30, equipment not included. Four-day certification classes are $325, and you can set up various expeditions with groups. **Frenchie's Diving Services** (north end of town behind Chocolate's Gift Shop, tel. 022/22–34) is a locally owned dive shop, where two dives at the main reef run $50, including equipment.

➤ **FISHING •** For a tranquil day on the clear, calm reef waters far from shore life, try a day of reef or flat fishing. Gaze upon 20-foot manta rays gliding just beneath the water, or catch barracuda, grouper, snapper, jimmyhan kingfish, and dozens of other smaller tropical fish on the reef. On the flats, you can land the bigger guys like tarpon, bonefish, and the rare prize marlin. **Rally Badillo** (tel. 022/21–90) will take a group of three out for six to seven hours of fishing for $100. Ask around town if you want to hitch a ride out with a local fisherman.

➤ **SNORKELING** • For a mere $8 per day, you can spend hour upon glorious hour exploring the barrier reef. If you've never been to the tropics before, you'll be wowed by the insane array of multicolored fish. The peacefulness of life beneath the waves is so spectacular that sometimes it takes a huge force of will to drag yourself out of the warm, womb-like water. The great thing is that snorkelers have almost as much opportunity to see what the reef has to offer as divers, because sea life is concentrated near the surface.

You can take your pick of boat operators—motor or sailboat, Rasta crew or not. Sailing is a slow and easy way to see the reef, and Rasta crews party it up on the boat. Reef trips from the caye run $8 per person, and an all-day excursion taking in the Hol Chan Reserve, San Pedro for lunch, and another stop on the way back is $13 per person. Equipment rental is an extra $3. **Island Sun** (tel. 022/22–15) and **Sunrise** (tel. 022/21–95) both have sailing trips. **Gamusa** and his mellow Rasta crew are famous for all-day sailing festivities. You can reach Gamusa at the blue house on Front Street or through the Pinx bar.

➤ **SWIMMING** • The best swimming is at the split. The water is clear and blue, and the dock is a cool place to spread out a towel. When the island fills up, so does the relatively small dock. If you want to splash around with fewer people, try one of the many public docks on the east side of the island.

Lighthouse Reef

Two main attractions dominate Lighthouse Reef: the Blue Hole and Half Moon Caye Natural Monument. Most people come here either on live-aboard dive trips or day trips; try **Sunrise** (tel. 022/21–95) on Caye Caulker to arrange camping trips. Made famous in the '70s by Jacques Cousteau, the **Blue Hole** is actually a cavern in the huge underground cave system that snakes throughout the entire reef. The sea punctured the roof of this huge karst sinkhole, forming a 400-foot shaft into the depths below—the name comes from the intense, deep blue water caused by the depth of the shaft. The attraction of diving the Blue Hole isn't the sea life but the spacey moonscape littered with gigantic stalactites and underwater cave formations. The coral reefs surrounding the sinkhole are a spectacular snorkeling spot.

Lying at the southern end of the lagoon, **Half Moon Caye** was established in 1982 to protect the breeding ground of the red-footed booby, a complacent bird who won't budge even if you walk right into it. This particular group of boobies is unusual because 90% of the birds are in the adult white-color stage, rare in the Caribbean. You can observe their nests from a platform constructed by the Audubon Society. The western side of the island, with dense vegetation, is covered in soil made rich by guano from the thousands of nesting birds. The eastern half is mostly sand and coconut palms. Snorkeling in the area is spectacular, with visibility sometimes up to 200 feet. If you want to camp, register at the Lighthouse and make sure to bring your own water and food because the island has no facilities.

Western Belize

Sometimes the jungle gets so loud you can barely hear yourself think. The songs of thousands of birds mix with insects that chirp, others that scream, and still others that sound like buzzsaws. When storms pass overhead, thunder cracks like hell's gates have opened up. When rain doesn't come, the air hangs heavy with anticipation. Excuse the grandiose verbiage, but attempting to describe western Belize is like making a list of descriptive clichés about a Tarzan movie: dense virgin jungles, tumbling jade-green rivers, lush forests, verdant valleys. Western Belize, commonly called the Cayo district, is the second-most-popular tourist destination in the country—many visitors have blown off the beach scene altogether after a taste of inland Belize.

Long an agricultural and farming center, the land has only recently been valued for its beauty (and therefore its potential to draw tourists). Riverside property was worth 13 times more in 1993 than it was three years before, and everyone plans to build cabanas on their property. Government regulations and wildlife protection programs may curb overdevelopment, but the big-bucks potential of tourist growth makes this a fragile scenario. With the advent of development, the days when only the rich could afford a holiday here are coming to an end; new low-cost camping, palapas, and cabanas are always springing up.

Much of the Cayo district is inaccessible; only one expedition has ever made it over the Maya Mountain divide to the southern reaches of the region.

Those with the fever to backpack into the spectacular Maya Mountains and Mountain Pine Ridge will be bummed. Camping is strictly regulated, and permits are always required. Extended camping expeditions can be arranged, but only with established resorts and tour operations that charge exorbitant prices (thanks, ya weenies). With this in mind, it may work best to use San Ignacio as a base for exploring the region and/or spend a few days at one of the reasonably priced ranches in the ridge (*see* Lodges and Ranches, *below*).

This area is extremely rich in Mayan relics; almost everyone in the Cayo has found mounds (piles of dirt that indicate unexcavated ruins) or pottery shards on their property. It's hard to imagine how the Maya were able to erect thriving trade centers amid wicked jungle virtually uninhabitable by modern man. Another marvel is the ancient metropolis of Caracol, perched on a mountain plateau far from any sort of waterway. How did a civilization that didn't use the wheel move goods without water transport? Mysteries like this make the alien-infiltration stories in Von Däniken's *Chariots of the Gods* seem almost plausible.

San Ignacio

At the center of the majesty of western Belize sits the modest town of San Ignacio. "Cayo," as Belizeans call it, is filled with good food, cheap hotels, and a diverse population. It's such a great place to chill out that if you hang around for a while, you may find roots growing from your feet—and judging from the number of expatriate gringos in town, it must happen all the time. People here are so friendly that you may find yourself overbooked with dinner invitations. Since it's near the Guatemalan border, Spanish is the dominant language and mestizo the dominant population; you'll also find plenty of Mayans, Creoles, Mennonites, Sri Lankans, Chinese, and a burgeoning influx of people from Hong Kong as the British colony prepares for its reversion to China.

Outdoor activities (of the nature variety) are the reason to come here, but you'll also find a couple of artificial things worth seeing. Check out the **Hawkesworth Bridge** straddling the river between San Ignacio and her sister city, Santa Elena. Built in 1949 and modeled after the Brooklyn Bridge, it's the only suspension bridge in Belize. A cool **mural** depicting the history of Belize (on the wall below the Government building) was painted by local artists. **Market day** is Saturday in the building near the bus lot.

BASICS

➤ **CHANGING MONEY** • **Belize Bank** is on Burns Avenue at Waight Street, and **Atlantic Bank** is on Burns beneath the Belmoral Hotel (both open weekdays 8–1, also Fri. 3–6). If pinching pennies, your best bet is the officially illegal—but unofficially accepted—black market. Ask around at local restaurants; sometimes they'll change small denominations themselves, and they can always point you toward other black marketeers.

➢ **PHONES AND MAIL** • Make phone calls at **BTL**, on Burns Avenue north of Eva's (open weekdays 8–noon and 1–4, Sat. 8–noon). The **post office** (open weekdays 8–noon and 1–5, Sat. 8–1) is above the police station in the government building next to the bridge.

➢ **VISITOR INFORMATION** • **Eva's Restaurant** (22 Burns Ave., tel. 092/22–67) is the unofficial tourist bureau of the Cayo district, as well as the center of town for travelers, tourists, and locals. Look for Bob Jones (the owner)—he's the closest thing to a demigod any traveler can ask for. Bob knows everyone, everything, and every rock in the region. Let him know your budget scenario and desired activity list, and he'll steer you in the right direction. He can help keep prices down for organized excursions by hooking you up with other travelers.

COMING AND GOING Batty and **Novello** buses go to Belize City (2½ hours, $2), the Guatemalan border town of Benque Viejo del Carmen (½ hour, 50¢), and Belmopan (45 minutes, $1). The first bus to the border leaves at 9 AM; to go earlier, take a taxi for $3 (bargain!). The last bus from Benque to San Ignacio leaves around 4 PM. The bus lot is behind the Belmoral Hotel in the marketplace.

Once in town, go straight up Waight Street (on the left of the Belmoral) from the bus stop and you'll see Burns Avenue, the main drag. San Ignacio is on the west side of the Hawkesworth Bridge, Santa Elena on the east. Your feet will be enough to get you around town, and taxis are an option for destinations off the Western Highway. Taxis, which hang out in the bus lot and near the bridge, sometimes charge outrageous fares, so settle on a price before getting in. One of the best ways to explore the area outside town is by car, but costs are too high for most budget travelers (starting at $65 per day). If you have a big group and don't mind cramming in like circus clowns, you can swing it. The one car-rental agency in San Ignacio, **Maxima** (tel. 092/22–65), will rent you a car for $75 per day. Make sure you get a sturdy vehicle to handle the mountain roads. Hitching is fairly easy on main roads.

WHERE TO SLEEP The people of San Ignacio know an opportunity when they see one. Tourism growth abounds, so everyone and their dog is getting in on the action. Prices fluctuate drastically throughout the year, and proprietors will be much more flexible in the off-season (May–August), slashing rates to fill rooms. On the flip side, opportunistic owners may take advantage of desperate tourists as the season gets going; look and book early in the day. Many hotels will accommodate luggage storage and laundry needs if you ask. Santa Elena has two scummy hotels, both under $4, but San Ignacio's hotels are a better value. Most lodgings are in the triangular center of town around Burns, West, and Waight streets. **Central Hotel** (24 Burns) is clean, safe, has hot water, and charges about $11 a double. Camping is strictly regulated, and most "wild" places are privately owned. Your best bet is to camp in designated areas; a good selection of budget camping and cabana-style facilities are springing up along Branch Mouth Road, north of town.

August Guest House and Maya Hotel. Martha and John (once in Belize, you're on a first-name basis with everyone) run both hotels. The Augusts are extremely friendly and committed to providing a homey atmosphere at reasonable rates. They can also arrange tours and rent canoes. And, if you want to be a couch *patata* in tropical paradise, watch soap operas on the in-room cable TV. The Guest House has only two rooms available. You have access to a fully stocked kitchen, veranda, and family room for $15 for a double and meals are provided on request for a few bucks. The Maya Hotel is kitty-corner to the Guest House and offers a more spartan ambience (double with shared bath is $8). Rooms have a common sitting room, fans, and a small veranda, and you also have access to the kitchen over at the Guest House. *Guest House: 10*

West St.; 2 rooms with bath. Maya Hotel: 24a West St.; 8 rooms, some with bath. Tel. for both: 092/22–76.

HI-ET Hotel. This family-run establishment is one of the oldest and consistently cheapest hotels in town. They make you feel welcome and secure, so the HI-ET can be a good place for women alone (Junior and Beatrice are especially diligent about monitoring comings and goings in their living room). $10 doubles are clean and basic, with fans. Hang out on the porch swing and check out the action on the street. *12 West St., corner of Waight St., tel. 092/28–28.*

Venus Hotel. The best thing about the Venus is its distance from the blasting sounds of the Blue Angel disco, which thump their way through the center of town. This way, you have the option of dancing only part of the night away—then come here and crash in peace. Clean doubles with ceiling fan and shared bath are $11. *29 Burns Ave., tel. 092/21–86.*

➤ **CAMPGROUNDS AND CABANAS • Cosmos Camping.** This is the place to go if you're into the peace, love, and health food thang. Owners Denise and Chris gush with enthusiasm over their all-natural, Eden-like, unobtrusive spot on the Macal River. They have a kitchen for campers' use, and you can buy healthy snacks like homemade peanut butter, granola, and whole-grain bread. The nearby swimming hole sports a plank diving board and two rope swings.

The outdoor shower at Cosmos Camping has a loofah vine growing on it. Break the fruit of the vine open and, presto, instant body scrubber!

Camping prices are $1 per person plus $1 per camper/vehicle. They also rent palapa-style hammocks or tents for $3, or you can sleep in wooden boxes (weather protection, I suppose?) for $4. *½ mi from town on Branch Mouth Rd.*

Midas Resort and Camping. Close enough to town so that you don't feel trapped, yet secluded and affordable, Midas is a nice alternative to the more expensive jungle lodges. Choose between thatched-roof cabanas with shared bath for $25, or pitch your

Village Life Festival

Village Life Festivals have grown into the party of the week. Originally live weekly radio broadcasts that moved from village to village, the festivals have metamorphosed into raging cultural bashes. Each week, the festival celebrates  the local history and culture in the various townships. It broadcasts live music and commentary on Friends FM 88.9, the most popular spot on Belize's dial. Try to catch the greasy pole contest, in which local men climb on each other in their attempt to scale a slimy 15-foot pole, as a bottle of rum baits them to the top. It's tragic when a tower of seven comes sliding down in a pile. You might find yourself devising strategies for them with your meager knowledge of physics: "If they would only use two guys on the second tier, they wouldn't collapse under the weight. And if the guy at the top..." Depending on how squeamish you are, look for (or hide from) the duck neck break, which also involves grease—on a duck's neck. Locals on horses gallop by the strung-up greased duck and grab for its neck, trying to, you guessed it, break it. Not for animal lovers, but it's entertaining in its own special way.

tent anywhere on the property for $5 per person. Relax on their private sandy beach and take a dip in the Macal river. Your hosts, the Preston family, also rent canoes and arrange tours. *¼ mi from town on Branch Mouth Rd., tel. 092/31–72.*

FOOD The food in San Ignacio is as varied as the people who live here. There are four Chinese restaurants, and one of the best spots in town is a Sri Lankan joint. The restaurant at the San Ignacio Hotel is surprisingly affordable, with an excellent selection of fish dishes; the view of the valley is sublime, and rumor has it you can use the pool if you have a meal. Health buffs will be stoked to find **Fruit-a-Plenty** across the river in Santa Elena, as well as a produce market held every day under the bridge. On weekends, check out the great barbecue-fest in Santa Elena. It's been called the best 'cue in the world, and you can fill your belly for $1.25.

Eva's Restaurant and Bar. Home base for everyone in town—locals, tourists, and expatriate gringos alike. You'll hear wild adventure stories, teary tales of woe, and have conversations with local Mennonites. Stop in to see Bob (of course), but also for a bite to eat. Lots of Creole specialties, as well as typical snack food, go for around $3 per plate. Good breakfasts too—yogurt and granola! *22 Burns Ave., tel. 092/22–67. Open weekdays 6:30 AM–11 PM, weekends 6:30 AM–midnight.*

Maxim's Chinese Restaurant. Small and dark like all good Chinese restaurants, Maxim's will fill you up to bursting with their generous portions. Vegetarian fried rice, chop suey, and chow mein, as well as tasty meat and fish dishes, go for $3–$8. *Corner of Far West and Waight streets. Open daily 11:30–2:30 and 5–midnight.*

Serendib Restaurant. Excellent curries are served up at affordable prices in a quiet atmosphere. Spicy and filling Sri Lankan dishes go for $4–$8. *27 Burns Ave., tel. 092/23–02. Open Mon.–Sat. 9:30–3 and 6:30–11:30, closed 2 weeks in mid-July.*

CHEAP THRILLS Sandy Beach Rope Swing. More like an electrical cable, this is the best rope swing in the area. Multi-leveled and long, it's got an awesome swing-out velocity that doesn't hurt your arms. Watch your ass (figuratively speaking), and hold your feet up if you dare the upper levels. Local kids will usually be around to demonstrate. Also check out the 15-foot, tri-level rock jump. The preliminary climb is treacherous—you may want to follow locals up. *Walk under the bridge and follow the path to the right, heading south about ¼ mi; swing is on other side of river.*

Check out the **Macal River Car Wash** on the north side of the bridge. Belizeans come to dunk themselves and wash their trucks, cars, and tractors in the river. Many an unsuspecting river-bather has been taken by surprise by this local practice. It's also entertaining to check out a local **soccer** game, held every Sunday behind the bus lot. For the death-obsessed, San Ignacio has a spookily nice **graveyard** at the north end of town.

AFTER DARK Many restaurants double as bars. Locals, archaeologists, and tourists usually stop in at Eva's to see what's up and have a beer. Practically the only place left for British soldiers to drink is the **Red Rooster** (2 Far West St., tel. 092/30–16), where you can also get good ole American pizza and baked

"If you're hell-bent on some real dive bars, head into Santa Elena. If you're hell-bent on keeping your teeth intact, stay in San Ignacio."

potatoes. **JB's** is a good dive bar on the corner of Burns, Waight, and Hudson streets. If you're hankering for a game of pool, head over to **Dacak's** on Hudson Street. **Cahal Pech Tavern,** up the hill near the ruins, has the best view of the city. It's also got that out-in-the-jungle feel with an enormous thatched roof. Check in town for their live band schedule. **The Western Bar,** a huge cement monster by the river, blasts '70s disco in the main bar, and the owner has recently finished a romantic addition that's surprisingly sheltered from the din next door. On weekends, just about all the young people head for the open-air **Blue Angels Bar** on Hudson Street for live Caribbean music and dancing ($1 cover). If you're hell-bent on some real dive bars, head into Santa Elena.

OUTDOOR ACTIVITIES If you're here in the Cayo district, you probably didn't come to sit around town and read. The area's self-evident attractions are its natural beauty and wide range of wildlife. Lots of locals have some kind of adventure trip to offer, equipment to rent, or vehicle and guide service for hire. If you want to round up some snook, catfish, or other such critters in the river, call **Terry** (tel. 092/33–63), or ask for him at Eva's. The government is trying to rigidify the tourist industry, so things could change overnight; the day may soon come when asking for service providers by their nicknames at Eva's is a thing of the past.

➤ **CANOEING** • The gentle flow of the Macal River is perfect for a relaxing float. Myriad birds and reptiles populate the lush banks, and the river is a welcome respite from the oppressive heat. The going rate for rentals is $12 for a half day or $20 a full day (ask Eva's Bob or check with your hotel proprietor). A good canoeing option is a guided tour with local guides. **Toni** comes highly recommended—contact him at Eva's. For $12 a person, he and his partner will paddle you upstream, and they're experts at spotting wildlife along the banks. They might even scare out El Garobo, a monstrous iguana, for your viewing pleasure. Also try **Orlando** at Eva's, or **Float Belize** (2a Benque Rd., tel. 092/32–13), which is a little more expensive.

➤ **HORSEBACK RIDING** • The best option for budget travelers is **Easy Rider** (¼ mi out of town on Bullet Tree Rd.). Katie and Charlie organize trips around the jungle and to the ruins at Cahal Pech. Prices start at $20 for a half day and $50 a full day. **MET,** or Mountain Equestrian Trails (Mile 8, Mountain Pine Ridge Rd., tel. 092/31–80), is the granddaddy of horse trips in the area. They can arrange extended horse and camping trips throughout the area, even to Caracol. Unfortunately, the price tags of most of these trips are out of range for the average working stiff. Several lodges have horses too: **Las Casitas Lodge** will sometimes offer a free horse trip with the price of a room, and otherwise rents the beasts for $10 per hour.

NEAR SAN IGNACIO

XUNANTUNICH Also known as "The Pride of Belize," this site was a Classic-period ceremonial center. Its name means "stone maiden." Perhaps the best part of a visit to Xunantunich is the spectacular view of the surrounding forest from the top of El Castillo, the largest structure in the complex and the second-tallest human-made building in Belize at 132 feet—only Canaa at Caracol is taller. The frieze on the side of El Castillo is a re-creation in stucco. It's believed that a frieze such as this—with abstract designs, human faces, and jaguar heads—once ringed the entire temple. Three beautifully preserved stelae are on display. Not much is known about the history of Xunantunich except that it was abandoned after being hit by a massive earthquake around AD 900. As with most Mayan buildings, the architecture here is layered, with new buildings erected on top of old ones. It's currently being excavated, so new information may be uncovered in time. *Take the bus to San José Succotz. The hand-cranked ferry will take you to the other side of the river, where it's a 1½ mi hike through the jungle to the ruin. Open 8–5; the ferryman often takes lunch from noon–1 or he may leave at 4. Admission: $1.50.*

Across the road lies the traditional Mayan village of **San José Succotz.** Not much happens here on a regular basis, but huge traditional fiestas are held on March 19 and May 3. You can stay in Succotz at the **Rancho Los Amigos** (1 mi from Succotz, tel. 092/24–83) for $10 per person including meals; vegetarian meals are available.

PANTI MEDICINE TRAIL The Mayans were masters at utilizing the jungle's natural resources for their practical and medicinal needs. Named for the Mayan Dr. Eligio Panti, the trail leads you through the jungle along the banks of the Macal River, where you'll see medicinal plants and native hardwoods. The trail begins at Ixchel Farm, where Dr. Rosita Arvigo, apprentice to Dr. Panti, works and studies the jungle. Dr. Arvigo's services are pricey, but she'll take you along the trail if you make a reservation. The $5 self-guided tour is about as good. You can also hire one of the farm guides for $8 per person. You'll see natural contraceptives, cures for dysentery and malaria, and vines that carry fresh, sterile water inside. Check out Rosita's mail-order herb company and healthful-living seminars. From San Ignacio, follow the signs to Chaa Creek Cottages. The easiest way is to take a canoe down the Macal River and dock at Chaa Creek or Ixchell Farm.

BENQUE VIEJO DEL CARMEN Benque lies about 1½ miles from the Guatemalan frontier, and, as with most border towns, you'll want to hang out here as little as possible. From San Ignacio, you may have to take a cab to Benque (around $3) because many buses don't go to the border. Crossing the border is fairly painless in both directions—just make sure your papers are in order. This station issues only tourist cards, so if you need a visa, make sure you get it beforehand. Guatemala charges a $1 entry and exit tax, and the tourist card may cost up to $5. It's free to enter or exit Belize. If you must stay here overnight, **The Maya Hotel** (11 George St.) and **Oki's Hotel** (47 George St.) both have cheap rooms. The bus station is also on George Street. Many people take day trips to **Melchor De Mencos,** across the border, for the great market and cheap restaurants.

Mountain Pine Ridge

At the entrance to Mountain Pine Ridge National Reserve, the thick lowland jungle abruptly gives way to a quiet and far-reaching pine forest, and the road metamorphoses into a bright rusty red. You won't find many annoying bugs, or people either—at your feet lie over 480 square kilometers (185 square miles) virtually uninhabited by

The Mennonites

You'll know 'em when you see 'em. The men dress in suspenders and straw hats, and the women wear modest cotton dresses and cover their heads with scarves. The Mennonites converse in German or German-accented English, and maintain small, insular, agrarian communities in and around Cayo. A devout Christian denomination named after Menno Sims, the Mennonites evolved out of the 16th-century Anabaptists. Strict discipline, separation from the outside world, and conformity to scripture is essential. Migrating south, they reached Belize many years ago, and plan on eventually movin' on down to South America. Except for trading for farm products, the Mennonites are completely self-sufficient. Orthodox "horse-and-buggy" Mennonites are completely averse to modern technology, while other sects may drive cars and have a few whirring electrical appliances in their homes. The Mennonites are famous for their elegant hand-carved furniture, and they often sell it on the side of the road. Another main product is cheese; locals are sometimes resentful about the Mennonites' perceived monopoly on the cheese market. Other than that, the Mennonites are well received, and Belizeans treat them as just another one of the many groups of people who immigrated to Belize because it's so cool.

Spanish Lookout is a successful Mennonite farming community. Locals often refer to them as "Mechanites," because they believe that it's okay to use modern technology. Take a bus from San Ignacio to Holdfast Camp and walk or hitch the 5 kilometers (3 miles) to Spanish Lookout.

humans. The Maya mountains which dominate the ridge contain some of the oldest rocks in Central America. They're thought to be remnants of a Caribbean island that was pushed into the peninsula millions of years ago. This may account for the ridge's incredibly out-of-place ecosystem—pine forest smack in the middle of jungly Belize. Rivers and swimming holes abound here (a perfect opportunity for first-time skinny-dippers), as well as caves galore. Caracol, one of the most impressive Mayan sites in the country, is deep in the jungle on the Vaca Plateau. To see the ridge in one sweeping view, check out the **Fire Lookout Tower** in Augustine (you'll see signs for the bunkhouse underneath the tower). You're so high up that birds soar below you, often hanging in the air as if posing for your camera. **San Antonio**, a small Mayan village consisting of a cluster of huts right on Mountain Pine Ridge Road, is a good place to use as a mini-landmark. Access to the ridge is not as daunting a prospect as it once was, but you'll have to fork over beaucoup bucks (close to $100 to rent a car or a guide) and time (long treks to points of interest).

COMING AND GOING Without your own car, you have two ways to see Mountain Pine Ridge: Hire a guide or hitch. New laws regulating tour operations have made it illegal for anyone without a certificate to take tourists around the ridge, meaning the days of hiring a taxi into the ridge are over. The going rate to hire a guide and a 4x4 for the day is about $90. Most ranches have their own guides, but the cheapest option is to hook up with others in groups of five. Bob (San Ignacio's aforementioned budget-travel demigod) can put your name on a list and call up his bank of certified guides. This brings the cost down to about $18 per person.

Live and Let Live

Belize is at the forefront of a new conservation movement that's developing viable economic alternatives using existing jungle resources. People are realizing that it could be more profitable on a long-term basis to harvest what the jun- gle naturally has to offer than to hack down vegetation with short-term, slash-and-burn agriculture. One obvious advantage is that the unspoiled wilderness attracts tourist dollars. However, harvesting medicinal plants and herbs seems to be the most successful venture yet. Medical companies may pay big bucks for the thousands of yet-undiscovered plants that could possibly aid in treating diseases like AIDS and cancer. Plants and trees that the Mayan doctors have used for centuries are finally being taken seriously by the Western medical community. Plants like the wild yam, which already has 14 known uses, including contraception and anti-inflammation, are being sent to the United States to be chemically analyzed. Also studied is the "give and take" tree, which can stop blood flow; the gumbo-limbo, which provides a cure for poison wood rash; and the bark of the negrito tree, which cures dysentery and was worth its weight in gold in 17th-century Europe. Many of these plants are used in daily life by Belizeans. As a developing nation, Belize is taking huge economic risks with its alternative approach to conservation, tourism, and "comparative advantage." If the experiment works, the ticking clock of environmental destruction might move its hands back a little. If not, Belizeans will at least know they tried.

➤ **HITCHING** • If you want to hitch in, be aware that traffic is sparse. Because many vehicles on the road into the ridge are already hired out, they won't pick you up. A good option is to flag down one of the white Land Rovers with blue plates that belong to the forest service. If you want to stay overnight, the brown truck that takes workers in and out of the ridge every day can give you a ride, too. The truck leaves from San Ignacio in the early afternoon and returns from Augustine (forest reserve headquarters) in the early morning. The best place to hitch is at the junction of Mountain Pine Ridge Road and the Western Highway in Santa Elena. Another road into the ridge is near Georgeville.

➤ **BY CAR** • If you're lucky enough to have a car, make sure it's sturdy. The main road has recently been improved, and is now supposed to be an all-weather road. Because it's partly made of clay, however, it can get pretty slippery when it rains. Side roads are also dangerous when wet. As of this writing, a road is being built from Augustine all the way to Caracol.

WHERE TO SLEEP Setting yourself up for the night in the San Ignacio countryside or in the ridge can be tricky, expensive, or both, but the rewards are great. Many of the lodges and ranches in the area cater to the week-at-the-beach/week-at-the-ranch crowd and may get booked up far in advance during the high season.

➤ **CAMPING** • Camping in the government reserve area is allowed by permit only, and only at Augustine or at the forest gate. Some backpackers say that if you ask nicely at the gate, you'll have no problems. Others say that people with permits have still been turned away. To make things even harder, permits are available only at the forestry department in Belmopan. No food is available in the reserve, so make sure to bring your own. If you have a purifier, the multitudinous streams will provide ample water; otherwise, pack your own.

Some of the lodges around the area will let you camp on their land (ask around). Crystal Paradise Resort (*see below*) charges $10 per person to camp, including two meals. Rancho Los Amigos in San José Succotz also has camping. The upcoming Cayo Resorts near Blackman Eddy will also provide camping facilities. A few small cabins are also available for rent in Augustine. Permits and advance reservations are required, and the cost is $8 per person.

➤ **LODGES AND RANCHES** • If you deny yourself a few nights in the Cayo countryside, you're missing out on what this region has to offer. Some say that the birding in and around the ridge is the best it gets—ever. Even the cheapest lodge is a splurge, but the payback makes it affordable. Most lodges are family-run and usually serve home-cooked meals. A few lodges stand out as more reasonable than the rest. **Clarissa Falls** (5½ mi Benque Viejo Rd., tel. 092/24–24) offers basic thatched cabanas with shared bath and home-cooked meals for under $20 for a double. **Caesar's Place/Blackrock** (62 mi Western Hwy., tel. 092/23–41) has a good reputation with backpackers and a price scale starting at $23 per person. **Crystal Paradise Resort** (Cristo Rey, tel. 092/24–83), run by the Tut family, has cabanas starting at $55 for a double, or they'll let you camp for $10. They have a nice beach on the Macal River and even offer night birding with a high-power light. **duPlooy's** (San Ignacio, tel. 092/33–01) used to be one of those plush places that backpackers had never heard of. Now that they've added a guest house with six rooms and two baths, budget travelers can definitely swing it ($45 for a double with a shared bath and breakfast). Ken and Judy duPlooy run this homey, laid-back operation where your breakfast is delivered each morning to your porch, and you can have after-dinner drinks and conversation in the open-air, riverview bar. Check out Ken's extra-special orchid and vine collection, or dive into their swimming hole.

WORTH SEEING

➤ **HIDDEN VALLEY FALLS** • Spilling over a 1,600-foot cliff into a jagged jungle gorge, Hidden Valley Falls (a.k.a. Thousand-foot Falls) is the highest waterfall in Central America and one of the routine stops on any Mountain Pine Ridge tour. You can get a great look at the falls from a viewing platform up the gorge. Hint for photographers: The light is *ideal* in the morning, since as day fades shadows shroud the falls. You can also check out the view from the caretaker's cabin, where on a clear day you can see all the way to Belmopan. *Follow the clearly marked signs about 14 km (9 mi) off the main road. Admission: $1.*

➤ **RIO ON SWIMMING HOLE AND PICNIC SPOT** • About 3 kilometers (2 miles) from Augustine, the Rio On cascades over smooth granite rocks on its way to meet the Belize River, where together they form deep pools and bubbling falls. Get a massage from a thundering waterfall or use the slippery granite as a natural water slide. The site has covered picnic tables (to protect you from the elements) and an outhouse/changing room.

➤ **RIO FRIO CAVES** • From the swimming hole, the Rio On continues its journey through the largest river cave in Belize. Cathedralesque in its grandeur, the Rio Frio is the most accessible cave in the inaccessible Chiquibul cave system (the longest in Central America). The cave is cut into solid limestone and drips with stalactites; the Mayans apparently used it as a ceremonial center, but all the artifacts were excavated or washed away. Because the Rio Frio is tunnel-like (open at both ends), enough daylight filters through so that you don't need to carry a flashlight. *Follow the signs at Augustine. You can either take the 45-minute nature trail or go to the end of the dirt road and walk about 400 yards to the entrance.*

➤ **PACITBUN** • A little over a mile from San Antonio, Pacitbun is one of the oldest Preclassic sites in Belize. Once a massive ceremonial center with more than 20 pyramids and raised pathways, now the site looks like a bunch of dirt mounds—but they're *thousand-year-old* dirt mounds. Maya buffs will definitely get a kick out of it. A plaque at the site tells a cool story of the site's history. *Follow Mountain Pine Ridge Rd. and once you're past San Antonio, you'll see clear signs.*

➤ **CARACOL** • Since the discovery of Tikal in Guatemala, no other site had been uncovered to rival its size and scale of achievement. Enter Caracol. Deciphered hieroglyphs at Caracol tell stories of military victories over Tikal. Caracol, in fact, appears to have dominated the eastern part of the southern lowlands of Belize and Guatemala during the transition from the early to late-Classic periods. For this reason, Caracol has become the anthro hot-spot, with the potential to answer many questions and mysteries plaguing Mayan scholars. The discovery of a royal tomb in 1992 was probably *the* most important excavation of the decade. The site itself covers approximately 3 square kilometers (1.2 square miles) and includes 32 large structures and 12 smaller ones. Canaa, the largest pyramid at 139 feet, is the tallest human-made structure in Belize. Dates on stelae suggest that Caracol was occupied for an extremely long time, with a possible population of a whopping two million. Caracol means "place of the snail," either because it has so many snail shells scattered about or because of the winding, twisty road leading there. Caracol is deep in the wild Chiquibul wilderness on the Vaca Plateau and getting here is extremely difficult. A new road, which should make it tons easier, is under construction. Check with Bob at Eva's for info on access and cost.

Belmopan

Belmopan was conceived after Hurricane Hattie destroyed Belize City in 1961. It had the honor of being selected as the capital of Belize, not for its size or objective importance, but for its weather. The government wanted to create an administrative and cultural center that wasn't so vulnerable to the elements, so they headed inland. Unfortunately, no Belizeans followed. The result is lots of government buildings (government workers had no choice but to move), banks, embassies, police headquarters, a hospital, and relatively empty streets. Belmopan's population is now 6,000, but it's slowly (very slowly) filling up. Another natural disaster in Belize City may do the trick and send urbanites scurrying to Belmopan's well-planned but barren avenues and buildings. As a capital, Belmopan is clearly lacking; as a small city, it's pleasant. You won't want to stay here for long (you'd get bored silly), but a short stop to take in the tree-lined walkways and relax in the tranquil atmosphere is always nice. The main attraction in Belmopan is the **Archaeological Vault** (Independence Square, tel. 08/22–106). It's open Monday, Wednesday, and Friday, 1:30–4. The government's plans for a national Mayan museum have stalled due to lack of funds, so many of Belize's treasures are stored in this small vault in the Department of Archeology. Hundreds of exquisite artifacts (painted vessels, stone carvings, jade necklaces) lie in the open, so you can browse without facing any imposing museum-like glass windows. To see the exhibit, you must make an appointment two days in advance.

BASICS The **British High Commission** (34–36 Half Moon Ave., tel. 08/22–146) has its headquarters here. It's open weekdays 8–noon and 1:30–4. The **U.S. Embassy** also has an office here (tel. 08/22–617). **Barclay's** and **Belize Bank** (open weekdays 8–1, also Fri. 3–6) both have offices behind the market, near the bus station. **BTL** is by the satellite dish, and the **post office** is in the main square (marked by the ugly contemporary art piece). The **immigration office** (Half Moon Ave., tel. 08/22–423) charges $13 per month for visa extensions.

COMING AND GOING If nothing else, Belmopan is at the geographic center of the country. It lies at the junction of the Western and Hummingbird highways, and buses to all southern and western destinations stop here at some point along their route. Buses leave for the east, west, and south about every hour. **Batty** and **Novelo** buses go to San Ignacio (1 hour, 75¢) and Belize City (1 hour, $1.50). Buses arrive in Belmopan (also hourly) from Belize City, Cayo, and Dangriga. If you're going to hang out in town, orientation is plain and simple. Belmopan is arranged in a circle; cars drive around the ring road and on the spoke roads heading outward. The entire center is for foot traffic only, and it's most pleasant to walk around. Remember: Though at times it looks like you're heading into an open field, keep walking and you'll eventually get where you're going.

WHERE TO SLEEP AND EAT The only reason you'd need to spend the night in Belmopan is if you're comatose from heat stroke and in desperate need of an air-conditioned hotel with cable. The **El Rey Inn** (23 Moho, tel. 08/23–438) has clean rooms with private bath, hot water, and ceiling fans at $23 a double. The bonus is extra-friendly management. **Bullfrog Inn** (25 Halfmoon Ave., tel. 08/22–111) will set you back $35 for an air-conditioned double with bath plus a restaurant and cable TV. The Belmopan Convention Center (across from the bus station) and two new lodging monstrosities nearby cater to diplomats and business people on expense accounts—backpackers beware.

The **Bullfrog Inn restaurant** has a nice veranda, and the food is actually reasonable—they serve typical beans, rice, and fish or chicken for $4–$5. Most other budget eateries congregate around the bus station, where you can chow down on Belizean or snack food. **The Caladrium** (right in front of the bus station) has fresh juices; **Yoli's** and the **Belmopan Outdoor Cafe**, both one block away from the bus station (near the Shell station), have open-air bars.

NEAR BELMOPAN

GUANACASTE PARK This awesome little park is easy to get to, has plenty of well-marked trails, and is lots of fun. It's 3 kilometers (2 miles) from Belmopan at the junction of the Hummingbird and Western highways. Take any bus heading toward Belize City or Cayo and ask the bus driver to let you off at the junction. You can also do Guanacaste as a day trip from San Ignacio; buses leave about every hour and the ride takes about an hour. Named after the huge 150-year-old guanacaste tree in the center, Guanacaste Park was formed as a national reserve in 1988. Orchids, bromeliads, and cacti cling to the big tree, spilling down its trunk to the ground. Guanacaste wood is extremely tough and water-resistant, and has long been an excellent choice for dugout canoes and water troughs. This particular tree escaped canoe life because of its damaged trunk. The park is also home to a bunch of mammals, reptiles, and birds; due to its proximity to the road, though, you aren't likely to see many. Check at the visitors' center for info on habitats and ecosystems. Roaring Creek and the Belize River run into each other in the park. You can swim to your heart's content (the creek is clear and cold with a sandy bottom), and also get into some rope-swinging action where the creek flows into the Belize River. Facilities in the park include fresh water, restrooms, and picnic facilities. For more info on the park, contact the Belize Audubon Society (49 Southern Foreshore, Belize City, tel. 02/77–369).

BLUE HOLE NATIONAL PARK Not to be confused with the offshore Blue Hole, the inland Blue Hole is a popular swimming and picnic spot 19 kilometers (12 miles) from Belmopan on the Hummingbird Highway. The ice-cold swimming hole was formed by a collapsed karst-rock sinkhole, where water on its way to the Sibun River emerges from the immense underground cave system which snakes through the region (some of *The Mosquito Coast* was filmed on the banks of this river). The water in the swimming hole actually glows with an intense sapphire brilliance (I swear), and is ringed by sheer cliffs and dripping jungle. The river flows a few more feet and then plunges into another cave, which has incredible natural acoustics. If you decide to swim in this cave, stay at the far left edge because the water flows back rapidly into the cave system at the near edge—potential danger even for accomplished swimmers. To get to the Blue Hole, take a bus or hitch from Belmopan; traffic on the highway is fairly sparse, so be prepared to wait.

Southern Belize

Inaccessible and underrated, this is the part of Belize that many tourists either blow through or blow off. For this exact reason, southern Belize is closer to tropical paradise than other gringoized spots. It takes a certain amount of determination (a sturdy vehicle or cash) to reach the wildest terrain in the south, but the more difficult the trek, the more rewarding the experience. The southern landscape is awesome: Wild Maya mountains descend into thick jungle valleys riddled with caverns and cave systems. Sometimes the jungle canopy is so dense that the sun seems a vague memory, but the oppressive heat will remind you soon enough. As with most of Belize, you can feel thousands of hungry mosquitoes contemplating your tender neck. Vines crawl up trees and drip down the soaring branches, and if you shove your face up close, the vines look like a writhing mass of slimy reptiles. (Maybe the heat *is* affecting you.) The butterflies fluttering past your head are every trippy color of the rainbow, and wild limestone and karst mountains jut out of the immense, soggy swamps. Head to the top of some of the peaks on a clear day and you'll see the Cayes. It appears that construction has finally begun on a new Guatemalan border crossing, past San Antonio in the Toledo district. If all works out, tourist traffic could increase dramatically.

Here in the south are the largest concentrations of Garifuna and Mayan peoples. Much of the Mayan population is from the Mopan and Ke'kchi tribes, and most are refugees from Guatemalan repression. The all-out party day down here is **Garifuna Settlement Day** on November 19, when the Garifuna celebrate their landing in Belize. Southerners treat you like one of the family and are itching to show off their spectacular countryside. Aquaphiles will be happy to know that the cayes off the southern coast have prime snorkeling. Clouds of iridescent fish with wings, plumes, and bulging eyes wiggle by the endlessly waving fan coral. Placencia, with its long, sandy beach, is a choice spot to base yourself for off-shore caye exploration.

Dangriga

Built right on the coast at the mouth of North Stann Creek, Dangriga is the center of Garifuna culture, with the largest Garifuna population in the country. Depending on your temperament, Dangriga will either wag your tail or send you packing. Drugs and gangs have trickled down the coast from Belize City, and the streets take on a decidedly sinister air after the sun goes down. On the whole, nothing really exciting goes on here, but Dangriga is a cool little community with a rich cultural history if you take the time to ferret it out. The streets have a vague Western frontier feel with ramshackle wooden buildings alongside ornate colonial structures. The main drag starts out as Commerce Street on the north side of the creek, becoming St. Vincent south of the creek. The best time to come here is on Garifuna Settlement Day, when the community erupts in celebration and flaunts all its cultural finery. If you miss this party, you can get a tiny taste of the town's history at **Melda's Historical Museum** (21 St. Vincent St., tel. 05/22–266). It's open 9–noon and 2–5, closed Thursday and Sunday; admission is $1. Check out all the tools used in making the Garifuna cassava bread, as well as old appliances, drums, and clothing from Dangriga's past. **Garifuna Culture Tours** (c/o Carol Colin, 22 Magoon St., tel. 05/23–018) introduce visitors to local culture and crafts. Various itineraries take in the Hadut, a traditional meal; drumming and dance recitals with the Waribagabaga dancers; and visits to local drum maker Austin Rodriguez. Cost depends on group size, but most tours cost $50 minimum. You can also drop in on Austin Rodriguez at 32 Tubroose Street, where you can watch him making drums.

The Garifuna

The Garifuna (or Black Caribs) are a unique cultural and ethnic group, born when escaped and shipwrecked slaves mixed with the native Caribs, who gave them refuge on the island of Saint Vincent 300 years ago. Though they adopted the Carib language, the Garifuna remained African in culture, maintaining their musical and religious traditions despite the control colonial powers held over the island. In 1795, they rebelled against the British in the Garifuna Revolt; to punish them for their insolence, the crown deported them to the island of Roatán, off Honduras. From there, using dugout canoes, the Garifuna established fishing villages on the Bay Islands, as well as along the nearby coasts of Belize, Guatemala, and northern Honduras. In Belize, most of the Garifuna settled in the Stann Creek district. The 1980s sparked a revival of the Garifuna culture and Stann Creek was renamed Dangriga, meaning "standing waters."

The African-descended Garifuna spirituality so mystified and terrified Europeans that during the days of slavery, drums were banned throughout most of the Caribbean because of the power they supposedly possessed. Now, drumming and chants are a core part of the Garifuna community, coupled with fervent dancing and speaking in tongues. As young Garifuna are swept up by ganja, Marley, and modern Caribbean culture, some people wonder if the old ways will survive. "After it all, from Africa to the English, we're still here today," they say. "The language is on our tongues, we're born with it in our blood—100% Garifuna."

BASICS You can take care of most of your needs near the main drag. A **hospital** is near the coast on Court House Road. You can do **laundry** on Commerce Street, where Plum Street ends. **Barclay's Bank** and **Bank of Nova Scotia** are both on Commerce Street, north of the bridge. All have regular hours: weekdays 8–1, also 3–6 on Fridays. **BTL** (open weekdays 8–noon and 1–4) is on the corner of Commerce Street and Courthouse Road, across from the police station. The **post office** (open weekdays 8–noon and 1–4) is at the south end of town toward the coast, on the corner of Caney and Mahogany streets.

COMING AND GOING Buses from Belize City drop you off near the bridge in the center of town at the **Z-Line bus terminal** (8 St. Vincent St., tel. 05/22–160). Buses leave for Belize City five times daily until 3:30 PM. You can also catch a bus coming through from Punta Gorda, but in the rainy season it's anyone's guess when it might show. Buses go south to Punta Gorda at around 11 AM and 7 PM, and a bus to Independence leaves at 2:30 PM (three hours, $3). If you're making a beeline for the Cayes, head to the bridge and fish market, where you can hook up with someone heading out. **Maya Airways** stops in Dangriga on its way south to Placencia and Punta Gorda. The one-way price to Belize City is $30; buy tickets at the Treasure House travel agency (64 Commerce St., open weekdays 8–noon and 1–4) or at the Pelican Beach Hotel (near the airstrip at the far north end of town).

WHERE TO SLEEP For most travelers Dangriga is often just a stop on the way to somewhere better, but you can catch some shut-eye at a number of budget digs. At the old standby **Rio Mar Hotel** (at the river mouth on the sea, tel. 05/22–201), okay doubles with shared bath are about $13.

➢ **UNDER $15 • Catalina's Guest House.** Near the town center, this simple, clean house is run by a boisterous family. A whole bunch of chickens roosting in the outside tree add to the down-home atmosphere. Rooms are small, and the kids may wake up earlier than you'd like, but it's cheap and central. A double with shared bath is $11. *37 Cedar St., tel. 05/23–029. Go right off St. Vincent heading south; it's the blue house on the right, next to the bridge. 6 rooms, none with bath.*

The Hub Guest House. Next to the river in the center, this is where backpackers congregate. The sitting room with TV and VCR is a comfy spot to chat. The Hub also has a decent, cheap restaurant downstairs. Rooms are clean ($13 double with shared bath), and the management is chummy. *On North Stann Creek, tel. 05/22–397. South side of the bridge; you'll see it from there. 6 rooms, some with bath. Laundry, luggage storage.*

The Riverside Hotel. The renovated Riverside has a vague colonial charm, with a huge comfortable sitting room smack in the middle. It's right on noisy Commerce Street at the bridge, but most rooms are set back from the street, so you get the best of both worlds: It's central *and* quiet. Rooms are large and airy, and it's $10 per person. *135 Commerce St., tel. 05/22–168. 12 rooms, none with bath.*

➢ **UNDER $20 • Pal's Guest House.** The real plus about Pal's is its distance from town. On the south side of town with an ocean view, Pal's is a tranquil refuge from the chaos and hustlers that congeal around the bridge. Doubles start at $15 with shared bath, and you'll pay more for rooms upstairs, which have cable TV. The courtyard is pleasant, and the bathrooms are (gasp!) beautiful. Cheap rooms fill up mighty fast, so you may want to call ahead. *868 A Magoon St., tel. 05/22–095. Walk down St. Vincent to the southern bridge, turn left, and walk toward the coast. 9 rooms, some with bath. Luggage storage.*

FOOD All Dangriga restaurants are cheap and serve the same old chicken, beans, and rice. You can feast on excellent seafood when it's in season. Beware of the conch fritters—the bad ones are so oily your stomach will never let you forget it. The most popular restaurant in town is **Burger King** (no relation), on Commerce Street next to the bridge, where you can get some of the best conch soup this side of North Stann

Creek for about $3. They also serve burgers, breakfast, homemade ice cream, and fresh juice. Three reasonable and tasty **Chinese restaurants** are within two blocks of each other on Commerce Street: the Silver Garden, the Sunrise, and the Starlight. The **Sea Flame** (farther north on Commerce St. near Church Rd.) has unpredictable hours, but the seafood specialties ($5) are worth the possible wait. **Melly's Homemade Ice Cream** (Ramos Rd. at Commerce St.) has homemade pastries. Try the soursap ice cream to get your taste buds jumping.

Some of the best garnaches in the country are sold at a small stand on St. Vincent Street at Yemeri Road. Four of these goodies (25¢ apiece) are guaranteed to fill your belly. Most restaurants close 2–6 PM (the unofficial siesta time), re-opening in the evening. As usual, it's kind of up to the whim of the proprietor.

CHEAP THRILLS One of the coolest things to do in Dangriga is to take a walk up to the posh **Pelican Beach Hotel** and lurk about their clean beach and long dock. The walk takes you along the coast, through the graveyard, and past a park with swings and seesaws. Notice how the graves marked before 1961 are broken and twisted; Hurricane Hattie knocked down a block-wide piece of Dangriga and blew it down the coast and into the ocean, leaving only three houses standing. When you finally get to the hotel, have a Coke and lounge in the hammocks on the dock—truly a slacker move.

"Crack central" is totally surreal: Smoke from smoldering fires envelops the street, while figures crouched over pipes are backlit by a few dim streetlights.

AFTER DARK Dangriga has been infiltrated by druggies and drugs; "crack central," where all the addicts converge, is all the way inland in the southern part of town. Be cautious, and be aware that women will be harassed no matter how modestly they dress. Bars are characterized by the frontier-looking swinging doors. A few discos start jamming on weekends, and the **Roundhouse** (next to Pelican Beach) has live music every weekend. The whole town shows up to boogie.

NEAR DANGRIGA

HOPKINS Hopkins is a fantastic place to chill for a few days, or even to rent a house and stay for a few weeks. Built along a sandy, palm-lined beach about 15 kilometers (9 miles) southwest of Dangriga, this peaceful Garifuna fishing village is closer to the soul of the Garifuna community than any other spot in Belize. Villagers exude warmth and hospitality. **BTL** (open weekdays 8–noon and 1–4) and the **post office** (open weekdays 8–noon and 1–4) are in the community center in the center of town. Hopkins has only recently joined the ranks of the electrified; after years of empty promises and frustrating delays, villagers are finally enjoying the benefits of refrigeration, electric light, and running water.

You can stay at the **Sandy Beach Lodge,** the only women-owned cooperative in Belize, at the far south end of town. Ask anyone on the street to point you in the right direction, and they'll tell you, "the women are waiting for you." A double in a simple thatched cabin on the beach is $13. You can also stay at the **Caribbean View Hotel** for $10 per person. Ask for Carly at Gilford's store (go down the main road; when it swings left, continue straight and you'll see a Coke sign). As for restaurants, forget it babe; there ain't a one. People do sell supplies, and fishing boats go out periodically for fresh fish. You can arrange meals at Sandy Beach or inquire about eating with a local family. Boats from Dangriga head to Hopkins; ask at the river. Regular truck service leaves Hopkins at 6 AM and returns from Dangriga at 10:30 AM on Monday, Wednesday, Friday, and Saturday.

THE HUMMINGBIRD AND SOUTHERN HIGHWAYS The Hummingbird Highway connects Belmopan and Dangriga. It's a potholed mess, but it's one of the most spectacular bus rides in the country—definitely make the trip during the day. Coming out of Belmopan, the highway immediately begins to climb into the foothills of the Maya mountains. The thickly forested peaks have bizarre and irregular formations reminiscent of Dr. Seuss towers. You'll also pass Hershey's cacao-processing plant and, as you descend into the Stann Creek Valley, an enormous citrus plant (the valley is the heart of Belize's citrus industry). At the coast of Dangriga, the **Southern Highway** picks up. This long, bumpy, and unkempt highway is the reason why many people avoid the Toledo district. But (and this is a big but) don't let it scare you away from the south. As long as you can wing the hairy drive, it's totally worth it. The Maya mountains rise up to the west, and pine forest and citrus orchards line the road. The road terminates in Punta Gorda; the only way to get further south is by boat.

GLOVER'S REEF For a true deserted-isle experience, Glover's Reef is one of the best. With the opening of the **Glover's Atoll Resort,** budget travelers get a chance to try it out. Glover's is made up of a lagoon surrounded by a circular coral reef, with a few cayes dotting the southeast corner. Clear waters and pristine conditions guarantee amazing snorkeling, diving, and fishing. For $85 per week per person, you get a basic beach cabin, complete with kitchen, shower, and private outhouse (wow). The reef uses rainwater for drinking, and groceries or meals are available. Boats leave Sunday at 8 AM from the Sittee River (south of Dangriga), returning Saturday evening. The resort is closed September–November. For more info or to book a spot, call 08/23–180. You can also call the guest house in Sittee River (tel. 05/20–06), or write The Lomont Family, Box 563, Belize City, Belize, CA. You can stay overnight in Sittee River at the **Glovers Atoll Guest House.**

Placencia

Placencia is an idyllic beach resort town that gives you that island feel on a mainland budget. It sports pretty much the best sandy beach on the mainland, with the Caribbean on one side and mangrove swamps on the other. The town itself is situated at the end of an 11-mile sandy peninsula about two hours south of Dangriga. Placencia, thankfully, lacks all the plastic trinkets and con men that can often taint a resort. The main drag is a thin, winding sidewalk that meanders along the sparsely populated beachfront. Placencia is a good place to arrange off-shore excursions and inland adventures to the Jaguar Preserve or Monkey River area. Shop around town for the best prices; anyone with a boat or a car may be willing to do a trip. **Geno** (ask around) is already set up for tours if you're at a loss to find anyone. During the tourist season, this sleepy Creole fishing village can fill up, but low-key and laid-back are always the name of the game.

BASICS Placencia has no bank, but **Belize Bank** has a branch in Big Creek (on the mainland) open only 8–1 Friday mornings. **Wallen's Market** (at the curve in the road near the end of the peninsula) will cash traveler's checks. The **post office** and **BTL** (in the hut at the very end of the road at the pier, tel. 06/23–101) are open weekdays 8–noon and 1–4. **Janice Leslie** at the post office has official tourist information, or go see **Joan Christensen** at the Orange Peel (behind Wallen's Market, tel. 06/23–184); she's got a great map of Placencia and will cheerfully dispense all sorts of info.

COMING AND GOING Since none of the established companies wanted to run a bus to Placencia, Dougie decided to do it himself. **Dougie's bus** leaves Dangriga Monday, Wednesday, Friday, and Saturday at 2:30 PM (two hours, $3); he usually waits for the Belize City bus if it's running late. The bus leaves Placencia for Dangriga at 6 AM on Monday, Wednesday, Friday, and Saturday. If you come on an off-day or from the south, get off in Independence (a.k.a. Mango Creek), where you can hire a dory across the lagoon for about $15. To go for less, try to catch the mail boat in Big Creek; be nosy and ask around. You can fly on **Maya Airways** for $42 one-way from Belize City, landing on the airstrip in Big Creek. If you're stuck on the mainland side of the lagoon, you can call the post office to send someone to get you, but don't count on it after hours. Try not to let this happen, because accommodation on this side is overpriced and/or disgusting. Getting around Placencia is pretty straightforward: There's the road and there's the sidewalk. Everything is either toward the end of the spit or north up the peninsula. A drinking-water vat is in the center of town on the sidewalk.

WHERE TO SLEEP AND EAT Placencia is geared toward visitors, so you'll find a bunch of places to snooze. You can camp for $2 at **Mr. Clive's** (at the north end of town, right on the beach where the sidewalk ends). The town can fill up fast during the high season, especially on weekends, so book a room early in the day. **Conrad's and Lydia's Rooms** (tel. 06/23–117) is a comfortable, clean, and friendly place down the sidewalk from Clive's. They charge $11 for a double, and Lydia will cook breakfast on request. The **Paradise Hotel** (at the end of the spit past the post office, tel. 06/23–118) is a great deal at $16 per double: It's clean and friendly, and it has a veranda with an ocean view. For a funky alternative, **Dr. Ted** offers weekly house rentals. He charges $80 per week for a house that sleeps up to four people. Showers are rustic (basically buckets of rain water), and cooking facilities are equally simple. Inquire at Dr. Ted's Acupuncture on the road across from the baseball field.

Just about every restaurant in town is affordable, and they all serve excellent fish and seafood. Sometimes you'll have to wait up to 1½ hours to be served, but hey, it's the Caribbean. **BJ's Restaurant** (on the road at the north end of town) is cheap, and **Sonny's** has lip-smacking breakfasts. **Miss Lizzy,** above Jaime's Restaurant, has home-made yogurt and granola, as well as fresh juice.

AFTER DARK Before you go hunting for bars, head to the beach with a blanket and get loopy on a local Belizean rum like Duurley's or Cane Juice. Then you can hit the town. By far the best bar is the **Dockside** (on the water past Tentacles Restaurant). All the yachties hang out here, so it's a great place to meet seafaring adventurer types or hitch a ride to Belize City by sea. (Scam tip: Check under the Dockside bar for money dropped through the floorboards by drunks.) Locals also hang out at **Sonny's** and the **Kingfisher.** If you feel dancing fever coming on after a few shots of Cane Juice, the **Cozy Corner Disco** gets going after 10 PM (the best boogie nights are supposedly Wednesday, Friday, and Saturday).

OUTDOOR ACTIVITIES Placencia is the place to have a ball, outdoors-wise, for very little. **E-lees** (at the Paradise Hotel) has a little sailboat you can schlep around in for $3 an hour; they also rent snorkeling equipment for $3 a day. Ask here if you want to go water-skiing—one of the guys might take you out if you pay for gas (about $3 per gallon). **Kitty's Place** (tel. 06/22–027) has an actual dive shop where you can rent equipment and/or set up trips to the outlying cayes. They also rent bikes (not mountain) for $8 per day; a fun bike trip is up the peninsula to **Seine Bight,** a Garifuna fishing village. The **Orange Peel** has a tandem bike for rent, and kayaks are available at Kitty's or the post office. Rent a paddling dory for fishing expeditions into the mangroves.

Punta Gorda

The most an average traveler sees of Punta Gorda is the customs office and the bus station. It's often mistaken for a border town and therefore remains something of a secret. The pace in town is gentle but lively, and the people are amiable—all the traits of a town that hasn't been taken over by over-zealous developers or moneyed travelers. The abundant rainfall makes Punta Gorda one of the wettest spots on earth, and is the reason for the south's lushness and fertility. A Caribbean breeze usually picks up in the afternoon, breaking the stifling heat. A good place to wind down is on the ferry dock at sunset. The sun actually sets over the land, but if you're lucky, you can watch approaching lightning storms out at sea.

Punta Gorda is the capital of the Toledo district, the southernmost inhabited portion of Belize. The people on the coast are mostly Garifuna fishermen, with Ke'kchi and Mopan Mayan farmers inland. This far south, the barrier reef begins to break up, but several cayes off the coast are still cool for diving, snorkeling, and sunning. Inland from Punta Gorda rise jagged hills blanketed with jungle, rivers, and caves. The area is also rich in Mayan ruins. **Lubaantun,** the pride of the area, is easy to reach, and **Nim Li Punit,** with beautiful carved stelae, is less than a mile from the Southern Highway. **Uxbenka** and **Pusilhá** are more remote. Ask around in Punta Gorda about directions to these ancient spots.

BASICS The **post office** and **BTL** are in the big government building on Front Street, next to the police station. **Belize Bank** has a branch in the town square on Main Street. The **hospital** is at the south end of town on Main Street.

The **Toledo visitor information center** (at the ferry dock on Front St., tel. 07/22–470) is open 8–noon, closed Thursday and Sunday. It's run by Alfredo and Yvonne Villoria, who have all the info you'll need on the Toledo district: bus schedules, hotel and restaurant guides, and volumes of information on local culture, customs, and activities. They can arrange day trips into Mayan villages in the surrounding countryside, and longer, customized trips into the wilderness.

COMING AND GOING If you've got the bucks, **Maya Airways** (tel. 07/22–014) offers daily flights from Belize City to Punta Gorda for around $50 one-way. Hitching on the Southern Highway can be torture unless you're the patient sort; sometimes only one car will pass in two hours. Hitching around Toledo into the villages is easier, safer, and widely accepted. Drivers may ask for a small fee, so be prepared. It's customary to ask, "How much do I have for you?"

One of the biggest problems facing archaeologists in Belize is the uncontrollable looting of valuable Mayan artifacts. Teams of professional looters can get in and out faster than they could strip a car. Several impressive jade pieces were recovered in a Miami cocaine bust, and researchers are clueless about their origin and meaning since they were found out of context.

➤ **BY BUS** • **Z-line** runs buses to Punta Gorda from Belize City, Monday–Saturday at 8 AM, Monday, Wednesday, and Saturday at 3 PM, and Sunday at 10 AM. They return to Belize City daily at 5 AM and 11 AM. The **James** bus to Belize City meets the ferry on Tuesdays and Fridays at 1 PM. Hint for the uninitiated: Seats at the front of the bus are considerably more comfortable than those in the back, which'll bounce and rattle twice as hard. A five-hour drive in the back can turn into Mr. Toad's wild ride. Your eyeballs will begin to come out of your head, and on average, you'll bite your tongue three different times. Buses also run every day but Sunday to a few Mayan villages in the area. Buses usually leave Punta Gorda from the town square around noon, but check the schedule at the Toledo visitor information center. Wednesday and Saturday are market days, so buses are more frequent.

➤ **BY BOAT** • Ferries run from Punta Gorda to Puerto Barrios, Guatemala, on Tuesdays and Fridays. The boat leaves Punta Gorda at 2 pm, but you should arrive at 1 to get stamped out at the police station (the pier is across the street). You can buy a $6 ferry ticket at Maya de Indita Tienda on Middle Street. The ferry returns from Puerto Barrios at 8 am.

WHERE TO SLEEP Punta Gorda may be small, but it's prepared for any massive tourist influx. The 15-plus hotels in town are almost all within a budget traveler's price range. When searching for a hotel, be aware that the address system is fairly random. Numbers often don't correspond, street names are virtually nonexistent, and, above all, no one cares. If you arrive on the late bus, your chances of getting a hotel can be pretty damn slim. If Mahung's is full, you can keep dry till morning by crashing on a bench under the overhang of a big building near the town square. You can pitch a tent almost anywhere around town—if it looks inhabited, just ask the landowner. If you're thinking that the little covered piers (all along Front Street) might be a nice place to sleep for the night, give it up. They're actually outhouses.

"Our first absolutely rippin' thunderstorm in Punta Gorda started last week and hasn't stopped since. The concept of a 'higher power' (you know, God) really has meaning out here. I can't believe this much water can come out of the sky and not drown us. And then there's the lightning. I think that all the energy bouncing around definitely has an effect on people."—from a letter from T.S.

➤ **UNDER $10 • Wahima Hotel.** Right on the water, the Wahima is one of the best deals in town at $8 per double with shared bath. The rooms are dingy and the bathroom is "useable," but the fact that you're in an ocean-front pad makes up for anything. *11 Front St., tel. 07/22–542. On the north side of town near the Texaco station. Laundry.*

➤ **UNDER $15 • Nature's Way Guest House.** Backpackers stay here for a reason: It's got a stupendous ocean view, rooms (with bunk beds) are clean and airy, bathrooms are oh-so-nice, and breakfast is served on request. It's about a 10-minute walk from the center of town, and doubles with shared bath are $13. William "Chet" Schmidt (the "boss") is knowledgeable and helpful. He'll organize tours of the area or take you out on day trips to nearby cayes. Ask about his Village Experience programs, in which visitors can stay in cabins in various villages in the area. Chet also has a Hobie Cat and a windsurfing board for rent. Pick up their awesome map of Punta Gorda at the front desk. *65 Front St., tel. 07/22–119. Continue down Front St. past the broken-down house #87.*

➤ **UNDER $20 • Goya's Inn.** Centrally located across from the clock tower in the town square, Goya's has doubles with hot water and in-room TV for $18. Rooms are clean and airy, with ceiling fans and private baths. Hang out on the cool veranda and check out the goings-on in the square. *Main Middle St., tel. 07/22–086. Laundry.*

Mahung's. Mr. Mahung (what a guy) is the only person in town who'll open his doors to weary travelers arriving on the extremely late bus. Try to get a room at the back of the hotel; the ones in front are lower than the road and subject to wretched flooding. The rooms in back are worth the extra money ($18 for a double with private bath). The ones in front are $13 a double, and the shared bathrooms for the front rooms are disgusting. *On the corner of North and Main Sts., tel. 07/22–044.*

FOOD Punta Gorda can be an exciting culinary experience if you're into funky decor and sharing a table with strangers—many restaurants are in people's homes. They don't really keep regular hours, and usually serve whatever's on hand that's fresh. **Morning Glory Cafe** (on Front St., south side of town) is good for fresh juice and ice cream. You can get decent Chinese food at the restaurant in the **Miramar Hotel** on Front Street.

Lucille's Restaurant. Lucille cooks up whatever she has on hand, and she'll even fulfill requests if she can. Usually, it's basic Belizean fare: rice and beans, fried fish, pork chops, and chicken stew. A small plate goes for $2, a large plate for $4. If the place looks empty, just holler upstairs. *3 North St., off Main St. on the north end of town; you'll see the big sign.*

Man Man's Five Star Cook House. With a toothless grin and a languid air, Man Man serves up yummy, definitely five-star meals. A huge plate of meat or fish, rice and beans, salad, bread, and fruit is $4. It's recommended by Duncan Hines (yes, that one), and the enormous placard signed by the big brownie-man himself commends Man Man on the grub. Don't worry about the hours; Man Man is always open. All you gotta do is knock. *On Far West St. between King and Queen.*

AFTER DARK Punta Gorda isn't jumpin' with nightlife, but you can hang out in any number of watering holes. The whole scene's very casual; if you hear music and/or see people standing around, there's probably fun to be had and beer to be pounded.

Check out **Dreamlight** and **Bobby's Bar,** on Main Street across from Mahung's. At the south end of town, the **South Side Disco** has a black-light dance floor. If you're looking for mellow, the tropical **Olympic Bar** on Prince Street is a good place to find it.

OUTDOOR ACTIVITIES Mahung's rents **bikes** starting at $5 per day. Wallace Young (2 Front St., tel. 07/22–034) has a fleet of more expensive mountain bikes for rent. Check at the market to see if a local will take you out **fishing.** You can often pay for the trip with the fish you catch. Nature's Way is opening a juice bar at the ferry dock, where they'll also set up a **water sports** activity center with Windsurfers, Hobie Cats, canoes, and boats for rent. The ocean is fairly clean, and you can splash around at a basic **beach** at the north end of town.

NEAR PUNTA GORDA

LUBAANTUN Lubaantun ("the place of the fallen stones") is a late-classic period ceremonial center. A ballcourt and marketplace (basically indentations in the ground) sit peacefully in the jungle. Unlike most Mayan sites, where mortar binds stones together, Lubaantun was made by fitting stone blocks together like a giant jigsaw puzzle. The caretaker at the site is super-knowledgeable, and he'll usually show you around for free. Lubaantun is a mile from the village of San Pedro Colombia. Take the first right after the school, cross the river, and follow the sign.

Northern Belize

In the north, the terrain is absolutely flat. Sweeping fields of sugar cane, mangrove swamps, inland lagoons and waterways, lowland pine savannah, and stray patches of jungle make up the countryside here—strangely enough, it all blends together seamlessly. Some of the most interesting and ambitious nature reserves in the country are here, including the Community Baboon Sanctuary, Crooked Tree Wildlife Sanctuary, the Shipstern Nature Reserve and Butterfly Farm, and the wild and inaccessible Río Bravo Conservation Area. You'll also find some of the most important Mayan ruins in the country (Altun Ha, Lamanai, and Cuello), in addition to many smaller sites that are scattered throughout the region.

Until 1930, when the Northern Highway was built, northern Belize had closer ties to México than to its own country. This area is dominated by mestizos of Spanish and Mayan heritage who have retained their Spanish language. Most of these Northerners are descended from Mexican refugees who fled during the brutal Caste Wars that ravaged their country in the mid-19th century. Thousands were driven out of the Yucatán when the indigenous people rose up against their mestizo landlords in a bloody revolt that lasted over 20 years. The refugees brought with them the valuable sugar cane, which is still one of Belize's main exports.

Traveling in the north is uncomplicated but sometimes irritating. The wonderfully paved roads are blessed with regular bus service and steady traffic, so hitching isn't a pain in the butt. The irritating part is that buses to the more remote (and stunning) areas originate only in Belize City—so even though the Baboon Sanctuary and Crooked Tree are only a few miles apart, you have to bus it all the way back to the city and then catch another bus to your destination, because nary a bus runs between the two.

The far northwestern portion of Belize is home to the ambitious **Río Bravo Conservation Area,** a 202,000-acre tract of subtropical moist forest managed by a private organization called the Programme For Belize (1 King St., Belize City, tel. 02/75–616). The program holds the land in trust for the people of Belize, implementing research, conservation, and sustainable-yield forest programs. The conservation area is near the Guatemalan and Mexican borders, where it meets the Calakmul Biosphere Reserve and the Maya Biosphere Reserve to form a tri-national peace park. The park itself is full of wildlife; it also houses the massive Mayan center known as **Las Milpas,** which is emerging as an extremely important archaeological site. You aren't likely to get to Río Bravo unless you have access to a car or can afford expensive transport and lodging. You can sleep at the research center for $40 a double; if you're interested, contact the Programme headquarters in Belize City. Near the private settlement of Gallon Jug is one of the most exclusive resorts in Belize, the Chan Chich Lodge, where you can stay if you can afford the $130 doubles (yeah, right).

Corozal

As you approach the coast at the tip-top of Belize, gentle sea breezes seem to come out of nowhere, and the blue waters of the Caribbean rise out of the cane fields. Sugar production is no longer as important as it once was, but most of the mestizo population still works the soil. As the northernmost town in Belize, Corozal has a decidedly Latin feel. Unlike most Belizean towns, Corozal is grouped around a large plaza ringed with benches and topped off with the obligatory fountain. The clock tower keeps the time of day, and the mostly Spanish-speaking townspeople congregate in and around the plaza. The coast is lined with shady palms, and the sweeping Corozal Bay protects the shore and keeps the coastline peaceful and relaxing. Belizeans like to come to Corozal on holiday, and it's a pleasant stop for travelers on the way to México. Refugees from the Yucatán Caste Wars settled here in 1849, naming the town Corozal after the cohune palm tree, a Mayan symbol of fertility. In 1955, Hurricane Janet wiped out a large portion of the older wooden buildings, so most of the dominant cinder-block architecture dates from the late-1950s.

An easy walk from Corozal are the ruins of **Santa Rica,** which was probably occupied for over 3,000 years, beginning in 1500 BC. It was part of a trading center known as Chetumal, which at its height covered over 3 square kilometers (1.2 square miles). The only thing for visitors to check out is one temple with a few chambers and wall carvings. The caretaker is an interesting man who will give you a tour well worth the $2 charge. Head out on the highway toward Mexico and take the left-hand fork. Go past the hospital and turn right at the power plant.

COMING AND GOING All buses traveling between Belize City and Chetumal (the Mexican border town) pass through Corozal. Coming into Belize, buses from Chetumal drop you at the Mexican immigration post in Santa Elena. The buses then wait on the other side of the bridge while you go through the formalities at the Belizean post. You'll be given a free 30-day visa, and you might need to prove that you have enough money to stay a while (around $30 per day). Black marketeers on the Belize side offer a great deal: They'll change traveler's checks at BZ$2 to US$1 and will sometimes give BZ$2.18 to US$1 for cash. Best of all, they're perfectly legit.

The **Batty** bus terminal is in the center, near the plaza across from Belize Bank, and the **Venus** terminal is to the north, across from the Shell station. Buses run regularly in both directions, beginning at 5:30 AM. It takes only 20 minutes to get to the border and three hours to get to Belize City ($4). You can fly to San Pedro (Ambergris Cay) from Corozal on **Maya Airways** for $27. Flights leave daily in the high season, and mainly on weekends in the rainy season. Dories go to San Pedro from here, but the ride is long, treacherous, and expensive. Ask for the drivers at the market.

WHERE TO SLEEP Corozal has some of the best values in all Belize, as long as you avoid the big resorts like Tony's and the Adventure Inn. Most budget hotels are on or near the coast at the southern end of town. A cool lodging option is to rent a room from someone in town. For $5 a night or $20 a week, you get fixed up with a room and use of kitchen and laundry facilities. If you're interested, contact **Mattie** at Donna's Restaurant (#46 7th Ave., tel. 04/23–065).

➤ **UNDER $10** • **Capri Hotel.** This is the cheapest spot in town, and the rooms aren't as scary as the bar you'll pass through downstairs. A major bonus here is the veranda overlooking the sea. Nine dollars gets you a clean double with private bath, or you can get a double with shared bath for about $7, but the hygiene aspect becomes iffy. The bar supposedly closes at around 8 or 9 PM, but if a band is rocking in the rec room, don't expect to sleep before three in the morning. *14 5a Ave., tel. 04/22–042. From the bus station go south and toward the coast; it's a big building right on the sea. 30 rooms, some with bath.*

Nestor's Hotel. Though not on the coast, this hotel is a good deal for your dough. A nice, spiffy double with private bath is $10. Run by a Canadian and a Texan, Nestor's is neighborly and safe, with 24-hour security. Dell's restaurant downstairs has yummy eats starting at 7 AM daily. Breakfast is $2–$3 and seafood runs $5–$8. *123 5th Ave., tel. 04/22–354. 16 rooms, some with bath. Laundry, luggage storage.*

➤ **UNDER $20** • **Maya Hotel.** More expensive but worth the splurge, the Maya is right on the sea. Rooms are big and airy, with an inviting veranda, and the immaculate bathrooms even have hot water. The best deal is a double with one bed (woo, woo) for $16. If you want separate beds, the price goes up to $21. The restaurant downstairs serves whatever they have and/or whatever you want for about $5. *On the highway, south end of town, tel. 04/22–082. 17 rooms, some with bath. Laundry.*

FOOD Plenty of restaurants dot the town, distinguishable only by whether they serve Belizean or Chinese. Most dining spots serve reasonably priced, mediocre food; a few, however, are head and shoulders above the rest. **Donna's Restaurant and Bar** (46 7th Ave., tel. 04/23–065), open daily 6:30 AM–10:30 PM, was recently bought by some transplanted Americans. They serve Belizean specialties like cowfoot soup and conch fritters at okay prices. The chicken, rice, and beans is a tasty mouthful for only $3. Locals flock to **Rexo** (9 6th St. N, on the north end of town, tel. 04/22–392) for Chinese food a notch above the rest. **Crises Restaurant** (20 10th Ave., on the north end of town, tel. 04/22–984) is open daily 10 AM–11 PM. It's another local favorite, with typical fare for under $3. The **market** (at the end of 3rd St. and 2nd St. S, on the coast) has fresh produce and fish, as well as food stands.

OUTDOOR ACTIVITIES The rocky coast is swimmable at all points, and you'll find a picnic area at the north end of town. If you feel like rubbing your toes in some fine imported sand (it feels like walking in flour), go to **Tony's Resort** (head south out of town, it's on the left); it's a treat to sun your bod on soft stuff. They have an expensive seaside bar and restaurant, but you can loaf on the docks and the shore for the price of a drink. You can also rent jet-skis here for $25 per ½ hour.

AFTER DARK Night life here is usually mellow, but the place gets kicking every once in a while when a live band comes to town. The bar at **Capri Hotel** has a dance floor and a pool table if you're in the mood to rack 'em up. You can also dance the night away at an open-air disco on the beach, near the Capri Hotel. **Donna's Restaurant** is a friendly little spot to sip some alcohol. If you really want to get plastered, go across the street to **Bumpers,** where the mood is lively and hard-core drinkers come to throw punches.

NEAR COROZAL

4-MILE LAGOON The best swimming in the area is up the Northern Highway at this roadside lagoon. **The Quality Inn** here is only a restaurant, but apparently they throw the best party this side of the border. All the locals come to swim, drink, and frolic on a regular basis (ask for info in town). Party or no, it's worth a stop to splash around and have a beer. You can camp overnight on the inn's land for a small fee. Take any bus heading north and ask to be let off at the Quality Inn. If you miss the last bus back to Corozal, you can easily hitch.

CERROS This site across the Corozal Bay has a 73-foot temple right on the water. It's a late Preclassic center with tombs and ballcourts, but most of it is unexcavated. The pleasant boat ride across the bay makes the trip to Cerros worth it. If you ask around at the dock by the Corozal market, someone will take you out there for about $13. The ride takes about an hour (round-trip).

Orange Walk

The first thing you notice as you approach Orange Walk is the sugar cane—it's every-where. Fields of it run beside the road, stretching out to the horizon like wheat in Kansas. And the trucks—literally hundreds pass up and down the highway, piled high with long, brown stalks of raw sugar. When you pass the processing plants in the evening, the loaded trucks line the factory roads as far as the eye can see. Sugar used to be Belize's main export, and although citrus is fast becoming the big moneymaker in the south and west, cane is still king in the Orange Walk district. Concealed inside the cane fields is Orange Walk's other big money maker: marijuana. When sugar prices plummet, the drug industry keeps the town above water. Orange Walk isn't all that inviting, but it is a good base from which to explore Mayan sites in the area. Cuello is right outside town, and you can arrange tours to Lamanai here as well. Orange Walk, like Corozal, is constructed around a plaza in the Latin tradition. Unfortunately, this plaza isn't particularly charming, although the slice-of-life element is interesting. The biggest thrill here is swimming. The **Lamanai Inn** (Riverside Dr. on the east side of town) is a little thatched restaurant and swimming hole on the banks of the New River. You can also use the pool at Baron's Hotel for $3.

COMING AND GOING Orange Walk is a two-hour bus ride from Belize City, and another couple of hours from the border. Between Batty and Venus, buses leave about every hour in both directions, beginning at 4 AM. The last from Chetumal is at 6 PM and the last from Belize City is at 7 PM ($3 from Belize City). Traffic on the Northern Highway is brisk, so hitching shouldn't be a problem, but use caution—the drug trade is also brisk. Orange Walk is a fairly large town, but most hotels lie along the main drag, Queen Victoria Street. Taxi stands, banks, and bus stops are all grouped around the plaza. The New River is east of town, and Cuello is to the west.

WHERE TO SLEEP Accommodation is slim pickin's, but you won't find much rea-son to stay here for long anyway. The best value in town is **Taisan's** (30 Queen Victoria Ave., tel. 03/22–752), on the main road in the center of town. Bed down in a clean double with shared bath with hot showers for $13. The main drawback is noise from the road, but this is a petty concern considering the price and quality of the rooms. The only other budget bed is **Jane's** (6 Market Lane, tel. 03/22–526). Go through the park and turn right at the Belize Bank; dingy doubles minus the annoying traffic noise are $13. If you want to splurge, do it right at **Baron's Hotel** (40 Belize Corozal Rd., tel. 03/22–847) on the main road at the south end of town. The hotel is equipped with a restaurant, disco, and pool. Doubles are $24. If for some reason these are full, the cement blocks on Queen Victoria Avenue have doubles for about $20.

FOOD Believe it or not, it's hard to find Belizean food here. Chinese restaurants, however, are everywhere. All serve the basic fried rice, chop suey, and the like (with fried chicken thrown in for good measure) for $2–$3. The real reason to choose **Lee's** (11 San Antonio Rd., behind the fire station, tel. 03/22–174) is the air-conditioning. Lee's is open daily 11:30 AM–midnight. A string of snack stands line Queen Victoria Avenue at Cemetery Lane. **The Diner** (37 Clark St., tel. 03/22–131), one of the few Belizean restaurants in town, happens to be one of the best in the country. It serves excellent gourmet Creole food in an engaging atmosphere. Terri Oreo (the owner) will take requests or serve up homemade delicacies for $4–$10. Try a typical Belizean breakfast of fried jacks (crispy, fried dough), fish, and greasy-greasy (sweetened bread loaded with shortening). The Diner is underneath the Bullet Tree (it looks bullet-riddled). If you walk down Clark Street, people will point the way, or you can ask a cab driver.

NEAR ORANGE WALK

LAMANAI This is one of the most impressive sites in Belize and fully worth the time it takes to get here. The boat trip through the New River and New River Lagoon is in itself a pleasant day on the water, complete with birdwatching and a pretty good chance of seeing a crocodile. Lamanai means "submerged crocodile," and it's one of the only true Mayan site names known today. Pulling up to the riverbank at the site, you're confronted with a dense stretch of some of the only remaining jungle in the area. Emerging from the canopy, the 1,122-foot temple N10–43 offers a spectacular view of the surrounding countryside and lagoon.

Occupation at Lamanai ran from 1500 BC all the way into the 16th century, outlasting many other Mayan cities; it reached its height in the late Preclassic period. Temple N10-43, which has been crucial in understanding the development of the early Mayan civilization, is the largest Preclassic temple yet discovered. The 6th-century temple P9-56 has a beautiful 13-foot mask in front, and workers are now busy clearing a tunnel into the tomb underneath. South of the temple complex you'll find the ruins of two Catholic churches in the nearby village of Indian Church, a reminder of the repeated Spanish attempts to convert the 16th-century "Indians" to Catholicism. You'll also find the remains of a 19th-century sugar mill built by Confederates after the U.S. Civil War.

The Lamanai site is in a nature area known as the **Lamanai Reserve.** Several troops of chattering black howler monkeys hang about the ruins, and rare birds, such as the collared aracari, black vulture, and northern jacana, live here too. Getting to Lamanai is going to cost you some money. You can arrange tours in Belize City or Orange Walk. **Jungle River Tours** (20 Lovers Lane, Orange Walk, tel. 03/22–293) will arrange trips from either place for 1–6 people for $100. If you're not with a large group, Antonio and Herminio Novelo of Jungle River Tours will hook you up with other travelers. If you don't bring your own lunch, they'll provide one for about $10. Another option is to head to the village of Guinea Grass, where you can hire a boat to take you on the hourlong trip upriver. **Atilano Narvallez** (tel. 03/22–081) will get you to Lamanai for $75, which is the going rate. (If you're a smooth talker, sometimes you can bargain down.) Lamanai can also be reached through San Felipe, but the road is very seasonal and may be completely washed out during the rainy season.

Crooked Tree Wildlife Sanctuary

Crooked Tree was established in 1984, mainly to protect resident and migratory bird populations. During the dry season, thousands of birds congregate in the network of inland lagoons, logwood swamps, and waterways. The most famous visitor to the reserve is the rare jabiru stork; with a wingspan of 10 to 12 feet, it's the largest flying bird in the Americas. An incredible variety of other birds nest and feed in the diverse habitats of Crooked Tree: night herons, great blue herons, snowy egrets, snail kites, ospreys, and the black-bellied whistling duck. The swamp also houses other wildlife, such as black howlers, monelets crocodile, coatimundi, turtles, and iguanas. The best time to view the migratory birds is in the dry season between November and March. As soon as the rain begins to pour, they take off to drier climates.

The island village of Crooked Tree is in the center of the lagoon. It was one of the first inland villages established during the logwood era because it was accessible by boat, but only recently has it become accessible by land. The island is crisscrossed by a network of walking trails through the lowland pine savannah and along the lagoon. You need to sign in at the visitors' center, where you can get a plethora of info on the reserve.

Two legends try to explain the origin of the name "Belize." The Eurocentric one says that in 1603, Peter Wallace, said to be the first Brit on the Mosquito Coast, camped at the mouth of the Belize River before seeking Spanish treasure in Honduras. "Belize" is perhaps a perversion of "Wallace" (pronounced "Valeese" in Spanish). The Mayacentric one holds that the name Belize comes from a Mayan word meaning "muddy water."

COMING AND GOING Batty Brothers runs a bus to Crooked Tree (1½ hours, $2) which leaves weekdays from Belize City at 4 PM, returning mornings at 7 AM. The Saturday bus leaves Belize City at noon, returning at 4 PM the same day; on Sunday, it leaves Belize City at 9 AM and returns at 4 PM. **Jex Bus Service** also runs to Crooked Tree several times a day Monday–Saturday. The island lies at the end of a 3-mile causeway off the Northern Highway, so you could conceivably hop off any bus and walk.

WHERE TO SLEEP AND EAT Crooked Tree has community-ty-cooperative lodging; double rooms with local families are $13, and you can eat local cuisine with them for $3 per meal. Arrange your stay in advance with the **Belize Audubon Society** (tel. 02/77–369), or drop in at the **visitors' center** tel. 02/44–101), where they can set you up on the spot from 8 to 5. Crooked Tree also has four irritatingly over-priced lodgings ($65 a night). If you're interested, inquire at the visitors' center. If you feel like staying in the jungle off the island, accommodation is available at the local ranch for about $13.

OUTDOOR ACTIVITIES You have several options for exploring the Crooked Tree Reserve. For $13, you can hire horses for half a day, and if you want a guide to show you around, it'll be another $20. Boating on the lagoon is a pleasant way to spend the day and perfect for spotting wildlife. It costs $80 including gas to hire a motorboat, or a mere $10 for a paddling canoe powered by you.

Altun Ha

Just so you know right off, Altun Ha is a pleasant place to visit and a very important site, but unless you have your own wheels, it ain't worth the trouble. The site lies off the old Northern Highway, where bus routes have all but disappeared. Even if you hitch the 48 kilometers (30 miles) from Belize City, there's no place to stay in **Maskall,** the nearest town. A bus (sometimes a truck) leaves Belize City at 3:30 PM for the 1½-hour trip. It then returns from Maskall around 5 AM, which doesn't exactly make the perfect day trip from Belize City. If you're dead-set on checking out Altun Ha, do it on Saturday, when the bus leaves Vernon Street near the Batty Bus Terminal in Belize City at 11 AM and returns from Maskall at 3 PM. The walk from Maskall is about 3 kilometers (2 miles), so you'll have to haul ass. If you miss the bus and have a tent, you may be able to camp—ask the caretakers. Apparently, a new farm and guest house are under construction in the nearby village of **Santana**. Inquire at the Seaside Guest House (Belize City, tel. 02/78–330) to find out what's up. Admission to the site is $2.

Once thought peripheral to the Mayan empire, Altun Ha was actually an important link in coastal trading routes between the southern lowlands and the Yucatán. The site was also a minor ceremonial center during the Classic period, though settlement dates to around 200 BC. The central ceremonial precinct is made up of two plazas dotted with palm trees. Altun Ha has yielded some of the richest artifacts yet uncovered in the Mayan world. Temple A-1 (Temple of the Green Tomb) contained the remains of a Mayan book, as well as jade, jewelry, and hundreds of other artifacts. The tallest temple on the site is B-4 (Temple of the Masonry Altars). The Sun God's Tomb was uncovered in 1968; it contained a carved jade head (the largest ever found) of Kinich Ahau, the Sun God himself. Unfortunately, this famous head and other valuable objects are locked away where no one (not even if you're special) can see them.

GUATEMALA

3

By Courtney Heller and Ian Signer

Guatemala's appeal as a travel destination is its mind-boggling diversity of people, culture, religion, and landscape. With one of the largest indigenous populations in Latin America, Guatemala is home to more than 100 distinct ethnic groups who speak more than 20 languages, from the Afro-Guatemalan Garifuna of the Caribbean Coast to the Highland Quiché. Flanked by the Pacific and Atlantic oceans and bordering Mexico, Belize, Honduras, and El Salvador, Guatemala is, in the words of poet Pablo Neruda, the "sweet waist" of the Americas. The first stop on most itineraries through Guatemala is the Western Highlands, *the* center of *Indígena* culture. Hundreds of villages are strewn through the mountains, each with its own distinct style of brilliantly colored dress, its white-washed colonial church, and teeming market days. Here, the country is cut up by mountain ranges and towering volcanoes. In the far northern reaches of the country is the Petén, where dense jungles carpet the valleys, shrouding lofty Mayan temples (notably, Tikal), lost tombs, and the occasional thatched-hut village. Central and Eastern Guatemala (Alta and Baja Verapaz) are a microcosm of the country, running the gamut from Kekchí villages to Caribbean beaches, expansive farms, and dusty, frontier-like Ladino towns. The Pacific coast is one of the least attractive parts of Guatemala, littered with sleazy ports filled with drunken sailors and vacationing *guatemaltecos*. It's a breeding ground for mosquitoes, and the sun blazes relentlessly on the black-sand beaches—a gift from the volcanoes. Inland from the coast are marshy lowlands (oozing humidity) that are diced into large *fincas* (farms) growing sugarcane, bananas, and coffee. Lacing it all together is the nation's capital, Guatemala City, crammed with belching buses, cheap pensions, in-your-face pollution, and all the amenities a traveler could ever want—or want to pass up.

For all its culture and beauty, Guatemala has suffered enormous destruction and pain. The dark side of Guatemalan politics is readily apparent. From the *conquistadores* to the present day, Guatemala's indigenous majority has labored under the injustices of the ruling class. Guatemala is the battleground of Latin America's longest running civil war, which has claimed the lives of over 100,000 people—mostly poor rural Guatemalans, almost all killed by their own government. More people have been murdered in Guatemala than in any of its more widely publicized neighbors to the south. Like so many things here, though, the killing remains hidden, conveniently masking the U.S. government's history of support for the most ruthless of Guatemalan leaders.

Guatemala

N

| 0 | | 20 miles |
| 0 | | 30 km |

PACIFIC OCEAN

Champerico

Nueva Venecia

Río Samalá

Río Madre Viejo

Retalhuleu

SAN MARCOS

San Marcos

Huehuetenango

Coatenango

Soloma

Todos Santos Cuchumatán

Memostenango

Nebaj

Chajul

QUICHE

Taetic

Cobán

San Pedro Carchá

Lanquín

Cahabón

Semuc Champey

Río Cahabón

El Estor

Mariscos

SIERRA DE SANTA CRUZ

Los Amates

Lake Izabal

IZABAL

Sto. Tomás de Castilla

La Ruidosa

Mazatenango

Quezaltenango

L. Atitlán

Totonicapán

Chichicastenango

Santa Cruz del Quiché

Purulhá

Salamá

BAJA VERAPAZ

Santa Lucía, San Vicente Pacaya

Colzumalguapa

Chulamar

Río María Linda

Puerto Iztapa San José

Taxisco

La Democracia Monte Alta

Escuintla

Cuilapa

JUTIAPA

Jutiapa

Jalapa

Antigua

L. Amatitlán

Guatemala City

Mixco

Viejo

San Juan Sacatepéquez

El Progreso

San Diego

San Jícaro

Río Hondo

Río Motagua

El Jicaro

Zacapa

Guatán

Chiquimula

El Florido

HONDURAS

EL SALVADOR

San Salvador

PACIFIC OCEAN

Guatemala

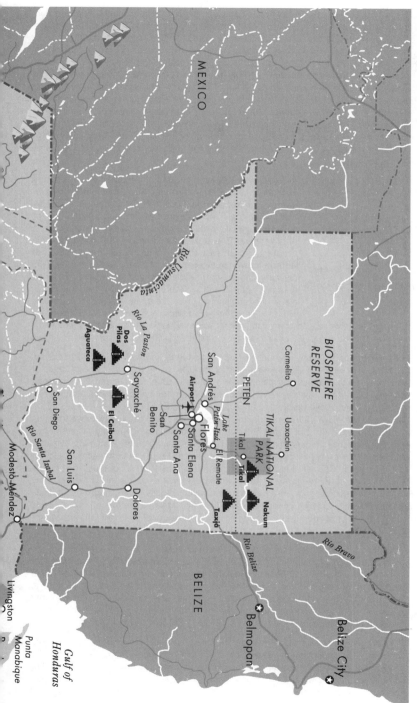

MEXICO

Río Usumacinta

Río La Pasión

Aguateca

Dos Pilas

Sayaxché

San Diego

El Ceibal

San Benito

San Andrés

Airport

Flores

Santa Elena

San Ana

Lake Petén Itzá

El Remate

PETEN

Carmelita

BIOSPHERE RESERVE

Uaxactún

Tikal

Tikal

TIKAL NATIONAL PARK

Nakum

Taxió

Río Santa Izabal

San Luis

Dolores

Modesto Méndez

Río Belize

Río Bravo

BELIZE

Belmopan

Belize City

Livingston

Punta Manabique

Gulf of Honduras

If you cast a blind eye to politics, Guatemala is the ultimate budget traveler's paradise. What might buy you a sleazy hotel room and greasy food for a week in London can buy you a month or two of comfortable rooms, healthy food, and thrilling adventures in Guatemala. More than anything, traveling here means preparing yourself for sights and events like nothing you could encounter in the First World: from a little girl sleeping in a cardboard box on the filthy streets of Guatemala City, to a view of the seemingly endless rainforest from the top of Temple IV at Tikal, to an incense-filled pagan shrine in a destroyed colonial church. Almost every place has a story to tell—of a bloody massacre, or a flamboyant Maya ruler, or a priest that used hymns rather than swords to conquer the native people. Today, modern and traditional, Ladino (people of mixed European and Indígena blood) and Indígena, rich and poor continue to coexist in a peace as rocky as when the Spanish first encountered the Maya almost 400 years ago.

The variety of landscape in Guatemala has kept pockets of people and their culture separated and distinct from one another. The Garifuna Afro-Guatemalans of Livingston, for example, live in a tiny town accessible only by boat, while the Pokom Maya of Tactic sit on a high mountain, surrounded by the Kekchí who make up the majority in Alta Verapaz. One trek around the country will throw you headfirst into at least a dozen thriving, distinct cultures, all with their own language, mode of dress, and traditions. This diversity can be both a blessing and a curse: In order to maintain their identity, Guatemala's many factions, especially the Indígena majority, continue to resist integration. This not only includes maintaining the old ways, but also refusing the new ones. In many rural areas, you may come across villagers who know only a minimal amount of Spanish, and few rural indigenous people can read or write.

"It's still a communal culture," says a Peace Corps worker in San Pedro Carchá. "If one child goes to school, that's enough for the entire community."

Guatemalans have a long relationship with exploitation and war. As early as 600 BC, the great city centers of the Maya rose out of this soil, using the sweat of thousands of laborers to build temples and palaces for a ruling class of priests and lords. Among the most dramatic of their achievements was Tikal, a brilliant city whose temples rise hundreds of feet above the thick, humid jungle. While Europe was in the throes of the Dark Ages, the Maya elite were drinking hot chocolate from the top of these towering architectural marvels. But in the 9th century AD, their great cities met a mysterious end. The immense centers that had once controlled nearly all of Guatemala began to crumble, and the people scattered into tribes that duked it out with each other until 1523, when the Spanish decided they wanted to join the fun. A hot-blooded conquistador named don Pedro de Alvarado played on old rivalries and with his meager army helped the warring Mayans defeat themselves. Today, indigenous Guatemala remains divided, but not conquered. The Quichés, Mam, Cackchiquel, Kekchí, and many other tribes continue to speak their languages and celebrate a culture that predates Columbus.

Alvarado established the Kingdom of Guatemala in Ciudad Vieja (the first of the country's ill-fated capitals) and repression of the natives went into full swing. Many of the conquistadores had children by Indígena women and a new class of mixed-blood Guatemalans emerged. Even today, the indigenous majority remains subservient to these Ladinos. This ruling class benefitted from the Spanish wealth that flowed into Guatemala, which at the time encompassed all of Central America, as well as the Mexican state of Chiapas.

In 1821, Ladino Guatemalans decided they were sick of Spanish rule and declared themselves the Independent Federation of Central America. Though independence granted new freedom and power to the colonists, it worsened the lot of the Maya. For the next century the Maya's lands were annexed and sold to huge plantation owners who made the indigenous people little more than slaves on their own land. In fact, some anthropologists claim that the unique traditional costumes of each village were actually introduced by the Spanish to identify their human "property."

By 1839, the loose ties of the Central American federation broke, and Guatemala began to take its present geographic shape (though it claimed Belize within its borders until 1990). The new government produced a series of unspectacular, and downright corrupt, dictators who looked after the interests of the small Ladino ruling class, all the while oppressing the indigenous majority. A ray of hope briefly shined through in 1944, when an army coup replaced the dictator Jorge Ubico with Juan José Arevalo, who gave an ear to the indigenous voices of his country. His successor, Jacobo Arbenz, continued reforms but went a bit too far for the reactionary right and the United States. He began redistributing idle land that belonged to the United Fruit Company (which, at the time, was the largest landowner in Guatemala) and used the company's tax returns (which vastly underestimated the true value of the land) to calculate compensation. United Fruit didn't like this one bit and immediately began a press campaign to discredit this first president who dared to challenge their power. They financed a coup by U.S.-trained Castillo Armas, and when it failed, went so far as to solicit American aid in the bombing of Guatemala City. (Although the extent of its involvement has been disputed, the C.I.A. is thought to have played a role.) Arbenz, tired and frightened, resigned from office and was forced into exile in Cuba. Armas took over and became the first in a string of dictators that dragged Guatemala to its lowest depths. By the 1960s, the *mano blanco* emerged, the first of many death squads that spread throughout Central America. Opponents of the government were murdered with a grim inevitability, and Guatemalan society became increasingly polarized.

But the most tragic time in Guatemala's history was the early 1980s, when the government began mounting ruthless "scorched-earth" counterinsurgency campaigns that destroyed hundreds of villages to flush out a handful of suspected guerrillas. As usual, those who suffered were the Indígena, who were raped, tortured, shot, mutilated, and often walled into their homes and burned alive. By 1985, the military had murdered 70,000 people and was responsible for the "disappearance" of 40,000. An additional 75,000 Guatemalans fled into Mexico to escape the violence. Though the wholesale butchering of villages has stopped, the military remains a constant presence, and anti-government guerrillas continue to operate, particularly in the Highlands. In 1985, Guatemalans elected Marco Vinicio Cerezo, their first civilian president in almost 40 years. He was followed by another civilian, Jorge Serrano Elías, who, for the first time, recognized Belize as a separate nation and appointed the first civilian head of the National Police in decades. These positive signs abruptly ended in May 1992 when Serrano seized authoritarian power and suspended constitutional rights in an apparent effort to quell growing political and economic protests. A few days later, the Guatemalan military forced Serrano from office and the government's human rights ombudsman, Ramiro de León Carpio, was named president. Although Guatemala's track record in politics sucks, Carpio may move the country in a better direction. We'll see...

Basics

See Chapter 1 for important info pertaining to Guatemala.

VISITOR INFORMATION

➤ **TOURIST OFFICES** • Tourism is one of Guatemala's biggest industries, raking in a chunk of the annual national income. The national tourist commission, **INGUAT** (Instituto Guatemalteco de Turismo), publishes colorful guidebooks and brochures focusing on the many natural and cultural wonders of Guatemala (and avoiding its unpleasant politics). You'll find branches in Antigua, Guatemala City, Panajachel, and Quetzaltenango, as well as in the airports of Guatemala City and Flores. In towns without an INGUAT office, a good place to go is the *municipalidad* (usually on or near the main plaza), which can point you toward hotels and comedors or private citizens who house and feed visitors.

➤ **VOLUNTEERING** • In general, if you're interested in volunteering and you're not hooked up with a specific program, you can travel to Guatemala and wing it. If you want to volunteer at a hospital or clinic, go to the smaller towns and ask around. The same goes for other areas of interest; you're sure to find some organization or hard-hit village that would welcome assistance.

Casa Guatemala is an orphanage on the banks of the Río Dulce. It's the ideal place for the socially minded to work with young Guatemalans who are really in need. Those who stay only a short time can expect to help with the daily chores, but long-term volunteers may get to work closely with the children. Call their main office in Guatemala City (17 Calle 10-63, Zl, tel. 02/225–517) for more info. The minimum volunteer time is two weeks.

The **Shawcross Aid Programme for Highland Indians** (Apartado Postal 343, Antigua, Guatemala, 03901) is a "non-profit, non-religious, non-political organization" to help out Indígena victims of violence during the early 1980s. Volunteers usually stay about three months, but sometimes longer, and they help provide technical assistance and materials to villagers. If you're interested, write first to make sure that the program is still alive and kicking.

Peace Brigades International (Box 1233, Harvard Square Station, Cambridge, MA 02238) has a six-month volunteer program for fluent Spanish-speakers who are at least 25 years old and have an interest in human rights. The program involves hanging out with and protecting the rights of at-risk social-justice advocates around Guatemala. You'll be trained in the United States beforehand. All living expenses are paid but you must provide your own airfare.

WHEN TO GO The tourist brochures that tout Guatemala as "The Land of Eternal Spring" are doubtlessly referring to the moderate, comfortable climate of the Western Highlands, where most of the tourists go. But honestly, Guatemala has such a varied geography that it's impossible to characterize the climate of the whole country. Guatemala is in a tropical zone, but it also has the highest mountains in Central America. The Petén (the far north) and Izabal are sweltering, rainy, and humid. At the opposite extreme are Quetzaltenango and Huehuetenango (northern Western Highlands), where the nights are downright freezing and you'll need a heavy sweater. In between are the cool, misty slopes of Alta Verapaz, all evergreen and drizzly. Over the mountains from here, in Baja Verapaz all the way to Zacapa, Chiquimula, and Jutiapa, it's dry and scrubby with never-green valleys. As you drop down to the Pacific coast, you're in for another stretch of hot, sticky, humid weather. Guatemala City and the Western Highlands are the only areas that experience a true dry season (October–May) and rainy season (June–September).

➤ **HOLIDAYS AND FESTIVALS** • In addition to all the major Catholic holidays, Guatemala celebrates the following: June 30, Army Day; August 15, Our Lady of the Assumption; September 15, Independence Day; October 20, Revolution Day. There's a festival for practically every day of the year somewhere in the country. Ask for the *Directory of Fiestas* at the Guatemala City INGUAT. Some of the most famous are Semana Santa in Antigua and the festival of Santo Tomás in Chichicastenago (Dec. 13–21). The national folklore festival in Cobán (end of July) is also great. For the market days and festivals of the Western Highlands towns, look in the Western Highlands section of this chapter.

MAIL It's really, really cheap to send mail home (about 5¢ for a letter to the United States), but you'll hear stories about letters getting lost before they even leave Guatemala. Mail usually takes 1–2 weeks to get to the United States. To receive mail, just have your pen pals put your name, Lista de Correos, the city, and the department (region). Sometimes, you'll be charged a small fee for each letter held in your name, and you have to show your passport or other ID to receive them. Post office hours all over the country are generally weekdays 8–4, although in Guatemala City the post office is open weekdays until 7 and all day Saturday.

MONEY The *quetzal* (also the name of the national bird) is one of the most stable currencies in Latin America. In fact, Guatemala is one of the few places in Latin America where the smallest unit of money (1 *centavo*) still has value and is readily used. There are 100 centavos to a quetzal. Prices quoted in this chapter are based on an exchange rate of Q5.1 to U.S. $1. The word *pesos* is sometimes used in place of quetzal, and *len* in place of centavos. Guatemala is one country where people *use* their money. Bills are ripped, torn, taped, and scribbled on, but still accepted everywhere. Though most wind up a sort of dingy brown, they usually retain some semblance of their original colors.

Most banks change American traveler's checks. No banks change Australian traveler's checks, and only one bank (**Banco de Guatemala** in Guatemala City) will change Canadian traveler's checks. You can get a cash advance on Visa or Mastercard from **Credomatic** (Edificio el Roble, 4 Piso 6-26, Zona 9, Guatemala City, tel. 02/317–436). Avoid getting 100-quetzal bills because everyone hates to accept them.

PHONES The national phone company, **GUATEL,** has offices across the country where you can make long-distance collect calls, credit-card calls, or local ones if there are no public phones in the city. Local calls cost 10 centavos (2¢). Hold the money above the slot and drop it in when the phone beeps. Always keep more coins ready. From most public phones you can reach an **AT&T** operator by dialing 190. This will give you direct person-to-person service only to the United States. The direct number to Canada is 198. In a few cities, there are **MCI** phones with a direct line to the United States. Using a calling-card number is cheaper than making a collect call. And you won't have to spend tons of time in the GUATEL office.

Unless you plan to reverse the charges, carry a small basket of change if you're making a long-distance call from a public phone. A call to the United States costs 15.27 quetzales (about $3) a minute and the largest coins accepted by pay phones are 25 centavos—that's 62 coins for 1 minute, folks!

VISAS Citizens of the United States and Canada need a tourist card ($5), but not a visa; citizens of Australia, New Zealand, and the U.K. require visas. A tourist card allows you 30 days of travel within Guatemala. You can apply for a renewal in Guatemala City at 12 Calle and 8 Avenida, Zona 1 (weekdays 8–4:30), but it may be more fun (and just as quick) to pop over to El Salvador or the ruins in Copán, Honduras. You have to be out of the country at least 72 hours before coming back in and getting a new "card" (actually, it's a stamp in your passport). Tourist cards are issued in the airport and at border crossings, as well as at Guatemalan embassies and consulates. If you are planning an extended stay, though, consider applying for a visa. The prime pass is a 90-day multiple reentry visa. Not only will this allow you a long time in the country, but you can reenter the country without having to pay for another tourist card. Apply at your local consulate and explain to them you're so interested in Guatemala that you need 90 days to really see all its wonders (and to spend money to help out the Guatemalan economy), and you may be able to get this valuable stamp.

COMING AND GOING

➤ **BY PLANE** • The cheapest and easiest way to get to Guatemala from the U.S. is by plane. Guatemala has two airports, one in Guatemala City (international and domestic) and one in Flores (domestic). Almost every airline arrives in the capital city, though you can take flights from Cancún (Mexico) or Belize City to Flores. Airlines flying from the United States include **American** (tel. 800/433–7300), **Continental** (tel. 800/231–0856), **United** (tel. 800/538–2929), **Aviateca** (tel. 800/327–9832), and **Taca** (tel. 800/535–8780). Round-trip airfares fluctuate from $300 to $600. Aviateca and Taca usually have the best deals, with $300 flights out of Miami. Flights to Guatemala City either pass through or originate in Los Angeles, Miami, Houston, or Dallas Fort Worth. If you're flying from Canada you'll probably connect in one of these cities. From Europe, weekly connecting flights usually stop in New York City, Miami, or México City. If you're coming from the United Kingdom, **British Airways** flies directly into Guatemala City. Other international airlines with direct service are KLM, Iberia, Mexicana, Lacsa, Copa, Aerovías, and Aeroquetzal (the last two are Guatemalan airlines which, in addition to Aviateca, also fly to Flores). Iberia has direct service from Madrid to Guatemala City for about $1,400 round-trip.

You can easily fly to most Central American capitals from Guatemala City. **Aerovías** (tel. 305/885–1775 in the U.S.) and **Tropic Air** (tel. 02/45–671, Belize City) fly to Belize City for about $125. (Call to make sure Aerovías is still flying.) Aviateca, Guatemala's biggest airline, flies from Guatemala City to San José, Managua, and Panamá City.

➢ **BY BUS** • If you want to bus it from the United States to Guatemala, **Greyhound** stops at all U.S.-Mexico border towns. From there it takes about two days to México City. At the capital, you can catch a **Cristóbal Colón** bus (tel. 52/5542–7263) that goes to the Guatemalan border, connecting with a bus that heads to Guatemala City. The entire trip (from the U.S.-México border to Guatemala City) can take 4–5 days (or longer) and costs about $150–$200. It's definitely a long haul and recommended only if you have lots of time on your hands and are hankering to see all of México. You can bypass México City completely by traveling on the Interamerican Highway along México's coast. The coastal trip is longer but it saves you from México City hell. The two main border crossings to enter Guatemala from México are La Mesilla and El Carmen. From either crossing, it's about 7 hours through the Western Highlands to Guatemala City if you take a pullman (private) bus, and much longer by public bus.

Most buses to neighboring Central American countries leave from Guatemala City. **Melva Internacional** leaves daily once an hour from Guatemala City to San Salvador (5 hours, $6; *see* Guatemala City, By Bus section, *below*). A good way to get to México from Guatemala City is to take a bus to Huehuetenango and then catch a connecting bus from there. **Velaquez** (*see* Huehuetenango, *below*) has buses that leave from Huehuetenango to La Mesilla (2 hours, $1.25). To bus it to Honduras, catch a **Rutas Orientales** bus from Guatemala City to Chiquimula (if you want to visit Copán) or Esquipulas, and from there take a microbus to the border. Microbuses leave regularly 5 AM–6 PM (*see* Esquipulas, *below*). The trip takes 10 minutes and costs about a dollar. From Esquipulas, the El Salvadoran border is one hour away, and costs about $1. To get to Belize, **Pinitas buses** depart daily from the Hotel San Juan in Santa Elena (in the Petén) to Belize City ($10, 7 hours). At the border the bus connects with a Novelo bus. For $10 more, minibuses (that are much more comfortable) do this same route to Belize City. *See* Santa Elena for more info on minibuses.

Boats head to Punta Gorda (in southern Belize) from Puerto Barrios (on Guatemala's Caribbean coast) Tuesdays and Fridays at 7:30 AM. The trip takes 2 ½ hours and costs about $6. *See* Puerto Barrios for info on where to buy tickets.

➢ **BY CAR** • If you decide to drive through México, make sure your car can take a beating, and leave yourself tons of time to do this road trip. Gas is quite expensive. You could pay up to $500 in gas driving from the México-U.S. border (Tijuana) to Guatemala City and the whole trip can take up to a week. An added expense are the toll roads, that set you back $4–$5 each time. You can try taking *libre* (free) roads, but these will sometimes take you hours out of your way and then you're paying for the extra gas anyway. The best (and most popular) route into Guatemala is to follow the Interamerican Highway along the coast of México, entering Guatemala on its western border (through La Mesilla) and then going through Huehuetenango to Guatemala City. Another direct (and popular) route starts out in Brownsville, Texas, going along the

Gulf coast to Veracruz, and then to the Guatemalan border. It's uncommon to enter Guatemala from its northern Petén region because the Petén is isolated, roads are horrible, and resources (for fixing a car, etc.) are few and far between. You need to get car insurance for both Guatemala and México (available at the border). Also, at the border entering Guatemala, officials will fumigate your car and make you foot the bill. This doesn't happen when returning to México. No matter what route you take, make sure to tote spare car parts, tools, and a mechanics manual so that you can take care of car breakdowns on your own.

➤ **BY TRAIN** • U.S. Amtrak and Southern Railways go as far as the U.S.-Mexican border. From there you can catch a Mexican train to the capital. South of México City, the trains are exceptionally slow, unreliable, and unsafe. After what seems like an eternity, they'll haul you to Guatemala where you'll encounter an even skankier train system (*see* Getting Around, *below*). The only saving grace is that trains are extremely cheap so if you're really counting pennies, it's a cool thing to look into.

GETTING AROUND

➤ **BY BUS** • Everyone rides the bus in Guatemala. Buses don't follow exact schedules (and it's unlikely that any driver would stick to one anyway). Private (or pullman) buses are direct and don't stop at as many corners as the public buses, but they're expensive ($6–$12 a ride) and more prone to be robbed. Public buses are packed till people smash up against the windows. It's fairly easy to figure out the bus system. Tickets can be purchased aboard, and signs advertising the main destinations are on the front of the bus. A bus will stop anywhere along the road. Whistle, wave, or pound the sides of the bus to get the driver's attention. Bus lines connect all the major cities with the capital, and you'll be able to reach almost any major destination in less than five hours (except for Tikal, which is 15 hours away in the heart of the isolated Petén). Prices generally run 40¢–50¢ per hour, depending on the destination and the condition of the road. Intra-city buses cost about 8¢.

➤ **BY TRAIN** • Trains are a dying breed in Guatemala. Only two routes are offered: one to the Caribbean Coast and the other to the Mexican border. The trains run excruciatingly slowly and the trip is tiresome, but tickets (thank God) are cheap. If you have a whole day to kill and then some, the train to Puerto Barrios via El Progreso, Zacapa, and Quiriguá leaves three times a week at 7 AM from the capital and the fare is less than $3. The return trip is the following day at the same time. To reach Tecún Umán at the Mexican border, trains leave Tuesdays at 9:30 AM and cost $1.50. Trains are consistently late (if they get there at all), so check out the latest schedules in Guatemala City at 18 Calle and 9 Avenida, Zona 1. The number is 02/83-030.

"Guatemala sometimes has only one train running and I watched it topple off the track in Puerto Barrios. It's just not Eurail."—I.S.

➤ **BY PLANE** • Aviateca has daily flights to Flores (near Tikal) from Guatemala City. To Flores it's $60 each way at the height of the season, but only around $25 during June price cuts. Tapsa and Aerovías also fly to Flores. Because it's a long, long (17–20 hours) bus ride and not always the safest road, you should definitely consider flying if your wallet says it's okay. Besides Flores, there is no other domestic service.

➤ **BY MOTORBIKE** • Traveling by motorbike is an excellent way to see Guatemala and bikes are easy to rent. In Guatemala City or Antigua you can rent bikes for a day, week, or month, for about $15 a day. A deposit is usually required. Don't worry about licenses or anything—as long as you can ride the thing and have the money, you're set.

➤ **BY BIKE** • Where there is little traffic, Guatemalans often use bicycles. However, bicycles aren't very prevalent in the more developed areas of the country, because many roads have little or no shoulder, hairpin turns, steep up-and-down grades, and obnoxious macho drivers. If you're in shape, this is still a great and economical way to

Scrunched in a bus with rap music blasting, Guatemalan bus-goers take it all in stride. In most places in the world, people would be complaining, "turn that horrible music off!" and "get that animal's butt out of my face!" When a pineapple rolls off the top shelf and bonks someone on the head, they laugh and pick it up. Back home, everyone would be ready to sue for damages.

cruise around Guatemala, but you need a sturdy mountain bike and you need to be able to fix your own flats. If you get tired of biking, you can always throw it on the roof of a bus until you recuperate. In the main cities, you can usually find a place that will rent out bikes, but normally just for the day ($5). In Antigua, you can rent bikes for up to a week. If you want a bike for an extended period you might be able to work out a deal with the bike-rental owner, or you may have to buy one or bring one from home.

➤ **BY CAR** • For obvious reasons, it's great to cruise the country in a car. You can check out a lot more of Guatemala in a much faster time and you don't have to rely on Latin time schedules and buses that never show. Gas can be expensive, though, and many roads really suck (if roads to your destination even exist). One exception is the amazingly smooth Interamerican Highway. Be sure to ask locals which roads to take and not take; they often know which roads are the current favorites of hijackers and bandits. Another problem with having a car in Guatemala is that vandalism and theft are rampant in the big cities—to be safe, look for guarded parking lots or hotels with lots. Guatemala City has awful traffic, and on a Friday afternoon you can be stuck in a traffic jam for hours. Renting a car usually comes to $40–$50 a day. Guatemala City has a bunch of car rental places, as do other major cities. Before driving anywhere, be sure to get auto insurance because it covers you if you're involved in an accident with a Guatemalan.

➤ **HITCHING** • Hitching is one of the best ways to get around Guatemala (and the *only* way in many of the more isolated areas). But here everyone—both gringos *and* Guatemalans—pays for the ride. It's good to find out the average price of a ride to your destination before you hop in the back of a truck. Military and police checkpoints have large speed bumps and often require drivers to stop—a perfect opportunity to ask for a ride. Some of these checkpoints are conveniently located at major crossroads like **La Cumbre** (between Alta and Baja Verapaz) and **Los Encuentros** (2 hours from Guatemala City toward the Western Highlands). Also, the roads in many areas are so bad that a slow jog will be enough to catch up and ask for a ride through the window. Hitching is called *pedir jalón* or *hacer jalón*.

WHERE TO SLEEP Guatemala is the land of cheap sleeps: Simple rooms with shared (public) bath are $1–$2; cleaner, more open rooms with patios are $3–$4; rooms with private bathrooms will run less than $5; and under $10 will get you ice water, a towel, toilet paper, shampoo, and hot water. INGUAT requires hotels to display the latest "approved rates," which are the maximum amount any establishment can charge for its rooms. A 17% tax is always added to the listed price. Look behind the front desk or on the door in your room for the rates. In small villages where there are no hotels, search out the *alcalde* (mayor), who can usually set you up in an empty office or church courtyard if there are no private homes.

Most of the camping in Guatemala is free. Guatemalans don't often camp, but a good number of hippie and other tourists do, so you won't get looked at funny. If you camp and cook your own food, you can live on about $2 a day. The big cities rarely have campgrounds—Panajachel and Tikal are the main exceptions. Tikal is one of the few places where you're charged to camp (about $6). Campers will have the most luck in Cobán and the Alta Verapaz region. In Cobán itself is the Parque Nacional Las Victorias, with 82 green hectares (203 acres) perfect for exploring and camping. Cobán's surrounding villages also offer tons of parks where you can camp for free. San Pedro Carchá, Lanquín, and Tactic all have palapa-covered campgrounds (*see* Near Cobán, *below*), and you can find similar camping possibilities throughout Alta Verapaz.

FOOD The standard dishes everywhere are rice, beans, eggs, cheese, tortillas, *carne asada* (roast beef), and chicken. Luckily, many areas also have delicious regional specialties, and in all the major cities you can chow down on a variety of eats from Mickey D's to Spanish paella. Many street stands sell ridiculously cheap food; just keep an eye out for the hygiene—if it's grilled right in front of you, it's probably okay. A hot empanada or tamale runs about a nickel, a piece of chicken with tortillas 25¢, and a hot beef sandwich 50¢. Another cheap option is *comedores,* simple restaurants (which are literally *everywhere*) that generally serve only *comida típica,* a basic menu of beans, rice, and meat. If you're going to get the runs, it'll probably be from a comedor. The most you can do is watch them prepare the grub and not eat anything that's obviously spoiled. Although some tap water is safe—sometimes you can smell the chlorine—you are strongly advised to **not drink** nonbottled water because it's a risk. Fruits and vegetables rarely accompany *comida típica* meals, and when they do it's often in a boiled-down, vitaminless form. But most Guatemalan markets are wonderful, with tons of fruits, vegetables, and other goodies. Don't be afraid to barter here as hard as you would for a handicraft. A well-balanced lunch of bread, nuts, fruit, and juice can be bought at a market for under a buck.

➤ **TIPPING** • Tipping is optional and not expected. Most Guatemalans don't tip unless it's really good service or an obviously fancy restaurant. Leaving a couple of quetzales is usually much appreciated and hardly a drain on the budget.

OUTDOOR ACTIVITIES Guatemala's varied topography and tremendous diversity of climates give you a lot to do outside. One of the easiest and most rewarding activities is **hiking.** In the Highlands, you can hike through countless mountain villages. You can almost always find a hike to suit your ability—from serious mountain treks to half-hour strolls on flat footpaths. Around Todos Santos, three hours from Huehuetenango, hiking is really the best way to enjoy the breathtaking greenery, and a number of easy-to-find trails crisscross the area. Also, hiking up volcanoes is popular among tourists and locals. Make sure to heed the warnings of this guidebook and of locals because there have been many robberies on volcano trails. In the Petén and in Central and Eastern Guatemala, you can explore remote **caves,** like the caves of Lanquín (near Cobán) and the caves of Actun Can, south of Santa Elena. **Rafting,** especially on the Río Cahabon (near Semuc Champey) is a fantastic adventure. Not only do you crash through whitewater rapids, but you can also check out ancient Maya cities that lie just off the river's banks. Check into rafting adventures through **Transpetén Tours** (*see* Travel Agencies in Flores and Santa Elena, *below*) or **Maya Expeditions** (*see* Travel Agencies in Guatemala City, *below*). For **water sports,** try Lake Atitlán. Although this area is a humongous tourist magnet, prices are still fairly cheap. You can rent a boat or kayak for $2 an hour, or for the whole day. If you're bent on doing some killer surfing or snorkeling, your best bet is to head to Belize or El Salvador.

Guatemala City

The enormous contrasts in Guatemalan society are laid bare in the capital's sprawling tangle of grimy streets and fume-choked alleyways. The split between rich and poor slaps you in the face the moment you begin exploring the neighborhoods. The elite glide above multitudes of beggars, street vendors, and shoe-shine boys, wiling away their days in shopping malls, and spending quetzales in denominations that the poor have never seen—all the while guarded by armored police and security guards. If the "two Guatemalas" mix, it's only out of necessity or accident.

Though few people want to hang out here, Guatemala City is the crossroads of the country, and you'll find yourself here at one time or another. Besides modern shopping facilities, you'll have hot water, comfortable hotels, and a whole slew of restaurants, all at cheap prices. The contrasts that keep this city in a constant buzz manifest themselves in a variety of sights, from the oh-so-modern, abstract office buildings, to

Guatemala City

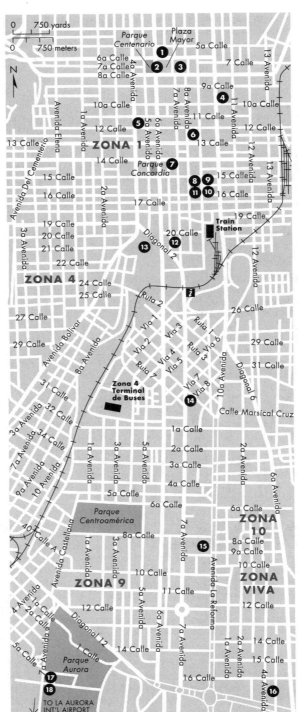

0 ⊢———⊣ 750 yards
0 ⊢———⊣ 750 meters

N

Exploring

Catedral
Metropolitana, **3**
Centro Cultural
Miguel Angel
Austrias, **13**
Iglesia Yurrita, **14**
Museo de Historia
Nacional, **18**
Museo Ixchel, **16**
Museo Nacional de
Arqueología y
Etnología, **17**
Museo Popol Vuh, **15**
Palacio Nacional, **1**
Plaza Mayor, **2**

Lodging

Hotel Belmont, **8**
Hotel Capri, **10**
Hotel
Centroamerica, **11**
Hotel Chalet Suizo, **7**
Hotel España, **9**
Hotel Fuente, **12**
Hotel Lessing
House, **5**
Hotel Spring, **6**
Pension Mesa, **4**

the Torre del Reformador (a dime-store replica of the Eiffel Tower), to the happening Sunday market at the Plaza Mayor.

Troubles in the highlands have driven people into the city, now packed with over 2 million residents—approximately one-fourth of Guatemala's population. Ironies abound: Women in traditional dress pawn plastic windmills or chewing gum, and marimba bands compete with rock music blasting out of modern shops.

The traditional and the cosmopolitan have been thrown together in Guatemala City. It's not unusual to see a huipil-clad indigenous woman holding hands with her sister, who's decked out in tight jeans and a Playgirl shirt.

When the old capital in the Panchoy Valley (La Antigua Guatemala) was devastated by an earthquake in 1773, the Spanish searched for a new location protected from such a hellish fate. They chose a nearby valley, which centuries before had been the center of the Mayan highlands, Kaminal Juyu. As the northernmost city in the Kingdom of Central America, Guatemala City linked the countries of the south with Mexico City, and became the wealthiest and most important center of the region. However, the new capital wasn't spared the fate of its sister city and was nearly leveled by earthquakes in 1917 and 1918. The colonial majesty that was once touted as the jewel of Central America was destroyed forever, replaced by futuristic architecture and charmless streets swimming with neon signs. Guatemala City is now an architectural curio cabinet, collected with no sense of style or subtlety, and certainly no continuity.

As you walk through the city, you can literally taste the third world, and the flavor is not a pleasant one. However, the city does serve as the country's heart, offering almost any luxury available in the United States at a fraction of the cost. People from even the most distant villages come here to sell their wares; the markets, though not as charming as those in the highlands, are among the most impressive in the country.

BASICS

AMERICAN EXPRESS The American Express office will hold mail and cash personal checks for cardholders as well as replace lost or stolen cards. *On the corner of Av. La Reforma and 9a Calle, Z9, below the glass Banco del Café building, tel. 02/340–040. Take Bus 82 from 10a Av., Z1. Open weekdays 8:30–4:30.*

MONEY Zona 1 has a lot of banks: **Banco de Guatemala** (7a Av. and 22 Calle), on the border between Zona 1 and Zona 4, and **Lloyds Bank** (8a Av., 10–67) are two of the biggies. To avoid waiting in long lines, check out banks further from the center of Zona 1. In Zona 4 the banks are immense, gleaming structures with unusual statues and fountains; try them if you don't mind passing through a small army battalion with hefty guns (a.k.a. bank security). Banks may be hesitant to change cash other than dollars. If you run into this problem, just zip over to the **black market.** Money-changers here offer a slightly lower exchange rate than the banks, but will deal in Canadian dollars, Mexican pesos, and every Central American currency. Go to 7a Avenida in Zona 1 between Calles 13 and 11 and you'll be approached by hordes chanting "dólares, lempiras, pesos..." Be careful—it's easy to get ripped off. Some hotels change money, but it's a service for guests only, and they charge a hefty commission.

EMBASSIES Guatemala continues to face political turmoil, so it's a good idea to check in with your respective embassy to catch up on recent news or warnings. This is especially important if you'll be traveling in the backcountry of Quiché, Petén, or other areas of guerrilla activity.

United States. *Av. La Reforma 7–01, Z10, tel. 02/311–541. Open weekdays 8–noon and 1–5.*

Canada. *7a Av. 11–59, Z9, tel. 02/321–411. Open Mon.–Thurs. 8–4:30, Fri. 8–1:30.*

United Kingdom. Australians, New Zealanders, and other Commonwealth affiliates can get help here with lost passports and other problems. *7a Av. 5–10, Z4, Edificio Centro Financiero Torre II, 7th Floor, tel. 02/321–601. Open Mon.–Thurs. 8:30–12:30 and 2–4:30, Fri. 2–4:30.*

LUGGAGE STORAGE Neither the airport nor the bus stations of Guatemala City have luggage-storage services. However, most hotels will be happy to keep your bags if you slip them a few quetzales or if you spend the night there. Some places will lock your bags up tight, others will just throw them into some dusty corner, so check it out first.

MAIL The main **post office** is in a beautiful pink and white colonial building on the corner of 7a Avenida and 12 Calle, Zona 1. You can buy postcards, paper, and envelopes on the street just outside. If you want to receive mail in Guatemala City, have it addressed to *Lista de Correos, Ciudad de Guatemala.* You can pick up your letters in room 110 on the ground floor. *7a Av., 12 Calle, Z1, tel. 02/26–101. Open weekdays 7–7, Sat 8–6.*

Telegrams are a popular means of communication throughout Guatemala. To reach the telegram office (open 24 hours), turn right just inside main post office building.

MEDICAL AID **Centro Médico Hospital** (6a Av. 3–47, Z10, tel. 02/65–061) and **Herreta Llerandi** (6a Av. 8–71, Z10, tel. 02/66–771) have doctors who speak English. For tampons and condoms (and other things of that nature) you can stop by one of the many branches of **Klee Pharmacies.** There's one on 6a Avenida at the corner of 9a Calle (tel. 02/23–905). **Godoy Pharmacies** also have several branches (one at 21 Calle 1–87, Z1, tel. 02/29–240). Pharmacies take turns staying open 24 hours a day so you'll always find a 24-hour pharmacy every few blocks.

PHONES GUATEL has offices throughout the city. Their main office is by far the most crowded—you might want to bring a few Dostoyevsky books to read while you inch to the front of the line. If all you're going to do is make a collect call to the United States, use the AT&T USA direct-dial phone. It's a black device off the main seating room. *8a Av., 12 Calle, Z1, tel. 02/20–498. Open weekdays 7–midnight.*

Another option (though the connection is a little less dependable) is to call from a regular **pay phone.** The ones in the main post office (right next to GUATEL) are on a pleasant patio and have a far smaller line than GUATEL. **MCI** has several phones which connect immediately to a U.S. operator—you don't even need to dial. One is in front of the U.S. embassy, and another in front of INGUAT (*see* Visitor Information, *below*).

Making Sense of Guat City Addresses

Guatemala City is arranged on a simple grid: Avenidas are major thoroughfares running north–south and calles run east–west. Each is numbered sequentially based on its distance from a central point (often the main plaza—though in Guatemala City this is located between 5–6 Calle and 5–7 Avenida). An address will list either the calle or the avenida first, based on which street the entrance faces. Say you're looking at the address 7a Avenida 19–44 Zona 1. This means the main entrance is on 7a Avenida between Calles 19 and 20 in Zona 1; the building number is 44. Now, how about 17 Calle 8–46 in Zona 1? You'll find the main entrance on 17th Calle, halfway between Avenida 8 and 9, building 46.

TRAVEL AGENCIES A fairly complete list of tour operators and the services they provide is available at INGUAT (*see* Visitor Information, *below*). Prices and packages vary widely, from $24 city tours to $1,000 jungle expeditions. Following is a list of a few companies that cater to people who want to get way off the beaten track.

Tropical Tours offers ecological and archaeological expeditions, complete with vegetarian fare. *4a Calle 2-50a, Z10, tel. 02/323–748.*

Maya Expeditions is run by Tammy Ridenours, an American adventuress who will take you white-water rafting to obscure archaeological ruins and/or diving in remote areas. *15 Calle 1-91, Z10, tel. 02/562–551.*

Izabal Adventure Tours offers specialty tours for travelers who want to discover the natural riches of Guatemala. They have ecotourism itineraries designed to please everyone from nature photographers to orchid growers to entomologists. *7a Av. 14-44, Z9, Edificio la Galeria, oficina 35, tel. 02/240–323.*

VISITOR INFORMATION INGUAT will give you all the propaganda you could ever want, as well as advice on bus routes and hotels. Exhibitions by Guatemalan artists are on the ground floor of their main office. *7a Avenida 1–17, Z4, Centro Civico, tel. 02/31–133. Catch any bus marked "terminal" from any even-numbered street. Get off at the Teatro Nacional and walk toward the towering buildings to the east. INGUAT is at the little blue "i" on the other side of the bridge across 7a Av. Open weekdays 8–4:30, weekends 8–1.*

The **Guatemalan telephone directory** has a section for tourists in both English and Spanish; it includes banks, transportation, and a list of festivals and sights in Guatemala City and throughout the country. Look in the pink pages near the front.

COMING AND GOING

If you're traveling in Guatemala, you'll have to pass through Guatemala City (whether you like it or not) at some point. The Interamerican Highway runs right through, so you can easily zip in and out if you have an intense aversion to big cities. Hitching is dangerous and difficult but buses run so frequently that all you have to do is stand at the side of the road waving desperately and they'll pick you up.

BY BUS Each part of the country is served by different bus companies. Most don't cross borders, although you can easily transfer buses and continue into Mexico, El Salvador, Honduras, and Belize. Listed below are the major cities and the bus companies that serve them.

Antigua. Transportes Unidos (4a Av., 18 Calle, Z1, tel. 02/24–949) leaves daily every ½ hour 7–7 (1 hour, 50¢).

Chichicastenango. Veloz Quichelese (20 Calle and Av. Bolivar, Z1) goes daily every ½ hour 5 AM–6 PM (3½ hours, $2.50). Buses stop at Chimaltenango on the way.

Cobán/Biotopo del Quetzal. Escobar/Monja Blanca (8a Av. 15–16, Z1, tel. 02/534–869) leaves daily about every hour 4 AM–5 PM (4 hours, $4).

Esquipulas. Rutas Orientales (19 Calle 8–18, Z1, tel. 02/536–714) buses leave daily every ½ hour 4 AM–6 PM (4 hours, $3). This company also has indirect buses to Honduras; make the connection in Chiquimula or Esquipulas and then catch a bus to Honduras.

Quetzaltenango. Transportes Galgo (7a Av. 19–44, Z1, tel. 02/23–661) leaves seven times daily between 5:30 AM and 9 PM (4 hours, $3). This company also has connections to México.

Monterrico. Cubanita (Terminal de Buses, Z4) goes three times daily (5 hours, $3).

Panajachel/Atitlán. Rebulli (21 Calle 1–34, Z1, tel. 02/516–505) leaves daily once an hour from 5 AM to 4 PM (4 hours, $1.50).

Petén (Tikal, Flores). Fuentes del Norte (17 Calle 8–46, Z1, tel. 02/537–282) leaves five times daily (14 hours, $7; $10 for direct service that will save you time). You need to reserve a seat. This company also has buses to Belize.

Puerto Barrios. Litegua (15 Calle 10–42, Z1, tel. 02/27–578) goes daily once an hour between 6 AM and 5 PM (6 hours, $6). Litegua is undoubtedly the most luxurious bus company in Guatemala.

San Salvador. Melva Internacional (3a Av. 1–38, Z9, tel. 02/310–874) goes daily once an hour 5:30 AM–4:30 PM (5 hours, $6).

BY PLANE **La Aurora International Airport** (for all international and domestic flights) is in Zona 13. An **INGUAT** office (open daily 6 AM–9 PM) and **Bank Quetzal** (open daily 6 AM–9 PM) are both in the airport. **GUATEL** is on the second floor and Budget, Avis, Dollar, and Hertz rental-car agencies have offices here.

The following domestic airlines fly to and from the Petén: **Aviateca** (10a Calle 6–20, Z1, tel. 02/81–479), **Aerovías** (Av. Hincapié, 18 Calle, Z13, tel. 02/319–663), and **Tapsa** (Av. Hincapié, Hangar 14 at the Aeropuerto, tel. 02/314–860). In May and June, Aviateca cuts most of its airfares in half.

➤ **AIRPORT TRANSPORT** • The easiest and cheapest way to get to the airport is by taking either Bus 5 from Zona 1 on 4a Avenida or Bus 83 from Zona 1 on 10a Avenida. Just make sure that the sign in the front window says AEROPUERTO. Leaving the airport, take the bus just outside the terminal (either Bus 5 or 83) and it'll drop you off in Zona 1. If you have tons of luggage, you may want to splurge on a taxi. INGUAT publishes an official list of authorized fares from the airport to various locations in the city. A taxi (with up to four passengers) to the budget hotels of Zona 1 costs about 35 quetzales ($7), 125 quetzales ($25) to Antigua. Taxis aren't allowed to charge more than these fares, but you may be able to barter for less. If you have a super-early flight (before 6 AM) or a flight after 9 PM, you'll have to take a taxi since buses aren't running.

GETTING AROUND

All the major cities of Guatemala have the same basic plan—a central plaza from which numbered *calles* (streets) and *avenidas* (avenues) radiate out to the distant sections of town. In the larger cities, these grids are divided into several zones (*see* box).

Coke and Pepsi (Burrrp!)—the Voice of a New Medication

In a land where the water is often unsafe to drink, and milk and juice are expensive and hard to come by, American soft drinks have become the beverage of choice. Even in the tiniest, remotest village you can buy a Coke. In one town, local healers traditionally had patients drink water and then spit it out, as part of a ritual to flush evil from the body. That was until the Pepsi salesman came along. "Look, you can see our product cleanses the body of evil," he said as he gulped down a soda. Moments later came the burp of evidence that the spirits were actually leaving the body. Pepsi is now incorporated into this pre-Columbian ritual. Uh huh.

If you can master this system in Guatemala City, with 21 zones of up to 30 calles and avenidas each, you'll instantly be able to find any address in any major Guatemalan city (no money-back guarantee).

BY BUS By far the most entertaining and economical way to see Guatemala City is through the dirt-coated windows of a public bus. Doors of Guatemalan buses are literally always open. Your best bet is to wait on a street corner and hope that the bus you want hits a red light. Or, when you see it barreling down the street, stick out your hand, with an optional whistle or hiss, and the driver will stop (or, rather, do a California roll) as soon as he can. Fares to all sites within the city are 10¢. Buy tickets from the attendant on board; just take a seat and he'll come around.

To Handle Guatemalan Cities, You Have to Get in a Zone

In large cities like Guatemala City, the grid system of avenidas and calles gets wacky and out of hand, so it's divided one step further into zonas (zones). Because Guatemala City has 21 zonas, you absolutely have to know what zone your address is in. Even a taxi driver can't find the corner of 5a Avenida and 7 Calle because 21 corners in the city have that exact address. You'll probably spend most of your time in the zonas listed below.

- Zona 1 is a crowded tangle of beggars, street vendors, shops, restaurants, and budget accommodations. The National Palace, Mercado Central, Catedral Metropolitana, Plaza Mayor, and Parque Concordia are all here.
- Zona 2 is the place to go if maps turn you on. Take Bus 45 or 46 to the Mapa En Relieve, a relief map that shows the country at a scale of 1:10,000. It's the only point of (questionable) interest in Zona 2.
- Zona 4 is where you'll find INGUAT, the bus terminal, the National Theater, and the main food market.
- Zona 7 is basically the Guat City 'burbs. Here you'll stumble upon a few grassy hills that are the ruins of Kaminal Juyu, an extremely important but sadly neglected Maya Center. If you want to go picnicking, check out these few blocks of greenery.
- Zona 9 is where you'll find the American and Canadian embassies, as well as the Popul Vuh Museum. You can recognize Zona 9 by the huge Torre del Reformador, a bad imitation of the Eiffel Tower in the middle of 12 Calle 7a Avenida.
- Zona 10, home to The Museo Ixchel, also has upscale bars and discotheques where the rich have their fun. Big open spaces and immense mansions characterize this zone.
- Zona 13 is dominated by the Parque Aurora, which combines a military base, a zoo, the international airport, and three national museums.

Infinite routes snake through the city, and each bus has its own peculiar variation, but the routes listed below should get you anywhere you need to go in the city. To make sure a particular bus is going where you're going, check the sign in the lower left corner of the front window. Good places to wait on 4a Avenida for Bus 17, on 5a Avenida for Buses 45–6, and on 10a Avenida for Buses 82–3.

Bus 17 will take you from 4a Avenida in Zona 1 to Zona 7 and the ruins of Kaminal Juyu. Be sure to look for the sign in the window, because not all 17 buses pass the ruins.

Buses 45 and **46** go from 5a Avenida Zona 1 to the Mapa en Relieve of Zona 2.

Bus 82 travels from 10a Avenida to Avenida La Reforma in Zones 9 and 10, and on its way passes INGUAT and Zona 4.

Bus 83 also passes through Zona 4, but heads to and from Parque Aurora, stopping at the airport and zoo.

BY CAR Parking and traffic are such a nightmare that you may want to reconsider having your own wheels. To park, look for a guarded parking lot or garage near the city center. You can either rent a car at the airport or at one of the numerous agencies in Zonas 9 and 10. If you're going way off the beaten track, a four-wheel drive is a must. **Avis** (12 Calle 2–73, Z9, tel. 02/31–690) and **Budget** (Av. La Reforma 15–00, Z9, tel. 02/316–546) are just two of the many rental agencies.

BY TAXI You can hire taxis at Plaza Mayor, Parque Concordia (15–14 calles between 5 and 6 avenidas), and the main bus terminal in Zona 4. Most city rides cost $3–$4, but you should always agree on a price before jumping in—there ain't no meters.

BY FOOT To get a mouthful and eyeful of smoggy Zona 1, you absolutely have to walk. Grab your most comfortable shoes and join the throngs of people on avenidas 5a and 6a, south from the Plaza Mayor. The crowded streets are overflowing with fruit stands, blue jeans for sale, watches, weavings, pornography, and plastic toys. Above all, watch your belongings: Lots of poor people with nothing may want your somethings.

WHERE TO SLEEP

Most budget hotels are in Zona 1. Though it's one of the more run-down, scuzzy parts of town, it's jammed with restaurants, stores, and nonstop action. All hotels must register their prices with INGUAT, and they should have their approved rates posted in quetzales or U.S. dollars. Many of the cheapest digs only have double rooms, which they'll offer to a single traveler for a lower price. "Laundry facilities" often means just a washbasin and clothesline. All hotels in Guatemala City are most crowded at the end of December, in August, and during Semana Santa. The towering hotels of Zona 9 and 10 cost *mucho dinero,* but are always fun to check out for a night or two if you want to soak your feet and watch TV, or take a joyride on one of their elevators. The city has no student housing per se, but you can check the first floor of INGUAT (*see* Visitor Information, *above*) for the occasional student-exchange program.

➤ **UNDER $5** • **Hotel España.** Simple but clean (there's actually toilet paper in the bathrooms), this hotel has a central lounge where you can watch TV or schmooze with other guests. As with all the hotels on 9a Avenida, avoid getting a room near the street because it's a major bus route. Doubles without bath are $5, with bath $6. Definitely the best of the cheapos. *9a Av. 15–59, Z1, tel. 02/300–502. 82 rooms, some with bath. Luggage storage, laundry, fresh towels daily.*

Hotel Fuente. Characteristic of the cheapest hotels in Guatemala City, the rooms are large but musty, and hot water is provided by an electric heater attached to the showerhead (after all those years of making sure not to bring your hair dryer in the bathtub...). Get a room with private bath to avoid the backed-up and seatless toilets of the *servicios generales* (public bathrooms). As with most places of this caliber, the rooms are secured with a padlock, and for extra safety you can bring your own. Right next to the Galgos bus station, this is a good place to crash if you've got an early morning bus to Quetzaltenango or the Mexican border. *7a Av. 20–16, Z1, tel. 02/23–723. 8 rooms, some with bath. Laundry, luggage storage.*

Pension Mesa. Known affectionately to many backpackers as "the mesa," this hotel has a dormitory-like atmosphere that is very youth hostelish. The rooms and bathrooms are not the cleanest in the world (though you may enjoy reading all the interesting graffiti covering the walls), but beds come cheap—$2.40 each in the public dormitory. This is an unmatched place to meet other young travelers. Join in a game at their Ping-Pong table or check out the bulletin board listing everything from dentists to jungle excursions to personal messages. *10a Calle 10–17, Z1, tel. 02/23–177. 27 rooms, none with bath.*

➤ **UNDER $10** • The following hotels all offer hot showers and purified drinking water.

Hotel Belmont. Rooms are dark 'n' dingy, but the place is brightened by the abundant plantlife in the hallways. Rooms near the back of the hotel are very quiet. The sweet maid may ask you if you know her relatives in New York City—no matter where you're from. Doubles without bath are $6, with bath $7. *9a Av. 15–30, Z1, tel. 02/511–541. 72 rooms, some with bath.*

Hotel Capri. The rooms are small, musty, and plain. A TV lounge with comfy couches invites you to hang out with other guests. The luggage storage looks especially safe—it's in a locked room near the front desk (watched by several desk clerks). Get a room away from the street (heavy-duty bus noise); rooms near the top offer a view of the city. Doubles without bath are $9, with bath $10. *9a Av. 15–63, Z1, tel. 02/28–191. 52 rooms, some with bath. Luggage storage, laundry.*

Hotel Centroamerica. This hotel lies in the heart of the red-light district—at night you'll have to share the sidewalk with prostitutes and beggars. Other than that, it's a real find. Guests are greeted with a mint on the pillow, free shampoo, and wonderfully clean towels. Rooms are spotless and bright, and most face onto a central corridor with fountains and hanging ferns. Doubles without bath are $8, with bath $12. Maxipads, aspirin, Band-Aids, and other last-minute necessities are theoretically available from the dusty cabinet by the front desk. *9a Av. 16–38, Z1, tel. 02/26–917. 58 rooms, some with bath. Luggage storage, laundry, money-changing.*

Hotel Lessing House. Several blocks from the Plaza Mayor, this hotel has fairly clean rooms decorated with handwoven textiles. Rooms to the left as you walk in have windows and are brighter than those across the hall. Doubles with bath are $7. *12 Calle 4–35, Z1, tel. 02/513–891. 8 rooms, all with bath. Luggage storage, laundry, wheelchair access.*

Hotel Spring. Most rooms open onto a bright central patio, with tons of greenery and plenty of comfortable tables and chairs for sitting, reading, writing, or chatting. A small kitchen serves breakfast and lunch at moderate prices ($1–$2), and you can buy soda pop and beer at the front desk. Plain doubles without bath are $8, with bath $10. It's a great place to meet other travelers. Reservations are recommended because it's always packed with Peace Corps volunteers. *8a Av. 12–65, Z1, tel. 02/26–637. Take Bus 82 from 9a Av. to Calle 13. 27 rooms, some with bath. Luggage storage, TV rental, money-changing.*

➤ **UNDER $15** • **Hotel Chalet Suizo.** If you get your jollies from cleanliness, this place has *got* to have the cleanest bathrooms in Central America. The staff is extremely friendly and can give advice about everything in Guatemala. There's no courtyard for hanging

Be sure to pick up a map at the front desk of Hotel Chalet Suizo—it's one of the best you'll find of Guatemala City.

out, the pillows are so chunky you could eat 'em with a fork, and the hot water isn't dependable; but, again, you'll die for the clean bathrooms. Doubles without bath are $12, with bath $18. *14 Calle 6–82, Z1, tel. 02/513–786. Luggage storage, laundry.*

HOSTEL The first youth hostel in Guatemala is due to open in 1994. To find out if it's alive and kicking, contact the Asociación Guatemalteca de Albergues Joveniles (AGAJ). *7a Av. 1–17, Z4, Centro Civico, tel. 02/311–333.*

FOOD

Guatemala City is chock-full of international restaurants and fast-food joints. For the cheapest *comida típica,* check out the street vendors or the grimy comedores in the Mercado Central. Unless you have a hell of a strong constitution, however, it's better to eat in restaurants to avoid getting a nasty case of the runs. The majority of cheap and fairly clean restaurants are in the commercial district, just south of the Plaza Mayor on Avenidas 5a and 6a.

Vegetarians will go gaga at the huge piles of fresh fruits and vegetables in the central food market in Zona 4 (*see* markets listing under Shopping, *below*). **Frutti Licuados** (11 Calle 7–60, Z1) caters to vegetarians with a menu of fruit juices and quiche. Hang out while three cute, old men play marimba hits. **Señor Sol** (5a Calle 11–32, Z1) and **Comida de Vegetales** (8a Av. 11 Calle, Z1) also specialize in vegetarian food.

Pollo Campero, Guatemala's KFC, offers delicious three-piece chicken dinners for about $3 including coffee, salad, drink, and fries. They have branches throughout the city, including one on 5a Avenida near the Plaza Mayor in Zona 1 and another just across from Parque Concordia on 6a Avenida and 14 Calle.

By far your best value at lunchtime is to order a menú del dia, available at most típico restaurants from noon to 2:30. The line-up usually includes bread, soup, salad, beans, rice, a main dish (chicken, steak, fish), coffee, a drink, and dessert for less than $2. Ask for it, and the waitress will list the choices for the day.

UNDER $5 **Cafetería la Taverna de Zoila.** You'll recognize Zoila, near the bus terminal at the border of Zonas 1 and 4, by the indigenous woman outside grilling fresh tortillas. The interior is bursting with color. Ferns dangle from the ceiling and the walls are covered with mirrors, ribbons, and pictures of the Three Stooges. The *menú del dia* (menu of the day) is less than $1.50, and you can get *sopa de camarones,* a huge bowl of broth, spaghetti, and vegetables overflowing with fresh shrimp, for $2. *7a Av. 20–46, Z1, tel. 02/29–141. Just north of the big round fountain on 7a Av. between the main bus terminal and Transportes Galgos. Open Mon.–Sat. 8–7.*

Cafetería y Pastelería Royal. Right next door to Zoila, this place has a large menú del dia for the same price (less than $1.50), but it definitely lacks Zoila's liveliness and charm. You can't leave without trying their delicious pastries—check out the strawberry shortcake, Black Forest cake, or chocolate cream pie for less than 75¢, including coffee. *7a Av. 20–80, Z1, tel. 02/24–223. Open daily 8–7.*

Fu Lu Sho. This is one Chinese restaurant in Guatemala that's discovered there's more to Chinese food than rice and bean sprouts. The *carne de res con jenjibre* (beef with ginger), for $2, and the humongous plate of *camaron chow mein* (shrimp chow mein), for $2.50, taste as if they came straight out of China. The portions are gargantuan, and you should seriously starve yourself for a few hours if you're planning to finish all your food. Don't confuse this place with Fu Sun Lo, a mediocre Chinese restaurant nearby. *6a Av. 12–09, Z1, tel. 02/23–456. Open daily 10:30 AM–midnight.*

Kam Cheung Fat (Restaurante Buen Gusto Oriental). You can't miss this Chinese restaurant with the telltale algae-filled tank gracing the entrance. They serve a wide variety of average Chinese food at average prices, but come nightfall they cater to a crowd that's far from average. Yes, every night this place fills to the bursting point with that elusive bunch—Guatemala's gay male contingent. Especially on weekend nights the air fills with cigarette smoke and cologne, and there's far more drinking going on than eating. Over whistles and loud conversation, social butterflies flit from table to table to give a peck on the cheek or a handshake to old friends. It's also open later than just about anywhere else in Zona 1, so it's the perfect place to grab that late-night snack when you get a sudden attack of the munchies. *6a Av. 15–57, Z1, tel. 02/28–967. Open daily 10 AM–1 AM.*

Restaurante Cafetería Peñalba. This place serves comida típica four blocks south of Plaza Mayor. Try their huge breakfasts, including orange juice, two eggs, beans, tortillas, toast (with homemade jam!), and coffee for under $2. Also worthwhile are three tostadas filled with guacamole, salsa, and frijoles for 50¢. *6a Av. 11–71, Z1, tel. 02/29–082. Open daily 7 AM–10 PM.*

Restaurante Capri. Right next to Hotel Capri on 9a Avenida (same owners), this is yet another place to enjoy comida típica. The menú del dia is only slightly more expensive than at Royal or Zoila, and it's much better, with juicy chicken and vegetable-packed soup. Also yummy is a meal of *platanos fritos* (fried bananas), eggs, beans, and coffee for $1.75. *9a Av. 15–63, Z1, tel. 02/511–062. Open daily 7 AM–11 PM.*

Restaurant Piccadilly. If you're craving Italian delights, load up on the lasagna ($1.50), tortellini ($1.50), or a number of tasty pizzas. At the full-service bar downstairs you can get toasted for decent prices. *6a Avenida 11–01, Z1, tel. 02/514–268. Take-out food available. Open daily 6:30 AM–11:30 PM.*

> *Fast-food joints like Mickey D's, Burger King, Domino's, and Taco Bell are so popular with well-to-do Guatemalans that security guards have to let you in the jam-packed eateries. A burger and fries costs twice a rural worker's daily wage ($4).*

UNDER $10 **Delicadesas Hamburgo.** The atmosphere and food is reminiscent of a small-town U.S. diner. Steaks, shish kebabs, and chicken all go for around $4. Chow down on a mongo breakfast for $2. Come here for a late-night ice cream ($1), because most pastelerías close by 7 PM. Get a seat near the window to watch the nonstop action across the street in Parque Concordia. *15 Calle 5–34, Z1, tel. 02/81–627. Right across the street from Parque Concordia on the south side. Open daily 7 AM–10 PM.*

El Gran Pavo. Right between Plaza Mayor and Parque Concordia, El Gran Pavo ("The Big Turkey") has yummy food from all over México. Try any number of seafood dishes typical of Veracruz, as well as enchiladas verdes ($2), a variety of soups ($3), and Yucatecan fare. *13 Calle 4–41, Z1, tel. 02/510–933. Open daily 9 AM–1 AM.*

WORTH SEEING

Guatemala City presents the visitor with a tossed salad of curiosities scattered randomly throughout the city. These vary from the bright pink colonial post office in Zona 1 to the green hills of Kaminal Juyu in Zona 7 (though it looks more like a vacant lot than a major archaeological site).

PLAZA MAYOR This large plaza in Zona 1 (between 5a and 7a avenidas and 6a and 8a calles) is divided into two parks by 6a Avenida. To the east (toward the Catedral Metropolitana) is the Parque Central and to the west (with a huge amphitheater) is Parque Centenario. By far the most interesting time to visit the park is Sunday, when brightly clad indígena women sell *huipiles* (traditional woven or embroidered blouses) and *cortes* (woven wraparound skirts) from all parts of the country. You may also catch a third-rate salsa singer or a children's chorus in the amphitheater on the west side plaza.

CATEDRAL METROPOLITANA Built between 1782 and 1809, this cathedral is one of the few colonial buildings in Guatemala City that has survived the area's myriad earthquakes. It did suffer considerable damage, though, and the walls are riddled with cracks, making the interior look centuries older than it really is. For 5¢ you can buy a candle and place it in front of your favorite saint. Sunday mass is the best time to come and visit. *East side of Parque Central, between 7a and 8a avenidas and 6a and 8a calles.*

PALACIO NACIONAL The imposing National Palace was built between 1939 and 1943 under the orders of the egotistical President Jorge Ubico. After you get frisked and your bag is searched, you can wander at your leisure through the compound's lush vegetation and impressive fountains. Look for a guide near the top of the stairs on the second floor so you can check out the *salón de recepción,* a beautiful ballroom with a Bohemian crystal chandelier and a giant Guatemalan coat of arms, complete with a real stuffed quetzal. The Regional Telecommunications Center (on the second floor near the back) was reputedly the headquarters for organizing and directing the assassinations and "disappearances" of key political figures since 1966. Also check out the **Galas de Guatemala** (between the two entrances), which shows various photography exhibits. *On the north side of Parque Central, two entrances on 6a Calle, Z1. Admission free. Open weekdays 8–4:30.*

CENTRO CULTURAL MIGUEL ANGEL AUSTRIAS This cluster of buildings is dominated by the futuristic **Teatro Nacional,** which looks like it could have been dropped out of the air from Pluto. A number of military police guard the periphery, and one will

A Deadly Vanishing Act: The Desaparecidos of Guatemala

The term "desaparecidos" (the disappeared ones) was coined in the late '60s, when the Guatemalan government began its ruthless counterinsurgency program. To eliminate all traces of guerrilla activity, anyone under suspicion was kidnapped in the middle of the night and whisked off to a distant outpost for torture and interrogation. In the past 25 years, literally tens of thousands of Guatemalans (mostly poor, indigenous people) have "disappeared." Because they're not listed as officially dead, families can't inherit their property. Therefore, countless Indígena women and children flock to Guatemala City to sell their labor—and often their bodies. The traditional lives of the Maya are quickly being swept away, as widows of desaparecidos leave their backstrap looms for a grueling and alienating life in the city. In a letter (smuggled out of an army prison in 1984) to his wife, a disappeared husband captured the horror and tragedy of Guatemala's political situation: "I am on the brink of life and death because they accuse me of being a guerrilla. I am not the first or the last such case in this world; after a while you come to realize anything can happen. I am very sad because I only think of death, and the mother I will never hug again. A kiss for them all. Please face life like a real woman. You are not the first woman in the world to become a widow. Goodbye forever." (Excerpted from Guatemala: Eternal Spring, Eternal Tyranny by Jean-Marie Simon, published by Norton, 1987.)

take you to the top and show you inside the theater for a "voluntary" tip of 1 or 2 quetzales. The top of the theater offers the best view of the sprawling city. A short walk through a cement park will take you to the **Teatro del Aire Libre,** an open-air theater, right in front of the **Museo Nacional del Ejército.** Sitting in the bleachers of this military amphitheater, you can almost see the camouflaged guards in the round gun turrets, guarding the dictator of your choice as he shouts proclamations from center stage. Leaving the theater through the main parking lot to the right, you descend from this playground of the rich and powerful to a vomit-choked alley housing the desperately poor—yet another reminder of the capital's rich/poor dichotomy. *Take any bus marked TERMINAL and make your way up the hill to the funky blue and white Teatro. You can't miss it.*

IGLESIA YURRITA (NUESTRA SENORA DE LA ANGUSTIAS) One of the wildest buildings in Guatemala City, this overly ornate church with bizarre stained-glass windows and weird carvings looks like somewhere the Addams Family would go for Sunday mass. The church and the adjoining colonial home were built by the wealthy Yuritta family in the mid-19th century. If you're lucky, you may be able to get in to see the carved-wood interior. Try at 8:30 AM or at 4:30 PM, when the priest opens the gates to let people in for mass (he'll do it if he's in the mood). *Take Bus 82 to Z9 and get off at Ruta 6 between 7a Av. and Av. La Reforma.*

MUSEO POPUL VUH This private museum of ancient Mayan and colonial-era artifacts has an unlikely home on the sixth floor of a glassy modern office building. Take the glass elevator on the right to get to the museum entrance. You'll find Mayan pottery and a collection of dusty colonial costumes. At the entrance, buy a guidebook ($1) that explains all the pieces on display. The small library is open to anyone who wishes to study the ancient Maya in depth. Along with the Museo Ixchel (*see below*), the museum is slated to move soon. *Edificio Galeria Reforma, 6 Floor, Av. La Reforma 8–60, right across from the American Embassy, Z9, tel. 02/347–121. Take Bus 82 or 102 to Av. La Reforma. Admission: $1. Open Mon.–Sat. 8–5:30.*

MUSEO IXCHEL This private museum takes its name from the goddess of the moon and weaving, and it's devoted to cataloging and preserving the weaving traditions of Guatemala. The collection is small but well presented, and the various native textile and weaving techniques are explained by signs in both English and Spanish. This museum (along with the Popul Vuh museum) is due to move soon to a building in the Universidad de Francisco Marroquin. *4a Av. 16–27, Z10, tel. 02/680–713. Walk among tree-lined streets and opulent mansions from Av. La Reforma, Z9. Admission: $1; 50¢ with student ID. Open weekdays 8:30–5, Sat. 9–1.*

MUSEO NACIONAL DE ARQUEOLOGIA Y ETNOLOGIA If you have limited time in the city, come here: It's better than Ixchel and Popul Vuh combined. According to one of the few employees who take care of the massive collection, this museum is "perhaps as popular as Tikal itself." Because it's state-run, it lacks the fancy brochures and gift shops of the private museums, but most of the amazing artifacts are well presented in a logical order. The first part of the museum (the archaeology part) traces Maya history, from cave-dwellers through the Preclassic, Classic, and Postclassic periods. Some of the collection's many highlights include an intricately carved human skull, a replica of a wood lintel from Tikal, and some of the most famous stelae (upright engraved stone slabs) in the Maya world. Also extra special is a vault filled with jade masks, jewelry, and a reconstructed grave site of a Maya ruler. The pieces basically speak for themselves, but try to stay within earshot of vacationers with a professional guide, a service that many tour companies include on their city tours. The second part of the museum (the ethnology part) presents a fairly complete collection of men's and women's costumes from different villages, with a map showing the location of each village above the display case. *Salon 5, Finca La Aurora, Z13, tel. 02/720–489. In a large pink colonial building just south of the National Zoo. Take any bus with a sign in the lower left corner reading* AEROPUERTO *or* LA AURORA. *Admission: 20¢. Open Tues.–Fri. 9–4, weekends 10–noon and 2–4.*

MUSEO DE HISTORIA NACIONAL For the most part all you'll see is a mangy collection of stuffed mammals and birds in dusty glass cases. Turn to the left when you enter and look at the diorama of the quetzal (Guatemala's national bird and currency namesake) on the far wall. For a 50¢ "donation," someone at the front desk will take you to a small room filled with enough live poisonous snakes to kill an elephant. Gila monsters (stout, poisonous lizards) saunter around the room—you can even pet one—and a number of velvety tarantulas paw the glass of their small terrariums. The security guard, Isai, may even play a request on the guitar while you view the vipers. *Across the street to the south of the Museo de Arqueología y Etnología. Open Tues.–Fri. 9–4, weekends 9–noon and 2–4.*

CHEAP THRILLS

Sizzling comedores dot the periphery of grimy **Parque Concordia,** between 5a and 6a avenidas and 14 and 15 calles in Zona 1. You can sit and watch the preachers, magicians, tin-pan musicians, and fortune-tellers that make this park a happenin' spot. At night it becomes even seedier than during the day and you should avoid it.

FESTIVALS On August 15, Guatemala City celebrates the feast day of its patron saint, the **Virgen de La Asunción.** Both Semana Santa and the days near Christmas are busy, fiesta-filled times in the capital as well as in the rest of Guatemala.

SHOPPING

Guatemala City is the place to buy anything and everything you may have left at home. Most stores are closed on Sunday. Listed below are some of the best (and cheapest) places to buy traditional and other goodies.

PARQUE CENTRAL The north side of Parque Central comes alive with color every Sunday as Indígenas from all over the country haggle over intricately woven huipiles and cortes of all regional styles. It's not a tourist market and you'll see the traditional clothing still worn in the highlands. *On 6a Calle between 6a and 7a avenidas, right across from the National Palace. Traditional clothing on sale Sun. 8–6.*

If you lose your luggage, or just need that extra jacket, sweater, or raincoat, Ropa Americana stores sell high-quality secondhand clothing donated from the U.S. for 50¢ to $2 each piece.

MAIN FOOD MARKET This huge warehouse, near the bus terminal in Zona 4, is piled high with familiar and exotic fruit of all shapes and sizes. Inside, the air is sweet and heavy, and you'll probably be the only gringo pushing your way through the hordes of shoppers. Remember to buy only fruits you can peel—mellons, mangoes, bananas—or risk the consequences! You'll also see rows upon rows of new and old leather shoes, religious paraphernalia, and witchcraft items like love potions, blessed elixirs, and copal (the sacred incense used by the Maya). Be sure to check out the statue of the Virgin, whose presence blesses each sale, in the center of the marketplace. *In the large blue and yellow warehouse just north of the Z4 bus terminal. Take any bus marked TERMINAL, then make your way to Diagonal 2 between 5a and 6a avenidas.*

MERCADO CENTRAL This cement box looks more like a parking garage than a market, but once inside, you'll be ducking through narrow hallways bursting with woven backpacks, leather, silver, and more Grateful Dead clothing than you could ever want. Prices here are sometimes 50% cheaper (before bargaining) than in Antigua and Chichicastenango. Downstairs is a large market selling basketry, dried goods (here's where you get that famous Guatemalan coffee), meats (you'll know 'em when you smell 'em), and fruits. *7a Av. to 9a Av., Z1, just behind the Catedral Metropolitana. Open Mon.–Sat. 6–6, Sun. 9–noon.*

AFTER DARK

BARS **Bar Europa.** This bar is one of the few places in Zona 1 where you feel right at home in the friendly and open atmosphere. Food is served (less than $3 for a good meal), or you can hang out and nurse a beer at the bar. Cesar the bartender loves to talk with foreigners, and will watch your baggage for free if you can't leave it in your hotel and need to take that odd afternoon flight. *11 Calle 5–16, Z1, tel. 02/534–929. Right next to the large spiral driveway. Open Mon.–Sat. 8 AM–1 AM.*

El Encuentro. This bar is hidden in an unmarked room on the top floor of a shopping mall in crowded Zona 1. Head here to relax and talk with *amigos de ambiente* (Central America's largely hidden gay population). Sip a drink and listen to soothing light-rock hits by Karen Carpenter and Barbra Streisand. The owner, Mario, speaks excellent English and if this is your gig, you'll find him an invaluable source of information. *Centro Capitol, 6a Av. bet. 11a Calle and 12a Calle, 5a Nivel, Local 321, Z1. Go upstairs toward the movie theater on the left hand side of the mall. You'll hear music coming from a doorway with a Chinese screen. Open Mon.–Sat. 4:30–11.*

El Meson De Don Quixote. Full bar service and live music are topped off with an Andalusian setting. Come here for the colorful atmosphere but not for cheap prices. *11 Calle 5–27, Z1, tel. 02/21–741. Open Mon.–Sat. noon–1 AM.*

MUSIC The traditional music of Guatemala is played on the marimba, a wood xylophone with an African name that Guatemalans insist they invented first. **Frutti Licuados** (11 Calle 7–60, Z1) is a good place to hear live marimba music as you slurp a freshly made juice-shake. The **Mercado Central** often blasts marimba tunes. Along with American rock, Guatemala's most popular music is Dominican merengue and Caribbean reggae and *soca* (soul-calypso).

CLUBS If you'd like to get some cheap(er) drinks in Zona 1 before heading off to the discotheques of Zonas 9 and 10, try drinking in one of the restaurants in the center of town. **Picadilly** (6a Av. 11–01, Z1) and **Los Cebollines** (6a Av. 9–75, Z1) both offer full bar service. If you want to dance in a hip club free from the grown-up wannabes and dirty old men who flood the *discotecas* in Zona 1, make your way to Zona 10 (also known as *La Zona Viva*—the "Live" Zone), and be prepared to shell out the bucks, at least by Guatemalan standards. Drinks are $2–$3 a pop. Most clubs are clustered around the luxurious Camino Real Hotel (Av. La Reforma and 15 Calle, Z10). **El Jaguar** (tel. 02/334–633), a disco within the hotel itself, offers your typical flashing colored lights, overpriced drinks, and crowded dance floor. To make the most of your money, come on a Tuesday night, when the music is salsa caliente and the drinks are two for one until 10 PM.

Come to **Pandora's Box** to boogie down with same-sex couples of the younger generation. Disco balls flash overhead as people pack the dance floor and rock out to the latest American pop hits. With your $6 cover charge, you receive two tickets that you can exchange for any two drinks at the bar until 1 AM. The place usually keeps rocking until 3 AM. Live shows add to the party atmosphere. *Ruta 3, 3–08, Z4, tel. 02/322–823. Open Fri.–Sat. 9 PM–3 AM, or until the place empties out.*

Near Guatemala City

Lake Amatitlán is a polluted, tacky spot that Guatemalans head to on weekends. You can take a boat around the lake where all you'll see are charmless vacation homes. Take any bus marked AMATITLAN from the main bus terminal.

SAN JUAN SACATEPEQUEZ Though it's less than an hour's bus ride from the capital, San Juan Sacatepequez is another world. It remains far off the beaten gringo trail that leads most foreigners through Antigua, Panajachel, Chichicastenango, and the villages to the west. If you come during the week, you're sure to stand out among the pigs, chickens, fried foods, and women with huge baskets of goods balanced delicately on their heads. The air rings with the guttural sound of Cakchiquel, and you may be hard-pressed to find someone who speaks Spanish. Everywhere you'll see the unique huipiles of San Juan Sacatepequez, with bold geometric designs of primarily lavender and yellow, embroidered on multicolored handwoven cloth. To get to the main market, go to 7a Calle in Zona 3, just across from the main church where the buses stop. Follow 7a Calle down a steep cobblestone hill, and then turn right on 5a Avenida to the main market, which continues to 8a Calle, Zona 4. To buy traditional huipiles and their accompanying cortes, try **Venta de Ropa Típica** (6a Av. 5–09). It's a good idea to bring your own lunch because there are not a whole lot of eateries. To get here, you can take a bus from the Terminal in Z4, but a safer bet is to take a city bus (30¢) to El Trebol (the clover leaf), then stick out your hand and catch a bus marked SAN JUAN SAC.

From May to June, the market in San Juan Sacatepequez sells Sanpopos de Mayo, giant roasted ants with salt and lemon. Just a tip: Make sure you remove the head and wings before you chow down.

MIXCO VIEJO Perched on a plateau overlooking the secluded highlands north of Guatemala City, the sparkling temples and paved ballcourts of Mixco Viejo (admission: 10¢) are so beautifully restored they don't deserve the title "ruins." Here, over 120 pyramids, palaces, and temples glisten with silvery mica, and from the top of any one you can peer off steep cliffs into cultivated fields far below. This dramatic city was once the capital of the Pocomam Maya, who occupied it until their conquest in 1542. The city is a formidable fortress, surrounded on three sides by sharp precipices, and is accessible only by a single causeway that winds steeply up a mountain on the north side. Don Pedro de Alvarado launched several full-frontal attacks in his attempts to conquer the city, but never succeeded. Unable to win the city fair and square, he wound up sneaking in a secret entrance and murdering all its inhabitants by night. Spared the moist heat and enveloping jungle of the Petén, the abandoned city remained largely intact. Its greatest damage occurred in the earthquake of 1976. The Guatemalan government has put a tremendous amount of effort into Mixco Viejo's restoration, and a library and museum showcasing its beauty are due to be completed by 1994 (it already has flush toilets). Only one bus a day traverses the winding, unpaved road that passes the entrance to the ruins, and it doesn't return until 3 AM. But anyone who dares to make the journey will be well rewarded. Three roofed enclosures overlook the ruin and each has its own barbecue pit; you can camp for free. Though people will try to convince you otherwise, you do not want a bus for Mixco, which is basically a Guatemala City suburb. Catch the bus (80¢) that leaves between 9:30 and 10 AM for Pachalum from the terminal in Zona 4 and make sure it passes "las ruinas de Mixco Viejo"—all but one bus to Pachalum don't. You'll arrive at the ruins in the early afternoon and then you're on your own until 3 AM, when the bus returns to Guatemala City. If you miss the bus and decide not to camp, you should leave the ruins a couple of hours before dark, because there's pitifully little traffic out here. Try and flag down a car or truck (your only option besides walking). If you can make it back to San Juan Sacatepequez, you can get a bus back to Guatemala City. The last bus leaves San Juan at 7 PM.

Western Highlands

The **Western Highlands are one of the** wealthiest regions of Indígena culture in all of Latin America. This beautiful region of mountains and volcanoes is the home of the living Maya, whose ancestors settled here thousands of years ago. Some villages still follow the 260-day Tzolkin Mayan calendar, and at any Mayan ruin in the highlands you'll see ashes and incense from recent prayer ceremonies scattered everywhere. Highland villagers survive on subsistence farming and they cart to market what little is left over. The women weave in blazing hues and incorporate elaborate designs of animals, flowers, and abstract symbols into the cloth. At one time, these patterns related personal info like marital status, the number of male children in a family, and what village the owner was from. Sadly, these details are being tossed aside as the international market for Guatemalan textiles grows in leaps and bounds. Tourist demand for típico clothing is so great that villagers are willing literally to sell the clothes off their back to make a buck. Then they buy western clothing for themselves because it's cheaper. The back-strap loom is also speedily being replaced with gleaming sewing machines so garments can be churned out faster to meet tourists' demands—handmade, intricate huipiles sometimes take as long as half a year to weave. Despite this new atmosphere of tourism, some symbols on Indígena clothing have yet to die: If the women's aprons are strung with jagged edges, for example, it means they're from the mountains.

On a map of Guatemala, the Western Highlands look like they're only a hop, skip, and a jump away from the capital. But the moment you begin your trek to the highlands, it feels like one hell of a journey: the air gets remarkably cooler; crossroads have no signposts; unpaved roads and mountain switchbacks criss-cross the region; and the mountains are terraced into small fields of corn, coffee, sugar cane, and vegetables. Temperatures can drop to near freezing at night, but at such high altitudes you also can get burned to a crisp by the sun during the day. The rainy season begins in May and lasts until October. However, with a good umbrella and a devil-may-care attitude about getting wet, the rain should not put a damper on your holiday.

Besides festival time, market day is a hoppin' 24 hours for the entire village. Families stuff fruit, vegetables, weavings, and household goods onto their backs and truck the whole shebang to the village center. Because most people work the fields all week, market day is as much a social gathering as a shopping and selling spree. Markets start in the wee, chilly morning hours with some vendors rarin' to go the night before. Bargaining and transactions are carried out in hushed, amicable tones. The momentum wanes around late afternoon when everyone crowds the buses to get home before the sun disappears.

Spanish is the predominant language in Guatemala, but a large percentage of the Indígena population continues to speak their own languages and can't understand Spanish. Around Lake Atitlán, Cakchiquel, Mam, and Tzutujile are spoken, but the Quiché dialect, which stems from Santa Cruz del Quiché and dominates the language scene all the way to Quetzaltenango, is the most common of all. Before the Spanish arrived in Guatemala, rival tribes spoke different languages, with the Quiché empire emerging as the strongest. The unobtrusive ruins of the Quiché capital of Utatlán lie fallow just outside the city of Santa Cruz del Quiché. The Spanish easily conquered the divided tribes, and shortly thereafter established their colonial capital in Antigua. The Spaniards constructed Antigua to reflect its importance as an administrative, cultural, and religious center. Today, Antigua is a quiet, relaxing spot with dreamy colonial ruins and cobblestone streets.

Wander into any of the self-contained, thriving villages and you'll see Indígenas who, physically, look like they've leapt right off a Mayan stela from Tikal.

The Western Highlands

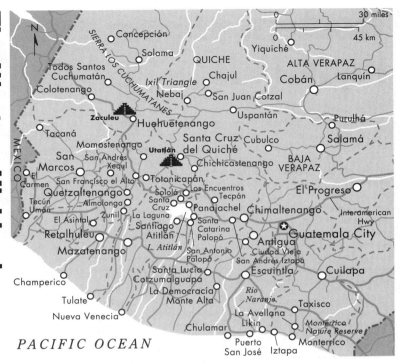

By the time the Spanish left in 1821, the colonial infrastructure had become cemented into the indigenous lifestyle. No village was complete without a white-washed adobe church, and the local pagan customs were tolerated by few authorities within the Catholic Church. Nevertheless, the two religions eventually fused into one. Today, both Catholic and pagan rituals play a significant role in the life of a town. In Chichicastenango, Indígena ceremonies are openly displayed on church steps; other forms of pagan worship are kept under wraps.

As rich as these highland communities may be in history and culture, the indigenous people are an exploited and persecuted race. Ladinos dominate the government and the military, and racism is rampant. Not surprisingly, much of Guatemala's antigovernment guerrilla activity from the '70s until the present has been centered in the highlands. Since the insurrection hasn't brought the promised freedom, though, Indígenas have become increasingly disenchanted with the guerrillas. The guerrillas try to avoid confrontations with the military when villagers may be caught in the crossfire so it's unlikely that travelers will be in any grave danger.

The Interamerican Highway cuts north through the highlands until it reaches the border of México. All buses travel this highway and **Los Encuentros** (about 2 hours from Guat City) and **Cuatro Caminos** (about five hours from Guat City) are two pit stops along the way, where buses unload and collect passengers. Almost every bus traveling through the highlands will stop at either of these two junctions.

Antigua

Set in a valley surrounded by the looming (and sometimes spewing) Agua, Acatenango, and Fuego volcanoes, Antigua was Guatemala's colonial capital from 1543 to 1773. Great pains have been taken by the local government to preserve its colonial charm—hanging signs are forbidden, which leaves the streets free from the clutter of

Antigua

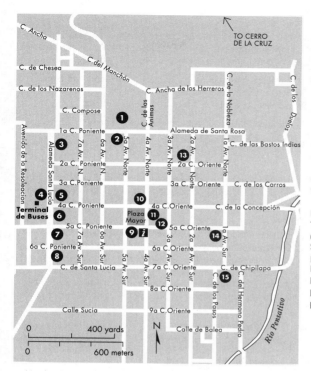

Exploring

Ayuntamiento, **10**
Casa Popenoe, **14**
Catedral de
San José, **11**
Convento de
las Capuchinas, **13**
Iglesia de
San Francisco, **15**
La Merced, **1**
Mercado Central, **4**
Museo de Arte
Colonial, **12**
Palacio de los
Capitanes
Generales, **9**

Lodging

The Annex, **8**
Casa de
Santa Lucía, **6**
Hospedaje
El Pasaje, **7**
Pensión El Arco, **2**
Posada Refugio, **5**
Posada Ruiz, **3**

advertisements. Antigua's streets follow a strict grid pattern. Massive churches, serene monasteries, and colonial mansions from the 17th century line the cobblestone streets. Travelers and urbanites flock to Antigua to relax, taking refuge in the tranquil, small-town atmosphere. By Guatemalan standards, Antigua is very clean; hotels have plenty of hot water and bathrooms are stocked with toilet paper. The *Semana Santa* (Holy Week) celebrations are Antigua's biggest event of the year. Thousands pour in from all over and the area explodes with magnificent parades. The celebration begins on Palm Sunday and ends on Good Friday. Make reservations months in advance because Antigua is *the* tourist hot-spot during that week.

Antigua was the third capital of Guatemala, after Iximché and Ciudad Vieja. It was called (but not in one breath) La Muy Noble y Muy Leal Ciudad de Santiago de los Caballeros de Goathemala. Antigua had its heyday in the mid-18th century, with a population of over 50,000, a university, one of the first printing presses in the region, and a newspaper. All this collapsed in 1773 when two earthquakes severely damaged the town and the capital was moved to Guatemala City. Today, hundreds of cool ruins scattered throughout the city can be explored on foot.

Antigua is famous for its Spanish-language schools, and hundreds of international students stay for weeks at a time. With so many students, retired Americans, wealthy Guatemalans, Ladinos, and indigenous people living together, it's a cultural swap meet. Tourists dress in embroidered huipiles and carry colorful bags stuffed with Guatemalan trinkets, while Indígenas often wear solid colors, blue jeans, and high heels. Antigua's slow pace is sometimes overshadowed by bus loads of tourists: As the first stop on the gringo shopping trail, Antigua is often mobbed by westerners on an adrenaline rush from their first contact with indigenous people.

With a slew of budget hotels and restaurants, Antigua is a popular meeting-ground for travelers. This is a good place to network and exchange tips with other backpackers. After a few days, however, Antigua may get a little too cozy.

BASICS

➤ **MONEY** • You can cash traveler's checks or change money at several banks surrounding Plaza Mayor. **Lloyd's Bank** (corner of 4a Calle and 4a Av. Norte) is open weekdays 9–3. **Banco Agro** (4a Calle) is open weekdays 9–6 and Saturday 1–6.

➤ **EMERGENCIES** • A **Policía** station is in the Palacio de los Capitanes Generales on the southern side of Plaza Mayor. The officers speak broken English at best, so bring a translator if your problem is serious and your Spanish is *muy mal.*

The **Hospital Pedro de Betancourt** is on an unnamed street, but it's easy to spot because of the line of people outside the door. *Tel. 0320/301. From Alameda Santa Lucía, turn right on 5a Calle Poniente and then make the first left; it's just after the Ministry of Education.*

If you think you're going to die waiting in line at Pedro de Betancourt, head straight to **Laboratorio Clinico Pasteur.** For $1.20, the clinic will get to the bottom of any stomach ailment you have. *6a Calle Poniente. Open weekdays 7:30 AM–1 PM and 3–6, Sat. 7:30–1.*

➤ **LANGUAGE SCHOOLS** • Antigua is internationally famous for its Spanish-language schools; over 30 are scattered throughout the city. The **Centro Linguístico Maya** (5a Calle Poniente 20) and **Projecto Linguístico Francisco Marroguín** (4a Av. Sur 4) are extremely popular. For under $100 a week, most schools will give you private tutoring plus room and board with an Antiguan family. A note of caution: Some families may house more than one student, which can be a serious deterrent to learning fluent Spanish.

➤ **PHONES AND MAIL** • GUATEL. *Corner of 5a Av. Sur and 5 Calle Poniente, at the southwest point of Plaza Mayor. Open 7 AM–midnight.*

Post office. *Alameda Santa Lucía on the corner of 4a Calle Poniente opposite the bus staion. Open weekdays 8–4.*

➤ **VISITOR INFORMATION** • If you're not armed with specific questions, all you'll receive from Antigua's **INGUAT tourist office** is a glossy brochure and an overpriced map ($2). Friends and family can mail you letters via the INGUAT office, which will hold them "indefinitely." *At the corner of 4a Av. and 5a Calle in the Palacio de los Capitanes Generales, tel. 0320/763.*

If you want more information, **Casa El Condo** has English books on Antigua and detailed maps. A well-stocked bookstore is **Un Poco de Todo,** on 5a Avenida facing Plaza Mayor. Also check notice boards in many budget hotels and restaurants for current tidbits on the city. If you want to hook up with people to climb a volcano, or even leave a note for a fellow traveler, the most widely read notice board is at Doña Luisa Xicotencatl (*see Food, below*).

COMING AND GOING All public buses come and go from Antigua's bus terminal, on the corner of Alameda Santa Lucía and 4a Calle. Buses leave every ½ hour to Guatemala City (45 minutes, 50¢) and several buses leave daily to Panajachel (2 hours). If you want to explore the highlands, take a bus to Chimaltenango (30 minutes, 25¢). Chimaltenango is the gateway to the highlands and from there you can catch a bus to anywhere. If you're driving to Antigua from Guatemala City by car, follow the Interamerican Highway to San Lucas Sacatepéquez, where you'll see the turnoff for Antigua. The entire road is well paved and the 45-kilometer (28-mile) drive takes less than an hour.

GETTING AROUND The best way to get around Antigua is on foot. You can take care of most of your needs around Plaza Mayor, which has plenty of banks, pharmacies, restaurants, and tourist shops. It's pretty easy to orient yourself here as long as you remember that you're operating within a simple grid. Calles are called *poniente* (west) from the bus station until they pass through Plaza Mayor, where they change to *oriente* (east). Alternately, avenidas run *sur–norte* (south–north) with Volcán Agua as a land-mark in the southern direction. The numbering of streets and avenues is also in a grid format. In the dead center of town is Plaza Mayor (4a Calle–4a Avenida–5a Calle–5a Avenida). These four blocks don't receive the east–west, north–south treatment.

WHERE TO SLEEP Keep in mind that the cheapest pensions are within one or two blocks of the bus station. In general, don't hesitate to bargain over a price on a room; hotel managers will often try to charge you a few extra quetzales.

➤ **UNDER $5 • Hospedaje El Pasaje.** Only 3 blocks from the bus station, this *hospedaje* (lodging) has doubles for $4. The rooms are painted different colors and the linens are flealess (an exceptional advantage). An awesome terrace on the roof invites you to meditate at sunrise. *Alameda Santa Lucía, at the corner of 5a Calle Poniente. Coming out of bus station, turn right and go 2 blocks. 16 rooms, none with bath. Laundry.*

Posada Ruiz. Right near the bus station, charmless, and often half empty, this place is saved by the presence of Norma, the proprietress, who breathes life into every room. She and her daughter are eager to converse and giggle with travelers in the front office. Doubles are $4. The beds are uncomfortable and the rooms are really noisy because of the busy street. *Alameda de Santa Lucía 17. Take an immediate left out-side the bus station and walk 3 blocks; it's on the right side of the street. 11 rooms, none with bath. Laundry.*

The Annex. Three blocks from the bus station, this tiny hotel is exceptionally clean. No sign marks the spot, but it's easy enough to find. Doubles are $4. Keep in mind that, because of its size, The Annex fills up quickly. *6a Calle Poniente, at the corner of Alameda de Santa Lucía; first door on the right-hand side. 6 rooms, none with bath.*

➤ **UNDER $10 • Casa de Santa Lucía.** If you want to spend a little more money, here's the place to do it. The hotel is luxuriously decorated, colonial-style. All rooms have their own baths, so if you're nursing a sick stomach you can have some much-needed privacy. Doubles are $7. *Alameda de Santa Lucía, between 4a Calle Poniente and 5a Calle Poniente. 14 rooms, all with bath. Laundry.*

Pensión El Arco. This pensión is quiet, secluded, and away from the low-budget lodg-ing area. The manager keeps the place spotless and the bathroom has hot water. Dou-bles are $6. *5a Av. Norte, bet. 30 and 32. From Plaza Mayor walk toward Arch of Santa Catalina; it's on the left. 9 rooms, none with bath. Laundry.*

Posada Refugio. Probably because it's right across the street from the bus station, this hotel is extremely popular with travel-weary backpackers. Where you enter, the corridor is dark and the prospects seem bleak, but for the price and location it's a good deal. Doubles with bath are $6, $4 without. Check the sheets before sleeping in them—they may not have been changed since the last person used them. *4a Calle Poniente 30. 30 rooms, some with bath. Laundry.*

FOOD Antigua is well known for its international restaurants, serving everything from Japanese food to good ol' American hamburgers. Shell out a few extra quetzales and your reward will be edible and crunchy vegetables or yummy teriyaki chicken over steamed rice. Comedores serving comida típica for less than $1 are in the Mercado Central, directly in front of the bus station.

Cafe Capri. This mauve-colored café has an Americanized menu with a cheeseburger, fries, and a milkshake for $3. Beware of the chicken sandwich, which is actually two globs of mayo and chicken bits (I think) on soggy "Bimbo" bread (Mexican Wonder bread and, yes, that's the brand name). What can you expect for 75¢? *4a Calle Poniente 24, 1 block west of Plaza Mayor.*

Doña Luisa Xicotencatl. This is the most popular place in town for travelers and locals to hang out, sip Guatemalan coffee, eat a pastry, and peruse the popular notice board. The prices are a bit steep but worth it: Luisa, the owner, was a nutritionist in the United States and she bakes her own bread. For $2.50 you can get healthy with home-made granola and fresh fruit. Salads are under $4. *4a Calle Oriente. Starting at Plaza Mayor, walk 2 blocks east.*

El Jardín. Facing Plaza Mayor so you can people-watch while eating, this cubbyhole of a restaurant offers great prices and decent American food (but, contrary to the name, no garden). A hamburger will cost you all of $1, and a plate full of beans and rice (there's no escaping this dish) is only $2. *5a Av. next to Plaza Mayor, across from the Cathedral.*

Sueños de Quetzal. Not the best restaurant (or the best prices) in town, but the only all-vegetarian one. You can get moussaka for $3.50 and salads for $3. Chill on the small balcony and watch the street action. *4a Calle Oriente, across the street from Doña Luisa.*

Wiener Cafe and Restaurant. This restaurant attracts mostly tourists and serves unexciting dishes. However, from the terrace on the top level you can see the Fuego, Acatenango, and Agua volcanoes in one brilliant panoramic view. *Alameda de Santa Lucía, 1 block past the Central Market. Closed Tues.*

Zen Restaurant. Japanese food in Guatemala? Who would have guessed shrimp and vegetables over steamed rice ($3) would exist in the land of the frijole? Good-sized portions and a welcome break in the diet típico make this place very appetizing. *3a Av. Norte 3, a yellow building between 3a Calle Poniente and 2a Calle Poniente. Open Thurs.–Tues. noon–10 PM.*

WORTH SEEING The best way to experience Antigua is to meander through town, checking out side streets and climbing around colonial ruins. Plaza Mayor, in the center of town, is a great place to start. It's also the perfect spot to stretch out on one of the many park benches and laze away the day. Facing the south side of the park is the **Palacio de los Capitanes Generales.** Once home to colonial rulers in charge of the kingdom of Guatemala, it now houses a police station, a bank, and the INGUAT tourist office. To the north, directly opposite, is the **Ayuntamiento,** the city hall until the capital shifted to Guatemala City. It's now the **Museo de Santiago** (open Tues.–Sun. 9–4), a boring museum with cheesy paintings of Mayans and a collection of Spanish weapons, torture tools, and metal chains for self-flagellation. Under the same roof is the **Museo del Libro Antigua,** which displays the first printing press in Central America. To the east is the **Catedral de San José,** which was destroyed in the 1773 earthquake. Though partially restored, the ruins' gigantic crumbling walls and fallen columns look more like a Hollywood set from *Clash of the Titans* than a reminder of the glory days of the Spanish empire.

Museo de Arte Colonial. The exhibit of antique colonial furniture is excellent and worth a look—you'll really get a feel for life in colonial Antigua. *5a Calle Oriente 5, one block east of Plaza Mayor. Open Tues.–Sun. 9–4.*

Casa Popenoe. If you're totally intrigued by colonial decor, check this place out, too. In 1932, Señor Popenoe restored the mansion and fully decorated it with authentic furniture and art from the 17th through the 19th centuries. *1a Av. Sur and 5a Calle Oriente. Open Mon.–Sat. 2 PM–4 PM.*

Iglesia de San Francisco. The attraction of this church is neither its grace nor beauty (it has none), but the remains of Pedro de Betancourt, the most beloved of Guatemalan holy men. After an intense religious experience with a wooden Virgin Mary who came to life before his eyes, Pedro settled in Antigua and founded a hospital and a school. He became a great healer of the people, curing hernias and returning stolen oxen. The church is now a shrine for the sick and desperate, and draws believers from all parts of Central America in need of a miracle or two. Decorating the walls are marble, wood, and metal plaques, and photographs and letters thanking Hermano Pedro for his divine intervention. Don't miss the **Museo de San Francisco** (50¢), which has the skull Hermano Pedro meditated over, the rags he wore, tokens of gratitude, and a stash of abandoned crutches. *7a Calle Oriente, between 1a Av. Sur and Calle del Hermano Pedro.*

Convento de las Capuchinas. This is the largest and best-preserved convent in Antigua. The Capuchin nuns arrived from Madrid in 1726, and their new convent quickly grew in size because, unlike at other convents, the women did not need to pay dowries to undertake the religious lifestyle. *Corner of 2a Av. Norte and 2a Calle Oriente. Open Tues.–Sun. 9–5.*

La Merced. Spanning an entire block at 6a Avenida Norte and 1a Calle Poniente, La Merced is a massive church with the most elaborate facade in town. Unfortunately, due to earthquake damage and a subsequent quick-fix restoration job, the interior lacks the same intricate molding that graces the front. It's barely worth the 5¢ to peek your head in. As you leave, walk along 5a Avenida Norte to catch a glimpse of the beautiful **Arco de Santa Catalina,** framing Volcán Agua far off in the distance.

Mercado Central. Adjacent to the bus station lies the busy marketplace that titillates the senses. With a plethora of fruits, vegetables, and meats on display, you may well be assaulted by some rather unpleasant smells, but it's a culturally valid stench.

CHEAP THRILLS On Sundays, one of the best ways to get sweaty with Antiguans is to catch the local soccer tournaments behind the central market, starting at 10 AM and lasting well into the afternoon. If you don't want to play, cheering from the sidelines can be just as entertaining.

AFTER DARK Guatemalans love to drink, and they drink hard. It's not uncommon for the men to pass out on bar tables until their wives search the taverns and drag them home. This is probably the reason for all the AA (Alcoholics Anonymous) clinics around town. Bar hours tend to fluctuate depending on the mood of the owner, but generally no place is kicking until 10 PM. A recent law says that bars (especially those infested with gringos) must close by midnight. It remains to be seen if this law will be strongly enforced.

➤ **BARS** • **Cafe Picasso.** A popular place with yuppie travelers, this bar plays country music that will make you forget you ever left your home on the range. *7a Av. Norte, between 2a Calle Poniente and 3a Calle Poniente.*

La Bota Tejara. Although it's located amid all the other gringo-infested bars, "The Texas Boot" is a local hangout. After a few drinks, you'll be enthusiastically testing out Spanish words on the regulars. *7a Av. Norte, across the street from Cafe Picasso.*

La Chimenca. This bar draws an international crowd with its blaring music. Occasionally bands are featured. *On the corner of 4a Calle Poniente and 7a Av. Norte, 2 blocks east of Plaza Mayor.*

OUTDOOR ACTIVITIES

➤ **HIKING** • A 20-minute hike leads you up to the **Cerro de la Cruz,** where you can look down on all of Antigua. Due to a number of robberies, policemen are stationed from 7 AM to 5 PM at separate points along the path. From Plaza Mayor, take 4a Calle Oriente until Calle de la Nobleza; turn left. For more strenuous hikes, trails lead to the rim of Volcán Agua and within a few meters of the active Volcán Fuego. Don't climb alone: Several people have been assaulted on the trails. With a guide and a group of people, there shouldn't be a problem. Guides advertise on notice boards and charge around $15 per person. If possible, arrange to climb Fuego in the late afternoon, so you can see it spit fire into the air and light up the night.

➤ **BIKING** • Rent a mountain bike for an hour, day, or week. You can cruise to nearby villages like Santa María de Jesús, about 10 kilometers (6 miles) south of Antigua (follow 1a Avenida Sur all the way out of town) or blaze your own trail through surrounding coffee fincas and tiny *pueblos* (towns). *Bike rental at La Casa de Las Gargolas, 5a Av. Norte 14. One hour costs $1, 24 hours is $5, and a week is $5.*

NEAR ANTIGUA

CIUDAD VIEJA This run-down village has such an entertaining past that it's worth a look. It's footnoted in the history books for being the original site of the first capital, Santiago de los Caballeros. Our favorite conquistador Pedro de Alvarado brought his wife Doña Beatriz to a newly built mansion in the city; he soon left her to continue his pillage of the New World. Along the way, he was crushed by a horse. When the news reached Doña Beatriz, she went wacko, painting all the mirrors and furniture in her stately home black. She also commanded the officials to appoint her governess—the first female leader of the Americas. However, her rule was short-lived. A storm that had been raging for several days caused one side of Volcán Agua to erode. The water stored up in the mouth of the crater flooded the capital, killing Doña Beatriz on her second day in office. Buses leave the Antigua station every 30 minutes and cost 15¢.

Just a few miles past Ciudad Vieja lies **San Antonio Aguas Calientes,** a well-known weaving community. If you're interested in learning the art of backstrap weaving, ask one of the women in the plaza about a teacher and a price.

SAN ANDRES IZTAPA Iztapa, about 45 minutes from Antigua, is relatively unknown to tourists. Not so for many Indigenas, who frequently visit in order to pay homage to **San Simón** (a.k.a. Maximon), the drinking and smoking saint (*see* box). The color of the candle planted at Maximon's shrine reveals the worshipper's desire: Red means love, green is luck in work, and black wards off enemies. Love problems seem to plague most of the believers—the temple is always crowded with lit red candles. To get to **La Casa de San Simón,** go one block past the church and turn right. Walk two blocks to the greenhouse on the left before the hill.

TECPAN AND THE IXIMCHE RUINS A full morning's venture from Antigua is Tecpán and the Iximché ruins. If you didn't know better, you'd never suspect that **Tecpán,** a town reminiscent of Sleepy Hollow, has a long and bloody history. In 1524,

San Simón

Images and effigies of San Simón, the smoking and drinking saint, are found in indigenous towns all over the country, including Santiago Atitlán, San Jorge La Laguna, San Andrés Iztapa, Zunil, and Nahualá. In each town, the idol is differently dressed and made up, usually with a hat teetering on his head. Regardless of how he looks, San Simón enjoys a stiff drink and a puff on a cigar before he starts spinning his magic. He's known to be nonjudgmental, granting the wish of anyone who approaches and believes in his powers. San Simón likes hard alcohol and cigarettes best (big surprise), but money, eggs, and candles are also showered on the idol in exchange for his help in personal matters. Because the Catholic church frowns on pagan practices, San Simón is usually kept under wraps; but, in some places, he's fairly accessible to (believing) travelers—ask around for directions. As a tourist, it's important to be highly respectful of Indígenas praying to San Simón. Picture-taking is not recommended.

when Pedro de Alvarado first arrived in the area, the Cakchiquel tribe was ruling from its own capital at Iximché, 5 kilometers (3 miles) outside town. In order to defeat the rival Quiché tribe, the Cakchiqueles allied themselves with the Spaniards, only to have their confidence betrayed later on. The Cakchiqueles then deserted Iximché; the Spaniards, with designs of their own, tried to establish their very first capital at nearby Tecpan. The Cakchiqueles spoiled these plans by attacking the Spanish settlement using guerrilla tactics. The Spaniards finally got the hint and closed shop. In 1530, Ciudad Vieja was crowned the new capital—out of the reach of the Cakchiqueles. Today, hardly a trace remains of the Spanish influence.

Tecpán itself is small and quiet, with very few tourists—the big and perhaps only reason to head here. The Iximché ruins are about an hour's walk past Tecpán. You'll see signs to Iximché all along the bumpy, dirt road that few cars travel. The site feels and looks sterile, with a freshly machete-mowed lawn, perfectly reconstructed ball courts, and tiny pyramidal structures. If you've seen a zillion ruins already, this place won't push your buttons. However, the isolated surroundings are relaxing, and your only desire will be to lay down under a shady tree and daydream about Iximché's glory days.

Buses leave periodically for Tecpán from Chimaltenango. It's about an hour bus ride, and Iximché is another hour's walk. From Panajachel or Guatemala City, buses leave several times a day. The archaeological site is open 9–5 and admission is 20¢. A museum houses a few artifacts and a topographical layout of Iximché.

Panajachel and Lake Atitlán

Panajachel's setting is highly dramatic, bordered by three volcanoes that drop off into the crystalline waters of Lake Atitlán. During the late '60s and '70s, Pana rightfully earned its spot on the worldwide gringo trail alongside such standards as Kathmandu in Nepal and Goa in India. During the tumultuous 1980s, as Guatemala's internal problems escalated into civil war, many of Pana's drifters left the country.

Today, Lake Atitlán is attracting a new type of traveler to its shores. Mingling with the aging hippies is a younger group of U.S. and European entrepreneurs, who have started up restaurants, motorcycle shops, and outfits for exporting Guatemalan textiles and clothing. Water sports like kayaking and waterskiing are up for grabs, and weekend visitors arrive in hordes for picnic and beer-drinking sessions. Even the smaller villages have adapted to the new shop-o-rama climate, as they incessantly hawk local *artesanías* (crafts).

You think you can come to Panajachel and avoid other travelers? The city is known to locals as "Gringotenango."

Despite its changing face, Panajachel and the surrounding area still have the best climate in the Western Highlands. The heat radiates an almost tropical feel, with temperatures becoming pleasantly warm (enough to get a suntan) during the rainy season. A number of brisk-to-strenuous mountain hikes dot the area, most leading to breathtaking views of the lake.

BASICS

➤ **MONEY** • **Banco Agrícola Mercantil.** *On the corner of Calle Principal and Calle Santander, next to the bus stop. Open weekdays 9–3, Sat. 9–1.*

The **black market** changers hang out around the bus stop across from Banco Agricola Mercantil. The exchange rate is pretty much what the banks offer, so the only reason to take a back-alley trip is to avoid bank lines and bank hassle.

➤ **EMERGENCIES** • The **police** station is near the end of Calle Principal, in a one-room shanty with only a desk and an antiquated typewriter. On Calle Los Arboles is a **clinic** (tel. 502/0621–111) with an English-speaking doctor. Call to make an appointment. If you're in a money pinch and don't want to pay the consultation fee, do as the locals do and head to **Pharmacy Prisy** (Calle Principal, 4 blocks before market).

➤ **PHONES AND MAIL** • **GUATEL.** *On Calle Santander, midway between the lake and Calle Principal. Open daily 7 AM–midnight.*

The local **post office** is opposite the police station on a side street facing the church. You can mail packages from here, but it's safer to send your boxloads of Guatemalan goodies from **Get Guated Out** (Calle Los Arboles) or **The Pink Box** (off Calle Santander).

➤ **VISITOR INFORMATION** • The main reason to stop by the **INGUAT** office is to get the scoop on bus and boat arrival and departure times. The schedule is posted outside, so you don't even need to stop by during office hours. *Calle Principal, where most buses stop. Open Wed.–Sun. 8–noon and 2–6, Mon. 8–noon.*

For miscellaneous information (rooms for rent or a random airplane ticket for sale), check the notice board at **Al Chisme**, on Calle Los Arboles.

COMING AND GOING

➤ **BY BUS** • Buses depart from just outside the Mayan Palace Hotel on Calle Principal, right next to INGUAT. Panajachel has direct buses to Guatemala City on the Rebuli line (3½ hours); Antigua (3 hours; take Rebuli bus to Chimaltenango and switch there to Antigua); Chichicastenango (1½ hours); and Quetzaltenango (2½ hours). For Huehuetenango (4 hours), take the bus to Quetzaltenango and ask to be let off at Cuatro Caminos; buses to Huehuetenango pass this point hourly. These lines don't run past mid-afternoon; if you miss your bus you can always catch a bus to **Los Encuentros,** from where buses run later to all of these destinations.

If you're ready to pack up entirely and head for Mexico, the journey takes fewer than 5 hours. To La Mesilla or San Cristóbal, catch the Rebuli line to Los Encuentros, and then take the El Condor line that leaves for the border at 6 AM, 10 AM, and noon. If you're heading to El Carmen or Talismán, take any bus for Cocales. At Cocales, change to the Galgos line heading for the Mexican border.

You can take buses to many spots around the lake. To Solotá, buses and minibuses leave every half hour. A 9 AM and a 5:30 PM bus head to Santa Catarina Palopó (½ hour), San Antonio Palopó (1 hour), and San Lucas Tolíman (1½ hours). **Minibuses,** stationed at the corner of Calle Principal and Calle Santander, randomly circulate between these villages.

➤ **BY BOAT** • Launches leave for **Santiago Atitlán** every hour 7–3; to **San Pedro La Laguna,** the boat leaves every two hours until 2 PM. These times are approximations; relax Latin-style and don't get bothered when departure times slide by.

GETTING AROUND
After the exhilarating descent into Panajachel (disrupted only by the sight of three phallic highrises), the bus stops in front of the INGUAT tourist office. Panajachel's main street, **Calle Principal,** runs through downtown, where the central market, church, post office, police, and city hall are all located. If you continue out of town, the road leads to the villages of Santa Catarina Palopó and San Andrés Palopó, where it finally comes to a dead end. Budget hotels and cheaper restaurants are on **Calle Santander,** which can be followed to the lake. **GUATEL,** on Calle Santander halfway between the lake and where the buses stop, is a good landmark to help orient yourself. **Calle Rancho Grande,** the other semi-major street, runs parallel to Calle Santander.

WHERE TO SLEEP
Hundreds of rooms that cater to those with a thin wallet are advertised in Panajachel. Rooms vary in size so always check before you pay to make sure you're not sleeping in a closet. Simplicity is the word to describe most hotels' style and decor. A hot shower will cost you 25¢ and is worth every penny. Many hotels

are on no-name side streets, but, with all the homemade signs that litter Calle Santander, you'll have no trouble finding them.

Anexo Santa Elena. Two blocks past GUATEL, the entryway of this small hotel is crowded with blossoming tropical flowers and beautiful (but caged) chirping birds; you'll feel like you're walking into grandma's garden. Rooms are light and airy (a rarity in these parts), and a small courtyard is equipped with a laundry basin. Doubles are $5. The only shortcoming is that the hot showers feel lukewarm, with the occasional ice-cold spurt that'll knock the wind out of you. *2a Calle. 8 rooms, none with bath. Laundry.*

Hospedaje de Londres. This cheap hotel is never full. Although dark and drab, Hospedaje de Londres is *the* cheapest of the cheap in Panajachel; doubles are $1.25. Rooms are quiet because it's a little bit off the main road. Be careful of the cockroaches—one might try to nest in your hair while you sleep. *On an alley off Calle Santander just past GUATEL; look for the advertisement. 8 rooms, none with bath.*

Hospedaje Vista Hermosa. Simple, clean, and very quiet rooms surround a courtyard. A table and some chairs on the second floor are sheltered by a plastic covering, so it's a super-comfortable nook on rainy days. Some rooms are windowless, so make sure you ask or check. Doubles are $3.25 plus a $3 deposit for the key. *2a Calle, two blocks past GUATEL. (The street name is more difficult to spot than the hospedaje sign.) 16 rooms, none with bath. Laundry.*

Mario's Rooms. One budget hotel always seems to be more popular with backpackers than the rest; in Panajachel, Mario's is the place. Its location halfway between Calle Principal and the lake (with vendor stalls right across the street) contributes to Mario's appeal and makes it very accessible. Rooms are bright and clean, and doubles cost $5. A café in the front section of the hotel has great food and two shelves of mostly romance novels for sale. *Calle Santander, just past GUATEL. The bus stops at the intersection of Calle Santander and Calle Principal; take Calle Santander in the only direction it goes. 12 rooms, none with bath.*

Villa Martita Hotel. Hidden behind a small grove of trees, this place has a charm that is severely lacking in most hospedajes. Rooms are sunlit and an adorable garden sits out front. The owner operates a small café out of his kitchen and, best of all, the showers are really, truly hot. Doubles are $5. *Calle Santander, two blocks up from the lake. 4 rooms, none with bath.*

➤ **CAMPGROUNDS •** Panajachel has two designated camping sites. A private campground on the west side near Hotel Visión Azul has special amenities like water and electrical hookups. The other spot is on the public beach on Río Panajachel. It's just after the bridge on the road to Santa Catarina Palopó; make the first right onto a small and ugly shore. The beach ain't flat or smooth and you may be damn uncomfortable. If you want a tent to come back to, don't leave it for a second.

FOOD Pana provides several ways to escape the comida típica grease. Often, the cafés owned by gringos cater to the gringo palate and diet. A couple of snack shops on Calle Santander sell refreshing smoothies of papaya and pineapple. You can also buy a loaf of bread from a local hippie, get vegetables from the central market, and concoct your own sandwich. The comedores on the lakefront that cater to weekend strollers and beer-guzzling tourists are surprisingly expensive. **Comedor Los Pumpos** has live marimba music on the weekends.

➤ **UNDER $5 • Mario's Restaurant.** Right in front of Mario's Rooms, this café/restaurant has the largest servings for the cheapest prices in all of Pana. It's super popular with hotel guests, other travelers, and locals. *Desayuno completo* (served at any time of day) includes two eggs, beans, freshly baked bread, fruit, and oatmeal for $2. If you think you're going to still be hungry, chow down on a humongous crepe stuffed with fruit and yogurt ($1.50). *Calle Santander, right in front of Mario's Rooms, just past GUATEL.*

Restaurante Vegetariano. A vegetarian's delight and probably the best dinner in town—the owner cooks up a complete meal, different each night of the week, for only $2. On Saturday night the menu includes mint soup, excellent lasagna, beet salad, artichoke-carrot salad, and bread. *At the fork of Calle Santander and Los Arboles, on the Los Arboles side.*

➤ **UNDER $10** • **Al Chisme Restaurant.** If you have money and want gringo company, come to Al Chisme. Expatriates and tourists congregate on the patio soaking up the sun. Lunch and dinner specials, like chicken in tarragon sauce and pasta primavera with salad and homemade bread, go for $5. *Los Arboles, on the side that branches to the left from Calle Principal. Closed Wed.*

Circus Bar. Better known for its nightlife and occasional live band, this bar also has a complete menu of pizzas ($3–$4), pastas, and meat dishes. Puppets dangle from the ceiling and old circus posters decorate the walls; you may find yourself staying longer than you expect and spending more than you want. *Los Arboles, next door to Al Chisme. Open daily 11:30–midnight.*

AFTER DARK With all the foreigners, Panajachel has a happening nightlife. For live music and a party atmosphere, the **Circus Bar** (on Calle Los Arboles, next to Al Chisme) stays open as long as patrons want it to. If you're hankering for a game of Ping-Pong, try **The Last Resort,** a full-service bar on the side street just before Mario's Rooms on Calle Santander. Locals mainly head to the **cantinas** (on Calle Rancho Grande or any small side street), where they partake in some serious drinking. Al Chisme and **Bombay Cafe** (on Calle Los Arboles) are great digs for an after-dinner coffee and sweet. If you want to catch a flick, the **Grapevine** (on Calle Santander) has its own screening room with cushioned benches.

OUTDOOR ACTIVITIES As Panajachel evolves from an isolated Guatemalan village into a booming lakeside resort, water sports are becoming more popular, giving Lake Atitlán a Club Med feel. It's easy to rent a kayak or boat for an hour ($2) or a day. If the contrived atmosphere gets to you, take a walk to a set of *miradores* (lookout points) and see the lake in its entirety. Follow the paved road toward Sololá just past the hilltop village of San Jorge until you get to the waterfall. For a more challenging hike, a 3-hour trail takes you to the isolated village of **Concepción,** with its whitewashed colonial church. You'll probably be the only tourist in town. From Panajachel, take Calle Los Arboles to the very end of the street (about a mile past the central market) until the road forks, with a metal bridge to the right and a dirt trail leading to Concepción on the left.

You can actually trek around the entire perimeter of Lake Atitlán in less than a week. The journey is tough and tiring, but getting off the gringo trail is very rewarding. Take plenty of water and food for those nights that you don't make it to a village with a comedor or hospedaje. If you don't want to sleep outdoors and you get stuck somewhere, you can always approach the mayor of any village and ask him about an available bed. Don't take any valuables with you, because robbery at gunpoint has recently been reported in the area.

AROUND LAKE ATITLAN

After you've had your fill of Pana, jump on one of the many launches that ferry people and goods across the lake. If you're prone to seasickness, take a boat ride in the morning when the water is smooth as glass. By early afternoon, Xocomil (a biting wind that, according to the Indígenas, burns out sin) begins to act up, making the boat trip feel like a roller-coaster ride. Less commercial than Pana, the nearby villages radiate their own individual style, displaying variations in dress, custom, and dialect. Most smaller villages lack hospedajes and comedores.

SANTA CATARINA PALOPO AND SAN ANTONIO PALOPO A short walk from Panajachel, these sister villages are surprisingly traditional. The women fix themselves up
in identical garb: stunning red huipiles embroidered with delicate figures, worn with
long, navy-blue skirts. The men also have a style all their own, with pants designed
with geometric motifs and calf-length woolen wraparounds fastened by leather belts or
red sashes. Life consists of farming, weaving, and attending church services. An
adobe colonial church marks the center of each town. The
church steps are used as a social meeting ground, where all
passersby are sure to stop for a while. If you plan on walking
to either town from Panajachel, take Calle Principal toward
the central market. A sign on a building wall indicates the
road leading to Santa Catarina Palopó (4 kilometers [2½
miles]) and San Antonio Palopó (8 kilometers [5 miles]).

*The villagers of San
Antonio Palopó are a wee-
bit camera shy and tend to
duck out of sight just as you
prepare to shoot. Don't take
it too hard. Their children
don't see the light of day
until they have reached their
first year, because their faces
are kept covered to ward off
evil spirits.*

SANTIAGO ATITLAN Surrounded by San Pedro, Tolíman,
and Atitlán volcanoes, Santiago Atitlán is the second-
most-visited lakeside village after Panajachel, and endures
constant facelifts to maintain its once-genuine traditional
beauty. Ironically, the result is that it often looks run-down
and dirty. A pathway from the lake leads up to the plaza and
the courtyard of the main church. The road is lined with
artesanía shops selling woven items, wooden animals, and
other handmade crafts. In some shops you might see the
women working on looms, where they weave traditional gar-
ments in soft shades of pink, purple, red, and blue. Many women sport a "halo," a 12-
yard-long headband wrapped around the head that looks like a sun visor.

On a darker note, Santiago Atitlán has seen its share of politics and death. The villagers are known for their spirited rebellions. As a result of a so-called guerrilla convention in 1981, the army set up camp in town. Many of the Santiago villagers that
were murdered or have "disappeared" through the years have been considered political victims. In 1990, 12 people died in a massacre; the army left Santiago in 1991.

Semana Santa is Santiago's most spirited occasion. Good Friday is highlighted by
simultaneous Christian and pagan rituals. The villagers dress in their very best and
crowd the central church to witness an icon of Christ being raised upon the altar,
surrounded by tropical fruits, gourds, cacao beans, and flowers. Later, the icon is
paraded around the streets along with the smoking and drinking San Simón. Here in
Santiago Atitlán, the San Simón idol is a wooden statue decked out in silk scarves and
wearing sneakers. If you want to ask a favor of this pagan god, he's under the protection of the *cofradía* (a religious society). For precise directions on how to contact the
cofradía, ask at the fire station. If you're sleeping in town, **Hospedaje Chi-Nim-Ya**
(near the boat dock) is decent and cheap. Eat at one of the many comedores or grab a
bite at the market.

Bird-lovers can check out **Pato Poc Nature Reserve** on the outskirts of town. For $3,
rent a boat to search out the elusive poc (or Atitlán) grebe, an awkward water bird that
can't fly and exists only here. Pocs once numbered in the hundreds, but with the
introduction to the lake of the black bass (which eats baby birds), the pocs are now an
endangered species.

SANTA CRUZ LA LAGUNA As you move west along the northern shore from Pana,
boat traffic decreases and the blue water becomes way more inviting. This mountainside village, a 20-minute hike from the shore, remains isolated and virtually
untouched by western influence. A whitewashed colonial church in the center of town
faces the city hall and medical clinic. The women gather around the public wash basin
to gossip and scrub their laundry. The villagers are shy, but if you stick around a while
they'll warm up to you.

Within the village, **Hospedaje Hernandez** is a three-room hotel; ask at the yellow house above the public wash basin for a room. If you want a little luxury, a German-owned hotel on the lake has everything a backpacker could dream of. Four bucks will set you up with a soft mattress, a private dock to sunbathe on, and filtered water in your room. Dinner is quite an occasion, in which a five-course meal is presented with freshly baked bread for $3.50.

SOLOLA Guarding the lake from on high, Sololá is culturally worlds away from Panajachel. Because few tourists stick around Sololá (they're all in a hurry to get to the lake), it has retained its own character and style. Admittedly, there's nothing in particular to see here but the people themselves. Most of the men and women wear their traditional garb, the designs of which can be traced back to pre-colonial days. Friday is market day, when everyone is decked out in all their splendor. It's purely an indigenous market for the exchange of fruits and vegetables, meats, and materials. The streets around the central plaza are blocked off for the event.

The men of Sololá look like Technicolor cowboys, with red pin-striped pants, an authentic, multicolored cowboy shirt, and a big ol' hat.

Facing the central plaza is the typical white church without which no Guatemalan town is complete. A **post office, GUATEL,** and a **Banco de Guatemala** lie nearby. Buses headed to Panajachel via Sololá come and go throughout the day. Plenty of buses are headed to Los Encuentros, where you can easily transfer (*see* Panajachel Coming and Going, *above*). Minivans from Sololá also cart people to and from Los Encuentros and Panajachel.

Chichicastenango

Because everyone likes to shop, Chichicastenango is one of Guatemala's número uno tourist attractions. Empty for most of the week, on Thursday and Sunday Chichi bumps and grinds with enthusiastic gringos and locals. Vendors set up shop while the dawn mist still lingers on the cobblestone streets. The market here is proof that the joy of shopping is infectious. It's hard to resist temptation when you walk through aisle upon aisle of kaleidoscopic Guatemalan goodies for sale. The possibilities are endless: gorgeous huipiles from Nebaj, made-for-tourist "típico" clothing, wooden masks, wool blankets, woven bags, baskets, machetes, *metates* (a corn-grinding stone), jade, pottery, and everyday necessities from soap to cassette tapes to produce. Although the city tries to centralize the frenzied shopping activity around the plaza, surrounding streets are inevitably blocked off by the overflow. If it's any kind of reassurance, the town is famous for accommodating masses of people on market day.

The Cakchiquel people once lived here, before they upped stakes and established their capital at Iximché. When Pedro de Alvarado and his gang destroyed the Quiché capital of Utatlán, the survivors fled to the old Cakchiquel town. The Quichés renamed the place Chugúila (above the nettles) and then Tziguán Tinamit (surrounded by canyons). Eventually, Alvarado's Mexican troops christened it Chichicastenango. (Nowadays, the only tribute to the Mayan names is the exclusive Hotel Chugúila and Restaurant Tziguán Tinamit.)

The fusion of Catholic and pagan practice adds a funky twist to this touristy locale. In 1540, while Chichi was under Spanish influence, **La Iglesia de Santo Tomás** was built right on top of a Mayan altar. From the beginning, the indigenous people easily converted their pagan deities into Catholic saints. Many of the symbols overlapped, such as the Mayan cross and the crucifix. Today, Mayan rituals unfold on the church steps. At the base, a small fire continually burns throughout the day, as believers kneel and pray quite vocally. Afterwards, alcohol is splashed onto the steps to ensure that their wishes are heard. These ceremonies are always carried out in a fog of sticky-sweet incense smoke. All of the worshippers recognize the Catholic God as their main deity, praying fervently to the idol inside the church. Pine needles cover the church floor, while corn husks, candles, and flower petals are arranged around the different altars. Every type of decoration, from Christmas cut-outs to Chinese lanterns, hangs from the ceiling. It's best to use the side entrance to the church so you don't disrupt the rituals on the steps. Once inside, you'll have to etch the scene forever in your mind, because picture-taking is taboo.

Chichi is an anomaly of sorts in that the Catholic Church openly accepts local pagan rituals. Unfortunately, the Mayans are not totally free of persecution. The shrine to the deity **Pascual Abaj**, on the hilltop outside of town, is often wrecked by zealous Christians. Every time this happens, the elongated stone face is salvaged and believers continue their daily rituals. *Brujos* or the local shamen preside over these ceremonies, and the villagers recite special prayers and offer candles, food, alcohol, and sometimes a slaughtered chicken. You can check out this fantastic spot by following 9a Calle until you see signs that point out the narrow footpath up the mountain. The serious rituals take place at odd times.

In Chichi, the Catholic Church and an elected Indígena council work hand-in-hand to administer the city. The church oversees the general interests, while the council handles the day-to-day matters. Even the religious leaders, known as **cofradías**, are locally appointed. To be selected as a cofradía is the most prestigious position in town. Like most good things, however, it comes at a heavy price. The cofradías have to pay (out of their own pockets, mind you) for all of Chichi's holiday celebrations and fiestas. Cofradías are easily distinguishable by the elegant costumes and headpieces they don on market days and for special processions. The wooden staff they tote is topped by a magnificent silver sun medallion.

Chichi is considered the Holy City of Quiché, and thousands of people turn up for the town's grand fiesta December 13–21, when the area explodes with parades and dances. The **Dance of the Conquest** is a ceremonial skit representing the Spanish conquest of the Indígena. You can also check out the **palo volador** (flying pole) ceremony, in front of the Santo Tomás. A 60-foot pole is erected, with ropes wound tightly around the pole from top to bottom. Professional (and oh-so-brave) villagers secure themselves to the free end of the rope and fling themselves into the air from a platform on top of the pole. They loopily spin down the length of the pole until they land on the ground.

BASICS **Banco del Ejército** is the only bank in town that has hours to complement the weekend market. *6a Calle, take 5a Av. from the central plaza toward the Arco Gucumatz and turn right. Open Tues.–Sun. 9–noon, 2–5.*

GUATEL. *7a Av. and 8 Calle A, 2 blocks behind Santo Tomás. Open daily 7–7.*

Post Office. *7a Av., 2 doors up from GUATEL (after the pig market). Open weekdays 8–noon, 2–6.*

COMING AND GOING Direct buses head to Guatemala City (4 hours, $1.50) and Quetzaltenango (2½ hours, $1). If you're heading out of the department of Quiché, the quickest option is to catch any bus heading to Los Encuentros, where you can get an onward connection. Buses zip back and forth all day long between Chichi and Santa Cruz del Quiché (15 minutes, 25¢) and to the little villages along the way. Since you'll find no designated bus stops in Chichi, you get to test your skill at flagging down buses.

Chichi is spread out in the typical Guatemalan grid format, but it's tricky to figure out because Chichi is very hilly. The town is so small, though, that you never feel truly lost. The principal street is 5a Avenida, where you'll see the Santo Tomás church and the Arco Gucumatz. The majority of hotels, restaurants, and tipíco stores spreads out from the central plaza to 6a Avenida and 6a Calle.

WHERE TO SLEEP AND EAT Although it's a tourist haven, Chichi isn't well prepared to handle the onslaught of budget travelers. The few cheap hotels tend to fill up quickly on Wednesday and Saturday nights, the days before the big markets. If you can't get a room, don't panic. Santa Cruz del Quiché, 15 minutes away by bus, has several low-budget hotels that don't fill up quite so fast (see below). If you're truly down and out in Chichi, you can bed down on the street, next to the vendors. They set up their stalls at the crack of dawn, so if you don't want a hand in your pocket or curious eyes staring down at you, it's best to start your day with them.

Hospedaje Salvador (5a Av., 2 blocks from main plaza) is a three-story budget hotel with a labyrinth of steep staircases. It's one of the cheapest places in town ($4 for a double without bath), so don't be surprised to see fleas jumping in and out of your sheets. **Hospedaje Giron** (7a Calle, 1 block north of main plaza) and **Posada Santa Marta** (5a Av., 1 block past Arco Gucumatz) are a hell of a lot nicer for a dollar more (about $5 for a double), but they have fewer rooms. For a luxurious budget hotel go to **Posada El Arco** (4a Calle 4–36), where you're given fresh towels, soap, and a piping-hot shower. Doubles are $10. From Arco Gucumatz walk up the stairs and turn left; it's a two-story building with green doors.

You'll also notice a serious lack of restaurants (not counting the comedores, of course) in Chichi. Meat dishes dominate the specials at the few restaurants. **Restaurante El Mash** (6a Calle, 2 blocks north of plaza) has a full menu with chicken or beef for about $3. **Restaurante Tapena** (5a Av., 1 block north of plaza) serves average food like hamburgers for about $1, and a line-up that includes fried chicken, soup, salad, and french fries or tortillas for $3.50.

WORTH SEEING The **Regional Museum** is overshadowed by Chichi's markets but still worth a look. The museum (open Wednesday–Monday 8–noon and 2–5) is a one-room exhibit to the left of the Santo Tomás church in the plaza. Amazingly well-preserved Mayan pots with the original paint on the sides, huge jade beads, stone figurines, and two pieces of finely designed gold jewelry that escaped the Spanish meltdown of precious metals illustrate the glory and wealth of the Quiché capital of Utatlán (see Near Santa Cruz del Quiché, below). These priceless artifacts were all donated by villagers to Father Rossbach, the main priest in Chichi in the early 20th century.

CHEAP THRILLS The indoor vegetable market opposite the Regional Museum is an enthralling sight. Purely for locals doing their weekly grocery shopping, it's small enough for you to get a close look at how bargaining is really done. The upper-level balcony is a great place to take pictures from without giving offense. If you're into sunrises and the early morning mist that weaves in and out of the silent streets, climb the steps to the top of **Arco Gucumatz** on 5a Avenida, where you can gaze into the steep valley below.

Santa Cruz del Quiché

On the ride to Santa Cruz, 15 minutes from Chichicastenango, the unnerving mountain switchbacks give passengers a bird's-eye view of terraced farm plots. After this heart-stopping ride, Santa Cruz del Quiché is quite a disappointment, lacking Chichi's luster. Catch the ruins outside town, peek quickly at the city's goings-on, and move on to more vibrant villages. This ho-hum scene comes as a surprise, since Santa Cruz del Quiché is the capital of the department of Quiché and was a hotbed of activity during the height of the guerrilla insurrection in the 1980s. Army camps surround the town, and soldiers frequently parade through the streets. Graffiti is sprayed everywhere on city walls and army garrisons, with messages that ask for peace and an end to repression. But the days of Indígena rebellion are fading fast. A feeling of tranquility prevails, as the indigenous population is integrated and becomes Ladinoized. The process is slow but undeniable, with a proliferation of western clothing stores that are transforming Quiché into the land of "Ropa Americana." The colonial church, made from the stones of the ruined Quiché capital of Utatlán, houses a memorial to crusading priests who were killed in the area during more violent times. **Banco de Guatemala** is at the corner of the plaza at 2a Avenida and 3a Calle. **GUATEL** and the **post office** share the same building a block up on 3a Calle.

COMING AND GOING Santa Cruz del Quiché is shortened to "Quiché" on the bus plaques above the front window. Buses come and go all day long from the **bus terminal** on 1a Avenida, 4 blocks south of the plaza. Buses start leaving for Guatemala City (4½ hours, $1.50) at 5 AM. Although it's a "direct" bus, this only means you don't have to change buses to get there. But you will stop at Chichicastenago, Los Encuentros, and Chimaltenango along the way. Direct buses go to Quetzaltenango at 8:30 AM, 1 PM, and 2 PM. If you miss these, catch one of the buses to Guatemala City and get off at Los Encuentros. From Los Encuentros, you won't have to wait long for your connection.

From Quiché's terminal, follow 1a Avenida north 4 blocks, turn left on 6a Calle, and you'll reach the central plaza. Keep an ear open for the loud Latin music that blares onto the plaza 12 hours a day.

WHERE TO SLEEP **Hospedaje Tropical.** The seedy, dark rooms pick up lots of noise from the bus station a block away. But it's so close to the terminal and has such cheap rates ($1 a bed) that it fills up frequently in spite of itself. *1a Av. at 9a Calle. 8 rooms, none with bath. Laundry, wheelchair access.*

Posada Calle Real. Here you'll find the best beds in Quiché. The rooms themselves are average, but the mattresses are luxuriously soft with starched, clean, pressed sheets. This posada has the only hot showers in town. A double goes for $4. *2a Av., 2 blocks below the main plaza. 16 rooms, none with bath. Laundry, wheelchair access.*

If sleeping in a cell doesn't intimidate you, you can check and see if the local jail has an available bed or two. Men's beds fill up, but you can count on the women's being empty.

➤ **CAMPING** • You can camp for free at Utatlán, 3 kilometers (2 miles) outside town. Sometimes the gates are locked (it's all up to the guard), but, if you're feeling daring, you can always scale the damn thing. There's no water and no nearby tiendas, so carry all your sustenance on your back.

FOOD Meat dishes, hamburgers, and french fries dominate your options here and, of course, you can gorge on beans and rice anywhere. **Restaurante Maya Quiché** (2a Av. on the plaza) serves chicken prepared every which way (in cream, in lemon sauce, etc.) for $2.50. **Cafeteria Los Antojitos** (on the corner of 6a Calle and "0" Av.) has hamburgers for $1 and fried chicken plates for $2. **Restaurante Calle Real** serves a decent daily special of salad, pasta, meat, and tortillas for $2.50. No sign marks the place, but the restaurant is an extension of Posada Calle Real (*see* Where to Sleep, *above*).

NEAR SANTA CRUZ DEL QUICHE

RUINS OF UTATLAN These ruins have a zillion names—or rather, a zillion spellings of the same name. Call 'em Utatlán, Cumarcaj, Gumarcaaj, or Kumarcaaj and everybody will know what you're talking about. What *is* known for sure is that Pedro de Alvarado's Mexican troops named the city Utatlán. When Alvarado killed Quiché hero Tecún Umán in 1524, the city leaders decided to retaliate. They invited the conquistador to Utatlán with plans to trap him and take their revenge. Unfortunately, Alvarado was not stupid or naive enough to believe that the Quichés would welcome him with open arms. All it took was a few spies to confirm his suspicions. Alvarado agreed to enter Utatlán as long as the Quiché leaders visited his camp first. Sadly, the leaders fell into their own trap and were burned to death. Later, Alvarado leveled Utatlán to weaken the Quichés further. Today, the glory days of the Quiché kingdom barely shine through. The ruins consist of a few pint-size temples, grassy mounds, and an intact ball court.

Few tourists head this way, so beating the crowd is not a major concern. However, villagers still worship at one of the temples, as evidenced by the melted candles and ash in the wall altar. A cave that at one time connected Utatlán to Quetzaltenango (but has long since been destroyed by earthquakes and the like) is the local brujo's favorite spot for carrying out pagan rituals. The floor is covered with pine needles, an occasional chicken feather, and charred fire circles.

The Ixil Fight for Their Way of Life— and Their Lives

The Ixil Triangle has a terrible and painful history. During the Spanish conquest, the village of Nebaj was completely annihilated in an attempt to break the Ixils' spirit; the survivors were forced into slave labor. Even after Guatemalan independence, many Ixil villagers were transplanted to work on large fincas, or plantations, where conditions paralleled medieval serfdom.

The continued isolation and repression of the communities in the Ixil Triangle made it an area ripe for rebellion. The birth of the Guerrilla Army of the Poor (Ejército Guerrillero de los Pobres, the "EGP") occurred with the organized killing of an Ixcán landowner in 1975. Although the EGP was not the only guerrilla movement in the country, they had the most impact on indigenous groups. The EGP enlisted whole families to provide information, food, shelter, and supplies, and also to harass the local army units.

What prompted many Indígenas to join the guerrilla movement was a need for protection from a blatantly murderous military. As more and more villages were occupied by army troops, indigenous villagers began to "disappear." Reports stated that, within the first year, the bodies of 32 community leaders in Nebaj, 40 in Chajul, and 28 in Cotzal were discovered, horribly dismembered or tortured to death. This was in 1977—only the beginning.

During the early 1980s, when the guerrilla war intensified, the Ixil were caught in the crossfire. Thousands of villagers lost their lives, crops were destroyed, and entire aldeas (villages) burned to the ground. Survivors of these attacks fled to the mountains to join the growing population of refugees, who had little food and no protection. As a result, when the military introduced development programs called Fusiles and Frijoles (Bullets and Beans) and Techo, Trabajo, and Tortillas (Shelter, Work, and Tortillas), many Indígenas decided to return peacefully in exchange for housing and food. Basically, there was no choice. The army had begun making large sweeps of even the most isolated areas to capture the guerrillas.

In Santa Cruz del Quiché, walk from the bus station toward the central plaza and turn left on 10a Calle. The cobblestone street turns into a dirt road leading straight to the archaeological site. The walk through the countryside is sweat-free, lots of fun, and takes about 30 minutes.

Ixil Triangle: Nebaj, Chajul, Cotzal

A weather-worn road, not even wide enough for two cars to pass, wends its way into the Cuchumatanes mountains. The road eventually dead-ends in the Ixil Triangle, home to the Ixil people and the only place in Guatemala (and the only place in the world) where Ixil is spoken. The triangle is in a wild and untamed portion of the country: Jagged mountain peaks reach extreme heights, and *aldeas* (tiny villages) are tucked away in lush, green valleys. Farther north is the sparsely populated tropical jungle known as the Virgin Zone. The heavy fog and mist of the Ixil Triangle are romantic, but it's the people that give the area its haunting beauty. More than anywhere in the country, the villagers in the triangle have had to weather terrible persecution, degradation, and oppression by foreign invaders and hostile governments. Miraculously, they have remained a proud and traditional clan, which clings tightly to its indigenous heritage.

The majority of villagers can't understand Spanish and communicate in Ixil; the soft, rhythmic Ixil words sound as foreign to the western ear as aboriginal tongue-clicking. The women wear magnificent, colorful skirts and delicately embroidered huipiles. The headdress is a long, brightly colored ribbon with pom-poms. The men have converted to western dress, but during religious holidays and fiestas (like August 12–15 in Nebaj), the older men wear blood-red bolero jackets with black silk embroidery. Because the cost is now too high for the villagers to make these jackets, they are sacredly passed down from relative to relative. Festivals and funerals are notorious for drinking binges. Alcoholism is a problem that afflicts both men and women; you'll see villagers passed out on the streets who may not move for two days.

Nebaj, Chajul, and Cotzal are the three principal villages in the northern highlands. Nebaj is the region's metropolis, enjoying an economic prosperity unknown in the other villages. Although it has no bank, Nebaj has a new hospital with modern facilities. The central plaza boasts a fountain with a funny little elf statue propped up on one side. Facing the plaza is the large colonial church, beckoning worshippers, who crawl on their knees to the altar. The town cemetery, easily identified by the colored tombstones, offers another look at the fusion of Catholicism and paganism. Incense and candles are frequently burned in front of burial stones. A shack in the older section of the cemetery is filled with wood crosses and ash remains, and sometimes food and flowers are spread on the dirt floor.

On market days (Thursdays and Sundays in Nebaj) villagers walk from all across the northern region balancing their entire livelihood on their backs or heads. Chajul (on Friday) and Cotzal (on Wednesday) also have busy market days. No bus services Chajul; the walk takes up to 4 hours from Nebaj and less than two from Cotzal. If a truck passes, wave it down and jump in back.

COMING AND GOING You can reach Nebaj or Cotzal from Santa Cruz del Quiché; a bus leaves twice a day at 9 AM and 10 AM. One goes to Nebaj (3 hours) and the other continues on to Cotzal (5 hours). A direct bus to Nebaj also leaves from Chichicastenango, stopping briefly in Santa Cruz. Bus schedules are mere approximations, so it's wise to get there early. Since so few buses pass through the Ixil Triangle, they're always crammed with people, live chickens, and sport an entire mini-market on top. Expect unexpected delays—anything from the guerrillas to the army to eroded roads (or all three) can detain the bus for quite a while. If you want to visit the aldeas, be prepared for exhausting hikes over surrounding mountains. A few roads head out in different directions from Nebaj, but buses never travel on them. If you're lucky, you can hitch a ride in a passing car, but don't count on it.

WHERE TO SLEEP AND EAT Nebaj is the only village in the region that offers food and accommodation. The minute you step off the bus, a swarm of children will surround you, hoping to guide you to a hospedaje for a quetzal. All hospedajes are within a block or two of the central plaza. **Tres Hermanas,** the closest and the oldest hospedaje in town, is owned by elderly spinsters. Two blocks down are **Hospedaje Kariari** and **Hospedaje El Rinconcito;** both offer brighter rooms and hot water. If you want to splurge ($3 for a double), the **Ixil Hotel** is the fanciest spot in town, having hosted the likes of the U.S. ambassador and his wife. You can eat at the Ixil's restaurant, have a typical Guatemalan meal at Tres Hermanas, or check out one of the comedores in the daily market. If you plan to visit Chajul or Cotzal or any of the aldeas, you'll have to ask around to rent a room and find a meal. It's not difficult and it makes for quite an adventure.

OUTDOOR ACTIVITIES If you base yourself in Nebaj, plenty of short hikes will keep you busy. You'll find two sets of gushing **waterfalls** about an hour outside of town; take the road to Chajul and turn left before the bridge. If you do cross the bridge, you can walk to Chajul, but the round-trip hike makes for a very long day (if you don't catch a lift). If you're curious about the model villages, **Acul** is quite close and very pretty, with lots of planted trees, a simple church, and a superb cheese factory visible in the distance. Acul is an extremely relaxed model village, without marching soldiers or barbed wire. A road leads directly to Acul, but it takes much longer than the mountain trail, which has the bonus of great views of both Nebaj and Acul. The trail is steep and tiring but well worth the pain. Follow the road past the cemetery and ask along the way for the path to Acul.

For Many, "Model" Villages Are Comfortable Prisons

The inauguration of "model villages" has been the government's most recent attempt to keep tabs on the Ixil people. These experimental communities vary: some allow villagers complete freedom, others are surrounded by barbed-wire fences with army watchtowers nearby. Acul (see **Outdoor Activities,** *above*), a 1½-hour walk from Nebaj, was one of the first of these planned communities. There are now more than 30 such villages in the Ixil Triangle. On the whole, the model communities offer more conveniences than the villagers previously had. Houses with metal roofing and wood paneling are better suited to the cold and rainy seasons than the typical thatched ceilings and mud-brick walls. Schools, health clinics, churches, and potable water systems are often constructed, too. However, the severe culture shock of living in such a structured community has caused depression among many villagers. Most families have long since been split up, and war-weary refugees find it difficult to cope. Given minuscule plots of land, they walk for up to 2 hours to reach their little patch of land, where they spend hours clearing with only a machete and tilling with a hoe. Sadly, what's left of the traditional lifestyle is slowly being worn down as the indigenous people of Guatemala are forced to become "model" Ladino citizens.

Quetzaltenango

In the heart of the Western Highlands, Quetzaltenango is the second-largest city in Guatemala. Ideally positioned a few hours from Guatemala City, the Mexican border, and the Pacific coast, Quetzaltenango is a mondo transportation hub. Fortunately, Quetzaltenango lacks the traffic and scummy, crowded streets that weigh down the capital. Instead, it sits deep in a valley with a perfect view of the majestic Volcán Santa María. The surrounding hills produce vegetables, corn, and, of course, coffee. Don't expect the "eternal spring" label to fit the bill here—rainy days and cold nights are the usual in this city. Travelers are lured to the area by the luxurious hot springs and the high-quality fabric that's churned out locally. Tons of shops throughout the city sell woven goods. The first Sunday of each month is the main market day and the Parque Centroameríca becomes a shopper's heaven. You can also watch weaving in progress at many of the small villages in the area. **Salcajá,** 9 kilometers (6 miles) away, produces a special cloth (*jaspé*) woven from tie-dyed yarn. Quetzaltenango is also the choice place to study Spanish, with lots of awesome programs and, just as importantly, few tourists.

Originally part of the main Kingdom, the city was taken over in the 14th century by the Quichés, who called it Xelaju. Later, when Pedro de Alvarado's troops renamed all the defeated Quiché cities, Quetzaltenango was born. Today, the city is more commonly referred to as Xela, in remembrance of its roots. Not far from here is where Alvarado defeated the famed Tecún Umán. With the death of this Quiché warrior in 1524 the rest of Guatemala quickly slipped into Spanish hands.

Early in the 19th century, Quetzaltenango was as mighty as Guatemala City; on its own, it decided to form political ties with Mexico. President Carrera did not like this one bit and pulled Quetzaltenango and the surrounding region into the Central American Federation in 1840. When the city tried once again to separate in 1848, ideas of independence were silenced with brute force. This didn't slow down the heartbeat of Xela for a minute. In the 1900s, during the coffee boom, the city climbed to new levels of prosperity. Around this time, President Manuel Estrada Cabrera (1890–1920) built the various neoclassical structures around town to encourage wisdom and education. Although it's hard to say if these monuments were a source of inspiration, Quetzaltenango prides itself on being an intellectual center. In 1902, everything changed when a disastrous earthquake shook the living daylights out of Xela. The city was eventually rebuilt, but it never again generated enough momentum to rival Guatemala City.

BASICS

➤ **MONEY** • Nearly every bank in Guatemala has a branch on Parque Centroameríca, so you would imagine there wouldn't be much of a line to change money. Nah. The **black market** is elusive but nevertheless functioning in this city of intellectuals. The best way to find a dealer is to poke your head in one of the appliance stores around Mercado La Democracia (*see* Worth Seeing, *below*). You're sure to get a wink, a smile, and some valuable information, if not a transaction.

Banco del Cafe. *12a Av. and 6a Calle, just a few doors down from Banco de Guatemala. Open Mon.–Thurs. 8:30–8, Fri. 8–8, Sat. 10–2.*

Banco Immobilario. *4a Calle 12–00, at 12a Av. Open weekdays 9–5:30, Sat. 9:30–2.*

➤ **PHONES AND MAIL** • Two **GUATEL** offices serve Xela. The office in Zona 1 is on 12a Avenida and 7a Calle at the southwest corner of the park. The other GUATEL is in Zona 3 on 15a Avenida, one block before Parque Benito Juárez. The hours for both are daily 7 AM–midnight.

Post office. This is an elegant but weathered neoclassical building with stone columns and decorative molding. Nowadays, the inner terrace is a basketball court, with the office itself at the far end. *4a Calle and 15 Av., 3 blocks west of the Parque Centroamerica. Open weekdays 8–4.*

➤ **LANGUAGE SCHOOLS** • Tons of language schools are in Quetzaltenango, and for most you don't need to make reservations in advance. Snoop around a little, because some of the better schools have accredited teachers and boast social and environmental weekend activities. The following programs are super-popular and come highly recommended by students; both fill up quickly during high tourist season (December–January and June–August) and it might be worthwhile to call ahead.

I.C.A. has excellent private Spanish classes and "ICAmigos projects" that include reforestation in water conservation zones, health education programs, and support for bilingual schools of indigenous languages and Spanish. *1a Calle 16–93, Z1, 09001, Quetzaltenango, tel. 0/616–786. In the United States, 900 Frances #351, Richardson, TX 75081, tel. and fax 214/699–0935.*

Proyecto Lingüístico Quetzalteco de Español also has an intensive language program and organized activities. *5a Calle 2–40, Z1, Quetzaltenango, tel. and fax 0/612–620. In the United States, tel. and fax 502/961–2620.*

➤ **VISITOR INFORMATION** • You can buy maps, posters, and videotapes at **INGUAT**, but don't expect any fascinating tidbits about the city—all you get is regurgitated brochure lines. *7a Calle next to La Casa de Cultura (attached to Museo de Historia Natural) at the south end of the park. Open daily 8–noon and 2–6; Sat. 8–noon.*

COMING AND GOING

➤ **BY SECOND-CLASS BUS** • A prolific number of second-class buses zoom everywhere imaginable from the Minerva Terminal on 6a Calle, Zona 3. If you're coming from another region, your bus will always pull into this station; you know you're nearing it when the bus turns off onto a dirt road filled with so many potholes that the bus crawls at a snail's pace. Besides the thousands of parked buses and aggressive bus hustlers, there's also a market at the terminal. To transfer to a local bus, walk through the market alley and turn left on 4a Calle until it crosses 25a Avenida. Buses to Zona 1 have a "parque" sign in the window.

Buses leave hourly to Guatemala City (4½ hours, $2), Huehuetenango (2½ hours, $1), Retalhuleu (2 hours, $1), and San Andrés Xequl (15 min, 25¢). Buses also head hourly to Zunil, San Francisco El Alto, and Momostenango via Cuatro Caminos. To reach La Mesilla (the Mexican border), catch a bus to Huehuetenango and from there grab a connecting bus. Direct buses head to Chichicastenango only on market days (Thursday and Sunday). Otherwise, take a bus heading to Guatemala City and change at Los Encuentros (2 hours) for either Chichi or Santa Cruz del Quiché.

Almolonga and Totonícapan buses depart from both the Minerva Terminal and the smaller bus depot near Parque Centroamerica. For Almolonga, go to the corner of 9a Avenida and 10a Calle (2 blocks east of the park and 4 blocks south). Buses heading to Totonícapan leave from 10a Avenida and 8a Calle.

➤ **BY PRIVATE BUS** • Galgos has more routes and departures than any other private company. Buses leave for Guatemala City (4 hours, $3) six times a day between 3:30 AM and 4:45 PM. Buses leave from Guatemala City for Quetzaltenango seven times a day between 5:30 AM and 7 PM. Galgos is the only line that travels to the Mexican border at Talsman (7 hours, $5) via Retalhuleu (1 hour, $2) and Tecún Umán (5 hours, $4). *Ticket office and terminal on Calle Rodolfo Robles 17–43, Z1, tel. 0/612–248. From Parque Centroamerica, take 12 Av. north and turn left on Calle Rodolfo Robles.*

Lineas Américas travels between Quetzaltenango and Guatemala City ($3) five times a day between 5:15 AM and 8 PM. *The ticket office and terminal is on 7a Av. (Calzada Independencia), Z2, tel. 0/612–063.*

Rutas Limas goes only to Guatemala City (4 hours, $3) at 5:15 AM, 7:15 AM, and 2:15 PM. *Main ticket office and terminal at 2a Calle and 7a Av. (Calzada Independencia), Z2, tel. 0/612–033. Smaller ticket office on 11 Av., Z1 next to Pensión Bonifaz, 1 block above Parque Centroamerica.*

GETTING AROUND All local buses passing by Parque Centroamerica (Zone 1) eventually end up at the Minerva Terminal (Zona 3). Look for "terminal" displayed in the bus window. All the action happens in and around Parque Centroamerica, so, if you need anything at all, make a beeline here. Banks, cheap and ritzy hotels, restaurants, and the few tourist attractions are all within this 'hood.

WHERE TO SLEEP Budget hotels speckle every corner of the city. The greatest variety of accommodations is around the park. The sophisticated and wealthy stay at the **Pensión Bonifaz** (4a Calle at the north end of the park) for $40 a pop, while budget travelers get a pretty meager choice of dark and grimy rooms in direct range of an odious bathroom scent. For $2, you can always breathe through your mouth.

➤ **UNDER $5** • **Hotel Colonial.** This rickety, run-down place has decent rooms with the usual: a desk, a chair, a bed, and a window. The bathrooms are primitive, bordering on unsanitary. A long porch on the second floor is nice for gazing out at the city's rooftops. Doubles are $3.50. Believe it or not, this hotel is better than most of Xela's cheapo spots. *3a Calle, behind the Pensión Bonifaz and 1 block down. 10 rooms, none with bath. Laundry.*

Hotel Radar 99. One block west of the plaza, this sparsely furnished budget pad has second-floor rooms that surround a tiny courtyard. Bathrooms are fairly clean with hot water. Doubles are $5. *13 Av., 1 block west of the park and 1 block north. 15 rooms, none with bath.*

Pensión San Nicolás. One block north of the plaza, this pensión is the cheapest place in town for a reason. Beds ($1) are hard as hell, rooms are huge and gloomy, and bathrooms are gross and smelly. All rooms have four beds. *12a Av. bet. 4a and 3a Calle, 1 block north of the park. 23 rooms, none with bath. Laundry, wheelchair access, car park.*

Pensión Victoria. Two blocks west of the plaza, this hotel has enormous rooms with high ceilings and 15-foot doors that can feel hauntingly empty. Beds are as hard as the wooden frames they're built on—you may as well sleep on the floor. Most rooms have three or four beds at $4 per bed. *6a Calle, 2 blocks west of the park. 13 rooms, none with bath. Wheelchair access.*

➤ **UNDER $10** • **Casa Kaehler.** This casa is an old favorite (it's been around for 20 years) and serves up that extra bit of comfort so appreciated by budget travelers. The colonial-style building has a courtyard, big private rooms, and clean bathrooms with hot water. Unfortunately, the three rooms available to the public are usually full. Doubles are $7.50. *13 Av. 3–33, 1 block west and 1 block north of the park. 3 rooms, 1 with bath. Laundry.*

Hotel Capri. Often filled up with traveling Guatemalan families as well as the occasional backpacker, this hotel has a bunch of plain rooms. Each room has a private bathroom, and doubles are $5.50. A popular comedor (with pretty good local eats) is in the front part of the hotel facing the street. *8a Calle 11–39, behind the Museo de Historia Natural, 1 block below the park. 20 rooms, all with bath. Wheelchair access.*

➤ **UNDER $15** • **Hotel El Centro.** If you want to splurge, here's the place to do it. You'll get a hot bath, sunlit rooms, filtered water for brushing your teeth, and a few of the rooms even have television sets. (Don't get too excited, because TV airtime is filled with really bad Mexican soap operas.) By Guatemalan standards, the rooms are spotless, and the bathrooms have clean towels and soap. Doubles are $12. *10a Calle and 12a Av., 3 blocks south of the park. 8 rooms, all with bath.*

FOOD If your life revolves around your next meal, then you've hit the jackpot in Quetzaltenango. Not big on comida típica, restaurants cater mostly to the international palate. You can feast on savory eats like pizzas baked in clay ovens, finely brewed Guatemalan coffee, and creamy cheesecake. For goodies like pastries and quiches, plant yourself at either **Cafe Baviera** (5a Calle and 13 Av., 1 block west of the park) or **Cafe Berna** (16 Av. facing Parque Benito Juárez), which serves the most excellent freshly baked bread. **Bake Shop** (150 feet from Terminal Minerva, on the opposite side of the street) serves delicious chocolate-chip and coconut cookies.

The cheapest way to eat healthfully is to shop at the fruit and vegetable market in the Minerva Terminal or at the mini-*mercado* (market) in the southern corner of Parque Centroamerica or even at Mercado La Democracia (*see* Worth Seeing, *below*). The Xelac Cooperative makes excellent cheese, available at Super Mercado La Selecta, 1 block from the park on 4a Calle.

➤ **UNDER $5** • **Cafeteria Utz' Hua.** This is one of the few places where you can munch on comida típica. The scant menu (look on the wall) includes a daily special for $2.50. For $1, you can feast on a too-filling meal of chicken, rice, potatoes, and corn tamales. *12a Av. 3–02 at the corner of 3a Calle, 1 block north of the park. Open daily 8–8.*

Deli-Cafe. This cute, tavernlike restaurant has decent food at cheap prices. The menu is unoriginal, but at 50¢ for a chicken sandwich, who's complaining? You can also get tacos for 50¢ and crêpes (more like pancakes) with fruit or ham for $1.50. Wash down the whole shebang with a beer. *14 Av. bet. 4a and 3a Calle, 1 block northwest of the park. Open daily 7 AM–9 PM.*

Pizza Ricca. If you're craving pizza with rich sauce, gooey cheese, a thin crust, and any topping you can think of, you're headed in the right direction. All pizzas are baked in clay ovens and take 15 minutes to be served—just long enough to salivate all over yourself. Cheese pizzas are $2 and salads with avocado and cucumber are $1. *14 Av. 2–42 bet. 4a and 3a Calle. 1 block north of the park. Open daily 11:30–9.*

Restaurante Shanghai. Guatemalan chefs do the Chinese thang in this restaurant, which has vinyl seats and a Denny's-like atmosphere. The red Chinese columns and painted dragons give it a kind of exotic touch. You can get duck, shrimp and, of course, wonton soup for $1.50. *4a Calle 12–22, west of the park. Open daily 9–9.*

➤ **UNDER $10** • **Cafe Restaurante Royal Paris.** This eatery is by far the best place to dine in town. A menu of delicious salads, fish, and chicken is complemented by an artsy decor and old jazz tunes. Spaghetti carbonara ($3.50), fillet of fish ($4), and César salad ($2.50) will all make your taste buds happy. A full-service bar and Latin guitar on the weekends make Royal Paris popular with the twentysomething crowd. *16 Av. 3–05, Z3, facing Parque Benito Juárez. Open daily noon–midnight.*

WORTH SEEING The one thing Quetzaltenango lacks as a big city is traditional tourist attractions. You'll see lots of neoclassical architecture (you know the type— stone columns and intricate ceiling molds). This style makes **Parque Centroamerica** the most stunning plaza in Guatemala. As you walk through the park, you'll catch a glimpse of **Pasaje Enrique,** a crumbling old building with "beware of falling glass" signs posted on the inner passageway that leads to 13 Avenida. Originally, it was planned as a shopping center for the rich and famous, but without a Robin Leach crowd only a bar and an ice-cream shop could drum up enough business to survive. The **Cathedral's** old facade (at 11 Avenida) features life-size patron saints looking down on the rest of us sinners. The church itself has been recently rebuilt; even though it's pretty as far as churches go, it's no Notre Dame.

La Iglesia de San Nicolas (15 Av., Zona 3, on the east side of Parque Benito Juárez) tries hard, with flying buttresses and a baroque design. It looks out of sync with the city's mix of Greek and colonial structures, but this sort of hodgepodge style is what gives Quetzaltenango its own peculiar flavor.

For shopping, head to the **Mercado La Democracia,** which is geared toward city residents. The four-block area is lined with stores that are over-stocked with household goods, appliances, and produce. To get here from Parque Centroamerica, walk three blocks down 4a Calle and turn right on 15 Avenida, following it for 6 blocks; make a right on 1a Calle.

AFTER DARK If you're a night owl and nothing short of Valium will conk you out before midnight, **Café Restaurante Royal Paris** (*see* Food, *above*) doesn't lock up till then. **El Garage** (near the Royal Paris) is a popular disco for the gay and hetero crowd. It only gets hopping on weekend nights, 9 PM–2 AM, and the cover is a buck. In the same vein, check out *Music Center* (12a Av., below Calzado Minerva) where college students from San Carlos hang out, and beer is about $1.20. Finally, if all you're craving is chips and a dark tap beer, **Taberna de Don Rodrigo** (14 Av. on the east side of the Teatro Municipal) can fill your need. It's open daily 10–10.

OUTDOOR ACTIVITIES An hour's walk from town, the **El Baúl** lookout point has a wicked view of the entire valley. If you happen to have access to a car or motorcycle, cruise up there at night. You'll probably be joined by a local or two who know it as the most beautiful drinking spot around town. *From Parque Centroamerica, take 5a Calle east for 3 blocks and turn left on Diagonal 3. Walk 8 blocks and turn right at the El Baúl sign.*

Baños Los Vahos is a natural sauna where you can sweat it out. A smart indígena woman, who knows a tourist attraction when she sees one, runs the little hotel and comedor on top of the sauna rooms. You just might pass on the cold shower, as the air will chill you to the bone in no time. *Take a bus heading to Almolonga and ask the driver to let you off at Los Vahos. Follow the dirt road up the mountainside and make the first right. It's near the top; when the road forks, veer left. $1 for the steam bath.*

NEAR QUETZALTENANGO

ZUNIL AND FUENTES GEORGINAS The little town of Zunil is 8 kilometers (5 miles) below Quetzaltenango off the highway that heads to the Pacific Coast. Zunil sits at the bottom of the now-extinct volcano of Zunil. Its claim to fame is the nearby luxurious hot springs that bubble to the surface from the volcanic base. Zunil itself, surrounded by the most fertile land in the valley, is a radiant highland village. Mud and adobe houses are arranged around a white-washed colonial church that marks the center of town. The local cemetery (at the top of the hill on the outskirts) is lined with tombstones painted in soft, airy pinks and blues. Monday is market day, and women with flashy purple shawls crowd the church steps hawking a multitude of fruits and vegetables that come straight from their own little gardens. Not more than a block away is San Simón himself (or rather, the idol of him). Here in Zunil, to help San Simón take a shot of liquor, he's set in a rocking chair. The brujo pours the alcohol while another person tips back the chair. Since pagan practices do not sit well with the Catholic Church, Mister Simón is kept under wraps in the basement of a large tienda. Nevertheless, most of the Indígenas in the area faithfully pay their respects. The idol has also become a tourist attraction; gringos are charged a 50¢ entrance fee. Ask around if you want to see him.

The **Fuentes Georginas** hot springs, 10 kilometers (6 miles) above Zunil, are set against a natural stone wall. Oversized, lush tropical plants shield the springs and a Greek goddess statue from the sun's harsh rays. For 50¢, you can frolic in the water to your heart's content. You can also spend the night in one of the adorable bungalows, where doubles are $10. By the weekend, the main pool is not only crowded but the water is also a little murky—similar to a kiddie pool by day's end. The best time to visit is on Tuesday, since the springs are closed Monday for cleaning. The fate of Fuentes Georginas is now in question because the Guatemalan government allowed a Mexican company to drill directly below the springs, with the intent of building a hydroelectric plant. Since the project began, the hot springs haven't been as hot (more tepid), and the water level is dropping. This 50¢ fantasy may soon disappear.

Taxis parked in front of the church in Zunil will transport you to the fuentes for $3 a person. If you're up for a brisk trot, the 10 kilometers are pleasant and walkable. From the Minerva Terminal in Quetzaltenango, buses leave every half hour to Zunil via the town of Cantel. A bus depot in Zona 1 (corner of 10a Calle and 9a Av.) has buses that head solely (and more directly) to Zunil via Almolonga.

SAN ANDRES XEQUL Fifteen kilometers (9 miles) north of Quetzaltenango, San Andrés Xequl is a magical town in every sense of the word. Mud-brick houses topped with Spanish-tile roofs cluster in one corner of the valley, surrounded by corn fields. In the middle of this rural beauty is a funky neon-yellow church decked out with blue angels, green vines, and two lions to spice up the facade. In a country where earth colors predominate, the church of San Andrés Xequl is like a surreal dream on a fantastic mushroom trip. Near the Casa de San Simón, down an unmarked dirt road, is supposedly a university for brujos—a school to teach promising young boys the long-kept secrets of Mayan magic. Taught by older brujos, graduating students become witch doctors, giving out advice, interpreting dreams and unusual occurrences, and practicing white magic.

To get to this pueblo, take any bus heading to Cuatro Caminos and ask the driver to let you off at San Andrés Xequl. The bus will drop you off a kilometer out of town.

TOTONICAPAN The one reason to visit Totonicapán is if you have an overwhelming desire to see ceremonial Indígena costumes that are stored in a large warehouse, ready to be rented out at a moment's notice for traditional dances. Totonicapán is basically an artisans' town and many of the ceramic pottery, wooden masks, and woven skirts that you see in the highlands come from here. The best time to visit is on Tuesday when the market livens up the streets. From Quetzaltenango, hourly buses head directly to Totonicapán, or you can take a bus to Cuatro Caminos and wait for a connecting bus.

SAN FRANCISCO EL ALTO To round off your Guatemalan shopping spree, hit the Friday market in San Francisco El Alto. A market to end all markets, this one fills the central plaza to bursting point and spills onto a nearby field and surrounding streets. Enthusiastic sellers and equally enthusiastic shoppers from all over the highlands congregate to exchange goods and cash. You won't find anything different here than at other markets, but the town's hilltop location makes it one of the more beautiful spots to shop. True to the town's name (El Alto, "the high one"), every street appears to drop off into a hundred-foot ravine carpeted with corn stalks. The ideal place to do some camera clicking is from the church roof in the plaza. For 20¢ you can climb the belltower from where you can gaze dreamily down on the entire valley.

If you want to spend a few days here, rooms six through eleven at the **Hotel Vista Hermosa** (3a Av. off the Central Plaza) have stunning views of the volcanoes around the Quetzaltenango valley. Doubles are $3. Hourly buses depart from the Minerva Terminal in Quetzaltenango.

Momostenango

After a brutally slow, hour-long ride from Quetzaltenango in a bus that can't get out of second gear, you'll see Momostenango poking its head out of a thick pine forest. It's *the* wool capital of the country and zillions of blankets and jackets are woven, dyed, and washed in this isolated town before being sent to other markets. The **cooperative** on the main street leading into town has quality goods at decent, fixed prices. It's open Monday–Saturday 8–1 and 2–6 and Sunday 8–noon. Momostenango is one of the few remaining villages that adheres to the ancient Mayan calendar, a 260-day Tzolkin year. The first day of the new year is marked with a religious ritual called the Ceremony of the Eight Monkeys. Indígenas from all over the highlands pour into town to celebrate with an all-night prayer session in the church. At the break of dawn, a procession winds its way up to special altars hidden in the hills. Shamen and brujos then conduct intense ceremonies in a cloud of incense smoke as Indígenas place beautiful ceramic pieces on the altars. The **Cerro Palcom** altar is strewn with ceramic shards, melted candles, and corn husks. It's a five-minute walk up the hill on 2a Avenida; turn right and you'll see the altar at the far side of the park.

At the hot springs, modesty is respected as the women wash themselves in ankle-length dresses; the men and women bathe in separate pools.

Hospedaje Palcom (at the corner of 1a Calle and 2a Av.) is the best place to get your shelter and sustenance. It has an excellent comedor—you'll eat especially well if you ask for the same meal the family is about to sup on. And, as long as you take a room upstairs, Palcom is the nicer of the two hospedajes in town.

Direct buses leave for Momostenango from the Minerva Terminal in Quetzaltenango. Buses also leave from Cuatro Caminos until 2 PM. The last bus from Momostenango to Quetzaltenango leaves at 3 PM.

Huehuetenango

Huehuetenango is a laid-back town with a surprisingly high Ladino population. Teenage couples scoot around on mopeds and the one theater in town features raunchy American "B" films that nobody has ever heard of. The main plaza is hemmed in by an old church, a clock tower, and a weird pink shell-shaped bandstand on the second floor of the Municipalidad. Bushes are carved into bizarre shapes of people and animals. Just a few blocks east on 1a and 2a Avenida, the streets sizzle with action—very different from the sluggish atmosphere in the plaza. The main indoor market (which starts on 2a Avenida) is lined with vendors selling colorful típico goods. Buses and people pack the streets during the day and car horns, music, and crowd sounds are everywhere.

Huehuetenango is closer to the Mexican border than to Guatemala City, and it has a strong affinity to the neighboring country. In preconquest days, the Mam-Maya kingdom was a powerful force dominating much of the Western highlands. Not until much later did the Guatemalan Quiché Indígenas push their rival tribe up into the Chuchumatanes mountains and even as far north as Chiapas, Mexico, where the Mam language is still widely spoken. Today Huehuetenango lies near the tidy grounds of the ancient Mam capital of **Zaculeu.**

During the '70s and '80s, at the height of the guerrilla insurrection, many Guatemalans crossed the border into México. Thousands still live in Mexican refugee camps, waiting for a change that will allow them to return to their homeland.

BASICS If you plan to visit the more isolated villages to the north, Huehuetenango is the last place to cash traveler's checks and take care of banking needs. **Banco del Agro** (2a Calle on the north end of the central plaza) is open Monday–Saturday 9–8. The **police** station is at 5a Avenida and 6a Calle. The **GUATEL** (open daily 7 AM–midnight) and **post office** (open daily 8–4:30) are conveniently located side by side on 2a Calle east of the central plaza. The post office is in the back of the building. The **Mexican Consulate** (5a Avenida, on the central plaza) issues tourist cards for $5 that can save you hassle time at the border. It's open daily 9 AM–noon and 3–5.

COMING AND GOING Huehuetenango is just off the Interamerican Highway and buses from everywhere in the highlands pull in and out all day long. The easiest spot to catch a bus to Huehuetenango is from Los Encuentros or Cuatro Caminos. You can also get a lift from the steady stream of trucks that zoom down the highway. If you're tired of sitting in contorted positions on second-class buses and want leg room for the 5-hour trip between Huehuetenango and Guatemala City, take a first-class bus. Buy tickets a day in advance so that you are assured a luxury seat.

Huehuetenango itself is small enough that you can easily master the grid format. The center of town bursts with hotels, restaurants, bus depots, and markets. You'll find 'em all between 1a and 7a Avenida, and 1a and 6a Calles. The central plaza is on 5a Avenida with 2a, 3a, and 4a Calles running perpendicular to it.

➤ **BY FIRST-CLASS BUS** • **Los Halcones** (7a Av. 3–62), 2 blocks west of the central plaza, has buses that leave for Guatemala City ($4) at 7 AM and 2 PM via Los Encuentros. Buses leave Guatemala City for Huehuetenango at the same time. **Rapidos Zaculeu** (3a Av. 5–25), 2 blocks east of the central plaza, leaves for Guatemala City ($4) at 6 AM and 3 PM returning at 3 PM and 8 PM. **Velaquez** (1a Av. near 2a Calle), east of the central plaza, has first- and second-class buses. The first-class buses go to Guatemala City ($4), leaving at 3 AM and 10 AM and returning to Huehuetenango at 8:30 AM and 5 PM. The second-class bus travels to La Mesilla (at the Mexican border) at 2:30 PM and returns at 7:30 AM (2 hours, $1.25). **El Condor** (5a Av.), 1 block north of the central plaza, doesn't offer the same level of comfort and the buses are often filled to bursting. Buses head to Guatemala City ($3) via Cuatro Caminos and Los Encuentros five times a day. Buses return from the city to Huehuetenango 5 times a day. Buses to La Mesilla (2 hours, $1.25) leave 4 times a day and return to Huehuetenango 5 times a day.

➤ **BY SECOND-CLASS BUS** • Although there is a new bus terminal on 6a Calle (2 kilometers from the central plaza), it hasn't caught on yet and not one of the bus lines has relocated their offices. Even arriving buses will drop you off at the central plaza. Buses head to La Mesilla, Quetzaltenango, and Guatemala City all day, 5 AM–5 PM. To go to Retalhuleu and the coast, take a bus headed to Guatemala City and transfer at Cuatro Caminos. Transfer at Los Encuentros to head to Lake Atitlán and Chichicastenango. Transfer at Chimaltenango to go to Antigua.

WHERE TO SLEEP Compared to the rest of Guatemala, Huehuetenango is isolated and unspoiled by bands of tourists. Weirdly enough, the town has a budget hotel on almost every street. You can always deluxe-out at **Hotel Zaculeu** where doubles cost $12. When the rare tour bus hits Huehue, it's always parked in front of this hotel. Most budget digs cost about $2.

➤ **UNDER $5** • **Hotel Central** This is a wildly popular backpacker spot because the buses stop directly in front. Loud, annoying street noises filter in constantly (especially in room #4 that faces the street). Doubles are $4. Linens are scummy and buzzing with fleas, but they're really no worse than at any other budget hotel. *5a Av. 1–33, 1 block north of the central plaza. 17 rooms, none with bath. Laundry, wheelchair access.*

Hotel Maya. Behind the main church, two blocks east of the central park, this hotel is enormous. Rooms are nondescript (one bed and one window) but clean. Doubles are $3.50. *3a Av. 3–55, near Mansión El Paraíso. 31 rooms, none with bath.*

Pensión Astoria. One block east of the central park, this pensión has rooms that are cheap (doubles are $3) and extremely safe (a guard watches the pensión at night and gates are securely locked). Mattresses, however, are wretchedly flea-infested. Sheets will be changed daily if you ask. Hot showers are lukewarm at best. *4a Av. 1–45. From the central plaza take 2a Calle east and make the first left. 18 rooms, none with bath. Wheelchair access, breakfast comedor, car park.*

➢ **UNDER $10** • **Hotel Gran Shinulá.** One block from the main indoor market on 2a Avenida, this place has grimy rooms with the occasional bug mashed onto the wall. A steady dose of street noise keeps you up at night, but every room has a private bath (it's an extra $1 for hot water) and the mattresses and rooms are actually sprayed for fleas. Bathrooms are a godsend. Doubles are $8. The comedor serves breakfast and dinner. *2a Av., 2 blocks east of the central plaza. 45 rooms, all with bath.*

Hotel Mary. Across from the post office and GUATEL, this hotel has spotless rooms with waxed floors. The rooftop terrace sports a view of Huehue's rooftops, the surrounding mountains, and a bull's-eye shot of GUATEL's antennae and satellite dish. Doubles are $6. Comedor on the second floor has okay grub. *2a Calle 3–52, 1 block east of the central plaza. 40 rooms, some with bath.*

FOOD Huehue is not going to win you over through your stomach. The town has its share of comedors, but few restaurants offer any variety. For breakfast, most hotels have their own comedors that serve up the standard oatmeal, eggs, frijoles, cheese, and tortillas for a buck. If you're craving real chocolate, Pringles chips, or even canned tuna fish at 2 AM, make a beeline for the 24-hour store at the corner of 1a Calle and 3a Avenida. Ice cream lovers behold: The store carries Mars and Musketeer bars filled with rich vanilla ice cream, imported all the way from Illinois, USA.

Cafe Restaurante Jardin. This tiny joint offers one of the biggest menus around. Take your pick between Central American, Mexican, Huehuetenangoen, and *la casa comida* (home-cooked food). Try chicken pepín—a local dish of chicken prepared in an oily sauce—for $3. Because of the long open hours, teenagers bring their dates here in the evening. *4a Calle at 6a Av., 1 block west of the central plaza. Open daily 6 AM–11 PM.*

Cafeteria Las Palmeras. Popular with Huehue residents, this is one of the best comedors in town. For $2 they'll whip up a filling plate of chicken, beef, or chorizo; soup or salad; frijoles; and tortillas. *5a Av. at 4a Calle on a corner of the central plaza, across from Banco de Guatemala. Open daily 6:30 AM–11 PM.*

Pizza Hogareña. Come here for that hole-in-the-wall feel (only six tables in the front room). The cheese on the pizza is excellent—quite unlike the typical Guatemalan cheese that's salty and crumbly. A large cheese pizza is only $3.50 and hamburgers, salads, and fruit drinks are similarly priced. *6a Av. 4–45, 1 block off the central plaza between 4a and 5a Calle. Open Tues.–Sun. 9:30–10:30.*

Restaurante Regis. One block east of the central plaza, this homey restaurant is decked with cheery tablecloths and fake flowers. Full meals with *bistec* (steak), grilled fish, or shrimp go for $4. Hamburgers and sandwiches are only $1. *2a Calle, across from the post office. Open daily 9 AM–10 PM.*

NEAR HUEHUETENANGO

ZACULEU Zaculeu was originally built around AD 600 by the Mam tribe. The site for the city was chosen for its strategic location, with natural barriers on three sides. It's hard to imagine how two small ravines and a river could act as a defense mechanism against the Spaniards in the 16th century. Unfortunately, it worked too well. The Spanish troops, led by Pedro de Alvarado's brother Gonzalo, realized they could not take Zaculeu by force and chose to starve them out. Within two months, the Mam surrendered.

The site has a few step pyramids, a ball court, a well-manicured lawn, and a skimpy two-room museum. At first sight, Zaculeu looks bare. The Mam Indians didn't decorate their structures at all—this leaves little to marvel at except their size. The reconstruction job sponsored by the United Fruit Company is so exact that the temples have spanking-new plastered walls and the intentionally unrestored mounds look contrived. The sterility of this Indígena ghost town squelches the urge to romanticize about ancient civilization. Several roads lead to Zaculeu but count on a full half-hour walk whichever way you go. One route is to follow 4a Calle westward out of town until the road forks. Take the dirt road to the right, and make another right at the next dirt road you come across. Signs point out the way. The site is open daily 8–6 and 2–5.

CHIANTLA Perched on the mountain above Huehuetenango, Chiantla is famous for its Virgen de Candelaria. Pilgrims (some crawling on their hands and knees) arrive en masse to pray to her in the colonial church. The Virgen is beautifully capped in silver and legend has it that a Spaniard, Señor Almengor, gave the Virgen to Chiantla as a gift after she saved his life in a mining accident. Buses leave from 5a Avenida in front of Hotel Central every half hour and drop you off near the town's church.

Todos Santos Cuchumatán

By bus, it takes three hours to travel the 20 kilometers (12 miles) separating Huehuetenango and Todos Santos—this long, bumpy, uphill ride is probably one of the best ways to experience the tremendous height and mass of the Cuchumatanes mountains. The winding dirt road is too narrow for an oncoming bus to pass and the ride can be especially gut-wrenching when one side of the road drops off into a 200-foot ravine. If heights scare you, grab a seat on the right side of the bus where you can stare at a solid, rocky mountain wall. The stunning scenery alternates between a green carpet of vegetation and barren frost-covered plateaus. Since the bus churns up the mountain only in second gear, you'll have plenty of time to memorize every last bit of vegetation. The climate high in the Cuchumatanes varies drastically—you'll get a sunburn during the day and freeze your ass off at night.

In the town cooperative, huipiles with old designs are sold dirt cheap, because the women of Todos Santos refuse to be out of fashion.

Todos Santos is a traditional town, and the villagers are decked out in vibrant garb. The men saunter around in candy-cane pants with cutoff gaucho shorts worn over the pants, and pin-striped shirts with long embroidered collars, reminiscent of the huge collars of the '70s.

Mostly an agricultural town, Todos Santos is deserted during the week. On market day (Saturday), however, the streets hop with rhythm, people, and noise. The only other time Todos Santos sees so many faces is during the rambunctious fiesta week, October 31–November 5, when highlanders swarm into the town to do some serious celebrating. A hot event is the annual horse race on November 1. The men ride all day long from one side of town to the other, stopping briefly to wet their throats and get hammered. By the end of the day, few riders are still in the competition and some only because they rope themselves to the beast.

The ancient Tzolkin calendar is partially observed in Todos Santos and religious rituals still take place at the Mayan ruins of Tojcunanchén. Follow the trail behind Comedor Katy and walk up the hill. The wooden crosses next to the mounds are scorched black from all the fires that have been lit around them. If you fall in love with Todos Santos (which you probably will), you can sign up at the language school and extend your visit. Proyecto Lingüístico de Español/Mam Todos Santos will set you up with a family; you attend classes at their newly constructed building (3 blocks from the main plaza) and learn Spanish or Mam.

Buses to Todos Santos leave Huehuetenango from Pensión San Jorge at the corner of 1a Avenida and 4a Calle at 4 AM, 11:30 AM, and 12:30 AM, and return at 5 AM, 6 AM, and 1 AM.

WHERE TO SLEEP AND EAT When you step off the bus, you may be offered a room in the home of one of the villagers. If not, **Nicolas Geronimo Ramirez** will rent you a room, feed you, teach you weaving, and sell you the handmade purses and huipiles that she has made herself. Her home is just above the Comedor Katy on the edge of the plaza. **Hospedaje Tres Olguitas** is close to the market, has a cozy atmosphere, and the rooms are fairly warm. For a buck you can get a much-appreciated steam bath. Eating options are limited to the local haunt **Comedor Katy** or the comedor in Hospedaje Tres Olguitas.

NEAR TODOS SANTOS CUCHUMATAN

The ideal way to experience the beautiful countryside around Todos Santos is to walk. Take any trail leading to the several nearby villages, and you'll catch a great glimpse of the highlands. On some of the trails you must trek over mountain passes, trudge across streams, and work up quite a sweat. Most of the villages themselves are pretty boring, so it's a case of the means (the trails) justifying the ends (the villages). **Mash** is a cute, traditional village 6 kilometers (4 miles) from Todos Santos. Follow the road below the plaza and you should reach it within an hour. **Tzunul**, a little further away, is on the road leading to Concepción. This two-hour walk has some exquisite nature spots. Follow the same road to Mash but turn right where the road forks off to the Todos Santos cemetery. A four-hour hike will get you to **San Juan Atitán**, a highly traditional village where both men and women dress in the same style as hundreds of years ago. Leave early in the day if you plan to day-trip it. Pick up the trail at the Tojcunanchén ruins above Comedor Katy. Follow it to the top of the ridge and, instead of walking along the summit, take the tiny path straight down into the valley. You'll walk through a ranch and over two more hills before you reach town.

The Pacific Coast

If you're dreaming of a white, sandy coast, gentle waves, and kickin' back in a hammock sipping a margarita, then the Pacific Coast is the last place to look for it. La Costa Sur (as locals call it) is the armpit of Guatemala. Its black-sand beaches absorb the gross, sticky heat, and the ocean currents are swift and dangerous. The few built-for-tourist beaches will quickly shatter any illusions of coastal beauty that you may have had. The Pacific Coast is actually quite short, and in a car you can easily drive from the border of México to El Salvador in a day; plenty of buses rumble down this route, too.

The coastal climate leaves a lot to be desired—it's hot, humid, and muggy as hell—but the mosquitoes and cockroaches sure love it. Malaria is not uncommon in these parts; if you hate the idea of popping pills every week, make sure you have plenty of protection. Anything containing 75% or more of DEET (a bitchin' ingredient in insect repellent) should do the trick, but the stuff is so potent that it eats through watchbands and glasses. The black-sand beaches from near Monterrico all the way to the El Salvador border are by far the closest to dream material, with clean, isolated beaches. Beyond Monterrico, accommodations are nonexistent and the roads impassable (especially during the rainy season). Inland from the coast are swampy marshes and tons of greenery. Most of the cotton, sugar, and coffee fincas in Guatemala operate amid this humid vegetation inland. The larger plantations sometimes employ thousands of workers; many are Indígenas who migrate from the highlands to earn money during the planting season.

Retalhuleu

Retalhuleu is the prettiest city on the Pacific Coast and that's not saying much. Relatively clean and mellow, it's an important commercial center and the capital of the region. Wealthy Guatemalan farmers live in enormous Spanish-style estates. Unlike other Guatemala ricos, the wealthy here don't hide their homes behind ugly cement walls. In the center of the main plaza is a colossal colonial church with giant wooden doors framed by two fetching little fountains and tropical flowers. A few of the main buildings surrounding the square (modeled after ancient Greek architecture) look incredibly out of place but are undeniably eye-catching. Taxis, taco stands, banks, and a **post office** line the plaza streets. **GUATEL** is one block away on 6a Calle. If you're desperate for fresh fruit or vegetables head to the **Mercado San Nicolás** (10a Calle between 7a and 8a avenidas) or the bus terminal market.

COMING AND GOING A mere two hours from the Mexican border, Retalhuleu is one of the main pit stops for all buses headed to the border towns of Tecún Umán and El Carmen. Most buses stop at the Mercado San Nicolás. Buses leave every hour to Guatemala City (3 hours, $2.50), Tecún Umán (2 hours, 75¢), and Quetzaltenango (1½ hours, 75¢). Mercado San Nicolás is a short three blocks east of the central plaza, but you can always walk to the bus terminal on the western side of the plaza to catch buses already en route. Take 5a Calle west until you are forced to turn right and continue on until you reach the terminal. It's set in a big parking lot surrounded by fruit and vegetable stands and a whole lot of tiendas.

The **train** passes through town twice a week on its way to Tecún Umán from Guatemala City and back. It allegedly arrives on Tuesday around 3 PM on its way to the border and returns on Wednesday at 10 AM. Because the trains are frequently crippled, it often doesn't make it to its final destination and certainly never on time.

WHERE TO SLEEP AND EAT The main hotels—Posada de Don José, Hotel Astor, and Hotel Modelo—cost an arm and a leg in budget-speak. The rooms have private bath, ceiling fans, and screened windows and cost $6 per person. For cheap sleeps, try **Hotel Pacifico** ($2) where you stay in a cement sweat box of a room with no fan, no screen, used linens, and a bathroom all the way down the hall. All these hotels are near the central plaza.

For a quick snack, try the taco stands on 5a Avenida just off the plaza. You can sup on Chinese seafood at **Restaurante Fu-'Kuai** (5a Calle on the central plaza). For about $4 you get decent, fresh seafood with crunchy vegetables and mushrooms. Also check out the endless choices under "chaw mein" or "chap suey." If you're hankering for a burger or a pizza, try the decently priced **Pizza Rondinella** (5a Calle, 3 blocks north of the plaza). A medium pizza with all the fixin's costs $3–$5.

NEAR RETALHULEU

BORDER TOWNS Even if you arrive late, there's no reason to linger overnight in either **El Carmen** or **Tecún Umán**. Both are nasty border towns and you can always catch a bus heading to another spot—anywhere is better than staying here. If you don't already have a visa, you can purchase a tourist card from one of the official looking chaps; it'll last you 30 days and costs $10. If you are driving your own vehicle, the Guatemalan border patrolmen will insist on fumigating it inside and out. This service is not free of charge either. Fortunately, when returning to Mexico, the same sterilization process is not mandatory.

ABAJ TAKALIK If you're a budding archaeologist in need of a little inspiration, the ruins of Abaj Takalik might do the trick. A team of archaeologists at work on the site have their hands full trying to reconstruct ceremonial temples and decipher the enormous stone stelae left by the Olmec tribe. Overlooked pottery shards and broken pieces of obsidian knives dating back to AD 800 are scattered throughout the ruins. Not much is known about this particular site except that a few of the stelae are older than those found at Tikal. The site itself is spread out over 9 square kilometers (3½ square miles) with artifacts scattered on five separate sugar and coffee fincas. Tragic as it may sound, only the Finca Santa Margarita has been willing to set aside land for excavation purposes. The other four fincas refuse to make concessions. Coffee sells a whole lot better than history and the site is being lost to the plow.

If you don't have your own wheels, it's a pain to get to Abaj Takalik. From Retalhuleu, jump on a bus to the Mexican border via Coatepeque and ask to be let off at El Asintal. From there it's a long walk, so wave your thumb frantically for a lift into El Asintal. Abaj Takalik is 4 kilometers (2½ miles) past El Asintal. One of the Spanish-speaking field workers will show you around the ruins. If your interest hasn't waned by the end of the tour, ask him to show you the two stelae by the river a kilometer away. One of the stela is still a place of worship for the locals and it's surrounded by melted candles and incense ash.

TULATE Three hours from Retalhuleu by bus, Tulate has one of the only decent beaches in the area. The black sand can get scalding hot and the ocean tide is a little rough for a casual swim, but it's clean and unpolluted. Right across from the Canal de Chiquimulilla, this one-street beach town has wall-to-wall comedores, ready to serve up fresh fish and cold drinks. Accommodation here is sketchy at best, with no screens and only a reed mat to sleep on—no different from the floor. Buses run every hour to Retalhuleu, with the last one leaving at 5 PM.

Puerto San José

Once a thriving port, Puerto San José is now a rotting corpse with scavengers trying to feast on the last morsels of tourism. It's a raunchy town with several unpaved streets, scary low-budget hotels, and shacks of cantinas that accommodate raging weekend parties. Concerning the scummy streets: Either there is an incredibly high illiteracy rate or people just don't care, but trash is always piled up under the *"prohibido botar basura"* (littering is prohibited) signs. If you're stuck in this hole, **Pensión Veracruz,** before the bridge on the main strip, has some sleazy but cheap rooms at $3 for a double. **Hospedaje Marvin,** across the bridge, is a much cleaner pad at $10 a double. **GUATEL** is at the top of the main road and **Banco Metropolitano** is midway down the main road.

North of Puerto San José is **Escuintla,** a large and fairly important town only because of its position as a mega bus stop. All buses from Guatemala City headed to the Pacific Coast stop in Escuintla.

NEAR PUERTO SAN JOSE

LIKIN Ten kilometers (6 miles) east of Puerto San José, directly on the coast, is the swank beach town of Likin. Here, wealthy Guatemalans build sumptuous vacation homes and zoom around on their speed boats. Likin is a resort town right out of Palm Springs, with over-sized homes and planned, superficial landscape. Instead of golf courses, Likin has cute canals. The entire time you're frolicking at the pretty beach it's nearly impossible to imagine that you're in Guatemala. No bus stops at Likin, but any bus heading toward Iztapa will let you off at the Likin gate entrance if you ask. Everyone entering Likin is subject to the security guards' scrutiny. Those driving Mercedes won't have a problem.

IZTAPA Down the road from Likin is the beach town of Iztapa—and it's about as unlike Likin as you can get. Less uppity, pint-sized Iztapa has unpaved roads and run-down tiendas and cantinas. The Canal of Chiquimulillo lies between Iztapa and the beach proper. Two hotels dominate the town. **Club-Hotel,** complete with its own swimming pool, has doubles for $16 a night. **Hotel Brasilla** has doubles for $5. It's a low-budget warehouse where none of the rooms has screens; you'll be slapping at the blood-suckers all night. Comedores are everywhere and they all seem to have a juke-box cranked to the highest decibels.

MONTERRICO Fifteen kilometers (9 miles) east of Iztapa, Monterrico is the beginning of the finest stretch of beach on the Pacific Coast. The isolated black-sand beaches are clean and fun, and stretch all the way to El Salvador. On Easter weekends, hordes of Guatemalans litter the area. Monterrico is becoming popular and high-priced hotels are being built. **El Bauley Beach,** four blocks from the main strip, is owned by an ex-Peace Corps American woman, and has $7 doubles with mosquito netting and views of the ocean. **Hotel Las Margaritas,** at the end of the main sandy road, has doubles for $3. This and other pensións fill up quickly on weekends with beach-loving, beer-guzzling Guatemalans.

You can reach Monterrico in two ways. The logical route is to leave from Iztapa and cross the canal. But, since the dirt road is often washed out, you are frequently forced to go back to Escuintla and then head south to Taxisco. Buses leave every half hour from Escuintla to Taxisco. From Taxisco, buses head to La Avellana and Monterrico every hour.

Tikal and the Petén

Although they comprise almost one-third of Guatemala's total area, the flat, humid jungles, swampy *bajos* (lowlands), and tropical savannahs of the Petén are almost forgotten by the Guatemalan people. The same remoteness that allowed the Maya city-state of Tayasal (buried under present-day Flores) to evade conquest until the late-17th century has kept this an isolated frontier whose largely untouched tropical forests still hide all sorts of wildlife and countless Mayan ruins. With no gold to plunder, few natives to exploit, and a hot, sticky climate, the Petén had little to hold the Spaniards' (and later the Guatemalans') interest. The few people who lived here were mostly natives, who scratched out a meager existence with little help or interference from officials in the far-off mountains to the west. Life in the Petén remained humdrum until the late 1800s, when the discovery of *chicle* (the natural resin base for chewing gum) suddenly made the previously untapped forest flow with "white gold." From the tile streets of Flores to the brothels of San Benito, the *chicleros* (gum workers) brought new life into the Petén. But in the end, the chicle camps remained isolated outposts. Not until 1970 did the government construct a dirt road linking the vast Petén to the rest of the country, and this bouncy, pothole-riddled excuse for a highway still remains largely impassable at the height of the rainy season.

Abandoned and ignored by the rest of the country, Peténeros are independent people who remain distinct from their fellow Guatemalans. Most towns in the Petén are nothing more than a collection of thatched huts sprouting from the forest along a lonely dirt road. Peténeros pride themselves on their toughness, self-reliance, and knowledge of the jungle. Here, the meat of the day is jungle fowl, venison, armadillo, or tepisquintle (a jungle rodent), and the people continue to make their living from chicle, xate (pronounced shah-tay; a broadleaf palm used in floral arrangements), and other gifts of the forest. Peténeros also have a strong sense of unity born out of their communal isolation. The divide between Indígena and Ladino melts in the humid heat. It's as common for a Ladino to learn Kekchí as it is for an Indígena to learn Spanish. Few gringos venture past the ruins of Tikal but those who do may wind up getting involved in a crazy, giggling card game, invited to dinner, or taken on a boat ride to a far-off Mayan ruin.

"Back in the city you have your stores, your shops, your hospitals. Life is rich here, too. We have everything: supermarket, pharmacy, all right next to us, growing from the ground."—German Magallón (chiclero and a guard at the ruins of Uaxactún, Petén).

The Petén was not always the isolated expanse it is today. At the height of Maya power in AD 600–800 (the Late Classic period in Maya-speak), feather-crowned rulers dripping with jade sat atop pyramids which still tower over the forests. Unfortunately, the ecological destruction which may have hastened the downfall of the Classic Maya has begun once again to tear at the green shields of Petén. Dusty cement towns such as

Sayaxché and Santa Elena are growing at a frightening pace; as each new dirt road emerges, its sides are quickly lined with ramshackle huts and piles of fresh garbage. Fish still manage to survive in huge Lake Petén Itzá, despite the lethal suds from bathers and launderers. "It does no harm, it's a big lake," one Peténero told me, with the conviction of a frontiersperson who takes the vastness of the Petén for granted. Today, environmentalists from the Petén and abroad are making an effort to save what some call "the lungs of the Americas."

Flores and Santa Elena

Though a causeway has connected Flores to the mainland since 1970, it remains a geographic and cultural island—a bastion of civilization against the deep-green jungle that spills into Lake Petén Itzá. The cement-tile streets, grill windows, and orderly stucco houses offer a sense of calm and tranquillity in this frontier zone.

Flores is old and established, and has had a chance to settle, mellow out, and relax. It can't grow anymore; in fact, it's shrinking—the tiny island is slowly being reclaimed by the rising waters of the lake. Flores dates back years before colonial times, to 1221, when a ruler of Chichén Itzá (a Mayan site in Mexico's Yucatán Peninsula) stole the bride of one of the lords of the nearby city of Izamal. Hunac Ceel, the ruler of Mayapán (also in the Yucatán), sacked Chichén and drove the Itzás south into the Petén, where they settled on the shores of the lake that still bears their name. They built a new city called Tayasal on the island. Cortés stopped here once in 1525, just long enough to drop off a sick horse, a strange new beast that was venerated as a god by the Itzás. When the horse bit the dust, they built a stone effigy in its likeness, and locals say that, on a clear day, you can still see it at the bottom of the lake where it was dropped centuries ago. Except for a few priests, the Itzás didn't see another European until 1697, when the forces of Martín de Ursua conquered this last outpost of Mayan independence. His conquest took a single day, and was perhaps helped by the fact that 1697 was the beginning of a new cycle in the Mayan calendar that was prophesied to be accompanied by momentous changes. Ursua spent the next day destroying all the idols; supposedly there were so many that it took an entire day for his men to smash them all. Then he promptly renamed the city Nuestra Señora de Los Remedios y San Pablo de los Itzás (Our Lady of Refuge and Saint Paul of the Itzás)—a mighty big name for a darn small island. The more manageable name of Flores was bestowed upon the town in 1831, in honor of a Guatemalan official killed in Quetzaltenango in 1826.

The peace of Flores is broken before you even get halfway across the causeway connecting Flores with her sister city of Santa Elena on the mainland. Santa Elena displays the bustling action of a true frontier town, in all its energetic, unabashed, and obnoxious glory. You can feel Santa Elena growing: From the noisy airport to the grimy market, it buzzes with new construction and fortune-seekers. Most people catch only a fleeting glimpse of Flores and Santa Elena on their way to Tikal. But, if only for their history and the fact that they represent two very different sides of the Petén, these two towns deserve at least a day of full attention.

BASICS

➤ **MONEY** • Just down the hill opposite the main church in Flores, the **Banco El Credito Hipotecario de Guatemala** (Calle Rosario and Av. Santa Ana, tel. 0/500–628) is open Monday–Thursday 8:30–2, Friday 8:30–2:30. You can also change money at most hotels and restaurants. **El Faisan** (*see* Food, *below*) offers good rates.

➤ **PHONES AND MAIL** • The **central post and telegram office** (open weekdays 8–4) in Flores is just off an alleyway to the right of the main church. **GUATEL** (7a Av., Santa Elena, tel. 0/811–399) is open daily 7 AM–9 PM. Slip into their air-conditioned office where you can make national or international calls—or just escape the heavy, humid air outside.

➤ **TRAVEL AGENCIES** • **San Juan Travel** runs all the minibuses in town and can arrange a trip virtually anywhere imaginable—for a price. *In the Hotel San Juan in Santa Elena, tel. 0/500–042* (see *Where to Sleep,* below). *Open daily 8 AM–noon and 2 PM–6 PM.*

Explore arranges expeditions to El Ceibal ($40 for one day), El Ceibal and Aguateca ($120 for two days), Dos Pilas ($150 for 3 days), and Yaxchilán ($125 for one day). Believe it or not, these trips are good deals. Boat fare alone from Sayaxché to El Ceibal is at least $20 per person. *On Calle Centroamerica in Flores, tel. 0/500–655. Open weekdays 8–noon and 2–6.*

Transpetén Tours offers white-water rafting tours in the Petén area. Check for their latest bargain river trips to Mayan sites. *Santa Elena, tel. 0/500–501. Open weekdays 7 AM–noon, 3–6.*

➤ **VISITOR INFORMATION** • Literally dozens of hotels, restaurants, and travel agencies offer "free visitor information," but the only place where you're guaranteed an unbiased view is the **INGUAT office** in the airport in Santa Elena (tel. 0/500–533).

COMING AND GOING

➤ **BY BUS** • First of all, it's practically a rule of thumb in Petén that gringos are charged double to ride the public buses. (In the highlands and Guatemala City, gringos fork over the same amount as Guatemalans.) In Petén, not only are there no official fares that you can depend on but INGUAT actually authorizes the "gringo price." Listed below are the gringo prices. You can catch all buses from the bus terminal in Santa Elena, smack dab in the middle of the central market (*see* Getting Around, *below*). For information on transportation to Tikal, *see* Coming and Going in the Tikal section, *below.*

Buses head to **Sayaxché** (2½ hours, $2); to **Poptún** (4 hours, $3); to **El Naranjo** (7 hours, $4) at 12:30 PM where you can catch a boat to the Mexican border; and to **Melchor de Mencos,** at the Belizean border (4 hours, $3). Most buses list all these destinations on their sign, but you may have to ask around until you find the one you want. **Fuentes del Norte,** just west of the bus terminal, and **Maya Express** (Calle Principal de San Benito and Santa Elena, tel. 0/500–157) will bump and jostle you to Guatemala City in a grueling 15- to 20-hour ordeal for about $10. Buy your ticket at least one day in advance. If you're heading to Río Dulce (8 hours, $8), take Fuentes Del Norte to Guatemala City and get off on the way.

➤ **BY MINIBUS** • By far the most comfortable and inexpensive way to get to **Belize City** or **Chetumal** is by minivan. Rather than pack onto a crowded bus where you'll have to switch bus lines and undergo the chaos of unloading and reloading at each border, you can hop on a minibus that will whisk you straight to your destination in relative comfort and style. Minibuses zip to Belize City ($20) and Chetumal (you pass through Belize and are dropped at the Mexican border for $30). From Belize City you can connect with a boat to the Cayes, and from Chetumal connect with a bus to Mérida or Cancún. All the minibus info you'll need is in the travel office at the Hotel San Juan (*see* Where to Sleep, *below*).

➤ **HITCHING** • Hitchhiking is one of the best (and only) ways to get around this sparsely populated frontier. Outside Flores, Santa Elena, and Tikal, visitors are rare and most drivers are happy to pick up a needy stranger. Since all roads in the Petén lead to Flores, you should have no trouble hitching a ride here. Be prepared to offer some money or buy a drink for the driver in exchange for his trouble. Between Santa Elena and Tikal, only a minibus or a regular bus (both cost $2) is likely to pick you up.

➤ **BY PLANE** • Because Tikal is such a popular tourist destination, a considerable number of planes fly into and out of this otherwise remote region. **Aviateca, Tapsa,** and **Aerovías** have flights to and from Cancún and Chetumal (Mexico), Belize City, and Guatemala City. Fares from Guatemala City usually hover around $50 one-way, but if you shop around you may be able to get a flight for as low as $30. The cheapest time to buy tickets is in May and June, which is considered the "low" season. A comfortable 30-minute flight is well worth the cash—your other option is the long, bumpy bus ride over unpaved roads.

GETTING AROUND Flores more than fills a tiny island on Lake Petén Itzá; ever since the lake rose in 1978, many of the outermost houses sit half submerged in warm, green water. One street goes around the island, met by cross streets radiating out from a circular central plaza in the center of the island. On the south side is the *relleno* (causeway), a dusty path that connects the city to the mainland. When it hits Santa Elena, the relleno becomes 7a Avenida, the main north–south street in Santa Elena. About 3 blocks south, this crosses the main east–west street, Calle Principal de Santa Elena. This street leads west into San Benito where it becomes Calle Principal de San Benito. Though these towns may look big on a map (and by Petén standards, they are), they are little more than crossroads and most businesses carry no proper address—simply their name, the town, and Petén.

➤ **BY BUS** • One bus route serves Flores, Santa Elena, and San Benito; buses run about every ½ hour. To catch a bus to the airport, the best place to wait is at the corner of 8a Avenida and Calle Principal in Santa Elena. Buses that run this route are either yellow school buses or have a sign saying URBANO. The fare is 10¢.

➤ **BY CAYUCA** • Before Flores was connected to the mainland, these small boats were the only way to get on and off the island. Today, *cayucas* continue to ferry people to and from San Benito, San Andrés, and San José (small communities on the lakeshore). These trips are infrequent, and most boat operators now cater mainly to tourists, taking them to the attractions around the lake (*see* Lake Petén Itzá, *below*). Cayucas tend to leave from behind Hotel San Juan II in Santa Elena. Follow the lakeside road to the west of the causeway and you'll see boats on the far side of the hotel to your right. Expect to pay $5–$12 for a trip that hits the sights around the lake.

WHERE TO SLEEP The Petén is undeniably the tropics and in many hotels you'll have to deal with insects and a powdery brown dirt that coats everything. Mosquitoes are rather clever creatures, and they've discovered a great spot to gather: It's where everyone inevitably has to go and where you're particularly vulnerable to attack. Yes, the bathroom. In general, hotels in Flores are cleaner, more luxurious, and slightly more expensive than in Santa Elena. If you can't get into the places below, **El Mesón de Don Quixote** and **El Jade**, just to the left of the causeway in Santa Elena, offer simple rooms with shared bath. They charge about $5 for a double.

➤ **UNDER $5** • **Hotel El Tucan.** You sleep in a communal bungalow right on the shore, where a bed goes for $3 a night. This is the cheapest deal on Flores, and sleeping in the same room with other travelers will make you all very chummy very fast. Besides the bungalow, separate rooms are available at $6 per double. *Go on the causeway to Flores; go through the first alleyway and turn right. El Tucan is on Calle Centro America on the right-hand side, tel. 0/500–577. 7 rooms, none with bath.*

Hotel Leo Fu Lo. This hotel offers one thing most places of a similar price don't: an electric fan in each room. In the sticky, humid air of the Petén, this alone makes the hotel worthwhile. Rooms are clean and overlook the lake. Doubles are $5. *Santa Elena, just to the left of the causeway, overlooking Lake Petén Itzá. 24 rooms, some with bath. Laundry, luggage storage.*

➤ **UNDER $10** • **Hotel El Itzá** and **El Itzá II.** These two sister hotels on Flores offer fairly clean (and bug-free) doubles with private bathrooms for $7. *On a side street off Calle Centro America on the south side of the island, tel. 0/500–686. 8 rooms, all with bath. Luggage storage.*

Hotel San Juan. This hotel is touted as the tourist information center for all of the Petén. From here you can catch a minivan to Tikal (which is worthwhile if you can gather enough people to split the cost), buy airline tickets, or exchange money at a bad rate. Rooms on the newly renovated right side of the hotel are infinitely cleaner and brighter than those in the old wing. New rooms have a fan, a television, clean private bathrooms, and screens on the window; doubles on this side cost $10. In the old wing, dusty and cobweb-filled doubles cost $5. *2a Calle and 7a Av., Santa Elena, tel. 0/500–562. One block south of the causeway. 50 rooms, some with bath.*

➤ **UNDER $20** • **Casona de La Isla.** If you're sick and tired of dealing with the dust, heat, and bugs, Casona de la Isla is a welcome escape. The clean rooms are (amazingly) insect free, and each one has a private bath with hot water. You can sunbathe on the lovely green lawn and splash around in the lake off their dock. Doubles are $19. *Flores, tel. 0/500–662. It's on the road closest to the waterfront, on the far west side of the island. A bright pink building with shiny white trim. 27 rooms, all with bath.*

➤ **CAMPGROUNDS** • You'll find an excellent camping area on the shores of the lake in the small town of **El Remate,** halfway between Santa Elena and Tikal. **El Mirador del Duende,** if not the best place to camp in Central America, is doubtless one of the most interesting. Built in Mayan style out of local materials, six individual bungalows sit atop ancient platforms overlooking Lake Petén Itzá. The owners see this spot as a lifelong experiment in adopting ancient Mayan techniques to build shelter and grow organic food. Hammocks are provided, and for $3 per person you can enjoy a bungalow overlooking the lake, swimming, relaxing, and getting in touch with your spiritual self. They cook three meals a day, all organic and vegetarian, of course. To get here, take a bus toward Tikal; it's on the right-hand side of the road across from the lake, about 1 kilometer south from the road leading to Biotopo Cerro Cahui (*see* Near Flores and Santa Elena, *below*).

You can sling a hammock for free at a large shelter in the Biotopo Cerro Cahui. It's right across the road from **El Gringo Perdido** nature lodge (which offers camping for $2), and you can walk over and use their swimming and sunbathing areas on the shores of Lake Petén Itzá. They'll even watch your stuff in the restaurant if you don't want to leave it at the campsite. For directions, *see* Near Flores and Santa Elena, *below.*

FOOD In Flores and Santa Elena the difference between a restaurant and a comedor is crystal clear. Comedores (mostly by the market in Santa Elena) are smoky and filled with grime, dogs, bugs, feces, and who knows what else. You'll find a few comedores that are OK. **La Estheria** (in Santa Elena, right next to the market) cooks up some pretty good fried chicken, black bean soup, tortillas, and sour cream for 2 bucks.

Flores restaurants cater almost exclusively to the tourist crowd, and all of them must have used Tarzan as their interior designer. Off the causeway to the left are places with names like **La Jungla** and **El Jacal,** which have bamboo walls, thatched roofs, and the pelts and heads of various endangered species splayed on the walls. **El Gran Jaguar** sports wooden menus lined with real jaguar skin. Not only can you enjoy the dried fragments of Petén wildlife on the walls, but you can also taste some of the exotic creatures for yourself. Go for a plate of armadillo (with its distinctive flavor) or *tepisquintle,* a large jungle rodent that is deliciously marinated with vegetables or eaten *a la plancha* (grilled). It's yummy and doesn't taste rodent-y at all. Though the tiki-room decor is overkill, the food in these jungle joints all costs around $6 and is considerably better than the characterless restaurants in Santa Elena which charge about the same prices.

➤ **UNDER $5** • **Tienda y Cafetería "La Union."** Pasta lovers' alert! You can chow down a hearty plate of the best spaghetti around for $2—a very welcome sight after too many platefuls of rice and beans. The cafeteria is connected to a store that has a chummy family atmosphere. Watch the adorable kids buy candy and play jacks while you pig out on pasta. *In Flores follow the streets closest to the water until you see the yellow sign that says Tienda y Cafetería with a tiny "La Union" written beneath it. It's* on the northwest side of the island across from Posada El Tayasal. Open daily 8 AM–10 PM.

➤ **UNDER $10** • **Bar/Restaurante El Faisan.** This place has a super comfy and happy feel about it. Checkers, backgammon, books, and other curiosities are behind the bar and they're happy to lend them out. Try tepisquintle for $5 or delicious, fresh fish from the lake for $6. *Flores, tel. 0/501–322. From Santa Elena cross the causeway and follow the dirt road to the left. El Faisan is just past the thatched roof of El Jacal to the right.*

Cafe Bistro Chez Michel. In the hodgepodge of jungle bungalows, you'll be surprised to find this bastion d'elegance. The owner (and the food) is très French, the ambience quiet, and the air cool (the air-conditioning alone is reason enough to eat here). If you want a real international experience, try the tepisquintle cooked French-style for $6. You can get other French delicacies for a similar price. *Calle 30 de Junio, Flores. Across from the hotel La Casona de la Isla. Open daily 11–4 and 6–10.*

Restaurante El Tucan. In the middle of the Hotel El Tucan, this restaurant offers a chance to come face to face with local wildlife. As you look out over the lake, you're likely to be approached by one of their parrots, an oversized turkey, or the resident toucans, which hop from table to table looking for handouts. The restaurant carries the usual fare, as well as some funky Euro-Mexican food that looks like it should taste Mexican but doesn't. Enchilada dinners go for about $4 and a plate of spaghetti is $3. *Calle Centro America, Flores, tel. 0/500–577. Go through the first alleyway after the causeway in Flores and turn right. You'll see it just ahead on the right on Calle Centro America. Full bar.*

AFTER DARK The main plazas of Flores and Santa Elena are where everyone congregates but, if you're looking for more, try the **Discoteca La Eclipse** (on Calle Centro America west of the causeway) which opens at 9 and fills with dance enthusiasts who rock to merengue, reggae, and punta. It's only $1 to get in.

The nightlife around here is mostly mosquitoes, bats, frogs, and moths.

NEAR FLORES AND SANTA ELENA

EL PETENCITO El Petencito is a small zoo where elusive Petén animals pace around their tiny cement cages. The zoo charges a $1 entrance fee, which is more than worth it, because up the hill from the incarcerated animals you'll find the most killer **waterslides** (*resbaladeros*) in Central America. These three cement chutes were designed with pure excitement (not safety) in mind, and will give even the most avid thrill-seeker the adrenaline rush of a lifetime. Though you may wind up filtering half the lake through your sinuses, nothing beats the feeling of shooting down at breakneck speeds and then getting thrown through the air into the tropical water, emerging to see nothing but jungle surrounding you. The 60-meter slide on the left is particularly dangerous (and exciting) because it hurls your body around a hairpin curve before sending you flying over the water. If you're alone, you'll have to look for the two taps on the ground by the right-hand side of the slides. You can only divert water to one slide at a time, so pick your poison and go for it. Remember, you're taking an extra risk if you go at the height of the dry season when the lake is at its lowest (late April or early May), so you may want to walk down the steps to the water's edge to check the depth before jumping in. El Petencito is on a small island just east of Flores. You can rent cayucas to take you out there for a few dollars.

BIOTOPO CERRO CAHUI On a small peninsula jutting out into the water on the north shore of Lake Petén Itzá, this parcel of relatively untouched forest was established as a haven for the Petén turkey, a regal bird that looks more like a peacock than a Thanksgiving Day dinner. One large trail circles the park and then climbs to the top of a hill, where an A-frame shelter offers a magnificent view of the lake. The park is largely surrounded by human settlement, and the wildlife here is shyer than at Tikal, where the beautiful turkeys strut nonchalantly in the open fields between the parking lot and official campground. If you want to take the long, beautiful ride across the lake from Santa Elena by cayuca, prepare to shell out the bucks because it's a long way. A quicker and considerably cheaper option is to catch a bus or minivan (about $1) bound for Tikal from the central market in Santa Elena and get off halfway (1 hour) in the town of El Remate. Follow the signs to the Gringo Perdido, a resort which sits on the lakeshore just across the road from the park entrance. It's about a 3-kilometer (½ hour) walk from the main road along the lakeshore.

EL MIRADOR Way, way north of Flores is El Mirador, a vast site that rises up out of the swampy bajos about 7 kilometers (4 miles) from the Mexican border. This was the largest center of the Preclassic period, before Tikal had risen to its full glory. The long trek to El Mirador begins in the town of San Andrés, just across the lake from Flores. From there, you need to find a ride to Carmelita, a full day's ride to the north. At Carmelita, you should be able to hire a guide to take you out to the ruins.

Tikal

Every Maya enthusiast (and average joe) the world over must make a pilgrimage to Tikal, the greatest Mayan site yet discovered. Smack in the middle of the 575-square-kilometer (222-square-mile) **Parque Nacional Tikal,** the towering temples are ringed on all sides by miles of virgin rain forest. This nature spot is super for checking out birds, butterflies, plants, monkeys, and flowers that spend their entire lives hundreds of feet above the forest floor in the dense canopy of trees.

Way back in 600 BC, the first Maya settled on a patch of high, dry ground surrounded by soggy Petén swampland. Not only was this prime piece of real estate spared the floods of the bajos, but it was also rich in obsidian, a volcanic glass perfect for chipping into razor-sharp tools. Little by little, the population grew, and by 200 BC some major works of architecture (including a version of the North Acropolis) began to take shape. By the time of Christ, the Great Plaza had been built, but Tikal was still dominated by the city of El Mirador, far to the north. It didn't swell to full power until the Early Classic period (see box, below), when a leader known as Jaguar Paw (who appears on monuments dating to AD 292–320) sired a lineage that would build Tikal into a city rivaling any of its time. By AD 500, it's estimated that Tikal covered over 47 square kilometers (18 square miles) and may have had a population of 100,000.

Tikal, by this point, had established jurisdiction over a large part of the Mayan world. In about AD 426, a ruler called Caan Chac ("Stormy Sky") ascended the throne. Under Stormy Sky, Tikal became an aggressive military and commercial center that dominated the surrounding centers with a power never before seen in Mesoamerica. Why was Tikal such a hot spot? Besides being rich in obsidian (black volcanic glass), the bajos were used for intensive agriculture, providing food for the city's huge population. These swamps also protected the elevated city from attack and allowed the leaders to spot any approaching enemy miles before they reached the city center. Tikal also occupied a strategic trading position where two river systems drain—one to the northeast and the Caribbean, and one to the west of the Gulf. This gave it strong ties to two powerful centers: Kaminal Juyu in the Guatemalan highlands, and Teotihuacán, far to the north, near present-day Mexico City.

In AD 553, Tikal suffered a major setback when Lord Water (ruler of Caracol, a site in southwestern Belize) began to conquer the Petén. By AD 562, Water had reached Tikal, where he captured and sacrificed their king. The city didn't recover until AD 682 when Ah-Cacao ("Lord Chocolate") rose to the throne. He and his successors commissioned the construction of most of the great temples that exist today.

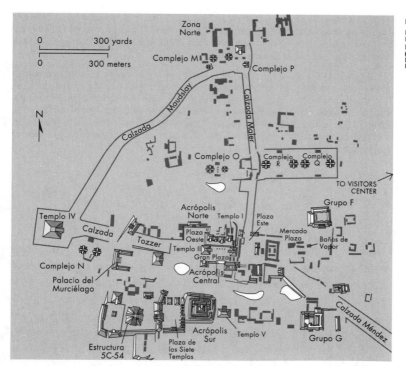

The son of Ah-Cacao continued to commission great temples and palaces, including Temple I, dedicated to his dear old dad, whom he buried right beneath it. He ordered the construction of Temple IV, the tallest temple at Tikal, and by the time of his death in AD 768, Tikal was at the zenith and would remain so until its mysterious abandonment in around AD 900 (*see* box, *below*).

For almost 1,000 years, Tikal sat in the jungle, while the green, humid mass slowly engulfed it. The conquistadors must surely have passed the overgrown ruins, which by that time looked like tall, rocky hills. The natives who occupied the area certainly knew of its existence, but not until 1848 did an official expedition set off to unearth Tikal. The first significant archaeological events didn't get cooking until 1877, when Dr. Gustav Bernoulli commissioned local people to remove the carved wooden lintels from across the doorways of Temples I and IV. These items headed to Basel, Switzerland, where they're shown off in the Museum fur Volkerkunde. In 1881 and 1882, Alfred Percival Maudslay (a pioneering English archaeologist) made the first map showing the architectural features of this vast city. He began unearthing the major temples, and recorded his work in dramatic photographs (copies of which you can see in Tikal today). His work was continued by Teobert Maler, who came in 1885 and 1904. Today both Maler and Maudsley have causeways named in their honor.

Up to this point, access to the site involved a long, hellish journey by foot or horse-back on chiclero trails. In 1951, the Guatemalan Air Force cleared an airstrip near the ruins. After this, large-scale archaeological work began. Today, Tikal is known to include some 3,000 unique buildings.

COMING AND GOING The stretch of asphalt between the airport in Santa Elena and Tikal is the only paved road in the Petén, and was specially designed to ferry tourists to Tikal as quickly and comfortably as possible. So sit back, give your butt a break, and enjoy a quick and painless journey.

➤ **BY BUS** • You can catch a bus to Tikal ($2) at the bus terminal in the center of the main market in Santa Elena (across from the Hotel El Diplomatico off Calle Principal). Two buses head out daily, one at 6 AM and the other at 1 PM. Buses leave Tikal for Santa Elena at the same times.

➤ **BY MINIBUS** • Considering that you pay $2 each way to go on the crowded, undependable public bus, it's worth spending the extra buck to get a minibus to Tikal. The small vans are more comfortable, quicker, and leave at a variety of times throughout the day. You can buy tickets at the Hotel San Juan in Santa Elena (*see* Where to Sleep in Flores and Santa Elena, *above*). Tickets are $6 round-trip. You're free to set an open return date on a round-trip ticket if you plan to spend several days in Tikal or head north to Uaxactún and Río Azul.

The Mystery of the Maya: Where'd Everybody Go?

*The question in every Maya-buff's mind is: How the hell did the Maya disappear? Between AD 800 and 900, the Maya's thriving cities and immense ceremonial centers rapidly declined and were subsequently abandoned. When 19th-**century explorers first discovered the Maya centers, their overgrown and crumbling states revealed that birds and spider monkeys had been the only inhabitants for countless years. Archaeologists have put forth a slew of theories in an effort to explain why they disappeared.*

The most recent, and most popular, proposition is that increasingly destructive warfare disrupted the ecological balance that Maya farmers had maintained for centuries in the fragile tropical forest. Siege warfare may have caused people to concentrate in urban centers—farmers abandoned their farms, leading to exploitation of the forest for food. As the Maya undermined their ecosystem, their civilization collapsed as well. Current archaeological excavations may prove or disprove this theory, but so far no data exists.

Detrimental changes in climate or rainfall have also been suggested. Although heavy rainfall may have been a factor, the study of a swamp at Tikal revealed that no drastic climatic changes have transpired in the past eleven thousand years.

Another theory of why the society disintegrated is that peasant and working classes revolted against the priests and elites, who demanded higher food production and became too remote from the rest of the population. However, new findings show that the lower classes probably shared in many of the ceremonial activities. If this was the case, peasants and workers could have aired their concerns through methods other than rebellion.

Abducted by aliens? Attack of the killer mosquitoes? Slipped and fell on decaying banana peels? List your theory here!

WHERE TO SLEEP Tikal is far from the nearest civilization; since it takes at least two days to really enjoy the ruins, your best option is to camp or, if that's out of the question, to stay in one of the overpriced hotels. The **Jaguar Inn** across from the museum has $40 bungalows and $8 tents—both are pretty scummy. The electricity in the facilities throughout the ruins shuts off at 9 PM.

Posada de la Selva. The white-tiled bungalows of this hotel are remarkably clean, and for the neat-freak this is definitely the best option. Singles without bath are $15. Doubles are $40 without bath, and $60 with. Rooms with private bath have hot water. *The hotel closest to the park entrance. 44 rooms, 32 with bath.*

Tikal Inn. If you must stay in a hotel, this inn is definitely the best value. Rooms are big, clean, and secure (padlocks on the doors). There's even a pool, so you can enjoy a soothing swim after a sweaty day at the ruins. Doubles without meals are $30. *The lodging farthest from park entrance, just off parking lot close to the runway. 11 rooms, all with bath. Luggage storage. 9:30 PM curfew.*

A User's Guide to Mayan Chronology

Historians divide the Maya past into three main periods: the Preclassic, the Classic, and the Postclassic.

• The Preclassic (2,000 BC–AD 250). The Preclassic period is characterized by the influence of the Olmec, a civilization centered on the Gulf Coast in the present-day states of Veracruz and Tabasco in Mexico. During this period, cities began to grow, especially in the Southern Highlands of Guatemala and El Salvador. By the Late Preclassic (400 BC–AD 100) the Maya had already developed their mathematical, calendrical, and hieroglyphic-writing systems—the most advanced in pre-Columbian America.

• The Classic Period (AD 250–AD 900). During the Classic period, Mayan artistic, intellectual, and architectural achievements literally reached for the stars. Vast city-states were flanked by satellite centers, connected by a vast number of paved roadways (called sachés), some of which exist today. The great cities of Palenque (Mexico), Uaxactún (Guatemala), Quiriágua (Guatemala), and Copán (Honduras) were just a few of the powerful centers that controlled the Classic Mayan world. But none matched the majesty and power of Tikal. By AD 850, the great city centers had begun to lose control of their empire (see box, above).

• The Postclassic Period (AD 900–AD 1697). The Maya of the Postclassic were heavily influenced by the growing powers in central Mexico. Their architecture, ceramics, and carvings lost much of their former integrity and began to copy Mexican designs. Though still dramatic, Postclassic cities such as Mayapán, Chichén Itzá, and Uxmal pale in comparison to their Classic predecessors. When the Spanish landed in Yucatán in 1511, they found the Maya scattered, feuding, and easy to conquer.

➤ **CAMPING** • The official campgrounds are a few thatched-roof shelters on a field just opposite the main parking lot. Nothing fancy, but an awesome bonus is that this is the main hangout for the rare Petén turkey. Spend your afternoon soaking in the sun and playing with these strange birds. Unfortunately, this is one of the few national parks in Guatemala where you can't camp for free; you actually have to pay up the wazoo. It's $6 per person to sling a hammock or tent. Another option is to sling a hammock in the garbage dump behind the Jaguar Inn for $2 per person.

➤ **ROUGHING IT** • Although it's illegal, it's still fairly easy to camp in the ruins themselves; if you're successful, you not only save the cost of camping, but also the $6 entrance fee for the next day. Many a young explorer has tried to sleep on top of Temple IV only to be rudely awakened in the middle of the night, fined, and sent out of the park. If you find a secluded spot away from the most popular temples (I, II, IV and the pyramid of El Mundo Perdido), you're less likely to get caught. If you'd rather camp outside the park and walk into the ruins early in the morning before the guards arrive, try some of the small paths along the runway going away from the parking lot. Most lead into a small forested area where you can easily pitch a tent among the mosquitoes and army ants.

FOOD At any one of the lodgings listed above, you'll pay $5 for a meal which you can buy at a comedor for $3—and the comedores are clean and slop on huge portions. **Comedor Tikal** serves the usual rice and beans, has fast service, and is closest to the park entrance. If you'd like something other than comida típica, your only choice is the **Café Restaurante del Parque Tikal,** which offers a variety of beef and pasta dishes at high prices (over $6 for filet mignon). Restaurants are all near the park entrance, which is at least a 45-minute walk from the closest ruin. It's a good idea to pack a sack lunch so you don't waste time traipsing to and from the temples just to grab a bite to eat.

WORTH SEEING First things first. When you fork over the $6 entrance fee, make sure to get your pass stamped so you can stay in the park an extra two hours (until 8 PM) and watch the glorious sunset. It takes two days to really see all the temples, pyramids, and stelae but the fleet-footed athlete can easily visit all the major pyramids in a single day. Take a sack lunch to tide you over and tote a flashlight—not only will it help you find your way back after dark, but it helps to explore some of the eerie, dark temple passageways that sometimes contain awesome masks and painted carvings.

Great Plaza. Just after the guardhouse, you'll stumble upon the well-kept lawn of the immense Great Plaza, surrounded by four tremendous structures. The Great Plaza is the very center of Tikal, geographically and in importance. Tikal basically began in this plaza more than 2,000 years ago, and the present-day site is the result of successive plazas built on top of earlier ruins. To your right as you face north is Temple I; to the left, closing off the plaza to the west, is Temple II; in front of you are the temples of the North Acropolis; and behind you is the Central Acropolis.

Temple I. Also known as the Temple of the Great Jaguar (after a symbol on one of the carved lintels), this temple was built in honor of Ah-Cacao (Lord Chocolate) by his son in about AD 700. Temple I is the best example of traditional Mayan temple construction, with a pyramid structure, wide stairs leading to the top, a sturdy platform, an elevated roof, and nine terraces (nine was a sacred number to the Maya). The stairs are known as a "construction stairway," because they were built first and used by workers to transport blocks and mortar to construct the rest of the pyramid. The beautiful wood lintels throughout Temple I are built from the rot-resistant zapote tree. Deep underneath the temple is the tomb of Ah-Cacao himself—you can see a reconstruction of it in the museum.

Temple II. Right across the plaza is this slightly smaller but equally spectacular structure. A three-tiered pyramid sits on a platform; inside Temple II (just like in Temple I) three rooms are connected by narrow hallways. As you climb the steps on the outside of the pyramid, you'll notice a wonderful echo—a testament to Mayan architectural genius. The acoustics were supposedly so precise that rulers could whisper to each other from the tops of the two temples unheard by anyone in the plaza below. The back of Temple II is one of the best places to watch flocks of parrots, toucans, and trogans (green relatives of the quetzal).

The North Acropolis. This group of small pyramids, stelae, and masks is perhaps the most complex structure in the Mayan world. Its foundations go back to 100 BC, with successive layers built upon layers until it became the massive structure it is today. This is a fantastic spot to flick on that flashlight and descend into a series of tunnels that hide two 10-foot-tall, long-nosed masks, still sporting some of their original paint. This structure used to house a number of bizarre archaeological treats long since removed, including a red stela (you can see it in the museum) and the tomb of a priest who took not only a turtle and a crocodile, but also nine human servants with him.

The Central Acropolis. Just on the other side of the great plaza, this is a maze of courtyards, temples, and palaces. Past the main plaza to the west is **Temple III.** Climb to the top and check out the cool restored wood lintels over the doorways. Directly south from here is **El Mundo Perdido** (the "Lost World"), a complex of some 38 buildings. In the center, ringed by low palaces, rises the **Great Pyramid,** the oldest Mayan structure at Tikal. On the north side are huge, eroded masks shaded by palapas, and you can climb the wide stairs between them to the dusty platform at the top. The summit looks different from the other pyramids, most of which have a little room rather than just a flat platform. This is a bitchin' place to watch hawks soaring above the forest canopy.

Temple IV. Northwest of El Mundo Perdido, this temple is, at 212 feet, the largest structure ever built by an ancient people of the New World. This humongous structure is still largely covered in jungle, and the ascent takes you scrambling over roots and up wooden ladders to the main platform. From here, a metal ladder brings you to the roof comb and undoubtedly one of the most beautiful views in the entire world. You'll be able to see the largest pyramids (Temples I and II, the Great Pyramid, and Temple V) rising up over a green expanse of jungle that seems to stretch forever.

Temple of Inscriptions. If you've got more time to spend at Tikal, head for this building (Temple VI) at the far southeast end of the city center. A beautifully carved stela lies at the bottom, but the temple itself is run-down, so it doesn't have as many clear inscriptions as the name would suggest.

Silvanus G. Morley Museum. To check out the many goodies that were found inside the temples at Tikal, visit this museum, which exhibits exquisitely carved pieces of bone and jade, as well as beautiful pottery and a replica of the tomb of Ah-Cacao (found under Temple I). *Between the Jaguar Inn and the Jungle Lodge, near the entrance. Open weekdays 9–5, weekends 9–4. Admission: 40¢.*

Uaxactún

Uaxactún has sustained waves of foreign invasions and still manages to remain a true frontier town of thatched-roof huts and small-town friendliness. Uaxactún is the domain of true Peténeros, who continue to make their living in partnership (rather than competition) with the surrounding forest. Everyone with more than a passing interest in the northern frontier should head in this direction. Also, the temples here are among the most impressive ruins in Petén outside Tikal. As the mayor will proudly tell you, "Uaxactún is closer to heaven, for it is here that the Mayans chose to watch the movements of their sacred stars." Behind the huts south of the runway you'll find Group E, the Maya observatory. Climb the large temple near the gate (stopping to see if you can tell which giant masks are bats and which are jaguars), then look east. You'll see three small temples, each carefully placed so that the sun rises over the one furthest south at the winter solstice (December 21), over the one furthest north at the summer solstice (June 21), and over the middle temple and its two stelae at the spring and fall equinoxes. Groups A and B, on the north side of the runway, have several large temples and palaces to explore. To the west is the place where the Mayas got the building materials for their temples and stelae. It looks strangely abandoned, as if the carvers suddenly dropped their saws in mid-slice and never returned. To get to Uaxactún, start in the early morning from Tikal because you'll have a much better chance of catching a ride. If you're feeling particularly energetic or are just sick of waiting, you can begin the 6-hour walk through the jungle, past Tikal. The road is well marked and easy to follow.

The mayor of Uaxactún is chummy with the stray gringo who comes into town. She'll take them aside and declare, "I'm the mayor, we'll just have to get you a wife (or hubby), a little home, and you can move in with us right here." This is the type of place where everyone is amazed that there are people who don't cook over a fire or wash clothes by hand in hollowed-out logs like they do.

Río Azul, in the far northeastern corner of Petén where Belize, Mexico, and Guatemala meet, is the destination for adventurers who want to continue north from Uaxactún into Mexico. These ruins are very large but still unrestored. However, they're connected to Uaxactún by a barely passable dirt road, so you may be able to hitch a ride here, or at least to Dos Lagunas where the road splits off to Río Azul.

WHERE TO SLEEP AND EAT Once you get into the town of Uaxactún, you'll see one or two small stores and a bar—basically bamboo huts with small signs. Believe it or not, travelers sleep and eat in the villagers' private homes. For a scrumptious meal where the food just keeps on coming, ask for the house of **Doña Urbana.** Your meal comes complete with full-on rural Central American ambience, including kittens rolling around at your feet, children playing in the dust, a full dose of local gossip, and cannibalistic chickens that are happy to wolf down any remains of their former nest-mates. **Doña Rosa** also offers food to visitors. She's shy about asking for money, but offer to pay accordingly. You can also eat at the house of **Doña Juanita,** an old Mexican woman who rents out hammocks in her home for $1 a night. If you'd like a little more privacy, ask the *alcalde* (mayor) to set you up in the new **Hospedaje El Chiclero,** where you can sleep for $2 a night.

Sayaxché

After a 3-hour roller-coaster ride over the bumpy road west from Santa Elena, the bus comes suddenly to a screeching halt right where the road sinks into the waters of a wide river. Look across and you'll see the blink-and-miss-it town of Sayaxché. Sayaxché is the political and commercial center of the southwestern Petén, where boats pick up fuel and supplies for the small towns deep in the swampy interior. This is the best (and only) spot to base yourself for visiting the ruins in this part of the Petén, most of which are only accessible by boat. Though none have been restored to their former glory, the sites of Aguateca, El Ceibal, and Dos Pilas all offer any aspiring Indiana Jones an incredible adventure within wet, mosquito-filled forests that are even deeper and darker than those around Tikal. You can't change traveler's checks anywhere in this tiny town, so make sure to do all your money transactions in Flores (or Santa Elena) before heading here. You can change cash at a tienda at a lousy rate.

Sayaxché is no tourist center, but you'll find a few cheap places to bed down after a grimy day in the jungle. **Hotel Guayacan** is the most expensive lodging in town ($6 for a double without bath), but it's also the cleanest and most luxurious, with a cool patio overlooking the river. **Hotel Mayapán** has cheap $3 doubles that are clean and quiet. The following eateries offer (in addition to food) free advice to tourists and can arrange all sorts of trips. Julian, at **Restaurante La Montaña,** offers regular trips to Ceibal, Aguateca, and Dos Pilas. He can also arrange lodging at Posada Caribe, on Río Petexbatun, within walking distance of Dos Pilas. The cost is $30 per person a night, including meals. Roberto Giron, at the **Restaurante Yaxkin,** also gives advice and help to foreigners.

To get to Sayaxché, take a bus from Santa Elena (2½ hours, $2). In Sayaxché, you can hunt around for a supply boat on the river to take you to Río Usumacinta, Yax-chilán, or the Mexican border. Halfway between Santa Elena and Sayaxché is **La Libertad,** a one-comedor town with an army checkpoint and a petrol station. Here the road splits off to the Mexican border and it's a great place to hitch a ride. Also, petrol trucks leave from here for Alta Verapaz, and you can join them on their long journey.

NEAR SAYAXCHE

EL CEIBAL Pull out the insect spray and lather up: The ancient site of El Ceibal lies deep within a humid stretch of jungle swimming with blood-sucking beasts. The extremely well-preserved stelae are amazing. Almost all the stelae depict rulers with mustaches and straight noses jamming on carved, guitar-like scepters in a style which is definitely non-Mayan. Archaeologists suggest that this site was actually ruled by Toltecs from Mexico. El Ceibal takes its name from the ceiba trees, which were sacred to the ancient Maya, who believed they held up the heavens. The cheapest way to get to El Ceibal is to ask in Sayaxché for any vehicle bound for El Paraíso. For less than 50¢, the driver will drop you at the head of the trail; from there it's a 2-hour walk to the ruins. You can easily hitch back that afternoon for the same price. If you'd like a more comfortable ride, you can rent a boat (about $50 for a six-person group) in Sayaxché to ferry you down the Río de La Pasión to the ruins. From where the boat drops you off, it's another ½-hour trek on a thin path through the jungle to the ruins. Though you'll hear howler monkeys and birds, it's difficult to see any animals through the thick vegetation. You can camp in the thatched shelters near the park entrance for free; as usual, bring some extra food and drink to share with the guards.

DOS PILAS At its height around AD 700, Dos Pilas was one of the most important Maya centers of the Petén, and, in alliance with Ceibal and Aguateca, its power rivaled that of Tikal. One of the site's most interesting features is a hieroglyphic staircase that records the capture of a Dos Pilas ruler by Tikal in AD 643. Dos Pilas is only accessible by boat. After traveling an hour up the Arroyo Petexbatún ($40 round-trip per boat), you'll be dropped at Paso Caribe, where you can hire a guide (and maybe even a mule) to take you the 12 kilometers (7 miles) to the site, where you can rap with the archaeologists and pitch your tent for free. Guides usually charge $10–$15 a day.

South from Flores

Two routes head south from Flores to Guatemala City. One is a two-day bus trip that heads south to Sayaxché, before continuing on to Raxruja, 5 hours away; after four bus changes, you eventually reach the city. It's a hairy, scary ride, but a real adventure. The other route goes south from Flores toward Lake Izabal. It takes about 10 hours to the town of Modesto Méndez, and another 5 hours to Guatemala City. Until 1970, this trip involved a week-long trek on horseback, across rope bridges and tiny footpaths. The government finally got around to bulldozing a road, but it remains one of the worst stretches in Guatemala—just wide enough to hold a rickety public bus. Buckle down, cushion yourself with a few chickens, and prepare for the ride of your life. At the town of San Juan, about 1½ hours south of Flores, the bus enters the foothills of the Maya mountains and the fun begins. The kamikaze bus driver begins barreling through the largely uninhabited jungle, tackling hairpin turns and monster potholes at full speed. If you're in a real hurry, your best option is to take an overnight express bus, where you can get a real seat. But why endure 20 straight hours of hell when you can stop and relax in Finca Ixobel, a bustling gringo farm/lodging spot? Before reaching the Finca, you pass Poptún, a cute Petén town where you can ask about staying at the Finca at **Restaurante Fonda Ixobel** (tel. 0/507–363). Definitely make a point to eat here—they serve up some of the most delicious food in all of Guatemala. The road is slowly being improved, so not far in the future you (and your behind) may be able to enjoy the miles of jungle and grass huts without the horrific bounce.

FINCA IXOBEL In the cool pine forests just south of Poptún is gringo paradise. Treat yourself to tossed green salad made with vegetables and herbs straight from the gardens of this working farm. Play volleyball, shoot some hoops, or take a dip in the sumptuous swimming hole. "The Finca" is so popular with young travelers that the moment you hop on a bus asking for Poptún, someone will immediately kick in, "so, you're going to Ixobel?" You can camp under a thatched palapa or in one of their tree-houses for under $3. The coed dorm has beds for less than $4. The latrines are the deepest in the country, and the shower water is wonderfully hot. The **river cave expedition** (offered by the Finca and more than worth the $2.50) takes you slipping over a jungly mountain and through a fern-rimmed entrance, where an underground river flows through caverns. With candles in hand (and shoes to protect your feet), you plunge into the water and swim through the cool caverns, finally arriving at a waterfall where you can jump over stalagmites into a deep pool far below. You can also go inner-tubing ($10), on a jungle trek, or horseback riding. To get here, take one of the Fuentes del Norte buses that run between Guatemala City and Flores; ask to be dropped at Finca Ixobel. It's $6 from Río Dulce and $3 from Flores. The farm is about a kilometer walk back from the main road.

Near the Finca is **Naj Tunich,** a cave with Mayan paintings. A few of these beautiful paintings depict erotic scenes, which is rare for the prudish Maya. Because of uncontrollable looting, the cave was closed to the public. Ask at the Finca whether it has reopened.

Central and Eastern Guatemala

While most visitors stream to the artsy boutiques of Antigua, the market at Chichicastenango, or the gringo-drenched shores of Lake Atitlán, few visitors head to Central and Eastern Guatemala. Who knows why? These highlands pack in so many worlds that you may suffer culture shock at each bus stop. From the reggae beat and Creole seafood of the Caribbean coast to the mariachi bands and cacti of the dry cattle-ranching hills of Zacapa; from the mist-covered forests and waterfalls of Alta Verapaz to the blasting night clubs and brothels of Puerto Barrios, Central and Eastern Guatemala is a perfect example of multifaceted Guatemala. Speak a few halting words of Kekchí in the main market of Cobán, tap on an African drum in Puerto Barrios, or light a couple of candles at the shrine of the Black Christ in Esquipulas—such actions are sure to bring out the hospitality and curiosity of locals who talk to few foreigners. Chiquimula is the ridin', ropin', ranchin' center of the Eastern Highlands and *the* transport hub for the area. It's dusty and boring but you'll probably only have to see it through the grimy windows of your bus.

Outdoor buffs will find that the region offers unmatched natural spectacles. Among the most beautiful are the dramatic cliffs that line the Río Dulce; the caves of Lanquín, where the river gushes out in a white fury and evening brings thousands of bats; the turquoise pools of the natural bridge at Semuc Champey, considered by many to be the most beautiful spot in all of Guatemala; and the spectacular scenery between Chiquimula and Esquipulas. If you're hankering to get off the gringo trail and do some exploring, Central and Eastern Guatemala is a great place to start.

Central and Eastern Guatemala

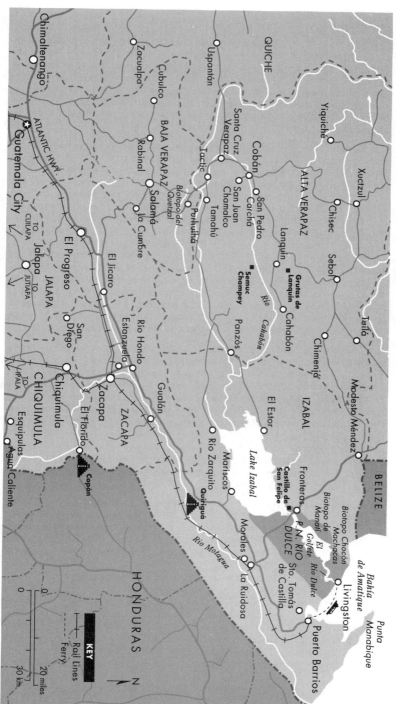

153

Cobán

In a cool, misty valley, Cobán is kept forever green by *mus mus ha'b* (also called *chipi-chipi*), an on-and-off drizzle that keeps everything at a calm, slow tempo. The population here is almost completely indigenous; although the huipiles and cortés look as close to European clothing as they can get, local Kekchí and Pokom cultures continue to run strong. Around Cobán are innumerable Indígena villages, each with its own ruin, cave, or colonial church. The *monja blanca* (the national flower) grows everywhere in the misty surrounding forest and the quetzal (the national bird) lives in the moss-covered trees.

The demure nature of modern Cobaneros offers few clues about the not-so-distant past, when they were one of the most feared and ruthless tribes of the Americas, the Rabinal Maya. When the Spanish arrived in the early 1500s, the Rabinal were still at war with their bitter enemies the Quichés, who had been fighting them for over 100 years. After the conquistadores had dealt with the Quichés, they tried to do the same to the Rabinal, but Rabinal warriors sent the Spanish packing. Spaniards renamed this region Tezulutlan, "The Land of War." But if these lands could not be won through brute force, why not ideology? Fray Bartolome de Las Casas, known as a crusader against the maltreatment of Indígenas by the Spanish crown, made it his mission to convert these heathen souls. In 1537, he struck a deal with his compatriots: If Spain would keep its military forces out for 5 years, he would win these lands for the crown. He started by translating religious hymns into local languages. This aroused several chiefs' interest and by the end of a year he convinced a number of communities to move into Spanish-style villages. He kept on evangelizing, and by the end of the allotted time he had conquered the formerly invincible Rabinales without raising a single sword, and the lands were renamed the Verapaces, the lands of "true peace."

Cobán didn't begin really to grow until the turn of the century, when German immigrants flooded in, establishing vast coffee fincas that still cover the surrounding hillsides. They transformed the city of Cobán from a mostly Indígena outpost into an isolated and wealthy "colony" that had little contact with the capital, or the rest of the country. Cobán hosted traveling performers from far off Germany and wealthy finca owners financed art, music, and culture. But Cobán's days of glory were short-lived. With the onset of World War II, the U.S. government pressured Guatemala to expel the Germans, many of whom were outspoken proponents of Hitler. But you can still see some faint traces of German influence: Some "Indígenas" have striking blond hair, and the cafés have paintings of the Alps on their walls and serve European pastries. Cobán continues to host one of the largest cultural events in the country, the National Folklore Festival, at the end of July.

Unfortunately, even this land of "true peace" has been shattered by the counterinsurgency campaigns of the late '70s and early 1980s, and many of the local Kekchí people have fled north to the Petén to escape the violence. In some remote regions, people continue to live in military-controlled "model villages" similar to those in the neighboring department of Quiché, and the region has witnessed military violence as brutal as any in the country. On May 29, 1978, a large group of Kekchí Indígenas gathered in the town of Panzós, Alta Verapaz, to protest the expropriation of their land by the military. After they assembled in the local soccer stadium, soldiers opened fire on the crowd, killing over 100 unarmed men, women, and children. Their bodies were thrown into two mass graves that had been excavated just outside town the day before. National and international outrage followed the massacre, and over 100,000 protesters gathered in Guatemala City in outrage. This event is often considered a landmark in Guatemala's political history; after this brutal killing, the government sank to even lower depths of corruption and the violence intensified, reaching its peak in the early 1980s.

Today Cobán is peaceful; unless you're here for the Folklore Festival, you'll be ready to move on after a few days.

BASICS

➤ **MONEY** • A number of banks are right in the center of Cobán behind the main cathedral. Most don't change traveler's checks or foreign currency. The **Banco del Ejercito** (2a Av. 1–47, Z3, tel. 0/511–078) has long lines, but also long hours. It's open weekdays 8:30–8 and Saturday 9–2.

➤ **EMERGENCIES** • The **policía** are at 1a Calle, 5a Avenida, Z2, tel. 0/511–225. **Red Cross** ambulances are at 3a Calle 2–13, Z3, tel. 0/511–459. The **regional hospital** is at 8a Calle 1–24, Z4, tel. 0/511–315.

Farmacia Carvi (1a Calle 4–53, Z4, tel. 0/513–094) is the one 24-hour pharmacy in town. It's down the hill behind the cathedral on the main road toward San Pedro Carchá.

➤ **PHONES AND MAIL** • **GUATEL** (1a Calle and 3a Av., Z1, tel. 0/511–498) is right off the main square—you can't miss the huge, glowing, white and blue sign. It's open daily 7 AM–midnight. **Correos y Telegrafos** (3a Calle 2–02, Z3, tel. 0/511–140) hides out in an unmarked building behind the main market. It's in a building with brick-rimmed windows right across the street from the Guatemalan fast-food marvel, Pollo Campero (let your nose do the walking). Look above the glass doors for the dimly painted words: Correos & Telegrafos. The mail section is open weekdays 8–4 and the telegrams part is open 24 hours.

➤ **VISITOR INFORMATION** • The **visitor information** office is right off the main plaza, behind a tiny playground next to GUATEL, and it's open weekdays 8–12 and 1–5. Besides a map and a couple of brochures, you can get a humongous list of all the things to see and do in Alta Verapaz. They also organize one-day tours to the Caves of Lanquín and Semuc Champey (*see* Near Cobán, *below*) for about $20 per person in a group of 4–5 people.

The Acuña family offers friendly advice on all the hidden corners of Alta Verapaz and can arrange adventures to hard-to-reach sites. Call Sean or Anita Acuña in Cobán at 0/511–268.

COMING AND GOING

➤ **BY BUS** • Cobán is served by Monja Blanca/Escobar (4a Av. and 2a Calle, Z4, tel. 0/511–952), right near the public bus terminal. They have a fleet of pullmans that regularly make the 5-hour trip to **Guatemala City.** These are first-class buses with assigned seats, so buy a ticket in advance. Second-class buses run to **Uspantán,** in Quiché (5–6 hours, $2), at 7 AM and 10 AM from San Pedro Carchá, passing Cobán a ½ hour later. A similar service to **Sebol** (a transport hub for buses to the Petén) also leaves from the nearby town of San Pedro Carchá. Buses run every few minutes to San Pedro Carchá and San Juan Chamelco, as well as all the other nearby small villages. Buses to **El Estor** (near Lake Izabal) leave from the main bus terminal in Cobán. This terminal, a dusty lot in front of the gymnasium, is just down the hill to the left of the church.

➤ **HITCHING** • If you're coming from Salamá or Biotopo del Quetzal, you should have no problem finding a ride. **La Cumbre,** a major junction where the road splits going to Alta Verapaz, Baja Verapaz, and Guatemala City, is a good place to scout out a ride. The junction near Tactic where the road splits to Cobán and El Estor is another safe bet.

GETTING AROUND Cobán is so small you'll have no problema finding your way around. The main plaza is a triangular park set on top of a ridge with a strange concrete pavilion in the center. 1a Calle is the main road that comes in from Guatemala City and runs out to San Pedro Carchá. Here you'll find the bulk of hotels, shops, and restaurants. Just behind the cathedral (running perpendicular to 1a Calle) is 2a Avenida. Down the hill to the right are the post office, the main market, and Pollo Campero; to the left, the street drops steeply down to the gymnasium, the main bus terminal, and another market.

WHERE TO SLEEP The hotels listed below all have friendly service and display their INGUAT-approved rates so you'll avoid the arbitrary "gringo price" that is unfortunately (and illegally) charged at some of the other budget lodgings. It's sometimes hard to find rooms during the fiestas in the beginning and middle of August.

Hotel Central. The medieval shields that grace the walls ringing the patio of this quiet hotel recall the town's German roots. Unfortunately, the patches of fungus that cling to the walls of most of the rooms may bring problems to asthma or allergy sufferers; otherwise, the place is spotless and quiet. The service is fast and friendly, too. Doubles are $5.60. *1a Av. 1–79, Z4, tel. 0/511–442. It doesn't have a sign, but you can easily find it right next to the Cafe San Jorge just to the left of the cathedral. 13 rooms, all with private bath and hot water.*

Hotel La Paz. Just like the name ("peace") says, this is a tranquil dig set well off the main road. The small but charming and spotlessly clean rooms open onto a flower-filled courtyard. Whether you get a room with a private bath or choose to use the equally clean public one, you'll pay the same $3 person. *6a Av., Z1, tel. 0/511–358. Walk on 1a Calle toward Guatemala City for about 2 blocks from the central park. Turn right where you see the Hotel Cobán Imperial; La Paz is just down the hill on the left. 15 rooms, some with bath.*

Hotel Nuevo Monterrey. The rooms in this hospedaje-type place are remarkably clean and spacious. Unlike at the Cobán Imperial next door, the rooms lack such extravagances as cable TV and rainbow sheets, but they are further off the main street and much quieter. Doubles are $4.60 with a cold public shower and clean public toilet. For a private bathroom with lukewarm water it's about $6 for a double. *6a Av. 1–12, Z2, tel. 0/511–131. Follow 1a Calle toward Guatemala City; you'll see the Hotel Cobán Imperial. Nuevo Monterrey is right next to it on the side street to the right. 18 rooms, some with bath.*

➤ **CAMPGROUNDS** • Campers are in for a real treat. Cobán's surrounding villages offer tons of parks where you can camp for free. In Cobán itself is **Parque Nacional Las Victorias,** where 82 green hectares (203 acres) are yours to stake out. An official camping area is right near the automobile access road next to the main offices. Ask here for permission before you pitch your tent. The office is open weekdays 8–4. Further within the park, countless picnic shelters and palapas beckon the creative camper. San Pedro Carchá, Lanquin, and Tactic all have palapa-covered campgrounds (*see Near Cobán, below*), and you can find similar camping possibilities throughout Alta Verapaz.

FOOD Cobán has a number of regional specialties of which it is (rightly) proud. The most famous is *Kak'ik* (also spelled *Cacic* or called *Caldo de Chunto* or *Caldo de Chompipe*), a delicious turkey soup packed with a leg, a wing, a breast, and tons of delicious internal goodies. It's usually accompanied by another regional specialty, *tamales.* These hot corn dough treats wrapped in banana leaves can be found almost anytime at the market or bus stop for pennies apiece. Local drinks reflect the products grown in the region: cacao, coffee, cardamom, and sugarcane. *Boj,* a liquor made from cane, has a cool history: A long time ago, a demon was wooing a harp player; to make her play extra well, he took her sugarcane juice to drink. But before he gave it to her, he pricked his finger and a drop of blood mixed with the sweet liquid. According to the legend, this was the first cup of Boj. Even today, it is said that men are driven to fight when they drink too much because they're filled with "the blood of the devil."

A number of delicious, clean food stands are just off the central park. One of the best is **Empanadas Argentinas,** right in front of GUATEL, where you can get hot chicken or beef *empanadas* (turnovers) for 30¢ each.

Cafeteria Mus Mus Ha'b. This spot doubles as a small tienda, so the comings and goings of shoppers always liven up your meal. The family that runs this joint is super-friendly and provides tourist information. Come on Thursday to enjoy a bowl of their homemade Kak'ik ($2.60; it's only served one day a week). For dessert, try some *nue-gados,* sugary clumps of bread balls for 10¢ each. *On the corner of 1a Calle and 5a Av., Z1, no tel. Walk on the main road toward Guatemala City; you can't miss the huge sign painted on the side of the building. Open daily 6 AM–10 PM.*

Cafeteria San Jorge. This place offers stupendous Guatemalan food at low prices and is one of the most popular spots with Cobaneros. Come at lunch time for an extra-special menú del día, with corn, vegetables, avocado, rice, delicious soup, and a main course ($2.40 for chicken and $2.80 for beef). If you're lucky you may be able to chow down on the best Kak'ik in town for $3 a bowl. *1a Calle 1–79, Z4, no tel. Just across the street from the cathedral on the left-hand side. Open Mon.–Sat. 8–8.*

Restaurante El Refugio. Dishes are elegantly presented and served at reasonable prices. As the waitpeople rush to open the door to the bathroom, to pull out your chair, or refill your glass every three sips, you may wonder: Is this good manners, annoying, or just plain entertaining? Try *pavesa* (a hearty bowl of French-onion-like soup), which will fill you up for only 90¢. As well as turtle soup and other local favorites, they offer a small selection of pasta and salads for the herbivorous traveler. *2a Calle 1–34, Z2, tel. 0/511–338. Follow la Calle behind the cathedral, turn left on the first street down the steep hill toward the main bus terminal. It's in the large wood building on the first corner to your left. Open daily 11–11.*

➤ **DESSERT/COFFEE HOUSES** • Cobán is *the* coffee capital of Guatemala, and is home to a handful of places where you can sit and sample a warm cup of one of the local blends while you watch the chipi-chipi.

Cafe El Tirol. At last! This is a real café where you can get that Guatemalan coffee everyone talks about—in over 34 different flavors. Take your pick from an espresso with chocolate and caramel, or even with vanilla ice cream, both for 70¢. Or, try Krup-nik (80¢), with honey, lemon, and vodka (to counteract the caffeine). *1a Calle 3–13, Z1, no tel. Right across the street from the Posada Hotel on 1a Calle. Look for the small sign (just past the Budget Rent-a-Car) and turn into the driveway. The café is just to your right. Open daily 7 AM–9 PM.*

WORTH SEEING El Calvario church is only a short walk from the prosperous modern markets of central Cobán, but as you zigzag up the hill toward the church you'll enter a world far away in time and culture. The cobblestone path to the top is bordered by a series of small shrines, each hiding a cross darkened with ash. The offerings inside include feathers, hair, or coins stuck to the crosses and walls with gobs of wax. If you sit awhile, you may see families muttering prayers in Kekchí to the gods. The church at the top offers another chance to see bloody sculptures of Christ and devoted wor-shippers kneeling in the flicker of candles. The view from the top of the hill is one of the best in the city. Just next to El Calvario is **La Ermita de Santo Domingo de Guzmán.** This is the clubhouse for Cobán's cofradía, religious officials elected each year.

The **cathedral** in the center of town is interesting not for its architecture but for some weird tidbits inside. Near the altar is an Englishman's account of his travels to Cobán at the beginning of the century. To the right of the cathedral is the **convent,** one of Cobán's oldest surviving buildings (from the late 1500s), which recently sheltered hundreds of Kekchí Indígenas who fled from their war-torn villages in the early 1980s.

GUATEMALA

FESTIVALS The National Folklore Festival draws people from all over Guatemala, and features folkloric dances and typical foods from every part of the country. One of the most important parts of this festival is the election of the **Rabin Ajau,** the winner of a "beauty pageant" involving a parade of all the traditional costumes from the villages of Guatemala. The Folklore Festival usually takes place in the last week of July. It's held in the national gymnasium behind the main bus terminal. Tickets go for $3–$4.

Just after the National Folklore Festival is the fiesta celebrating Cobán's patron saint, Santo Domingo de Guzmán. It's celebrated in Indígena style, featuring fireworks, presentations by the cofradía, and lots of marimba music. This is the time to enjoy *El Baile de Los Venados,* the deer dance. Locals dress in bright red costumes and don masks of hunters, dogs, jaguars, bears, and, of course, deer. The fiesta runs August 1–6, with the principal day being the 4th.

AFTER DARK Le Bon Discoteca (3a Calle 3–38, Z3, tel. 0/511–673) is across the street and down one block from Pollo Campero. The boogie-ing begins around 10 PM (they open at 8) and goes on till 3 AM. The red light and stream of scantily clad women wandering down from upstairs suggests this is more than just a disco, but Cobaneros also come here in couples and the atmosphere still manages to be pretty classy. Cover charge is $1.

OUTDOOR ACTIVITIES For hiking, jogging, camping, or picnicking head to **Parque Nacional las Victorias.** This huge city park was once a German coffee finca, but has since become an ecological reserve for preserving the native plant life of Alta Verapaz. A tiny corner of the park is accessible by car, but this is nothing compared to the web of hiking trails that extend far into the mountains above Cobán. This park is close to the center of town and the perfect place to camp. The gates are only open 8–5, so be sure to get in before five if you plan to spend the night. To get here, walk past El Calvario and La Ermita and the park entrance will be on your right. A large sign with a map of the extensive trails greets you as you enter.

You may have a hard time seeing the elusive quetzal, but don't worry about seeing the national flower, the lovely monja blanca. In the **Vivero Verapaz** orchid nursery, Otto Mittlestaet and his wife Concha have raised these and countless other varieties of floral wonders under the shade of giant tree ferns since 1981. It's illegal to export any orchids from Guatemala so you'll have to take home photos and memories of these beauties. The best time to visit is from October to February when most of the flowers are in bloom. The Vivero lies 1 kilometer out of Cobán on the old road to Guatemala City. After crossing the bridge, take the second dirt road to your right. Look for the small artificial pond and giant tree ferns to the right. The Mittlestaets will happily guide you through their prized plants for 40¢ from 9–noon and 2:30–5 Monday–Saturday. On Sunday, it's open only in the morning.

NEAR COBAN

BIOTOPO DEL QUETZAL "MARIO DARY RIVERA" As the road winds up into the mountains north of Baja Verapaz, the climate takes a turn as dramatic as those in the twisting road. These cool slopes are home to Guatemala's national bird, *Pharomacrus moccinno* or, in lay terms, the quetzal. This brilliant green creature has been important since ancient times, when it was incorporated into one of the most important religious cults of Mesoamerica, *Kulkulcán,* which means the feathered serpent. Today, this bird continues to be the most important national symbol, and you'll see its image plastered everywhere—from effigies hanging in bus windows to the national currency. To native Mesoamericans, killing a quetzal was an offense punishable by death, and the bird still remains under legal protection. Unfortunately, the habitat it depends on for survival is quickly falling to the axe. The Biotopo del Quetzal is intended to give the bird a permanent sanctuary. This huge reserve stretches up and over a steep hillside and offers two meticulously cleared trails from which you can observe moss,

158

lichens, bromeliads, and orchids growing in the cool misty forests. Quetzals are extremely elusive birds, but your chances of seeing one are best in the early morning or late afternoon. In the breeding season (February–May) you have a better chance of getting a glimpse of the birds. The park is open daily 6 AM–4 PM. You can camp for free on one of five small, grassy camping plots. Each has an adjoining picnic table and barbecue pit. There's a small swimming area beneath one of the waterfalls near the park entrance. **Hospedaje Los Ranchitos**, right next to the reserve, offers a fun, communal room with a public restroom for $1.80 a bed. They serve comedor-type meals for around $2. The reserve is 4 kilometers (2½ miles) from Purulhá on Carretera del Atlantico (Kilometer 161). Ask the bus driver to drop you at the entrance. From Guatemala City it's about $2.50 for the 3½-hour trip on the Monja Blanca bus service. From Cobán, it's about 45 minutes and costs about 60¢. It's easy to hitch in either direction from the reserve.

GRUTAS DE LANQUIN About 1 kilometer outside the town of Lanquín, the Lanquín river appears above ground, gushing out of huge dark caverns in a spectacular white roar. You can explore the huge caverns on an established trail using iron railings to help keep your footing as you check out huge stalactites and stalagmites. Bring a good flashlight because many trips have come to an unhappy end in the slick caverns. For your safety (and to make their lives easier) the municipio of Lanquín is planning to cover the cave entrance with a gate. To have them open the gate and switch on the lights ($2 per person), ask at the policía nacional in the municipalidad in Lanquín. One of the best times to visit the caves (even if you're not going in) is in the evening, when thousands upon thousands of bats spill out of the caverns. You can camp for free under two large palapas (with barbecue pits) at the site. The caves are just off the main road, 1 kilometer before you reach Lanquín. If you're camping have the bus drop you here; if not you should continue to the nearby town.

The town of Lanquín itself is a small community of Kekchí Indians. The three churches in town reflect the indigenous influence—no pews, and altars covered with candles and sacrifices of flowers, food, and incense. **La Divina Providencia** is your one-shop-stop in Lanquín, packing a hotel, comedor, pharmacy, and tienda all under one roof. Simple rooms with a clean public bath go for about a buck per person. Hearty meals are served in the adjoining comedor for $1 each. The generator in Lanquín starts up at 6 PM and goes off only 3 hours later at 9. Buses to Lanquín (3½ hours, 90¢) leave the main terminal in Cobán at 6 AM, 1 PM, and 3 PM, and return at 6 AM, 8:30 AM, and 3 PM from the main plaza of Lanquín. Come early to get a seat.

SEMUC CHAMPEY Reputed to be the most beautiful spot in Guatemala, Semuc Champey is a must-see. Trickling through the forest, tiny rivulets of water flow down and fill a series of crystal-clear turquoise pools that cascade into one another. But, swim upstream to the edge and the calm is broken by the Río Cahabón which plunges into dark caverns below the pools in a turbulent white fury. Local guides warn, "Don't fall in, it'll take 40 days for the body to come out the other side." Downstream, the waters emerge in an equally forceful rush, plunging on through the valley below. If you can't bear to leave, you'll find a few benches and an area to pitch a tent.

To get here, follow the main road through Lanquín, past the main plaza and municipalidad, and begin winding your way through the hills. Ten steep kilometers (6 miles) and about three hours later you'll reach a bridge across the Río Cahabón. Follow the small footpath to the right and at this junction you'll be charged 40¢. Then, voilà, you made it. A bathing suit is a must.

TACTIC Though only 30 minutes from Cobán by bus, Tactic is another world. The people here are Pokóm, with a dress and language distinct from their Kekchí neighbors. The town is set on a hill, and above it, at the top of a dirt path, is the church of Chi-Ixim. The path bustles with women balancing full baskets of corn on their heads, or men carrying loads of firewood strapped to their backs. Behind the church are the ruins of the fortified city of Chicán, the Pokóm's former hangout. One of the weirdest things that draws visitors to Tactic is **El Pozo Vivo** (The Living Well). The well may look like a big zero—just a small pond off the highway. But look closely, and you'll see the mud at the bottom oozing and bubbling. As you watch, leaves and rocks move, disappear, and reappear. Legend has it that the well only comes to life when it hears people approaching. The guard swears he's snuck up and caught the well unmoving. For added excitement, try this yourself. Be vewy, vewy quiet and then spontaneously shout and, hmmmm, the well starts to move. Buses leave for Tactic (½ hour, 40¢) every ½ hour from the main bus terminal in Cobán. You can camp at the Pozo Vivo for 40¢ per person; the entrance fee is 5¢.

Livingston

Situated at the mouth of the Río Dulce where it enters the Gulf of Honduras, Livingston might as well be a Caribbean island—the only way to get to or from the town is by boat, and the culture is closer to that of Jamaica than the rest of Guatemala. Livingston is home to the Garifuna or Black Caribs, descendants of slaves brought to Central America by the British. If you've been to Belize, you'll notice the cultural similarities. On May 15, a festival celebrating the arrival of the Garifuna on the coast of Guatemala rocks the town. A number of ships reenact the original voyage from Roatán (an island off Honduras) and, after they arrive, the town rejoices with traditional music and dancing. If you're not here at the same time as the festival, settle down under a coconut palm and relax, as reggae, ganja, and the soft lick of waves slow the clock to the *tranquilo* pace that draws visitors to this laid-back community.

"My first Livingston friend who taught me Garifuna was Chente, a man with one leg, a graying beard, medium dreadlocks going blond at their tips, and a laid-back (and mostly toothless) yellow smile."
—I.S.

BASICS Livingston has no banks, but several places will change dollars at a hefty commission. **Almacen Monica** (up the hill from the pier on the left) offers the best rate in town—skimming off 5%. A **GUATEL** office (open daily 7–7) and a **post office** (open weekdays 8–noon and 2–4) are right next to each other, halfway up the hill from the pier on the right.

COMING AND GOING The only way to get to or from Livingston is by boat, which you can take from either Río Dulce (Fronteras) or Puerto Barrios. The cheapest and easiest way is to go from Puerto Barrios. Boats leave Puerto Barrios every morning at 10:30 AM and 5 PM, except on Sunday when the first boat leaves at 10 AM sharp. For a mere 70¢, this 1½-hour trip may be the cheapest boat ride in all of Guatemala. Arrive well in advance to stake a spot on the boat, because sometimes they randomly kick people off. The boats from Livingston to Barrios at 5 AM and 2 PM are equally popular. From Río Dulce, the "mail boat" (which has nothing to do with mail) leaves at 6 AM on Tuesdays and Fridays, returning from Livingston at 9:30 AM. The trip takes three hours and costs $6. On the return trip from Livingston to Río Dulce, the boat makes a stop at the *aguas calientes* (*see* Near Livingston, *below*).

GETTING AROUND Livingston is divided into different barrios, which more or less follow the few streets in this tiny town. As you walk toward town from the pier, the first street to the left is Barrio Marco Sanchez Díaz, where you'll find the most budget hotels. If you continue up the hill on the main street (Calle El Centro), you'll reach the center of town, which is bursting with *almacénes* (department stores), comedores, and restaurantes. Calle El Centro takes a sharp turn to the left before Cafetín Lili, and leads past still more eateries toward African Place. If you keep walking straight past Cafetín Lili you'll end up on the beach.

WHERE TO SLEEP

➤ **UNDER $5 • El Chiringuito.** This isolated spot is paradise. On the quiet shores of the warm Caribbean sea, relax in a private bungalow complete with both a bedroom and a fully furnished lounge. A sparkling toilet and shower await, with filtered water pure enough to drink straight from the tap. The Spanish owner is a friendly fount of information who also whips up some of the best seafood in town. The solitude—the hotel is a 10-minute boat ride from town—is its best and worst aspect, and worth it only if you're going to be in Livingston more than a couple of days. For 1–2 nights it's $2.50 per person per night; for two weeks it's about $1.50. You can pitch a tent under the palapa here for $1 a night, or sling your own hammock absolutely free. *Hire a boat on the pier in Livingston (about $4 for the 10-minute ride) or hike along the beach almost all the way to the Siete Altares, a 40-minute trip including wading across a river. 4 bungalows. Laundry, luggage storage.*

➤ **UNDER $10 • Hotel El Vajero.** This hotel has a few more cucarachas and an ickier public bathroom than the others, but makes up for it with comfortable beds, a really nice staff, and large bright rooms (with fans) all on the water. Doubles are $5.50 with bath. *Barrio Marco Sanchez Díaz, no tel. Turn left on the first road as you walk toward town from the dock; it's the third hotel on the left. Laundry, luggage storage.*

The African Place. Modeled along the lines of a Moorish palace, with tile floors, Islamic archways, grilled windows, and even an Arabian stallion, this spot has doubles with bath for $8. Despite the gaudy decor, the rooms are clean and the public bathrooms have toilet seats. *Barrio El Centro, no tel. Follow the main street up from the pier and keep going as it makes a sharp left before Cafetín Lili. It's the white castle at the end of the street. 16 rooms, 6 with bath. Laundry, luggage storage.*

➤ **UNDER $20 • Hospedaje Alida.** Perched on a hill overlooking the water in a quiet, untouristed part of town, this hospedaje has a cool deck and spotless rooms. A kind, puritanical family keeps the place alcohol-free. Doubles are $16 with bath. Hon-

Creole Cooking Is Great When Tortillas Leave You Flat

Creole cooking on the Caribbean coast is like nothing else in the country. Coconuts, bananas, and mounds of fresh seafood will tantalize even the most tortilla-jaded taste buds. If you play your cards right, you may be able to escape tortillas entirely, as meals often come with small bland rolls called pan de coco (bread made with coconut milk). Creole goodies include:

• Tapado *is a bouillabaisse of vegetables, shrimp, crab, boiled green plátanos, and fish.*

• Rice and beans *(in Creole, "Rays an' Beenz") are not your typical rice and beans. You'll be wowed instead by a mix of red beans and rice cooked in coconut milk with vegetables and spices.*

• Jujuto *(called Hu Hu Tu) is a fish soup cooked with coconut milk. You eat it not with a spoon, but with fried balls of mashed plátanos.*

• Sopa de caracol *is a soup made with conch. It's supposed to be great for lower back muscles, which need to be loose and wiggly for salsa dancing and any other sweaty activities that involve tons of hip action.*

eymoon bungalows go for $20. *Barrio La Capitania, tel. 481–567. Walk through the gate that's past the entrance to the expensive Tucan Dugú (just to the right when you get off the pier). It's down the road on the right.* 6 rooms, 4 with bath; 3 bungalows, all with bath. Laundry, luggage storage.

➤ **CAMPING** • **Biotopo de Manatí** (*see* Near Livingston, *below*) has palapas where you can sling a hammock or pitch a tent for free. The mosquitoes here are vicious, so come prepared. To get here, hire a boat in Livingston and have them leave you at the reserve (it should be less than $7 person with a group). Either arrange to have the driver pick you up at a later date or hook up with a group of day visitors (several boats arrive daily). At **El Chiringuito** (*see* Where to Sleep, *above*) hammocks are free and it's $1 to pitch a tent.

FOOD Livingston is not only one of the best places to get fresh seafood, it's also a bastion of Creole cooking. And, once you get some, you'll be rushing back for more. **Cafeteria Coni** (Barrio San Francisco across from the African Place) is the best place to munch on Creole eats. Try the Jujuto for $4. Be sure to place any requests early (as much as a day in advance), because many of the dishes take hours to prepare. **Cafetín Lili** (El Barrio Barrique, on the main road toward the beach) serves good seafood and vegetarian dishes on a patio overlooking the street. Tapado and other specialties are about $5. If you need to satisfy your sweet tooth, the women on the street sell snacks like *dulce de coco* (a sticky coconut goodie) or *dulce de leche* (a light brown fudge).

AFTER DARK Cool down, mellow out, and let your soul drift to the throbbing beat of reggae and punta that turns Livingston into one big party every weekend. The place to start is **Restaurante/Discoteca Raymundo** (Barrio El Centro, tel. 481–548), just up from the pier on the left. Weekend nights are the best and the entrance fee is only 20¢. At midnight, when the management kicks everyone out, there's a mass pilgrimage to the beach, where a thatched-hut disco keeps going till early morning.

NEAR LIVINGSTON

Livingston is the base from which to see all the sights of the Río Dulce, Guatemala's widest river. To get to all the places listed below, you'll have to rent a boat. A group of eight people should be able to go to the Biotopo, Aguas Calientes, Río Dulce, and the Castillo San Felipe for $6–$7 each.

"A boat pulled onto the beach, and straw-hatted women instantly swarmed around it. The boat was overflowing with mean-looking barracuda. The women, knee-deep in water and haggling in Garifuna, elbowed each other and snatched the best barracuda, tossing them into their colorful shopping bags."—I.S.

LOS SIETE ALTARES Just north of Livingston, these cool falls trickle into a series of tiered aquamarine pools, forming "seven altars" in a brilliant green cathedral of towering rain forest. They're only a 15-minute boat ride from Livingston, but the hour walk is an experience in itself. Head north along the beach, passing the thatched Garifuna huts that line the shore. After ½ hour of walking, you'll get to a small (but deep) river: the Río Keveche. Cross on the sand bar just off-shore. You'll come to a small **Serpentarium** and **Entomology Museum,** where you can check out incarcerated specimens and schedule jungle expeditions—including a boat trip and village visits for about $20. Continue up the beach, and just as it peters out, you'll see a small footpath to the left; pull out your sturdy shoes and begin the hike to the Altares. As you climb over the slippery rocks, each waterfall seems more beautiful than the last. You may think you've reached the top, but keep on trucking, and you'll come to rocks set over a deep pool where you can leap into the water.

BIOTOPO DE MANATI AND AGUAS CALIENTES When the boat turns inland to the río, brace yourself for some spectacular tropical scenery. As the river narrows, the land rises on both sides to form dramatic cliffs covered in jungle. At the base of one of the cliffs, a sulfur spring emerges, the **Aguas Calientes,** creating a warm spot in the water where you can swim. As you continue up the river, the cliffs slowly open into the large Golfete, where flocks of egrets race beside your boat. At the north end is the **Biotopo de Manatí.** The lagoons of the reserve are the hideout for elusive manatees, which are unlikely to make an appearance. To get an idea of what they look like, imagine Roseanne Barr as a mermaid. A small nature center (complete with mounted wildlife) is in the Biotopo, and you can trek along a short trail through the park. You can also camp for free (see Where to Sleep, above).

FRONTERAS ("RIO DULCE") This settlement, often referred to as "Río Dulce," is actually two towns (El Relleno and Fronteras) located on opposite sides of an obnoxious concrete bridge that arches over the Río Dulce. Though little more than an oversized bus stop, this is the last bastion of civilization before the road heads off into the remote reaches of the Petén. Everything you'll need is in Fronteras, on the north side of the bridge. **Hotel Del Río** (just under the bridge) offers okay doubles with bath for $5. Snack at one of the many comedores along the main road.

LAKE IZABAL AND CASTILLO DE SAN FELIPE The largest lake in Guatemala, ringed with forest and green mountains, is now a hideaway for wealthy, mansion-dwelling, yacht-sailing Guatemalans. On the shores of Lake Izabal, the Spanish established the port of Bodegas (now called Mariscos), from where they shipped out all their Guatemalan booty. English pirates, greedy for their own piece of the pie, sailed the Río Dulce to raid the galleons. To protect themselves, the Spanish built Castillo de San Felipe, an awesome stone fortress complete with a moat, drawbridge, dungeons, turrets, and rusty chains and cannons. With your $1 entrance fee, you'll receive a cute cartoon sheet explaining the history of pirates, prisoners, and noblemen. The castle adjoins a park, where you can swim or picnic along with many Guatemalan families. Hire a boat in Fronteras ($3 round trip) for the five-minute ride, or walk 4 kilometers (2½ miles; it takes about an hour) from Fronteras. Just head north along the main road, then follow the signs (the road to the castle is on the left).

Puerto Barrios

Puerto Barrios is the capital and the largest city in the department of Izabal, which means "the place where they make necklaces." Today, more necklaces are worn than made here, along with fishnet stockings, cheap perfume, and the too-red lipstick preferred by the many prostitutes who work this Guatemalan port. The town was founded in the 1880s by president Rufino Barrios (the "Great Reformer"), but it wasn't until 1908, when the United Fruit company used its power over the railroads to bring business here, that Puerto Barrios boomed with commercial activity. The boom is long since over, but the rusting railroad cars, dilapidated warehouses, and paint-chipped wood buildings give this town a run-down, comfy feel. The few blocks of sleaze near the market and bus station give way to simple wood shacks, green lots, and old stilt houses. In this section of town the people are as warm as the tropical air. A simple "buenas noches" will almost unfailingly make even the most hard-faced ship worker smile, and don't be surprised if you get invited into a house or two to enjoy some Creole grub. Other than a quick look around and some shmoozing with the people, though, there's little reason to spend much time in Puerto Barrios. But the nonstop nightlife may make it worth at least one evening before heading off on the morning boat to Livingston or back to Guat City.

BASICS

➤ **MONEY • Banco G & T** (open weekdays 9–8 and Saturday 10–2) is on 7a Calle between 6a and 7a Avenidas.

➤ **EMERGENCIES** • The **national hospital** (tel. 483–071) is outside town on the north side, toward Santo Tomás. The Red Cross (tel. 48–03–15) runs **ambulances,** and the **police** can be reached at 48–03–85.

➤ **PHONES AND MAIL** • **GUATEL** (open daily 7 AM–midnight) is on 8a Avenida 10a Calle near the main church. Look for the cement tower with a cross on top. The **post office and telegrafos** (6a Calle, 6a Av.) are in the center of town. The post office is open weekdays 8–4:30, and the telegraph office is open daily 24 hours.

COMING AND GOING No visitor information office exists, but you can get info on transportation at the pier and the bus station.

➤ **BY BUS** • **Litegua** buses (tel. 481–172) shuttle to and from Guatemala City. You can choose between *corriente* buses (6 hours, $4.50), which leave every hour, or *especial* buses (5 hours, $6), which leave seven times a day. The bus station is on 6a Avenida, between 9a and 10a calles. You can store luggage here for 20¢ per bag.

If you're bound for Petén, you'll have to change to a **Fuentes del Norte** bus at La Ruidosa (50 minutes from Puerto Barrios, 60¢). Don't get confused with another bus company called Fuente del Norte (not Fuentes)—it's centered in Bananera/Morales and runs luxury buses to Esquipulas and Chiquimula. You can catch second-class buses (just outside the Litegua station) bound for Chiquimula (5 hours, $2.75); from there you can transfer to buses to Copán (in Honduras) and Esquipulas (6 hours, $3.50).

➤ **BY BOAT** • The main *muelle* (pier) is at the end of 12a Calle, on the edge of town, where you can catch boats to Livingston. Regular boat service also heads to **Punta Gorda**, in Belize (2½ hours, $5.50). Get tickets from **Agencias Líneas Marítimas** (open weekdays 7–noon and 2–5), near the pier. Boats leave every Tuesday and Friday at 7:30 AM and it's a good idea to buy a ticket at least a day in advance. If you'd like a cheaper option, try asking around at the pier. A large freighter or supply boat may be able to take you along.

GETTING AROUND If you get here by bus, you'll be plunked in the center of town, across from the main market. Follow the blasting music and you'll get to the center of Puerto Barrios' action on 6a–7a Calle and 6a–7a Avenida. Slimy bars, one cool dance club (*see* After Dark, *below*), and a number of 24-hour restaurants fill the area. If you arrive at the pier, walk down 12 Calle (the street leading inland toward town) and turn left when you get to the railroad tracks at 6a Avenida. To get around, even budget travelers may want to consider taking a **taxi** through the less reputable downtown streets and the main shipping area. Taxis hang out by the main market and bus station, and charge about $1–$2 per person to go to the pier, Hotel Del Norte, or the motels.

WHERE TO SLEEP Two types of lodging dominate Puerto Barrios. In the center are the cheapest places where simple, grimy rooms come complete with drunken sailors, painted women, late-night noise, and a rude staff fed up with dealing with the whole thing. Your best option is the moderate hotels that cater to the ships' staff. Most are located between the main pier and the center of town; you'll pass 'em on the way to and from the boat.

Hotel Nineth. Shabby, turquoise cubicles are hardly the *"cuartos higiénicos"* (sanitary rooms) advertised on the sign, but this place is quieter and cheaper than the others nearby, and it's still fairly central (near the bus station). Doubles are about $3. *7a Av. bet. 9a and 10a calles, tel. 0/480–209. Walk from the bus station toward the church, past Hotel Xelaju, and turn right. Go through the grilled gate; the office is on the left. 48 rooms, none with bath.*

Hotel y Restaurante La Caribeña. This hotel has a reception desk, a cafeteria, maids in pink uniforms, and rooms that are quiet and safe—but the atmosphere is sterile and motel-like. Doubles with bath are $7. *4a Av. bet. 10 and 11 calles, tel. 0/480–384.*

Go toward town from the pier and turn left on 4a Av. It's down 2 blocks on the left side. 42 rooms, 33 with bath. Luggage storage.

Hotel Del Norte. If you're gonna splurge, do it here. This hotel has clean rooms (with bed linen changed daily) and an atmosphere to die for. This building once catered to the banana bigwigs in the early 1900s. Its wood porches overlook the best park in town; they're a great place to plant your buns and watch the huge ships as they leave the nearby main dock. Doubles are around $15. 7a Calle 1a Av., tel. 0/480–087. Follow 7a Calle toward the ocean; at the very end you'll see the huge hotel to the right. 37 rooms, 16 with bath. Luggage storage, laundry service.

➤ **ROUGHING IT** • The park near the center of town is grimy and unsafe, but another park right in front of the **Hotel Del Norte** is where young lovers come to make out all night. You can do some smooching yourself or just crash on one of the cement benches overlooking the Caribbean Sea. The covered pavilion in the center is a prime spot to cozy up if it's raining. Follow 7a Avenida to the end and you'll see it.

FOOD By a long shot, the best place in town to chow down on seafood is **Embajada de los Pescadores** (3a Calle, 4a Av., tel. 0/48–03–41). Order their sopa de mariscos ($4) and prepare to get wet as you plunge into the huge bowl of seafood. All around you are the sounds of Guatemalans crunching on shrimp or trying to suck the last piece of meat from a crab leg. From the center of town, walk down 7a Avenida (look for the bank G & T sign) toward the Hotel Del Norte. Turn right at the vacant lot a block before reaching the hotel, and follow the street with wood shacks. You'll see the Embajada on your left in a two-story concrete building. It's open daily 8–8. If you just want a quick bite to eat, head to **Cafetería Amy** (6a Av. 8a–9a Calles, tel. 0/480–982), a cute comedor where you can get a hearty meal for $2. **Filipino Restaurant** (7a Av. bet. 6a and 7a calles) has delicious lumpia (spring rolls).

AFTER DARK Puerto Barrios has a bustling (if somewhat seedy) nightlife, centered around the bars and nightclubs at 6–7 calles and 6–7 avenidas. As well as the houses of ill repute, you'll find two movie theaters, some video arcades, and one of the most happening dance clubs in Guatemala. Here, as in Livingston, the sounds of reggae and punta dominate, but salsa, merengue, and American rock are thrown in to satisfy the more mixed crowd.

Tropical House. Rising out of the teeming bars and pick-up joints is Tropical House, the hottest dance club in Puerto Barrios. Under flashing disco balls, people writhe to the latest tropical hits on the packed dance floor. The club often hosts live bands on weekends. 6a Av. bet. 6a–7a Calles, no tel. Follow the music and the smell of cheap perfume; Tropical House is in the two-story building on the same side of the block as Restaurant Cafesama. Admission: $1–$2. Open Wed.–Sun. from 8:30 PM until whenever.

La Canoa. A slightly older, mostly Garifuna crowd enjoys the sound of punta music in this small but bouncing club with a tiny dance floor. Walking down dark 5a Avenida late at night can be scary, so you may want to take a taxi. 5a Av., 1a–2a Calles, no tel. Follow 5a Av. south toward the water. La Canoa is in a small hut that doubles as a bar/club. Punta dancing Fri.–Sun. 7:30 PM–1 AM.

Quiriguá

Set in the midst of a banana plantation, Quiriguá may not be the largest Mayan site you'll visit, but it's certainly the most bizarre. In the main plaza, huge monoliths (covered with thatched palapas) rise out of a neatly trimmed lawn. Check out the intricate 3-D carvings that grace the largest stelae in the Mesoamerican world—right next to acres upon acres of bananas.

Quiriguá was established in AD 250–300 as a satellite center to Copán (50 kilometers [31 miles] south), and remained under its power until AD 725, when a ruler named Cauc Sky decided he'd had enough. By AD 737, he had captured and beheaded 18 Rabbit, the ruler of Copán, and Cauc Sky began erecting the monoliths as a testament to his own glory. Most still sport his face (though a little worn and nose-chipped). His son, Sky Xul, inherited the throne, but he was soon usurped by Jade Sky, who took Quiriguá to its greatest heights around AD 800. He was responsible for erecting the Central Acropolis. As with the other Classic centers, Quiriguá was mysteriously abandoned around AD 900. Nobody paid much attention to the site until 1840, when John Lloyd Stephens, an American explorer, was so taken with the site that he wanted to dismantle it and ship it home to the U.S. as a souvenir. (He had already bought Copán for $50 in 1834 with the same intention.) Luckily, the asking price for Quiriguá was considerably higher, and the site remained.

In 1909, the United Fruit Company bought the land surrounding Quiriguá to add to its growing empire. The company grew so mighty that it controlled the railroads, commerce, and politics of Guatemala for half a century—company officials even went so far as to organize a coup when President Arbenz began giving some of their unused land back to the Guatemalan people in the early '50s. Today, you can still watch exploitation in action, as workers toil in the humid heat for 12 hours a day at minimal wages. The Guatemalan government began restoration here in 1975, and in 1979 the site was declared a heritage of humanity by UNESCO.

To get to Quiriguá, take any bus that runs between Puerto Barrios and Guatemala City. Buses to Chiquimula and Esquipulas also pass the site. It's about $1.50 for the 3½-hour ride from Puerto Barrios. When you get dropped at the dirt road that leads to the site, you can store your backpack (or other luggage) in the back room at the large tienda on the main highway. From the highway, it's less than an hour's walk, but you can easily catch a ride with a truck heading past the site; give the driver a quetzal. A bus (20¢) also runs this route. Be sure to get the bus to the ruins, not the one to El Progreso, which will only take you halfway and drop you off in the middle of the banana plantation. Camp for free at the two thatched palapas in the parking lot; you may even be able to use the cooking fires at the nearby comedor. Ask the guards if you can use the bathrooms just inside the park entrance. Admission to the site is 20¢, and it's open daily 8–5:30.

Zacapa

Right after you cross the bridge over Guatemala's Río Grande, the first thing you see is the large military base, with the ironic slogan "The National Army, fighting for peace in Guatemala." It's not necessarily any more striking than the other bases around the countryside, but it was here that the government first began the heinous "scorched earth" counterinsurgency tactics that have continued to wreak havoc since the late '60s. General Carlos Arana, who rose to the presidency in 1970, earned the nickname "The Butcher of Zacapa" for the gallons of blood he spilled here. The old Colonel is quoted as saying "If it is necessary to turn this country into a graveyard in order to pacify it, I will not hesitate to do so." Well, he did. On the pretext of eliminating an estimated 300–500 guerrillas, he massacred over 10,000 rural Guatemalans in the provinces of Zacapa and Chiquimula during the late '60s and early '70s. The base still stands, but the bloodshed has long since moved to the Northwestern Highlands, leaving Zacapa to dry in the cactus-dotted plains. Other than their rodeo-like fiesta in the first week of December, the only thing worth visiting in Zacapa is **Los Baños De Santa Maria** (open daily 6–6), a set of natural hot springs in an old wooden building, where you can relax in a tiled tub. To get there, you can either walk the 4 kilometers (2½ miles) north of town (ask directions) or take a taxi for about $4. Admission is 20¢. (Slip the guard a quetzal or two and he'll let you enjoy the baths after hours.)

Esquipulas

CENTRAL AND EASTERN GUATEMALA

The road from Chiquimula twists through pine forests and cliffs, emerging on a high ridge overlooking a wide valley below. As you descend into the town of Esquipulas, you instantly feel the sense of peace and spiritual power that has drawn pilgrims here since pre-Columbian days. Before the conquest, the Maya came here to worship at a shrine that originally came from nearby Copán. The peace this shrine brought to the valley was so strong that the native people chose to surrender to the Spaniards without spilling a single drop of blood. The Spanish called it Esquipulas, which means "place where the flowers abound." Flowers still abound, but now they lie at the feet of a new shrine—**the Black Christ**—that draws the faithful from all over the Americas. In 1595 sculptor Quirio Cataño brought the carved image here from his workshop in Antigua.

He was commissioned to make an image out of dark mahogany wood, which the colonial administrators thought would be more easily accepted than the usual European crucifixes. From the beginning, the image was accorded miraculous powers. But not until 1737, when don Pardo de Figueroa (then bishop of Guatemala) was cured of a chronic illness, did the image emerge as one of the most powerful Christian shrines in the Americas. Figueroa ordered the construction of a huge white basilica, and his body is buried beneath its beautiful silver altar.

"Up close, the Black Christ looks cold and twisted, hung on a round silver crucifix and surrounded by hundreds of flickering candles. The devout kiss the small statues (which sit at the bottom of the Christ) with passion. One woman lovingly grabbed the Black Christ around the waist, as if he were her lost child."—I.S.

Masses in the Basilica of the Black Christ are among the most spectacular in the country. At the end of the weekly 5 PM mass, a small group of monks sing Gregorian chants in the candle glow as the sun sets outside. Masses take place Monday–Saturday at 6:30 AM, 11 AM, and 5 PM, and on Sunday and religious holidays throughout the morning and at 5 PM. The **Church of Santiago Apostól** is where people who actually live in Esquipulas come to worship, and this is the town's true cultural heart. Inside are some interesting statues, particularly the one of Christ entombed (and at the same time carrying the cross above his entombed body) at the back of the church.

From the dozens of ratty pensions to the photographers who sit at the base of the basilica to snap a Polaroid of you, it's obvious that the Black Christ is not only the spiritual but also the economic heart of this community. The **central market** bursts with souvenirs—this is where the bus drivers get those gearshift handles that have an image of Christ encased in plastic. Cotton candy and hot dog stands are scattered among stalls packed with cheap plastic rosary beads, bumper stickers, pennants, and baskets of *pandel señor* (a nasty bread said to have miraculous powers). The best and least expensive selection of medals, crucifixes, rosaries, and postcards is in the Basilica's own store (just to the right of the church) open 8–6 daily. The Black Christ is said to be at its most powerful in the week of January 15. During this time, the town swells with tens of thousands, who crowd the hotels and choke the streets with cars and buses. Even the poorest villages scrape together enough funds to send at least one representative to pray for their well-being.

COMING AND GOING Esquipulas is served by **Rutas Orientales** (Campo de la Feria, tel. 0/431–076). The main office is under the Hotel San Vincente in the main bus terminal; another office is on Doble Vía, to the right of the Basilica. Buses run every half hour to Guatemala City (4 hours, $3.50) from 2 AM to 6 PM. Second-class buses leave regularly for Chiquimula (1 hour, 80¢) throughout the day. **Microbuses** (75¢) also run regularly between Esquipulas and Chiquimula. Microbus is the only way to get to the nearby borders of **Honduras** or **El Salvador**. No timetable exists, but these vans leave regularly starting around 5 AM and continuing until about 6 PM. A trip to Honduras

GUATEMALA

(crossing the border near Agua Caliente) takes a mere 10 minutes, but costs about 80¢. The El Salvadoran border is one hour away, and costs the same.

GETTING AROUND The dominating features of Esquipulas are the two main churches. The basilica sits on one edge of town; it's connected to the Church of Santiago Apóstol (on a hill at the end of town) by Calle Real (also called Calle Principal or 3a Avenida). Right in front of the basilica is a large, two-way street called Doble Vía, which connects the main highway with the dusty bus terminal below the Cine Galaxia.

WHERE TO SLEEP The good news is that there are dozens upon dozens of lodgings in Esquipulas at ridiculously low prices. The bad news is they all suck. Insects crawl through holes in the grimy sheets and straw mattresses, the rooms are small, and dark and unmentionable horrors lurk in the murky waters of the servicios generales. **Hotel Lemus** (Doble Vía, tel. 0/431-156) is just about the best of the cheap, offering semi-clean public restrooms and a sheet you can sleep on for $1 per single, $2 per double ($2 and $4, respectively, with private bath). It's across the street from the basilica toward the main highway. **Hotel San Vincente** (which leads a double life as the Rutas Orientales Bus Terminal) is the super-saver option. Beds are 60¢ each with general bath (nasty!), or $1 a night for a bed in a five- to 10-person room with a slightly less nasty bath. You can expect all these prices to at least double during Semana Santa and the first two weeks of January, when even the innkeeper at the rattiest pensión may have to turn you away like Mary and Joseph. For fancier places where you can rub elbows with rich Guatemalans, try **Hotel Los Angeles** (2a Av. 11-94, Z1, tel. 0/431-254) or **Hotel El Peregrino** (2a Av. 11-70, Z1, tel. 0/431-206), which charge $3.60 per person with baño general, $5 with baño privado. These and other posh hotels are all on the street just to your right as you face the basilica.

FOOD

➤ **UNDER $5** • **Cafeteria La Rotonda.** You can't miss this huge round soda fountain just off the road that comes in from the main highway. Sit on a bar stool and munch on some juicy chicken ($2 with salad and fries) or order a burger ($1-$2) through one of the glass take-out windows. Its location on a dusty lot that doubles as the second bus terminal does nothing to enhance the ambience, but it's very popular with locals and draws a steady stream of people from 9 AM until about 10 PM. *Doble Vía, no tel. On the two-way road running in front of the basilica toward the main highway. Open daily 9 AM–10 PM.*

Comedor Lorena. This comedor is 10 minutes from Esquipulas in a town called Agua Caliente, right across from the Honduran border. Whether or not you're headed for the border, the trip is worth it to enjoy some of the best comedor food ever spread on a tortilla. A huge fish with a hearty green salad, potato salad, beans, rice, tortillas, and FRESH cheese is $3. (Beef is $2.50.) This place is frequented by Honduran and Guatemalan border guards, as well as a fair number of Esquipultecos. *Take a minivan from the main bus terminal (under Cine Galaxia) bound for Honduras. Most drivers know this comedor and will drop you right at the door, just off the main highway. The fare should be between 40¢ and 60¢ (for the 10-minute ride). It's easy to hitch to the Honduran border or back to Esquipulas. Open 6 AM–9 PM daily but lunch or dinner is best.*

➤ **UNDER $10** • **Restaurante Los Arcos.** No matter whom you ask, Los Arcos is always cited as the best restaurant in town. It offers a waterfall, free lemonwater, and cloth napkins in a too-white shopping mall atmosphere. It's fairly popular with wealthier pilgrims, who fork out $3 for a salad, $5 for a filet mignon, and $7 for seviche. The bathrooms here have got to be the cleanest in eastern Guatemala—soap dispenser, electric hand dryer, and all the comforts of home. *Calle Doble Vía, in front of the basilica, tel. 0/431-124. Open daily 9 AM–10 PM.*

FESTIVALS Besides the big festival from **January 1 to 15, March 9** is when the people of Esquipulas celebrate the day Quirio Cantaño brought his blessed sculpture to their city. The 400th anniversary of this date (in 1995) should be an extra-special celebration. The town of Esquipulas has its fiesta July 21–28, celebrating its patron saint, Santiago Apostól. The event is in festive Ladino fashion, with parades, salsa dancing, and crazy contests like relay races where grown men push cars around town with balloons in their mouths and potato sacks on their feet.

OUTDOOR ACTIVITIES For a bird's-eye view of Esquipulas and the surrounding valley, climb to the top of **Cerrito de Morola,** a hill which rises up out of the center of town. To get to the Cerrito, walk from the basilica to the Church of Santiago Apostól. Directly in front of the church, make a left; when the road ends, make a right. Follow the cobblestone street that zigzags up the hill, passing shrines depicting the passion of Jesus. Keep going till you get to the final shrine, the crucifixion, where the cobblestone ends. Up the steep steps to the left is a candle-filled walk-in shrine dedicated to Our Lady of Fatima, and a tremendous view of the valley below.

According to legend, it was in the **Cueva de las Minas** (Cavern of Las Minas) that the Black Christ was originally seen by villagers. What is certain is that villagers mined stones from these caverns to build the inner sanctum of the basilica. The faithful come to leave candles and other offerings. To get here, walk down 2a Avenida behind the basilica (and past the huge and cool-looking graveyard). Go up the side of the mountain, and the path will lead you down to the caves right on the other side.

The **Piedra de los Compadres** (The Stones of the Godparents) has an interesting, if lurid, history. More than two hundred years ago, a group of young people and their godparents began the long pilgrimage to Esquipulas by foot. As the journey continued, they got to know each other better and better, and, just before they reached town, their relationship got just a bit *too* close. In the middle of their sin, they were turned to stone, and here they sit to this day. It's basically just one rock set on top of another but pilgrims come and light candles to ponder those carnal temptations. The rocks are in Aldea Belen, outside town on the road that goes straight past Santiago Apostól.

HONDURAS

By Jeff Tyler

4

Honduras has been overlooked by most travelers to Central America.
Though woefully distinguished as the *original* "banana republic," it has usually been
overshadowed by headline-grabbing violence in neighboring countries. But its unassuming posture is great for visitors. In fact, Honduras is considered one of the safest
spots in Central America by frequent visitors. The beautiful rain forests and beaches
aren't (yet) bursting out of travel brochures, so adventurers have plenty of opportunity
to enjoy the diverse flora and fauna in virtual solitude. Many of Honduras's national
parks are jungly rain and cloud forests; at these high altitudes the air is cool, rain is
abundant, and thick canopies of tropical vegetation shelter monkeys, jaguars, pumas,
quetzals, parrots, and macaws. Day hikes and tranquil boat trips bring exquisite
scenery within easy reach no matter where you are in the country. The absence of
well-worn paths means you have a better chance to see animals and birds that shy
away from hordes of humans. Tourism is still a novelty, and foreigners are generally
welcomed by locals. The flip side of Honduras's lack of beaten tracks is, well, the lack
of beaten tracks. Few things outside big cities are set up for tourists, so dose up on
the patience pills when traveling in less-developed parts of the country.

Hondurans hope that someday their ecotourism industry will boom like Costa Rica's.
Drawing people here to experience the beautiful *naturaleza* depends on it still being
beautiful, and there's a national movement trying to ensure that natural wonders are
developed in a nature-friendly way. The mood is optimistic. One day I was hiking
through La Tigre national park near Tegucigalpa with a young Honduran. My companion surveyed the lush vegetation and the hawks circling in the afternoon sky. "*Este
pais tiene alas, y va a remontarse,*" he said, summing up the general belief held by
most about the tourist industry. "This country has wings, and it's going to fly." Sadly,
short-sighted logging and ranching operations have eaten away many woods at lower
elevations. But little by little, this antiquated school of thought is changing, and virgin
forests are surviving at higher elevations. As tourists visit in greater numbers, locals
are discovering that the forests can be more profitable intact than when broken down
and sold in pieces. The government has taken steps to preserve the natural landscape
by creating over 40 national parks and wildlife reserves.

Land use has always been a source of conflict in Honduras, as natural resources are
the bounty in an otherwise poor country. Jesuit Superior Antonio Ocaña, who has been
working with *campesinos* (rural folk) for over 20 years, summed up the conflict in saying, "Sometimes it's a violent fight. Sometimes it's a legal fight. But it's always at the

171

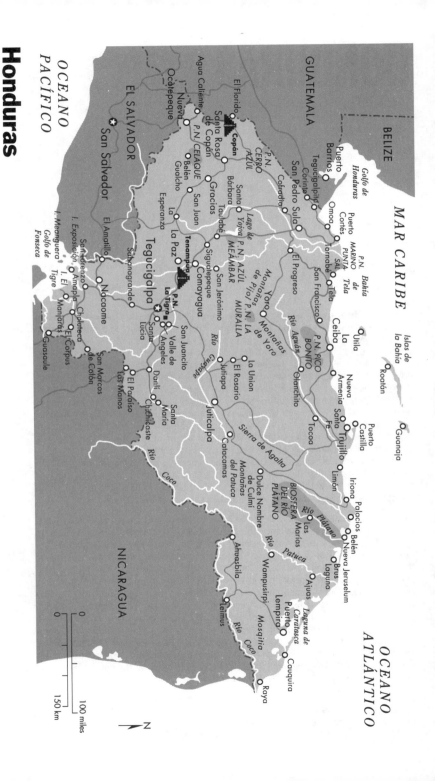

Honduras

OCEANO
PACÍFICO

OCEANO
ATLÁNTICO

MAR CARIBE

GUATEMALA

BELIZE

EL SALVADOR

NICARAGUA

Golfo de
Honduras

Islas de
la Bahía

Puerto
Barrios

San Salvador

Agua Caliente
Nueva
Ocotepeque
El Florido

Teguciqalpita
Corinto

Omoa

Puerto
Cortés

P.N.
MARINO
de
PUNTA
SAL

Tela

Utila

Roatán

Guanaja

El Amatillo

Ocotepeque

Santa Rosa
de Copán

Copán

P.N.
CERRO
AZUL

P.N. CELAQUE

Belén
Gualcho

Gracias

San Juan

La
Esperanza

Santa
Bárbara

Taulabé

San Pedro Sula

Cofradía

San Francisco

Lago de
Yojoa

P.N. AZUL
MEÁMBAR

El Progreso

Siguatepeque

San Jerónimo

Comayagua

Montañas
de Pijol / P.N. LA
MURALLA

Yoro

Montañas
de Yoro

Río Aguán

P.N. PICO
BONITO

La
Ceiba

Santa
Fe

Nueva
Armenia

Trujillo

Tocoa

Puerto
Castilla

Limón

Iriona

Palacios

Belén

Nueva Jerusalem

I. Meanguera
I. Exposición
Amapla
I. El
Tigre
I. El
Monjarás

Golfo de
Fonseca

San Lorenzo

Choluteca

El Corpus

San Marcos
de Colón

Guasaule

Nacaome

Sabanagrande

Tegucigalpa

La Paz

Tenampua

P.N.
La Tigra

Santa
Lucía

Valle de
Ángeles

San Juancito

San
Angeles

El Paraíso

Danlí

Los Manos

Santa
María

Chichicaste

Río Guayape

La Unión

El Rosario

Juticalpa

Catacamas

Juticapa

Olanchito

Santa
Bárbara

Sierra de Agalta

Dulce Nombre
de Culmí

Montañas
del Patuca

BIOSFERA
DEL RÍO
PLÁTANO

Las
Marías

Río Patuca

Río Plátano

Ahuasbila

Wampusirpi

Río
Patuca

Ajuas

Brus
Laguna

Laguna de
Caratasca

Puerto
Lempira

Cauquira

Raya

Leimus

Río Coco

Mosquitia

Río
Coco

Bahía
de
Tela

Brus

Nueva

Santa

Pidiana

N

0   100 miles
0   150 km

expense of the poor." For the most part, Honduras is still an agrarian society where a plot of land equals survival; yet 4% of the country's landowners control 56% of the farmland, and the disparities are increasing. If campesinos lose their land or are unable to make a living in the country, they often head for the city. Unfortunately, few jobs await them. Rapid urbanization has spurred the development of miserable shanty-towns around Tegucigalpa, the capital, and San Pedro Sula, the industrial giant in the north. Tegucigalpa's newspaper, *El Heraldo,* printed the following description: "Every morning breaks differently for the 600,000 residents of Tegucigalpa. About 200,000 live in squalor, in hovels, under bridges, amid garbage, worms, sacks, and cartons, without power or money to alleviate the situation." At the same time, a small but visible minority of Hondurans drive European luxury cars and look like they just spent the day in Manhattan shopping at Saks. The dichotomy between rich and poor is impossible to ignore; however, the disparities of wealth here aren't as severe as in some other Central American countries. The truth is, people are more uniformly *poor* in Honduras than elsewhere.

The despair you may feel about Honduras's in-your-face social problems may be partly assuaged by the country's beauty, sights, and the spirit of the people. Lying in the jungles of western Honduras, the ancient Mayan city of Copán is one of the pinnacles of Mayan achievement. The amazing pyramids, stelae, and other goodies left by this highly advanced civilization are a must-see. The north coast is another inspiring destination, with miles of sandy, palm-fringed beaches and the wonderful Garifuna people, descendents of slaves originally brought to the Caribbean from Africa. Visit their villages, listen to their great music, and eat their amazing food and you may think you've found the true meaning of life. The waters surrounding the Bay Islands off the north coast are a diver's or snorkler's wet dream. The islands have a distinctly Caribbean feel, very different from mainland Honduras. Due to the influence of the British, English is the tongue of the isles. Mountainous central Honduras has a couple of national parks and reserves well worth the effort it takes to reach them, and the southwestern Gulf of Fonseca sports a few cool beach villages among the mangrove swamps. If you look at a relief map, the northeastern part of the country is all green—this is the Mosquitia jungle, bona fide backwater and terra incognita. The area is penetrable only by plane or river transport, so it's expensive and time-consuming to travel here.

Remember the lilting George Bush declaration, "there was no quid pro quo"? He was talking about Honduras. According to "no quid pro quo," the greatly increased U.S. aid to Honduras in the 1980s was not directly exchanged for letting the contras train on Honduran soil. Just because two things were done at the same time doesn't mean anything. It was probably just a "quid pro nada" and then a totally separate "nada pro quo." Don't be so paranoid.

Columbus landed near Trujillo on the north coast in 1502, "discovering" the American mainland. The Classic Mayan civilization at Copán had peaked and declined centuries before. When the Spanish arrived in full force in the 1520s, the Mayans had spread out through the countryside, but other indigenous societies were thriving, especially the Lencas. Resistance to colonization was fierce, and Lencan warrior Chief Lempira united different tribes against the conquistadores. To return the favor, the Spanish invited Lempira to a peace conference and assassinated him when he showed up—thus providing Hondurans with their first national hero and the namesake of their currency. After breaking indigenous resistance, the Spanish established an inland capital in Comayagua and began the usual systematic looting of natural resources. Indígenas who survived the warfare and introduction of foreign diseases were forced to work on Spanish plantations and in gold and silver mines. As the colonial era progressed, other European countries were loathe to allow the conquistadores an unrivaled monopoly on New World wealth. The British settled the Bay Islands and the Mosquitia region along the east coast. From these strategic bases, pirates raided Spanish ships bound for home loaded with loot. Despite repeated attempts, the Spanish couldn't oust the English, who maintained territories in Honduras until 1859.

Decades after Independence (1821), the United States began looking at Honduras as a "backyard" garden to be cultivated. In a drive for economic development, the Honduran government opened the door for U.S. investment—and unwittingly to foreign exploitation revisited. Honduras offered concessions to foreign investors in hopes of bringing capital into the country. Mining operations were subsidized by the government, and huge stretches of fertile farmland were given to banana companies in return for building roads, railways, and other infrastructure. The companies indeed modernized the country with their doings; but at the same time, the roads and trains were for the exclusive use of the companies to ship their goods to their port. Many government officials and the traditional aristocracy were themselves involved in export businesses, motivating them to protect their private interests. Special kickbacks and favors from the companies only sweetened the deals. As resources were thrown toward helping the exporters prosper, little money or energy was left over to develop other regions and sectors of the economy.

As bananas became the premier industry, national politics slowly but surely became subservient to moneyed interests—thus the term "banana republic."

As United Fruit (later called United Brands) and Cuyamel Fruit established strong footholds in the 1910s, each was able to exert political influence to make sure bananas turned a steady and unregulated profit. The two giant corporations often put employees in local government positions; Cuyamel president Sam Zemurray sponsored a 1911 coup to reinstate a buddy of his, ex-president Manuel Bonilla. Once in power, Bonilla repealed an export tax on bananas. Keen, huh? Since the gringo corporations didn't view themselves as foreign guests, but rather as rightful proprietors, U.S. military forces were "rightfully" used a number of times to protect "their" land. In 1935, General Smedley Butler candidly admitted, "I served 33 years as a member of our country's most agile military force, the Marine Corps. During that period, I spent most of my time being a high-class muscle man for Big Business, for Wall Street, and for the bankers. In short, I was a racketeer for capitalism . . . I helped make Honduras 'right' for the fruit companies."

In 1954, banana workers went on strike; with the support of most of their compatriots, they brought 60% of the national economy to a halt. Impressively, strikers gained increased benefits and wages, and formal recognition for labor unions. The banana companies couldn't afford to totally crush the strike and piss everyone in the country off, but they were far from thrilled at having their authority challenged. When, that same year, left-leaning Guatemalan president Arbenz went a step further and began redistributing company-held lands, the CIA reportedly helped stage a coup to try and oust Arbenz. Honduran president Gálvez allowed Honduras to be used as a base from which to mount the attack on Guatemala—so much for a region-wide uprising against the imperialists.

When the U.S.-backed Somoza regime in Nicaragua fell from power in 1979, the gringos again sensed trouble in their backyard. The United States moved quickly to forestall any more popular revolutions in Central America. The *contras,* opponents of the Sandinista regime in Nicaragua, were trained and based primarily on Honduran soil. Overnight, Honduras became an army barracks, as the Reagan Administration flew in men, arms, and millions of dollars in "assistance." U.S. financial backing beefed up the Honduran military; they had always had tremendous influence in the country, but with the newfound finances the armed forces became virtually all-powerful during the 1980s. Their might was used to silence national dissidents, labor leaders, and peasants' organizations; human rights violations soared as the state used bloody intimidation tactics to make civilians stop trying to change the status quo. When the contra war ended, so did the big U.S. checks. The military still holds a great deal of power,

and Hondurans are cautious about criticizing them. Nonetheless, human rights violations have dropped off considerably in the 1990s.

Basics

See Chapter 1 for more information.

VISITOR INFORMATION The tourist bureau, **Instituto Hondureño de Turismo (IHT)**,
provides general and idealized info (unless you come prepared with specific questions). They have offices in the capital, San Pedro Sula, La Ceiba, Roatán, and Copán
Ruinas. Although national parks are steadily becoming more accessible to visitors, IHT
really doesn't help much in this arena. If you're persistent, they can usually find some
info about outdoor activities or at least provide a good reference. From abroad, write to
the office well in advance of your trip (months). The main office is in the capital—
write to Instituto Hondureño de Turismo, Barrio Guanacaste, Box #3261, Tegucigalpa,
Honduras. Or call 22–6618 if your Spanish can cut the mustard.

WHEN TO GO The north coast is hot, humid, and fairly wet year-round. The rainy
season along the coast runs June–January, with heavy rain September–December. The
Mosquitia shares the coastal wet season, but it gets a bonus dry month from around
mid-August to mid-September. The rainy season in the cooler, mountainous interior
lasts from May to November. One of the hottest regions is the coastal plain near the
Gulf of Fonseca on the Pacific; during December and January it's more tolerably hellish. This area adheres to roughly the same rain schedule as the interior.

➤ **HOLIDAYS AND FESTIVALS** • **April 14:** America's Day; **May 1:** Labor Day;
September 15: Independence Day; **October 3:** Soldier Day; **October 12:** Columbus
Day; **October 21:** Armed Forces Day.

Every town has an annual celebration for its own **patron saint.** Festivities usually last a
week, including games, competitions, music, food, and the crowning of the fair's
queen. Any Garifuna village festival is also worth attending (*see* individual towns for
dates, or pick up a schedule at the tourist bureau). Pilgrims from all over the country
converge on the tiny town of **Suyapa,** near Tegucigalpa to celebrate the patron saint
for all of Honduras, the Virgin de Suyapa. Festivities and religious services last for a
week around the saint's day, February 3. **Carnival** (middle and late May) in La Ceiba is
a kick-ass fete, where people parade in costumes and dance to live music in the
streets. May 15 (the day of La Ceiba's patron saint San Isidro) and the following weekend are the highlights.

MAIL Any **correo** (post office) can send a letter internationally. To the United States,
a letter takes 7–14 days; to Europe, 10–15; to Australia, 15–20. Postage costs
20¢–30¢. You may wish to send letters or packages to the United States with **Urgente
Express** (found in most towns); it's not a lot faster, but at least it's registered. The
correo will hold mail for up to six months addressed to "Your name, Lista de Correos,
(town and department), República de Honduras, Centroamerica."

MONEY The unit of currency is the *lempira,* which is generally pretty stable. Notes
come in one, two, five, 10, 20, 50, and 100 lempiras. 100 *centavos* make a lempira,
and centavo coins come in denominations of one, two, five, 10, 20, and 50. The current exchange rate is 5.50 lempira to U.S.$1. Most banks in larger cities will change
major international traveler's checks. U.S. dollars are the most easily convertible currency in Honduras; almost every bank (except in the tiniest towns) will change dollars
even if they don't change traveler's checks. The currencies of neighboring countries
should be changed at the borders, since most banks inside the country won't do it.
Most of the multitudinous **Bancahsa** branches give cash advances for Visa cards. **Cre-
domatico,** with offices in Tegucigalpa, San Pedro Sula, and La Ceiba, gives cash
advances for Visa or MasterCard. Unless otherwise stated, banks are open weekdays
8–11:30 and 1:30–4, Saturday 8–11:30. Bigger cities have a **black market,** which is

technically illegal but unofficially accepted—marketeers are quite conspicuous with their calculators, big wads of dollar bills, and "change money?" mantras. Their rates are usually exactly the same as banks, sometimes better and sometimes worse, and bargaining isn't out of the question.

PHONES All but the dinkiest towns have a **Hondutel** office, where you can make intracountry and international calls. A local call at a pay phone costs 10 centavos for three minutes. Call 123 to reach an **AT&T USA Direct** operator to make collect or credit-card calls to the United States (accessible from most phones in the country).

VISAS To enter Honduras, everyone needs a passport and a round-trip airline ticket. Nationals of the United Kingdom don't need visas. Citizens of the United States, Canada, Australia, and New Zealand do; visas can be obtained abroad, at the airport when you arrive, and sporadically at border customs stations when entering the country by land. Visas are good for 30 days and can be extended monthly for up to six months at the *migración* (migration) offices in Tegucigalpa, La Ceiba, San Pedro Sula, Santa Rosa de Copán, Siguatepeque, La Paz, and Comayagua. After six months, you must leave the country for three days before you can enter and start the process again.

In the United States, visas cost $10, available from the Honduran Embassy (Suite 957, 1511 K St. NW, Washington, D.C., 20005, tel. 202/1638–4348) and consulates. The Honduran embassies in Britain (115 Gloucester Pl., London, WIH 3PJ, tel. 071/486–4880) and Canada (151 Slater St., Suite 3–A, Ottowa, Ontario, KIP 5H3, tel. 613/233–8900) also issue visas. You can also get visas at Honduran embassies in other Central American capitals.

COMING AND GOING

➤ **BY BUS** • No buses run directly into Honduras from neighboring countries; you must always get off at a border station, walk across, and pick up a connecting bus on the other side. The same goes for exiting the country en route to Nicaragua, El Salvador, or Guatemala ($2 exit tax). Border hours are usually 8–noon and 2–5, and connecting buses generally leave frequently. You can pass through either El Florido or Agua Caliente to reach Guatemala; El Poy or El Amatillo for El Salvador; and El Espino or Las Manos for Nicaragua.

➤ **BY PLANE** • Tegucigalpa and San Pedro Sula both have international airports; Taca, American, Continental, and Tan-Sahsa (the national airline) serve both airports. Iberia, Spain's national airline, flies into San Pedro only. Direct flights connect Honduras with Los Angeles, San Francisco, Miami, New York, New Orleans, México, Madrid, and other Central American capitals. From Britain or Australia/New Zealand, you have to transfer in Spain or in the States. When flying out of Honduras you have to fork over $10 for the departure tax.

➤ **BY BOAT** • Cargo and fishing boats run between the United States, other Central American countries, and Honduras. If you have the time, you can hitch a ride for a fraction of the cost of a plane ticket. Since these aren't official passenger ships, you'll probably sleep on deck or on the floor. Check around local docks to find out who's going where and when.

GETTING AROUND

➤ **BY BUS** • Buses are the primary mode of transportation in Honduras, and they go almost everywhere. They're very cheap (around $1 for every hour of the journey), although expect to pay more for buses to remote destinations. Buses are amazingly efficient, considering that half of them are secondhand U.S. school buses. They often come with free entertainment in the form of itinerant salesmen hawking miracle concoctions that cure death and impotence. If you need to stop midway and are unfamiliar with the area, ask the conductor to tell you when to get off. Unless they're absolutely packed with people buses will pick you up along the roadside if you wave them down.

➤ **BY TRAIN** • Train service exists only between San Pedro Sula, Puerto Cortés, and Tela on the north coast. The trains are antique, take at least an hour longer than buses, but cost a little less.

➤ **BY PLANE** • Domestic flights with the national airline, Tan-Sahsa, are cheap by international standards. Here are some examples of routes and one-way fares: Tegus–San Pedro Sula ($19), Tegus–La Ceiba ($23), Tegus–Roatán ($31), San Pedro Sula–Roatán ($21).

➤ **BY BIKE** • Many Hondurans bike around town. Their cycles are usually old and broken down, so there are lots of shops for basic repairs. Mountain bikes are becoming more common these days, but if you have a super-fancy bike, consider bringing spare parts from home. Honduras is loaded with mountains, so be in good shape if you hope to peddle everywhere. Motorists don't expect to see bikers outside towns, so wear conspicuous clothing and do the lights-and-reflectors thing religiously.

➤ **BY CAR** • Upon entering the country you have to buy a driving permit, which needs to be renewed regularly. Driving a hefty 4x4 is best, especially if you hope to get to remote parks and reserves—muddy roads entrap lesser cars, and many of the country's mountains would laugh heartily at a VW bus. Main highways are all paved and painless, and the Interamerican Highway runs through the southwest near the Gulf of Fonseca. You can rent cars at the airports or elsewhere in Tegus, San Pedro Sula, and La Ceiba. In the cities, park your car in a hotel garage to keep it away from thieves.

➤ **HITCHING** • Hitching is easy in Honduras; in remote parts, where buses are infrequent, thumbing is a way of life. Truckers are the most likely folks to pick you up, and most of your rides will be bumpy ones in the back of pickups. Some drivers exhibit an entrepreneurial spirit, using their trucks as taxis, and you'll be expected to pay.

WHERE TO SLEEP All but the tiniest villages have accommodations of some sort. Aside from the occasional cockroach, rooms in budget hotels are usually quite clean, often sharing a communal bath. Basic rooms run $2–$4 per person. If there isn't a hotel in town, you can probably find a *hospedaje,* low-key and less official establishments. In very remote spots, like parts of the Mosquitia, priests, teachers, and local cantina owners will often help you find a place to sleep. If you're determined not to stay in hotels, bring a tent and sleeping bag, and get as far away from the general population as possible. Beaches are usually a safe place to crash. It's a very poor country, and people assume that all gringos have money, so take care when roughing it.

FOOD Cheap plates are about $1.50, nice meals about $4. *Comedores* have the cheapest sit-down meals. A *plato típico,* usually the cheapest thing on the menu, includes some combination of rice, beans, eggs, meat, tortillas, and cheese. *Baleadas* (tortillas with beans and cheese) are very cheap, as are *nacatamales* (corn, meat, and sauce wrapped in banana leaves). Vegetarians can order baleadas or a plato típico without meat. Seafood along the coast is cheap and wonderful—conch soup with coconut milk shouldn't be missed, and *pan de coco* (coconut bread), a specialty of the Garifuna, is divine. Chinese restaurants are everywhere, and most towns have a market selling seasonal fruits. Street-vended food is usually delicious and filling, but sometimes the food can be somewhat less than fresh. Don't be paranoid, but do trust your judgment.

Most Hondurans are as concerned as you about cholera and purify their water in some way. Still, never feel shy about asking if the ice in your Coke was made with *agua purificado.* Soft drinks (*refrescos* or *frescos*) are available everywhere. The four national beers are all cheap and taste pretty decent. *Licuados* are fruit juices mixed with water, and *batidos* are fruit drinks made with milk. Both are delicious, but the latter is safer unless the milk is unpasteurized. Good orange juice (*jugo de naranja*) is sold in small milk cartons, available everywhere.

➤ **TIPPING** • Nobody tips in restaurants; who knows which came first, the prevalent bad service or people not tipping. If a tip is expected (in some swanky places it is), it's often calculated into your bill.

OUTDOOR ACTIVITIES Honduras's natural beauty rivals Costa Rica's. Day-trippers can find several parks with easy hikes, and the super-zealous can cut trails into the unknown with a machete. Honduras is heaven for the intrepid traveler who doesn't mind the sweat and patience required to reach the virgin heart of a pristine cloud forest. All hikers should beware of poisonous snakes and jaguars; though seldom seen, they are dangerous when threatened. Be prepared to get wet, since it rains in cloud forests and rain forests throughout the year (gee, that's logical!). Honduras also has lots of great caves, many of which haven't been fully explored. Bring lights and mountain-climbing equipment, since most caves descend deep into the earth. Scuba-diving and snorkeling are so bitchin' here that many people come to Honduras just for these sports. From the Bay Islands, divers can reach an extension of Belize's barrier reef (the second largest in the world). Establishments on the islands are equipped to handle both expert and novice divers; dives cost around $35 dollars, and one-day courses for virgins $50–$100.

Tegucigalpa

Tegucigalpa gets mixed reviews from travelers and Hondurans alike. You could rag on its funkiness all day long: It's smoggy, it's crowded, and, as capital cities go, there's not a whole lot to do. On the flip side, a visit to Honduras may seem incomplete without visiting Distrito Central, the hub of political life for the vast and sparsely populated country. The city of one million people sits in a high-altitude (3,000-foot) valley, surrounded by beautiful pine-forested mountain ranges. If you're looking in the right direction, and a smog-belching bus hasn't just passed by, you might even take a deep breath and exclaim, "Aaah, nice city!"

The name Tegucigalpa is the compound of two words from the language of the area's indigenous people. *Teguz* (hill) and *galpa* (silver) refer to the prosperous mining industry that began soon after colonization in the mountains around the city. As the wealth increased, so did the city's size and importance, and eventually it grew down from the hills and across the Río Choluteca. It became the country's capital in 1880; the same year, the Gran Hotel Central opened as Tegucigalpa's first public lodging. It had hammocks for the travelers and on the patio was a sign reflecting the contemporary style of life: DON'T LAY ON THE HAMMOCKS WITH YOUR SPURS ON!

Never intended as the country's seat of authority, the city retains many characteristics of a small town, with narrow, winding streets and brightly colored houses built into the hillsides. The lack of city planning would be okay if it *was* still a small town, but the population is steadily growing as landless peasants relocate here from rural areas. The result is a slum of shanties—the so-called "misery belt"—notorious for its vile sanitary conditions, lack of water, electricity, and other supposed conveniences of city living. The huge population has created a need for modern public transportation, which hasn't yet materialized. The traffic situation is nightmarish: No city buses have mufflers and car horns are always honking, creating an incessant din. If you didn't bring a handkerchief, invest in one here: They're ideal for filtering out the crap from passing traffic. Whenever possible, take side streets; it's not only a chance to see the underbelly of the city, but also to get away from major bus routes.

Many people visit "Tegus" (TAY-goose), as it's called locally, purely for practical purposes. They come to get government documents or obtain visas at the embassies. The Peace Corps, along with many other international agencies, has their main offices here. Foreign travelers fly into the capital and then leave quickly for more beautiful parts of the country, while others return to Tegus from the remote wilderness to pamper themselves with real beds, hot water, and a pepperoni pizza.

Tegucigalpa

Exploring

Iglesia San Francisco, **12**

Iglesia Los Dolores, **4**

Museo Nacional, **1**

National Theater (Teatro Nacional), **6**

Parque La Merced and Antiguo Paranito Universitaria, **10**

Parroquia de la Inmaculada Concepción, **8**

Plaza Morazán (Parque Central), **11**

Lodging

Cafe Allegro, **16**

Hotel Goascorán, **5**

Hotel Granada, **14**

Hotel Granada Anexo, **13**

Hotel Imperial, **3**

Hotel MacArthur, **2**

Hotel Ritz, **7**

Hotel San Pedro, **9**

Hotel Tegucigalpa, **15**

BASICS

AMERICAN EXPRESS The local representatives are housed at **Mundirama Travel Service**. They cash and sell traveler's checks, and for cardholders will cash personal checks, sell insurance, and hold mail for up to four months. *Col. Palmira, Edificio CIICSA, Av. Rep. de Panamá at Av. Rep. de Chile, tel. 32–3943. Open weekdays 8–noon and 1–5, Sat. 8–noon.*

MONEY U.S. dollars and traveler's checks are the easiest, and sometimes the only, exchangeable currency. Most banks exchange money; try **Banco de Honduras** (Edificio Soto, right near Parque Central, tel. 22–1152). Most banks in the capital are open weekdays 9–3, but **Bancahsa** (Av. Cristobal Colón at Calle Los Dolores, tel. 22–9296) is also open Saturdays 9–11. Visa cash advances are available sporadically at different banks, but are always given at **Credomatic** on Boulevard Morazán. The **black market** thrives in Tegus, and marketeers will often take traveler's checks. As one tourist official told me, "We don't need late-night banks, because the people are always open." It's a slight overstatement: Though money changers proliferate on Calle Peatonal and in front of the Plaza Hotel, they often close up "shop" on weekends.

CONSULATES **Belize.** *Calle Diapa, tel. 32–0001. Open weekdays 8–3.*

Canada. *Edificio El Castaño, Blvd. Morazán, tel. 31–4538. Open weekdays 8:30–12:30.*

Costa Rica. *Col. Palmira, 1a Calle 704, tel. 32–1054. Open weekdays 8–noon.*

El Salvador. *Col. San Carlos 219, tel. 32–1344. Open weekdays 8:30–noon.*

Guatemala. *Col. Tepeyac, tel. 31–1543. Open weekdays 9–2.*

Nicaragua. *Colonia Lomas del Tepeyac, tel. 32–9025. Open weekdays 8–noon.*

Panama. *Col. Palmira, Edificio Palmira, tel. 31–5441. Open weekdays 8–1.*

United Kingdom. *Col. Palmira, Edificio Palmira, across from Hotel Honduras Maya, tel. 32–5429. Open weekdays 9–noon and 1–4.*

United States. *Av. La Paz., tel. 32–3120. Open weekdays 8–5.*

EMERGENCIES Red Cross for **ambulance** (tel. 37–8654); **police** (tel. 199); **female police** (yes, there's a difference, tel. 37–2184); **fire** (tel. 198).

IMMIGRATION Come to this *migracíon* office to extend your visa. *Barrio La Ronda, next to Hotel La Ronda, tel. 22–7711. Open weekdays 8:30–noon and 1–4:30.*

LAUNDRY Laundromats are scarce and often go out of business. Luckily, owners or maids in almost any hotel will *lava ropa* (wash clothes) for a few lempira. Another option is **Super Jet** dry cleaning—they'll get the funk out and give you clean clothes within a day, possibly within the hour (55¢ for about two pounds). *Av. Gutemburg 1724, across from Hotel Tegucigalpa, tel. 37–4154. Open weekdays 8–6, Sat. 8–noon.*

MEDICAL AID **Hospital y Clínica Viera** (Barrio La Ronda, Calle Dionisio Gutierrez, tel. 37–3156) accepts walk-ins around the clock and has a few English-speaking doctors. If you want to know exactly which parasites have taken up residence in your body, get your blood analyzed at one of the safe, clean clinics around the corner on Calle Finlay, off Avenida Gutemburg. Pharmacies are everywhere, and **Farmacia Rosna** (½ block from Parque Central on Calle Peatonal, tel. 37–0605, open 9 AM–7 PM) has some English-speakers on staff. No pharmacies stay open 24 hours, but the tourist office has a list of those closing as late as 10 PM.

PHONES AND MAIL **Hondutel** (402 Av. Cristobal Colón) is open 24 hours to send telegrams, faxes, and make international calls. The **post office** (open weekdays 7:30 AM–9 PM, Saturday 7:30–3) is nearby on Avenida Barahona at Calle El Telégrafo.

TRAVEL AGENCIES Different agencies have specialty fares for particular destinations, so check around. Mundirama (*see* American Express info, *above*) has a good reputation, and **Trek de Honduras** (Edificio Midence, across from Parque Central, tel. 37–0623) is unique in organizing adventure trips. Trek's treks make remote regions of Honduras more accessible, but, like most organized tours, they certainly aren't cheap.

VISITOR INFORMATION The tourist offices in town have friendly, eager staff without the resources to do a lot of good. For example, the office doesn't stock an up-to-date map of the city. **Instituto Hondureño de Turismo** is in Barrio Guanacaste on Avenida Gutemburg (tel. 22–2124). There's also a tourist kiosk in Parque Central. Both offices are open weekdays 8:30–4:30. Look in hotel lobbies for *Tegucigalpa This Week*, which gives tips (in English) about goings-on around the capital. If you're planning back-roads hiking or mountain-climbing anywhere in the country, visit the **Instituto Geográfico Nacional** (Barrio La Bolsa, across the southeastern bridge from Comayagüela). Spend some time checking out their huge array of nifty topographical maps, ranging from the cute and touristy to 50,000 scale. Allow time if you want to buy a map, because for some odd reason you have to go to a separate office building, pretty damn far away, to pay for it.

COMING AND GOING

BY BUS No single bus station connects the capital with the rest of the country; different destinations are served by individual stations. Unless otherwise noted, all the stations listed below are in Comayagüela.

➤ **TO/FROM THE NORTH** • **El Rey** (Av. 6a at Calle 9a, tel. 37–6609) has buses to San Pedro Sula (4½ hours, $3), stopping in Comayagua and Siguatepeque on the way. Buses leave once an hour 2:30 AM–7 PM. **Norteños** (Av. 7a, between Calles 12a and 13a, tel. 37–0706) does the same route hourly 4 AM–4 PM, taking up roughly the same amount of your dough and time. **Traliasa** (Calle 12a, between Avs. 8a and 9a, tel. 37–7538) leaves at 6 AM for Tela (5½ hours, $6) and La Ceiba (7½ hours, $6.50). **Sultana** (Av. 8a and Calle 12a, tel. 37–8101) goes to Santa Rosa de Copán and La Entrada (near Copán) once daily at 3:15 AM (8 hours, $4).

➤ **TO/FROM THE EAST** • **Aurora** (Calle 8a between Avs. 6a and 7a, tel. 37–3647) leaves for Juticalpa (3 hours, $2) and other locales in the eastern-mountain department of Olancho every hour 4:30 AM–5 PM. **Discua Litena** (Col. John F. Kennedy, Tegucigalpa, tel. 32–7939) runs to Danlí (2 hours, $2), and from there a minibus goes to El Paraíso and the Nicaraguan border.

➤ **TO/FROM THE SOUTH** • **Mi Esperanza** (Calle 24a and Av. 6a, tel. 38–2863) goes to Choluteca (3 hours, $2) hourly, 4 AM–6:30 PM. This station also has buses to San Marcos de Colón (5 hours, $3) six times daily, 4 AM–4 PM; from San Marcos it's a quick taxi or minibus ride to the Nicaraguan border at El Espino. A number of bus companies go to Nacaome near the Gulf of Fonseca and on to El Amatillo at the Salvadoran border (2½ hours, $2); they leave frequently from near the Mercado Zonal Belén in Comayagüela, 6 AM–4:30 PM.

HITCHING Locals don't thumb many rides, but patient and nonscraggly-looking foreigners will probably find success, especially with truckers. Hitching karma will be with you if you head for the outskirts of town. Take the Río Grande bus and get off at the Texaco station just before the airport to find drivers fueling their tanks for the journey south. The Miraflores bus line runs a little beyond the city on the road to Danlí, where you can get off and start a-thumbin'. To go north, catch a city bus headed east on Calle 9a in Comayagüela and get off at any place that takes your fancy.

BY PLANE Seven kilometers (4 miles) outside Tegucigalpa, **Toncontín International Airport** has been nicknamed the "Stop and Drop," referring to the steep descents made onto a short runway. Change money at the bank (open 8–4), and make international or domestic calls at Hondutel (6–6). The tourist office is supposed to be open 6–6, but may be closed for reasons unknown. The airport closes at dusk. Airlines have ticket agencies at the airport, and some also have them in town. **American Airlines** (Edificio Palmira, across from Hotel Honduras Maya, tel. 32–1347) and **Continental** (Toncontín airport, tel. 33–7676) both have direct flights to the States. **TACA** (Edificio Interamericana, Blvd. Morazán, tel. 31–2469) flies throughout Latin America. **Tan-Sahsa** (Toncontín airport, tel. 33–3333 or 33–1134) flies internationally as well as to San Pedro Sula for $13, La Cieba for $17, and Roatán for $29 (one-way prices).

➢ **AIRPORT TRANSPORT** • Many taxi drivers who hang around the airport are typical shysters who take advantage of fresh-off-the-plane travelers: Don't pay more than $3 per person for a ride to town. If you get tired of haggling, walk down to the street and catch one there, because prices drop dramatically. Better still, take the Las Lomas bus in front of the airport to the town center for 5¢. To return to the airport from downtown, take the Río Grande bus from Avenida Gutemburg.

GETTING AROUND

Most things of interest to the traveler are either near the city center or outside the city limits. Tegucigalpa is a hilly maze of different neighborhoods that most foreigners will never visit; *barrios* are usually older and more centrally located neighborhoods than *colonias*. Barrio El Centro has the Parque Central (Plaza Morazán) and other things of interest to the traveler. As long as you know which barrio or colonia you're in, getting where you need to go is pretty easy. Few maps sold in town have details like street names. Familiarize yourself instead with the city's landmarks: Hotel Honduras Maya, Parque Central, the Río Choluteca bridge, and Mercado San Isidro across the bridge in Tegus' sister city of **Comayagüela**. Locals will refer to these landmarks when giving directions.

As one salesman explained, "It would be useless to put names on the maps, since we change the names of streets every two weeks."

BY BUS Tegus has myriad bus routes that can take you to the edges of the city and back for 5¢ each way. Some bus stops are marked by signposts, but the most reliable indicator is a bunch of people standing by the curb looking expectant. Buses start running at 5 AM and stop around 9 PM. Lines and routes are too numerous to list here, so get a bus schedule from the tourist office in Parque Central. Locals use buses like North Americans use cars, so they're quite knowledgeable about the system; most are willing to hold your hand and show you which bus to get on. From Parque Central you'll find a city bus going almost anywhere in the city.

BY TAXI After 9 PM, taxis are basically the only transport option. Day and night, taxis ask if you want a ride by honking. If you take them up on it, discuss the price immediately. All prices should fall in the $1–$2 range. If the driver seems unimpressed by your spunky declarations about how much you'll pay, ask to be let out at the corner—it usually closes the deal. Certain taxis are *colectivos,* where five people going in the same general direction share a ride. It's a good compromise between the expense of a normal taxi and the inconvenience of a bus. Look for lines of people in the side streets around Parque Central, or yell out your destination when a half-full taxi honks at you.

BY CAR Driving in Tegus is no fun. Parking is generally a bitch, traffic snarls are frequent, and many streets are one-way and have no street signs. If you already have a car, the Hotel Granada Anexo and Hotel MacArthur both have parking garages, where you can park safely while you explore the city on foot or by bus. Rental cars are not cheap (at least $40 per day), but they make day excursions easy. If you have a large group and want to go off the beaten track, they can actually be money-savers. A number of agencies base themselves at the airport, and some have offices at the Hotel Honduras Maya.

WHERE TO SLEEP

The best budget accommodations are within a block or two of Parque Central. The area is bustling with businesspeople and school kids during the day, and in the evening the whole town stops by to hang out and chat. It's usually quite safe, though women alone at night should, as always, be super-cautious. Convenience is the area's big plus: Most notable sights are within walking distance and you can catch a bus to almost anywhere from the Parque. Staying in Comayagüela is a suitable option if you arrive late or need to leave early from one of the bus stations. Also, Comayagüela has lots of working-class neighborhoods where you can get a feel for how residents of the city live. Otherwise, except for the market, Comayagüela holds little attraction. Though relatively safe by day, even Hondurans consider the area dangerous at night.

The real authorities on budget hotels are the underpaid Peace Corps volunteers, who have a *serious* lodging-info grapevine. Their office is up the hill past the Hotel Honduras Maya on Avenida República de Chile. Remember, they aren't a tourist office; to meet some volunteers, hang around in one of the neighborhood bars or restaurants, particularly the Hungry Fisherman. When asking Tegucigalpans for directions to a hotel, telling them the street address won't get you what you need; refer to landmarks and ask for the name of your hotel. To find out about **camping** options, *see* Near Tegucigalpa, *below.*

TEGUCIGALPA

➤ **UNDER $5** • **Cafe Allegro.** Half a block up from the Peace Corps office, the Allegro is full of volunteers and backpackers. It's got a large TV with cable, a private bar, and a piano. The owner Jorge speaks five languages and writes about Honduras for some of our rival guidebooks; nonetheless, he's a great info source. Each communal room has a fan and two bunkbeds. It's overpriced for dorms ($5 per bed), but it looks new, well cared for, and has an excellent restaurant. *Av. Rep. de Chile 360, tel. 32–8122. Walk west on Av. Cervantes from Parque Central, continuing up the hill where the road becomes Rep. de Chile. It's on the left just after stoplight at top of the hill. 20 beds, none with bath. Luggage storage, laundry.*

Hotel Imperial. If dirt cheap is what you want, cheap dirt is what you get at this hotel behind Los Dolores church. The beds here sag and the showers may not work during the day. Rooms with private showers are better maintained. The restaurant serves decent meals all day. Doubles are $3, $5 with private bath. *Barrio Dolores, Calle Buenos Aires, tel. 22–1973. From pedestrian street Calle Peatonal, walk north on Calle Los Dolores past the church, turn left on the first street. 15 rooms, some with bath. Wheelchair access. Luggage storage.*

Hotelito Goascorán. On the left when you're facing Iglesia Los Dolores, this new hotelito isn't spotless but it's tolerable. Though all rooms are doubles, haggle with the friendly owner for a single's price if you're solo. Doubles are $4, with bath $5. *Peatonal Los Dolores 617. Same directions as the Imperial but go to the left of Iglesia Los Dolores. 10 rooms, some with bath. Wheelchair access. Luggage storage.*

Hotel Tegucigalpa. Rooms here vary from cramped prison cells without window panes, blighted by the noisy street below, to larger rooms on the basement floor where you're lulled to sleep by the peaceful sound of the river. Be prepared for the dinge factor: Halls are dimly lit, and the communal showers need a good dose of Ajax. But the neighborhood is good, with the tourist office right up the block and lots of restaurants and cinemas close by. It's $3 for basic doubles, $5 with bath. *Barrio Guanacaste, Av. Gutemburg 1645, tel. 37–3847. Take Lomas bus from airport, or walk 10 minutes northeast from Parque Central. 26 rooms, some with bath. Wheelchair access. Luggage storage.*

➤ **UNDER $11** • **Hotel Granada.** This centrally located hotel is one of the most popular with budget-minded backpackers and Peace Corps volunteers alike. The beds are firm, and the communal showers are squeaky clean. It's just down the street from

Hotel Tegucigalpa, and right near the heart of the town center. The laid-back manager suggests that groups make reservations. Doubles are $5, $8 with bath. *Barrio Buenacaste, Av. Gutemburg 1401, tel. 37–2681. Same directions as Hotel Tegucigalpa. 46 rooms, some with bath. Luggage storage, laundry.*

Hotel Granada Anexo. As the name *Anexo* (annex) may suggest, the first Granada did so well that the owner opted for a sequel. Well-dressed foreign professors and businesspeople stay here. Just up the hill and around the corner from its predecessor, the annex maintains the same standard of quality, including good mattresses and high marks for overall cleanliness. The added attraction of the annex is that all rooms have showers and telephones, and the lobby has a big TV with cable. Singles are $6, a double is $10, and triples are a bargain at $12. *Calle Subida Casa Marta, off Av. Gutemburg, tel. 37–7079. Same directions as Granada senior but 1 block west. 48 rooms, all with bath. Luggage storage, laundry.*

➢ **OVER $10** • **Hotel MacArthur.** Hotel MacArthur's not cheap, but it's worth it. Quality screams at you from the lobby, to the bed, to the bathroom. It's the only yelling you'll hear because they've posted a sign telling people to please stay quiet. The manager is a friendly and very helpful gent, and the location, ½ block from the police station, couldn't be safer. It's the place to come for a comfy, peaceful splurge ($21 for a standard double, $24 with air-conditioning, $3 more for TV with cable). *Barrio Abajo, Av. Lempira 454, tel. 37–9839. Behind Iglesia Los Dolores, walk a block down Calle Buenos Aires, turn left on Av. Lempira. 45 rooms, all with bath. Luggage storage, laundry, safe deposit boxes, parking.*

COMAYAGUELA **Hotel Ritz.** A block away from the Mercado San Isidro, the Ritz is a good spot to meet travelers from other Central American countries. Each room is distinctly decorated, ranging from gaudy to conservative. The communal bathrooms are clean, but watch out for the infamous electric water heater in the shower that can give you a bigger jolt in the morning than your first cup of joe. The terrace café on the roof serves all meals and has a terrific view of downtown Tegus and the hillside shanties. Basic doubles are $6, $8 with bath and air-conditioning. *Calle 4, between Avs. 5a and 4a, tel. 22–2769. Walk south from the market or north from bus terminals. 23 rooms, some with bath. Luggage storage, laundry by maid.*

Hotel San Pedro. Hotel San Pedro is a huge complex conveniently located next to the bus station for San Pedro Sula and a block from the Juticalpa station. The rooms are minimalistic—a bed, a nightstand, and a light bulb. It seems there are more maids than clients, but they still need to hire more help to tame the mildew in the communal shower. The hotel's in one of the better parts of Comayagüela, but still be cautious at night. A simple café serves all meals. Doubles are $4, $7 with bath. *816 Av. 6, between calles 8 and 9, tel. 22–8987. Buses 7, 8, and 35 connect the hotel with Parque Central. 74 rooms, some with bath. Luggage storage, laundry.*

ROUGHING IT On Carretera Tapias, near the stadium, the **Parque Club de Leones** is a designated campground during big sporting events and normally functions as a parking lot and a market on Saturdays. You can probably sleep unobtrusively in a corner here and not be bothered; if questioned, say you thought it was a campground. In a pinch, you might crash above the stadium in the woods around Parque a la Paz. Let one eye sleep while the other keeps watch for both police and thieves. The couple of bucks you'll save by not staying in a hotel probably isn't worth the anxiety.

FOOD

U.S. fast-food has a strong foothold in the Honduran capital. The popular Pizza Hut near Parque Central has a salad bar stocked with very fresh produce AND CLEAN LETTUCE YOU CAN EAT! Apparently, the set-up is notable even by international standards: One ex-Peace Corps volunteer actually dreamed of the salad bar when he was stateside! Fast-food joints are cool for what they are, but the cheapest and most traditional meals are found in small hole-in-the-wall establishments. Lots of good ones are downtown, near the Parque Central. The restaurants listed below are well respected and clean, though even cheaper meals are available, especially if you pick something up in one of the many sidewalk food stalls. In the northeast end of town, along Boulevard Morazán, you can find cuisines ranging from Japanese to Argentinean to French. As you can probably tell just by looking, quality and prices ascend as you move east along Morazán.

NEAR PARQUE CENTRAL **Al Natural.** Set in a courtyard shaded by exotic trees, this patio restaurant offers welcome relief from the hot sun. It's relaxing if you don't mind the shrieks of caged tropical birds crying for freedom. In addition to ambience and many typical Honduran plates, they offer some vegetarian dishes: a hearty sandwich ($1.50), good *crema de cebolla* (onion soup) for $2, and yogurt with honey, granola, and fruit ($2). *Calle Hipolito Matute, tel. 38–3422. Directly behind the cathedral in Parque Central. Wheelchair access. Open 8:30 AM–6:45 PM.*

Brik Brak. Open 24 hours, Brik Brak is the Denny's of Tegus. This coffee shop can tide you over till breakfast after a late night out, or fill your belly before an early bus. A good variety of Honduran and American standards fill the menu. Pancakes are $1.50, a cheese sandwich $2, and filet mignon costs a whopping $5. Service can be tediously slow, so let your voice be heard. *Calle Peatonal, tel. 32–4742. Just off the Parque Central. Wheelchair access.*

Repostería Duncan Maya. Duncan Maya is a great spot to get a cheap meal with local flavor. A typical Honduran breakfast is $2, and the tasty and filling plato del día costs $3. *Av. Cristobal Colón 618, tel. 37–2672. One block east of Parque Central. Wheelchair access.*

Terraza Don Pepe. While the saintly WC is pretty enchanting (*see* box), many pilgrims come for the good food. The beefy *carne asada con chimole* is the house specialty ($2.50), and the *burra cubana* (Cuban donkey), consisting of beef, egg, bananas, and sour cream, is yummy too ($1.75). The Latin bands that play at night are bearably sappy. *Av. Cristobal Colón, tel. 37–1084. Walk west 2 blocks on Av. Colón from Parque Central. It's just past the mini Empire State Building. Breakfast, lunch, and dinner.*

The owner of Terraza Don Pepe boasts that his restaurant was the site of a "miracle." A statue of the patron saint of Honduras, the Virgin of Suyapa, was stolen from a local cathedral and "miraculously" appeared in Don Pepe's men's room, which is now enshrined.

NEAR BOULEVARD MORAZAN **Cafe Allegro.** When the owner Jorge went to Italy to learn how to cook, he brought a little bit of the Mediterranean home with him and now gives pasta a Honduran accent. The restaurant is a little expensive, but the tasteful candlelit patio atmosphere is ample compensation. Fettucine with mushroom sauce is a favorite at $3.50, and ice cream dribbled with your choice of liqueur ($2) finishes the meal off right. Be sure to check out the ceramic pieces adorning the room; they're some of the nicest craftworks in town, and Jorge brokers them for his artist friends. *Av. Rep. de Chile 360, tel. 32–8122. Walk 10 minutes from Parque Central up Rep. de Chile to the top of the hill. It's just past the stoplight on the left. Breakfast, lunch, and dinner.*

El Patio. El Patio looks more like a carnival ride than a restaurant: A large model of Captain Hook overlooks a fountain guarded by mock Mayan sculptures, and strolling guitarists serenade drunken carnivores. The traditional Honduran barbecue is scrumptious and uniquely presented: Beans are warmed over a bowl of cinders, and a multitude of condiments are served separately. *Pincho Grande de Res*, a mystery-meat shish kebab, is affordable at $3.25. Most meat dishes cost $5–$7. *Way out on Blvd. Morazán, tel. 32–9648. Over ½ hour walk from town (take a taxi). Wheelchair access. Open 11 AM–1:30 AM.*

Mike's. Mike's is a good place to bring a date. Not only are the tables nicely set, with cloth napkins folded like fans in the water glasses, but the menu is written in English so you can make a good impression by knowing what you order. Mike's is popular with travelers and Peace Corps volunteers, and the fare is mostly steak and seafood. If your date orders the sea bass in garlic sauce ($5), leaving you pinched for the taxi ride home, try the jalapeño steak sandwich for $3. *Blvd. Morazán, tel. 32–0017. A long walk up Av. Rep. de Chile, go left on overpass and up several blocks (it's appropriate to splurge on a taxi). Wheelchair access. Open 11 AM–2 AM.*

Most restaurants use agua purificado in food preparation and in drinks— locals are as apprehensive as you about getting cholera—but it doesn't hurt to ask anyway.

DESSERT/COFFEE HOUSES If your sweet tooth needs a fix, stroll into one of the numerous *reposterías* and munch on some terrific pastries. Ice cream joints are equally abundant, especially around the pedestrian street Calle Peatonal. The Italian gelato-style ice cream in the shop across from Pizza Hut is great. **Librería Paradiso** is a bastion for bohemians and the only true coffee house in town. If you want to find local intellectuals and students to talk with, this is the place. Three cozy rooms are decorated with paintings by local artists, and a small bookstore sells quality literature including several books in English by Guillermo Yuscarán, an American expatriate writer living in Honduras. A splendid coffee laced with cognac costs $2, and they also have other novelties like croissants and crepes. *Av. Paz Barahona, tel. 37–0337. 3 blocks east of Parque Central, just past the Shell station. Open daily 10 AM–8 PM.*

WORTH SEEING

Tegucigalpa is not a cultural magnet. Sights of interest seem to exist more by accident than by any calculated design. For example, the numerous old churches around town were never intended to be tourist attractions, though many travelers spend days exploring the old Christian embassies in the New World. You could chart a course, beginning with the oldest church in town, **Iglesia San Francisco,** founded by Franciscans in 1592, and church-hop across the river into Comayagüela, finishing up with **Parroquía de la Inmaculada Concepción,** near the market. Old-church enthusiasts should note that the national shrine is not in the city, but in nearby Suyapa. Most sights lie within walking distance of downtown.

PLAZA MORAZAN, A.K.A. PARQUE CENTRAL Parque Central is like a social club without exclusive membership, crowded day and night. People congregate here to chitchat with friends, hunt for the "perfect" lottery ticket, have their shoes polished, and listen to free afternoon concerts. In the Plaza and all the way up the pedestrian walkway Calle Peatonal, street vendors hawk their wares while moneychangers and clients haggle over rates. At the top of the park, **Cathedral San Miguel** has stood as a tribute to its architect, Gregorio Nacianceno Quiroz, since its completion in 1782. At night, floodlights make the outside look particularly heavenly; inside, the ornate gold altarpiece shines under its own power.

IGLESIA LOS DOLORES As the name indicates, this 16th-century church is dedicated to suffering (*dolores* are sorrows); it's a religious theme that poverty-stricken Hondurans can identify with. Most of the interior decorations depict the Crucifixion, though some paintings seem anachronistic (look at the symbolism used in the dome above the main altar and see for yourself). Stranger still is the presence of neon lights around Mary's countenance. *Walk 2 blocks down Calle Peatonal, turn right on Calle Los Dolores.*

MUSEO NACIONAL The home of former President Lozano has been converted into this museum of national history and anthropology. Honduras boasts few indigenous groups that still maintain traditional societies. The museum supports a growing trend toward protecting indigenous cultures, validating their importance to the country by recognizing and highlighting the contributions of each distinct group. *Walk north along Calle Morelos, and take the first right quite a way past Av. Las Delicias, tel. 22–1468. Open Tues.–Fri. 9–5.*

THE NATIONAL THEATER The **Teatro Nacional Manuel Bonilla** (Corner of Av. Barahona and Calle La Concordia, tel. 22–4366) was established in 1915, modeled after theaters in Europe (Latin American upper classes of the time tended to be Europhiles). The theater schedules events almost every night, with diverse attractions ranging from ballet to folklore presentations to pop music.

PARQUE LA MERCED AND ANTIGUO PARANIFO UNIVERSITARIA A few blocks south of Parque Central, La Merced is another cool hangout with its own church that's worth seeing. It's also the site of a 19th-century (but now defunct) university; today its *paranifo* (auditorium) houses art exhibits and artistic performances. *Admission free. Open weekdays 8–8, weekends 10–6.*

CHEAP THRILLS

FESTIVALS During the second week of December, Tegus hosts an artisan and tourism fair that draws people from all over Central America who come to party and display their goods and services. One of the most important festivals in Honduras occurs in Suyapa, just outside Tegucigalpa (*see* Near Tegucigala, *below*). Locals and pilgrims come together to honor the Virgen de Suyapa, the patron saint of Honduras. The celebration runs from the second to the 11th of February, but the big day is the third.

LA PENITENCIARIA CENTRAL Haven't you always dreamed of going to prison in Central America? Unusual though it may seem, the public is welcome to visit and buy craft items from the inmates. Knock at the visitor's door and show the guard your passport, explaining that you've come for the market. Woodwork is the specialty, with especially nice guitars and violins in abundance. Few tourists pass through the gates so you can usually find the same prices locals pay, but haggle a little just in case. Your personal security is not a problem, since an official escort guides you from one workshop to the next. Inmates are glad to have company, and will gladly weave a hammock and spin an interesting tale at the same time. *Av. San Martin de Flores at Av. Molina. Follow Calle Bolivar south from Parque Central, turn left onto Av. Molina. Admission free. Open daily 8–5.*

AFTER DARK

Ninety-nine percent of Tegucigalpans aren't wealthy enough to indulge in nocturnal diversions; most night owls are from the few rich families, so trendy hangouts are able to charge a lot more than the average budget traveler can afford. To economize, drink in one of the restaurants near the town center before going to the more expensive clubs. During the week most bars close by 1 AM; however, weekend crowds usually won't arrive before 1 and don't leave till dawn. Buses don't run past 9 PM, so taxis are the only form of nighttime transportation. The infrequent but free musical performances in Parque Central are often better than anything you could pay to see. Pick up the current edition of *Tegucigalpa This Week* to find out what's showing at the numerous cinemas around town; tickets are usually about $1, and films are almost always in English with Spanish subtitles.

BARS The **Hungry Fisherman.** Mostly Americans stir the water here. The Hungry Fisherman is a second home for many Peace Corps volunteers. The bar has cheap beer and reasonably priced seafood at lunch. *Av. Rep. de Chile, across from Peace Corps office, tel. 32–6493. Open Mon.–Sat. 9–2 and 5–11, Sun. 10–2 and 5–10.*

Kloster. Set upon stilts, this second-story bar is good for watching people on the street below. Young, well-to-do patrons come to Kloster to be seen, while workers on the way home from the office stop in for a quick belt. *Blvd. Morazán, tel. 32–2255. Walk left on Morazán from Av. Rep. de Chile. Open Mon.–Thurs. 4 PM–1 AM, Fri.–Sat. 4 PM–3 AM.*

Taco Taco. Taco Taco is the liveliest bar in town, where socialites and juveniles in heat compete with the TV, stereo, and itinerant mariachi and salsa musicians for a chance to be heard. The only drawback is the location—you need to take a taxi from town. *Far east end of Blvd. Morazán, tel. 37–8684. Open Sun.–Wed. 11 AM–1 AM, Thurs.–Sat. 11 AM–3 AM.*

DANCING AND MUSIC Dance spots within the city limits come and go relatively quickly; since none has telephones, confirming their existence must be done in person. Take a cab to Boulevard Juan Pablo II, the party ghetto of Tegus. **Hunters** (Blvd. Juan Pablo II) has live music for an older set on Fridays, and hipper stuff on Saturdays. Next door at **Tropical Port**, a big sign asks customers to leave their guns at the door; maybe they're afraid someone will shoot the DJ since more disco is played than Caribbean music. Just up the hill, across from the Pizza Hut, **Backstreet** plays a mix of American and Latin tunes, and it's popular with U.S. military personnel stationed in the area. Within walking distance of town, **Sueños** (Blvd. Morazán at Calle Maipu) is a discotheque of some repute. Dance clubs charge around $2 cover.

Near Tegucigalpa

The small villages in the mountains surrounding Tegus are, in many respects, more interesting than the capital. Some towns are noted for their artistry or their houses, while others are good bases for hiking in the forests. The pace of life is slow, and people are more than willing to stop and chat about local traditions.

SUYAPA Just east of Tegus is Suyapa, the Honduran Mecca. Inside the 16th-century church is a tiny clay statue of the **Virgen de Suyapa,** the patron saint of Honduras. Legend has it that a poor farmer was sleeping in a field and in the middle of the night he felt a stick poking him in the back. Perplexed, he put the stick in his bag. When he arrived home, instead of the stick, he found the statue. Hondurans' devotion to the saint is intense; throughout the year visitors stream through, and on February 3, her saint's day, an army of festive pilgrims descends on the town. Overshadowing the small church is the **Basílica de Suyapa,** begun in 1954 and still under construction. The stained-glass windows of clear sky blue are moving, no matter what your faith. Down the hill from the basílica, the Universidad Nacional Autónoma de Honduras, or **UNAH,** is a small city in itself. If you're interested in meeting students, hang around here. A favorite student watering hole is **La Peña,** across the street.

➤ **COMING AND GOING** • The Suyapa–Mercado San Isidro bus leaves from the market in Comayagüela (5¢). A special bus going directly to the campus (also called *Ciudad Universitaria*) leaves from **Campo la Isla** near the national stadium.

VALLE DE ANGELES The name doesn't lie: Heavenly beings *would* stay in Valle de Angeles (Valley of Angels) if given the choice. The town, 25 kilometers (16 miles) east of Tegus, maintains a cheery colonial appearance of centuries past, and the countryside is even more beautiful than the town. Since foreign visitors are frequent, most locals speak a few words of English (especially those wanting your turo-dollars). Many people come to visit the old church in the park downtown, but artistry is the area's biggest attraction. The local craftsmen are known all over Honduras for their extraordinary woodcarvings, leatherwork, ceramics, and other crafts. Artisan shops are all over the place, and a **market** lies at the far edge of town where the bus stops (it's best on Sundays). A good cheap thrill is seeing *los artistas* in training at **CAAVA,** where masters teach novices the ins and outs of producing fine *artesanís* (open 8–4; obtain permission to observe the students at the *Dirección* office inside the college). The town has a cool **festival** on October fourth.

Valle de Angeles has only one hotel. Just past the church, **Posada del Angel** (tel. 76–2233) is a nice Spanish-style abode, though expensive at $12 for a double. A kilometer from town on the road to Tegus, the campgrounds at **Parque Nacional Turís-tico Valle de Angeles** *sometimes* offer space, toilets, and water to campers. Sounds flaky? Well, it is. It's a tentative organization, so check with the Boy Scouts in Tegus (tel. 32–0377) before venturing here for the night.

➤ **COMING AND GOING** • Headed toward the town from Tegus, buses leave every hour 6 AM–5 PM from behind the La Milagrosa church, a short distance from the U.S. embassy (1 hour, 40¢). To get to the stop from Parque Central, take the Lomas or San Felipe bus to the Esso gas station on Avenida República Dominicana. The last bus returns from Valle de Angeles at 5 PM.

SAN JUANCITO A boom town when the mining industry employed thousands, San Juancito struggles for survival now that all the precious metals are gone. It's a pretty little village of red-tiled roofs, but with less than nothing to do. It's only important as a starting point for the hike up to **Parque Nacional La Tigra.** If you get stuck here, ask around for the location of the no-name, no-address, no-phone hospedaje that I heard will put you up for a buck per person.

➤ **COMING AND GOING** • Getting here can be a pain in the ass, which is ironic since the government is trying to promote La Tigra as a tourist attraction. Direct buses leave the San Pablo market without any regularity and return at 3 PM, though you'd be wise to double-check the time when you arrive in San Juancito. Slightly more compli-cated (but way more reliable) is to take the bus to Valle de Angeles, where you can catch another bus or hitchhike to San Juancito. Hitching is easy, and the more fre-quent Valle de Angeles bus service allows flexibility. Another possibility is a direct bus that allegedly leaves around noon from Mercado Jacaleapa in Tegus. Buses also leave from this mercado to San Juan de Flores and Cantarranas, and pass the turnoff for San Juancito; tell the driver you want to get off there and be prepared to hitch or walk the 2 kilometers.

PARQUE NACIONAL LA TIGRA La Tigra is Honduras's best-developed natural attraction, but everything's relative; as of this writing, trail maps and general info for the public are still not available. This might cause dismay for some visitors, but hikers who don't want to fight through a jungle of tourists will be stoked to find this enviro-wonderland just 21 kilometers (13 miles) from Tegus.

El Rosario is the first of two entrances to the park. To get here, hike (about 1½ hours) up the steep grade that begins in San Juancito (*see above*). A little over halfway up the mountain, you'll find El Rosario, a ghost town left behind by a mining company. The old buildings are currently used by park officials, and you can get acquainted with the park and its natural inhabitants at the very small museum inside. The ranger station also has dorm-style lodging (30 bunks, $2 per night); bedding isn't provided, so bring a sleeping bag or something warm since temperatures drop significantly at night in the higher elevations. Meals are available ($1 per plate), as well as beer and soda. The other entrance, near **Rancho Quemado,** is within walking distance of El Hatillo and Jutiapa (take the once-daily bus from the Mercado Zonal Belén in Tegus to Jutiapa). This entrance also has a ranger station. If the prospect of leaving this pris-tine wonderland for civilization seems harrowing, spend the night in the forest. Small campsites are located close to fresh water. Bring a tent and definitely inform the ranger of your intentions.

La Tigra itself is a magnificent cloud forest with prolific dark-green vegetation. The forest is home to pumas, monkeys, quetzals and other wonderfully bizarre birds, and wild pigs. They blend in well with their surroundings, so spotting them requires great patience and some luck. Along the trails, you can find plenty of pure mountain water, which is generally safe to drink (ask at the ranger station to be sure). From El Rosario, you can walk to a waterfall in 1½ hours, or take one of numerous full-day hikes. Without much difficulty, you can hike over the mountain in ½ day to the Rancho Quemado entrance. From there, walk to Jutiapa and catch the infrequent bus back to Tegus (or just hitch). Many report that mountain-biking is awesome on the soft soil. The Rancho Quemado entrance may be a better place to start because the grade isn't so steep.

DANLI A two-hour bus ride from Tegus, this is the most interesting place between the capital and the Nicaraguan border. The town itself isn't much, but the nearby mountains provide a righteous outdoor playground. You can rent a horse from a nearby ranch for the trip up **La Piedra de Apaguiz,** and munch on fruit from the groves on the way to the summit. Otherwise, hike to the ancient Mayan-style bridge, **Paseo Los Arcos,** or to the waterfall at **Los Chorros. San Cristóbal** has potential for rock-climbing and gold-mining, but superstitious locals warn that the mountain is cursed! Danlí's streets are full of bicycles, and though nobody officially rents bikes, a couple of dollars and a deposit can persuade a young entrepreneur to lend you one for the day.

➤ **BASICS** • None of the streets is marked, so ask for offices by name. **Banco Atlántico** cashes traveler's checks weekdays 9–3, and Saturdays 9–11:30. **Hondutel** is open daily from 7 AM–9 PM and Sunday 8–8. The **post office** (on the street passing Parque Central) is open Monday–Saturday 8–noon and 2–5.

➤ **COMING AND GOING** • Catch a bus to Danlí from the Discua Litena station in Colonia John F. Kennedy in Tegus (departures every hour, 6–6, $1.50). Buses leave Danlí for the capital regularly from early in the morning until 5 PM. Minibuses run to the Nicaraguan border town of El Paraíso regularly during daylight hours, and into the evening on market days (1 hour, 50¢). Five buses run daily to Santa María from Danlí, 7:30 AM–4:30 PM (2 hours, $1).

➤ **WHERE TO SLEEP** • The **Hotel Gran Granada** (tel. 93–2499) is the best place in town. Rooms are expensive at $11 per person, but they have a pool. **Hotel Esperanza** (around the corner from the bus station, tel. 93–2106) has doubles for $6.50–$16, depending on the amount of comfort you desire. Since customers are scarce, you can bargain for lower rates at these and the many other hotels in town. To camp, head for one of many tranquil spots around **Santa María,** a two-hour bus ride away into the hills. Pitch your tent along the crystal-clear El Limón river, or along the equally beautiful river near the village of **Chichicaste.**

EL PARAISO AND NICARAGUAN BORDER An hour from Danlí, and an hour away from the border, El Paraíso is a stagnant hole, nothing more than a transfer station. A hotel is near the bus station, but you're better off crashing in Danlí. Frequent buses to the border at **Las Manos** run 6:30 AM–4:30 PM (50¢). The border is open 8–noon and 1–4.

Golfo de Fonseca

It's been said that the devil vacations in the sweltering gulf so he won't miss the comforts of home. Make no mistake, the Southwest is the hottest region in Honduras. The pace of life is slow—people have no choice but to take it easy when the thermometer pushes through the roof and the humidity kicks in. Locals swing gently in their hammocks, trying to stir the air without expending any energy. If you're okay about getting wet periodically, the rainy season, from June to November, is the best time to visit. Afternoon showers make it cooler and also revitalize the countryside to a healthy green. During the dry season, particularly March and April, the foliage is brown and ugly and even the water is on the verge of spontaneous combustion. The beaches here aren't great, but the water is a nice respite from the heat. Definitely worth checking out are the enchanting mangrove forests, home to all types of reptiles and birds. The little islands in the gulf are the emerald treasures of the south, though no one knows exactly who the booty belongs to. The islands of El Tigre and Exposición (*see below*) are incontestably the property of Honduras, and are unquestionably worth a visit. Other islands, such as Meanguera, are occupied by El Salvador (*see* El Salvador chapter). The possibility of fighting erupting over who owns the islands is talked about, but, ya know, people like to talk.

Choluteca

Choluteca is bland and uniform compared to surrounding villages, but here you'll find the conveniences of the district's largest city. In the dry months, notably March and April, the temperatures stay above 100 degrees Fahrenheit. Despite protests by locals to the contrary, there *are* interesting sites in town, however minimal. The houses of **Jose Cecilio del Valle,** an author of Central America's declaration of independence from Spain, and **Dionicio de Herrera,** an early Honduran president, both face the main park in Barrio Colonial. This neighborhood has lots of colonial architecture.

BASICS Numerous **banks** change traveler's checks; if you arrive after hours, Hotel La Fuente, 5 blocks northwest from the bus station, will change dollars and traveler's checks. **Hondutel** (Barrio El Centro, Av. Alavaro Contreras, tel. 82–0005) handles international calls, telegraphs, and faxes. It's open daily 7 AM–9 PM. The **post office** is across the street from Hondutel (open weekdays 8–noon and 2–5). For emergencies, call the **police** (tel. 199); **ambulance** (tel. 82–0232); **fire department** (tel. 198); or **Hospital del Sur** (Av. Bojorque, tel. 82–0231).

COMING AND GOING The two bus stations in town are not far from each other. The main station (on the corner of Blvd. Carranza and 3a Av. NE, tel. 82–0034) houses a number of lines; buses from here leave for El Amatillo every ½ hour 5 AM–6 PM ($1.50, 2 hours), and Cedeño hourly 6 AM–6 PM (½ hour, 75¢). About 1½ blocks north, the **Mi Esperanza** line (tel. 82–0841) has its own station and goes to Tegus hourly 4 AM–6 PM (3 hours, $2) and San Marcos 5 times per day (1½ hours, $1). Hitching rides to El Salvador or Nicaragua should be easy along the Interamerican Highway. Get an early start on the sun, or you may be a shriveled raisin before a car stops.

GETTING AROUND While relatively small, Choluteca is spread out. The main drag, **Boulevard Carranza,** runs roughly east–west, with a number of avenidas coming off it. Street names are prone to changing, and are commonly not even used; orientation by landmarks is the norm. At the west end of downtown, the **Mercado Nuevo** (New Market) is a few blocks south of Carranza near Avenida Valle; if you follow Valle a few blocks north from Carranza you'll hit the **Mercado Viejo** (Old Market). The bus stations are a few blocks north of the eastern end of Carranza. If a local doesn't have a bike, her only option is to walk or take a taxi. Don't pay more than two lempira (40¢) for any daytime taxi ride. Anyone out in this quiet town after 10 PM is living extravagantly, and is penalized as such by paying twice as much for a lift.

WHERE TO SLEEP Where you stay will be influenced by what you expect from Choluteca; the hotels near the bus station and the Interamerican Highway do well for those with road fatigue, while the hotels in the center near the markets are better suited for those seeking the town's primal essence. If camping is your game, **Gringo Jim** is the man to set you up with a place to pitch your tent. Check to see if water's available at the campsite before putting down money. To find Jim, ask a local taxi driver. If you're low on cash and need to rough it, the main bus station has no doors that lock, so you can sleep on a bench for the night. The only real threat is the senile old man who hangs out here in the mornings and likes to pinch foreigners.

➤ **UNDER $5 • Hotel Don Poco.** The restaurant is a better reason to come than the rooms, so sleeping around the corner and popping in for a hearty breakfast may be a good strategy. Average rooms all share a passable communal shower. Married couples, or those who can pass as such, get the best rates at $3 per room, while others will be forced to take two beds for $4. *Barrio Centro, near old market. 10 rooms, none with bath.*

➤ **UNDER $10** • **Hotel Lisboa.** The rooms here are only slightly cleaner than those of neighboring competitors, but the overall atmosphere is markedly better. Hammocks line the open courtyard, and a big TV receives cable from the States. If you have a car, you may want to go around the corner to **Hotel San Carlos,** which is run by the same manager as Lisboa and has off-street parking. A double with fan at either place is $6. *Barrio Centro, across from Mercado Viejo, tel. 82–0355. 31 rooms, some with bath. Wheelchair access. Luggage storage, laundry.*

Hotel Pacifico. Within walking distance of the bus station, Hotel Pacifico may be a good spot to catch some Z's. At $7 per double, all rooms have fans. *4a Av. NE, tel. 82–0838. 4 blocks northeast of bus station. 12 rooms, all with bath. Wheelchair access. Luggage storage, laundry.*

➤ **OVER $20** • **Hotel La Fuente.** It's a big jump in price for a small jump in quality. You'll pay $21 per double for luxuries like TV, air-conditioning, and a swimming pool. If you want to lay down less cash for your splash, sleep somewhere else and pay the few lempira to use the pool. *Near Interamerican Highway on north side of town, tel. 82–0253. 41 rooms, all with bath. Luggage storage, laundry, restaurant, pool, money exchange.*

FOOD Choluteca has nothing special by way of grub. You'll find a number of cheap, decent comedores around the hotels listed above. **Henry's** next to Hotel La Fuente serves filling shish kebabs and hamburgers and is considered tops by locals. The restaurant in Hotel Don Poco is simple and cheap; they serve comida típica and have no menus, so to find out the fare for the day ask "*¿Qué tiene?*"

Amapala (Isla El Tigre)

The island of El Tigre romances the imagination with tales of Sir Francis Drake's still-hidden pirate's treasure. More interested in profit than romance, 20th-century businesspeople moved the country's primary port on the Pacific from Amapala to the mainland. They left behind a city overshadowed by a dormant volcano and a U.S. military station. (To get an idea of how the place looks, flip over a two-lempira note and check out the picture.) Isla El Tigre is definitely one of the best places to visit in southern Honduras. Even though the quiet fishing village of Amapala has a bank, phones, and a Red Cross office, it feels isolated from the modern world, partially due to the lack of cars and smog. Except during Semana Santa, few tourists ever pass through.

COMING AND GOING The jumping-off point for the island is the tiny town of **Coyolito,** which has few amenities and no hotels. Only four buses a day run here from Choluteca and San Lorenzo, but hitching a ride in the back of somebody's truck is easy (though not always free). The road to Coyolito lies off the Interamerican Highway, a few miles north of San Lorenzo. Small, inexpensive ferries take people across to Amapala (or Exposición) whenever boats fill up.

WHERE TO SLEEP AND EAT The numerous *cantinas* that line the beach offer wonderful seafood meals for cheap. For (relatively) upscale food try the seaside **Miramar Restaurante.** Expect standard Honduran fare, buoyed by fish and shellfish. The sea air is eating away the paint at **Hotel Internacional,** the rooms have no fans, but you can't help but love it. The wind-blown atmosphere makes it a great place to finish that novel. The three rooms on the second story were designed to sleep entire families, and each room opens onto a balcony overlooking the bay. If the showers run out of water, the super-kind family managing the hotel will pull water up from an on-site well. Rooms are under $2 per person. To find the hotel, close your eyes as you leave the pier and you'll run into it. Since Hotel Internacional only has eight rooms, and no phone for reservations, you may need an alternative. During Semana Santa, lots of hospedajes open their doors. Though closed most of the year, one will take you in a pinch—ask around. Camping is tolerated on almost all beaches, and you can try to work out a deal with a local to get bathing water. For a few dollars, boat drivers are agreeable to dropping off campers on a small deserted island for the night, and returning to pick them up in the morning.

OUTDOOR ACTIVITIES Perhaps the most interesting characters on the island are the fishermen. Spend a day with one of them and the money spent to rent equipment might save you the price of dinner. Several beaches around the island are within walking distance of Amapala or you can rent a boat to take you. Bring the sunblock and don't expect much surf. A half-day hike to the summit of the mountain rewards you with a great view of the islands. Since the United States has a military base here, you're supposed to get permission to walk up the mountain from the mayor's office; you can always play dumb—at your own risk.

Elsewhere in the Gulf

CEDENO Cedeño is more like a local swimming hole than a beach resort—the barnyard meets the beach, roofs are made of palm leaves, and local pigs sniff at the waterside. To avoid mobs of Hondurans frolicking in the surf, don't come here during Semana Santa. Whenever you visit, you'll find the beaches south of town more inviting, since locals often dump trash in the water near town. Buses run hourly to Cedeño from Choluteca, and two or three per day connect the beach town with Tegus. Set upon stilts above the tiny waves, the **Miramar** and **Los Arcos** are both restaurants and hotels. They serve best in the first capacity, as guests of Los Arcos report waking up in the unventilated rooms dripping with sweat and finding no water for a shower. Rooms at both places are about $6.

PUNTA RATON Punta Ratón is another beach town, 1½ hours from Choluteca. The town is similar to Cedeño, but smaller. No hotels, but you can camp on the beach and eat at the small comedores. Innocent tortoises draw some spectators, but everyone should watch out for the scorpions that are said to hang out on the beach and around town.

PUNTA CONDEGA AND LA IGUANA These two unofficial reserves are home to all things scaly or amphibious. Punta Condega is a tortoise sanctuary, where mothers come to deposit their eggs. A recent publicity campaign to protect baby tortoises has improved the life expectancy of these shelled creatures and provided tourists with more living specimens to gawk at. La Iguana is a swamp-like area that is home to tortoises, caimans, iguanas, snakes, and other bizarre tropical reptiles. Both sites are easily accessed from the tiny, remote village of **Guapinole**. To get here, hitch a ride or drive southeast from Monjarás, on the road to Cedeño. The people at Guapinole's only hospedaje are valuable sources for acquiring a canoe for the trip downriver to Punta Condega, or for getting specific directions to La Iguana. Punta Condega can also be reached by canoe from Cedeño (ask around when you're there).

SAN LORENZO This seaside town is one of the better spots to rest along the Interamerican Highway. Considering it's Honduras's only major Pacific port, San Lorenzo is surprisingly tame; rowdy bars full of drunken sailors are conspicuously absent. The sea resembles a river delta, with wide channels separated by islands overgrown with forest-green moss. Though unattractive spots for swimming, the waterways offer great birding. The Hotel Miramar (see below) rents boats, though for the price of your first-born son. You can also talk to the folks at **C.O.D.D.E.F.F.A.G.O.L.F.** (hell of an acronym, hey?), 1½ blocks west of the

San Lorenzo shuts down around 10 PM so people can wake up refreshed for another exciting day at the shrimp-packaging plant.

park, where they work to protect the gulf's environment. In addition to finding a cheap boat for you to rent, they also have info on points of ecological interest on the islands and the mainland, and can get you a guide for remoter excursions.

➤ **COMING AND GOING** • San Lorenzo is pretty much due south of the capital, which makes it a regular stop on the way to Choluteca or San Marcos. While some buses from the capital will take you directly to San Lorenzo's center, many of the bigger buses only stop on the highway outside town. The stop for smaller minibuses to El Amatillo or San Marcos is downtown. Buses frequently pass both places from early morning to mid-evening.

➤ **WHERE TO SLEEP** • The kind, elderly owners of **Hotel Perla del Pacifico** (Barrio Centro, one street west of main bus stop, tel. 81–2385) had the foresight to install a water reserve, so when the city runs dry your shower won't. Doubles with bath and fans are $8. You'll know the **Miramar** (Plaza Marina, near the shrimp-packaging plant at the waterside, tel. 81–2138) is the fanciest place in town because the children who beg for a living never stray far from the door. Sit with the town's upper crust on the patio that juts out over the water while you try to ignore the social problems knocking at the front door. All rooms are $13 and sleep three people; some have private baths, and most have air-conditioning.

➤ **FOOD** • Working-class folk eat at the restaurant next to the shrimp-packing factory, where low-cost meals obviously have the locals' stamp of approval. The restaurant at the Miramar Hotel (*see above*) has food that your stomach can trust, though your wallet may be skeptical. Fish is a norm, but they also have burgers and other meat dishes. The same owner has an air-conditioned place right near the main park, across from the church. It's one of the nicer-looking restaurants in the area, with a menu similar to the Miramar's. Locals salt everything heavily. When having coffee, double-check the bowl where you just put your teaspoon—it's probably not sugar, but salt.

ISLA EXPOSICION Isla Exposición has been set aside as a nature reserve, and has flora and fauna extinct in other parts of the Gulf of Fonseca. Escape into the wilderness for a few hours and try to spot the caiman believed to inhabit the island. The island has no hotels, so camp on the beach—you need the permission of the mayor's office in Amapala. Boats depart for Exposición from Coyolito (*see* Amapala, *above*) whenever the captain sees a big enough cash incentive.

EL AMATILLO This border town is a little more elaborate than others, probably due to the heavy traffic along the Interamerican Highway between Honduras and El Salvador. These border officials keep longer hours than others, 6 AM–9 PM. After 5 PM the exit tariff increases, but otherwise you'll pay $2. If you just want to visit the market on the El Salvador side, a less expensive arrangement can be made for day trips. **Hotel Los Arcos** on the Honduras side has doubles for $6 a night.

Western Honduras

For 2,000 years, the Maya lived here near the Guatemalan border, and during their Classic period they created the superb art and architecture of Copán. The Lencas, who are believed to have co-existed with the Maya, have been the predominant tribe in the area since the Maya's decline. When the Spanish arrived in the 16th century, the Lencas weren't thrilled at the prospect of becoming slaves. Indeed, they made great efforts to kick Spanish butt. But after the Lencan chief Lempira was murdered, the Spanish took control and made Comayagua the colonial capital. Until the discovery of Copán by archaeologists in the 19th century, the far west was considered a backwater in relation to other areas of the country. Even today, western Honduras doesn't feel like a densely populated region. Cities of the West are small, and many retain a colonial appearance, with cobblestone streets and whitewashed Spanish-style houses. The people are more outgoing here than in many parts of inland Honduras, and conversations come easily. Hiking is prime—a number of national parks beckon the adventurous, and the caves in the area are some of the best in the country.

Comayagua

Eighty-two kilometers (51 miles) northwest of Tegus, Comayagua is the city that refused to die. During the 300 years that it was the capital of Honduras, the town survived an earthquake, a savage fire at the hands of invading Guatemalans, and the nearly mortal blow of the capital being moved to Tegus in 1880. Most tourists come to pay respects to the corpse of Comayagua, as history is more prominent in these streets than in any other Honduran city. The churches, originally founded by the Spanish to stabilize the territory, now support the small tourist trade.

BASICS Banks are easy to find downtown, and most cash traveler's checks. **Hondutel** (behind the cathedral) is open 24 hours for calls; fax services are available 7–noon and 2–4. Next to Hondutel, the **post office** is open weekdays 8–noon and 2–5, Saturdays 8–1. The office of **COHDEFOR** at Recursos Naturales (1 kilometer past Comayagua toward San Pedro Sula) is not a tourist office, but they have advice about camping and how to reach the mountains. For emergencies, call the **ambulance** (tel. 72–0290); **police** (tel. 72–0080); **fire department** (tel. 72–0291); or **hospital** (tel. 72–0094).

COMING AND GOING Buses to Tegus and San Pedro Sula pass Comayagua hourly in each direction from around 5 AM to 8:30 PM daily. Most buses don't enter the city but leave passengers at the Texaco station just outside town. It's a short walk to the closest hotels, but you may want to take a taxi if you're headed directly downtown and/or have lots of baggage (about 50¢ for the few-minute ride). Frontage Road (also called **Boulevard**) leads off the Carretera del Norte (Tegus–San Pedro highway). If you follow the frontage road toward town for about a kilometer, the city center will be a few blocks to your right (east). Once in town, getting around is pretty easy. Most things of interest are in the central, or "old" part of town, wherein lie the Parque Central, many of the churches, and most basic services. The center has numbered calles running east–west and avenidas north–south. The main **market** is a few blocks south of Parque Central, between 1a and 2a calles north and 1a and 2a avenidas.

WHERE TO SLEEP **Hotel Libertad.** The rooms at Hotel Libertad are passable, but you'll want to pass on the rancid showers. None of the rooms has fans. On the positive side, it's very cheap and close to the major sites ($4 double). *Facing Parque Central, tel. 72–0091. 18 rooms, none with bath. Wheelchair access. Luggage storage, laundry.*

Hotel Emperador. Close to the bus stop, this is one of the nicer hotels in town. Aesthetics have an influence on the prices, so if you can do without carpeting and a balcony, an air-conditioned room is only a buck more than a basic sweat lodge. The airy doubles are $9. *On the right a couple of blocks north of Texaco on frontage road, tel. 72–0332. 38 rooms, all with bath. Luggage storage, laundry.*

Hotel Quan. A long walk from the bus stop but only a short walk to town, Hotel Quan has nicer rooms than the budget places you'll pass on the way here. Rooms, some with fans, cost $2–$6. *End of the frontage road, turn right before road crosses river, tel. 72–0070. 27 rooms, some with bath. Wheelchair access. Luggage storage.*

FOOD Near Parque Central you'll find lots of cheap eateries, frequented by younger and/or poorer locals. Vegetarians will be pleased with a big plate of vegetables and noodles at the Chinese joint. A more formidable set of eateries lines the frontage road (Boulevard) to the highway.

Fruty Taco. Popular with young Comayaguans, this place has some of the tastiest food in the Parque area. Under black velvet and neon lights, consume tasty 60¢ tacos and a delicious fruit drink for 40¢. *Southwest corner of Parque Central. Open 9 AM–10 PM.*

Pajaro Rojo. "The Red Bird" has one of the most comprehensive menus in town. The atmosphere is formal, but the prices are good for everything except the gourmet dishes. You can get Honduran standards like a filling plato típico for $2.50, and vegetarians should try the spaghetti for $2. A worthwhile splurge is the paella for two ($10), and, if you've just come into an large inheritance, try the lobster thermidor (*langosta termida*) for $11. The live music played every night is borderline cheesy. *On Boulevard, up a couple of blocks from the highway, tel. 72–0690. Open 11–10, closed Mon.*

WORTH SEEING

➤ **CHURCHES** • Being a former colonial capital, Comayagua abounds with *iglesias* (churches). Most churches are within a block of each other. Starting at the north end of town, on 7a Calle North, **Iglesia de La Caridad** (1730) sits on the periphery of town because it was designed as a church for "Indians" and "Negroes." A statue of the black virgin still sits on the altar. Three blocks southeast, across from the archaeology museum, **Iglesia San Francisco** (1574) was part of a Franciscan attempt to gain a foothold in the new territory. Two blocks south, the **Cathedral** (1685-1715) is the most ornate church in town. Someone even talked Phillip II of Spain into donating the Moorish clock in the Alhambra to this New World cathedral. Over 800 years old, it isn't much to look at from the outside, but climb the clock tower steps and check out the inner mechanics. **Iglesia La Merced** (1550), 3 blocks southeast, was the first church in town.

➤ **MUSEO COLONIAL** • Across from the Cathedral, this museum resides in one of the first universities in Central America, founded back in 1632. Today, the museum holds a collection of 15th- to 18th-century relics and paintings from the local churches. The curator is a friendly woman who's happy to share her knowledge about the artifacts. *In Casa Cural. Admission: 60¢. Open daily 9:30–noon, 2–4:30.*

➤ **MUSEO DE ARQUEOLOGIA** • A number of Lenca artifacts found in Cajon are on display, but it's mostly pictures and a rock or two. The people here can also give info about little-known ruins in the area. *Admission: 30¢. Open Wed.–Fri. 8–noon and 1–4, weekends 8–noon.*

NEAR COMAYAGUA

Montaña de Comayagua Parque Nacional is only 13 kilometers (8 miles) from the city but still virtually wild. Adventurers can find a pristine cloud forest and places to camp, but bring water, food, and possibly a machete to hack through the bush. A minibus leaves the Parque de la Merced in town for **La Sanpedrana,** from where it's a hard 4-kilometer (2-mile) walk to the forest. With a car, take the road north toward San Jerónimo, and turn off to the village of Río Negro. From here you can walk through the forest to a town on the other side in a full day. It's a difficult hike, but the views are great. You may find a local to put you up on either side of the forest, but bring a tent nonetheless. About 10 kilometers (6 miles) south on the road to Tegus lie the ruins of an old Lenca fort, **Tenampua.** With untrained eyes, you'll see very little besides mounds of earth and the remnants of some walls. Still, archaeologists find the site fascinating. For more details about the work going on here, talk to people at the Museo de Arqueología in Comayagua.

Lago de Yojoa

Just an hour south of San Pedro Sula, Lake Yojoa is a popular recreation spot for families and young people alike. Trees draped with Spanish moss grow out of the water, and the marshy areas are havens for all sorts of bird life. The warm, clear water offers a boomin' swim. Fishing equipment is available at hotels for a few lempira. Great hikes are offered by the surrounding mountains; a trip to the top of **Maroncho,** the highest in the area (9,059 feet), is a three-day round-trip endeavor for serious climbers. Buses to Tegus (3 hours) and San Pedro Sula (1 hour) pass the lake hourly. Buses will drop you off at **Hotel Los Remos** on the southeastern tip of the lake or at La Guama, where buses toward Peña Blanca pass Hotel Agua Azul. The contractors who built **Hotel Los Remos** (southeastern tip of the lake, next to the highway) may have been smoking some of that wacky weed, as evidenced by the funhouse-esque, lopsided rooms. This minor shortcoming is easily made up for by the beauty and serenity of the location and the kindness of the English-speaking owners, who rent rowboats, motorboats, and rooms for $6 per person. The beautiful wooden deck at **Hotel Agua Azul** (a short bus ride from La Guama toward Peña Blanca; in San Pedro Sula, call 52–7125) has a great view of the lake. The rooms are nice, nothing special, and a little expensive ($12–$20 per room). What makes the hotel appealing is Enrique, an English-speaking naturalist who manages the conservation agency **Ecolago** out of the hotel. Except in hotels, you won't find any real sit-down restaurants. Around the lake are plenty of little fish-fry huts; you might want to worry about the cleanliness, but generally the fish will be fresh.

NEAR LAGO DE YOJOA

PARQUE NACIONAL CERRO AZUL MEAMBAR This national park is in the process of being developed, and a visitor's center should be up and running by the time this book hits the shelves. Hiking on the Lago de Yojoa side of the park is strenuous and often wet, while the trails closer to Siguatepeque to the east offer milder hiking. On either side, you can explore lush virgin forest that has rarely been seen by gringos (yet!). Though no hotels have yet sprung up near the park, local villagers have been known to take in strangers. The park has several entrances. From La Guama on Lago de Yojoa, hitchhike up to the dam at Santa Elena, and continue on to Los Pinos. The future may bring a hospedaje here for park visitors. Trails lead out of Los Pinos into the forest. Another entrance lies 10 kilometers (6 miles) past Taulabé on the highway. Cross the bridge over Río Varsovia, and hitchhike 20 minutes to Cerro Azul. You can reach the top of the mountain and some waterfalls from here. From Siguatepeque, a truck leaves the central market daily for Los Planes de Meambar. From there, head on to Los Cedros, a coffee-growing village on the edge of the pine forest. Camping is possible in all these locations. Bring water, warm clothes, and be prepared for rain. Aldia Global (tel. 73–2539) can provide more info, as can Ecolago at Hotel Agua Azul (*see* Where to Sleep, Lago de Yojoa, *above*).

Santa Bárbara

Thirty-five kilometers (22 miles) west of Lago de Yojoa (as the crow flies) is this medium-size city dominated by mountains. The town itself is famous for its woven handicrafts, but many visitors use it only as a base for exploring the nearby mountains and caves. To the east is the second-highest mountain in the country, **Montaña Santa Bárbara;** if you're serious, you can climb to the 9,000-foot summit in a few days. You can also hike to the dilapidated **presidential palace** on the hillside near town. A tunnel is rumored to run down from the palace to the town church, but don't expect to find anything more than a panoramic view from the ruin. Buses leave San Pedro Sula for Santa Bárbara 6–6 daily (2 hours, $2); they return to San Pedro Sula hourly 4 AM–5 PM.

BASICS Hondutel, near the main plaza, is open daily 7 AM–9 PM. The **post office** next door is open weekdays 8–noon and 2–5. No banks in town will cash traveler's checks, but **Banco Atlántico** does exchange cash.

WHERE TO SLEEP AND EAT When you're hungry, look for **Doña Ana**, past the church toward the hill. You won't see a sign out front because all the locals know where to find the best food in town. All meals are $2 per plate—just ask for food and you'll get the day's dish. **Doña Mirna** (near Banco Atlántico) has cheap tacos and enchiladas, and vegetarians can have a banana with beans and cheese for 30¢.

Hospedaje Rodriguez (Barrio Abajo, on the street behind the church) has no room service or valet parking, but what do you expect for $1.25 per person? All rooms are basic but acceptable, and $3 doubles come with private showers. All 19 rooms at **Hotel Santa Lucía** (Barrio Abajo, tel. 64–2531) have fans and cost $2–$3 per person, depending on which frills you want. **Boarding House Moderno** (tel. 64–2203) and **Hotel Ruth** (tel. 64–2632) both have air-conditioned rooms. Ruth is a modest hotel with $9 doubles. Moderno, a block past the church, offers hot water, nice wooden fixtures, the nicest ambience in town, and prices to match (around $15 double).

OUTDOOR ACTIVITIES Parque Nacional Santa Bárbara is wonderful but difficult to reach. Colectivo pick-up trucks leave Santa Bárbara daily for villages on the outskirts of the park. In the towns of Santa Rita de Oriente, La Cuenta, and El Aguacatal, you can rent horses to get you to the park. Bring a good map and a compass, but hiring a local guide is much safer. A good three-day hike through the cloud forest begins in El Aguacatal and crosses the park to San José de los Andes. There are some excellent spots for camping along the way, but bring water since you'll find none on the limestone mountain. Be prepared for rain and beware of sinkholes in the limestone. Contact the local **COHDEFOR** office (tel. 64–2519) in Santa Bárbara for directions, local guides, maps, and maybe a ride. You can also write ahead to **ASECOVE** (Box 28, Santa Bárbara) for info. They may put in a real office in town soon.

The caves around Santa Bárbara are amazing. These limestone tunnels are some of the deepest in the world—**Pincaligue** is known as the Devil's Cave because of its incredible depths. Talk to ESNACIFOR in Siguatepeque for maps and info about local caves. Also, several natural hot springs dot the region; off the road to San Pedro Sula, try the springs at **Bañario Santa Lucia**. Remoter but better springs are near **La Arada**, a little town also noted for crafts like baskets and hats. It's an hour walk to the hot springs from town; ask locals for directions to the *aguas termales*.

La Entrada

A smelly little armpit of a town with all the charm of a bus stop, "The Entrance" is an unavoidable transfer point for many. Everything lies along the highway: the bank, a flea market selling clothes and other junk, and lots of fill-your-mouth, pray-for-health snack shacks. Bus drivers with discerning palates eat at **Comedor Guitty** (tel. 98–5060), which serves all meals at $2 a plate. If you must stay in town for the night (poor thing), **Hotel Central** (tel. 98–5084) has doubles with communal showers for $6. **Hotel Tegucigalpa** has doubles with fans, showers, and TV for $15. If you're around in the afternoon and have nothing else to do, check out the **Museo Arqueológico,** open daily 1:30–4 (admission: 50¢); it's pretty bunk, consisting basically of rejects from the museum out at the site.

COMING AND GOING Buses stop in front of the station just south of the turnoff to Copán. Buses to Copán Ruinas (2 hours, $2) leave every 40 minutes 5 AM–4:30 PM daily. Buses to San Pedro Sula (2½ hours, $2) leave every ½ hour 5–5. Buses to Santa Rosa de Copán (1 hour, $1) leave every ½ hour 6:30 AM–6 PM. Buses to El Paraíso leave every two hours 7:30 AM–5 PM ($1.25).

Copán Ruinas

Copán Ruinas's main attraction is obviously the Mayan ruins, 1 kilometer away, but you can't avoid being charmed by the town itself. The clock-tower chime sounds like a funky cowbell, children gather in the church on Sunday to sing, and an amplifier carries their songs all the way to the soccer field where athletes practice another of Honduras's religions. The town radiates from the Parque Central, with residences continuing up the hill. Locals live pretty comfortably due to the tourist trade, and welcome the hordes of foreigners who come to experience the ruins of Copán, the Paris of the ancient Mayan world. During the third week of December, a **festival** celebrating Honduran culture attracts artists and artisans from across the nation. Copán celebrates its patron saint San José during the third week of March.

BASICS **Banco de Occidente,** across from Parque Central, changes traveler's checks. The Hotel Maya (*see below*) will change dollars or quetzales. **Hondutel,** next to Museo Copán, is open for calls 7 AM–9:30 PM daily. The **post office** next door is open weekdays 8–noon and 2–5, Saturday 8–noon. The **police** station is a block from the Hotel Marina on the road toward Guatemala. Cruz Roja for **medical emergencies** is next to the Hotel Honduras at the eastern entrance to town.

COMING AND GOING Buses leave La Entrada for Copán Ruinas about every ½ hour from early morning until 4:30 PM ($1.25, 2 hours). Buses to La Entrada from Copán Ruinas leave every 40 minutes 5–5. Direct buses to San Pedro Sula ($3, 5 hours) leave at 4 and 5 AM daily. To reach the Guatemala border at El Florido (45 minutes, $1), wait at the bus stop across from the soccer field or head past Parque Central to the bridge on the west side of town, where you can hitch or catch a bus; minibuses and pickup trucks leave hourly 7:30 AM–3 PM, and buses sometimes leave as late as 4 PM. Getting a connecting bus once over the border can be tricky, so start early.

WHERE TO SLEEP

➤ **UNDER $10** • **Hotelito Copán.** Rooms ($3 per person) here are standard, but you get a private shower; for the same price at other hotels you have to share a skanky communal bathroom. If you're driving, they've got a safe place for parking. *Turn left as you enter town from the east, go down 2 blocks. 14 rooms, all with bath. Wheelchair access. Luggage storage, laundry.*

Hotel Posada de Raul. These digs are the best deal in town. The rooms are generic, but the attraction here is hot water in one of the communal showers and seats for the toilets (que luxury!). At $4 for doubles, you can't do any better. *Across from Hotel Marina. 28 rooms, none with bath. Wheelchair access. Luggage storage, laundry.*

➤ **OVER $10** • **Hotel Brisas de Copán.** Hotel Brisas has a tidy, residential atmosphere. The two rooms without baths for $3 per person fill up quickly. The other rooms are much nicer, with private showers, hot water, fans, and a somewhat prohibitive price ($12 double). The friendly owner has a few horses for rent. *Up the hill from the soccer field. 11 rooms, some with bath. Luggage storage, laundry.*

Hotel Maya Copán. The charming owner changes U.S. and Guatemalan cash, cooks in the restaurant, and would even sell you the hotel if she could figure out how to do it without sharing the profit with her husband. Weary travelers often buy a bottle of rum at the mini-mart and drink it on the second-story terrace. All this intrigue and decent rooms with a hot shower go for $6 per person. *On the corner of Parque Central. 20 rooms, all with bath. Wheelchair access. Luggage storage, laundry, money exchange.*

Hotel Marina Copán. You'll forget about the ruins as you spend your time excavating Marina Copán's swimming pool, restaurant, bar, and gift shop. The beauteous rooms have air-conditioning, hot water, and TV with U.S. cable. The receptionist speaks wonderful English, so you can be sure you heard the price correctly ($45 double). *On the corner, across from Parque Central. 40 rooms, all with bath. Luggage storage, laundry.*

> **CAMPING** • Out near the ruins, officials will let you camp on the grass near the parking lot. See if you can make your way past the first fence, where you'll be surrounded by lots of trees and a more pleasant atmosphere. Use the tourist center's rest rooms for your morning grooming.

FOOD **Llama del Bosque.** A virtual jungle of plants and birds, this place is great for breakfast and is a favorite watering hole of locals at night. The large menu has all types of dishes and prices; beef and chicken plates cost $3, and burgers are just $1. Vegetarians will spend $3 on spaghetti with cheese. *2 blocks from Parque Central, past Museo Copán. Breakfast, lunch, and dinner.*

Tunkul Bar. Almost deserving of a category unto itself, the Tunkul Bar caters to the needs of Westerners. On the premises they operate an affordable Spanish-language school and an adventure agency, **Go Native Tours,** offering local and longer-distance trips. Their expeditions are out of most backpackers' price range, but for a trip into the Mosquitia, the convenience of an experienced guide may be worth the bucks. The place is busy, but your meal will arrive before you've had a chance to soak up all your options. They serve soups, salads, and even a vegetarian plate ($4). If you haven't eaten in two days, try the beef or chicken burrito for $3 and you'll be satisfied for the next two. *1 block from the park. Open daily 11:30–3 and 6–midnight.*

WORTH SEEING Here you are at the most popular tourist attraction in the country. To avoid the sightseers who pour off their tourist buses and cram the old Mayan metropolis, visit in the early morning. The ancient city lies an easy 1-kilometer walk away on the road east from Copán Ruinas. The admission price for the ruins has risen dramatically and now stands at $6. The price covers admission to the Principal Group, Las Sepulturas, and **Museo Copán** in town. Though most of the museum's descriptions are in Spanish, the ancient tools and artwork speak for themselves. The *El Brujo* (the witch) exhibit is especially interesting, displaying the skeleton and religious artifacts of a Mayan spiritualist. The ruins and museum are open daily 8–4. The site's tourist office gives better info on Honduras in general than about Copán, but it does have a souvenir shop where serious ruin-ites can invest in a guidebook. English-speaking guides loiter around the ticket office, but they're expensive unless a big group splits the cost. Try to haggle—maybe it's a slow day. The site's official snack bar is more expensive than **Comedor Mayapán** across the street (decent sandwiches for $1).

Copán isn't as large or old as some of the Mayan cities in Guatemala, but you'll still marvel at the abundance of ancient artistry. (For more info on the development of Mayan civilization, *see* Mayan Chronology box in Guatemala chapter.) Copán was at one time home to more than 20,000 people, and many theories, some plausible and some idiotic, are in circulation about its decline and abandonment (*see* Abducted by Aliens? box in Guatemala chapter). For over 100 years, archaeologists have been excavating arduously, but significant discoveries have only been made in the last 25 years. What authorities do know comes from hieroglyphics of the Classic period, AD 426–800, when the city's construction and power were at an apex. Because new structures were built on top of existing ones, the great temples and buildings visible to the general public date only from the last few generations of rulers.

Luckily, some of the more prolific builders recorded the history of Copán's rulers in their artistry. Copán's glyphs and art tell tales of kings, wars, and heredity. The first dynastic ruler during the Classic period, Great Sun Lord Quetzal Macaw, came to power around AD 435. Archaeologists believe the early kings represented themselves as divine beings embodied in human form, which gave spiritual justifications for their power. Over time, the kings were no longer seen as deities but rather just mighty, kick-ass mortals. Changing artistic motifs between earlier and later generations of governments supports this theory. Very little is known about Copán's kings until the rise of the 12th ruler, Smoke Jaguar (628–695), who developed Copán militarily, commercially, and artistically. His successor, King 18 Rabbit (695–738), continued Copán's artistic adornment until he was beheaded in the nearby city of Quiriguá. His execution

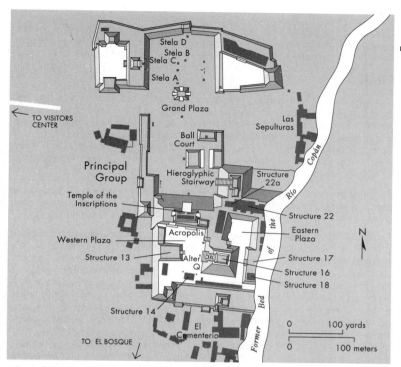

Stela D
Stela B
Stela C
Stela A

Grand Plaza

TO VISITORS
CENTER

Las
Sepulturas

Ball
Court

Principal
Group

Hieroglyphic
Stairway

Structure
22a

Río Copán

Temple of the
Inscriptions

Structure 22

Acropolis

Eastern
Plaza

Western Plaza

N

Structure 13

Alter
Q

Structure 17

Structure 16
Structure 18

Structure 14

TO EL BOSQUE

El
Cementerio

Former Bed of the

0   100 yards
0   100 meters

shook Copán's political structure. The next king, Smoke Monkey (738–749), tried to stabilize power during his short reign by using artistic themes consistent with his predecessor. Around this time, according to archaeologist Barbara Fash, artistic themes shifted from cosmology and fertility images to those of warfare. The king's authority was increasingly being challenged by powerful noble families in the area. Smoke Monkey's son, Smoke Shell (749–763), tried to justify his power by playing up the historical importance of great warrior kings in Copán's leadership. For instance, his Hieroglyphic Stairway elaborately emphasized the supremacy of Copán's rulers in battle. The 16th king, Dawning Sun (763–820), continued to glorify warfare in his architecture, but it seems he was too late: By this time, Copán and its political authority were in decline.

The ceremonial and governmental structures are known collectively as the **Principal Group.** As you enter the site you'll find the **Grand Plaza** to the left. The stelae standing about the plaza were monuments erected to glorify contemporary kings, and some on the periphery are for King Smoke Jaguar. The most impressive group in the middle of the lawn was dedicated to 18 Rabbit. Pay your respects to Dr. John Owen, an archaeologist who died at the site in 1893 and was buried in front of Stela D. Besides political propaganda and ego-boosting, these monuments may have had spiritual significance, too, since sacrificial vaults have been found near many stelae.

The primary **ball court** is between structures 9 and 10. The second largest of its kind in Central America, it was used for more than simple entertainment or exercise. Players had to keep a hard rubber ball from touching the ground, using the large macaw statues as markers for keeping score. The game may have symbolized the sun's battle to stay aloft and resist falling into night. Losers didn't graciously say, "It's Miller time!" or call for a rematch—they were put to death. King 18 Rabbit is thought to have been a great competitor, and some experts speculate that he lost a game and that's why he was taken to Quiriguá to be sacrificed. The **Hieroglyphic Stairway,** under the huge canopy, contains the single greatest collection of glyphs in the world. Erected by King Smoke Shell, the 63 steps immortalize the battles, deaths, and the inaugurations of Copán's kings, paying special respect to King Smoke Jaguar. Unfortunately, the history cannot be read chronologically since an earthquake knocked many steps free. They couldn't be put back in order so were replaced in a purely aesthetic arrangement.

The **Acropolis** was partly washed away by the river, which has since been routed away from the ruins. The last great king-builder, Dawning Sun, was credited with the construction of many of these elevated buildings. He had structure 16 decorated with images of war and death, and structure 18 was his tomb. The most important building on the Acropolis was 22-A, erected by Smoke Monkey. Called Popol Nah, or "mat house," this structure was like a committee room where rulers met with nobles to make decisions and perform ritual dances.

The **Western Plaza** is thought to have represented the underworld. Structures do appear symbolic of something, with doors that lead into blank walls. At the side of the plaza, Altar Q shows 15 of Copán's rulers passing power down to King Dawning Sun.

El Bosque and **Las Sepulturas** were private residences. While the architecture is nowhere near as impressive as in the ceremonial buildings of the Principal Group, it's important to archaeologists investigating the daily routine of the average Joe living in Copán. El Bosque lies in the forest off the trail to the Principal Group. Las Sepulturas lies 2 kilometers down the road, and appears to be the more revealing example of Mayan society. Excavations have shown that the Mayans had a highly stratified social system, where the elite owned multiroomed houses, while a separate ethnic group, possibly Lencas, lived as servants to the rich. Evidence indicates that women outnumbered men, which leads experts to conclude polygamy was practiced by the upper classes. With this portrait of Mayan society, another explanation for their disappearance could be proposed: Copán's women and the Lencas got fed up with the Mayan men and ran away to live together in blissful sin.

AFTER DARK The "tunkul" is a Mayan musical instrument, believed to be the predecessor of the marimba. The Tunkul Bar (*see* Food, *above*) plays anything but ancient music. The large tape collection and TV with cable make the bar an oasis for visiting archaeologists and travelers lonesome for a taste of home. Yummy drinks and happy hour prices (6–7 PM daily) are enough to make an alcoholic take up residence under the corner table. Down the street, **El Patio** draws the town's youth out for discomania. It opens every Saturday night, sometimes.

OUTDOOR ACTIVITIES Trucks leave from in front of Hotel Paty, next to the soccer field, for the one-hour trip to nearby **hot springs**. For **horseback riding,** do some bargain hunting—many hotels and entrepreneurs around the ruins rent the beasts. Guides are available, but they won't do much for your budget. Do it solo by asking someone for directions for the walk along the river or to **Los Sapos,** a site with Mayan statues of toads. A full-day hike runs from **Cabañas** near Copán Ruinas to **Dulce Nombre Copán** along a little-used road; from Dulce Nombre Copán you can hitch the final leg into Santa Rosa de Copán. Pilgrims often walk over the mountains from Copán Ruinas to the shrine in Esquipulas, Guatemala. The route is also used by smugglers, so take care. The hike is rumored to take one full day, but be prepared for a night just in case. You can rent a horse in Copán Ruinas for the journey. Since the mountain pass has no border station, have your passport stamped with a Guatemala tourist visa when you arrive in Esquipulas.

NEAR COPAN RUINAS

EL FLORIDO This Honduras-Guatemala border is frequented mostly by people who just want to visit Copán for the day. If this includes you, tell the officials at the Guatemalan *and* Honduran sides, who'll give you a temporary visa for several days in

Honduras. Regular entries and exits cost $2, and the station is open 6 AM–5 PM daily. The last bus from the border to Copán Ruinas leaves at 4:30 PM, and the last bus from the Guatemalan side of the border going inland leaves at 3:30 PM.

Santa Rosa de Copán

Hondurans and visitors alike are full of praise for Santa Rosa. Everyone likes to make excuses to come visit, because the town offers the amenities of a city while maintaining the casual charm of a village. Don't let the bus stop on the highway dispirit you; the city itself is set back in the pine-covered hills. The climate is mild, the streets are cobblestone, and the people are friendly and talkative. Everyone in Santa Rosa seems to be hard at work. Tobacco is grown all over western Honduras and they roll it up in Santa Rosa. **La Flora de Copán Fábrica de Tabacos** is one block west of the Plaza Central. This cigar factory will give you a free tour, and the little tienda sells stogies to take home (open daily 7–11:30 and 1–4:30). Leatherwork shops are all over the place—quality high, prices low. Belts and purses are cheap, but saddles are a real deal: Handcrafted saddles go for $100 (⅕ the U.S. cost).

BASICS Most **banks** are within a block of Parque Central and most change traveler's checks. **Hondutel** (across from Parque Central) is open daily 7 AM–9 PM for calls, 8–3 daily for faxes. The **post office** next door (open weekdays 8–noon and 2–5, Saturday 8–noon) will keep poste restante letters for three months. The **COHDEFOR** office (tel. 62–0212) works toward preserving the parks and wooded areas in the region, and has good info about the region (though it depends on who's working that day). To find the office, walk down a block from the park to Bancahsa, then go left four blocks. Peace Corps volunteers may have good advice, too (see Where to Sleep, below). For emergencies, call the **police** (tel. 199); **ambulance** (tel. 195); or **hospital** (tel. 62–0107).

COMING AND GOING Buses leave Santa Rosa daily for San Pedro Sula ($2, 3½ hours) every ½ hour 4:30 AM–5:15 PM. Buses to Nueva Ocotepeque leave about every three hours, 6 AM–5 PM daily (3 hours, $2). Buses to Gracias (2 hours, $1.25) leave every two hours 7:45 AM–5:30 PM. If you're looking at a map, don't be tricked into thinking the road through Gracias is the quickest route to Tegucigalpa; the mountain road between Gracias and La Esperanza is terrible and has poor transit connections. You're better off going to San Pedro Sula and down to the capital from there. From Santa Rosa's bus stop, it's a pretty long walk into town, and taxis cost around 50¢ per person. Once in town, it's very easy to get around. The center is small, and follows the grid pattern. The **Parque Central** is near the intersection of 1a Avenida and 1a Calle.

WHERE TO SLEEP

➤ **UNDER $2 • Hospedaje San Pedro.** San Pedro is the cheapest place in town and definitely off the beaten path. Most customers are elderly Hondurans, and rooms go for $1.25 per person. Since the place doesn't have a shower, you need to be flexible about washing. Try the bucket and some water—it'll get you there. *Barrio Merced, 2 blocks east of Parque Central. Wheelchair access.*

Peace Corps House. This hostel's the best deal in town, but it isn't always an option. The house is primarily for volunteers in the area, but they allow outsiders if space permits. If you're starved for reading material, their book exchange is worth a visit in itself. The bunk beds have sheets and are $2 per night, and the showers have hot water. *From behind the church, walk 3 blocks through the street-food vendors and down the hill. It's on the right-hand corner (unmarked), with an elevated sidewalk. Ask neighborhood kids where the gringos live. 7 beds and 2 couches, all share bath.*

➤ **UNDER $8 • Hotel El Rey.** If you need to stay close to the bus station, walk down the road a few meters to El Rey. Parking's in the back, a restaurant's in the front, and basic doubles with bath are $7. *On the highway, tel. 62–0602. 20 rooms, all with bath. Wheelchair access. Luggage storage, parking.*

Hotel Rosario. If you're a hypochondriac, you'll feel comfortable at Hotel Rosario since the owner runs the pharmacy next door, too. The rooms were done by the same interior designer who did all the budget lodgings in Honduras. What it lacks in style it makes up for in cleanliness and safety. Doubles are $6, or $8 with bath. *3a Av., 2 blocks east of Parque Central, tel. 62–0211. 20 rooms, some with bath. Wheelchair access. Luggage storage.*

➤ **CAMPING** • **La Montañita** park isn't officially open all night, but tell the people at COHDEFOR you intend to camp and they probably won't mess with you. The park, about 5 kilometers (3 miles) from town, wasn't designed for campers, so bring all your own necessities, including water.

FOOD Santa Rosa has lots of good options for lunch and dinner. All the good places are closed for breakfast, so just hit any comedor for a morning meal. For snacks, try the street vendors in the shacks behind the church. The better restaurants are all conveniently located on the same street, restaurant row, two blocks downhill from the church.

Chiky's. Though hidden behind a fence and parking lot, this modest patio restaurant shouldn't go unnoticed by any budget eater craving Mexican food. Chiky's owner is super hospitable, and claims to make his hamburgers in a unique fashion. It's a good place to have a few beers, and the best place to eat tostadas and tacos (65¢ each). The chilaquiles ($1) are very popular, too. *Walk down restaurant row, turn right after Flamingo's restaurant, go down 2 blocks. Open daily 10–10.*

Rincón Colonial. The menu is Honduras típica, but somehow standard dishes achieve extraordinary flavor. The service is great, and the owner will often leave you in control of the cable TV so you can watch movies or news in English. Most beef, chicken, and fish plates cost $3. The *brochetas de Res* ($3) is an especially delicious beef shish kebab. *1 block down restaurant row, tel. 62–0457. Open daily 10 AM–11 PM.*

AFTER DARK Restaurant row can get pretty lively on weekends, but you may want to wet your whistle somewhere else to save money on drinks. **Auto-Pollos,** a block away, is a parking lot/restaurant that rocks hardest during afternoon beer time. The proprietor keeps an eye on people's cars while they relax after a day's work. Too bad the owners can't watch the road for their customers, too, since many leave blind drunk. Disguise your staggering as dancing at the nearby **Discotheque Classic** on Friday and Saturday nights ($1 cover).

Gracias

Gracias is a pleasant little mountain town that served as the nation's capital before it moved to Comayagua centuries ago. The fortress of San Cristobal, built by president José Maria Medina, looks down upon the city. The town itself has little to offer today, but it serves as a good base for visiting **Celaque National Park.** The park covers 27,000 hectares (66,717 acres), with mucho pine trees on the ascent to the cloud forest at the summit of the principal mountain. Celaque means "bank of water" in the Lencan language, and the name is appropriate since 10 major rivers come from the mountain and provide the water supply for surrounding towns. Gracias celebrates the festival of Santa Lucia December 11–14. The highlight of the fair is the dance "El Guancasco," a typical Lencan dance that survived the colonial era. **Hospedaje Corazón de Jesus** is as cheap a sleep as you'll find at $1.25 per person. The place is dirty and the beds are lame, but it's only 2 blocks up from the bus station. The reception desk for Hotel Erick (1 block from Parque Central, tel. 98–4036) is in the general store, which is always full of candy-seeking kids. The clean $5 doubles have fans and hot water. The owner is very friendly and will let you leave your backpack here while you climb the mountain. Some righteous **hot springs** lie several hours' walk from Gracias;

ask around for directions. Otherwise, cars can take you here for $4 per carload. The springs have been developed for visitors, and the entrance fee is 25¢.

BASICS Banco Occidente changes traveler's checks. **Hondutel** is open 7 AM–9 PM daily. The **Correo** next door is open weekdays 8–noon and 2–5, Saturdays 8–11. For emergencies, call the **police** (on the corner of the park, tel. 98–4436) or the **hospital** (tel. 98–4425). The office of **COHDEFOR**, next to the police station, has info about the national park. If you plan to spend the night at the visitor's center in Celaque, you need to pay and get the key at this office.

COMING AND GOING Five buses leave Gracias for Santa Rosa, 5:30 AM–4 PM daily. Getting to La Esperanza is much more difficult. You need to catch a ride in the back of one of the pickup trucks that shuttle people back and forth to San Juan. From San Juan, only one bus leaves a day for La Esperanza, at 11:30 AM. If you arrive late, try to hitch with one of the few cars headed that way. The scenery is spectacular as you wind up through the mountains, but the road is hellish and you should allot a full day for the journey.

NEAR GRACIAS

CELAQUE NATIONAL PARK Celaque National Park is considered to have the best cloud forest in the entire country. Full-time inhabitants include white-faced monkeys, toucans, quetzals, pumas, and many of their furry or feathered friends. It's most hospitable in the dry season, when you can find a car to take you up to the trail head, about ½ hour from the visitor's center. During the rainy season, be prepared to get your feet wet since you must cross a swollen river twice in order to reach the summit. Hiking to the summit from town takes basically a full day—more in rain, less in shine.

Two hours from town, the visitor's center makes a good base camp, where you can stay for $1 per person. Get the key from COHDEFOR in Gracias. The center has 17 beds, a shower, latrines, gas lamps, and cooking facilities. Bring food from town. It gets cold at night so bring a sleeping bag or something warm for cover. The cabin sits next to a roaring river, surrounded by pine trees and the caretaker's coffee plants. Even if you aren't planning to climb the mountain, you'll love the tranquil night you spend at the center. Continuing up the mountain, you'll find two other cabins near the top, each with four beds. The cabins shouldn't be locked, but check with COHDEFOR to confirm this. The park has several camping sites, with showers, running water, and latrines available at some. Fresh water is available, so you needn't carry tons from town. Though the water is reported to be perfectly compatible with gringo stomachs, you should probably boil or treat it anyway. If you have the time and energy, extend your camping trip into a 3- to 4-day trek through the park to **Belén Gualcho** on the other side.

La Esperanza

La Esperanza, about 90 kilometers (56 miles) southwest of Siguatepeque, is a cute colonial town set in a stunning valley. The forested hills surrounding the town, complete with waterfalls and lakes, are great for mellow hikes. The valley is clocked at almost 4,950 feet above sea level, and it can get cold at night, especially during winter. La Esperanza merges with the town of Intibucá, and together they share a groovy **market** where Lenca women gather daily in their brightly colored scarves to buy and sell vegetables and crafts. On the hill behind the town, Iglesia La Gruta has a panoramic view of the valley and surrounding mountains. If you work up a sweat getting to the church, the *baños publicos* are a natural shower coming out of a rock. Since these waters are close to the church, you should plan on bathing in more than just what God gave you.

BASICS The Parque Central is the place to go for practical needs. Three **banks** are within a block of the park. **Hondutel** on the corner is open daily 7 AM–9 PM. The **post office** is open weekdays 7–noon and 2–5, Saturday 7–11.

COMING AND GOING Buses for Tegus leave daily at 5:30 AM, 9 AM, and 1 PM from the station one block over from the main market (5 hours, $3). Buses to Yamaranguila and Gracias leave from the other side of the market. The bus toward Gracias only goes as far as San Juan, where you'll need to transfer buses. You may be better off hitch-hiking, though the road between La Esperanza and Gracias is pathetic and the infrequency of passing vehicles can be exasperating. The journey will take at least a full day. On the other hand, the views from the back of a pickup truck in the high mountains are breathtaking.

WHERE TO SLEEP AND EAT Bathless rooms at **Hotel Mina** (1 block from the market, tel. 98–2071) are $2 per person, and shower gluttons pay $3 (hot water included). The hotel's comedor serves okay meals for about $1.25 per plate. The two-story **Hotel Solis** (tel. 98–2080) feels like a quaint bed-and-breakfast. Doubles are $8, and the kitchen serves all meals for $1.25 per plate. It's on the same street as the market stalls, 1 block down.

Nueva Ocotepeque

If you arrive in Honduras late in the day from El Salvador or Guatemala, you may be forced to spend the night here since the last bus headed inland leaves mid-afternoon. The place is small and bland, but as transit hubs go, you could do worse. You can always find a money changer who speaks four languages—colóns, quetzales, lempiras, and dollars.

BASICS **Banco Occidente**, a block from the bus station, changes traveler's checks. **Hondutel**, one block southeast from the bus station, is open daily 7 AM–9 PM. The **post office**, behind Hondutel, is open weekdays 8–noon and 2–4. For **police** assistance, call 63–3199.

COMING AND GOING Buses leave for the Guatemalan border at Agua Caliente 6 AM–4 PM daily (½ hour, $1). Buses to the Salvadoran border at El Poy leave every 45 minutes 6:30 AM–7 PM (½ hour, 25¢). The last few buses won't do you a lick of good, since the border closes at 6 PM. To go north, a few buses leave in the morning for San Pedro Sula. Perhaps more convenient is taking the bus to Santa Rosa de Copán (3 hours, $1.25), which departs hourly 6 AM–3 PM. From Santa Rosa, buses leave every ½ hour for San Pedro Sula, or you can stop in La Entrada and catch a ride to Copán Ruinas.

WHERE TO SLEEP AND EAT Elementary but cheap rooms at **Hospedaje Ocotepeque** are $2 for one person, $3 for two people, and $4 for three (none with bath). It's on the main street next to the bus station. **Hotel Sandobal** (1 block from the bank, tel. 73–3098) is the nicest joint in town and has a great restaurant, too. It's a block off the main street, so the rooms are insulated from the traffic din. The $8 doubles all have private showers with hot water. The cheap comedores along the main street have food sufficient to keep your bod going, as do the stands near the bus station. Bus drivers think the air-conditioned restaurant in Hotel Sandobal is the best in town. Highlights include pancakes ($1), a chicken plate ($2), fish plate ($4), and asparagus soup ($1).

NEAR NUEVA OCOTEPEQUE

GUATEMALAN BORDER AT AGUA CALIENTE The border is open 6–6 daily ($2 exit or entry fee). Buses from the border to Nueva Ocotepeque run constantly 8 AM–6:30 PM, (½ hour, 60¢), and the reverse trip is done 6 AM–4 PM. If you're going into

Guatemala, stop in the church across the border in Esquipulas to check out the figure of the Black Christ.

SALVADORAN BORDER AT EL POY Though things have quieted down in El Salvador, you should check the current conditions before crossing here since the area was once (and could be again) a civil war hot spot. The Honduran side of the border is open 6–6 ($2 exit or entry fee). Buses leave the border constantly for Ocotepeque 8–7 daily (½ hour, 25¢).

GUISAYOTE NATURE RESERVE The road between Nueva Ocotepeque and Santa Rosa is the highest paved road in Honduras and passes through the Güisayote nature reserve. Have the bus driver drop you off at the visitor's center (no more than a billboard with info) and spend the day hiking in the cloud forest. Some of the park has been damaged by clear-cutting, but the center of the park has virgin forest with all the exotic cloud-forest animals you'd expect. Some ruins have recently been found in the forest, where it is believed pre-Columbian locals fought off a Spanish attack. Take advantage of the easy access to this park, bring some water, and be prepared for rain.

San Pedro Sula

Comparisons between Tegucigalpa and San Pedro Sula are unavoidable. As the country's second-largest city, San Pedro is content to be the industrial and financial capital of the country, leaving political administration to Tegus. San Pedro is the bustling commercial center for the coffee, lumber, banana, and sugar trades. Over the years, it's been slammed by numerous floods and fires, which have wiped out all visible colonial vestiges. Perhaps as a result, the city is well organized, constructed more for function than aesthetics, and streets are well labeled. San Pedro has a more affluent air than Tegus, with downtown high rises and modern architecture. San Pedro also has hotter air, broiling in the summer while the climate in mountainous Tegus remains endurable. San Pedro has good accommodations and all the other necessities, and it's a great base for day-trips in all directions.

Many travelers enter the country here en route to the palm-fringed beaches of the Caribbean coast.

BASICS

AMERICAN EXPRESS The office offers standard services to card holders: holding mail, cashing traveler's and personal checks, and replacing lost or stolen checks or cards. Some of the staff speak English. The mailing address is Box 795, San Pedro Sula. *Housed at Mundirama Travel Service, 2a Calle near 3a Av., across from the cathedral, tel. 53–0490. Open weekdays 7:30–5, but financial services are available only while banks are open (9–3).*

MONEY In the park and on the adjacent pedestrian street, money changers do everything to make themselves conspicuous. They change traveler's checks and cash at more or less the official rates of exchange, and they keep longer hours. Competition is fierce, so bargain-shop and watch out for counterfeits. If you want more security, most banks around the park will change dollars weekdays 9–3.

CONSULATES United Kingdom. *Terminales de Cortes, 4a Av. at 4a Calle NO, 2nd floor #29, tel. 53–2600. Open weekdays 7:30 AM–11:30 AM.*

United States. The U.S. uses the basement of Centro Cultural San Pedro as a consulate, but only on the first Friday of every month (?!). *3a Av., between Calles 3a and 4a NE, tel. 53–3911.*

EMERGENCIES Police, also known as FUSEP (4a Calle, between Avs. 3a and 4a SO, tel. 52–3171); **female police** (3a Av., bet. Calles 9a and 10a, tel. 52–3184); **ambulance** (8a Calle, between Avs. 8a and 9a SO, tel. 57–5069). The **hospital** (7a Calle, bet. Avs. 9a and 10a, tel. 52–3411) has some English-speaking doctors.

LAUNDRY If the maids in your hotel don't do laundry, try **Lava Facil.** A medium load costs about $2. *7a Av. at 5a Calle NO, tel. 52–7040. Open Mon.–Sat. 7–5, Sun. 8–noon.*

MEDICAL AID Pharmacies stay open later than 10 PM on a rotating basis, and many post the table for late-night pharmacies in their windows. The tourist information office has a list as well. The owner of **Farmacia San José Centro** (2a Calle, between Avs. 5a and 6a SO, tel. 53–3509) speaks English. The store often has tampons and other hygiene luxuries, and they're open weekdays 7:30–6, Saturday 8–noon. Up the street from Farmacia San José, **Optica Boyell** (2a Calle, between Avs. 6a and 7a SO, tel. 53–1121) carries Bausch and Lomb products for contact lenses (open weekdays 8–noon and 2–6, Saturday 8–noon).

PHONES AND MAIL Hondutel (4a Av. at 5a Calle SO) is open 24 hours; two telephones have direct lines to operators in the United States for credit card or collect calls. Local calls cost 10 centavos (2¢), but the phones are lousy and the queues are long. For local calls, you're better off paying a little extra to use the phone in a hotel. The main **post office** (1a Av. at 9a Calle) is open weekdays 7:30 AM–8 PM, Saturday 7:30–noon.

TRAVEL AGENCIES Cambio C. A. specializes in ecotourism, with canoe trips into the Mosquitia and to national parks. The company says they're environmentally sensitive, and their trips are more adventurous than many guided tours. The excursions aren't cheap, but the convenience and organization are priceless to some. *1a Calle, bet. Avs. 5a and 6a, tel. 52–7335.*

VISITOR INFORMATION The **Instituto Hondureño de Turismo,** three blocks behind Gran Hotel Sula (which is on Parque Central), is easy to miss because it's on the third floor, so look up. The office is worth finding because they're well stocked with info on the whole country, but as of yet have no maps of San Pedro Sula. *Edificio Inmosa, 4a Calle between Avs. 3a and 4a NO, tel. 52–3023. Open weekdays 8–4.*

COMING AND GOING

BY TRAIN Trains take twice as long as buses but cost half as much. The train to Puerto Cortés (3 hours, 50¢) leaves San Pedro Sula at 6:45 AM and returns from Puerto Cortés at 3:15 PM. If you're headed to Tela, take the 6:45 AM train that leaves a couple of times a week for Baracoa (1½ hours, 25¢), and transfer to the 8:30 AM train for Tela (2½ hours). The train leaves Tela for the return trip to San Pedro Sula at 1:45 PM. The Tela train has first- and second-class seats (55¢ or 40¢).

BY BUS While the city has no central bus station, all the individual stations are relatively close to one another on the south side of the town center, not far from the hotels. **Hedman Alas** (3a Calle, bet. Avs. 7a and 8a NO, tel. 53–1361) has buses to Tegus (4½ hours, $3) leaving five times a day 6:30 AM–5:30 PM. **Saenz** (9a Av. bet. Calles 9a and 10a SO, tel. 53–1829) has buses to Tegus (4½ hours, $2.50) every ½ hour 2 AM–5:15 PM. **Copanecos** and **Toritos** share the station at 6a Av. bet. Calles 8a and 9a SO (tel. 53–1954 or 53–4930). Both companies serve Santa Rosa de Copán (4 hours, $2), leaving every ½ hour 4:30 AM–5:15 PM. If you're heading for Copán, you can take this bus as far as La Entrada, and transfer there. **Etumi** has direct buses to Copán Ruinas (5 hours, $3) at 11 AM and 1 PM. Etumi buses come and go from in front of Hotel Palmira on 6a Calle, between Avs. 6a and 7a SO. **Impala** (2a Av., bet. Calles 4a and 5a SO, tel. 53–3111) goes to Puerto Cortés (1 hour, $1) hourly from 6–6. Take the bus to Río Lindo (2 hours, $1) with **Tirla** (in the parking lot on 2a Av.

bet. Calles 5a and 6a). Tirla leaves hourly 6:30–5, and can drop you just a short walk from the Pulhapanzák waterfalls. Buses to El Progreso and La Lima share the same parking lot (2a Av., bet. Calles 5a and 6a SO, tel. 53–1023). Buses to La Lima (½ hour, 30¢) and El Progreso (1 hour, 50¢) leave frequently 4:30 AM–10 PM. Transfer at El Progreso for Tela. Buses to La Ceiba ($3, 3 hours) leave from the same station every ½ hour 5:30 AM–6 PM. Buses to Nueva Ocotepeque and the border at Agua Caliente ($4, 8 hours) leave the station at 4a Avenida at 2a Calle SO at midnight, 6 AM, and 10 AM. A 2 PM bus only goes as far as Nueva Ocotepeque.

HITCHING The cheapest way to get to hitching spots on the outskirts of town is to take Bus "Route 1" from 1a Calle at 2a Avenida SO. This bus travels along Avenida Circunvalación, which makes a loop around the city. Ask the driver to let you off at the *salida* (exit) for Puerto Cortés if you're headed that way, or Tegus if this is your destiny. To reach the north coast beaches, walk down 1a Calle a mile or so before flagging down passing cars.

BY CAR If you come to San Pedro with a car, take it to a hotel with a private, secure garage so you'll still have it when it's time to leave. If you want to rent a car, multitudinous agencies have offices at the airport and downtown. Consider renting a 4x4, since the areas not served by public transportation are usually on potholed, dirt/mud roads.

BY PLANE The **Ramon Villeda Morales Airport** is open daily until dusk, but the two banks for changing money are open only 9 AM–3 PM. Not to worry; "businesspeople" wait just outside the airport door to change your money. The airport is served by Tan-Sahsa, Lacsa, American, Continental, Taca, and two charter services, Serpico and Isleña. Tan-Sahsa, the national airline, has flights to Roatán for $21, and to Tegus and La Ceiba for $18 (one-way fares).

➤ **AIRPORT TRANSPORTATION** • The airport lies 15 kilometers (9 miles) outside town. Taxis into the city cost $4–$8; take a regular taxi rather than a yellow cab and you'll save $3. To save more money, walk past the parking lot exit and hitch a ride (quite easy to do) or walk 1½ kilometers to the main road and take a bus into town for 25¢. To get to the airport economically, take a bus toward El Progreso and get off at the airport entrance (15 minutes, 25¢). From there, hitch, walk, or take a cab the last 1½ kilometers to the terminal.

GETTING AROUND

The city is laid out in a grid of intersecting calles and avenidas. Since the numbers of streets repeat themselves, the city has been divided into sections: NorOeste (northwest—NO), SurOeste (southwest—SO), SurEste (southeast—SE), and NorEste (northeast—NE). If arriving by bus, you'll be in either the SO or SE part of town. To get your bearings, walk north to 1a Calle and the Parque Central. The park is the center of town, bordered by 1a Calle and 3a Avenida SO, and the Hotel Gran Sula across the street is a prominent landmark. The train station is right downtown on 1a Avenida and 1a Calle. It's probably in this section (SO) that you'll spend your time. "Abajo de la linea," SE below 1a Avenida, is considered a dangerous neighborhood, especially at night. Around the perimeter of the city runs **Avenida Circunvalación,** which has other names at different points in the city—including 10a Avenida, 17a Avenida, and 17a Calle. San Pedro has some city buses, but they usually go only by day to the places you want to visit by night. Nonetheless, Bus 3 goes to Zona Viva from 3a Calle, between avenidas 3 and 4 NO. Bus 1 goes to Avenida Circunvalación from 1a Calle at 2a Avenida SO. The happening night-spot district, **Zona Viva,** is on the outskirts of town, near Avenida Circunvalación. Other than taking a bus, take taxis for $1–$2 a pop.

WHERE TO SLEEP

Hotels are omnipresent in the SO part of town. Cheaper accommodations than those listed below do exist, especially for couples. Matrimonial beds in some of the hospedajes around 6–7 avenidas and 4–7 calles SO cost around $2. Be aware that these places are frequented by prostitutes, and you may be kept awake by the couple next door, who'll seem to be having too much fun to be married.

➤ **UNDER $5** • **Hotel Brisas de Occidente.** This is the best place in town for the money, and everybody knows it—it's a second home for Peace Corps volunteers. The rooms are clean, and most are large with lots of light. All rooms have fans, a table, and comfy chairs. The price is a wonderful $2 per person. *5a Av. at 7a Calle SO, tel. 52–2309. 32 rooms, none with bath. Luggage storage.*

Hotel Brisas de Copán. Rooms are tidy, but the bathrooms will be someone's Herculean task to clean. The second-floor rooms with balconies allow you to see who's making all the noise in the street. The people hanging out on the corner are a mixed blessing: They stay up late so you may, too, but the presence of men and women in the streets makes an otherwise dubious neighborhood more secure. Rooms are $2 for two people. *6a Av. at 6a Calle SO. 13 rooms, none with bath. Luggage storage.*

➤ **UNDER $10** • **Gran Hotel San Pedro.** Businesspeople who can't afford the expensive Gran Hotel Sula come here. The hotel offers rooms with an extensive price range, so backpackers will feel at home, too. All rooms have fans, and the more expensive rooms have TV, telephone, and air-conditioning. The cheapest rooms without bath are barely big enough for the beds ($3 per person); more expensive rooms run $9–$12 for a double. *3a Calle bet. Avs. 1a and 2a SO, tel. 53–2655. 127 rooms, some with bath. Luggage storage, restaurant.*

Hotel San José. Hotel San José is virtually brand-new, and the owner beams with pride about the immaculate establishment. Purified water and a TV are in the lobby for your drinking and viewing pleasure. All rooms have fans, and for $3 more you get air-conditioning. With several rooms on the ground floor, this is virtually the only decent hotel that is wheelchair accessible. Doubles are around $8. *6a Av., bet. Calles 5a and 6a SO, tel. 57–1208. 42 rooms, all with bath. Wheelchair access. Luggage storage, laundry.*

➤ **UNDER $20** • **Hotel Ambassador.** If you're looking for a nice place with five-star billing, park your car in the Ambassador's private garage and rent an air-conditioned room with a balcony looking out on the hills. All rooms have hot water and phones, and classier rooms have cable TV. Doubles run $10–$18. *7a Calle at 5a Av. SO, tel. 57–6825. 32 rooms, all with bath. Luggage storage, restaurant, parking.*

Lots of people rough it in this city. Unfortunately, most of them are about 13 years old and have no choice. You'll find them shoeless and barely clad sleeping in doorways. Watch long enough and you'll see someone rifle through their pockets. You can expect this (or worse) sleeping on the streets.

CAMPING Camping is allowed on any soccer field, but you need to get permission from city hall in Parque Central. If you arrive too late or just can't be bothered, you probably won't have trouble except for an occasional soccer ball coming through your tent flap.

FOOD

You'll find lots of U.S.-style fast-food right around the park and west on 1a Calle. If you need a familiar taste, **Pizza Hut** has several locations; the one on 1a Calle at 16a Avenida has a salad bar (open daily 11–11). The Gran Hotel Sula's **Cafe Skandia,** across from the park, is open 24 hours serving waffles ($2), club sandwiches ($2), and chef's salad ($4). Zona Viva is full of people on weekends and always crowded with restaurant-goers. You can find both cheap comedor food and fine, expensive dining from 10a Calle on up 17a Avenida.

➤ **UNDER $5** • **Mi Rinconcito.** At this little log cabin you'll find little log tables inside and a patio out back. Fruit drinks and shakes are the specialty, with all different flavors in a huge cup for $1. Generic breakfasts, lunches, and dinners cost $1.25. Vegetarians can have pupusas con queso (tortilla baked around cheese) for 30¢ each. *1a Calle, bet. Avs. 6a and 7a NO, 1½ blocks west of the park. Open Mon.–Sat. 9–9.*

Restaurante Madrid. The ornate decoration resembles a cheap eatery in Spain, and many people come here to hang out and talk. Breakfast is only $2, and the Spanish dishes are a welcome change from beans. Spanish tortilla ($2), paella ($4), and flan ($1) will fill you up, and the espresso and cappuccino will jump-start your nerves. *In Parque Central. Wheelchair access. Open daily 8 AM–10 PM.*

➤ **UNDER $10** • **Don Juan's.** It would be a shame if the formal ambience of this Canadian restaurant scared you off; the prices aren't exorbitant and the selection of international dishes is mighty. The menu has English subtitles. The Indian-style shrimp with curry ($7) and the Hungarian goulash ($2) are among the favorites. Leave room for peach Melba ($2) or a crepe Suzette ($2). *17a Av., tel. 52–7355. 10-minute walk up from Zona Viva. Open Mon.–Sat. noon–2 and 6–11. Wheelchair access.*

➤ **UNDER $15** • **Pat's Steak House.** The menu says the beef is cheap here because the owner is a cattle rustler, but the cheap cows must have been stolen by someone else because this place costs *mucho dinero.* All that aside, it *is* the best steak house in town. Each dinner is served with a potato and soup or salad; pepper steak is $10, and the Surf 'n' Turf is $11. *17a Av. at 5a Calle SO, tel. 53–0939. Several blocks up from Zona Viva. Open Mon.–Thurs. 11–12:30 and 6–11, Fri. and Sat. 6–midnight. Wheelchair access.*

WORTH SEEING

For a city its size, San Pedro has surprisingly few cultural or historical sites. Check with the tourist office for the current whereabouts of a meandering archaeological exhibition, which is as yet without a permanent home. The **cathedral** on the park is the most important, though still unexciting, church in town. Built in the 1950s, the neo-colonial structure epitomizes the unhistoric nature of the city. Not far from the city are a few outdoor spots worth checking out. Walk (far) or take a taxi up to **Mirador Bella Vista,** near the monstrous Coca-Cola sign on the mountain, and you'll get boomin' views of the city and beyond. On the northern edge of town, you can hang out in the forested **Parque Presentación Centeno** near the Río Las Piedras. The **artisan's market** (6a Calle bet. Avs. 8a and 9a NO) is open daily; mornings are the busiest and most interesting time to visit. In addition to the regular vegetable stands and street-food vendors, artisans gather here to sell baskets, woodwork, wicker shoes, and leather goods. Along 6a Calle SO and running east from 4a Avenida, a more general market meets people's practical needs. You can find a few exciting bargains here, in addition to clothing and shoes for all occasions. Every Saturday, the **Exposición Artisanal y Comidas Típicas** (exhibition of typical art and food) is held in Parque Central. *Sopa de Mondongo* and *Yuca con Chicharron* are two culinary specialties—don't ask what they are, just try them for the adventure. The **festival** honoring the town's patron saint, San Pedro, is during the last week of June. The fair, Semana Sanpedrana, rocks on with horse races, art exhibits, song and dance competitions, and beauty contests for both females and cattle.

AFTER DARK

If you're bashful or have a working conscience, close your eyes. Those of you still peeking should know that an invitation to a "nightclub" usually means visiting a glorified brothel where men bribe women to dance by buying them drinks. This is a typical night out for many men in San Pedro. If you want to see how men pass their evenings somewhere less pressure-filled than a straight-out whorehouse, try one of the semi-raunchy stripper clubs. **Night Club Vegas** (Zona Viva, tel. 57–6371) is pretty easygoing. Of course it's still macho-oriented, but it's often frequented by couples. Local papers list what's showing at the many **cinemas** around town

BARS **Wilmer's Bar.** Wilmer's is a regular's bar, but if you speak Spanish, you'll find yourself welcomed as an instant regular. Foreigners are a familiar sight here and won't feel uncomfortable. Tease the owner and he might dance on the bar. Snack foods are served free with each beer. *7a Av., bet. Calles 2a and 3a SO, tel. 57–9381. Wheelchair access. Open Mon.–Sat. 2 PM–2 AM, Sun. 1–7 PM.*

Turtle eggs are sold in some clubs to men who believe the eggs enhance their sexual prowess (the only real sexual repercussions involve the turtles, whose populations are thinning out).

Sopa de Cardan. This bar is as typical as they get. Business-people come here directly after work to unwind over a bottle of *guaro,* Honduran moonshine with a label. Beers and drinks come with free *Sopa de Cardan,* a frijole soup with fried pork. Tourists don't come here, so if you drink a guaro and some soup, you're "in" with the locals. *3a Av., bet. Calles 2a and 3a NE. Open daily 8 AM–10 PM.*

Corsel Negro. The big gay bar in town died with its owner, and now all the gay clubs are private. This bar has a mixed crowd, and anyone will feel comfortable here. The bar itself has little to offer, but the owner Miguel and the bartender Yovanny are gay and can possibly help you get in the private clubs. *13a Calle SE, tel. 52–5075. Open daily 7 PM–whenever. Take a taxi since it's a long walk from downtown.*

MUSIC AND DANCING The Zona Viva, with wall-to-wall bars and restaurants for several blocks, rocks hard on weekends. After the dinner rush, the music gets louder, bands strike up, and most everything on waitpeople's trays is liquid. You'll need to take a taxi, because it's a very long walk from downtown.

Terrazas. This disco is popular on weekends with a well-dressed, young crowd, but happy hour ($1 drinks) only runs Tuesday–Thursday 7–8 PM. Weekend prices aren't bad—$2 each for all sorts of mixed drinks. *10a Calle at 15a Av. SE, $2 cover on weekends. Open Tues.–Thurs. 6:30–midnight, Fri. and Sat. 6:30–?.*

Confetti's. At the other end of town from Zona Viva, several discos hover around the exit for Puerto Cortés. Confetti's is the most popular, and enforces a minimal dress code (dress "nice"). The dance floor is small but air-conditioned. The crowd usually arrives after midnight. *Av. Circunvalación at the salida de Puerto Cortés. Weekdays $2 cover, weekends $3. Open daily 7 PM–?.*

Black and White. Black and White is a Garifuna bar that specializes in "punta," a distinct Honduran dance music. A fun place to dance with friends, the club thumps with the Caribbean rhythms. Take a taxi, because the neighborhood is dangerous. *8a Calle, bet. Avs. 1a and 3a SE. Open weekends 7–?.*

Near San Pedro Sula

LA LIMA Famous for banana growing, La Lima is just past the airport, 15 kilometers (9 miles) outside San Pedro. Many travel agents, like **Maya Tropic Tours** in the Gran Hotel Sula, offer banana plantation tours (in English) for $25 per person. The companies may let people wander around on their own, and you can probably pay someone less than $25 for an unofficial tour.

EL PROGRESO Most people stop here only to change buses for Tela. Yet, it's worth mentioning that this town is the capital of the Jesuit community in the country. These priests are the most outspoken and valiant defenders of the poor in the country. They're always doing 15 things at once, but corner one for a minute and you'll find out a lot about the ins and outs of the country's politics. If you spend the night here, **Casa Blanca** (across from the Tela bus station, tel. 66–0143) has very basic $3 doubles, all sharing bath. You won't need an alarm clock since the buses will wake you up. **Porky's** bar in Zona Rosa is rumored to be a popular transvestite hangout. **Hondutel** (open 7–noon and 2–9 daily) and the **post office** (open weekdays 8–3, Saturday 8–11) are both just past the park toward the bus stations. Banks and cheap restaurants abound on the streets connecting the two bus stations, which are two blocks apart. Buses to San Pedro Sula (1 hour, 50¢) leave every 5 minutes 4 AM–10 PM. Buses to Yoro ($2, 3 hours) leave from the same station 4:30–4:30. Two blocks down, buses to Tela ($1, 2 hours) leave every ½ hour 5 AM–7 PM.

PULHAPANZAK WATERFALLS Pulhapanzák, the most famous waterfall in the country, is an easy day-trip from San Pedro Sula or Lago de Yojoa. Swim in the tranquil pools below while you look up at the gushing falls. Try to come midweek, since you'll have to share the beauty with everybody else on the weekend. The bus to Río Lindo (*see* Coming and Going in San Pedro Sula, *above*) leaves you a short walk from the falls.

CUSUCO NATIONAL PARK This cloud forest is only two hours from San Pedro if you have a car, but it's a bitch of a hitch if you don't. In either case, take the southwest road toward Copán and turn northwest at the town of Cofradía. Go until you reach Buenos Aires, the last town where you can buy food and water. Twenty minutes after the road splits you'll find the park office on the left. You can pitch a tent here and use the water near the office. Hikes vary from several hours to a couple of days; one goes all the way to the coast. See if you can spot one of the armadillos for which the park is named. As always, be prepared for rain. Talk to Fundación Ecologista (3a Av., bet. Calles 9a and 10a NO, tel. 53–3397) in San Pedro for trail maps. If they can't help you find a ride, Cambio C.A. (*see* Travel Agencies in San Pedro, *above*) offers pricey tours of the region.

Caribbean Coast

Though banana companies and the tourist industry think they've laid claim to the Caribbean coast, this is really the domain of the Garifuna. Descendants of African slaves who shipwrecked in the Caribbean and escaped to the island of St. Vincent in the Lesser Antilles, they mixed with indigenous Caribs. In the 18th century the British removed the Garifunas to the island of Roatán, and many of them eventually migrated to the mainland, inhabiting the coastline from Belize to Nicaragua. Nearly 80% of the Garifuna still live in Honduras. Most live in thatch-roofed huts next to the sea and survive by fishing.

Their music, dancing, and native language portray a distinct West African influence. The older generation voices concern that the culture is slipping away—the young speak Spanish rather than Garifuna, and due to rampant unemployment they often move to the United States or urban areas of Honduras, abandoning their past. The Garifuna are intensely vital and passionate; 80-year-olds can still sing and dance a young Westerner under the table. Some of their songs are filled with motifs of poverty and loss, while others are more like oral history put to music. Behind occasional veils of sadness lie some of the most profound beauty and love for life that you'll ever see.

The whole country flocks here during Semana Santa, and all hotels fill up. Another damper on your visit could be the rain—occasional showers will soak through your shoes and dampen your socks all year, but the rain gets dire from mid-October to December. It can fall for days without end, and flash floods can occur in the mountains. Unless you have gills, this isn't the best time for hiking and camping.

Puerto Cortés

Not directly connected to the eastern Caribbean coast by road, Puerto Cortés is off the beaten tourist path. The town, 57 kilometers (35 miles) north of San Pedro, is the country's biggest and busiest port. It's surprising, then, just how sedate Puerto Cortés is; aside from nearby beaches, the town has little to offer visitors. The city is laid out in a grid, with the main plaza at 3a Avenida and 4a Calle.

BASICS Hondutel is open 24 hours a day, and the **post office** next door is open weekdays 8–noon and 2–5, Saturday 8–noon. Both are on 1a Calle, between avenidas 1 and 2. For changing money, try either **Banco Atlantida** or **Banffau,** both near the park. For emergencies, call the **police** (tel. 55–0420 or 199); **ambulance** (tel. 195); or the **hospital** (tel. 55–0562).

COMING AND GOING

➤ **BY BUS** • **Impala** and **Citul** (tel. 55–0466) both have stations on 3a Avenida, a block from Parque Central. Both lines run buses to San Pedro Sula at least every hour 4:30 AM–late evening ($1, 1 hour). Buses to Omoa (30¢, 45 minutes) leave from across the street from the Citul Station on 2a Calle hourly 6 AM–7:30 PM.

➤ **BY TRAIN** • To reach the train station, walk down 2a Avenida, and turn left at the dead end; it's beside the dock gate labeled Porton 3. The train also stops closer to the town center, next to Porton 7 at the docks. The train for San Pedro leaves around 3:30 PM and the train to Baracoa, the transfer point for Tela, leaves around 5 AM. The people hanging out by the dock gate can tell you if the schedule has been revised.

➤ **BY BOAT** • Ships pull out to sea for destinations around the world, and you could conceivably find a ride to Singapore if you had time to wait. Boats go to Roatán almost daily, to Belize a couple of times a week, and occasionally to the United States. For more info, go to Porton 7, the dock gate, and talk to the sailors. Sit patiently through the information-costs-money routine, and eventually they'll probably enlighten you about the schedules for free.

WHERE TO SLEEP The hotels along the docks are cheapest, but they're pretty dirty and often frequented by prostitutes. The rooms a block over are nicer and sometimes equally cheap.

Hotel Colón. The rooms are clean but nothing special, and sailors complain that the beds are old and beaten up. All rooms share a decent common bath; doubles are $3, or $4 with a fan. *3a Av. near 2a Calle Oeste, 5 blocks from the park. 23 rooms, none with bath. Wheelchair access. Luggage storage, laundry.*

Hotel Formosa. Rooms here vary in quality and price. Most are at the upper end of the scale, with air-conditioning and private baths. Several basic rooms share a super-clean communal bath. All rooms are well kept, have fans, and cost $3-$12. *3a. Av. bet. Calles 1a and 2a, tel. 55–0853. 2 blocks from the park, 1 block from buses. Wheelchair access. Luggage storage, laundry.*

FOOD **Cafe Viena.** The name is Austrian, the interior decoration is Greek, and the food is típica Honduran. They also have a good selection of fish—snapper prepared to your liking is $4, and conch salad is $5. *2a Av., across from the park, tel. 55–0438. Wheelchair access. Open Mon.–Sat. 9–noon and 5–midnight, closed Sun.*

Restaurante Tuek San. The Asian food here is prepared without a lot of heart, but they also serve pretty good típica plates and fish dishes. Vegetarians will have good luck here, with vegetable soup ($2) or Chinese-style rice ($3). *2a Av., across from the park, tel. 55–1060. Wheelchair access. Open daily 8 AM–10 PM.*

NEAR PUERTO CORTES

Travesía, a small Garifuna fishing village just eat of Puerto Cortés, has the nicest beaches around. Take the bus from Parque Central (30¢, 25 minutes). **Omoa,** 15 kilometers (9 miles) west of Puerto Cortés, has the Fuerte San Fernando de Omoa, a defunct Spanish fortress built in the 18th century. Check out their big guns 9–4 daily (admission: $2). The beach down the road has funky sand, but the bay flanked by mountains is far more idyllic. Buses run from Puerto Cortés 6 AM–7:30 PM (30¢, 45 minutes), and return until 6 PM.

If you want to go **west to Guatemala** but can't be bothered to head inland to an official crossing, take the "Jungle Trail" west from Puerto Cortés. **Río Cofo** is a nice beach, where the cool river meets the sea, on the road to **Tegucigalpita** (note the *-ita*). Once you get to Tegucigalpita, change buses for **Corinto,** where you can walk to **Cacao** and the Guatemalan border. Remember to get your passport stamped in the next town.

Tela

Lots of people know Tela is beautiful. It's the most visited Honduran beach town, but it's still mellow and uncrowded (with the exception of Semana Santa, when Hondurans flock in and prices go up). Life here is easy and fun. Beautiful beaches, delicious seafood, and nearby wildlife reserves entice many travelers to stop over for a week, a month, or even call their home country quits. The town once bustled with business when the United Fruit Company was based here. The company built houses along the coast west of the Río Tela, also known as **Tela Nueva.** East of the river, the old town, **Tela Vieja,** houses most of the hotels, restaurants, and important stuff for travelers. The tranquility on both sides of the river may not last—foreign developers plan to build mega-hotels to capitalize on this unspoiled paradise. Yikes.

BASICS Everything you'll need is within a couple of blocks of the main street in Tela Vieja. **Hondutel** (4 Av. near 8a Calle) is open daily 7 AM–9 PM. The **post office** next door is open weekdays 7–noon and 2–4:30, Saturday 7–noon. **Bancahsa** on the main street changes traveler's checks. **Laverdería El Centro** (Av. Guatemala, just off the main street) will wash and dry a big load of laundry for about $3. For urgent matters, call the **police** (tel. 48–2079); **ambulance** (tel. 48–2121); or **hospital** (tel. 48–2073).

COMING AND GOING

➤ **BY BUS** • Buses come and go from the station at 9a Avenida at main street. Hop on a bus to El Progreso (2 hours, $1) leaving every ½ hour 4:30 AM–6 PM; from there you can catch a bus to San Pedro Sula. Buses to San Pedro leave El Progreso until about 6 PM. Buses leave for La Ceiba ($1.25, 2 hours) every ½ hour 4:30 AM–6 PM.

➤ **BY TRAIN** • Getting around en route to San Pedro by train is cheaper but takes longer than the bus. Trains for Baracoa (2 hours, 30¢) leave Tuesday, Wednesday, and Saturday at 1:45 PM. Trains for El Progreso (2½ hours, 30¢) leave Monday, Tuesday, Wednesday, and Sunday at 1:45 PM.

➤ **HITCHING** • Coming north from Tegus, you'll save about an hour if you bypass San Pedro Sula. Take the road north at La Barca, which is basically a gas station at a fork in the road. Try to arrive early, since little traffic passes during the day. A ride on this road will take you to El Progreso, where you can get a bus to Tela or walk out of town to continue hitching.

WHERE TO SLEEP All hotels listed below are near the beach and close to the bus station. Surprisingly, places farther from the beach aren't any cheaper than those catching the sea breeze.

Boarding House Sara. Set back one block from the west end of the beach, Sara's is a backpacker hot-spot. Rooms in the main house ($3 per person) are a little stuffy and not mosquito-proof, but the cabaña next door is wonderful, with a refrigerator, a patio with hammocks, and a living room. The English-speaking owner says he only rents the three-room cabaña as a whole, but you can probably haggle one of the rooms for $3–$4 per person. The kitchen facilities in the main house are open to all, and the managers will prepare you a meal with advance notice. *Av. Cuba at Calle Herrera, tel. 48–2370. 18 rooms, none with bath. Luggage storage, laundry.*

Hotel Roberto. Right across from the bus station, this is one of the cheapest hotels in town. Rooms are small, clean, and all have fans. The hotel is crammed between two lively bars, but they turn the music down around midnight. Doubles sharing bath are $5. *Across from the bus station on main street, tel. 48–2290. 25 rooms, some with bath. Wheelchair access. Luggage storage, laundry.*

Hotel Playa. The afternoon music from the evangelical church across the street may be the only thing that keeps Hotel Playa from being an utterly relaxing place to stay. All rooms ($6 double) have nice wooden furniture, fans, and clean private baths. Purified water is in the lobby, and saltwater is a block away in the sea. *1 block off the west end of the beach. 14 rooms, all with bath. Wheelchair access. Luggage storage, laundry.*

➤ **CAMPING** • The **Lancetilla Botanic Garden** has a fickle policy for overnight guests. The Garden officially closes at 3:30 PM, but usually if you come in earlier you're allowed to stay. Sometimes you'll be welcomed to set up camp, and sometimes they'll tell you it's not possible. Check with the management for today's ruling.

FOOD Tela has some of the best seafood on the north coast. The *sopa de caracol* (conch soup), often prepared with coconut milk, is delicious. The local coconut bread rocks on.

Luces Del Norte. Renowned among the traveler set, this enclosed-patio restaurant serves up pretty good grub. Conch soup ($3) and pork chops with french fries ($4) are both popular; shrimp prepared to your liking is $5, and yummy omelets are $2. *Av. Panamá, 1 block from the beach. Wheelchair access. Open daily 7 AM–10 PM.*

Restaurante Cesar Mariscos. Cesar, at the west end of the beach in old Tela (sort of hard to find), has terrific seafood dishes. As sea breezes mix with the cool sounds of rock and salsa, munch on shrimp in curry sauce ($6), Cesar seafood salad ($7), or the conch soup, which is a great deal because they don't skimp on the conch meat ($3). *Av. Uruguay, just off the beach, tel. 48–2083. Open daily 9 AM–11 PM. Wheelchair access.*

Tia Carmen. Come early because the food, the cheapest in town, sells out quickly. The *baleadas*, a concoction of tortillas, beans, eggs, and avocado, are great (50¢). *Av. Honduras at 8a Calle, a block from the Parque Central. Breakfast and dinner only.*

Garifuna-Speak

Garífuna is a dialect, rather than a written language. In recent years, several linguists have attempted to record the language. Here are a few basic words and greetings, which will be enthusiastically received no matter how poor your pronunciation. Idabinya—How are you?; Ugodiati—I'm fine; Buitibunafi—Good morning; Buitirabonweyu—Good afternoon; Gundatina Nasubu Dirunibu—Pleased to meet you; Buitibu—You're beautiful; Tankéy—Thank you; Iyo—Goodbye.

AFTER DARK Multi Disco Napoles (at the western end of main street, near the bridge) attracts mostly teenagers. If a live band is playing, a more diverse crowd usually shows up. They charge a 50¢–$2 cover depending on the event. **Tourist Centro Lancetilla** is considered the best disco around; it's a kilometer outside town near the Lancetilla Botanic Garden, doesn't have live music, and is open only Saturday and Sunday evenings. The architecture blends in attractively with the environment, and it has a nice outdoor patio.

OUTDOOR ACTIVITIES The beaches around Tela are jammin', but the beach directly in front of Old Tela isn't the best. Hike west down the beach to find better sands, or cross the bridge to New Tela and enjoy the beach in front of Hotel Telamar. The hotel often has volleyball games, or you can use the pool for $1 per day. Having a bike in Tela is very useful, especially if you want to visit attractions outside town. Hotel Telamar rents bikes for $2 an hour; bargain for a day rate, or ask around town for someone who wouldn't mind being a pedestrian for the day for a few bucks. Hotel Telamar also rents horses, and galloping rides on the beach at sunset may go down in your book as one of those perfect-moment deals.

NEAR TELA

Before starting out to one of the parks listed below, talk with a volunteer at **PROLANSATE** on the main street, a tourist office specifically geared toward promoting the local wildlife reserves. Their office is the best equipped in the country, chock-full of info about most national parks throughout the country. The office is open whenever the Peace Corps volunteer who runs it is home.

PARQUE NACIONAL PUNTA SAL Chill with the dolphins and turtles in the sea, or white-faced monkeys and toucans in the forest. This is one of the most geographically diverse parks in the country, with mangrove swamps, rain forest, lagoons, and coral reefs. Though from Tela you can see the point to the west on which the park sits jutting out into the ocean, it's laborious to reach. **Alix Bonilla** (tel. 48–2880) offers an excursion that includes deep-sea fishing, diving, and a visit to the park, but it's only affordable if you have a group. Alternatively, hitch a ride with the cargo boat that leaves every other day from Hotel Atlantico in Tela to Río Tinto on the far side of Punta Sal. In Río Tinto, **Hotel Suyapa** has cement-box rooms with passable beds for $2 per person. Take a fishing boat from Río Tinto to the point, or walk directly into the forest. Alternatively, catch a ride with the cargo truck leaving the Shell gas station in Tela at 7:30 AM Monday–Saturday to the beautiful Garifuna village of **Miami.** You can always find someone to take you on a canoe ride in the lagoon, and if you've got the equipment, it's possible to camp in the park.

PUNTA ISOPO RESERVE This is perhaps a more rewarding trip than Punta Sal, since the area is virtually free of visitors. A trip to the forest is also an inexpensive adventure. To do things right, bring lunch, water, and insect repellent. You can take a bus from Tela's Parque Central to El Triunfo de la Cruz, a little Garifuna village near the park. It's a decent walk from Triunfo to the park, so hiring a bike in Tela is a great idea. In Triunfo, make a right when the road dead-ends into the beach, and follow the dirt road to Laguna Río Platino. Take a short 50¢ canoe ride to the other side. Walk along the beach, and just before you reach the next lagoon you'll find a gate into the forest. When you get here look for Jesús (hey-ZOOSE), who has a couple of *cayucos* (dugout canoes) for rent for $1 per day (but be careful of his gnarly dogs). The cayucos are difficult to balance with more than one person in them. Paddle for ½ hour up Laguna Jicaque until the channel becomes very narrow and flanked by lilies. You'll run into **Cerro Sal Si Puedes** ("Leave If You Can Hill"); follow one of the trails up into the hills if you can ignore the somewhat ominous, taunting name. White-faced and howler monkeys hang out here, and toucans and parrots come around late in the afternoon. You can also find the *sangre* tree, whose sap looks like blood.

LANCETILLA BOTANIC GARDEN This *jardín botánica* was founded by the United Fruit Company in 1926 to test the adaptability of trees and plants imported from around the world. The setup, with over 1,000 varieties of plants marked by name, country of origin, and date of introduction, is interesting even if you fell asleep in botany class. Those marked in black are poisonous. Ask the guard to show you where the *coca* (i.e., cocaine) plant is; some visitors have been allowed to sample the stimulating leaves, but no promises. The nearby river has a great pool for bathing. Behind the garden is a biological reserve, which is the watershed for Tela, and an awesome hiking trail runs through this rain forest. The entrance to the garden is a kilometer west of Tela along the highway, and the actual garden is another 4 kilometers (2 miles) from the entrance. You can take any westbound bus to the entrance and walk the rest of the way, but biking is the easiest way to go. It's open daily 8–3:30.

La Ceiba

The huge Pico Bonito (8,000 feet) and the coastal mountain range rise majestically behind you as you look out on the Caribbean Sea. As the third-largest town in the country, La Ceiba lacks the easy pace of neighboring towns, but offers the comforting amenities of a bona fide city. Sixty kilometers (37 miles) east of Tela, it's smack in the middle of the north coast and is a good hub for visiting nearby Garifuna villages, the Cayos Cochinos, and the Bay Islands. It's the only place to get planes into the Mosquitia, and is the cheapest gateway to the Islands. The nightlife here is head and shoulders above anywhere else on the coast, and when they do Carnival, it's a fantastic party by anyone's standards. Dancing in the streets, live music, beauty pageants, and general merrymaking last a full two weeks. The highlight is May 15, the day of their patron saint San Isidro.

BASICS Most **banks** in town cash traveler's checks. **Hondutel** (2a Av. at 6a Calle) is open 24 hours for calls, and has two direct lines to the States. The **post office** (open weekdays 8–5 and Saturday 8–noon) is on Avenida Morazán near Hospital D'Antony, several blocks south of the road to the bus terminal. The **visitor information** kiosk in Parque Central has decent maps of the city (open weekdays 7:30–11:30 and 1:30–5, Saturday 7:30–11:30). To wash your grungies, go to **Laundry Wasserv** (1a Calle, Barrio La Isla, 4 blocks from bridge). They're open daily till 6 PM and charge $2 for a standard load. For emergencies, call the **police** (tel. 199 or 43–0895); **ambulance** (tel. 43–0707); or the **hospital** (Calle de Estadio, tel. 42–2195).

COMING AND GOING

➤ **BY BUS** • The bus station on Boulevard 15 de Septiembre is a 20-minute walk or a 50¢ taxi ride from Parque Central. Buses going long distances park in the station, while buses to nearby communities park out front. Buses to Trujillo (3 hours, $3) leave every 1½ hours 4 AM–3:30 PM. Take the Trujillo bus to get to Tocoa. Buses to Olanchito (2½ hours, $2) leave hourly 6:30–5:30. Buses to Tela (2 hours, $1.25) leave every ½ hour 4:45 AM–6 PM. Buses to San Pedro Sula ($3, 3 hours) leave hourly 5:30 AM–6 PM. The bus to Tegucigalpa (7 hours, $7) leaves daily at 6 AM. Four buses a day run to La Unión (1½ hours, 50¢). Buses to Sambo Creek (45 minutes, 50¢) leave hourly until 4:15 PM. Buses to Nueva Armenia (2 hours, 75¢) leave irregularly.

➤ **BY BOAT** • Boat departures fluctuate, so you'll need to speak to someone in the office of **Capitania de Puerto** at the edge of the pier to double-check these times. The boat to Utila (3 hours, $5) leaves at 10 AM on Tuesday. Boats leave for Roatán (4 hours, $8) at 8 PM on Wednesday and Friday. The boat to Guanaja (5½ hours, $12) leaves Wednesday at 8 PM. A cargo boat to the Mosquitia leaves twice a month bound for Puerto Lempira. It takes four days to reach Lempira ($24), but you can jump ship in Palacios, Brus Laguna, or other points along the way. You might be able to buy meals on the ship, but bring some sleeping equipment and be prepared to sleep on the floor; by no means is this the Love Boat.

➤ **BY PLANE** • The **Golosan Airport** is 6 kilometers (4 miles) from downtown. The big, special airport taxis cost a bundle; take a regular, collective taxi for around $2. If you walk to the entrance of the airport, you can catch an occasional public bus into town (6¢). Public Buses 1er de Mayo and El Confite stop at the Avenida San Isidro side of Parque Central en route to the airport (6¢); colectivo taxis make the same run for $2. Several companies have flights to the islands, and most have ticket offices near Parque Central. The following prices are for one-way fares: **Isleña Airlines** (tel. 43–2326) has flights to Utila Monday–Saturday at 6 AM, 3 PM, and 4 PM for $10. Daily flights to Roatán ($17) leave hourly 6 AM–4 PM. Flights to Guanaja ($20) depart Monday–Saturday at 6 AM, noon, and 4 PM. **Aero-linea Sosa** (tel. 43–1399) has the same prices as Isleña but a slightly different schedule. **Tan-Sahsa** (tel. 43–2070) has flights to Roatán ($17) Monday–Saturday at 6 AM, Sunday at 7:15 AM. Flights to San Pedro Sula ($19) and Tegucigalpa ($23) leave at 6 AM. Isleña Airlines also has flights to Palacios ($30) and Puerto Lempira in the Mosquitia ($50). Planes to both destinations leave Monday–Saturday at 8 AM.

GETTING AROUND The town may look big initially, but after wandering around for an hour it'll seem very manageable. **Avenida San Isidro** is the main drag running past the park. The pier is 1 block south of where San Isidro hits the sea. Between San Isidro and Avenida 14 de Julio are the market stalls, and most of the banks and airline offices. Just over the bridge to the east is **Barrio Las Isla,** a Garifuna neighborhood with several nightclubs. A taxi around town shouldn't cost more than 50¢. Public buses "Colonia" and "Miramar" stop on the Avenida La República side of the park on their way to the bus station. **Casa Detari** (Av. San Isidro at 13a Calle, tel. 43–2471) rents mountain bikes for about $4 per day.

WHERE TO SLEEP The cheapest rooms in town are along the tracks leading to the pier, and you get drunks for neighbors as part of the bargain. Safer but colorless hotels abound between Avenida San Isidro and Avenida 14 de Julio.

Hospedaje y Billares Murillo. It's the safest of the dirt-cheap hotels, and very few drunks call the sidewalk outside home. The rooms are big but simple, the shared baths are dirty but livable ($3 double—bargain!). A pool hall is downstairs in case you get that late-night urge to shoot a game. *Av. La República, next to the train tracks running to the pier, tel. 42–2485. 13 rooms, none with bath. Luggage storage, laundry.*

Hotel Amsterdam 2001. The friendly Dutch owner speaks several languages, and heartily receives European backpackers. If you're traveling alone, the cheapest rooms are overpriced; they make you buddy-up with other travelers and thus pay private-room prices for a hostel-like environment. If you're traveling in a group of five, you can monopolize a room. The few private rooms for couples are a pretty good deal. The hotel's in a safe area, only yards away from the beach, a laundromat and a *terrific* restaurant with lots of fresh veggies. Down side: no fans. Beds are $5. *1a Calle and Av. Paz Barahona, 4 blocks past the bridge into Barrio La Isla. 4 rooms, some with bath. Wheelchair access. Luggage storage.*

Hotel Granada. Hotel Granada is the best hotel for the bucks. It's in the center of the market district, their small comedor does basic meals, and the lobby does cable TV. All rooms have overhead fans and decent showers. A nice double is $7, and a triple with air-conditioning is $11. *Av. Atlantida near 6a Calle, tel. 43–2451. 58 rooms, all with bath. Wheelchair access. Luggage service, laundry services, cantina.*

FOOD La Ceiba has lots of cheap and ethnically diverse restaurants, but surprisingly few spots for seafood. **Mi Delicia** (Av. San Isidro at 11a Calle) is popular with locals because you can get a wide variety of big meals, breakfast through dinner, for about a buck.

El Colonel Hotel Restaurant. One of the town's fancier restaurants, El Colonel is considered by many to be overpriced. Nonetheless, it may be the only Thai food in the country. Chicken breast in Thai sauce is $5, Thai beef $6, and a good shrimp and chicken soup $4. *Av. 14 de Julio, 2nd floor of the hotel, tel. 43–1954. Open daily 7 AM–10 PM.*

Restaurante Palace. The dining room is air-conditioned, and the food here is authentic and delicious. A marvelous conch prepared with vegetables in oyster sauce costs $5, and cheaper entrées, like sweet-and-sour beef with tomato and pineapple ($4) or chicken chow mein ($3), are equally good. Vegetarians can have one of several tasty rice or chop suey dishes. *9a Calle bet. Av. San Isidro and Av. 14 de Julio, tel. 43–0685. Open daily 11–3 and 5–11. Wheelchair access.*

Restaurante 2001. Don't leave town without eating here. The American owner is sensitive to health concerns, so all the vegetables here are stomach friendly. All meals in this seaside restaurant come with salad and coconut bread, and pasta is the specialty of the house. The fettucine Alfredo ($4) is delectable, and the chicken fajitas ($3) are popular, too. *1a Calle and Av. Paz Barahona, 4 blocks across the bridge into Barrio La Isla. Lunch and dinner only.*

AFTER DARK La Ceiba has plenty of nightclubs, mostly in Barrio La Isla. **D'Lido** (1a Calle, just past the bridge) has lots of funky lights and a beach-front patio, but locals complain of nagging prostitutes that frequent the disco. It's open nightly, from 10 PM on ($1 cover). **Black and White** (Av. 5 de Septiembre and 3a Calle, Barrio La Isla) is very popular on weekends. The club plays all types of music, but the young people are crazy for rap. Occasionally patrons get the pleasure of live bands. Tuesday and Wednesday feature happy hours with 50¢ drinks, and they're open every night except Monday. **Coco View** (off 4a Calle, in Barrio Porterito, on the town center side of the bridge) is the best disco if popularity is an accurate measure. They play all types of music for folks on the crowded but air-conditioned dance floor. The party starts late; arrive after 11 PM and you'll still be early. Coco View is open Thursday–Sunday and charges a $1 cover.

OUTDOOR ACTIVITIES

➤ **BEACHES** • The beach at **Playa La Barra** starts where Barrio La Isla stops, and continues until interrupted by the Río Cangrejal. La Barra is okay, but you can take an eastbound bus to nicer **Playa Peru** or **Cuyamel.** When going to Playa Peru, ask the driver to let you off at Río Maria. Walk 20 minutes up the river to find a waterfall and great pools for bathing. If you want any privacy at all, come midweek.

➤ **ANIMAL WATCHING** • The **Cuero y Salado** wildlife refuge is one of the few places in the world set up for the protection of manatees (sea cows). In addition to sighting the gentle and adorable sea cows, once mistaken for mermaids by early explorers, visitors may see white-faced monkeys, several species of heron, and other birds along the canals. Cars aren't allowed in the park, and all transport is by boat. Adults pay $10 to get in, and the $32 for transportation and guides can be split by up to 15 people. Talk to **FUCSA** (1a Calle near Av. Atlantida, tel. 43–0329) for more info.

➤ **HIKING** • Rising up green and lush behind La Ceiba, **Parque Nacional Pico Bonito** has some amazing virgin rain forest. Just after sunrise is the best time to see birds. Beware of snakes and jaguars, too, though most people say you'd be lucky even to see one. The mountain is quite steep, but you can climb almost to the top without special equipment—for the last part of the ascent, mountain-climbing gear is *highly* recommended. A trip up to the summit and back down takes about nine days. For those only interested in coming down, **Cambio** (across from Parque Central, tel. 43–1399) will drive you partway up and give you a thrilling raft trip down the rapids of Río Bonito ($75 per person).

To reach the park, take public bus "1er de Mayo" to the village of **Armenia Bonito** at the edge of the park. Walk to the campsite owned by the university (CURLA). This spot will house the future visitor's center, and a number of trails lead into the forest from here. Another option for getting to the park is to take the bus toward Tela and get off at **Río Zacate.** Walk along the river until you find the waterfall; trails from here lead into the park. Camping is allowed wherever you can pitch a tent or lay down a bedroll, but drinking the water is iffy (at best). Call COHDEFOR in La Ceiba (tel. 43–1033) for more info.

NEAR LA CEIBA

A number of Garifuna villages are easy to explore from La Ceiba. The best time to visit **Corozal,** 10 kilometers (6 miles) east, is during their annual fiesta during the second week of January. Come prepared to party like it's 1999. **Sambo Creek,** 16 kilometers (10 miles) east of Corozal, is an easygoing village, nestled between an unspoiled beach and lustrous green mountains. Lodging is available, and sometimes you can find a boat ride to the Cayos Cochinos. Buses to both communities leave from in front of the station in La Ceiba.

Trujillo

Needless to say you won't be the first traveler to visit Trujillo. Columbus set foot on the American mainland here during his final voyage. Legend has it that he thanked God for delivering him from the *Honduras* (roughly, "deep waters"). That first footprint laid the path for the Spanish to establish the country's first capital in Trujillo. Others followed, sniffing out money and power. British pirates staked out the bay and raided the coastal towns from time to time to snag gold bound for Spain. In 1860, the tragi-comic American filibusterer William Walker launched his final attack in Trujillo as part of his quest to control Central America. The attempt proved futile, and earned him a front-row seat before a firing squad. Today's travelers generally come without such a bogus attitude and find great tranquility here in one of the lesser-visited coastal towns. The city center rests upon a hill, with a great view of the bay and surrounding beaches. Down the hill to the west, **Barrio Cristales** is a lively Garifuna neighborhood. To the east lies "the future," typified by a monster hotel project under way.

BASICS **Banco Atlantida** on Parque Central changes traveler's checks. **Hondutel,** 2 blocks south of the park, is open daily 7 AM–3 AM. The **post office** next door is open weekdays 8–noon and 2–5, Saturday 8–11. For **police,** call 44–4038; the **hospital** (tel. 44–4093), a block east from Parque Central, has an English-speaking doctor on staff.

COMING AND GOING Buses don't all stop in the same area. Most headed east park a block from Parque Central, on the road to Hondutel. Buses to Tocoa (1½ hours, $1.25) leave frequently 7 AM–4:30 PM; buses to La Ceiba (4 hours, $3) depart every two hours 2 AM–2 PM. Any of these buses will pass through **Corocito,** where you can hitchhike or pick up a bus to Limón. Buses to nearby Garifuna villages stop in front of the Granada restaurant; three a day run to Santa Fe (45 minutes, 60¢) and other villages. The bus to Tegus parks up the hill three blocks south of the town center, next to the Cementario Viejo (old cemetery). Buses to the capital (8 hours, $7) leave at 4:30 AM and 9 AM.

WHERE TO SLEEP The affordable places to stay are around the town center. **Hotel Central,** on the Parque Central, is cheap ($3 per person) but definitely a bit run-down. Up in the hills toward Villa Brinkley (*see below*), ask around about rooms with kitchen facilities that rent cheaply by the week or the month.

Hotel Mar de Plata. The rooms are clean, simple, concrete cells with thin mattresses and fans. These are the cheapest decent rooms in town ($5 double). The manager is very easygoing, and lets you use the stove to cook up some grub. *Walk 1 block south of the park and several blocks east. It's on the corner at the hilltop before the descent into Barrio Cristales. 5 rooms, none with bath. Wheelchair access. Luggage storage, laundry.*

Hotel Trujillo. A 10-minute walk from Parque Central brings you to this very clean and comfortable hotel. All rooms have fans, and it's a good deal at $10 for a double with bath. *Calle 18 de Mayo, up the hill near the Cementario Viejo, tel. 44–4202. 18 rooms, some with bath. Luggage storage, laundry.*

Villa Brinkley. The nicest hotel in Trujillo sits up in the hills, looking out on the whole bay. Every room shares a piece of this panorama on private terraces. Rooms have gorgeous woodwork, sunken showers, two double beds, and a futon. It's affordable only if you put five or six people in a room; the base price is $28 for one person, and $4 for each additional person. *From the west side of Parque Central walk 15 minutes south into the hills, tel. 44–4444. 20 rooms, all with bath. Luggage storage, restaurant, pool.*

FOOD Directly below the town center, a row of open-air restaurants serves basic plates, fish, and chicken, for $2. In the Garifuna neighborhood of Barrio Cristales, similar meals at street comedores are about $1.50 per plate. Prices are higher at the downtown restaurants, but the quality is better. **Restaurante Granada** (1 block south of the park) is a local favorite, with savory conch soup ($3), garlic shrimp ($5), and calamari ($4).

Bahía Restaurante and Bar. A couple of kilometers west of town near the airport, Bahía is popular with foreigners, especially Americans. The patio has a beautiful sea view, and the seafood is prime. Prices are a little higher than at other restaurants, but all plates are big and come with beans, rice, salad, and french fries. Fried fish ($4) and lobster ($15) are pricey, but a yummy bowl of chili con carne is only $2.50. *Next to the abandoned airport runway, tel. 44–4770. Wheelchair access. Open daily 7 AM–10 PM.*

El Pantry. El Pantry has dishes for all tastes and budgets. A breakfast of either French toast, waffles, or banana pancakes costs about a dollar. The filet mignon with bacon and mushrooms is tasty ($4), and the pizzas are plenty for one person or two ($4 for a veggie combo). The owner boasts of having the best margaritas outside México, and he may well be right. *Barrio Central, a block southwest of Parque Central, tel. 44–4856. Wheelchair access. Open daily 8 AM–11 PM.*

Villa Brinkley. The restaurant in this fancy hotel, looking across the bay, is a delightfully affordable surprise. The breakfast buffet ($3) lets you loose on a big spread of crepes, eggs, bacon, and fruit. The lasagna ($4) makes an excellent dinner, and most other dishes are around $6, like the inventive *Pesacado Villa Brinkley* (fish in cream and peanut butter sauce). All dinners are served with soup, hot buttered bread, iced tea, and coffee. *A 15-minute hike into the hills from the west end of the park, tel. 44–4444. Wheelchair access. Breakfast and dinner only.*

WORTH SEEING Just behind Parque Central, the **Fortaleza de Santa Bárbara** looks out over the bay. The Spanish used this fort to fend off pirates. The ruins are unspectacular in themselves, but you can kick back with a great view. It costs 10¢ to get in, and it's open daily 8–noon and 1–4. Three blocks south of Restaurante El Pantry is the **Cementario Viejo**. The gate may be closed, but generally it's not locked. Just inside is the grave of filibusterer William Walker. The only other word on his tombstone besides his name and the date of his death is "fusilado," a nice and tidy Spanish word meaning "executed by firing squad." If you continue down the road to the west, signs will lead you to the **Museo Arqueologico y Piscina Rivera del Pedregal.** This museum has an eclectic collection of bric-a-brac, including old muskets, ancient sewing machines, early photos of Trujillo, and turtle shells. They have a large collection of supposedly Mayan statues and pottery, but nothing in the gallery is properly labeled, and, to the dismay of archaeologists, the owner refuses to say where the statues were found. If the museum leaves you wanting, wander down to the network of river-fed pools out back, since it's included in the price of admission (50¢, open daily until 6). Some of the pools are murky and moss covered, but others are cool, clear, and inviting.

AFTER DARK You might want to look in the relaxed **Bar and Restaurante Paradiso,** across from Hotel Mar de Plata, to see what is showing on the cable TV movie channels. There are several unimpressive discos around town, made conspicuous by their sonic volume. The best of the bunch is **Black and White** in the Garifuna neighborhood of Barrio Cristales to the west of town. Everybody comes here weekend evenings to dance punta. The cover charge is about $1. Across from Black and White, facing the sea, is **Cocopando.** It's a dark shed crammed with dancers, and they have a great traditional punta band, with three drums, maracas, and a tortoiseshell xylophone. Cocopando is open only Wednesday and Saturday nights; admission is $1. Wander the streets of Barrio Cristales and you may find a traditional Garifuna dance troupe practicing; people of all ages dance and sing to the accompaniment of a pulsing rhythm section. This is the original punta. Be humble and respectful, and you may be invited to join in.

OUTDOOR ACTIVITIES A guy next door to Bahía Bar and Restaurante (*see above*) rents snorkeling masks and fins for $1. Take advantage of the afternoon winds by renting a Windsurfer here for $4 an hour. They also rent Jet Skis and have motorboat tours, but not for cheap. The **Capiro** and **Calentura** national parks rise up just behind town, with great expanses of tropical rainforest and exotic birds. The same road that runs past Villa Brinkley goes into Calentura. The Capiro forest is south of the airport. The adventure-tour agency **Cambio** (around the corner from the park, tel. 44–4044) sometimes rents mountain bikes to aid your exploration of the forests. Five kilometers (3 miles) east of Trujillo is the gigantic **Laguna de Guaimoreto.** Some visitors to the lake report feeling a spiritual reverence, as if they've entered nature's cathedral. This place is paradise for birdwatchers. Cambio and the Bahía Bar offer tours here, but you'll do just as well finding someone along the lagoon with a canoe to rent, and then you can paddle anywhere you want.

NEAR TRUJILLO

Puerto Castilla is a large port across the bay from Trujillo. Cargo boats set off from here for the United States and destinations around the world. Check around the docks to see if any are taking passengers. Buses leave the town center for Puerto Castilla. **Santa Fe, San Antonio,** and **Guadalupe** are Garifuna villages listed here in descending order of proximity to Trujillo. Santa Fe, 10 kilometers (6 miles) west, has beautiful beaches and some of the best people on earth. You'll be stoked if you make it here for the annual festival during the second week of July. *Everybody* dances until the sun comes up, apparently thrilled just to be alive. The other villages are less touristed and harder to reach. The Garifuna are great people to hang out with, so the effort is worth it. For transport info, *see* Coming and Going, *above.*

LIMON Limón is a beautiful Garifuna village by the sea. The beach is awesome, but sometimes windy. Though only a couple of hours east of Trujillo, the village is rarely visited by tourists. The locals are a little bit reserved, but they open up with time. Change all the money you'll need before you head out this way; there's only one hospedaje in town, and **Hondutel** keeps very irregular hours. Some buses come to Limón directly from Trujillo and Tocoa, but more than likely you'll have to stop in Corocito to transfer buses, or hitch. Buses leave Limón for La Ceiba daily at 3 AM. Buses to Tocoa leave at 5 AM, 7 AM, and 1 PM daily. If you want to visit a really remote village, take the 4 PM bus east to **Iriona** (4 hours). This coastal town, right on the edge of the Mosquitia, has some extremely basic accommodations.

Bay Islands

Islanders today live much like they have for hundreds of years. They speak a very distinct style of Caribbean-accented English; for work, they fish; for fun, they eat, dance, and gossip. But this culture is getting watered down as the tourist industry draws more and more mainland Hondurans looking for work. While many on the islands are still ardently faithful to Caribbean strains of religion—complete with superstitions, ghosts, and smokey torchlit ceremonies—evangelical movements, like the Seventh-Day Adventists, are making noticeable inroads. Spanish is now heard almost as much as English on Roatán, if not more. Utila, the westernmost island and the closest one to the coast, is still predominantly English-speaking and culturally the best preserved. The islands are heavenly to the eye, with beautiful beaches and teal-blue water. The world's second-largest reef system extends from Belize down to the islands, and 95% of the species of coral found in the Caribbean are found around the islands; scuba-diving and snorkeling are *very* popular sports here. Though supply and demand has led to increased prices over the past few years, you can still find diving and accommodations that don't break your bank, especially on Utila.

British pirates used the isles as bases for raids while Spain was in power, and the English kept the islands as territories until the mid-19th century.

When Columbus arrived on Guanaja (the easternmost island) during his last voyage, the Bay Islands (Islas de la Bahia) were populated by the indigenous Pech. The Spanish eventually solved this, and some of their colonial labor needs, by moving the Pech off the islands and into mineral mines and onto plantations. In the 18th century, the British moved the Garifuna from St. Vincent to Roatán, the largest of the islands. Except for a settlement in Punta Gorda that survives today, the Garifuna didn't much care for the island and emigrated to the mainland.

Roatán

Only about 65 kilometers (40 miles) from end to end, Roatán is the biggest, busiest, and most-populated island. Most villages are on the water's edge, but many Americans have settled on Roatán in the past few years, and they're constructing houses throughout the island. Roatán is getting expensive, but you can still find rooms and meals for prices comparable to mainland rates. The capital is Coxen Hole, sometimes called "Roatán." The west side of the island, where lots of mainland Hondurans live, is more developed; life in the east hasn't been affected much by tourism, and full-blooded islanders here are friendly and chatty. The east end has climbable mountains with fabulous panoramic views of the sea. **Punta Gorda** is a Garifuna village on the far northeast corner of the island, where locals play punta on Saturday nights. The town has no official lodgings, but you can usually find a room for rent by asking around.

BASICS Take care of practical needs in Coxen Hole. **Bancahsa** on main street cashes traveler's checks and gives advances on Visa cards. In the alley next to Bancahsa, a path leads up the hill to **Hondutel**. The office is always busy, so come early to make calls (open daily 7 AM–9 PM). Across from the bank, the **post office** is open weekdays 8–noon and 2–5, Saturday 8–10:30. The **tourist office** (open weekdays 8–11 and 2–4) is halfway between the highway and the town center, on the dirt road to Coxen Hole. If you're interested in environmental stuff, several other agencies in this same building can give you info. **Roatán Hospital** (tel. 45–1227) is off the main road a couple of blocks. The **police** station (tel. 45–1138) isn't far off main street, but it's well hidden—ask directions.

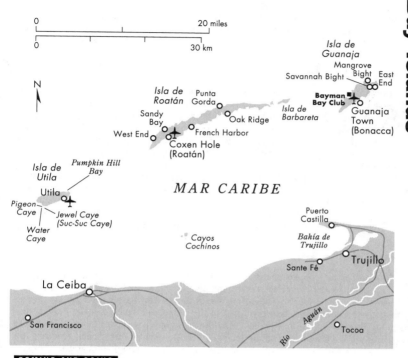

Bay Islands

COMING AND GOING

➤ **BY PLANE** • Airplane is the easiest way to reach the island, with flights daily from Tegus, San Pedro, and La Ceiba. It's good to make reservations as soon as you know what you're doing, since flights fill up quickly. **Isleña** (tel. 45–1088) has two flights daily to San Pedro Sula ($21) at 7 AM and 1 PM. About eight flights leave daily for La Ceiba ($16) 7 AM–5 PM. **Tan-Sahsa** (tel. 45–1085) has a daily flight to San Pedro ($21), continuing on to Tegus ($30), leaving at 6:30 AM. **Sosa Airlines** (tel. 45–1154) has flights to Guanaja ($15) Monday–Saturday at 1:30 PM. *See* Tegus, La Ceiba, and San Pedro Sula, *above,* for info on getting to the island.

➤ **BY BOAT** • Most boats don't have fixed schedules. The one exception, a boat to La Ceiba (4 hours, $8), leaves from next to the office of Capitania de Puerto in Coxen Hole at 11 AM on Sunday—arrive a few hours early. Three boats a week leave for Puerto Cortés (15 hours, $15). Authorities in Coxen Hole say no fishing boats run to Guanaja or Utila, but authorities on the other islands say differently; check around the docks, or just hire a private boat. To get the latest info on boat departures, check with the **Capitania de Puerto** (tel. 45–1262), near the small park on main street and the Warren Supermarket.

GETTING AROUND The island has one main road running east to west. The west is paved, and the east soon will be too. The road gets a lot of traffic considering the island's size. In addition to all the taxis trying to pass each other, the road is full of pedestrians, so be careful if driving. Sandy Bay and West End, the most popular spots for divers, are west of the airport and Coxen Hole; French Harbor, Oak Ridge, and Punta Gorda lie to the east. **Taxis** are very convenient and not too expensive. A ride from the airport to Coxen Hole costs about $1, or to West End about $8. A bus connecting the airport to Coxen Hole (10 minutes, 50¢) leaves infrequently. **Buses** serving the island originate in Coxen Hole. Buses to Sandy Bay (20 minutes, $1) and West End (½ hour, $1) leave from next to Warren Supermarket 6–6. Buses to French Harbor

(20 minutes, $1) and Oak Ridge (45 minutes, $2) leave every half hour 6–6. The station is toward the west end of Coxen Hole, across from Paragua disco. The island's mountainous, twisting roads and great seaside paths make for great dirt bike riding. **Amigo** (across from the airport, tel. 45–1498) rents motorcycles for $25 a day.

COXEN HOLE

Roatán's capital is a transport hub, a necessary stop for basic practicalities, and the least attractive town on the island. People are less friendly here than in smaller communities around the island, and the crack cocaine trade means theft is on the rise. It's not a hellhole, but it just doesn't compare to other places nearby. Roatán doesn't have much nightlife, so most everyone who wants to go out at night comes to Coxen Hole for the disco. **Paragua** (open nightly except Monday), on main street, occasionally has live bands on Saturday night, but the music is usually canned. Hotels on main street are more expensive than the ones on the periphery of town. The rooms at **Hotel Allen** (on main street just past the Paragua disco, tel. 45–1243) are bland but clean, and all have fans ($6 double). The owner is an interesting man, with a large collection of shells and African statues. Vegetables are abundant and cheap; augment what you buy at the marketplace with groceries from the **Warren Supermarket** on main street.

WEST END

The most beautiful part of the island, the West End, hasn't gone unnoticed. Large numbers of visitors come to snorkel and dive in the turquoise waters and lounge in hammocks on the beach. The cash value of the scenery hasn't been lost on anyone either, so it's the most developed part of the island, and being built up more all the time. Buses leave Coxen Hole for West End 6–6 every day except Sunday. Taxis cost $8 to or from Coxen Hole, and hitching is definitely worth a try. Thank goodness the tourism development isn't rudely ostentatious or overpowering, and campers can still pitch a tent and enjoy serenity on the cheap. The idyllic beach at **West Bay,** 4 kilometers (2 miles) south, is only minimally developed; it's an easy walk, or hire a horse from Jimmy's hotel at the south end of the beach in West End; boats also go to West Bay ($1) from Foster's and Vivian's (*see* Where to Sleep and Eat, *below*).

WHERE TO SLEEP AND EAT Inexpensive food in the West End doesn't come in many forms. The **nameless comedor** across from Tyll's Dive Shop has breakfast plates for $3, and burgers and sandwiches for about $1. At the south end of the beach, **New York Restaurant** has a nice second-story porch looking over the water. Chicken and fish plates are around $4, and spaghetti is only $2. Follow the beach to the southern end of town to find **Jimmy's,** a double-decker hammock-hostel. Jimmy rents snorkeling equipment and horses, and charges $3 per hammock. Set back from the beach at the south end, the **Sam Miller Inn** isn't very visible, so ask directions at the New York Restaurant next to Jimmy's. Rooms are basic and without fans, but the ambience is good (plenty of reefer-smoking travelers) and they have a kitchen for use. Dorm-style beds and hammocks are $2, and doubles are $5. **Foster and Vivian's** (midway down south side of beach, tel. 45–1008) is the social center of West End life. The wooden bungalows, set back from the beach, all have two big beds, fans, and private baths ($30 for up to six people). The restaurant in front is expensive, but portions are big and quite tasty. The owner also has a tree house in West Bay, with a hammock and bed 40 feet up in a ceiba tree ($10 a night).

OUTDOOR ACTIVITIES Aside from the expensive resorts, West End is the best place to hook up with dive boats. "Hole in the Wall" is a popular dive site. Lots of moray eels hang around "Blue Channel" and "Eel Garden." Upon request, dive boats can take you a little farther to the dramatic walls of "Valley of the Kings." Most dive shops offer PADI certification courses. Prices are usually quoted in dollars, and most shops charge around $25 a dive. **Roatán Divers,** near the entrance to the town, is the oldest independent dive shop on the island. The owner, Tino, is actively involved in reef preservation. **Ocean Divers** (next to Foster and Vivian's, tel. 45–1497) has equipment for underwater photography. **Tyll's Dive** also rents windsurfing boards for $5 an hour. If snorkeling is more in line with your budget, rent stuff from a dive shop and swim out to some reefs from the beach. Or, Roatán Divers offers snorkeling from a boat for $5.

SANDY BAY

The beach at Sandy Bay, about 5 kilometers (3 miles) northeast of West End, isn't as good, but the diving and snorkeling are excellent. The reef here is under protection, giving divers a living museum to visit. **Anthony's Key Resort** will take out nonguests, if they're certified, for $25 per dive. Down the road, **Sun Rise Dive** (tel. 45–1475) has similar prices. Most dive shops in the area rent snorkeling equipment for $5. **The Carambola Botanic Gardens**, across the highway from Sandy Bay, offers scenic walks among the chirps of birdlife. **Bailey's Key** at Anthony's Key Resort has a nature trail, bird sanctuary, and sea turtle pond. If you don't have time to visit these animals in the wild, you can come here 8–5:30 daily.

The town has only a few hotels; most are quite expensive, and the few exceptions aren't easy to find. Go up the hill to **Beth's Hostel** (tel. 45–1266) and look out over the sea and the hills from the breezy deck hammocks. Miss Beth is extremely allergic to smoke, and won't take smoking guests. She can pick up guests from the airport ($5) if they call. Guests stay downstairs, sharing a cooking stove, dining area, laundry, and bath ($8 per person). Finding the place is a trick; walk east from Anthony's Key Resort past the school, ask around for directions, and walk uphill on a dirt path. Farther down the beach, **Miss Effie** (tel. 45–1233) has rooms with private baths for $10 per person. Her rooms are often full with long-term boarders.

FRENCH HARBOR

French Harbor, the primary fishing community on the island, is a quiet town a few kilometers east of the airport. **Bancahsa** changes traveler's checks. **Fantasy Island** (tel. 45–1191), a deluxe resort a couple of kilometers east of town, rents canoes, sailboats, kayaks, and Jet Skis. **Celebrations Disco,** just past the town entrance, is touted by some as the best butt-shaking joint on the island. **Hotelito Brooks,** in the center of town, is the cheapest place to stay. The $4 doubles are plain, have no fans, and showers only get water at night. Since they only have matrimonial beds, two male travelers are forced to get separate rooms (homophobia reigns supreme). In the center of town near Romeo's restaurant, facing the bay and boat docks, **Hotel Joee's** (pronounced Joey's) falls somewhere between the cheapest hotels and the unaffordable resorts. The only remarkable feature, besides the restaurant that serves good seafood, is the option of having a fan or air-conditioning. Rooms with fans and communal bath cost $12, with air-conditioning and private bath $20. Up the hill from Joee's, **Comedor Marissa** has a daily plate for $2. Try the **French Harbour Yacht Club** (on entrance road to town) for a medium-priced meal with a great bay view. You can have French toast for breakfast ($3), shrimp ($8) at other meals, or a good but expensive pizza ($8 for a one-person pie).

OAK RIDGE

The last bus stop to the east, this tranquil, low-key fishing village is considerably more attractive than French Harbor. A cove cuts between lush, green hills, and houses sit on stilts above the water. The only places to stay are on the nearby caye, which is serviced by boat taxis (50¢) from the dock near the bus stop. **Bancahsa** on the mainland changes traveler's checks. **Hotel San José** is the only cheap place to stay on Oak Creek Caye. Clean (though stuffy) rooms sharing a bath with the adjoining room are $5 per person ($1 more with fan). The **Reef House** has bungalows that cost about twice as much, but with the bonus of kayak and windsurfing equipment for guests. The **Road House** (near the end of the caye, tel. 45–2271) has burgers and hot dogs for $1.25, a plate of the day for $2, and on weekends they have special ice cream and barbecue. Ask here about boat trips and snorkeling expeditions.

Guanaja

Guanaja is covered with green hills and what's left of a pine forest. The island is almost completely surrounded by coral reefs, which must have been a bitch for Columbus when he landed here en route to the mainland. Aside from visitors to the two big resorts, and swarms of sand flies, few creatures come to the island these days. **Guanaja Town,** also know as **Bonacca,** is on a small caye off the mainland. Since there are no cars, only shallow boat canals, Bonacca has been called the Venice of Honduras. It's an appropriate analogy if you've seen the Italian town where the canals are nearly devoid of water and full of trash and sewage. Unless you have camping equipment, or a fat wallet with a resort's business card in it, you'll probably stay in overpopulated Gaunaja Town. The winding streets and bridges make Bonacca seem like a fun-house maze, but it's so small you can't get lost. Follow the street from the pier until it ends; the street going left and right from here is the main walkway, along which are most hotels and restaurants. **The Coral Restaurant** is the primo hangout for locals, foreigners working on the island, and dive masters. **Cafe Fifi** across the street is another popular spot for an afternoon drink. If Mr. George (*see* Where to Sleep, *below*) isn't feeling grumpy, he's an excellent source for info on Guanaja and its history. The whole town turns out at the disco on weekend nights, especially after the Sabbath ends on Saturday night (lots of Seventh-Day Adventists here). The **Mountain View** disco has a sign out front with a different name that says the club is private; ignore it. Everyone is welcome, and there isn't even a cover charge (open Tuesday–Thursday till midnight, weekends until 2 or 3).

BASICS Bancahsa and **Banco Atlantida** (both on main street) change traveler's checks. **Hondutel** (also on main street) is open 7 AM–9 PM. For medical needs, go to the **clinic** across from the Seventh-Day Advent Church. They won't treat minor ills on Saturday, the Sabbath, but they're always open for emergencies.

COMING AND GOING

➤ **BY BOAT** • Cargo and fishing boats arrive most frequently from Roatán, sailing 2–3 times a week. About once a week, a boat comes from La Ceiba, and less frequently from Trujillo and Puerto Lempira. These boats don't have regular schedules, so you'll need to check at the docks. Boats return to the above destinations with the same regularity. Stop by the office of the Capitania de Puerto, on the pier across from the Isleña office, for info.

➤ **BY PLANE** • Isleña has flights from La Ceiba ($20) leaving Monday–Saturday at 6 AM, 12:30 PM, and 4 PM. Planes fly back to La Ceiba, for the same price, at 6:30 AM, 1 PM, and 4 PM. Sosa Airlines flies to Roatán ($15), then continues on to La Ceiba ($20); planes leave Guanaja Monday–Saturday at 1:30 PM.

GETTING AROUND Boats wait at the airport for each incoming plane, with rides to Guanaja Town offshore. Similarly, a boat will always be at the dock in Guanaja Town just in time to get you to your departing flight. The ride between town and the airport costs about $1. The price of gas for boats is high, and the expense is passed on to customers. For example, a boat taxi charges about $25 per trip between Guanaja Town and Savannah Bight. If you adjust your schedule, you can take public boats for virtually nothing. Collective boats leave the pier in Guanaja Town for **Savannah Bight** (60¢), at the east end of the main island, at 7 AM, 11 AM, and 6 PM. A boat taking the employees of Bayman Bay Club from Guanaja Town to the resort leaves the Zapata gas station at 7:30 AM; you can hitch a ride for free to the main island. The boat takes employees back to Guanaja Town between 4 and 5 PM if you want a lift back.

WHERE TO SLEEP Guanaja isn't really set up for backpackers. The deluxe resorts on the main island, **Bayman Bay Club** and **Posada del Sol,** both charge around $125 a night per person, including all meals, two boat dives, and unlimited shore diving. If you didn't mortgage your home to pay for your trip, you'll be staying out on Guanaja Town caye where they charge only double mainland prices. Mr. George of **George's Inn** (left on main street from the pier) is one of the Guanaja's more colorful characters. He has the cheapest rooms in town (hot, stuffy doubles $8), but unfortunately only three of them. Look for Mr. George choking on a cigar in the window of Cafe Fifi below the inn. All rooms at **Hotel Carter** (above Banco Atlantida, go left on main street from the pier) have fans and private showers. They're a good deal if you have two or three people to split the price, since a bed for one is $10 and it's only a dollar more for each additional person up to three. **Days Inn,** on the far side of the caye from the pier toward Fire Point, has clean but elemental rooms with fans and private baths (doubles $12). **Hotel Alexander** (go left on main street from the pier until you hit the sea) is the nicest place on the caye. It's $25 per person for a very simple seaside room with a terrific view (wheelchair accessible).

FOOD The real chefs all work in the main island resorts, but that's a long way to go for a meal. Guanaja Town's restaurants won't satisfy a gourmand, but the food is cheap. Saturday is a difficult time for your stomach since many restaurants close for the Sabbath. During the rest of the week, **Restaurant TKO** (right of main street from the pier) has fast, decent food. Pancakes with two eggs costs $2, burritos are 60¢, and meal plates are $2.25. They're open 7:30 AM–9 PM, closed Saturday. **Glenda's Restaurant** is the town diner, where locals listen to country music, drink beer at the counter, and watch baseball on the tube. Glenda's serves up good plates of beef, chicken, fish, or breakfast for $3. An oasis for weekend eaters, it's open daily 8 AM–11 PM. Look for a bamboo fence between Cafe Fifi and Banco Atlantida (no sign).

OUTDOOR ACTIVITIES

➤ **DIVING** • Surrounded by reefs, Guanaja has plenty of great diving sites. **Volcano Caves** and **Black Rock Caves,** off the far north end of the main island, are carved from black volcanic rock and considered tops. Dive masters may not want to make the trip unless they have a group, since it takes a lot of gas to get here. Closer to Guanaja Town, **Jim's Silver Lodge** has an abundance of eels. Hugo Cisneros, of **Dive Freedom Dive Shop** (tel. 45–4180), will take you out diving for $25 per air tank. Find him at the **Coral Restaurant** with the other dive masters. Bayman Bay Club and Posada Del Sol, the resorts on the main island, will take divers out if they don't have prior commitments with guests.

➤ **HIKING** • The main island has some great day hikes, including adventurous journeys up into the mountains to cemeteries left by the island's indigenous inhabitants. An option for exploring the island without spending lots of cash is to take the morning collective boat from town to Savannah Bight (60¢), and then hike 40 minutes across the island to **Mangrove Bight.** Walk west along the beach until you reach the mouth of the river. From here it's an easy hike to a refreshing waterfall. Continue down the beach to the Bayman Bay Club to catch the boat leaving between 4 and 5 PM to take employees back to Guanaja Town. You can also take the 7:30 AM boat from Guanaja Town to Bayman, and walk up the beach to the falls. Bring lunch and lots of insect repellent to ward off the sand flies.

➤ **BEACHES** • You can catch one of the above-mentioned boats to the Bayman Bay Club, which is surrounded by good beaches. If the resort isn't full, they'll rent you sea kayaks ($15 a day) and snorkeling equipment. When locals go to the beach, they head for **Michael Rock,** just east of Bayman Bay. Great beaches lie on either side of the promontory.

Utila

The smallest of the Bay Islands, Utila has evaded any full-scale resort development and caters mostly to young backpackers. The island has the cheapest diving certification classes in Central America. Utila is like a small town, and the islanders are chatty tellers of tales. Utila has plenty of interesting and colorful residents. Gunter, owner of **Gunter's Gallery,** makes jewelry, wood carvings, and hand-painted postcards; sells yogurt; makes dive trips; and helps rent keys. Shelby McNab is president of **BICA** (Bay Island Conservation Association) and runs **Gable's Health Club;** he's convinced Robinson Crusoe not only lived, but lived on Utila. The **Casino** (main street, across from the bank) is open as a bar nightly and as a disco on weekends. Be prepared to shift gears a lot, since the DJ mixes country music, reggae, and fast-paced punta willy-nilly.

The beaucoup sand flies on Utila can be maddening—coconut oil is said to be an effective repellent.

Pumpkin Hill Bay has a nice beach and some caves for exploring. One cave has a freshwater spring for bathing, and another big cave runs through the mountain to the beach (it's difficult to find the mouth through the foliage, so bring a flashlight). Pumpkin Hill is 5 kilometers (3 miles) from the town center, along the path leading from the bank—take a bike if you can, so you can whiz along the insect-filled trail. (The island's oldest community was built on the nearby cayes to avoid being sucked dry by insects.) Boats run to **Jewel Caye** and **Suc-Suc Caye** daily, leaving from behind Henderson's Market around 1 PM ($2). You can catch a boat to **Water Caye** from Diver's Place. The boat leaves at 9 AM, returning around 2 PM ($7 including snorkeling gear). Things aren't really set up to explore the cayes as more than a day-trip, but the beaches are happenin' and you might find a room for the night by asking around.

BASICS Serving as a bank as well as the landmark for the middle of town, **Bancahsa** changes traveler's checks. Continuing down the main street away from the airport, you'll find **Hondutel** tucked away off the street next to the bay (open weekdays 7–noon and 2–5, weekends 7–11 AM). After Hondutel closes, Ron at **Cross Creek** charges just slightly more and you can make calls until around 8 PM. Next door to Hondutel are the **post office, police** (tel. 45–3145), and the **port authority** (tel. 45–3116). The **Community Medical Clinic** across the street is open weekdays 8–noon. The **tourist information center,** between the airport and bank, is open whenever they feel so inclined; if you see someone on the porch, ask for a map or whatever advice you need and they can open the little blue kiosk.

COMING AND GOING The airport is in the process of being moved inland so planes will have more room to land. Until then, the landing strip is a five-minute walk from the town center. The main road, which runs from the airport all along the shore, has most of the town's hotels and restaurants. Aside from the intersection at the bank, Utila is a one-lane town.

➤ **BY PLANE** • Three planes a day leave La Ceiba Monday–Saturday for Utila ($10); same deal for the Utila–La Ceiba run. To get to Roatán you'll have to fly back to La Ceiba, but buy the ticket in Utila for $20.

➤ **BY BOAT** • The *Starfish* sails for La Ceiba (3½ hours, $5) Monday at 4 AM. Look for the sign along the main street. The boat to Puerto Cortés leaves Sunday at 4 PM. The boats to Roatán don't have a schedule, but they make the voyage 2–3 times a week. Talk to the Capitania de Puerto (tel. 45–3116), next to the police office, for more info.

WHERE TO SLEEP You can't take a baby step on main street without seeing a ROOMS FOR RENT sign. Most of these spare rooms in people's homes are small, simple, and quite cheap ($1–$3). Out on **Diamond Key,** a nice house has hammocks for about $3 a night, and also rents more expensive individual cottages. You can rent a whole key with a private house for $50–$60 per day. If you like nude sunbathing, rent a key because it's against the law to go au naturel on the main island. Talk to Gunter for details. On the main island, the owner of **Blue Berry Hill Hotel** (tel. 45–3141) rents rooms and cabins, gets fresh water for his guests, and likes to help people find the caves at Pumpkin Hill. The windows in the rooms don't have screens, but what do you want for $2 per bed? To get there turn off main street at the bank and follow the road to Pumpkin Hill for a few minutes. If you're taking a diving certification course at **Cross Creek Divers and Hotel** (off main street, turn off at huge sign and cross bridge to lagoon area, tel. 45–3134), your room is free. Regular rooms ($3 per person) are basic but have fans and 24-hour electricity. **Hotel Trudy's** (main street, tel. 45–3195) is everybody's favorite place to stay, and with good reason. Set right on the bay, the rooms here are cared for and have fans to keep the sand flies away, at least until midnight when the electricity goes off ($4 per person, $7 with bath). **Laguna del Mar** (main street, tel. 45–3108) is new and pretty expensive. The rooms (doubles $7, $14 with bath) are clean, have 24-hour electricity, and snorkeling equipment is free for guests.

FOOD Food here's cheap and plentiful. Several comedores have good $2 plates of the day. The restaurant at Laguna del Mar on the main street, while not terribly inexpensive, has good pancakes and cereal for breakfast. **Mermaid's Corner,** in the same house as the blue tourist-info place, has yummy take-out pizza ($6) and lasagna ($9)—either one could fill three growling backpacker bellies. At **Selly's,** locals serve themselves drinks when they arrive so they don't die of thirst. Consider giving a hand in the kitchen if you're hungry, otherwise you may wait 2–3 hours for your meal. If you have the patience, go for the fish—a great slab of barracuda costs $4. Turn toward Pumpkin Hill at the bank and follow the signs. Locals go to **Tropical Sunset Restaurant** (just behind the bank, off main street, tel. 45–3219) when they dine out. The portions are small, but the menu has a good variety. The conch soup ($2) and fried shrimp ($5) are both good, and this is the only joint in town with ice cream.

OUTDOOR ACTIVITIES

➤ **DIVING** • The diving here is awesome. The water's warm, the visibility's good, and the marine and coral life are spectacular. Most shops offer all types of dives: caves, wrecks, night dives—you name it—and they work with divers of all skill levels. The competition for diving dollars is fierce, so some outfits entice divers with fringe benefits. **Utila Dive Center** offers a room for the night if you dive with them for the day. They also have underwater photography equipment and can develop any type of film. **Cross Creek** offers a free room if you take their certification course. Cross Creek, Diver's Place, and Laguna del Mar also rent snorkeling equipment. **Utila Divers** also takes out divers. Prices with all diving outfits are about the same, and are likely to rise since they're rock-bottom now. The reef next to the airport is excellent, and the reef at **Blue Bayou,** a mile along the shore from the town center, is decent.

Remember that coral is alive, and walking on it can kill it, so be very careful entering and exiting the water.

➤ **PADDLING** • The island's cut in half by a canal, where you can often spot migratory birds chillin' in the mangrove forest. Walk along the shore until you hit the canal, and hire a dugout canoe at Blue Bayou Hotel for $3. You can paddle the channel to the north side and hike through the coconut groves to Turtle Harbor.

Cayos Cochinos

The Cayos Cochinos (Hog Cayes) are two islands and 12 cayes just off the coast near La Ceiba. The surrounding waters are crystal clear, home to the best protected, and possibly most beautiful, coral reefs in the Bay Islands. Unfortunately, all the islands and cayes are privately owned. Most owners take a dim view of trespassers, sending would-be campers away as soon as a boat touches shore. There are two exceptions. **Plantation Beach Resort** (Cachino Grande, tel. 42–0974), a secluded dive resort, charges $125 per person per day for accommodations, three buffet meals, three boat dives, and unlimited shore diving. If this sounds like your dream holiday, call **Hondutours** (La Ceiba, tel. 43–0457) for information on charter flights to the island. The more affordable option is **Chauchuate**, a small caye used as a fishing hole by the Garifuna from the village of Nueva Armenia on the mainland. The island's owner permits fishers to work from here, and, so far, has tolerated a few, low-key travelers and campers. The locals will almost always accommodate you, usually in a palm-thatched hut where you can hang a hammock. Prices vary, but expect to pay around $2. A meal of fish and tortillas will cost about $1.25.

Snorkeling equipment isn't readily available, so consider bringing your own. Soon another option will be available in the Hog Cayes. Henrick and Susan Jensen have recently acquired a caye. They plan to run a "hippy tour," with a boat taking a few backpackers from Utila to their island for a couple of days of snorkeling. Accommodations are basic, and you must be a relaxed spirit to inquire. Look for them in Utila. To get to Chauchuate from La Ceiba, take the only bus going to Nueva Armenia (1½ hours, $1) at 11:30 AM. You'll probably have to spend the night at the hospedaje in Nueva Armenia, since the sea is too rough in the afternoon for the boats to cross. Some people avoid this problem by paying for a 4 AM taxi ride from La Ceiba (1 hour, $16). Dug-out wooden boats leave Nueva Armenia around 6 AM. When some captains see foreigners, they jack the price up a little. If you can get a ride with a cargo boat, it's only around $2.

Olancho and the Eastern Mountains

It's the wild, wild west with a different compass heading. Olancho, the largest district in the country, includes most of Honduras's inhabited eastern frontier. Gold prospectors still come looking for that elusive strike, and stalwart men maintain a macho-desperado mentality, which is paid for in blood. Most men who can afford it carry a gun, either in a blatant side holster or concealed on their body. Long-standing family feuds bring these weapons out of hiding with alarming regularity and lamentable consequences. The attitude of residents toward outsiders varies widely; you may be greeted with a hostile, distant air, or welcomed with bubbling hospitality. Women would be ill-advised to travel alone in Olancho, and even in groups should be very careful going out at night. Men should exercise caution as well; always avoid doing anything that might threaten a man's ego. Avoid drunks, especially the pistol-packing ones. Outside the cities, you can find peace in the beautiful verdant woods, especially the wondrous Agalta and La Muralla national parks.

Juticalpa

The capital of the department and the biggest city in eastern Honduras, Juticalpa is more "civilized" and relaxed than some of its smaller neighbors. The town itself is pretty much yawn central, though it has a nice Parque Central with lots of trees and meandering paths. Multitudinous rivers and mountains in the surrounding area are well worth exploring (*see* Near Juticalpa, *below*).

BASICS **Banco de Occidente,** on Parque Central, is the only bank that changes traveler's checks. **Hondutel,** 1 block toward the hills from the park, is open 24 hours for calls. The **post office** next door is open weekdays 8–noon and 2–5, Saturday 8–noon. For emergencies, call the **police** (tel. 95–2028) or the **hospital** (tel. 95–2030).

COMING AND GOING The bus to Trujillo (8 hours, $5) leaves the main terminal at the edge of town at 4 AM. The bus to La Unión (3 hours, $2) leaves from across the street from the main bus station at noon. Since these two buses leave only once a day, you'd be wise to confirm that the schedules haven't changed. Buses to Catacamas (1 hour, 60¢) leave hourly from early morning till 8 PM. Buses to Tegus (3 hours, $2) leave the main station hourly until 6 PM. When you arrive by bus, take a taxi 2 kilometers to the town center. Everything you'll need is within a few blocks of the park, which is a good thing because taxis are the only public transport option.

WHERE TO SLEEP AND EAT **El Rancho,** behind the main church, and **El Rodeo,** two blocks from Parque Central, are both good for lunch and dinner. Fish or meat plates run $2–$3. **Restaurant Asia** on the main square serves pretty good, heaping plates of Chinese food for $2–$4. **Hotel Juticalpa** (1½ blocks northwest of Parque Central) is plain ol', plain ol', plain ol'. Not much can be said for the place besides the price, $1.50 per person. **Hospedaje Regis** (2 blocks west of Parque Central) is nothing more than a place to crash and lay your pack, but for the rock-bottom price ($2 per person) you get a private bath. The rooms at **Hotel Antunez** (1 block west of Parque Central, tel. 95–2250) that share the communal shower—the cheapies—are ordinary and a bit noisy. Doubles start at $5. For a few "lemps" more you can enjoy a fan, a private bath, and hot water. The salon has a TV, and the restaurant serves all meals.

NEAR JUTICALPA

CATACAMAS About 40 kilometers (25 miles) northeast of Juticalpa, Catacamas isn't far from the western edge of the Patuca national reserve. Surrounded by mountains, the city stretches out like a big suburb from the town center (which is recognizable by its paved roads). Locals here aren't especially receptive to foreigners, but they aren't hostile either. During Semana Santa they're more free-spirited, and Hondurans from all around come to drink *coyal,* a potent sap from palm trees. When sugar is added, it becomes a fortified liquor affectionately called *pata de burro* (mule kick). Besides (or while) getting drunk on coyal, try **Fernando's Discotheque** for fun. It's disguised by a sign out front that says BALNEARIO MONUMENTAL, and it really is a former *balneario* (spa). Dance in the empty swimming pool amidst colored fountains for $1 on Saturday nights. Perhaps more interesting than dancing is talking with the owner Armando. He loves to hunt, fish, and hike, and it takes very little convincing for him to show you his favorite outdoor spots.

Local craftsmen turn out beautiful mahogany guitars and woodwork.

➤ **BASICS •** **Bancahsa** will only change cash dollars. **Hondutel,** a block from the park, is open daily 7–5. The **post office,** one block toward the mountains from the park, is open weekdays 8–noon and 2–5, Saturday 8–noon. The **police** station is 4 blocks toward the mountains from the park. En route, you'll pass the **ambulance** headquarters.

➤ **COMING AND GOING •** The Aurora bus station across from the park has buses to Tegus a few times daily (4 hours, $3). If you're only going as far as Juticalpa (1 hour), direct buses leave more frequently from the park's edge. Buses leave from the market for Dulce Nombre de Culmí in the morning and early afternoon (3 hours, $1).

➤ **WHERE TO SLEEP AND EAT •** The street one block over from the other side of the park has several choices for grub. Many locals say **El Rodeo** (tel. 95–4282) is the best place in town. They serve good shish kebabs for $3, a boomin' filet mignon for $4, and can make salads or special plates for vegetarians. The semi-enclosed patio restaurant is open 11:30 AM–midnight.

Hotelito San José, across from the park, has basic but survivable rooms that all share a mediocre communal bath. The price is right at $1.25 per person. **Hotel Oriental** (½ block from park, tel. 95–4038) distinctly smells of animals. Basic doubles are $2, $4 gets you the deluxe with bath. The **National School of Agriculture Dormitory** (tel. 95–4133), about 5 kilometers (3 miles) outside town, is a good place to meet Honduran students. $8 per person gets you three cafeteria meals, use of the swimming pool and sports facilities, and your bed in a 3- to 5-person room. The owner prefers you call to make a reservation, but it's not essential. Buses run to the school from the market in the morning, otherwise take a cab.

➤ **OUTDOOR ACTIVITIES** • **Parque Nacional Sierra de Agalta,** west of Catacamas, is one of the biggest cloud forests in Honduras. The park is unusual because of the dwarf forest at the top, where trees aren't more than 5 feet tall. You can hitchhike to **Talgua,** where some interesting caves tunnel deep into the ground. Some expertise (i.e., a guide) is required for a thorough exploration of the caves, some of which remain unfathomed. **Piedra Blanca,** inside the park but not far from town, has some climbable faces. Camping is permitted virtually anywhere, and the water in the park is considered drinkable. To find guides for Sierra de Agalta or to get more info, visit the COHDEFOR office (tel. 95–4204) in the city near Barrio Colegio.

LA UNION AND LA MURALLA NATIONAL PARK Northwest of Juticalpa, **La Unión** is a small, friendly mountain town that doesn't get many tourists despite the impressive park nearby. A couple of establishments glow dimly under a weak electrical current, but for the most part the town is cloaked by an air-raid–like blackout (stargazing here is incredible). A rustic **hospedaje,** with marvelous character, boasts a shrine to the Virgin Mary and shares a barnyard with rabbits and chickens. For $1.25 per person you get a plain, candlelit room. Buses from Juticalpa (3 hours, $2) leave around noon, and make the return trip from Parque Central in La Unión around 11:30 AM. Buses depart about the same time for **Olanchito** (3 hours, $3), where you can transfer to a bus to La Ceiba.

La Muralla has been called the equivalent of Costa Rica's Monteverde, and makes an excellent side trip for those traveling by car from Tegus to La Ceiba. The park is 14 kilometers (9 miles) from La Unión; you can hitch a ride in the morning with passing trucks or walk it in about three hours. The park has *so many* quetzals and other furry, scaly, and feathered cloud forest animals. You can camp next to the visitor's center about a kilometer into the park and use the toilets and campfire pits. Four kilometers (2 miles) outside town, in the mountains, the park service has set up a hostel with 30 beds. Electricity runs till 10 PM; the hostel has showers, and also a kitchen to cook the food you bring. Pay the $8 per night and get the key from the COHDEFOR office in La Unión, or make reservations with the office in Tegus (tel. 22–1027). The park is high on the priority list of national parks being upgraded, and several new campsites with latrines should be ready soon.

The Mosquitia

A mystique of impenetrability and adventure surrounds the Mosquitia. Almost no roads penetrate the area, but planes land on makeshift landing strips, and boats navigate the extensive system of inland waterways. The indigenous Garifuna, Pech, Tawahka, and Moskito cling tenuously to their culture and tend to view outsiders skeptically. Since 1992, over 50,000 landless peasants from overpopulated western areas have been camping out along the fringe of the Mosquitia, waiting for a chance to move in and claim some farmland in this remote and sparsely populated region. As the would-be squatters advance, the hunting grounds of the indigenous Tawahka and the forest itself are increasingly threatened. This migration has been slowed by the Río Plátano Biosphere, created in 1980 to protect over 525,000 hectares (1,297,275 acres) of land around the Plátano River. The government is in the process of creating a Tawahka reserve, which would link up with the Plátano Biosphere and a national reserve on the Nicaraguan side of the Mosquitia to form a giant barrier against deforestation.

The Moskitos, populating the coastline, are a fiercely independent people. They loathed the Spanish who tried to oppress them, so less pushy English sailors were able to gain a foothold in the Mosquitia, from which their pirates raided Spanish boats filled with gold. The British knighted a Moskito chief, creating a Kingdom of the Mosquitia with very loose ties to the throne in London. The Spanish were never mighty enough to take charge here, and Britain didn't forfeit control of the region until 1892 (and then only under pressure from the newly emerging hemispheric heavy, the United States).

To this day, many Moskitos feel more affinity for their historical ties to England than they do for their present-day countrypeople. One Englishman I met said that when locals learn his nationality, many ask, "So, when are you guys going to come back and kick out these Spanish?" Virtually autonomous for hundreds of years, the Moskitos have begun to lose their precious independence. During the Nicaraguan wars of the 1980s, the contras were based along the border here, and the U.S. and Honduran governments opened a number of military bases in the region. When the war ended, some infrastructure had been built that put those cartoon dollar signs in the eyes of a few developers. The infringement of Honduran businesspeople upon traditional ways of life has created a deep prejudice against the "New Spanish"; they're viewed with distrust and hatred, often branded as thieves and murderers.

Transportation in the Mosquitia can be expensive. Try to hook up with other travelers for your journey in, so you can split the cost of boat or plane rides. Since getting around relies so heavily on river travel, too much or too little water can really wash out your trip. January–April is the dry season here, while June–July and October–December means rain, rain, rain. A dry spell usually hits from mid-August to mid-September, when boating conditions are prime. **Isleña Airlines** has flights from La Ceiba to Palacios ($30 one-way) and Puerto Lempira ($50 one-way), both leaving at 8 AM Monday–Saturday. **Sami,** based in Puerto Lempira, has regular flights to and between smaller villages in the Mosquitia.

No banks have yet sprung up in the area, so bring whatever money you need *in lempiras.* In order to stay happy and healthy, bring rain gear, water purification tablets, antimalaria pills, a mosquito net, a flashlight, and tons of mosquito repellent. Crime is on the rise, so visitors should use their smarts out in the backwater (though travelers rarely have serious problems). There is undoubtedly travail and potential trouble involved in visiting the Mosquitia, but you'll be rewarded with experiences that are truly a world away.

Puerto Lempira

Puerto Lempira is having an identity crisis. Fifteen years ago, it was a small Moskito village. When the contra war broke out, its proximity to Nicaragua brought in foreign faces and politics. The shipping lanes changed and Lempira became the cargo port for eastern Mosquitia, and the Honduran military base imported soldiers' favorite vices (sex, drugs, beer). The strange and somewhat sad result is a village that thinks it's a city. The **hospital** is near the airport, and there might be a Hondutel in town by the time this book hits the shelves. The bank won't change traveler's checks, but the **Sami** office at the airport sometimes will. **Yampus** is a bar, disco, restaurant, and the center of town activities. The name means "ashes" in Moskito, after a disco that burned down in the same spot a few years ago. It's next to the pier on the lagoon, open nightly, and doesn't charge a cover.

➤ **BY PLANE** • **Isleña** flies to and from La Ceiba ($50) daily Monday–Saturday. **Sami** connects towns inside the Mosquitia. They fly Monday–Saturday from Puerto Lempira to Ahuas ($15), Brus Laguna ($23), Wampusirpi ($23), Belén ($28), and Palacios ($30). Sami also has occasional flights in between these towns.

➤ **BY BOAT** • A cargo boat stops in Puerto Lempira twice a month. It takes four days to reach La Ceiba but you can always hop off at smaller ports along the way. The price of $24 doesn't include meals, and bring sleeping gear unless you want to sleep flat on the deck covered with a banana leaf.

➤ **BY LAND** • One of the only roads in the Mosquitia leads into Nicaragua. A truck departs daily from Merendero Mavis Aracelly around 8:30 AM for **Leimos** (3 hours, $4); cross the nearby river and you're in Nicaragua. You need to get an exit stamp in Puerto Lempira if you want to be able to return to Honduras without real problems. The entrepreneurs at the Nicaraguan immigration office have reportedly charged up to $70 for an entrance stamp in your passport!

WHERE TO SLEEP AND EAT **Hospedaje Modelo** has no sign, but it's about two blocks from the airport, across from the pool hall (clean, $4 doubles). **Hotel Gran Flores** is big, visible, and overpriced. A passable room for two with a bath is $13, the only bonus being fans. The managers also run the hospedaje next door ($3 per person), which is basically a big sweat lodge. **Merendero Mavis Aracelly** is the cleanest and best place to eat in town but it's hard to find. Locate the sign for Cafeteria Delmy, and continue down this block, stopping at the corner house on the right. A typical plate costs $1.25. The truck to Nicaragua also leaves from here. **El Bambu,** on the same street, also has good, cheap food.

NEAR PUERTO LEMPIRA

Before the afternoon winds pick up, boats cross the Laguna de Caratasca for **Cauquira** ($2). Cauquira, just a short walk from the sea, doesn't have a hospedaje but you can sometimes sleep on the boat driver's floor. A cool excursion is to the **Isla de los Pajaros** (Bird Island) in the lagoon. Get a look at them while you still can; the feathered tenants are being evicted by their landlady, Mother Nature, as the island is steadily sinking into the lagoon. From Cauquira, you can hire a tuk-tuk boat to take you along the canals through the overgrown swamps under a fairy-tale–like tunnel created by the mangrove canopy. This is a great trip for bird-watchers; one birder reported seeing more birds on a day-trip here than he did in a week in Costa Rica. You can go as far as **Raya,** the last village before the Nicaraguan border. Ask the local priest or the cantina owner about finding a bed for the night.

Biosfera del Río Plátano

On its way to the coast, the Río Plátano snakes its way through some of the most beautiful terrain in the Mosquitia. Monkeys, toucans, parrots, herons, and spoonbills are easy to see from the river, but to see more fauna you need to enter the forest. From August to September and from March to April, migratory birds fill the trees, and if you've got a keen eye, you can see the reptiles which blend in really well with their surroundings. When hiking, be *very* careful of snakes near the riverside. Some of them, including the heinous *barba amarilla* (fer-de-lance), can bite your butt into oblivion. You'll need 4–5 days to adequately explore the area.

You can fly from La Ceiba to Palacios ($30) or from Puerto Lempira to Belén ($30). When you arrive in Palacios, take a morning boat to Belén ($4). If you miss this group boat, find people to split the cost of a private boat ($20 per trip). If you want to crash in Palacios, try a decent $2 room at **Hospedaje Feliz Marmol.** Or you can hire a cheaper boat to get you to the beach, and walk four hours to the village of **Nueva Jerusalem.**

Here you can spend the night at **Hospedaje Yosira,** where basic rooms cost $5 for two people. They serve all meals, with pretty tasty plates for about $1.25. Begin looking here for boat rides up the Plátano.

Boats upriver leave from Nueva Jerusalem, the next village of **Kury,** and the village at the mouth of the river, **Barro Plátano.** If luck is smiling on you, you can hitch a ride on a cargo boat upriver to **Las Marías,** a Pech community along the river, for $4. More likely, you'll have to hire a private boat. Getting to Las Marias with an outboard motor ($80 round-trip) takes 5–6 hours; a *tuk-tuk* boat, so called because of the sound the engine makes, takes 8–9 hours and costs $50–$60 for the whole boat. These prices are round-trip, and the price rises in accordance with the number of days you spend in Las Marías (you're paying for the driver's sustenance). It'll make sense to cut a half-now-half-later deal with the boat captain. With no tourist facilities whatsoever, you'll need to seek out someone with a bed to rent or just ask to sleep in the church. As far as eating, ask around to see if a household will prepare you a meal for a few lempira. From Las Marías, you can continue six hours upriver in a *pipante* (a dugout river canoe) to an archaeological site with cool petroglyphs at **Walpulbantara.** The origin of these ancient rock carvings is unknown, but they're fading fast, due to the lapping of the river's water. For an awesome side-trip before Walpulbantara, stop and walk up either **Sulawala** or **Waikauban** creek deep into the forest.

Many Moskitos speak little Spanish, if any. Your attempts to speak Moskito will be greatly appreciated. Try a few simple phrases: naksa—hello; nakisma—how are you?; pain (pronounced like in English)—fine.

Río Patuca

The Patuca river has much of the same flora and fauna as the Plátano, but it's more difficult to see from a boat since the river banks obscure the view of the jungle. Fly from Puerto Lempira to **Brus Laguna,** a village on a lagoon near the mouth of the river on a lagoon. Brus has a savannah climate, and the tributary leading to the Patuca river is impassable in the dry season. The village has a few hospedajes ($2–$5 per person), and you can find a ride in Brus to go upriver. An adventurous alternative is to fly to **Wampusirpi** from Puerto Lempira ($30), then take a motorized canoe up river to **Krausirpe,** a large Tawahka village. Hire a local guide (or two) for about $4 a day and continue up river to the **Suptowala Valley.** A footpath cuts through the dense forest, following a natural divide between the mountains; the 24-kilometer (15-mile) hike takes 2–3 days. When you get to the other side of the divide, you can take a boat down the Río Coco or walk several hours to **Ahausbila,** where you can pay for a 5-hour ride in the back of a truck to Puerto Lempira.

EL SALVADOR 5

By Tim Kessler

Many people ask themselves two basic questions before visiting El Salvador. First, "Is it safe to go?" and second, "How much time should I cut out of Guatemala, Costa Rica, or Belize in order to check out El Salvador?" Most people know little about El Salvador other than what they read in newspapers about the country's civil war. As long as the truce between the army and the Farabundo Martí Front for National Liberation (FMLN) rebels holds, most observers agree that El Salvador is a relatively safe place to travel. The pervasive military presence will nonetheless be disconcerting; you may get pulled aside for impromptu interviews with frosty soldiers or have your bags searched too many times for your liking, but right now you're likely to encounter far less overt political violence than in Guatemala or Nicaragua. If the civil war heats up again, forgo the trip; army and guerrilla forces are prepared to fight pitched battles in many parts of the country, including the capital.

Whether the country's history and social strife turn you on or off, El Salvador has some distinct advantages and disadvantages for the prospective traveler. The country isn't used to tourists, and has little specifically organized around tourists' needs, appetites, and interests, especially outside the capital. You'll find few fluent English speakers, electricity and water shortages are chronic, changing foreign currency and traveler's checks can be agonizingly slow and frustrating, and credit cards are shunned. Your visit will, however, be memorable; for those who honestly want to see, feel, touch, and taste a Central American country, El Salvador is the real McCoy.

"El Salvador's grisly history mocks the hopeful name passed down by the Spanish: 'The Savior'."

An appealing aspect of El Salvador, particularly from a budget traveler's perspective, is it's small size. The country is only 200 kilometers (124 miles) long from end to end, and bus rides between cities never exceed four hours. The major roads are well paved and reasonably maintained. The ease of transportation means you can really take advantage of El Salvador's wonderful diversity of people, places, landscapes, and climates. The country's topography is marked by several impressive volcanoes—some still marginally active—and a few sizeable lakes. The rich volcanic soil produces huge quantities of coffee, sugar, cotton, and fruit for export. On long stretches of pasture in the north and west, cattle and sheep graze behind endless miles of barbed wire. Hundreds of narrow rivers wind their way to the Pacific, though not one of them is naviga-

El Salvador

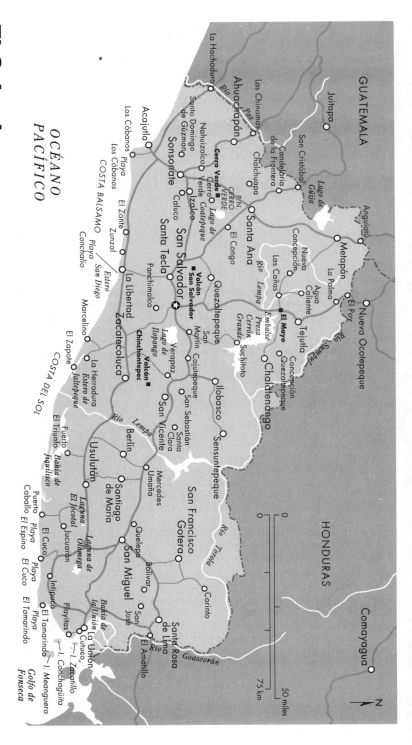

ble. The climate is hot and humid in most places, but some of the parks in higher elevations are refreshingly cool.

San Salvador, the mammoth capital city, offers the usual urban mélange of good and bad. It's wretched to the eyes (and often the heart), but it has plenty of rockin' nightlife, and bountiful day trips—volcanoes, lakes, beaches, huge climbable boulders, waterfalls, and artisan villages are within easy reach. Western El Salvador saw lots of bloodshed during insurrections earlier this century, but it was relatively calm during the recent civil war. You'll see far less militarization and mass trauma in the west than in other regions; it's a good thing, because it's really a beautiful area. Coffee-covered mountains are the backdrop for some of the country's best hiking, swimming, camping, and ambling. El Salvador's best-preserved archaeological site, Tazumal, is just a half-hour ride from Santa Ana, the hub city of the west. The Sonsonate department is home to

If you visit northern El Salvador, it'll be a sobering part of your travels; the grim realities of civil war and poverty are all too apparent.

several of the country's few remaining indigenous communities. The north and northeast, most notably the departments of Chalatenango and Morazán, are the most wartorn, least populated, and most impoverished areas in the nation. The major northern cities are highly militarized, and the FMLN rules in outlying areas. Chalatenango and San Francisco Gotera are both chilling, defeated cities. They're now totally subjugated by the government army, which knows all too well that the surrounding countryside hides a highly mobile and widely supported enemy. Expect a cool reception, military interrogations, and harder traveling conditions in these parts. The region has understandably been devoid of tourism, and locals are generally suspicious of outsiders.

San Miguel is the east's most important city. West of this metropolis, a rugged mountain chain stretches from Berlín to Santiago de Maria, where volcanic lakes, sulphuric baths, and some serious off-the-beaten-track camping and hiking await. The Pacific coast has a long string of good beaches—ranging from the quaint fishing village of El Tamarindo to the ritzy resorts along the Costa del Sol, to the surfing mecca of La Libertad. The rugged grandeur of the thinly populated northwest is largely ignored by Salvadorans, including the beautiful Montecristo cloud forest and wildlife preserve, and the stunning Lago de Güija.

El Salvador's natural beauty only makes its troubles seem that much more tragic. Its grisly history mocks the hopeful name passed down by the Spanish: "The Savior." You'll meet few people in this country whose lives haven't been affected by one of the longest and bloodiest civil wars of this century. It will never be known how many women, men, and children have lost their lives in resistance movements dating back to the Great Depression. The figure is well over 100,000. How El Salvador became the violent, terrorized nation that shocked the world during the 1980s is, frankly, a story of uninterrupted greed, corruption, and exploitation, beginning five centuries ago. The original Americans of what is now El Salvador were Mayan, numbering perhaps 100,000 at the time of the Spanish Conquest in the 16th century. Without the grand civilization seen in Guatemala, the *indígenas* (indigenous people) were easily defeated by the Spanish and entered the long nightmare experienced from México to the Southern Cone: destruction of customs, economies, culture, and religion, along with disease and slavery. For the first several hundred years, most indigenous communities retained enough land for traditional subsistence farming. However, early Spanish settlers gradually began siphoning off surplus production for European consumption. In the 19th century, *ricos* (the rich) began to seize the land itself, and large plots were consolidated into huge *haciendas* (estates) under the self-proclaimed ownership of Spanish bureaucrats, soldiers, and well-connected settlers. After Independence (1821) came two decades of civil war, in which the wealthy fought each other to retain or increase their rights over the land and people.

At the same time Europe developed a taste for an exciting new product: coffee. As Spanish settlers and other fortune-seekers immigrated to exploit the lucrative bean, subsistence farmers and their modest plots were quickly swallowed up by increasingly powerful coffee concerns. It worked out wonderfully for the new coffee magnates—the *campesinos* (peasants) no longer had their own land to work, and, lo and behold, the plantations needed sowing and harvesting! El Salvador's elite was overwhelmingly white (i.e., of Spanish descent), and the colonial social structure and division of labor left little doubt in the ricos' minds that the masses were something less than human, born to be controlled. Needless to say, the workers saw something wrong with this picture. Oppressive working and political conditions made it necessary for national oligarchs to employ force to keep the social structure intact, using at first private armies and eventually the national armed forces. With their immense economic power, the oligarchy was able to retain firm control of the state and military.

As coffee production further enriched the tiny minority of El Salvador's elite, they expanded into other profitable activities, like banking and producing tropical fruits. In 1881, the government declared an end to common lands—i.e., the legal basis for the sovereignty of traditional villages. From then on, even as the fertile lands of El Salvador vastly increased the country's wealth, most people sank deeper into the poverty of tenant agriculture. The political legacy of a landless multitude has perpetuated the remarkably violent history of El Salvador: Even today, most political strife in this densely populated country centers around the use and ownership of the limited amount of arable land. Inevitably, both the destruction of indigenous farming and the growing population of impoverished *ladino* (people of mixed indígena and European descent) campesinos led to protest. Generally small and unorganized, peasant insurrections in the late 19th century were put down with ease; but nothing lasts forever.

The Great Depression brought painful change to El Salvador. In the midst of plummeting coffee prices and frantic divisions within the ruling elite, a reformist landowner named Arturo Araujo led a coalition of urban progressives, workers, and peasants to political victory in El Salvador's first free election, becoming president in 1931. From the beginning, Araujo was pressured by the growing demands of desperate peasants—who were losing even subsistence work as plantations remained idle—and the growing intolerance of the oligarchs, who sensed real change in the political climate. Increasing tensions still further, the political activist (and avowed Marxist) Farabundo Martí entered the Salvadoran scene. His ideology and common-sense mobilization tactics

The Bull-Headed Gringo

"Walking down the street in San Francisco Gotera I heard a couple of guys yelling 'Gringo! Gringo! Fuera!' I hate it when I'm called gringo and told to fuera ('get out'), so I ignored them and continued walking. I didn't want any trouble with local Yankee-bashers. Better deaf and dumb than dead. They kept yelling at me and finally one said 'Camisa roja, fuera de la calle!' ('Red shirt, get out of the street!'). I turned around and found myself about three feet from a great big agitated bull with some serious fucking horns headed straight for my flaming red shirt. Some rancher herding his cattle to market didn't count on skewering some damn-fool gringo on the way. Reflexes are an amazing thing. I was on the sidewalk with my back against a wall before you could say the 't' in toro. I'm sure it all happened because I'm not a vegetarian and have built up some bad bovine karma." —from a letter by writer Tim Kessler.

attracted thousands of impoverished famers, workers, and students. The Latin American elites were terrified.

In January 1932, a series of municipal elections won by communist candidates was voided by a new, indignant leader, General Maximiliano Hernández Martínez. The General's army smashed an ill-fated Communist insurrection in the coffee center of Sonsonate with unprecedented brutality. The event, known simply as *la matanza* (the massacre), was a bloodbath that left 30,000 dead. In the town of Izalco, groups of 50 men were tied together by the thumbs and led to the wall of the Church of the Assumption, where they were shot. Victims were forced to dig mass graves for themselves before a machine gun dropped them into the hole. The roadways were littered with bodies killed indiscriminately by the National Guard. Campesinos learned a harsh lesson about the dangers of pressing for social change.

In the mid-20th century, the Cold War turned hot in Central America. President Kennedy's Alliance for Progress sought to bring stability to the region by diminishing communist appeal through direct-aid programs. Although these millions of dollars generated significant economic growth in the country, the wealth remained concentrated in the hands of those best able to manipulate political resources. Even as agricultural exports exploded tenfold in the 1960s, the Salvadoran people were left among the five most malnourished in the world. The number of peasants thrown off their land rose steadily from the early 1960s.

During this period, new economic groups within the cities, especially the growing professional and working classes, began pressing for liberalization. José Napoleón Duarte's Christian Democratic Party allied with the National Revolutionary Movement to challenge oligarchic power in 1972; Duarte's apparent electoral victory didn't stop the military from declaring victory for the oligarchs' candidate. Popular protest, ranging from civil disobedience to armed insurrection, came soon after. The military met these movements with counter-insurgency units, often under the tutelage of U.S. intelligence. The most infamous was ORDEN (a Spanish acronym meaning "order"), whose members drifted in and out of El Salvador's renowned right-wing death squads.

The 1979 Sandinista victory over the Somoza dictatorship in Nicaragua only heightened the level of panic and reaction among El Salvador's embattled elite. While peasants, workers, students, and intellectuals were all targets of right-wing violence, a particularly gruesome war was waged against the Catholic clergy, which had largely shifted from traditional conservatism to "liberation theology." Priests and nuns were found shot, raped, and mutilated. In March 1980, Archbishop Oscar Romero, one of the nation's leading human-rights advocates and an outspoken critic of government-led violence against the poor, was gunned down while delivering a sermon in San Salvador's cathedral. The judge put in charge of investigating the case narrowly escaped assassination himself. No killer was found, but many say the government and justice system didn't look too hard. Film director Oliver Stone took a pretty hard look at the life and death of Archbishop Romero in his movie *Salvador*.

In Catholic "liberation theology," poverty is no longer seen as the will of God, but rather as the design of rich people who want an unfair piece of the pie.

In May of the same year, a half-dozen guerrilla organizations united under the leadership of the FMLN. The armed insurgency was also joined by a political coalition, the Democratic Revolutionary Front (FDR), composed of reformers demanding an end to military repression. The FMLN-FDR has remained the political and military force of opposition in El Salvador for over a decade. In the 1980s, with tremendous U.S. support, Christian Democrat José Napoleón Duarte returned to the political scene as a moderate, a national hero, and a voice for democracy. However, he almost immediately proved incapable of controlling the army, the death squads, or the "Fourteen Families," who have constituted the country's oligarchy since the mid-19th century.

Colonel Roberto D'Aubisson, founder of the ultra-rightist ARENA party and suspected death-squad director, criticized Duarte's "weakness" in dealing with the communists, and conducted covert military operations against guerrilla supporters. Squeezed between the military's might and inflexibility on the one hand, and the surprising resilience and popular support of the FMLN on the other, Duarte presided over an agonizing civil war in which he could do nothing more than pay lip service to democracy while soliciting further U.S. funding.

President Jimmy Carter, long considered a communist by El Salvador's elite for his moderate human-rights position, left the White House in January 1981. President Reagan brought joy to the oligarchy in the form of unprecedented levels of U.S. aid, which, by many reports, funded a redoubling of repression in the country. The Reagan Administration proclaimed El Salvador one of the Central American battlegrounds against communism in the western hemisphere. Despite growing lefty-gringo criticisms of human-rights abuses committed with U.S. money, and even periodic rumblings within Congress, aid to Duarte's government continued at remarkably high levels. Guns, helicopter gunships, rocket launchers, and special counter-insurgency training were poured into El Salvador's military. The Salvadoran army "disappeared" people, decimated popular organizations, created an atmosphere of fear, and sent thousands fleeing the country for safer ground.

By some estimates, El Salvador's gross national product was doubled by U.S. aid during the height of military "cooperation."

In the late '80s, the conflict seemed endless. In November 1989, the FMLN shocked the Salvadoran government and army with its "final offensive," which involved pitched battles in the heart of the capital for almost a month. The army and air force indiscriminately attacked areas of FMLN support, dropping bombs over several densely populated (and poor) neighborhoods. After untold thousands of casualties, the FMLN had to withdraw. Both sides claimed victory in the battle, but the stalemate was painfully obvious. Beginning in 1990, perhaps as a unique case of diplomacy through mutual exhaustion and frustration, rebel-government negotiations started making unprecedented progress. After 12 years of a cruel war that killed over 75,000 (mostly civilians), a truce and comprehensive peace accord were made official in February 1992. Although many details are still to be ironed out, the basic idea is to demobilize the rebel forces while assuring them political rights and safety from army slaughter. An unusual plan to integrate ex-guerrillas into the national police force has been put forth, but as yet this hasn't gone too far. At the same time, the size of the Salvadoran army is to be drastically reduced. Already there have been mutual accusations of bad faith, truce violations, and so forth, but at press time actual fighting has not begun anew.

Today, no issue is more important to the lives of El Salvador's people than the potential of renewed warfare. While hopes run high for a lasting truce, many are doubtful that real peace can endure the intense political confrontation between battle-hardened guerrillas and the current right-wing ARENA government. Compounding the problem still further is the army, which has many characteristics of an autonomous state; it can nullify any diplomatic progress with a coup. For many Salvadoreños, the desire for peace competes with the desire for revenge. The simmering hatreds of this long war can't be eliminated by a mere U.N. resolution. But for all the naysaying and skepticism, the 1992 accord is being touted by the guerrillas as the world's first "negotiated revolution." With both sides thoroughly exhausted, the populace desperate to avoid more war, and U.S. aid cut to a trickle, all main actors in El Salvador have strong reasons to honor the fragile peace and learn to fight each other with politics instead of weapons. The FMLN was recently granted official status as a political party, and may freely participate in all elections. A sign of the new political climate is that you can visit their offices to chat, or buy their newsletter on the street. However, the original issues of the civil war—land, food, distribution of wealth—are yet to be seriously acknowledged by El Salvador's economic elite, much less resolved politically. It remains to be seen if those with power are willing to share the pie, and give a meaningful political voice to the mass of poor people who strive to break the chains forged five centuries ago.

Basics

For other, important information about El Salvador, *see* Chapter 1, Basics.

VISITOR INFORMATION

➤ **TOURIST OFFICES** • El Salvador doesn't have any send-away-for-the-brochure-type tourism bureau. The Salvadoran consulate nearest you may have some literature about traveling in the country, so look in a phone book and give them a call. Within El Salvador itself, **Instituto Salvadoreño de Turismo** (ISTU), the national tourist board, has a fairly well-stocked office in the capital and in a few other locations.

➤ **WORK AND STUDY ABROAD** • The **Miranda Language School** offers three different programs that include a combination of language classes, homestays with Salvadoran families, work programs, visits to rural communities, and learning about trade unionism in El Salvador. Fees range from $75 to $175 per week, sometimes including room and board, and your length of stay is flexible. *Mailing address: Aptd 3274, Correo Centro de Gobierno, San Salvador, El Salvador, Centroamerica, tel. 503/222–849; in the U.S. contact 415/885–5541.*

The **Marin Interface Task Force on Central America** has a number of work programs for people with technical skills in teaching, accounting, agriculture, medicine, solar energy, and construction. They require a minimum three-month commitment, and your work is generally done in rural settings. *20 Sunnyside Ave., Suite A303, Mill Valley, CA 94941, tel. 707/935–3882.*

Peace Brigades International runs much-needed and multifaceted programs aimed at facilitating nonviolent conflict resolution in El Salvador. You can join if you're over 25, speak fluent Spanish, have experience working with grassroots organizations and/or have spent a fair bit of time in the region. There's a mandatory training period before departure, and it's a minimum one-year commitment. Participants pay their own airfare, but living expenses are covered. *Contact Louise Palmer, Central America Project Director, 192 Spadina, Suite 304, Toronto, Canada M5T2C2, tel. 416/594–0429.*

WHEN TO GO During the wet season (May–October) you'll see plenty of rain. Expect a downpour at least once a day, and some days may get completely washed out—along with most unpaved roads. You get used to it, though, especially if you come prepared with the appropriate gear. The pluses of traveling in the rainy season include fewer vacationers, somewhat lower hotel prices, and by far the most important cultural event in the country, El Salvador del Mundo. Temperature-wise, the whole country is *hot* year-round; it's significantly more scorching in the Pacific lowlands than elsewhere, and San Salvador—situated at a high elevation—is comparatively cooler. Bank on it getting chilly at night when you're hiking and camping at higher elevations.

➤ **HOLIDAYS AND FESTIVALS** • Other than the normal Central American holidays (*see* Basics chapter), the most important public holiday is September 15, Independence Day. The festival of **El Salvador del Mundo** consumes the capital and the rest of El Salvador from August 3 to 6. **Patron saint festivals** vary from town to town (*see* individual cities).

MAIL The regular *correos* are cheap, very slow, and often unreliable. Do not send money, objects, or anything you really want to arrive home. It's a good idea not to send anything politically controversial if you want to keep it unseized and unburned. Normal "I'm doing fine" letters usually arrive eventually (in 2–3 weeks). Letters to the United States cost 10¢, to Europe and Australia 15¢. The best way to send important stuff to the United States is through one of the many express services. The two largest are

Urgente Express and **Gigante Express,** which are very safe, reliable, and usually get the stuff there within 10 days. They're everywhere in the country, operating in little branches (clothing stores, pharmacies) or larger offices. Sending a regular letter costs about $1.50, and a one-pound package about $6. If you want to receive mail at post offices on the road, have it addressed to: your name, Lista de Correos, name of city, name of department, El Salvador, Centroamerica. To have mail sent to the capital, it should say: Lista de Correos, Centro Gobierno, San Salvador, etc.

MONEY The currency of El Salvador is the *colón,* worth approximately 12¢. Some refer to it colloquially as the *peso.* The coins are confusing to use because some of the denominations are the same size; one colón looks like 10 *centavos* (Salvadoran version of pennies), a five-centavo piece is the same size as 25 centavos, et cetera.

Changing money in El Salvador can be tricky. The easiest way is with U.S. dollars, which are gladly accepted at major banks, and at dozens of *casas de cambio* all over San Salvador. If you carry only traveler's checks, make sure they're American Express, and, more importantly, that you carry the original receipt. Apparently there was a massive fraud several years ago with false checks, and no bank will change money for you without proof of purchase. You can use your Visa or MasterCard to get colones at a few banks; the best bets are **Banco Hipotecario** and **Banco de Comercio,** both of which have branches in many medium-sized and major cities. There's a sizeable commission charged, so it's not a cheap way to go.

PHONES Antel, the national phone company, has an office in virtually every city, town, and *pueblito.* Operators here can connect your international and domestic calls. Public telephones work like U.S. phones, and a digital display tells you how much money (time) you have left. Calling inside the country is fairly cheap, but if you plan to talk for a while bring a load of coins. You can reach an **AT&T USA Direct** operator by calling 190 from almost any phone in the country.

VISAS Citizens of all countries (except Central America) must get a visa to enter El Salvador. Although it's convenient to have all travel documents ready before you leave, you can also get your visa at the Salvadoran embassy in other Latin American capitals. It's cheaper than getting one outside the region, though you may have to wait a day or so for it. U.S. citizens must procure a lot of stuff to get a visa in the United States: proof of employment, an official police department "letter of clearance" (stating you have no felony record), a passport-size photo, and $15. No proof of return ticket is required. Almost all tourists will be given 15 days to travel upon arrival. If you need more, you must go to the immigration office in the capital (tel. 21–2111) on the second floor of the Centro de Gobierno, open weekdays 8–noon and 1:30–4. (Take Bus 29 from Alameda Juan Pablo II, but it's probably faster to walk from the center.) You'll have to spend $3 on photos and another $1.50 for God-only-knows-what paperwork, but you can do it all in an hour or two, depending on the crowd. To cross the border (both going in and out of the country), you pay 50¢–$1.25 on foot, $8–$17 by car, and there is a $10 airport departure tax.

Don't visit San Salvador's immigration office looking "loose"— i.e., wearing shorts, T-shirts, or sandals. Officials may decide they don't want to let a scruffy person through the door, and then where will you be?

COMING AND GOING

➢ **BY BUS** • Getting to San Salvador from Guatemala City is an easy six-hour ride along the Interamerican Highway via Santa Ana (around $5). Getting to the Honduran border at El Amatillo takes about five hours from San Salvador's Terminal de Oriente, and only ½ hour from the eastern city of Santa Rosa de Lima. The four-hour ride to or from El Poy, the Honduran border station due north of San Salvador, passes through some truly beautiful country (buses leave several times daily from Terminal de Oriente in the capital).

➢ **BY PLANE** • **TACA,** the national airline, has a very good reputation and flies between San Salvador and all other Central American capitals. TACA also flies from the United States, as do Pan Am and Continental. Most national airlines in the region have at least one daily flight to El Salvador. No one flies directly to and from Europe or the South Pacific; visitors from these places should transfer planes in Miami.

GETTING AROUND

➢ **BY BUS** • Buses are cheap. Short excursions (30–45 minutes) run about 15¢, medium ones (1–1 ½ hours) 25¢–50¢, and longer ones (2 ½–4 hours) 60¢–$2. Rates on weekends go up 20%. Most buses leave frequently (every 15 minutes is common). Certain destinations are served by only a couple of buses a day, so you should plan ahead and leave early in the morning. Buses rarely travel at night; final departures are usually between 4 PM and 6 PM, so try not to get stuck in a small town without a *hospedaje* (lodging) after the last bus has left. Also, don't plan to arrive by bus "just in time" for any important meeting, deadline, or border crossing. Times listed in the chapter are estimates—just getting out of San Salvador can take up to 45 minutes in heavy traffic. Also, many buses start and stop incessantly to pick up and drop off passengers with tons of cargo which must be loaded or unloaded from the roof. The **desvío** (highway junction) is a common element in Salvadoran bus travel. On many journeys, you'll take one bus to a desvío, get off, and then pick up another bus heading to your destination.

➢ **BY PLANE** • The national domestic airline, **Transportes Aéreos de El Salvador (TAES)**, flies between San Salvador and San Miguel, San Francisco Gotera, Santa Rosa de Lima, La Unión, and Usulután. Flying in El Salvador is rarely necessary and never economical—the country is tiny, most trips only take a few hours by bus, and you could drive across the country in about a day.

➢ **BY BIKE** • Biking isn't real big in El Salvador, but you'll see mountain-bike riders from time to time. A couple of places in the capital may be able to help with parts and servicing. Most of the country is mountainous, so get ready to pump those legs. A network of often rocky secondary roads can get you around without snarling you in traffic.

➢ **BY CAR** • El Salvador has top-quality highways, especially between major cities. The Interamerican Highway runs right through the middle of the country. Many smaller roads are markedly more primitive, but generally passable. You can rent cars in the capital and a few other places around the country; if you'll be doing a lot of off-the-beaten tracking, try to get a 4x4. You should have proof that you either own or have rightful possession of the vehicle. To drive, all you need is a valid U.S. or international driver's license; proof of insurance isn't necessary (though it is nice to have). Driving is on the right side of the road.

➢ **HITCHING** • Hitching's not a popular sport here. Buses are so cheap, leave so often, and cover so much territory that it usually isn't worth the effort. The exception is when you've missed the last bus of the day and need to get somewhere; even so, cars don't stop that often, and hitching after dark is risky due to guerrilla activity, army operations, and basic bad guys.

WHERE TO SLEEP
El Salvador doesn't have a single youth hostel. That's okay, because in most towns a decent clean room with bath costs $3–$6 per person. Unpleasant dives run $1–$3. These prices can double in popular beach towns. Hotels hail by many different names, including *hospedaje, posada, cabaña, casa de huespedes,* and hotel, but the name doesn't tell you a thing about the quality or price of a lodging. There are only a few sanctioned camping areas in the country, mostly in the west. You can always camp off-road, but the obvious precautions hold (avoid private property, robbers, rain, and the army).

FOOD Decent-sized meals with meat at typical restaurants or *comedores* run $1.50–$3 per plate, with simple "vegetarian" stuff being somewhat cheaper. Middle-class restaurants run $3–$4, and fancy places can set you back $6–$10. Meals at beach towns cost more. The most typical of the *comida típica* is the *pupusa*, a fried tortilla filled with beans, cheese, or *chicharon* (pork skin). Pupusas are traditionally served with pickled cabbage, and are the specialty of the house in *pupuserías*. Quick, tasty, and safe, they're a good way to fill up on the cheap (10¢–20¢ apiece). *Mariscada* is a delicious seafood soup. *Minutas* are icy, slushy drinks sweetened with honey—truly a godsend on hot afternoons, but they're often made with unpurified water.

One of the most common drinks in El Salvador is horchata, a rice-based beverage with varying degrees of sweetness; it's served everywhere in plastic bags. Don't be frightened by its dirty-dishwater coloring; it's very refreshing, though the water isn't guaranteed to be purificado.

➤ **TIPPING** • Restaurant service is an oxymoron here—don't expect much and you won't be disappointed. Tipping isn't practiced in any regular sort of way; but since the food is so cheap, 10%–15% probably won't hurt you too much and it'll certainly brighten someone's day. High-class restaurants may add a service charge to your bill.

OUTDOOR ACTIVITIES A big thing here is recreation parks called *turicentros*. They're all around the country and usually have swimming pools, ball fields, basketball courts, and grassy areas for picnicking or lounging. If the ocean is your game, head to the Pacific coast for tanning, surfing, and boating. The country also has a few lakes good for bathing and fishing. There's lots of good walking and hiking territory outside big cities; western El Salvador, especially Cerro Verde national park, is the place to go for serious camping and nature hiking.

San Salvador

Most travelers give El Salvador's capital about 15 minutes before writing the city off as a hellish urban monstrosity. Give the place a chance, if for no other reason than necessity, since the capital has services and resources unavailable anywhere else in the country. The city's central location makes it the logical jumping-off point for interesting day trips in every direction. While traveling in El Salvador, you're probably going to pass through here a few times and may even stay for a while. You'll never be more than 10 feet from someone wanting to sell you something, you'll sweat like a pig, and if you think you can taste the pollution in New York, in San Salvador you can eat it with a fork. Make your peace with it early. Accept it for what it is: an aspiring modern city in a developing country.

San Salvador is about 2,000 feet above sea level in a smog-trapping basin called Valle de las Hamacas ("Valley of Hammocks"), so named for the region's swinging history of earthquakes. The official population is about half a million, but that figure triples when you include outlying suburbs, shanties, migrants, and homeless people. San Salvador is easily the densest major city in Central America. It's been destroyed and rebuilt several times since its founding in 1525 and consequently bears hardly a trace of its colonial heritage. In October 1986, much of the capital was leveled by a strong earthquake that left over a thousand dead. The last FMLN offensive in the city (November '89), which claimed an untold number of lives, entailed ferocious urban gun battles and the use of aerial bombing by the government air force. All this worsened an already acute shortage of housing and infrastructure. This is especially true in some of the poorer suburbs, where guerrilla support runs high among the desperate population. You can still see the damage in the ghostly concrete and metal skeletons of buildings, "temporary" locations for key government services, and the endless shanties around the city's edge.

San Salvador

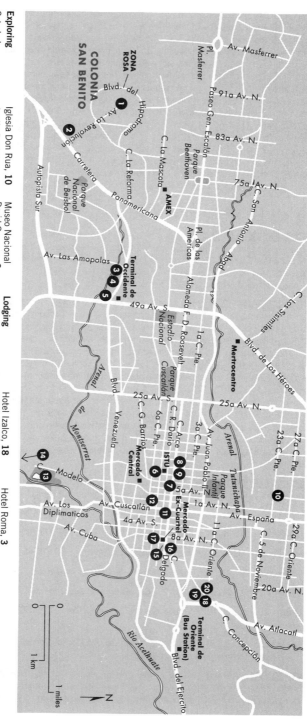

Exploring

Catedral
Metropolitana, **11**

El Parque
Zoologico, **13**

El Rosario, **17**

Iglesia Calvario, **12**

Iglesia Don Rua, **10**

Jardín Botánico
La Laguna, **14**

La Basílica del
Sagrado Corazón
de Jesus, **8**

Monumento de
la Revolución, **1**

Museo Nacional
David Guzman, **2**

Lodging

Casa de Huespedes
El Oso, **9**

Hospedaje
Santa Rosa, **19**

Hotel Bruno, **16**

Hotel Centro, **6**

Hotel Izalco, **18**

Hotel Occidental, **5**

Hotel Nuevo
Panamericano, **15**

Hotel Pasadena, **4**

Hotel Ritz
Continental, **7**

Hotel Roma, **3**

Hotel Yucatán, **20**

Despite San Salvador's sprawling, frantic appearance, getting around the city isn't too difficult. Buses are cheap, run frequently, and go everywhere. Like any metropolis, San Salvador can be dangerous. The problem is made worse by frequent power failures—always carry a good flashlight. Much more common than muggings or violent crime is petty theft. Cramped sidewalks make backpackers easy targets for pickpockets and pocket-slitters. San Salvador hosts relatively few tourists, so travelers stand out and are frequently singled out by the omnipresent street beggars asking for *limosna* (handouts). One of the more serious daily nuisances, especially during the dry season, is the lack of tap water. It frequently shuts off, usually when your hair is full of shampoo. Most hotels keep a *pila* (wash basin) filled for communal use when the tap is off, but keep a small basin of water ready for your basic morning grooming. Since over half of El Salvador's electrical energy is hydro-electric, power and water shortages go hand in hand. Widespread rumor has it that a director of the national power company is knee-deep in corruption (i.e., selling energy to the highest bidder), and is largely responsible for the shortage.

BASICS

AMERICAN EXPRESS They'll help replace lost or stolen cards and traveler's checks; for members they hold mail, let you receive faxes for free, or send them for a fee. *Centro Comercial La Mascota, first office on lower level, tel. 23–0177. From El Centro, take Bus 34 San Benito or 101 Santa Tecla, ask to be let off at La Mascota. Open weekdays 8–noon and 2–5.*

CHANGING MONEY Make sure you read about money-changing hardships in the Basics section, *above*. Even in the capital they have stringent restrictions on cashing traveler's checks. If you don't have the original receipt, shameless sobbing in a bank office might help, but your only certainty is the American Express office (*see above*), where you'll also get a fair exchange rate for AmEx checks. The **black market** for dollars isn't worth the hassle, since banks offer competitive rates; if the government starts to over-value the colón, the black market may become more appealing. The major banks in El Centro are along Avenida Cuscatlán; most change dollars as well as major traveler's checks. These banks have dozens of branches throughout the capital, as well as smaller casas de cambio, where you can change money during normal business hours. Opposite the domed cathedral, **Banco Hipotecario** changes money at the *Cambio* office, weekdays 8:30–5:30 and Saturday 8:30–1. Across from Hipotecario, **Servi-Cambio,** open weekdays 9–5 and Saturday 9–noon, usually has pretty fast service.

CONSULATES/EMBASSIES Embassies are generally open 8–5. Some take lunch breaks and close their doors, but it's a willy-nilly kind of thing.

Costa Rica. *Centroamericana Bldg., Alameda Roosevelt 3107, tel. 23–8283.*

Guatemala. *15a Av. Norte 135, near Calle Arce, tel. 22–2903.*

Honduras. *7a Calle Poniente 4326, Col. Escalón, tel. 98–0524.*

Nicaragua. *89a Av. Norte at 9a Calle Poniente, tel. 24–6662.*

Panamá. *Av. Las Bugambilias 21, Col. San Francisco, tel. 98–0773.*

United Kingdom. *4828 Paseo General Escalón, tel. 24–0473. Take Bus 52 from Alameda Juan Pablo II.*

United States. *25 Av. Norte 1230, tel. 26–7100. East of the Centro de Gobierno. Take Bus 29 from Alameda Juan Pablo II.*

LAUNDRY Washing clothes is a problem because of the eternal water shortage. Some pricier hotels have washing machines and a stiff charge to use them, while many others won't even allow use of the pila (try to bargain). It's pretty cheap to go to a pila house once in a while—in the meantime learn to like your body odor. One of the cheapest pila houses is **Lavadora Publica** (admission 5¢). *Near Terminal de Occidente, corner of Av. Rep. Federal Alemania and Calle 5 de Noviembre. Open daily 6 AM–5 PM.*

MAIL The central post office is just north of the Centro de Gobierno, east of Parque Infantil. It's open weekdays 8–5, Saturday 8–noon. A smaller branch is at Metrocentro on Boulevard Los Héroes.

MEDICAL AID San Salvador has several large hospitals with emergency and general medical services. Many doctors have received training in North America and speak fluent or at least functional English, but they won't necessarily be available right when you come. At the east end of the capital is the **Hospital General Florencia Nightengale** (Km 3½ on Blvd. de Ejercito, tel. 27–3344). To get there, take Bus 29 from the center or any east-bound bus from Terminal de Oriente. **Hospital Rosales** is at 25a Avenida Norte and Calle Arce, just west of the center. **Hospital de la Mujer** (81a Av. Sur and Calle Juan José Cañas, Col. Escalón, tel. 79–0133 or 98–1978) provides specialized medical attention for women.

PHONES Antel's main office in El Centro is at the corner of Calle Rubén Darío and 5a Avenida Sur (opposite McDonald's). It's open daily 6 AM–10 PM. A smaller, less hectic branch is in the Torre Roble in the Metrocentro on Boulevard Los Héroes. Making collect calls with Antel costs 50¢, and direct international calls are extremely expensive. Local calls start at 10 centavos (a penny or two). Don't be fooled by the huge Antel sign at Calle Rubén Darío and 23a Avenida Sur—it's just an administration building.

VISITOR INFORMATION At the **Instituto Salvadoreño de Turismo (ISTU),** the people are friendly enough, but they really don't do much more than shove a pile of maps and glowing turicentro descriptions at you. The pamphlets are hardly unbiased, but the details are worth having. Especially helpful is "Nuestras Bellezas Naturales" (Our Natural Beauty), with info about all the cool outdoor things you can do around the country. *619 Calle Rubén Darío, between avenidas 9a Sur and 11a Sur, tel. 22–8000. Open weekdays 8–4.*

COMING AND GOING

BY CAR A number of rental agencies have offices at the airport, but they're expensive ($45 per day for a basic car). For a better rate try **Sure Rent** (Blvd. de los Héroes at 23a Calle Poniente, tel. 25–1810).

BY PLANE The **international airport,** 44 kilometers (27 miles) south of San Salvador near Comalapa, has a post office, a bank, and a sometimes-open tourist office. TACA, the national airline, only flies internationally. A number of other airlines also fly between San Salvador, North America, and other Central American capitals. **Domestic flights** come and go at Aeropuerto Ilopango, 13 kilometers (8 miles) east of San Salvador (no tourist services available). Internal flights are made by Transportes Aéreos de El Salvador (TAES). From the capital they go to San Francisco Gotera, Usulután, La Unión, San Miguel, and a few other places. The TAES office is in the Edificio Plaza at 5a Avenida Norte and 19a Calle Poniente (tel. 27–0314), and they're open weekdays 9–4.

➤ **AIRPORT TRANSPORT** • The **domestic airport** is right on a main thoroughfare, and practically any bus will take you to Terminal de Oriente in town; just flag one down. The **international airport** is a 45-minute drive from the capital. Private taxis are very expensive, but the microbus *colectivo* service, **Acacya,** charges $3 per person. It leaves the airport at 6 AM, 7 AM, noon, and 3 PM for the capital. The Acacya office in San Salvador is at 19a Avenida Norte and 3a Calle Poniente, tel. 71–4937; the airport office phone number is 39–9271. A cheap way to get from Comalapa is to take a taxi to the desvío a few kilometers south of San Juan Talpa and wait for Bus 102 coming from La Libertad, which'll take you straight to the capital.

BY BUS The bus system is efficient and extremely cheap, and buses are usually crowded. Most lengthy rides leave from one of the two main terminals: **Terminal de Occidente** (49a Avenida Sur and Boulevard Venezuela) serves destinations more or less west of the city, and buses from **Terminal de Oriente** (where Avenida Peralta turns into Boulevard Ejercito Nacional) go north and east. Bus 34 goes between the two terminals and passes through the city center on the way. Following are some of the most popular bus routes from the capital. Most buses begin service at dawn and continue till late afternoon; never count on night travel (wartime habits fade slowly).

➤ **TERMINAL DE ORIENTE** • To San Vicente (1½ hours, every 10–15 minutes, 50¢); San Miguel (3 hours, every 15 minutes, $2); Usulután, (4 hours, several times per hour, $2); Chalatenango (2½ hours, several times per hour, 50¢); El Amatillo at the Honduran border (5 hours, five times daily).

➤ **TERMINAL DE OCCIDENTE** • To Sonsonate (1½ hours, every 15 minutes, 50¢); Guatemala City (5 hours, leaving frequently 5 AM–1 PM, $4); Santa Ana (1 hour, every 15 minutes, 50¢)—ask for the bus going *via Calle Nueva* (New Road) for a faster trip to Santa Ana.

GETTING AROUND

San Salvador isn't the most logically planned city, but it does have a logic: Familiarize yourself with it before trying to get around. If it helps, every Salvadoran city is laid out the same way. Avenidas always run north–south and calles east–west; addresses are often given as the intersection of an avenida and a calle. **El Centro** is the main square, with the Palacio Nacional, Banco Hipotecario, and the cathedral. The central avenida is called **Avenida Cuscatlán** south of the central calle, and **Avenida España** north of it. Likewise, **Calle Delgado** is the central calle on the east side, and it's **Calle Arce** to the west. Avenidas to the north or south are appended by *norte* or *sur,* and calles to the east and west with *oriente* and *poniente.* One main thoroughfare is undergoing a serious identity crisis. From El Centro moving east, 2 Calle Poniente becomes Calle Rubén Darío, then Alameda F. Delano Roosevelt, and finally Paseo General Escalón.

If you're in El Centro and need to go anywhere within about 10 blocks, go on foot. The traffic is so congested that a leisurely walking pace will probably beat a taxi. For longer trips, buses run faithfully from dawn until 7 or 8 PM, depending on the route. A ride is 10¢ before 6 PM, 12¢ after. Some minibus lines charge more. From El Centro, Bus 29 goes to Terminal de Oriente, Bus 34 goes between the two bus terminals and along Avenida de la Revolución to the ritzy San Benito/Zona Rosa neighborhood. Bus 101 goes right past the Calle de la Mascota on its way to Santa Tecla, and Bus 52 goes to the Colonia Escalón, ending in Plaza Masferrer. Taxis are plentiful and relatively cheap, but you should always settle on a price before taking a ride. A five-minute trip (without traffic) runs about $2. If you're far from your destination after 7:30 or 8 PM and don't want to walk, taxis are the only option.

WHERE TO SLEEP

The capital isn't a great place for budget travelers. You can get by if you're willing to rough it a bit, but you'll pay *dearly* for amenities that you might take for granted elsewhere. Unless things change drastically, you can usually expect to be without power until late evening, and water comes and goes throughout the day. Plan to use utilities in the early morning. Make a small investment in candles and matches, since it's pretty depressing to spend several pitch-black hours in your room. Be sure to ask hotel managers if the price covers 12 or 24 hours, since it's common to rent by day *or* night.

Travelers usually stay near one of the two bus terminals or in El Centro. Unless you simply must be in the middle of it all, El Centro is not the place to stay. In addition to being perpetually filthy, crowded, smoggy, and more dangerous than anywhere else, it's generally overpriced for what you get (a big exception is El Oso, *see below*). The main drag by Terminal de Occidente is Boulevard Venezuela, in a safe but industrial and ugly part of town. If you're spending more than a couple of days in the capital, you'll probably want to stay near Terminal de Oriente, an area with plenty of interesting after-dark diversions. A few minutes from El Centro by bus, the neighborhood can be rowdy, but it's not nearly as dangerous or scruffy as the center. A number of hotels are clustered on Calle Concepción near 20a Avenida Norte.

You can't camp legally in the vicinity of the capital, and it's futile to try to make your own campground; even the turicentros are patrolled, and proprietors make overnight visitors pay.

NEAR TERMINAL DE OCCIDENTE

➤ **UNDER $10** • **Hotel Occidental.** Only settle for this cheap run-down hotel if the two below are full. The bathrooms stink, and the rooms are small and dingy. Doubles are $7; its one saving grace are the hammocks. *3077 Blvd. Venezuela, tel. 24–3648. 14 rooms, some with bath. Wheelchair access.*

Hotel Pasadena. Hotel Pasadena lacks amenities, but it does have decent hammocks. Swinging in them is fun and keeps you cool. The $7 doubles are clean but shabby, and the bathrooms are passable but could use a good kick in the butt with Ajax. *3903 Blvd. Venezuela, tel. 23–7905. 16 rooms, all with bath.*

Hotel Roma. The clean, cheerful atmosphere inside contrasts with its *Amityville Horror* appearance from the street. Large, clean doubles with fans and baths are $7. The management is talkative and friendly, and the small restaurant serves cheap soft drinks and good simple meals. *3145 Blvd. Venezuela, 1½ blocks "uphill" from terminal, tel. 24–0256. 12 rooms, some with bath. Wheelchair access, laundry.*

NEAR TERMINAL DE ORIENTE

➤ **UNDER $10** • **Hospedaje Santa Rosa.** Rooms at Santa Rosa are old but clean, and all have ceiling fans ($5 double). The bathrooms are okay, but at night roaches roam, and beds are on the mushy side. The management's extremely friendly, and will try to give you a room away from the street if noise keeps you awake. *672 Calle Concepción, tel. 22–9290. 36 rooms, some with bath.*

Hotel Yucatán. Rooms in this huge, sprawling complex are the cheapest in this area at $4 per double. It's basic, but not gross. Ask the manager's permission to use the pila to wash clothes *before* you pay and he'll definitely say yes. *673 Calle Concepción, tel. 21–2585. 38 rooms, some with bath.*

Hotel Izalco. It's a little more expensive than the above two, but Izalco is much cleaner and more comfy. The beds are big and firm, and the bathrooms give you the minimum requisite feelings of hygiene and privacy. Doubles with ceiling fans are $8. *668 Calle Concepción, tel. 22–2613. 40 rooms, some with bath.*

EL CENTRO

➤ **UNDER $10** • **Casa de Huespedes El Oso.** Large, clean, and off the main streets so you escape the noise, this is the best deal in the center. The rooms, with good fans, phones, and clean baths, are a bargain at $4 per person. *11a Av. Norte 243, tel. 22–1213. Near the ISTU office, ½ block from 1a Calle Poniente. 30 rooms, all with bath. Laundry.*

Hotel Bruno. With basement prices and a basement atmosphere, Hotel Bruno is dark, dank, and depressing. The beds are tiny and uncomfortable, and the bathrooms are in shambles. But, hey, doubles are only $4. *531 1a Calle Oriente, near ExCuartel, tel. 22–3958. 22 rooms, some with bath.*

Hotel Nuevo Panamericano. The Panamericano isn't much of a deal at $6.50 per double. The beds are so-so and the rooms are small and scummy. It does have a nice patio where you can seek refuge from the prison-like rooms, and the restaurant serves meals until mid-afternoon for less than $3. *113 8a Av. Sur, ½ block from Mercado ExCuartel, tel. 22–2959. 22 rooms, all with bath. Wheelchair access.*

➤ **UNDER $25 • Hotel Centro.** It you have to stay in the centro, you might want to go whole hog and stay in Hotel Centro. It's clean and orderly, and the people are courteous. Rooms are small but immaculate, and have TVs and phones. The immediate neighborhood gets rough at night, but at $12 per person, it's the best you'll find. *410 9a Av. Sur, tel. 71–5045. Wheelchair access. Luggage storage.*

➤ **UNDER $35 • Hotel Ritz Continental.** Smack in the center of El Centro, the Ritz is pretty darn ritzy. The Motel 6-style rooms are spotless and have all the amenities, including hot-water showers. Live it up in a $33 double. *219 7a Av. Sur, tel. 22–0033. 80 rooms, all with bath. Luggage storage, laundry, restaurant.*

FOOD

Vegetarians may have a problem getting more than *frijoles* and *arroz* (beans and rice), but many places offer some kind of fruit or vegetable plate. The city's tap water tastes like a swimming pool, but is *relatively* safe (no guarantees).

➤ **EL CENTRO • Cafe Bella Napoles.** This busy watering hole for locals is a good place to escape the frantic streets of El Centro. They have a huge menu, with everything from tamales to sandwiches to salads. Two vegetarians can split a mushroom pizza for $3, and down-home folks will snork up the roast chicken with potatoes ($2). They also have a large bakery that sells scrumptious goodies. *113 4a Av. Sur, tel. 22–6879. Open daily 6:30 AM–8 PM.*

Koradi. There's hope yet for vegetarians. Koradi has no-nonsense food served by no-nonsense waitpeople. Try a soy burger for $1, or split a whole-wheat pizza with veggies for $2. Wonderful fresh juices (pineapple, tomato, or carrot) are 75¢. Healthy breads and pastries are baked fresh daily. *225 9a Av. Sur, near 4a Calle Poniente. Lunch only, noon–2 daily; bakery open 8–5.*

Restaurante El Pulpo. The name means "the octopus," and it's one of the few decent seafood restaurants that won't cost you a week's rent. It's in a lower-middle-class neighborhood in El Centro near a university, and the clientele is diverse and laid-back. You'll get large portions of fresh seafood for good prices: Shrimp with rice, fried fish, and an excellent *sopa de mariscos* (seafood soup) each costs $3, and draft beer is 80¢ per glass. *Corner of Calle Arce and 15a Av. Norte. Open daily 9–9.*

➤ **NEAR TERMINAL ORIENTE • El Nuevo Mais.** A mom-and-daughter team serves simple regional favorites to neighborhood folk in this down-to-earth place right in the middle of hotel row. Standard fare includes *carne guisada* (a variant of pot roast) and *chorizo* (pork sausage), each for $1. Vegetarians should try fried *pacaya* (a bitter veggie that wakes up with salsa) with rice for $1. Bonus: the restaurant has lanterns for riding out the nightly power outage. *678 Calle Concepción. Wheelchair access. Open daily 6:30 AM–8:30 PM.*

➤ **CENTRO COMERCIAL LA MASCOTA •** If you're near the ritzy San Benito neighborhood (or at the American Express office), the Centro Comercial La Mascota has several possibilities. To get here, take Bus 101 from 11a Avenida Sur in El Centro.

Chalet Don Pancho. Don Pancho is definitely the most charming thing in this ugly mini-mall. The three women here serve a variety of comida típica to as many locals as can fit at the six small tables in this tiny, open-air restaurant. Everything is made fresh, and all meals cost $1.25. Try a *torta mexicana* (cousin to a meat sandwich) or *sopa de res* (beef soup). *Centro Comercial La Mascota, next to American Express, bottom level. Open daily 7–5.*

➤ **ELSEWHERE** • **Metrocentro.** The Metrocentro shopping mall has an open-air, fast-food eatery with dozens of small restaurants. It's all here: Taco Bell, fish and chips, crêpes, Chinese. The average meal costs $2–$3, but prices can go much higher. *Take Bus 52 from Alameda Juan Pablo II to Blvd. Los Heroes. Open daily 7 AM–9:30 PM.*

9a Avenida Sur. Local eating with local flavor. You can choose from over a dozen pupuserías and comedores along this street. For a real (if smelly) treat, ask for lots of pickled cabbage on top of your pupusa. Pupusas cost about 15¢ each. *9a Av. Sur, between Calles 4a Poniente and Vasconcelos.*

Restaurante Queco's Tacos. At the beginning of the posh Paseo General Escalón, this wanna-be-Mexican joint serves terrific food at the best prices in the area. It's a good springboard for doing the nightlife later at Plaza Masferrer. The tacos (two for $2) are awesome, and vegetarians can have quesadillas for $1.50 apiece. *3952 Paseo General Escalón, ½ block west of Parque Beethoven. Take Bus 52 from Alameda Juan Pablo II. Wheelchair access. Open weekdays noon–10, weekends noon–11.*

DESSERT/COFFEE HOUSES **Cafe Don Pepe.** If you spend more than a couple hours touring El Centro, give yourself a break and drop in here for a cold drink, a pastry, or ice cream (it's not Haägen-Daz, but it's cold, sweet, and only $1). Food is also served, but it's marginal and overpriced. Oh yeah—it's got *air-conditioning,* so bring those postcards you've been meaning to write and chill (so to speak). *Corner of 4a Calle Poniente and 9a Av. Sur. Open daily 8 AM–6:30 PM.*

Casa de Licuado. Students and locals get okay pastries and small meals in this clean, unpretentious café. The real reason to come to Casa de Licuado is, lo and behold, the wonderful fresh-fruit licuados. You get a mongo glass for 50¢. Beware that the crushed ice they use in the licuados is from tap water. *15a Av. Norte between calles Rubén Darío and Arce. Open Mon.–Sat. 6–6.*

WORTH SEEING

CHURCHES Although San Salvador has nothing like the centuries-old colonial churches of other Latin American countries, several are strikingly cool. In El Centro, the crippled image of a huge gray dome is almost all that's left of the **Catedral Metropolitana,** where Oscar Romero was gunned down in 1980. It's still pretty impressive from a distance, which is good because repairs and seismic reinforcement keep all onlookers outside. In much better condition is **Iglesia Calvario** (at the end of 6a Calle Poniente, 1 block from Av. Cuscatlán). Its haunting, almost Gothic appearance makes it seem much older than it is. The double steeple of **La Basilica del Sagrado Corazón de Jesus** (at Calle Arce and 13a Av. Norte) is also being repaired, but you can still go in through the east door 8–6 daily to see the spectacular interior or attend mass. **El Rosario** is on 6a Avenida between calles 2a and 4a Poniente; Father Delgado, a major figure in Central American Independence, is buried here. The **Iglesia Don Rua** has a distinctive clock tower and stunning works of stained glass inside. It's a ways from El Centro, at 3a Avenida Norte and 23a Calle Poniente.

MUSEO NACIONAL DAVID GUZMAN This place has a hefty collection of artifacts, art, and literature from the colonial period and back to 1500 BC. If you're heading northwest to the Tazumal ruins, check out the stuff here from the site so you'll have a better idea of what you're looking at once you get there. *Take Bus 34 toward the Interamerican Highway, get off as soon as bus turns onto Av. de la Revolución. Admission free. Open Tues.–Sun. 9–noon and 2–5.*

EL PARQUE ZOOLOGICO With over 600 animals in residence, this park/zoo is pretty snazzy. The inhabitants seem to live in a relatively tolerable environment, though some probably still miss their mommies. *Take Bus 2 Modelo from El Centro near the cathedral. Admission: 15¢. Open Wed.–Sun. 9:30–5.*

MONUMENTO DE LA REVOLUCION Straight out of an Orwell novel, this monument to the liberation of Central American people is in San Benito, at the entrance to the wealthiest, most exclusive neighborhood in San Salvador. The irony of the placement of this statue is inescapable. *Take Bus 34 to the end of Av. de la Revolución.*

JARDIN BOTANICO LA LAGUNA In the bottom of an extinct volcanic crater, over 2,500 feet above sea level, La Laguna has a huge collection of the world's plants and flowers. It's a welcome respite from the city's unceasing gray and offers one of the city's few long, shady walks. *Take Bus 101-"C" from Calle Rubén Darío and 13a Av. Sur, get off at Antiguo Cuscatlán stop. Admission: 15¢. Open Tues.–Fri. 10–5, weekends 10–6.*

MARKETS City dwellers get all their daily staples at the huge **Mercado Central**—it's the real thing, and a good place to pick up basic articles for cheap. It begins at the Iglesia El Calvario, and it's open dawn to dusk. **Mercado Ex-Cuartel de Artesanía** (between Calle Delgado and 1a Calle Oriente at 8a Av. Sur, open daily 7:30–5:30) is the most interesting shopping area in the capital. You can bargain for handwoven textiles, ceramics, and other crafts, and you'll usually get decent prices.

AFTER DARK

After dark it's really DARK. Keep in mind that when you go out on the town at night, there's usually no electricity until late evening, and buses stop running at 7:30 or 8 PM. It's no fun to get caught on a long, dark stretch of street: Bring a flashlight, have a pretty good idea of where you're going, and be prepared to pay for a taxi back to the hotel. In residential neighborhoods, the power outage seems to generate lots of lantern-lit action, as crooners come out with guitars, accordions, and shameless voices to sing local favorites; make no mistake, this is drunken revelry and fistfights are not uncommon.

Should you venture into one of the capital's 500 tough-ass dive bars, be ready to leave should someone not like the way you look, dress, or smell. This is not your turf.

Travelers should think twice about going into the hundreds of small dive bars in the city unless they can handle themselves—and their Spanish—in tough situations. These boozy joints often have that universal someone's-about-to-get-killed ambience. Women especially should be careful, even in groups. Good music abounds in the capital. One bar that's cheap, loads of fun, and has great live music is **Los Pitufos** on Calle Concepción, attached to Hospedaje Santa Rosa (*see* Where to Sleep, *above*). The name Pitufos translates as "The Smurfs"—go figure. At the **Teatro Café** (in El Centro on the corner of Calle Delgado and 2a Av. Sur), local singers try their luck in late afternoons, and there's a makeshift musical talent show Friday evenings. For genuine nightclubs, go to the western section of the city.

BOULEVARD DE LOS HEROES Boulevard de los Héroes is the closest hot-spot to El Centro and has the most recognizable night-life atmosphere. To get here from the center, take Bus 52 to the big kiddie amusement park at the beginning of the Boulevard; a taxi back should be about $2. Beware that food and drinks are pretty expensive in all these places. **El Corral Steak House** (one block south of Hospital Bloom) is open till 1 AM with live rock music. Right across the street is **Las Torchas,** with good salsa and meringue music and a shakin' crowd of locals. On weekends, music begins about 7 PM and goes till 2 AM, with a $1 cover charge and $4 drink minimum. A little further down the street, get a taste of the upper-class at **Villa Fiesta,** with a $5 cover and $5 drink minimum. Sequined dresses and a machine-gun-wielding bouncer sum this place up; open till 2:30 AM on weekends. **Los Estratos** is the closest thing San Salvador has to a gay bar. Those in the know come to party down; however, machismo and homophobia being what they are, people are pretty conservative about displaying sexual orientation here or in any other bar in El Salvador. Los Estratos is on Boulevard de los Héroes near the hospital, a bit off the street, on the second floor.

PLAZA MASFERRER For more local flavor and less price shock than hanging out on the Boulevard, take Bus 52 to the end of Colonia Escalón to Plaza Masferrer. If you walk here from Parque Beethoven, you'll notice the ritzy wannabe U.S. restaurants along Paseo General Escalón. Don't worry, it's much groovier at the other end. Dozens of mariachi musicians stroll around this pleasant plaza till all hours. The plaza has no cover, it's all very casual, and the music is great. You can also rent an entire band for the night if you have a place to party. Just beyond the park is a cluster of crowded pupuserías where you can eat and guzzle on the cheap. The taxi back to El Centro runs $4–$5, which ain't bad considering the distance.

ZONA ROSA In the ritzy Colonia San Benito along the Boulevard del Hipodromo, the Zona Rosa is home to San Salvador's most exclusive and expensive nightclubs. Come to the **Underground Discotec** (237 Blvd. del Hipodromo) if you want to rub shoulders with El Salvador's beautiful people; wear something decent and be ready to spend some colones. Be aware that nonmembers are often turned away from clubs in this area. To get here from El Centro, take Bus 34 to the Monumento de la Revolución.

Near San Salvador

SANTA TECLA Santa Tecla, 13 kilometers (8 miles) west of the capital, was founded immediately after the catastrophic earthquake of 1854 as El Salvador's new seat of authority. Though it only held that honor for about a year, many people still call it Nueva (new) San Salvador. Today it's mostly a middle-class suburb, a nice get-away from the capital due to its cooler weather and slower pace, and the departure point for exploring nearby volcanoes. Santa Tecla's two central parks are next to each other; **Parque San Martín** is the pretty one, and **Parque Jose C. Lopez** is the one surrounded by the market. The town has a couple of fun things to do besides hanging out in the park and gabbing with locals. Near the entrance to the city is a large park with several basketball courts and soccer fields. Overnighters should head to **Hospedaje Guerrero** (Calle Daniel Hernandez 4–3, 3½ blocks from Parque Jose C. Lopez, no sign). It's *very* tidy and quite safe; small doubles with bath are $4 (11 PM curfew).

To get to Santa Tecla, take Bus 101 from 11a Avenida Sur in El Centro. The bus leaves every 10 minutes for the 45-minute trip (10¢). Pay a visit to the **Casa de la Cultura** (right-hand side of Parque San Martín at Calle Lopez) to discuss the state of latino culture with the dedicated and friendly director, or participate in an art class. It's open weekdays 9–noon and 2–5, Saturday 8–noon.

PANCHIMALCO The peaceful village of Panchimalco, 15 kilometers (9 miles) south of the capital, is surrounded on all sides by lush green mountains and dramatic jutting boulders. Descendants of the indigenous Pipil live a surprisingly traditional life here, and it's probably the most beautiful town within an hour of San Salvador. It's hard to believe the urban sprawl is so close—but it's a good thing it is, since Panchimalco doesn't have any lodging. The town's tranquil, cobblestone streets and simple buildings are dominated by a plain but elegant colonial church. The surrounding area is ideal for hiking, and if you haul yourself to one of the summits you'll be rewarded with spectacular views. Around the corner from the bus stop is the **Casa de la Cultura,** where you can learn about the town's pre-Columbian Mayan heritage. Panchimalco is a good side trip if you're going to Parque Balboa (*see below*), since it's just a few minutes from the park entrance. Take Bus 17 from 12a Calle Poniente in San Salvador's central market. The 45-minute trip costs 15¢, leaving a couple of times per hour.

PARQUE BALBOA To get to this nearby turicentro, pick up Bus 12 "Mil Cumbres" at Calle 29 de Agosto and 12a Calle Poniente. Bus 12 leaves frequently, the ride lasts 40 minutes, costs 15¢, and it's sardine city. The park is pleasant and green—a great place for a picnic. The area's big attraction, **Puerta del Diablo**, is a 45-minute walk from the entrance of the park. (The bus also goes directly here if you're not up for the walk.) "The Devil's Gate" is a pair of enormous boulders that you can climb for a spectacular view of Lago de Ilopango. It looks intimidating, but the stairs going up the rock are solid—if it's not wet and you've got decent shoes. If you forgot your picnic, pick up some lunch at one of the several good pupuserías right outside the park.

SAN SALVADOR VOLCANO Volcán de San Salvador is definitely visible from town (there it is, looming over there!). It makes a great day hike, and you'll get some cool views of the Puerta del Diablo and the whole Valle de las Hamacas. The crater of the lower peak is nicknamed **El Boquerón** ("big mouth"), and the higher one is called **Pichacho**. Circling the volcano takes a good two hours. If you've still got it in you, circumnavigate El Boquerón's crater. Getting to the volcano is a chore: Take Bus 101 from the capital to Santa Tecla, and then Bus 103 from there (leaving once an hour). The bus will leave you in the pueblo of Boquerón, and from there it's a bit over a mile to the crater.

LAGO DE ILOPANGO Filling a giant volcanic crater 15 kilometers (9 miles) east of the capital, Ilopango is the country's largest and deepest lake, with an area of over 120 square kilometers (46 square miles). Swimming is fine, but be careful because the water gets deep fast. You can rent bathing suits at the *ceviche* stands for 50¢ plus $1 deposit. Boat rides are expensive, about $4 per ½ hour. Coming to the lake on weekends is a mixed bag; it's way more crowded, but you'll have a better chance of sharing the cost of a ride on the lake. As you zip around, check out the ostentatious homes of El Salvador's rich and famous along the private shores, or go visit the island of Puntun. For about $12 you can go all the way to Los Cerros Quemados ("Burned Hills"), an island created by the most recent volcanic eruption (1880), home to a traditional **festival** December 15.

Getting to the lake from the capital is easiest from the **Apulo turicentro** (open daily 6 AM–6:30 PM, admission: 50¢). Apulo has a few hotels; doubles at both **Hotel Familiar** and **Hotel Malvinas** cost $5, but neither is very clean. Fresh fish is about $3 per plate at the little restaurants dotting the shore. Seafood thrill-seekers should try the mussel ceviche at the stands by the water, scraped right out of the shell before your eyes ($2 per cup). Toss in some of their nuclear *chile* and wash it down with a beer. Bus 15 for Apulo leaves from Avenida España and 3a Calle Poniente in San Salvador every ½ hour (1 hour, 15¢).

LOS CHORROS Los Chorros, 6 kilometers (4 miles) north of Santa Tecla, is *the* spot for San Salvador residents with the money and the time to get away. It's a beautiful natural gorge that lets you forget the visual brutality of San Salvador. A bunch of fresh springs and short cascades lie beneath volcanic cliffs, which are occasionally closed-off when the Salvadoran army uses them for combat training. (Do they know how to spoil a picnic or what?) When the park is just a park, spend the day walking around and swimming to your heart's content. The restaurant here is lousy, rather expensive, and home to more flies than you can shake a stick at—you'll be much happier bringing a picnic. The rooms at **Hotel Monteverde**, on the other side of the road, are okay but pretty expensive at $12 per night. Bus 79 for Los Chorros (45 minutes, 10¢) leaves the capital once every 10 minutes from 11a Avenida Sur and Calle Rubén Darío. Los Chorros is open daily 8–5; admission is 20¢.

Northern El Salvador

Northern El Salvador is rough territory. If you're mainly looking for relaxation and recreation, think twice before venturing into the region. The north is the poorest part of the country, and, not coincidentally, the most war-torn. Virtually every city north of Colima has been visited by the army and guerrillas, and some have been thoroughly devastated by the civil war. Even during the (hopeful) transition to peace, you should be prepared for a heavy military presence, especially near Chalatenango and San Francisco Gotera. If you have political interests, some people are willing to talk about their experiences, but many are understandably hesitant to discuss their ordeals, especially with a foreigner. In San Salvador, you're a tourist. In the North, you're an outsider.

If civil war hostilities are at a lull, your best bet for outdoor fun is hiking. North of Tejutla are miles of beautiful mountains, and the views from their summits are often terrific. Stay on a recognizable trail, and for safety's sake make sure you're not still poking around the hills after nightfall. Buses heading north from the capital are quite frequent and frequently quite crowded. To be safe, don't plan on traveling anywhere after dark. The locals have a saying: *Hay los que no trabajan, pero comen* (there are those who don't work, but eat). Translation: Thieves are afoot.

Hotels in northern El Salvador are scarce and generally awful, since towns don't get many travelers and aren't equipped to serve them. Make sure you know a town *has* lodging before you venture out with plans to spend the night. Camping is an option: Gorgeous, forested mountains, from Tejutla all the way to the Honduran border, are ideal for more experienced campers. Make sure you have a waterproof tent during the rainy season, because natural coverage is scant and nightly downpours are brutal. While official campgrounds don't exist, locals claim camping's no problem during peacetime. Don't camp anywhere near the city of Chalatenango, which is patrolled by a battalion of edgy soldiers. Obviously, don't camp if you hear of renewed combat—for that matter, don't go north at all.

North to El Poy

The **Troncal del Norte** is the paved highway that runs from the capital to the Honduran border at El Poy. Most bus transportation in this region centers around a highway intersection called **El Desvío de Mayo,** or simply El Mayo, about 1½ hours due north of the capital. From the El Mayo junction, you can take the road east to Chalatenango, west to Nueva Concepción, or north to El Poy. Buses don't pass very frequently here, so be ready to wait up to an hour and have your face shoved up against a basket of angry hens once you get on the crowded buses.

CHALATENANGO

With over 30,000 people, Chalatenango (55 km [34 mi] from the capital) is the largest city in the region. It's also one of the most war-torn. You can't ignore the military presence, and you should be on your best behavior to avoid uncomfortable interrogations. An FMLN stronghold only a few years ago, the city is now creepily silent and broken (spiritually and physically) under the army's constant watch. The people of Chalatenango are definitely poor, but with a sense of dignity not found in the urban squalor of the capital. Poverty, resistance, pride, and the scars of violence make this a difficult but worthwhile place to visit. The town's **patron saint festival** is June 24.

From the capital, take Bus 125 from Terminal de Oriente (2½ hours, every 20 minutes till 5:30 PM, 60¢). Arrive early to make sure you get a seat. **Antel** is 1 block past the park at the corner of Calle José María San Martín and 5a Avenida Sur. The central market is in the center at Calle José Maria San Martín and Avenida Libertad. **Hospeda-je Nuevo Amanecer** (near 894 Av. Fajarda) is the only lodging in town. Since the owners enjoy a monopoly, they can charge $5 for a little fleabag of a room with mushy beds, sheets whose smell may stay with you long after you've gone, and a communal bathroom permeated by a general funk. (Ask around about alternatives.)

NEAR CHALATENANGO Just 7 kilometers (4 miles) west of Chalatenango is the charming village of **Concepción Quetzaltepeque.** Although the civil war ravaged this place as well, the atmosphere is quite different from its larger neighbor's, and hardly a soldier is on the street. This alone is reason to come here, plus it's got cobblestone streets and a pretty church. For local artisanship, visit the home of Concepción Cayax (Kye-ash) in Barrio San Antonio. Ask around—everyone knows her house. She makes beautiful hammocks by hand for great prices, and can even customize one with words. To get straight here, take one of the infrequent buses from Chalatenango's terminal; or, take Bus 125 the short distance to the desvío for Concepción and wait for one of the pickup trucks that run frequently to the town. From the capital, take Bus 125 from Terminal de Oriente and do the same thing at the desvío.

Nearby are some excellent places to enjoy the great outdoors in virtual solitude. Several rivers have kick-ass swimming, and a multitude of beautiful, low mountains are within easy walking distance. The pueblito of **Llano Grande** has a commanding view of the mongo Cerron Grande mountain. Llano Grande is about 8 kilometers (5 miles) from town; ask around about the pickups that leave from the town center.

LA PALMA AND EL POY

The last city of any significance before you reach the Honduran border at El Poy is **La Palma,** 30 kilometers (19 miles) north of El Mayo and 8 kilometers (5 miles) south of the border. It's a tired, one-horse town that would be completely forgettable if not for its dozens of *talleres* (workshops), where artisans craft ceramic, cloth, and wooden goods to sell in the capital. You can observe the artists at work but don't bother looking in the miserable central market—artisans don't sell locally because it's not a huge tourist center (understatement of the century). Since La Palma is a small, insular town, some people may be defensive when they see outsiders poking their noses around. Check with the **Casa de la Cultura** (open weekdays 9–noon and 2–5), on 1a Calle Poniente just below the main square, for info on which talleres are cool to visit. **Antel,** a block from the park near the bus stop, is open daily 6 AM–10 PM.

La Palma's only **hospedaje** is a nameless atrocity, connected to the pharmacy next door to León Express on the main drag, ½ a block from the Centro de Evangelización on Calle Independencía. A double costs $3 and is dreadful—a teeny room with a corroded cot. Fortunately, an excellent alternative is a ½ hour up the main highway, just minutes from El Poy. **Hotel Cayahuanca** has a dozen clean, comfortable rooms for $3 without bath, $5 with. The owner, Juan, will talk with you for hours about his experiences with wine, women, the government, and the guerrillas. The little restaurant serves huge plates of good food (around $3), and you can wash your own clothes in the pila.

El Poy is a classic border town: filthy, tiny, and full of fast-talking money-changers. Don't plan on spending much time here. The exit fee is 50¢, $8 more for a car. Immigration is open daily 6–6. It's best to get here early to make sure you can catch a bus to Ocotepeque on the Honduras side. To reach La Palma, take Bus 119 from Terminal de Oriente (every hour from dawn until 3 PM, 4 hours, $1). From La Palma you can catch buses to Tejutla (1 hour, 50¢), El Mayo highway junction (1½ hours, $1), and El Poy (20 minutes, 25¢). Direct buses to El Poy also run from the capital a few times daily.

Northeast From San Salvador

SAN MARTIN

A very pleasant surprise just 18 kilometers (11 miles) from the capital, San Martín is a little town with a lot to offer. The first five minutes here will tell you this place was spared much of the war horror: The people move quickly, talk sharply, and laugh a lot. The surrounding countryside is beautiful and safe for hiking, and the nearby foothills have pretty views of the area. A real attraction for music lovers is **Master Music Light** (Corner of Av. Morazán and 4a Calle Poniente, open daily 8–7), which sells bootleg cassettes of good Latin, U.S., and British popular music for about $2 a pop. The owner, Nelson Hernandez, knows a lot about music and the area, and is glad to talk with travelers. To get to San Martín, take Bus 145 from Terminal de Oriente (every ½ hour until 5:30 PM, ½ hour, 15¢). You can also catch Bus 129 headed toward Suchitoto and tell the driver to let you off here.

WHERE TO SLEEP AND EAT Hospedaje El **Amigo** (5 Av. Colonia America, at the end of the block) has eight small, clean, well-ventilated doubles with *muy* comfortable beds for $5. The neighborhood is very lively and playful, with lots of cute kids playing street soccer. San Martín has a couple of great restaurants. **Restaurante El Mafufo** (4a Calle Poniente, ½ block from Av. Morazán) serves soup, sandwiches, and plates of comida típica, for less than $1. Vegetarians can depend on a venerable plate of rice and beans or a terrific seasonal fruit cocktail (50¢). On the other side of Avenida Morazán on the same street (now 4a Calle Oriente) is **Comedor Pupusería San Martín**, serving comida a la vista—i.e., go in the kitchen and see what looks good. Nothing is over $1 except the ceviche, made with fresh mussels, for $1.50.

COJUTEPEQUE

Don't be fooled by the dusty, God-forsaken cluster of buildings where the bus comes in; Cojutepeque is a happening city well worth visiting. To get here, take Bus 113 from Terminal de Oriente (every ½ hour until 6:30 PM, 45 minutes, 25¢) in San Salvador.

The town's main attraction is the **Cerro De Pavas** ("Hill of Turkeys"—however, there are no turkeys in sight unless you count the soldiers frumping around the site). To get there from Parque Central, walk through the long, narrow market along Avenida Raul Contreras. From there, several roads lead straight up to the top, a leisurely ½ hour walk or a heart-starting jog. At the summit you'll find beautiful views of Lago de Ilopango and the countryside, and the shrine of the **Virgen de Fátima**. Her statue was brought here in 1949 from Portugal, where the Virgin was first "sighted," and it was eventually declared a miracle sighting by the Vatican. Be on your best behavior, since locals and pilgrims come to this holy site for serious religious purposes. Not surprisingly, the army has made its presence felt on this strategic hilltop. The best views from the very top of the summit are off-limits, since that's where soldiers encamp. This grave insult to local tradition goes relatively unnoticed, a testament to the unspoken power of the military in the region. The Virgen's **festival** day is May 13.

WHERE TO SLEEP AND EAT Overnighters don't have a lot of choice. **Hospedaje Cojutepeque** offers six clean rooms, all with bath, and all below ground level. It's hardly a bargain at $7 per double. Bring plenty of candles to this cave, which is a half-block up from the main square. **Panadería "Fátima"** (317 2a Av. Sur, one block from the church) is possibly the best bakery in the country, serving wonderful, fresh-baked cookies, cakes, and breads. The posh **Restaurante Los Pichardos** (Av. Santa Ana, 2 blocks up the hill from the main highway where the bus passes, tel. 22–3238), becomes a live-music dance hall at night. Dinners are typically overpriced, and they charge a small cover.

Eastern El Salvador

Many towns in the east are basic El Salvador, and some have interesting artisan traditions, while the hub of the east—San Miguel—is your textbook Third-World metropolis. The region also has a couple of enjoyable, little-known surpirses; south of the main east–west highway is a rugged mountain chain that runs from Berlín to Santiago de Maria, where volcanic lakes, sulfuric baths, and great off-the-beaten track camping and hiking await. For many, the Morazán department north of San Miguel is a discomforting surpise; as one of the most war-torn, impoverished, least populated, and hottest areas in the nation, traveling here is rough, intense, and eye-opening.

San Vicente

Located 50 kilometers (31 miles) due east of San Salvador, just south of the main highway to San Miguel, San Vicente is a schizophrenic place. Half is charming and tranquil, with an elegant flair. The other half is dominated by a green, militarized compound, where black-booted soldiers carrying machine guns romp through the subdued city which they clearly control. San Vicente is worth visiting, but be on your guard; don't panic if interrogated, and keep your camera lens away from anything military.

The town doesn't have much by way of architecture, and even the church is ho-hum. The obvious exception is the unusual and somehow graceful clock tower right in the middle of the park, visible from several kilometers away. For a terrific view of the city from the top of the tower, find the park attendant to open up the gate so you can climb the stairs. He claims the lock is to prevent high-dive suicides, but it's probably a military precaution. Just off the park, you can't miss the enormous military compound that stretches a full block to 1a Avenida. On the other side of the park you'll find **Antel**, ½ block from the church, and the **post office,** down a bit further at Calle 1 de Julio and 2a Avenida Norte.

COMING AND GOING To reach San Vicente take Bus 116 from Terminal de Oriente in the capital, a 1½-hour trip for 50¢, leaving every 15 minutes until 5:30 PM. Bus 301 to and from San Miguel stops on the main highway a few kilometers outside town. From the town center, catch a local bus to get to the desvío where all buses pass (the walk is long but quite scenic).

WHERE TO SLEEP **Casa de Huespedes El Turista.** This is the budget traveler's first choice. I could go on all day about the towels, clean water, stylin' furniture, comfy hammocks, fans, nice bathrooms, TVs.... The friendly manager will let you do some laundry in the pila if you ask her nicely. $7 for a double is a bargain. *Corner of 4a Calle Poniente and 1a Av. Sur, tel. 33–0323. Follow the military barracks away from church for a block, left on Av. Maria de Los Angeles Miranda (becomes 1a Av.) and go 2 blocks. 18 rooms, some with bath.*

Casa de Huespedes German y Marlon. This hotel is at the bottom rung of the luxury ladder. You can sleep cheap in big, very shabby rooms with uncomfortable beds and dubious-looking ceilings ($3 double). *6 1a Av. Sur, tel. 33–0140, about a block past the military compound. 15 rooms none with bath. l0 PM curfew.*

Hospedaje Diamante. It's bare, simple, and relatively clean, but Hospedaje Diamante's big advantage is its proximity to Amapulapa and the volcano. Doubles are around $5. *69 2a Av. Sur, follow 2a Av. Norte from church toward volcano, look for sign at road fork. 5 rooms, all with bath.*

FOOD **Comedor Rivoly.** About as close as you're likely to come to dorm food, this cafeteria-style joint is fast, rude, and cheap. Chicken tamales are a good bet at 50¢ each; vegetarians will have to resign themselves to the usual rice and beans, although the potato salad here is pretty good. *15 1a Av. Sur, tel. 33–0492. Open daily 7 AM–8 PM.*

Restaurante Casa Blanca. If you want to treat yourself right, this upscale, chic restaurant is a pleasant, quiet spot frequented by upper–middle-class locals. Outdoor tables on a nice evening provide an easy, laid-back atmosphere. The house specialty, grilled shrimp and steak (or chicken), is great though it will set you back $7 (okay for two medium-sized appetites). Vegetarians can request chop suey without meat ($2.50). *13 2a Calle Oriente, tel. 33–0549. 2 blocks down 2a Av. Norte from church, make left on 2a Calle Oriente.*

NEAR SAN VICENTE

SAN SEBASTIAN Best known for its handmade textiles, this peaceful little town a few kilometers from San Vicente is slowly losing its fame to technology. However, you can still come here to see (and of course buy) excellent work done on wooden hand looms. You won't find any of the artisan work in the local market. It's all inside the many talleres around town, which make their living by selling directly to the capital. Worth checking out is the taller run by the **familia Mejilla Rodriguez** (8a Av. Norte and Calle Instituto Nacional, one block past the church dome and go left), which specializes in broadcloth and hammocks. You can watch the intricate process of stringing a hammock and buy one for a good price. There's not much else to do here except take a look at the several churches and visit the **Casa de la Cultura,** which has a good-size library. From San Vicente, take Bus 116 to Km 44 and wait for the 110 to take you the rest of the way. From the capital, take Bus 110 from Terminal de Oriente, a 1½-hour trip leaving every ½ hour for 40¢. The last bus leaves San Sebastián at 4 PM. The town's **festival** is in mid-January.

LAGUNA DE APASTAPEQUE This turicentro is on the opposite side of the main highway from town, about 5 kilometers (3 miles) from the desvío. This medium-size crater lake is reasonably pretty, and is ideal for serious swimmers. No lifeguard is available to save you if you're flailing, and it gets deep fast—over 300 feet in the middle. On weekdays you have the lake practically to yourself. The buildings and gardens are well maintained; a thatch-roof restaurant sells chicken for $2, fish for $3. *Bus 156 Santa Clara (only!) goes directly to the park, leaving infrequently from the corner opposite the military base. Alternatively, take any bus headed back to San Salvador and get off at the desvío and you'll see the sign for the turicentro; walk or hitch the 1 ½ km to the park. Admission: 50¢. Open daily 8–5.*

VOLCAN CHICHONTEPEC It's hard to miss this 2,200-meter work of nature. You can take several paths up, but try the one starting just past Amapulapa turicentro—anyone will know where it is. Give yourself several hours to go up (be realistic about your endurance), and bring plenty of water.

INFIERNILLO Approaching the base of Volcán Chichontepec from south of Verapaz you come to this beautiful, natural hot spring. Strong sulfuric fumes have made the affectionately named Infiernillo ("Little Hell") a popular medicinal retreat. During wartime people didn't come here because the FMLN heavily mined the area. The damn things have been cleared out and the folks are coming back, so you (with luck) shouldn't have any surprises.

From San Vicente to San Miguel

South of the main highway that runs from San Vicente to San Miguel are a number of scenic, serene, and inspiring places little known by tourists (or even many Salvadoreños). The area is rustically poor, the bus trips are rough, and you'll see a very different and refreshing side of the country.

BERLIN

Berlín lies south of the Mercedes Umaña desvío, about 60 kilometers (37 miles) east of San Vicente (about halfway to San Miguel). Visitors are routinely questioned by the national police here, so stay calm and play the dumb tourist. Spend the night at **Automotel Berlines** (4a Calle Oriente and 2a Av. Sur), a very simple, clean hotel where doubles are around $4. You won't find much to do in the town itself, but you can wander around a number of nearby forested mountains. You can hike to the massive hydroelectric power plant, **El Tronador** (The Thunderer), just over 5 kilometers (3 miles) from town. To get to El Tronador go to Canton de Zapotilla, a village just northeast of Berlín, and look for the signs. To get to Berlín, get off Bus 301 (which travels the main east–west highway) at the desvío near Mercedes Umaña, then take Bus 354 to town (½ hour from the desvío, leaving every ½ hour, 20¢).

The outside wall of Berlín's church has a mural commemorating the late Archbishop Romero with his unheeded words: "The only peace that God wants is based on truth and justice." Does this remind anyone of the 1992 Rodney King riot chants that were heard across the United States and beyond: "No justice, no peace"?

SANTIAGO DE MARIA

Santiago is possibly the most scenically located town in eastern El Salvador, and the ride alone makes a trip here worthwhile. Get a seat on the left side of the bus (if your're coming from Berlín) to enjoy breathtaking views of the Río Lempa and Honduras in the distance. This is coffee country, and the crop is grown all over the beautiful mountains around town. Somehow Santiago escaped the ravages of the war; the FMLN hardly had a presence here, and today it isn't militarized like so many other Salvadoran locales. The city is lively and attractive, and the people are fiercely proud of their *pueblo*. To get here from Berlín take Bus 348 (hourly till 5 PM, 40 minutes).

When in Santiago, give yourself at least a day to explore the surrounding countryside. To the east, several paths lead up the **Cerro Tigre,** a good hike with a commanding view of the town and valley below. To the west is **Volcán de Alegría** (take the bus halfway back to Berlín and ask to be let off in Alegría). The volcano has a crater lake known as the **Laguna de Alegría,** which is more for breathing than swimming; the sulfur fumes emanating from the volcanic rock are said to have medicinal value.

WHERE TO SLEEP AND EAT Hotel **Villahermosa** (4 3a Av. Norte, tel. 63–0146), the friendly pride-of-the-town hotel, comes complete with a terrace and pleasant garden patio. Rooms are clean and well maintained ($7 per double with bath, $5 without). **Hospedaje El Quetzal,** next door to Villahermosa, is an option if its wonderful neighbor is full or if you're on a tight budget. The atmosphere is a little creepy, and they lock the doors at 8:30 PM, but tolerably clean doubles go for $3.25 without bath. The clean, simple **Restaurante El Unico** (2 2a Av. Sur, right on the park) serves seafood and meat dishes for $2–$3. The owner swears he sells whole lobsters for $3 each when he's got some. Next door is an okay pizzeria with some vegetarian fare.

San Miguel

San Miguel is the hub of the east and, with almost 200,000 residents, the third-largest city in the country. It's big and busy, though without the hellish frenzy of the capital (or the charm of many smaller cities). It is a major commercial center: Industrial goods, household products, and consumer electronics are sold all over the city, giving San Miguel a warehouse ambience. Come here to get your bearings, buy something major, or even to relax—but don't expect much adventure or diversion, except possibly during the November 17–21 **festival** of the Virgen de la Paz.

For such a big city, sightseeing possibilities are minimal. The **cathedral** is large and imposing, but rather artless for an important religious building. A block behind it sits the **Antiguo Teatro Nacional,** a more elegant building where you might be lucky enough to see an event. You won't find much going on at night, and where there *is* action you probably don't belong (unless you're self-described riffraff). On weekends, you might catch a soccer game at the **Estadio Municipal,** at the end of 4a Calle Oriente (look for the tall lights). Check the paper or ask around for game times.

BASICS **Antel** (right on the Plaza) is open daily 6 AM–9 PM, and the **post office** is a couple of blocks down 4a Av. Sur at 3a Calle Poniente. A number of **banks** and **casas de cambio** lie along 2a and 4a Calles Poniente, opposite the cathedral; you can change dollars during normal business hours and Saturday mornings. The city **hospital** is pretty far west of the town center; to get here, either take the "hospital" bus from 4a Calle Poniente at the Plaza Central or a taxi. The facility is large and relatively well equipped, and has a limited English-speaking staff.

COMING AND GOING Bus 301 leaves every 15 minutes for San Miguel from the capital's Terminal de Oriente (3 hours, $1). From San Miguel, you can catch buses to virtually everywhere in the east. The bus station (6a Calle Oriente and 10a Av. Norte) is truly a mess. The following are all 1- to 1½-hour trips and cost around 50¢, with buses leaving several times per hour: Bus 373 to Usulután, 324 to La Unión, 328 to San Francisco Gotera, 330 to Santa Rosa de Lima, and 320 to El Cuco. Other buses go to smaller cities; ask for more info at the station.

GETTING AROUND Finding your way around town isn't very hard, as long as you're amenable to change. Avenidas run north–south, with the main one called **Avenida G Barrios** in the north end of town and **Avenida E Gavidia** in the south. Smaller, numbered avenidas are appended by "norte" in the north end of town and "sur" in the southern end. Calles run east–west; the main one is **Calle Chaparrastique** to the west and **Calle Sirama** to the east of the center. Smaller, numbered calles are "poniente" in the west section of town and "oriente" in the east. The **Plaza Central** sits between 2a and 4a calles on 4a Avenida Norte. The central **market** is always a zoo, and is a maze of pure mud after a good rain. The market begins in earnest at Calle Chaparristique near the cathedral, and extends south for several blocks. Everything you'll need to sustain your life and travels is within a few blocks of the town center.

WHERE TO SLEEP

➤ **NEAR THE BUS TERMINAL** • **Hotel Hispanoamericano.** Hispanoamericano's rooms are clean and well-kept, with good bathroom fixtures, firm beds, and fans ($7 per double). Relax with other patrons and watch cable TV in the lobby. *408 6a Av. Norte at 8a Calle Oriente, tel. 61–1202. 22 rooms, all with bath.*

Hotel Migueleño. This fairly new hotel has plenty of clean rooms ($5 per double) with great bathrooms, fans, and bottles of cold drinking water. Ask to use the laundry pila in the evening. *610 4a Calle Oriente, one block from bus station. 29 rooms, all with bath. 10 PM curfew.*

Hotel San Rafael. This pleasant, three-floor building has simple, clean rooms. Doubles ($5) all have baths, fans, decent beds, and hammocks. *704 6a Calle Oriente, one block from bus station, tel. 61–4113. 20 rooms, all with bath.*

➤ **NEAR THE CENTER** • The town center is more residential, quieter, and probably safer than most other parts of town. Unless you have lots of baggage, you can still walk here from the bus station.

Hotel Caleta. Hotel Caleta is the *Berkeley Guides'* choice for this city. For $7 per double you get lots of nice details: a flawlessly clean room and bath, comfy beds, fans, and pretty furniture. Best of all—no bugs! *607 3a Av. Sur, tel. 61–3233. 40 rooms, some with bath. 10 PM curfew.*

Hotel Modelo. A bit of a walk from the center in a quiet, pleasant neighborhood, the Modelo has clean, simple rooms with well-kept bathrooms for $6 per double. To enter, go around the side because the big front doors are practically facades. *208 17a Calle Poniente, just up from 3a Av. Sur, tel. 61–3122. 13 rooms, all with bath.*

FOOD **El Nilo.** Just a block from the bus station, El Nilo is a good place to stop for breakfast or lunch before moving on. The ceiling fans keep it cool, and the plastic tables keep it tacky. The food is typical and reasonably priced: burgers, sandwiches, meat, and chicken for $1–$2. A bright spot is its sizable bakery, with fresh breads, pastries, and donuts. Pineapple upside-down cake (*piña volteada*) is their specialty. *8a Av. Norte and 6a Calle Oriente, just a block from the bus terminal, tel. 61–3787. Open Mon.–Sat. 8–4.*

El Oasis. A neat little spot on a busy street, this is a great place to escape the ruckus of the center. Choose from a wide selection of very large, cold licuados ($1) and juices (60¢). The *huevos a la ranchera* are eggs and salsa with a ton of fresh vegetables (75¢). Vegetarian adventurers should try the *enrollado de elote* (corn on the cob made creatively) for $1.25. Sandwiches and burgers run about $1. It's the place to go during power outages because they have a generator. *104 4a Calle Poniente, down from the Plaza away from the cathedral, tel. 61–2250. Open Mon.–Sat. 7–7, Sun. 7–1.*

La Skarcha. This simple place is the best in town for local flavor and good value. A lively, rough-and-tumble bunch of regulars sits under the patiolike structure and watches Latin music videos on TV. The huge *gallina asada* (roast chicken) is only $2, as are most basic meat dishes. Vegetarians should point at a few fresh vegetables in the kitchen and the cooks will figure out what to do with them—they seem to enjoy a challenge. *616 4a Calle Oriente, 3½ blocks behind cathedral, tel. 61–3769.*

NEAR SAN MIGUEL

VOLCAN CHAPARRASTIQUE Standing 7,000 feet high, this babe is a serious climb. The volcano has been quite active during the last hundred years, and the last time it blew its top was 1976. Take the bus for La Placita, a ½-hour ride from the Farmacia San Miguel in the marketplace. Colectivo pickup trucks also make trips from the market.

LAGUNA DE OLOMEGA For most of the year, the laguna is little more than a large swamp, though it's always navigable and filled with fish. The best time to go is from August to October, when the heavy rains bring up the water level. Much of the surface is littered with an obnoxious plant called *nimfa*, which looks like a big head of lettuce. The laguna is the lifeblood for fishermen in Olomega and several villages on the other side, and fish is the main grub for miles around. Locals favor the tasty *guapote,* and the sturgeon-sized *tilapia* is also popular. You can cross the laguna in one of the boats that ferry passengers to and fro whenever boats fill up (50¢). The best time to catch a ride is in the morning before 8. Small villages nestle in the serene hills on the other side; **Olomegita** and **La Estrachura** are two of the larger communities. You can also stop by **Los Cerritos,** a little island where locals like to bathe. If you can't catch a regular ferry, make a deal with an independent or possibly rent a canoe and do your own exploring. The canton of Olomega has no hospedaje or real restaurants, though you can sometimes crash on the floor at the **Casa Comunal** (ask an employee). Some okay camping spots are on the other side, though the rains here are serious. Take Bus 384 from San Miguel (1½ hours, 50¢). From La Unión, take the bus toward San Miguel and get off at the desvío in **Carmen.**

North of San Miguel

The department of Morazán, like Chalatenango to the west, is large, sparsely populated, poor—and most definitely FMLN territory. Before traveling here, make sure that peace is the order of the day; the area saw some of the worst fighting of the civil war, and if active conflict returns, it'll surely affect Morazán. Be prepared for some major inconveniences, aside from the hellish heat and humidity. Compounding the nationwide power shortage, Morazán suffers the worst water shortage in the country. Don't expect that you will always be able to use sinks, much less showers. Carry a canteen for drinking water and refill it whenever possible. During the rainy season, several harsh downpours a day are common, so be prepared for water and mud.

SAN FRANCISCO GOTERA

It won't take you long to realize that something is seriously wrong here in the capital of Morazán department, 30 kilometers (19 miles) north of San Miguel. The government army has never been able to hold its own in the region, much less control it. Since it couldn't establish an entrenched power base, it did the next best thing: turned Gotera into a virtual military compound with more soldiers than you could shake a stick at. The cathedral is only a puny appendage to the massive military compound built right up against it. For safety's sake, resist temptations to take pictures of the curious armed vehicles, like the Ford pickups covered with sheets of welded metal to serve as tanks. Although you'll meet some friendly residents, you'll often feel the cold eyes of soldiers and locals upon you. Frankly, you're not a welcome visitor in Gotera—don't call attention to yourself more than your appearance already does. To get here, take Bus 328 from San Miguel (leaves every 20 minutes until 5:30 PM).

Gotera has a great Sunday **market**—look for the colorful mounds of hammocks in every size and material, going for some of the best prices anywhere. November 7–16 is the most exciting time to come, during the **festival** of San Francisco. The town plays the **lotería** in the center of the market area nightly at 6 PM (or whenever the power comes on). It's also neat to hang out with local kids in the side streets during the early evening. Little girls play hopscotch and boys play street soccer, hardly noticing the heavily armed soldiers sealed up in sand-bagged, camouflaged bunkers at either corner. It's quite a sight—the kids play their games while the grown-ups play theirs. Everyone here is obviously quite used to the situation, and their indifference can be more disconcerting than the military presence itself.

WHERE TO SLEEP AND EAT Hotel Arco Iris (25 Av. Morazán, tel. 64–0183) is the better of the two hotels on the main drag. $5 gets you a clean double with bath, fan, hammock, and a decent bed. The manager is quite attentive, seems concerned that guests are comfortable, and imposes a 10 PM curfew. **Hospedaje San Francisco** (23 Av. Morazán, tel. 64–0066) is less attractive than its aforementioned neighbor. Doubles with bath are around $5, or $3 without, but it depends on how business is going (bargain away). They do the curfew thing, too—9 PM.

Restaurante Bonanza (3a Calle Poniente at Av. Morazán, tel. 64–0306), just around the corner from the hotels, is the place to go for a serious meal. It's air-conditioned and caters to the few well-to-do folk of Gotera, so it's rather pricey. The fried fillet of fish is huge ($4.25), and the fried chicken is a bargain at $2. Grilled shrimp and cream of seafood soup are the house specialties, each for $6.25. **Comedor Malita,** across the street, is much cheaper. It's *comida a la vista* with the usual meaty options, but the cook says she'll put together a vegetarian medley if you ask ($1–$2 per plate).

SANTA ROSA DE LIMA

Aside from hot and wet, Santa Rosa is everything that Gotera is not: The military is practically absent and the people are open, laid-back, relaxed, and (more) welcoming. You won't get that look from people that asks "What are you DOING here?" The locals are used to strange faces because the town is close to the border town of El Amatillo. Santa Rosa really gets going August 25–31 during the **Festival de Agosto,** when bullfights, carnival rides, and general hell-raising abound. Travelers with a political bent might check out the FMLN Party headquarters at 2a Avenida Sur and 6a Calle Poniente. Who knows how your presence or questions will be received: Many in the FMLN appreciate foreign supporters, others hate all gringos categorically. Use your best judgment and don't be pushy. The large daily **market** has dozens of eating stands. **Antel** (Calle Giron and 4a Avenida Norte) is open 6:30 AM–9 PM daily.

WHERE TO SLEEP Santa Rosa is the last major Salvadoran town before Honduras, and a good place to stop for the night if you're running late. It has plenty of hotels, but the water shortage affects them all—expect bathroom inconvenience.

Hospedaje Mundial. Desperados can try this bargain-basement hospedaje for $1.50 per person. You even get free in-room showers during rainstorms (situate yourself under one of the drips coming through the ceiling) and fans (real). Entomologists will appreciate the variety of flying and crawling occupants. *6a Av. Sur and 6a Calle Oriente, behind the bus terminal. 20 rooms, none with bath.*

Hotel El Recreo. It has the most character, highest level of cleanliness, and best prices of all the hotels I saw. For $2.50 per person you get big, clean rooms with wonderfully firm double beds, boomin' overhead fans, and window screens to keep the bugs out. Managers Marta and Juana are a fun pair, and let you wash a small load of clothes if the pila has water. The lobby has a TV, phone (4¢ per local call), and great rocking chairs. The only drawback is the dreadful communal bathrooms, which are unavoidable in these parts. *Calle Giron and 4a Av. Norte, next to Antel (look for the antenna), tel. 64–2126. 11 rooms, none with bath.*

FOOD The family-run restaurant in **Hotelito Tejano** (Calle Giron and 6a Av. Norte, a block from Antel) feels like a large dining room in an old house (which it probably is). The people are friendly and attentive, and serve delicious and plentiful meat and chicken dishes for around $2. At **Comedor Nuevo** (6a Calle Poniente between Av. General Larios and 2a Av. Sur, near the bus terminal) a crowd of regulars bumps elbows at the close-together tables. It's a good place to meet people because you can't ignore whoever's sitting next to you. Basic steaks and chicken are $2, and the house specialty, *sopa de camarones* (shrimp soup), is a pretty good deal at $3.

NEAR SANTA ROSA DE LIMA

➢ **EL AMATILLO AND THE HONDURAN BORDER** • The Goascorán bus for El Amatillo leaves Santa Rosa's bus station every 15 minutes until 6:15 PM. The ½-hour trip costs 40¢. El Amatillo looks like the set for a Mad Max movie: It's that gray, dusty, and broken-down. Immigration will charge you 75¢ to leave on foot, and the Honduran side charges about the same to enter. After checking through El Amatillo, continue across the bridge—the **Río Goascorán** is the border—and finish the paperwork at the Honduras office. The immigration offices are open 6 AM–8 PM; if you want to catch a bus for the Honduran capital Tegucigalpa, or the nearest major city Choluteca, get across by 5 PM (meaning arrive by 4 just in case).

Pacific Coast

Surf El Salvador, dude! The Pacific coast of El Salvador is pretty groovy and laid back compared to many other parts of the country. If hostilities do start up again, though, this region will be affected along with the rest of the country: The cute little port towns will revert to high-security harbors for military and supply ships. Let's enjoy it while it lasts. The 320-kilometer (200-mile) coast is dotted with beautiful bays, tropical lagoons, and marshy areas that are home to an amazing variety of birds and other wildlife. But don't expect to find a secluded tropical paradise; towns take up most inhabitable stretches of sandy coast, and elsewhere rocky cliffs drop straight down into the crashing surf. A top-quality highway, Central America 2, runs the length of the coast. About mid-way along the highway is the big, boring town of Zacatecoluca (rhymes with "pack a Czech bazooka"), 60 kilometers (37 miles) southeast of the capital. The city itself is completely forgettable, but it's one of the best departure points for the exquisite Costa del Sol. The Pacific is *the* vacation spot for anyone in the country who can afford to vacation, so it can get crowded; time your visit right (i.e., come during the week) or accept the company gracefully, and your visit here will be quite relaxing.

La Unión

On the Gulf of Fonseca about 45 kilometers (28 miles) southeast of San Miguel, this nondescript port town has little to attract a traveler except access to nearby beaches and the Islas Salvadoreñas (*see below*). The beaches in town are bunk—don't even bother. If you're catching a boat out of town, note that the docks are actually a couple of kilometers outside the city in **Cutuco**. La Unión is slow, hot, and easy-going. As the country's second-largest port, shipping is the livelihood for many residents, while others are dependent on the large fishing industry. Luckily, the military's presence is confined to the local marina, about 1 kilometer from town.

Calle Generál Menéndez is the main drag, dividing the avenidas north (toward the sea) and south. Numbered calles run parallel to Calle Menéndez and the waterfront. A well-maintained and attractive church is at Calle Menéndez and 1a Avenida Norte, facing the large Plaza Central. The large **market** spans the block between 1a and 3a avenidas Norte along Calle Menéndez. Many **banks** downtown will change money. **Antel** is at 1a Calle Oriente and 5 Avenida Norte. **Gallo's Restaurante** (*see* Food, *below*) is THE place to party in this ho-hum town. If you're up for a hike, take one of the frequent buses to the nearby town of **Conchagua** and climb the 1,250-meter volcano of the same name.

COMING AND GOING The bus station is in the north end of town on 3a Calle Poniente, 1 block from the waterfront. Bus 304 from San Salvador's Terminal de Oriente will get you here in about four hours for about $2. Take Bus 324 to or from San Miguel or Bus 342 from Santa Rosa de Lima. Both trips take a little over an hour for 50¢, with buses leaving frequently. Bus 383 takes you to El Tamarindo (1½ hours). If you're headed to Honduras, take Bus 353 to the border at El Amatillo (2 hours, 75¢). To get to Las Playitas, take the hour-long ride on Bus 418 from the railway station at 3a Avenida Sur and 4a Calle Oriente, leaving once every 3 hours from 9 AM (50¢).

WHERE TO SLEEP **Hospedaje Anexo Santa Marta.** Don't confuse this with the original hospedaje (not "anexo") in the market, which is a disaster. This place isn't really appealing either, but it'll do in a pinch. The rooms are clean enough but have only one small bed, and the nonattached roof lets in bugs. How much can you complain when you're paying only $2.50 per room? *7a Av. Norte and Calle Generál Menéndez, tel. 64–4238. 15 rooms all with bath. 10 PM curfew.*

Casa de Huespedes El Dorado. Stay away from hotels near the market, except for this place (not to be confused with the grungy *Hospedaje* El Dorado). It's probably the best in town; for $5 per double you get clean towels, plenty o' water, and a fan. The rooms are big and so are the beds, private baths are scrupulously clean, and everything works. The hotel has its own water tank to use during rationing periods, and snacks and sodas are sold at street prices. *2a Av. Norte and Calle San Carlos, tel. 64–4724. 2 blocks from central market away from church. 12 rooms, some with bath. Laundry.*

Hotel San Francisco. This place covers all the basics in decent fashion: big rooms, big comfy beds, fans, private baths, towels, water, and pilas. A big plus is the second-floor balcony, perfect for chillin' with your sweetie or a beer (or both). The $5 rooms all have one double bed and one hammock; if you want air-conditioning, fork over $9. Ask for a room away from the street if noise bothers you. *Calle Gen. Menéndez between 9a and 11a Av. Sur, 4 blocks behind church, tel. 64–4159. 25 rooms, all with bath.*

FOOD **Comedor y Pupusería Marya** (Calle Genéral Menéndez at 11a Av. Norte) is a decent, family-run dive serving basic meat and chicken plates for about $2. Nearby, **Pollo del Campo** (5a. Av. Sur and Calle Genéral Menéndez) serves up big portions of good fried chicken for $1.50. Near the church, **Pastelería y Batijugos Claudita** (Calle Genéral Menéndez and 3a Av. Norte) serves good licuados ($1) and has a small bakery. Vegetarians can split a large cheese pizza here for $5.

Gallo's Restaurante specializes in Mexican food and seafood. The chicken fajitas ($4) are good, and the fish fillet ($5), prepared in garlic butter and white wine, is excellent. Vegetarians will enjoy the *enchilada Santa Rosa,* with melted cheese, guacamole, rice, and beans for $3. Gallo's is also the entertainment spot of La Unión, where strolling mariachi bands drop by after dark to play all night—put on your boogie shoes. The well-stocked bar makes this the place to tie one on, though you'll have to walk through a poorly lit and somewhat freaky area to get back to the main drag; consider taking a taxi home if *you're* lit and it's late. *3a Av. Sur and 4a Calle Oriente, tel. 64–4282. Open daily from 8 AM until all the people go home.*

NEAR LA UNION

PLAYITAS Traveling the few kilometers to Playitas or one of the nearby islands will make your visit to La Unión much more pleasurable. Playitas is just what the name advertises: a little beach. You can walk its length in less than five minutes. It's a simple fishing village, where you'll see far more pigs and chickens than people. **Tienda y Mariscos Rosita** is the best restaurant in town, serving a modest but tasty bowl of *mariscada* for $3. It's also a hospedaje, where a double with fan and bath is $3. Bus 418 to Playitas from La Unión leaves the railway station at 3a Avenida Sur and 4a Calle Oriente about once every 3 hours, starting at 9 AM (50¢). A direct ride would take little more than ½ hour, but you should count on double or even triple that, as the bus stops every few hundred meters to drop off passengers and their week's shopping. Infrequent pickup trucks also make the trip.

ISLANDS If you want to get to one (or more) of the nearby islands, you'll have to go with a fisherman—there isn't a tourist boat in sight. Prices will vary according to how good the boat owner's catch has been lately, his first impression of you, and your will to haggle. Most talk a very fast, mumbled, and slang-filled Spanish: Make *sure* you've got a mutual understanding before you get into the boat, and that the price is *ida y vuelta* (round-trip). Your best bet is to cut a half-now-half-later deal with someone who'll drop you off and pick you up. The best time to get a boat is early in the morning around 5 or 6, which means catching a pickup from La Unión at 4 AM or spending the night in Playitas. Most boats leave the islands in the late afternoon, around 4 PM; if you're not ready to return when they are, it'll mean camping out overnight. The isles make for some good freelance camping, since local authorities don't seem to mind. The islands all have plenty of lush vegetation, beautiful palm trees waving in the wind, and deserted beaches. The closest one to Playitas is **Zacatillo**; **Conchagüita** isn't too far either. Trips to these should run around $6. Farther out is **Meanguera** (about 3 hours by boat), which has a small fishing village with a hospedaje. Meanguera has been the object of a bitter territorial dispute with Honduras, and Salvadorans are mighty proud that their neighbor hasn't been able to take possession. On weekends, you might be able to catch a ride on one of the cargo boats leaving Meanguera for the scenic trip to La Unión. *If you're coming here from Honduras, make sure you have an El Salvador visa and proper entry documentation.* If found without, you'll have plenty of trouble, and probably a stiff fine.

La Unión to Usulután

EL TAMARINDO

El Tamarindo, on a sheltered bay 20 kilometers (12 miles) south of La Unión, is a delightful fishing village with minimal tourist facilities, which gives it more character than some of the highly frequented spots up the coast. Thousands of fish lie drying under the sun, destined for kitchens far and wide, and thatched houses line the paths that wind their way helter-skelter to the ocean. The beach itself is very inviting, with timid waves, fine sand, clean water, and great views of the islands. On weekdays you practically have this playa wonderland to yourself. Camping here may be difficult because the sandy area is narrow and your tent will practically be in the water. The hospedaje at **Tienda Yemlath** (on the main drag) has basic doubles for $3 each—an okay price, though the place is frequented by some unsavory types from town.

The normal way to get here is by direct bus from La Unión (several different buses, including Bus 383, make the trip), a 1½-hour ride. Beware of opportunistic drivers inviting you aboard the bus for Intipucá: It's faster but drops you off on the wrong side of the inlet of El Tamarindo. You'll have to walk over a kilometer and catch a ferry (10¢) to the other side. Hitching is pretty easy and quite common in these parts. Not far from Tamarindo is **Las Tunas,** another beach of the same character, though with a wealthier, more developed hotel strip a few kilometers away from the main village.

EL CUCO

El Cuco, 30 kilometers (19 miles) west of Tamarindo, is probably the most popular playa in El Salvador. The beach is humongous, with clean, fine sand. The strong waves and undertow are probably cool for surfers, though dangerous for casual swimmers. As of yet, no one rents surf boards or other fun-in-the-sun equipment. Disheartening (and potentially lethal) are the ridiculous drivers who vroom their vehicles up and down the beach. The only direct bus to El Cuco comes from San Miguel, a 1½-hour ride for 50¢. From La Unión, take the bus to Intipucá; from there take the bus toward San Miguel, which can drop you off at the desvío; wait for the El Cuco bus from San Miguel, which'll probably be packed to the rafters. From Usulután, take the bus toward San Miguel and get off at the desvío.

The lodging situation in El Cuco can be summed up in one word: heinous.

WHERE TO SLEEP AND EAT You can pitch a tent on the beach, or pay very little to stay in one of the seaside cabañas. If you want something more than that, you're in trouble. Hotel rooms are expensive (which is to be expected in a tourist hangout), but the amazing thing is the places are so disgusting and so obviously neglected. *Cuco* means ghost in Spanish, but it can also mean "the sly one"—an apt description of the owners who actually charge money for these hovels. Stay away from any places that use the word hospedaje, which are at best miserable shacks you wouldn't let your dog sleep in. The best place in town is the **Hotel Los Leones Marinos** (tel. 61–2870), which will relieve you of $10 for an utter shithole (dirt caked to the floor boards and *thick* spider webs in all four corners). Best of all, you don't get a mattress! A thin bedspread is graciously draped over the hard bed-board.

As long as you're a seafood fan, the food scene won't be so depressing. Along the road leading to the beach, stands sell fresh (and apparently pretty safe) fish concoctions for cheap. **Cafetín Ana** is typical of the small outdoor joints, where you can get a small fish artlessly tossed into salted oil for $2 or a bowl of decent mariscada for $2.50. The larger comedores have little character but serve somewhat heartier dishes for $3–$5.

Usulután

Lying 30 kilometers (19 miles) southwest of San Miguel, this former center of the Lenca civilization shows virtually no memory, opinion, or appreciation of its pre-Columbian past. Today, Usulután is a big, drab city that's a good jumping-off point for a number of coastal destinations. Almost everything you'll want can be found in or near the **Plaza Central**. At night you shouldn't stray far from the center: The streets empty by early evening and the surrounding area is only marginally safe. **Antel** (open daily 6 AM–9 PM) is just a block from the municipal building on Calle Grimeldi. The **Casa de Cultura** (Calle Malera, attached to the Municipal building) is worth a visit if for no other reason than chat with the friendly director, Herminio Jovel Guevara. (But don't expect any info about Lenca culture!) It's open weekdays 8–noon and 2–5, Saturday 8–noon. Death aficionados can visit the very colorful **cemetery** just outside the city (any westbound bus can drop you off).

COMING AND GOING Usulután is about two hours from San Miguel and three from the capital. Zacatecoluca is 1½ hours west on the route to San Salvador. Buses to and from these places run many times an hour. Infrequent buses go north to Santiago de María, and buses south to Puerto El Triunfo leave all the time. The bus terminal is at the end of 2a Calle Oriente, a five-minute walk from the center.

WHERE TO SLEEP Hotel España. By far the best place to spend the night, España gives you clean, big, and bug-free rooms. Prices for doubles run less than $7 with bath and $5 without, and, remarkably, the general baths are clean and work fine. The patio is covered with large plants, giving the place a pleasant, healthy aura. The in-house restaurant has a long table where guests have meals together or watch the tube. The cooks will make whatever they have, and plates average $2. *Calle Grimeldi, just off Parque Central, tel. 62–0378. 12 rooms, some with bath.*

Hotel Florida. The Florida is probably the fanciest hotel in town. You get nice clean rooms and decent service, but puny bathrooms. The outdoor hammocks are a pleasant touch, but rates should be lower than $8 per double. The little restaurant serves soft drinks, beer, and basic meals for okay prices. *26 4a Calle Oriente, tel. 62–0540. Follow 4a Calle Oriente straight down from bus terminal, look for big black metal door (no sign). 30 rooms, most with bath. 10 PM curfew.*

FOOD Plenty of simple outdoor stands line the park, and are good places to stop and enjoy a drink.

Itali Pizza. Clean and overflowing with plastic, Itali ties with Pizza Hut for the eatery with least character. Try one of the veggie-laden pizzas or a standard meaty combo ($5–$7), which will easily feed two hungry travelers. The licuados are also good. *5 6a Av. Norte, tel. 62–0364.*

La Pampa Usuluteca. Large, simple, clean, and close to the center, La Pampa gets the job done. Try a mixed drink for $1–$2 while you snack on excellent pupusas for 30¢ apiece. The house specialty is *pechugas de pollo* ($3), chicken breasts covered with melted cheese and a light tomato salsa—more than the standard dead bird. Vegetarians get beans, rice, cheese, egg, and banana for $1. *On the Parque opposite Banco Salvadoreño, tel. 62–0182.*

NEAR USULUTAN

VOLCAN DE USULUTAN Officials at Usulután's *alcaldía* (city hall) say it's not a good idea for foreigners to be wandering around the volcano without a local companion. The police, army, FMLN, and residents up there are evidently touchy about unknown faces. It's also a serious trek just to reach the base of the volcano: Walk toward the volcano up 9a Avenida Norte, which becomes Calle La Peña and enters the Canton de La Peña; keep walking straight. If you do make it up, good views of the countryside await.

PUERTO EL TRIUNFO The best reason to visit Usulután is its proximity to this little harbor and the delightful cluster of islands in the **Bahía de Jiquilisco.** To reach Puerto El Triunfo, take Bus 363, which leaves every 15 minutes from Usulután's terminal (1 hour, 25¢). If you're traveling west to Zacatecoluca or the capital, get off at the desvío and wait for a passing bus. Puerto El Triunfo itself is quite ugly. You don't want to swim here—ships dump their garbage willy-nilly, and the water reeks of the town's refuse. The **Hotel Jardín** (the big red and white building on 1a Avenida Sur, 1½ blocks from the park where the buses line up) has a dozen shabby but okay rooms for $4 per double with bath. Hotel Jardín's big restaurant serves standard seafood and meat dishes for $2–$4. It doubles as a bar, where local fishermen and drivers gather for some serious drinking; eat your spinach and be prepared to meet Bluto, or be incredibly polite to stay out of trouble. Near the park are a number of small stands and pupuserías. If you're not squeamish about drinking unpurified water, try an iced *fresco de arrayan,* a light, sweet, fruit drink that makes life worth living in the heat.

From Puerto's port, catch a boat to one of the nearby islands. None has hospedajes, but there's some good camping. The most populated is **El Corral de Mulas,** which isn't far from the relatively barren **Punto San Juan.** Several other islands in the bay all have cool beaches and clean, mellow surf. Best of all, it's possible to visit them on the cheap because local passenger boats charge only $1–$2 per person. If you want to return the same day, start early (6 or 7 AM) and make sure the boat makes a return afternoon trip. Otherwise, you'll have to shell out $10 or $15 to hire a private boat back. Rent a canoe from one of the locals to do some exploring on your own.

El Zapote and the Costa del Sol

The Coast of the Sun, Costa del Sol, begins at El Zapote (due south of Zacatecoluca) and extends northwest almost to La Libertad. Salvadorans come from every corner of the country to enjoy the beaches here, so don't expect a secluded tropical paradise with your own coconut grove. The several great beaches along the strip are all similar: clean, wide-open water, strong waves, fine sand, and lots of development. These 15 kilometers (9 miles) are among the richest in El Salvador—fabulous homes (easily mistaken for large hotels), lots of Mercedes Benzes, and sky-high price tags adorn the beaches. Be careful not to wander onto someone's private property: Many homes have private guards or attack dogs. If you've got the time, visit one of the nearby islands and their cool beaches, but it'll be taxing and expensive since no regular passenger service exists as yet. Try to water-hitch (offer a few bucks for the ride) or hire a boat at the Jaltepeque estuary, on the left just before El Zapote.

COMING AND GOING Bus 495 leaves for El Zapote from the capital's Terminal de Occidente at irregular intervals, more often in the morning. You can also catch Bus 133 toward Zacatecoluca and get off at the desvío to wait for Bus 193 from Zaca, which leaves from the main bus terminal there about five times a day (2 hours, 50¢). Some buses don't go all the way to El Zapote, terminating instead at the turicentro in Costa del Sol.

WHERE TO SLEEP The major hotels are both near El Zapote: **Hotel Tesoro Beach** and, closer still, **Hotel Pacific Paradise.** The parking lots of these luxury hotels look like German car dealerships. You won't pay less than $35 per person for a room, and their restaurants serve clean, heartless food for commensurate prices. The budget place to stay is the **turicentro** at Costa del Sol (around the middle of the strip). The cabañas are tiny and the mosquitos have a field day, but you can't do better for $3 a night. Try renting a hammock, covering up with a sheet, and lathering on the bug repellant, but accept that you'll lose about a pint of blood. During the day, the turicentro is packed with noisy families so you may want to go to less populated beaches nearby, but be back before closing (6 PM) or you'll probably get locked out. If the turicentro is full, a marginally acceptable option is down the road about 10 minutes toward El Zapote. The hospedaje at **Restaurante El Marisco** will do, if you can bear paying $6.25 for a sad little room with no bath or fan.

A good option for roughing it is to spend the night inside Bus 193 from Zacatecoluca; the last bus arrives around 6 PM and leaves at dawn. Look for it near the estuary. The drivers are generally pretty good natured and understand all too well the problem of being broke on the Costa del Sol. Drape yourself across a seat and snore away with the bus crew. If that fails, try one of the buses parked across from the turicentro (definitely a night to keep at least one ear awake).

FOOD The only way you're going to avoid starving and stick to a budget is by eating pupusas at the turicentro, since most everything else is 2–3 times normal prices. Less than a kilometer east of the turicentro are a couple of roadside restaurants which beat the prices at the main hotels. **Restaurante El Gran Chema** is big and busy, the seafood is good but not incredible, and a couple of choices are around $4 per plate. Next door, the family-run **Restaurante El Marisco** is smaller and mellower. Don't be fooled by the simple wood picnic tables and cute little kids taking orders—the joint's expensive. Make sure you get a price when you order, because the sky's the limit with a foreigner's check. A big plate of plain ol' fried fish is around $8, and passable meat and chicken dishes are $5.

La Libertad and the Costa Bálsamo

The Balsam Coast, Costa Bálsamo, runs from La Libertad northwest to Acajutla. The Balsam Coast is named for the region's indigenous but now-scarce trees and used to be the world's richest source of the medicinal resin. The Costa Bálsamo is within easy reach of the capital, so expect to share the sand, especially on weekends. La Libertad ("Freedom") is by far the most popular spot, though the beach here isn't as good as some lesser-known gems nearby. Unlike at most other beaches in El Salvador, surfers are as abundant here as rice and beans. East of La Libertad is **Playa San Diego** (Bus 102 from La Libertad), and to the west **Conchalío, El Zonte,** and the venerable **Zunzal** (Bus 80 or 192). Zunzal is the most famous beach on the Costa Bálsamo, considered by many to be the best surfing beach in Central America, and it regularly hosts hang-ten competitions. Zunzal has no hotels, but it's only a 15-minute ride from La Libertad.

Once El Salvador's premier shipping port, La Libertad has a new raison d'être—as one of the biggest fun-in-the-sun hotspots in Central America. The black volcanic sand tends toward the mucky, but the water and waves are awesome. Less experienced swimmers should watch out for the undertow, and everyone should keep their ears open for shark (*tiburón*) warnings. One of the more interesting events of the day is the return of the fishing boats to the pier, where they're hoisted up with a winch in a procedure that is sometimes scary and always entertaining. The pier itself is the site of the **market,** with oodles of fresh fish and shellfish. The big trawlers come in on Sundays and hold a colorful fish and crustacean auction. The turicentro in town has the usual restaurants, tiendas, swimming pools, and basketball courts. An added attraction is the ice cream distribution center nearby which sells a dozen kinds of yummy sorbet and other frozen delights (the Choco-Banana is awesome).

While you'll be stumbling over surfers all the time, surfboards themselves are hard to come by. The only game in town is at the **Condominio Playa La Paz,** a condo/surfboard repair and craftshop. It's on 4a Calle Poniente in the middle of all the restaurants, next door to Hotel Amor y Paz (the diviest dive in town). They don't always have boards to rent, but when they do it's about $2 per hour (or, make them an offer for the day). You'll probably have to put up a hefty deposit. **Antel** (2a Calle Poniente and 2a Av. Sur) is open 6 AM–9 PM. The **post office** is around the corner on 2a Avenida Sur. You'll find most of the hotels, restaurants, and action on 5a Avenida Sur, stretching south to the water and east along 4a Calle Poniente.

COMING AND GOING La Libertad doesn't have a bus terminal. The major bus routes generally come in on Calle Calvario heading west, or on 2a Calle Poniente heading east. From the capital, Bus 102 leaves every 15 minutes from Parque Bolivar at 4a Calle Poniente and 13a Avenida Sur, about an hour ride for 30¢. From Zacatecoluca, Bus 540 leaves only a few times per day before noon. Buses 80 and 192 to the beaches leave all the time from 4a Avenida Sur and 2a Calle Poniente.

WHERE TO SLEEP Fancy, expensive hotels abound in La Libertad, frequented by wealthy *capitalinos* taking long weekends. At the east end of town is the elegant **Hotel El Malecón de Don Lito** (tel. 35–3201) whose 15 rooms run $22/$33 for a single/double. It has a swimming pool right on the ocean. In the same class at the other end of town is **Hotel Los Arcos** (tel. 35–3490), a good place if you want some pricey solitude. To get here, take Bus 80 a few kilometers from town. Few possibilities exist for those with more modest budgets. Depending on room availability, the best bet is probably **El Retiro Familiar** (corner of 5a Avenida Sur and 4a Calle Poniente), which has 15 rooms ranging from gross to decent. Better rooms cost around $6 for a double without bath, but try to make a deal with the friendly manager, especially if you're staying more than one night. The general bathroom is okay. If you can't get a tolerable room there, check out **Hotel Puerto Bello** (tel. 35–3013), nearby at 2a Calle Poniente and 1a Avenida Norte. Many of its 25 rooms are also disasters, and price varies according to quality; the doubles for $6 are halfway decent, but that's as good as it gets (still no fans). The general bathrooms have functional and clean toilets, but the showers are cockroach city. Rooms are often rented for 12-hour periods, so make sure you know when you're supposed to leave or risk a rude awakening.

FOOD Munch on some (relatively) cheap seafood while you gaze at the ocean in the small restaurants lining 4a Calle Poniente east of 5a Avenida Sur. Mariscada runs about $3 and a decent portion of shrimp about $4. Vegetarians are generally left in the lurch, but the ritzier places will serve up a pretty good vegetable or fruit salad for a couple of bucks. Contradicting the sign, the owner of **Cafetín El Amigo** (2a Av. Sur just below Calle Calvario) says it's called Restaurante Concha Molina—maybe there'll be a convergence someday. Right in the center of town, the place has absolutely no character but a good bowl of mariscada is an amazingly cheap $2. If you're a shellfish novice, don't be ashamed to ask for eating instructions. Right on the water, **Chalet Sandra** (4a Calle Poniente) is big and clean, and the soft, airy Latin music will have you swaying in your seat. They serve mongo portions for less than the big shots nearby; very tasty appetizers of ceviche, shrimp, or oysters are $2–$3, and *arroz con calamar* (squid with rice) is a bargain at $4. Go off the deep end with a big stuffed lobster for $9.

Western El Salvador

The west is popular with both tourists and nationals for its dramatic natural beauty, the most famous examples of which are Cerro Verde and Lago de Coatepeque near Santa Ana. Small rivers and scenic waterfalls abound, too, especially near Sonsonate. Campers and hikers will certainly want to spend some time exploring this region, although heavy rains make it rough going July–October. The rural areas here are also home to the few indigenous communities that have survived in El Salvador. Their distinctive dress, language, and customs are dying out fast as urbanization and "progress" spread.

Although the FMLN was active all over the country, the west saw much less of the war (with the notable exception of the northwestern area around Metapán) than other parts of El Salvador. As a result, most of the west is better off economically than the war-torn northern and eastern departments. Its mild climate and fertile hills make it the coffee-growing center of the country and the source of a great deal of export-generated wealth. While the bucks certainly aren't distributed equally, agriculture provides subsistence work for thousands of campesinos and helps dissipate some of the class-based social strife.

Santa Ana

Salvadoreños call Santa Ana the *segunda ciudad,* the most important and largest city after San Salvador. The second city isn't particularly large, which tells you something about the scale of cities in the rest of El Salvador. With less than a quarter-million people, it doesn't display the urban frenzy of the capital, yet it's unquestionably the center for commerce and agriculture in this prosperous region. The otherwise placid city comes alive during its annual **festival,** July 17–26. You can tour the city in just a couple of hours, but it also makes a good base from which to explore several natural sensations in the area. Santa Ana is devoid of anything resembling a visitor-information center; the tourist bureau in the capital may have some brochures about *la naturaleza* in the west, but other than that you're stuck with us.

BASICS

➤ **CHANGING MONEY** • The major banks are clustered around 2a Avenida and Calle Libertad just a block from the cathedral. Changing traveler's checks can be a hassle even at banks that accept them in the capital. **Banco Salvadoreño** (corner of 2a Av. Sur and 1a Calle Poniente) does change American Express, Visa, and Mastercard checks. It's open weekdays 9–4 and Saturday 9–noon (like all major banks in town).

➤ **EMERGENCIES** • The central **hospital** (tel. 41–1736 or 41–1778), San Juan de Díos, is at 1a Calle Oriente and 13a Avenida Sur, about a 10-minute walk from the town center. It provides around-the-clock emergency treatment and specialized medical attention. The **police** station is at 4a Avenida Independencia (tel. 40–7827).

➤ **PHONES AND MAIL** • **Antel** is on the corner of 5a Avenida Norte and Calle Libertad Oriente, just behind the cathedral, open daily 6:30 AM–10 PM. The central **post office** is at 2a Avenida Sur and 7a Calle Poniente, open 8–4:30.

COMING AND GOING
From the capital, take Bus 201 from Terminal de Occidente. For a fast one-hour ride, make sure you get a bus *directo* via Calle Nueva (New Road), or you'll trudge through a dozen podunk towns for more than two hours before reaching Santa Ana. Buses run from early morning till about 6:30 PM, and the trip costs 50¢. From Guatemala, most buses to San Salvador pass through Santa Ana. Buses from Santa Ana to major western points include: 236 to Candelaria and the Guatemalan border at San Cristóbal, leaving until 5 PM (1 hour); 235 to Metapán with

some continuing to Angüiatú at the northern border (2 hours); 216 to Sonsonate, and 210 to Ahuachapán (both around an hour).

GETTING AROUND Santa Ana really has two "centers." The big *centro* radiates south from the cathedral for several blocks, and includes the central **market** (1a Calle Poniente between 6a and 8a Avenida Sur), an enormous covered building selling everything from fresh vegetables to Walkman radios. It's only a 15-minute walk from the **bus terminal** (10a Avenida Sur and 15a Calle Poniente) to the cathedral in the big center, or you can shuttle back and forth on local Bus 51 for 5¢, which runs frequently till around 7:30 PM. Further southwest is the second center, the area between Parque Menéndez (Calle Libertad and 10a Avenida Sur) and the bus terminal. This area is more residential and dotted with small businesses; it's also the best area to stay in terms of hotel prices and proximity to transportation.

WHERE TO SLEEP

➤ **NEAR THE CENTER** • Unless you have particular business to do in Santa Ana, proximity to the big center probably isn't a big deal. Most of the cool stuff lies outside town and is accessible from the bus terminal.

Hotel Colonial. Hotel Colonial is a small, rickety place with little going for it apart from its central location. The rooms are spartan and depressing though reasonably clean, and the beds have seen better days. The general bath is marginally clean, but it works. $6.25 for 24 hours is overpriced, but $3.25 for ½ day is about right, especially if you plan to vacate early. *4a Calle Poniente and 2a Av. Norte, near the cathedral. 5 rooms, none with bath.*

Hotel Libertad. Probably the best hotel in Santa Ana, Hotel Libertad still isn't anything to write home about. The rooms are large, clean, well kept, and all have good fans. There's nothing particularly charming about the place or management, and at $10 per room it's far from a bargain. *1a Av. Norte and 4a Calle Oriente, tel. 41–2358. One block from cathedral. 15 rooms, all with bath.*

➤ **NEAR THE BUS TERMINAL** • This area is both cheaper than the big center and just a short walk from transportation. Some people may be disturbed by the large number of prostitutes working the streets, but it's not a dangerous area as long as you stay in lighted places and around other people.

Hospedaje Livingston. The best overall value in town, Livingston offers large, clean rooms with functioning baths for $4 ($3 without bath). The rooms are rather dark, the mattresses are covered with plastic, and each room has only one big bed, but all the essentials for a decent night's sleep are here. *17 10a Av. Sur, tel. 41–1801. Between 7a and 9a Calle Poniente. 26 rooms, some with bath. Laundry pila.*

Hotelito Monterrey. If all other options are full—not unlikely—this place is near the terminal and has small, clean, but shabby doubles for $3 without bath. Judging from the look of the women hanging out in the lobby, this may be the only budget hotel in town that offers "room service" (nudge, nudge, wink, wink). *29 10a Av. Sur, between 9a and 11a Calle Poniente, tel. 41–2755. 14 rooms, none with bath.*

Hotel Nuevo Roosevelt. Only slightly better than those at Hospedaje Livingston, the small, clean rooms at the Roosevelt are less of a deal at $8 with bath and $5 without. All rooms have a large, mighty comfy bed. The lobby is pleasant and the building has a very formal feel to it. *8a Av. Sur at 5a Calle Poniente, a few blocks from Parque Menéndez, tel. 41–1702. 19 rooms, some with bath. Laundry pila. 10 PM curfew.*

Hospedaje El Carrousel. If you're leaving early in the morning, this might be the best deal. All rooms have one big bed, a fan, and a functioning yet grimy bath. Doubles cost $3 for 12 hours, but you can make a deal to extend that a bit (the $6 charge for a full day is foul). At night you share the room with cockroaches so big they can knock your toothbrush off the sink. *8a Av. Sur 55, tel. 40–0941. Between 13a and 15a Calle Poniente, right where buses enter the terminal. 12 rooms, all with bath.*

FOOD On Avenida Independencia Sur between 5a and 9a calles is a row of good, middle-class restaurants, including **Pollo Campero, Burger Queen, Toto's Pizza,** and a decent donut shop. Meals on this strip run $3–$5 per person. The restaurants are open till 10 PM or so, and the street is well lit. For a little more character and a little less plastic, try one of the following.

Pizza y Cafetería California. The wide variety of dishes at this clean, two-floor restaurant makes it a good place for diverse tastes. Plates include a quarter pound of meat or chicken for about $2.50. A great vegetarian pizza for two is $5 and comes loaded to the brim, and the sandwiches are tasty, too. *1a Av. Sur and 1a Calle Oriente, one block from the center, tel. 41–3139. Open daily 10 AM–8 PM.*

Restaurante Kiyomi. The Chinese food served here isn't exactly authentic, but it's not bad and the portions are generous. Fried wonton appetizers ($2) are fun to start with, and a decent chop suey for $3.25 will fill you up. Plates with fish, rice, and other stuff run $2–$3, a good value considering the heaping portions. Vegetarians can have a meatless chow mein for $3. *4a Av. Sur between 3a and 5a Calle Poniente, tel. 41–3849. Open daily 10 AM–8:30 PM.*

Tacos Mexicali. Here they serve straightforward, reasonably priced Mexican food in a pleasant atmosphere. The specialty soup is *frijoles blancos* (white bean with a pork base); meat-filled tacos run $2 per plate, and they even prepare rabbit. *1a Calle Oriente and 3a Av. Sur, near the center. Open Thurs.–Tues. 11:30–2:30 and 5–9.*

WORTH SEEING The gothic **cathedral** that dominates the main center is impressive both inside and out, even in its current state of disrepair. Next to the cathedral is the baroque **Teatro de Santa Ana** whose beautiful and well-maintained exterior belies the years of neglect inside. Completed around 1910, the building was converted into a movie theater during the Martinez dictatorship of the 1930s and remained so until 1979. By then, customer abuse, water damage, and lack of maintenance had destroyed much of the exquisitely detailed work. The Mexican government is now funding a restoration project which should be finished by the year 2000. Nonetheless, you can still appreciate much of the original work, and the technical process of restoration is interesting in itself. Occasionally, the theater hosts artistic and cultural events—inquire at the front desk.

NEAR SANTA ANA

CHALCHUAPA AND THE TAZUMAL RUINS The Mayan ruins of Tazumal ("Place of the Burned" in the Quiché language) are El Salvador's most important and best preserved pre-Columbian site. If you're coming from ruin-rich Guatemala or Belize, you may think the site lacks intensity; nonetheless, it's a cool day trip from Santa Ana. Only a small part of the 10-square-kilometer area has been excavated, and the digging continues. Artifacts are being discovered all the time, so chatting with one of the on-site archaeologists can be worthwhile. The site provides a glimpse into the lives of several indigenous civilizations dating from at least 3,000 years ago. Evidence suggests that the residents had trading partners in other parts of Central America and even México.

Until more structures are uncovered, the main attractions are the large pyramid and ball court. The pyramid, most likely a religious temple, can be climbed from several sides and offers an inspiring view of Chalchuapa and the surrounding countryside. The small museum at the site exhibits a number of relics found at Tazumal, though many of the best ones have been taken to the national museum in the capital. The photos and bilingual descriptions of the site's history and the restoration process are fascinating—lots of problems come up when you're trying to maintain the structural integrity of a stone building that is several thousand years old.

The town of Chalchuapa is pleasant enough, but of minor interest apart from the ruins. It doesn't make much sense to sleep here with Santa Ana so close, but the centrally located **Hotel Gloria** (Avenida 2 de Abril and Calle General Ramón Flores, tel. 44–0131) has eight clean rooms with private baths for $6.25. Grab a sandwich or a plate of comida típica at **El Gran Pollo**, right off Parque Central at the end of 1a Calle Poniente. They also have shakes and ice cream. From Santa Ana, take Bus 218 to Chalchuapa (½ hour, 15¢); the bus drives around the town then drops you off just a two-minute walk from the ruins (get off at the cemetery). From the center of town, it's a 15-minute walk to the end of 5a Calle Oriente (follow it past 7a Avenida Sur and keep going straight). The site is open Tuesday–Sunday 9–5; admission is free.

LAGO DE COATEPEQUE Set high in the mountains, Lago de Coatepeque is one of the most dramatic and beautiful sites in El Salvador. The climate is cool and fresh, and this enormous crater lake has some of the best swimming, sightseeing, food, and accommodation in the country. With an area of 26 square kilometers and a depth of over 1,000 feet, the lake hasn't (yet) been polluted by reckless commerce or development. Volcanic springs keep the temperature remarkably comfortable. Sit back and gaze at the enchanting Cerro Verde, or the looming Santa Ana and Izalco volcanoes. The only thing that mars the lovely atmosphere is the dozens of fancy homes that line the shore, making some of this natural wonderland hopelessly private (no trespassing). To get to the lake from Santa Ana, take Bus 220 from the terminal (1½ hours, 20¢). From the capital, take Bus 201 *ordinario* and get off at the crossroads town of El Congo (where Bus 220 stops).

If you're into it, look for the crab hunters using snorkeling gear in the shallow parts: A nice smile or offering a cold beer might get you some time gazing at the amazing variety of creatures and plants just beneath the surface. During the week you practically have the lake to yourself, although during the crowded weekends you have a better chance of sharing the high cost of a boat ride around the lake. Local fishermen give ½-hour rides for around $5. A ride to **Agua Caliente** island is 1½ hours round-trip and can't be done for much less than $20. As the name (Hot Water) suggests, volcanic springs beneath the surface here keep a small pocket of water at hot-tub temperature. Make sure to yell like Tarzan and fling yourself off the trapeze-like swing into the water.

➤ **WHERE TO SLEEP AND EAT** • You can eat cheaply at one of the simple comedores near the lake, but if you want to sample any of Coatepeque's delicacies—most notably *guapote* (bass) and fresh-water crab—you'll have to spend some real money at one of the hotels. Unless you have camping gear, you'll be staying there anyway. **Hotel del Lago** (tel. 78–2873) has very tidy rooms for $19 per double. If you eat here, pin down food prices before you order so you don't end up paying double the non-gringo price. Bigger and friendlier than Hotel del Lago is **Hotel Torremolino** (tel. 41–1859), with similar rooms for $15. They have a small, clean swimming pool in case you're hankering for chlorine instead of the fresh-water lake. The restaurant at Torremolino is tastefully decorated though pricey, and has a large dock where you can eat right on the water. Breakfast is the best value: Juice, eggs, platanos, bacon, and coffee for $2.50 will start your day off right. Continue the good feeling throughout the afternoon with a magnificent shrimp-stuffed avocado for $3. On Sunday afternoon, you can dance to *cumbia* (cousin to salsa) and romantic live music performed by the Orquesta Maya Club from Santa Ana (call 40–3507 to see if the schedule is the same). If you're lucky, in the evening you'll cross the path of a strolling mariachi band.

The best eating and sleeping deal on the lake is definitely at the government workers' resort **Centro Obrero**. It has simple but clean and pleasant accommodations, and an affordable restaurant. Technically, you need to get prior permission from the Ministerio de Trabajo in the capital (check with ISTU). If you don't, it's still worth a try, especially during the week. If the place is empty and the manager's in a good mood, you're in.

CERRO VERDE Nowhere in El Salvador will you experience nature like in Parque Nacional Cerro Verde. The name means green hill, but hill is an understatement. Over 6,500 feet above sea level, Cerro Verde offers spectacular views of the Santa Ana and Izalco volcanoes and Lago de Coatepeque. The thickly forested mountains make for awesome hikes. Cerro Verde is an extinct volcano, home to the most diverse community of plants, trees, and wildlife in the country (according to ISTU, there are 127 varieties of birds). The air is clean and crisp year-round, and the high altitude can bring a serious chill. From the parking lot, you can choose among several clearly marked trails. Some take you through thick pine forest, some to the top of volcanoes, and others to breathtaking panoramas.

Volcán de Santa Ana, the highest volcano in El Salvador (7,800 feet), is also known as Lamatepec ("Father Hill"). It's still active but hasn't spewed in quite some time. A walk to its crater takes about three hours from the Cerro Verde parking lot. Prepare for a strong rotten-egg smell, since you'll surely get a whiff of the sulphuric lagoon in the crater. From the rim of the volcano you also get a good view of the neighboring Volcán Izalco.

One of the world's youngest volcanoes, **Volcán Izalco** was born in 1770. A small hole near Cerro Verde shot up thousands of feet in less than a month, spewing out molten rock and flames with such violence that sailors dubbed it *El Faro del Pacifico* (lighthouse of the Pacific). It's now almost 6,000 feet high. After almost two centuries of continuous activity, Izalco suddenly went to sleep in 1957, but it may still have some serious fireworks left. Geologists say so much lava has poured down the volcano over time that the entire cone's surface is dead—even the meanest weed can't grow on the gray-black slopes. The climb from the Cerro Verde parking lot is laborious, not so much because of the height or distance but the difficult surface—loose sand, gravel, and lava. Be particularly careful coming down, and perhaps carry a staff to stop yourself from slipping.

➤ **COMING AND GOING** • Getting to Cerro Verde without your own car is frustrating. Frankly, you may not get enough time here unless you spend the night. From Santa Ana, Bus 248 leaves just twice a day, at 10:15 AM and 3:15 PM. It's the only direct route to Cerro Verde in the country. It's at least a two-hour trip, so the earliest you can arrive by bus is after noon. The last bus returns to Santa Ana at 5:30 PM, giving you about five hours, barely enough time to go up and down a volcano, and have a picnic. From San Salvador, take Bus 201 *ordinario* toward Santa Ana and get off in El Congo. Bus 248 passes through El Congo before 11 AM if it's going fast, so leave the capital by 9:30 to be on the safe side. From Sonsonate, take Bus 209 via Cerro Verde, which leaves you at the desvío 14 kilometers (9 miles) from the top. It leaves about once every hour. Thumbing a ride from the desvío is possible but not a sure thing, especially if you're in a group.

➤ **WHERE TO SLEEP AND EAT** • **Hotel de La Montaña** is the only game in town. It has luxurious rooms for $25, and also a spiffy and expensive restaurant. The hotel has a somewhat unfortunate history. It was built in the 1950s to have a bird's-eye view of the Izalco cone. Unfortunately, when construction was finished in 1957, so was the volcano's activity. Camping is permitted around the volcanoes, but park rangers are really concerned about your safety and ask that you keep your tent near the parking lot. If you just go up and make camp, it's unlikely they'll come looking for you. As for food, you'll find a low-cost comedor along the trail to the *mirador* (lookout) of the Santa Ana volcano, and tasty cooked vegetables are sold in the parking lot. Your best bet, though, is to bring a picnic lunch from the city.

Sonsonate

Founded in 1552, Sonsonate is one of the oldest cities in El Salvador. Today it's a major center for the coffee and cattle industries. Other than some fine colonial churches, you won't find much to see or do in the town proper. Good news: It's in the heart of a beautiful area and many amazing natural attractions await day trippers. As a commercial center, Sonsonate has everything needed to keep businesspeople comfortable, like clean accommodations and good restaurants.

Sonsonate is long and narrow, with the bus terminal at one end and the Plaza Central and market at the other. **Paseo 15 de Septiembre** is the long street that runs down the middle of town. **Antel,** just off the plaza at Avenida Rafael Campo and 2a Calle Oriente, is open daily 6 AM–9 PM. Bus 205 runs all the time to San Salvador (1½ hours), and Bus 216 to Santa Ana. You can take Bus 259 to La Hachadura at the Guatemalan border, but it's a lousy three-hour trip on a terrible road. Unless you have special business, it makes sense to exit (or enter) the country at Las Chinamas near Ahuachapán.

WHERE TO SLEEP If you want to stay near the bus terminal, choose one of the basic but clean places on 18a Avenida Sur a block from the station. **Hotel Florida** and **Hotel Los Angeles** both have doubles for around $5, a bit more with bath. If you're stretching your colones, try **Hospedaje El Rinconcito** (1a Calle Oriente and 16a Av. Norte) where the $2.50 doubles, and the general bath, are as nasty as you'd expect for the price.

Hotel New York. This is probably the hippest, though not the nicest, place in town. The management and clientele are a loud and free-wheeling bunch. Rooms are dark, poorly ventilated, and poorly constructed; just meet some people here and head outside. Doubles are $3 without bath and $5 with. *1-11 4a Calle Poniente, ½ block from the central market, tel. 51–0754. 8 rooms, some with bath.*

Hotel Orbe. Hotel Orbe is by far the best hotel in town. It has clean rooms, great beds, and winning bathrooms. $6.25 for a room with one big bed is worth it for a couple (or close friends), though the $9.50 doubles are pricey. *2a Av. Sur and 4a Calle Oriente, tel. 51–1416. Make a left after crossing bridge going away from the terminal. 32 rooms, all with bath. Restaurant.*

FOOD **Sabor Club** on the Parque has great licuados, shakes, and cheap lunches. The real attractions, though, are the novelty pupusas; they make shrimp, carrot, mushroom, raspberry (*mora*), and pumpkin (*ayote*) pupusas for about 20¢ each. One-half block from Antel is a wannabe Chinese restaurant, **Hilay** (Av. Rafael Campo 1–3, tel. 51–0116). The food is pretty good but not particularly Chinese, though the wonton soup ($2) is a good effort. Chow mein or chop suey plates with meat run about $3. Sonsonate yuppies frequent clean, plastic, and air-conditioned **Pizza Atto's** (right next to the bus terminal, tel. 51–3878) in a modernish mall. Loaded pizzas, including a great veggie combo, are big enough for two and cost $5–$8. Smaller appetites (or wallets) should try the melted mozzarella sandwich for $1.

NEAR SONSONATE

SALTO LAS VICTORIAS Two kilometers past the tiny town of **Caluco** are the Las Victorias waterfalls. The falls themselves are low, wide, and brown—certainly not the height of natural beauty. Just the same, the walk here takes you through a slew of glorious crop fields and tiny villages, and the *salto* (waterfall) will certainly cool you down. From Sonsonate, take Bus 432 from the terminal to Caluco. Follow the main trail past the soccer field for about 2 kilometers till you come to railroad tracks; cross them and go through the small village. It's hard to find the falls through all the thick vegetation, but prick up your ears and don't give up. If you're coming from the Atecozol turicentro, walk the short dis-

In the small village on the way to Salto Las Victorias, beware of the dogs, especially the Doberman from hell.

tance to the main highway, make a right and walk ½ kilometer to the desvío for Caluco. Wait for a bus or a pickup truck heading your way, or walk the 2 kilometers to the town.

LOS SALTOS DE SANTO DOMINGO DE GUZMAN The waterfalls near the small, indigenous village of Santo Domingo de Guzmán are perhaps the most dramatic example of the isolated natural beauty of the Sonsonate region. A word of warning: Despite information given in some guidebooks, and even by the tourism institute itself, these falls are *not* easy to get to. You'll have to stone-step across a river several times, and, depending on path conditions, you may have to walk in it for some distance. Camping is possible in some areas, but except for private crop and pasture land much of the ground is hilly and rocky—not tent friendly. Bus 246 leaves Sonsonate from Calle San Antonio 5-1 at the opposite end of town from the terminal, and it's at least an hour ride over a crude road to Santo Domingo Guzmán. Buses stop running mid-afternoon and passing pickup trucks become infrequent around the same time, so go early.

To get to the nearer of the two falls (known locally as **El Saltillo**), follow the main drag from the bus stop to the end and bear right; follow the road until you're no longer passing any buildings. You'll be on the right side of the river. Cross over to the left side by hopping rocks, and continue on through a small pasture (you may have to open a barbed-wire gate, but it's there to keep cattle in, not you out). From here, listen for the falls and be ready to traverse plenty of wet boulders and a couple of short but hair-raising precipices. The falls are an awesome sight. The water plummets more than 150 feet into the Río Tepechapa, forming a small pond at the bottom which is prime for bathing.

The truly adventurous can return to the main part of the river and follow it to the 300-foot **Salto La Quebrada** (a.k.a. *El Saltón*). Getting here depends on your physical dexterity and stamina. Follow the main river using either the foot-wide edge trails, the river banks, and, when all else fails, the river itself. From town, a competent hiker can make it in two hours. Since there aren't any signs you should constantly ask passers-by if you're heading in the right direction. Better still, you can hire a competent guide in Santo Domingo for a reasonable price. Abil Perez García lives in the house just next to the Iglesia Monte Horeb on the main drag; he does a good job and can make your day much less uncertain.

The Northwest

METAPAN

This town near the Guatemalan border has next to nothing to offer. But it's the only solid base from which to visit the beautiful Lago Güija or Montecristo wilderness preserve. Metapán's bus terminal is right on the main highway near the closed-down movie theater. **Antel** is on 2a Calle Oriente and 2a Avenida Sur. If you're headed out of the country, take Bus 211 or pick up Bus 235 in transit from Santa Ana for the 20-minute trip to Angüiatú at the Guatemalan border. Keep in mind that from the border it's an hour to Esquipulas and another four to Guatemala City, not including waiting around, so plan ahead.

A true bright spot in Metapán is the **Hotel California** (tel. 42–0164). It's not exactly life in the fast lane, but it does have seven very clean rooms with keen bathrooms and fans. All rooms are $4 and have one big bed. The owner is very helpful and friendly, and gladly lets you use the pila. The hotel is on the left side of the main highway, five blocks north of the bus terminal. If Hotel California's full, you'll have to settle for **Hospedaje Central** (2a Av. Norte and Calle 15 de Septiembre). It's not a bad deal, $3 for one big bed with bath and $2 without, but the whole building is rundown and dark. The management does keep the place really clean, though. **Deli Pizza** (right next to the main church on 1a Calle Poniente) has a clean, plastic, sterile ambience. They serve *only* pizza, though in every imaginable style. A veggie for two is $6, and a plain cheese pizza is $4. For more variety, try the large, open-air **Multidelicias** (2a Calle Oriente, tel. 42–0226). It has cheaper pizza than Deli as well as sandwiches, burgers, standard meat dishes, cakes, and ice cream. It's one block down from Mercado Municipal on the main highway.

MONTECRISTO WILDERNESS PRESERVE

Montecristo has the most pristine natural beauty in El Salvador, hands down. It's part of El Trifinio, a forested international park jointly operated by El Salvador, Guatemala, and Honduras. The range of animal and plant life is amazing, and the park offers sanctuary to a number of endangered species, like quetzals and spider monkeys. The most interesting part is the super-humid cloud forest, beginning around 7,000 feet. A journey here is a dark, wet odyssey amid huge trees and mysterious forest life. Although humid, it can get cold due to the altitude. Bring a jacket.

The reserve is closed April–September to ensure undisturbed animal breeding. From October to March you can see it all and camp as well. During the closed season, you may also be able to visit certain areas of the reserve with fewer animals. Call in Metapán to get the latest info, but this isn't a straightforward task. There seems to be a bureaucratic turf battle between the Department of National Parks in the capital (tel. 77–0622), which claims you must get permission from them to enter the reserve, and the Montecristo National Park office in Metapán (tel. 42–0119), which just tells you to bring $1.50 for admission and have a good time.

Getting to Montecristo is quite laborious—14 kilometers (9 miles) of 4x4-only road from Metapán, beginning just past the bus terminal. There's some talk of an organized transportation service in the future, but for now you'll have to ask around to hire a private vehicle. It won't be cheap. Bus drivers and their helpers often have good info. Tried and true hikers can just walk the distance. Unless you make it a day trip, you'll have to camp since no lodgings exist as yet.

LAGO DE GUIJA

Considered by some to be the most beautiful lake in the country, Lago de Güija lies in both Salvadoran and Guatemalan territory. It was a site of great religious importance to Toltec and Pipil tribes. Local legend has it that the lake was formed after several nearby volcanoes erupted and the lava flows altered the directions of several rivers which, in turn, flooded and destroyed a couple of nearby towns, Zacualpa and Güijar. This gave rise to lost-city tales and rumors of sunken treasure.

You can swim in the lake, though it gets pretty brown from mountain run-off. Lago de Güija has a number of curious sights, and a local fisherman can give you a good 45-minute tour around it for $8. This should get you as far as the island of **Tipa**. Nearby is **Cerro Negro**, not really a hill but rather a cluster of volcanic boulders that form something akin to a cave. Fishermen use it for protection during dangerous storms, or just to chill and have lunch. Visible from Tipa are the volcanoes of Chingo and Ipala, both near the Guatemalan border. Near the lakeshore is the island of **Las Figuras**, so named for the several hieroglyphics carved into boulders here. ISTU came several years ago and hauled away most of the good stuff to the national museum, leaving behind a bunch of dynamited rocks (thanks folks). During times of low water, the island becomes part of the shore and you can walk there. Farther out in the lake are rumored to be the ruins of the ancient town of Zacualpa.

To get here take Bus 235 from Metapán toward Santa Ana and get off at the village of **Desagüe**, a 20-minute ride for 20¢. Make sure to have the bus driver tell you where to get off since nothing on the highway will signal the village, much less the lake. To get to the lake from the highway, follow the road a short distance till you come to a fork.

Go right, follow the train tracks over a bridge, and bear right again. From there, ask anyone where the boats are; although very near, it's not hard to miss the shore. The walk takes about a half-hour.

NICARAGUA

By Gregory Smith

6

A few weeks into my trip to Nicaragua, I had had it. I had seen enough hope-
less disorganization, machismo, crippling strikes, heart-breaking poverty, pickpockets,
obnoxious drunks, and plain and simple unfriendliness. Sure, the land was stunning,
but I was no closer to getting to know Nicaragua's people than before my trip. The
frustration of trying to collect accurate, detailed information essential for a useful
guidebook in a country dizzy with rapid change was pushing me toward the edge of
insanity. Try taking down names and addresses in your next riot and you'll have an
idea of what I mean. In the end, however, I learned to accept that in a country reorga-
nizing itself from top to bottom, change is inevitable and chaos is the norm.

What will keep you going through it all are the mesmerizing beauty and diversity of the
Nicaraguan landscape; every place you go seems more beautiful than the last. Even
travelers who just zoom through on the Interamerican Highway will be impressed,
since the road winds through the wild, misty, northern mountains before descending
to the Pacific coastal plain, a world of lush foliage, volcanoes, enormous lakes, and
deserted beaches. To the east, on the Atlantic coast, the jungle blankets the land,
weaving a fragile, complex ecosystem that shelters exotic wildlife and communities of
indigenous tribes and Afro-Caribbeans.

The Nicaraguans themselves will keep you fascinated with their country. Fifteen years'
worth of war, economic chaos, and increasing social polarization may have worn away
some of their friendly exterior, but it has done little to diminish their passion, humor,
and instinct for living intensely. Though this generation of Nicaraguans has lived
through a decade and a half of terror and destruction, it's hard to argue that their
ancestors had it any easier. From 1502, the year of Columbus's "discovery" of the territory, to the present, the Nicaraguan experience has featured invasions, civil wars,
grinding poverty, and devastating natural disasters. No wonder that, by some counts,
nearly half the population are poets: The pain of such history can only destroy all hope
or inspire creative defiance.

To find some tranquility in Nicaragua's history, you have to look back beyond Columbus's arrival. Numerous tribes, all farmers or nomads, lived here in relative peace for
thousands of years. Nicaragua's fertile earth, large lakes, and prominent position on
the land bridge connecting México with South America, made it a natural settlement
for nomadic tribes heading north or south. The earliest evidence of human presence in
the area, the fossilized Acahualinca footprints in Managua, is nearly 10,000 years old.
According to scientists, the prints were probably made by people fleeing to Lake Man-

285

Nicaragua

HONDURAS

Comayagua

Tegucigalpa

EL
SALVADOR

San Miguel

Ocotal

Ciudad
Antigua

Somoto
El Espino

San Rafael
del Norte

Golfo de Choluteca
Fonseca
Punta
El Rosario
Punta Ñata   Potosí
Punta Cosigüina   **Volcán Cosigüina**
Mochipa
Estero Padre Ramos   Las Zorros
La Bocana
Jiquilillo

Estelí

Somotillo

Lago de
Apanas

Jinotega

Salto
Estanzuela

Río   El Sauce
Grande

Volcán
San Cristóbal

Matagalpa

Sébaco

El Viejo

Chinandega

Ciudad
Dario

Casas
Viejas

Esquipula

Volcán
Telica

San Jacinto

Volcán Cerro Negro
Volcán Momotombo

Santa

Corinto

León

Puerto Momotombo

Bo

Poneloya

La Paz
Centro

I. Momotombito

Lago de
Managua

Tipitapa

Puerto Sandino

El Velero

Managua

Nindiri

P.N. VOLCÁN
MASAYA

Masaya

Diriamba

Granada

Masachapa

Jinotepe

San Juán de Orien

Nandaime

Pochomil

I. Zapate

La Boquita Casares

OCÉANO
PACÍFICO

Huehuete

Moyogalpa

A.
Vol

Rivas

San
Jorge

C

Per
Bla

San Juán
del Sur

El Ostional

Coco

Río

N

0   50 miles

0   75 km

286

Nicaragua

Cabo Gracias
a Dios

Río Coco

Leimus

Waspam

Laguna
Bismuna

San Carlos

Río Wawa

Laguna
Páhara

Punta
Gorda

Bonanza

La Rosita

Puerto
Cabezas

Siuna

Laguna de
Wounta

Río Tuma

Río Grande

de MISKITOS

COSTA DE Matagalpa

MAR
CARIBE

Laguna
de
Perlas

Laguna
de Perlas

Punta de
Perlas

I. de Maiz
Pequeña

Islas del Maiz

I. de Maiz
Grande

Rama

Juigalpa

Villa
Sandino

Río Mico

Santo
Tomás

Río Escondido

El Bluff

Bluefields

Bahía de
Bluefields

Rama
Cay

Lago de
Nicaragua
Nica

Concepción
que
Ometepe
la

Morrito

Punta
Mono

San Miguelito

Archipiélago
de Solentiname

Bahía
Punta
Gorda

San Carlos

Castillo
Viejo

Río San Juán

San Juán
del Norte

COSTA RICA

agua to escape a volcanic eruption. Though their cultures never advanced to the level of the pre-Columbian civilizations of México and Guatemala (which explains the lack of impressive ruins here), the indigenous inhabitants of Nicaragua were highly skilled craftspeople, creating intricate stone carvings, pottery, and gold jewelry.

It was the gold, of course, that eventually drew the Spanish to Nicaragua. Columbus sailed down Nicaragua's Caribbean coast in 1502 and claimed the territory for the Spanish crown. The conquistadors eventually established two major colonial settlements—Granada, on the shore of Lake Nicaragua in the south, and León, on the northern Lake Managua. The invaders set the conquered tribes to mining gold for the Spanish treasury, but the gold reserves were quickly depleted. Granada, which had access to the Atlantic via the Río San Juan, remained prosperous as a trading and commercial center. León, however, didn't fare as well. An earthquake destroyed the city in 1610, and it was saved from complete obscurity only because it was named the capital of the colonial province.

When independence came in 1821, the two cities were sharply polarized along family and political lines. Granada was home to the Conservatives, who held to traditional pro-monarchy and pro-clerical views. Their rivals, the León-based Liberals, promoted anti-clerical policies and advocated a political arrangement based on the examples of the revolutions in France and the United States. The conflict between the two factions was to drive Nicaraguan politics for nearly a century, erupting several times into outright civil war. Meanwhile, both the United States and Britain coveted Nicaragua as a place to do business and as a possible site for a canal linking the Pacific with the Caribbean. The California gold rush in 1849 added to the pressure for an interoceanic passage, so the U.S. millionaire Cornelius Vanderbilt established the Accessory Transit Company to take passengers overland and by river between Nicaragua's two coasts.

The Liberals, in a risky bid to seize power, invited filibusterer William Walker to join them in a battle against the Conservatives. Walker, a lawyer and doctor from Tennessee, styled himself a crusader for U.S. supremacy in Latin America. He arrived in Nicaragua in 1855, fresh from his summary ejection from Baja California, México, after declaring himself president there. Walker landed with 56 troops recruited in the bars and brothels of San Francisco, gathered a few more Liberal recruits, and marched to Granada, taking it easily. The Liberals were finally in power, but they got more than they bargained for from Walker. He declared himself president of Nicaragua, and the United States immediately recognized his government. He then instituted slavery to gain favor with U.S. slave states, declared English the official language, and put the country up as collateral for a huge loan. Walker's ambition, however, soon got the best of him. He announced his intention to conquer the rest of Central America and, most fatally, seized Vanderbilt's transportation company for himself. Vanderbilt and the U.S. government turned against him, and he was defeated at Rivas in 1857, where he surrendered to the U.S. Navy to avoid capture by Central American forces. Never knowing when to quit, Walker returned to Central America in 1860 in an attempt to conquer Honduras, where he was captured and executed.

The bizarre tale of American William Walker, the late-19th century wanna be dictator of Central America weirdo, was the subject of Walker, *a film by Alex Cox, director of* Repo Man.

With the defeat of Walker in 1857, the Conservatives regained power and moved the country's capital to Managua, originally a tiny settlement of fishermen and farmers. Before long, the competing factions were again at each other's throats in a rapidly escalating civil war. The United States seized this opportunity and landed Marines in 1912 to occupy the country in the name of "protecting American lives and property." The Marines stayed until 1925, installing and ousting presidents at will. They returned in 1927 after feuding between the Liberals and Conservatives threatened another civil war. During their second occupation of Nicaragua, the Marines encountered fierce resistance from a guerrilla army led by Augusto César Sandino. Sandino, a fierce nationalist, had grown tired of U.S. domination of Nicaragua and entered an alliance with Liberal leaders to fight the U.S. invasion and restore the Liberals to power, believing they would ensure Nicaragua's independence. The Liberals, however, soon concluded a pact with the Conservatives at the urging of the U.S. ambassador, and Sandino and his men were left to fight the occupation alone.

The "crazy little army," as the U.S. press dubbed Sandino's forces, fought a brutal war with the Marines over the next six years, and Sandino's guerrilla tactics made out-right U.S. victory impossible. Taking heavy losses in a war that was increasingly unpopular back home, the Marines withdrew in 1935 but left behind a well-trained and well-equipped army, called the National Guard (*Guardia Nacional*), under the command of Anastasio Somoza García. The withdrawal convinced Sandino to lay down his arms, and a year later Somoza invited Sandino for talks in Managua. As Sandino left the meeting, Somoza ordered his troops to ambush the rebel leader and kill him. Sandino's death at the hands of Somoza, as well as his resistance to U.S. occupation, made him the country's most enduring heroic figure.

Somoza, either directly or through figurehead presidents, ruled the country ruthlessly for the next 20 years. In the process, he appropriated for himself and his family most of Nicaragua's prime property and commercial interests. As a loyal ally of the United States and a strong guarantor of stability, he enjoyed unwavering support from succes-sive U.S. administrations, Republican and Democrat. Franklin Roosevelt pithily summed up official U.S. policy with his remark about Somoza: "He may be a son of a bitch, but he's *our* son of a bitch." Somoza's venality provoked strong resentment among many Nicaraguans, and he, in turn, felt little affection for most of his people. His government made no effort to pro-vide the poor majority with health care, clean water, electric-ity, or education. Under his rule, Nicaragua continually placed at or near the bottom of the list of Latin American countries in quality-of-life indicators. Finally, in 1956, Nicaraguan poet Rigoberto López Pérez could take no more: He arrived at a diplomatic party in León disguised as a waiter and shot the dictator before he himself died in a hail of bullets. Somoza was succeeded by his older son, Luís Somoza Debayle, who ruled until his death in 1967; Luís' younger brother, Anastasio Somoza Debayle, then assumed the presidency. Can you see the pattern?

Touring a school for the poor in Costa Rica, Somoza commented impatiently, "I don't want educated people, I want oxen."

The corrupt and repressive Somoza dynasty continued to provoke widespread discon-tent. In 1961, Carlos Fonseca Amador, a prominent student leader, founded the *Frente Sandinista de Liberación Nacional* (Sandinista National Liberation Front), or FSLN, in honor of Augusto Sandino. Members of the FSLN, known as Sandinistas, campaigned against Somoza under constant threat of harassment, exile, torture, and death; this threat, as well as the FSLN's staunch socialist ambitions, kept their ranks small at first. But the younger Anastasio soon proved more clumsy and ruthless than his father. His greed especially began to irritate wealthy Nicaraguans, who wanted a larger share in the country's economy. Not satisfied with his already enormous wealth, the younger Anastasio went to the extreme of pocketing most of the relief money that poured into the country after the 1972 earthquake that leveled Managua and left 300,000 homeless. Some of the country's most prominent citizens then turned against the dictator, but their resistance was limited mostly to appeals for help to the U.S. ambassador. The Sandinistas, however, took a more direct approach and began mounting a serious guerrilla insurgency. With each Sandinista success, Somoza stepped up his campaign of repression against a populace he viewed with greater and greater suspicion. In 1976, Carlos Fonseca, the FSLN's founder, was captured and killed.

The increased repression and escalating guerrilla war provoked more active resistance to Somoza among Nicaragua's elite, who believed that peace would only come with the dictator's departure. One of the more prominent conservatives, Pedro Joaquín

Chamorro, publisher of *La Prensa,* Nicaragua's most popular newspaper, began openly calling for Somoza's resignation. In 1978, Chamorro was shot and killed by plain-clothes soldiers as he drove to work. His death sparked a national revolt, and nearly the entire country, including large segments of the wealthy elite, began supporting the Sandinista insurgency. The Sandinistas captured the national imagination with a daring takeover of the National Palace in Managua in 1978, where they held the 1,000-member National Assembly hostage, demanding a huge ransom and the publication and broadcast of their political program. Somoza had little choice but to grant their demands, and the country reacted in support of the FSLN with a crippling general strike. Still, Somoza refused to step down, ordering instead the indiscriminate bombing of cities held by the rebels and increased repression. The Carter administration in the United States, realizing Somoza wouldn't last and fearing a Sandinista takeover, desperately attempted to negotiate a solution that would ensure Somoza's departure while leaving the country firmly in the control of the National Guard and the conservative elite. Events, however, had gone too far. In June 1979, when the U.S. TV audience watched National Guard soldiers execute ABC newsman Bill Stewart in downtown Managua, much of the U.S. public began sympathizing with the Sandinista cause. Isolated and defeated, Somoza fled to Miami, taking with him his father's coffin and the national treasury. Two days later, on July 19, 1979, the FSLN marched victoriously into Managua.

In 1979, the Somoza dynasty came to an end. Its final patriarch, Anastasio Jr., fled to Miami with his father's coffin and the national treasury.

The costs of victory, however, were severe—tens of thousands dead or wounded, a bankrupt treasury, and the country's economy and infrastructure in ruins. Even with no further disasters, the FSLN's work seemed hopeless. Nevertheless, the Sandinistas began to reorganize the state and economy to serve the needs of the poor majority who formed the bulk of their constituency. They also left room for private enterprise, without which, they believed, a diverse economy would not be possible. Their early successes in raising living standards triggered a steady influx of international volunteers.

Disaster, however, wasn't long in coming, this time in the policies of Ronald Reagan. After his inauguration in January 1981, U.S. posture toward the Sandinistas changed from wary suspicion to active hostility. The new president and State Department thought the Sandinistas' leftist ideology, and the fact that they eventually turned to Cuba and the USSR for military and economic aid, foreshadowed a "domino effect" that would spread communism throughout the Western Hemisphere. Reagan's administration began organizing the remnants of the National Guard into a guerrilla army to harass the Sandinistas and prevent the realization of their socialist vision.

The Sandinistas' war with Reagan's *contras* (from the Spanish *contrarevolucionarios*) raged on throughout the 1980s, consuming Nicaragua's resources. It also forced a Sandinista alliance with the Soviet Union and East Bloc that was closer than the FSLN claimed it wanted. As revelations surfaced in the United States about contra brutality and CIA involvement in patently illegal acts, the U.S. Congress grew uneasy with Reagan's Nicaraguan policy and cut off funds to the contras. Reagan's obsession with the Sandinistas, however, proved too strong, and his administration organized an intricate covert network to supply the contras. The network included a clever scheme operation whereby profits from secret arms sales to Iran, supposedly a sworn enemy of the U.S., were used to fund the contras. When this operation became public in 1986, Reagan faced the most severe political scandal since Nixon's Watergate.

Nevertheless, U.S. support for the contras' cause continued; as the war dragged on, the people of Nicaragua began to express discontent with the Sandinistas. The regime was criticized by the Catholic hierarchy, which saw the Sandinistas as Godless communists, patently hostile to the Church's power and position in society (which wasn't far from the truth). Other Nicaraguans were put off by what they considered the inappropriate amount of power wielded by the party's directorate, which amounted to a small handful of educated men. This pissed off quite a few women, as well as rank-and-file party members who desired a more democratic organization. The Sandinistas claimed they wanted a more inclusive structure, but that the ongoing war prevented them from opening up the decision-making process. Hurricane Hugo, which struck Nicaragua's Atlantic coast in 1988 with devastating effects, only contributed to the country's problems.

The Nicaraguan elections in February 1990—part of a regional peace accord engineered by Costa Rican president Oscar Arias—proved decisive. The country's conservative elite, with support from the United States and Nicaragua's Catholic Church, united in a coalition with a broad range of political parties to promote the candidacy of Violeta Chamorro, widow of the martyred Pedro Chamorro, who was killed by Somoza in 1978. Chamorro's campaign for the presidency against Daniel Ortega, the Sandinista leader, benefitted from the widely held perception that only her victory would ensure an end to the U.S. war and economic blockade, a perception confirmed by U.S. President George Bush shortly before the elections.

Under these conditions, victory for Chamorro and her coalition, known as UNO (United Nicaraguan Opposition or *Unión Nicaragüense Opositora*), was practically assured. The FSLN suffered a resounding defeat in an election monitored by an unprecedented number of international observers. The Sandinistas, though stunned, followed through with an orderly transition of government to UNO. Once in power, Chamorro quickly found herself facing crisis after crisis. Confrontations between her government and Sandinista-affiliated labor unions over economic austerity policies have often turned violent. Her own coalition, united only in its opposition to the Sandinistas, has fallen into bitter in-fighting and has begun to unravel; some factions are now in a de facto alliance with the FSLN, while others, including Chamorro's own vice-president, attack her from the right. If this weren't enough, bands of former contras, in some cases allied with Sandinista militants, have rearmed to force the government to fulfill its promises of land and jobs. Other former contras roam Managua and the countryside, committing violent assaults and robbing highway passengers.

Through the crises, however, Chamorro has shown herself to be more astute and independent than most gave her credit for. Her decision to retain prominent Sandinista Humberto Ortega, brother of Daniel Ortega, as army chief incensed the rightists in her coalition, but it reassured the Sandinistas that Chamorro was willing to work with them and had no plans to use the army to harass the opposition as in El Salvador, Guatemala, and Honduras. Still, in order to receive

After the Sandinista takeover, the CIA became actively involved in a campaign of sabotage against key Nicaraguan ports and industrial facilities.

U.S. and International Monetary Fund assistance, Chamorro had to institute an economic policy of severe austerity and "structural adjustment"—featuring currency devaluations, reduction of import barriers, budget cuts, and privatization of the economy—that hit the poor majority with devastating effect.

Because of her policies, unemployment has reached crisis levels (some estimates put it at 70%), wages have fallen, and health care has been rolled back. The result is the reappearance and rapid spread of chronic malnutrition, cholera, measles, and other devastating health problems. Crime, delinquency, and alcoholism are also becoming chronic problems in the "new" Nicaragua. The economic siege has also decimated the nation's arts and culture, which flourished under generous Sandinista funding during the 1980s; most museums have closed, theater groups and dance troupes have disbanded, and the arts community is in total disarray.

With a "pro-business" government now in power, the rich, who fled to the United States to escape the Sandinistas' socialism, are flocking back, with their luxury cars, U.S. consumer habits, and hardened right-wing attitudes. Their *dinero*, however, is staying in Miami banks—you can never be too safe, after all. Many came back to reclaim businesses and property confiscated by the prior government and handed over to state cooperatives and *campesinos* (rural folk). The conflict over the legality of these confiscations is now one of the most divisive issues in Nicaraguan politics today. Prominent members of the U.S. Senate, most notably Jesse Helms, seized on the issue to order a freeze of U.S. aid until the Chamorro government returns all property to the former owners. The Clinton Administration, apparently satisfied with Chamorro's efforts, reinstated the aid.

The explosive political situation and rapid overhaul of economic and social arrangements have created a palpable, frightening tension in the country. Travelers are likely to experience this in the form of unfriendliness and, at times, open hostility. As for physical safety, the closer you are to large cities or the Pacific coast, the farther you'll be from eruptions of violence; this is basically a guerrilla war, fought mostly in remote jungles and mountains. Especially along the northern border with Honduras, where bands of "*re*contras" and government troops have been butting heads lately, the exact locations of battlegrounds change constantly. Keep up on the news of the day: Read the paper; talk to other travelers; and, if you have your ears open, you'll always hear Nicaraguans discussing this month's hot spot. You should definitely visit your country's embassy in Managua: Take lightly their suggestions to hop on the next plane out of the country or hole up in the Managua Sheraton, but pump them for info about current conditions. They send officials all over Nicaragua to do their duties, so they really know the difference between manageable tensions and downright danger. Also, consider registering with them before setting out into sticky areas. Anywhere you go, be especially careful in any encounter with drunks. The macho culture is at full strength in Nicaragua, which means many men will resort to violence at the least provocation, especially if they've had too much to drink.

Listing Nicaragua's problems like this may make it sound like a traveler's hell, and at times it is. But being aware of the situation only makes the idealism and intensity of many Nicaraguans that much more impressive. The people now face a present and future that look no brighter than the past. That so many Nicaraguans still live with hope and humanity is no small miracle. Hope never seems to die in Nicaragua, though no one could blame Nicaraguans if it did.

Basics

See Chapter 1 for important info pertaining to Nicaragua.

VISITOR INFORMATION

➤ **TOURIST OFFICES** • Instituto Nicaragüense de Turismo, or **Inturismo,** is the government tourist office. Their Managua office is about as good as it gets in Nicaragua—unfortunately, that's not very good. They spend most of their time organizing business delegations and have little info or patience for individual travelers. They sell maps and sometimes have other useful tourist publications. Inturismo has a few other offices around the country.

Marazul Tours in New York is probably the most knowledgeable U.S.-based travel agency working with Nicaragua. They can find cheap air-fares and help with hotel and rental-car reservations. *250 W. 57th St., Suite 1311, New York, NY 10107, tel. 212/586–3847 or 800/223–5334.*

➤ **RESOURCES FOR WOMEN TRAVERLERS** • Nicaragua's most visible and active women's organization, **AMNLAE** (Asociación de Mujeres Nicaragüense "Luisa Amanda Espinoza"), publishes a monthly magazine, *Nosotras,* on events and activities of interest to women (available at their office and in some bookstores). They can also help women in distress or those who just want further contacts in Nicaragua. They also maintain a list of *casas de mujeres* throughout the country where women can get medical aid, counseling, and other assistance. AMNLAE can also put travelers in touch with groups that represent homosexuals. *From the front gate of the Universidad de Centroamérica (UCA) in Managua, walk 1 block west and 1½ blocks south, tel. 02/75911. Open weekdays 9–5.*

➤ **VOLUNTEERING** • Many organizations continue to seek volunteers for development and work-brigade projects. Those with technical skills will have an easier time obtaining a position. In Managua, would-be volunteers should head to the **Casa Ben Linder** (3 blocks south and 1½ blocks east of the Estatua Monseñor Lezcano, tel. 02/664373), where an assortment of international and U.S.-based solidarity groups have offices. A few groups in the United States are still actively recruiting volunteers for work in Nicaragua. Try **APSNICA,** Architects and Planners in Support of Nicaragua (Box 1151, Topanga, CA 90290, tel. 213/455–1340), or **TECNICA** (3254 Adeline St., Berkeley, CA 94703, tel. 510/655–3838), which both help place professionals and technicians in volunteer jobs. The **Nicaragua Center for Community Action** (2140 Shattuck Ave., Box 2063, Berkeley, CA 94704, tel. 510/428–2146) organizes work brigades to live and work in rural areas twice a year in January and July. A three-week trip, which includes meetings with political organizations in Nicaragua and room and board with a family, costs about $400 plus airfare.

➤ **STUDYING** • Those wishing to study Spanish have a wide range of options. The Nicaraguan Ministry of External Cooperation has a language course for foreigners that includes lodging with a family plus excursions. In Managua, contact **MCE Escuela de Lenguas** (Plaza España, tel. 02/664099). **Nahuatli** (2330 West 3rd St., Suite 4, Los Angeles, CA 90057, tel. 213/386–8077) offers two- to eight-week language courses that include meetings with representatives from various political groupings in Nicaragua. The **Universidad de Centroamérica,** or UCA (Departamento de Lenguas, Apartado 69, tel. 02/70352, ext. 238), offers Spanish-language courses for foreigners three times a year in Managua. UCA is the cheapest option; an eight-week course costs $100. Some smaller schools also advertise in the classified section of the major Nicaraguan dailies.

WHEN TO GO Nicaragua's climate varies greatly between regions. The Atlantic coast and Mosquitia lowlands are piping hot and almost constantly rainy—the "dry season" lasts only March–May and still sees a lot of rain. The wet season in the cooler central mountain region is May–January, and in the scorching Pacific lowland zone (including Managua) it rains May–November. March and April are the hottest months along the Pacific, and some beach towns raise lodging prices for the larger dry-season crowds.

➤ **HOLIDAYS AND FESTIVALS** • July 19 is **Revolution Day,** celebrating the fall of Somoza. The FSLN puts on big rallies in major towns throughout the country, but the real party is in Managua, where tens of thousands gather in the Plaza de la Revolución. Every town, even the most humble hamlet, celebrates one or two **patron-saint festivals** (*fiestas patronales*) a year. The typical festival features fireworks, parades, beauty pageants, macho rodeos, dances, and lots of public (male) drunkenness. The most noteworthy festivals take place in Managua (August 1–10), León (last week of September), Granada (last two weeks of August), Masaya (end of September), and Jinotepe (third or fourth week of July). Most restaurants post a Victoria Beer calendar, which gives the dates of the country's patron-saint festivals; check it out for exact dates. Managua also hosts **El Repliegue,** usually during the last weekend in June. It's a decidedly nonreligious celebration of a tactical retreat by the Sandinistas during the last weeks of the revolution. Sandinista cadres led supporters in Managua on an overnight march to Masaya to save them from a National Guard onslaught. The annual celebration is a wild, drunken re-creation that will fatigue even the most party-hearty.

MONEY In Managua, you'll find casas de cambio everywhere ready to trade your dollars for córdobas. Most are private businesses offering better rates than state banks. No commission is usually charged to exchange cash dollars, but you'll pay about 2% (or more) to exchange traveler's checks. For a similar commission, many places will also give you dollars for U.S. traveler's checks. Outside Managua, the only official avenue of exchange is usually a state bank, often called **Banco Nacional de Desarrollo (BND),** which exchanges *only dollars* at official rates. Carrying U.S. dollars in cash (preferably in denominations of $20 or less) in Nicaragua is essential if you plan to leave Managua, since few places outside the capital exchange traveler's checks, and other currencies are not accepted. **Cred-o-Matic** (Multicentro Camino de Oriente, Managua, tel. 02/72362) is the only place in the country where you can use Visa or MasterCard to get a cash advance. Changing money through the black market (changers are called *coyotes*) is ostensibly illegal but widely practiced. Once I even saw a police officer giving a black marketeer change for a large bill so the coyote could complete his transaction. In reality, you'll get a rate that's no better than the best private rate, but when the only option in town is a state bank, the black market is often a better deal. Because the Nicaraguan currency is so unstable, prices in the book are given in U.S. dollars.

➢ **CURRENCY** • Nicaragua's monetary unit is the *córdoba,* divided into 100 *centavos.* There are no coins, just bills of 1 to 1,000 córdobas. Centavos come in small-sized bills of 5, 10, 25, and ½ córdoba (50 centavos). In rural areas, locals sometimes speak of *reales,* equivalent to 10 centavos (so 5 reales is 50 centavos or half a córdoba).

PHONES AND MAIL Telcor, the combined post office and telecommunications center in most Nicaraguan towns, is about the only option if you don't have access to a private phone, as you won't find a single pay phone in the country. You can make collect calls at any Telcor, but rates are very expensive (about $5 per minute to the United States). Most local calls are less than 10¢ a minute. Interregional calls (outside your city's telephone code) are about 60¢ a minute. To call a number outside your city, dial the city code and phone number. For example, to call Managua from León, dial 02 (Managua's city code) and the number. Going through the **AT&T USA Direct** operator (dial 64 in Managua or 02/64 outside Managua) is a cheaper way to make collect calls to the United States.

For mail, Telcor is cheap but inefficient. An airmail letter to the United States is about 50¢, but can take up to three weeks to arrive. Prices to Europe or Australia are slightly higher. To receive mail, have letters addressed to you at Lista de Correos, Telcor (town name), (name of department), Nicaragua. Most offices hold mail for three weeks, and you need I.D. to collect it.

COMING AND GOING

➢ **BY PLANE** • The following phone numbers are for the airline companies' offices in Managua. Four airlines provide service to and from the United States: **American** (Plaza España, tel. 02/663900), **Continental** (tel. 02/661030), **Aviateca** (tel. 02/662898), and **Nica** (tel. 02/31762). Service to and from Europe is provided by **Iberia** (Plaza España, tel. 02/661703) and **Aeroflot** (Plaza España, tel. 02/660565). Connections to Central and South America are provided by **Copa** (tel. 02/675438), **LACSA** (tel. 02/668270), **SAHSA** (tel. 02/664791), and **TACA** (tel. 02/660872).

➢ **BY BUS** • Two bus companies offer connections between Managua and other Central American capitals. **Ticabus** (2 blocks east of Cine Dorado, tel. 02/22096) has service to Tegucigalpa, departing daily at 6 AM (6 hours, $20 one-way); to San José, daily at 7 AM (7 hours, $35 one-way); and to San Salvador, departing daily at 6 AM (8 hours, $35 one-way). You have to buy your ticket the day before. **Sirca** (2 blocks south of the Distribuidora Vicky, tel. 02/763833) has buses departing for San José every Monday, Wednesday, and Friday at 6:30 AM (6 hours, $15 one-way). Tickets should be bought two days in advance.

➢ **BY CAR** • If you're leaving Nicaragua by car, you need to have a transit document (about $20) for your auto. Buy it when you enter Nicaragua, or at the headquarters of the **Policía de Tránsito** in Managua (Mercado Roberto Huembes, tel.

02/59318). If you're trying to leave the country without a transit document, you won't be allowed through the border post (I speak from experience).

➤ **VISAS** • Travelers from Great Britain, Ireland, the United States, Scandinavia, and some other European nations need no visa to enter Nicaragua. Just show up with a valid passport (with at least six months' validity remaining before expiration), and the immigration police will give you a visa valid for 90 days (30 for U.S. citizens). You can extend your stay twice in Nicaragua by visiting **Migración** in Managua (Km. 7 Carretera Sur, tel. 02/50014) and paying a $1 fee for every day you wish to remain. Visitors from other countries will have to obtain visas in advance at their country's Nicaraguan embassy or consulate. Most nationalities need only a valid passport, two photos, and $25 to get a visa. Though everyone entering Nicaragua is technically required to show proof of resources—at least $200—this requirement is rarely enforced. No onward ticket requirements are currently in force, but check before you go.

GETTING AROUND

➤ **BY BUS** • The best bargain in Nicaragua is bus travel; you can literally cross the country for about $4. Trips are usually about 60¢ an hour, though express buses can cost twice or three times that. Even the most far-flung hamlets are usually served by bus or passenger truck (except on the Atlantic coast, where few roads exist). Each town's market usually doubles as a bus depot. Most buses are vintage school buses from the United States, and overcrowding is a serious problem on popular routes.

➤ **BY TRAIN** • Trains, though slower and less comfortable than buses, are usually a little cheaper. Nicaragua's rail network is limited and dilapidated. The major rail line runs from León to Managua and on to Masaya and Granada. A line also runs north of León to several rural communities.

➤ **BY PLANE** • Plane travel within Nicaragua is expensive. Since the national airline, **Nica** (tel. 02/663136), offers no domestic flights, passengers are at the mercy of small private charter companies. A typical one-way fare from Managua to Bluefields on the Atlantic coast is $70. Some charter flights are also available from Puerto Cabezas and Bluefields to points deep in the coastal jungle.

➤ **BY BIKE** • Bike repair shops are common, but parts for high-quality or high-tech bikes are next to impossible to find. Managua has a few bona fide bike-rental shops, as well as places that sell them. Outside the capital, ask at repair shops about possible rentals or purchases. Getting around by bike is possible in the flat Pacific lowlands, but the heat is exhausting. In mountainous regions, be prepared for some *serious* mountains. Most buses will carry a bike on the roof rack for a small fee.

➤ **HITCHING** • Hitching in Nicaragua is getting more competitive; as the cost of living goes up, more people are thumbing to save bus fare. Pickup trucks are the best bet for rides. In general, the best strategy is to hitch on the outskirts of town on the road to your destination. Hitching for men is generally very safe, but women, even with their *amigas,* should exercise a caution approaching paranoia.

➤ **BY CAR** • Getting around by car is easy if you don't mind the adventure of chaotic traffic. A 4x4 is necessary to negotiate most roads during the rainy season. The Interamerican Highway is in need of serious repairs, but the only major hazard is other drivers. Gas costs about twice U.S. prices, but it's widely available on main roads. Managua is the only place to rent a car. U.S. companies are the cheapest; **Budget** has a good deal (offices at the airport and the Hotel Intercontinental, offering a tiny Daihatsu for about $25 a day.

WHERE TO SLEEP
Unless you're okay about living in absolute squalor, expect to pay $3–$7 per person for decent budget accommodations. Most basic hotels are called *hospedajes* in Nicaragua, though some refer to themselves as *casas de huespedes.* A typical one will have concrete floors, two or three small cot-like beds to a

room, and fairly skanky shared bathrooms. For First World amenities you'll pay First World prices ($20 and up per room).

Nicaragua has no formal campgrounds, and the countryside, with its thriving insect life and proprietary pitchfork-wielding farmers, is decidedly inhospitable to campers. Your best bet is the beach, but bring lots of bug repellent and guard your stuff carefully.

FOOD Beef, pork, and chicken are usually served grilled or covered in a ketchupy sauce. For more variety, you'll have to look in pricier restaurants. Seafood is available near the coast and is usually served covered in garlic (*al ajillo*) or tomato sauce (*entomatado*). *Gallo pinto* (literally, painted rooster), a mixture of refried beans and rice, is ubiquitous. *Sopa mondongo* is a tripe soup, only for the gastronomically adventurous. *Nacatamales* are a mixture of cornmeal, pork, tomato, and chile rolled in a corn husk. Many households sell homemade nacatamales on weekends—look for the HAY NACATAMALES sign. Finally, *baho,* a tomato and beef stew, is a typical entry on menus. Roadside stands and market food stalls (*comedores*) manage to serve filling meals of meat or chicken, rice, beans, and salad for $2–$3. In sit-down restaurants, where hygiene is (usually) less of a worry, the cheapest option is to order a *comida corriente*—a daily special featuring (what else?) meat or chicken, rice, beans, and salad—for $3–$4. Ordering off the menu can get expensive in a hurry: Prices start at $5 at the most humble restaurants and climb fast.

➤ **TIPPING** • Tipping is only expected at more expensive restaurants, where it's often included in the bill (look for *servicio* on the check). Since most servers receive only minimal compensation, even a córdoba or two would be a nice gesture at cheaper restaurants. Any stranger who offers to do you a favor (like watch your parked car) expects to be paid.

OUTDOOR ACTIVITIES Nicaragua's poor tourism infrastructure means that few organized opportunities exist for outdoor adventures. A few of the beach towns that see tourist traffic have facilities for renting surfboards, windsurfers, and scuba equipment, but the low supply means pretty high prices. The surfing on either of the country's coasts won't thrill serious surfers. Travelers can sometimes find people willing to rent their boats for deep-sea fishing expeditions, but no companies specialize in the trade. Still, the economic disruption of the last 15 years means that Nicaraguan waters have not been heavily fished, making it a good place to try your luck at landing something big. The volcanoes along the Pacific coast beg to be climbed, but don't charge up the slopes before finding out about trail conditions and volcanic activity. Climbers and hikers should visit **INETER** in Managua to get topographical maps of areas they plan to explore. *Complejo Cívico, Edificio "O", tel. 02/50281. From the National Stadium, take Bus 107 to the Complejo Cívico. Open weekdays 9–5.*

Managua

Grimier than grimy, uglier than ugly, and hotter than hell, Managua is at once grotesque and mesmerizing, impossibly frustrating, and unforgettably unique. Sitting on the polluted southern shore of Lake Managua, the city is a hopelessly chaotic sprawl of some 600 *barrios* (neighborhoods) that form no coherent whole. The city's "center," levelled by the 1972 earthquake that killed as many as 10,000 people, was never rebuilt: Anastasio Somoza Debayle, Nicaragua's most-hated native son, couldn't resist stealing the aid and relief money that poured in from abroad. Today, as a result, downtown Managua is a pathetic, surreal landscape of vacant overgrown lots, crumbling ruins that house homeless families, and a few lonely government buildings overlooking the devastation. Cities certainly exist that are less physically suited for tourism—like Beirut, perhaps—but you could probably count them on one hand.

Managua

Lake Managua

Exploring

Casa Julio Cortázar, **2**

Museo Huellas de Acahualinca, **3**

Museo Nacional de Nicaragua, **5**

Plaza de la Revolución, **1**

The Ruins, **4**

Lodging

Casa San Juan, **14**

Center for Global Education, **13**

Estancia La Casona, **15**

Hotel El Pueblo, **12**

TO LAGUNA DE XILO

El Triunfo

Pl. de la Revolución

R. Bermúdez

Dupla Norte

Dupla Sur

Train Station

Pista P.J. Chamorro

C. A. Espinoza

Stadium

C. J. Buitrago

Mercado Oriental

SEE DETAIL MAP BELOW

Hotel Intercontinental

Laguna de Tiscapa

Paseo S. Allende

Zeledón

Las Piedrecitas Park

Isreal Lewites Market

R. Ibarra

Carretera Sur

Av. W. Romero

Av. Bolívar

Av. Colón

Av. El Guerrillero

Santo Domingo

Av. C. Sotelo

Pista de la Resistencia

UCA

TO IVÁN MONTENEGRO MARKET

El Chipote

Nuembes Market

Pista de la Solidaridad

Carretera Masaya

Av. Vargas Barres

TO POCHOMIL

N

0   2 miles

0   3 km

Barrio Martha Quezada

Hospedaje Carlos, **9**

Hospedaje Meza, **8**

Hospedaje Norma, **7**

Hospedaje Santos, **6**

Hotel Morgut, **11**

Managua's Inn, **10**

0   300 yards

0   300 meters

N

C. Julio Buitrago

Av. Williams Romero

Fábrica El Triunfo

Av. Bolívar

TO HOTEL INTERCONTINENTAL

Cine Dorado

Tica-Bus Terminal

Still, for those who come here with extra reserves of adventure and patience, Managua, or more accurately Managuans, will slowly and steadily charm you. Far away from the center, in each of the city's barrios, life pulses with a dizzying intensity. Managuans, all one million of them, live life with a fierceness that few of the rest of us can ever match and that stubbornly defies the dreariness of their surroundings. For the adventurous traveler, there is more to see and do here than you'd think. Built for neither comfort nor speed, however, Managua will make you work hard to find her treasure. The timorous and the impatient should stay away.

Present-day Managua sits on the site of an ancient *indígena* fishing village whose inhabitants refused to submit peacefully to the Spanish. In return, the Spanish destroyed the village. Years later, after independence, Nicaragua's competing political factions, the Liberals and Conservatives, agreed to relocate the nation's capital from Liberal León to Managua, which lay roughly halfway between León and Conservative Granada. Soon the factions were fighting again, turning the capital into a bloody battleground in Nicaragua's ongoing civil conflict. Managua has weathered political violence again and again through the years, but none so serious as that which occurred during the Sandinistas' insurrection against the Somoza dictatorship in the 1970s. Near the end, with Somoza facing inevitable defeat, the dictator ordered the indiscriminate bombing of whole barrios. The city, already heavily damaged by the 1972 earthquake, could ill afford more destruction.

After Somoza's overthrow, the Sandinistas concocted grand plans for reconstructing the city, but, in many eyes, these were shelved as Reagan's war on Nicaragua made survival, not urban planning, the government's overwhelming priority. Not all was bleak in Managua, however, during the Sandinista years. The city became home to a burgeoning international population of volunteers, café socialists, artists, Latin American political exiles, and simple adventurers. Managua in the 1980s, by all accounts, was a magical cultural event. Managua in the 1990s is certainly less wondrous than it was a few years ago, but you'll still find magic here if you dig for it. Volunteers from abroad, especially from Europe, still come in droves to try to help Nicaragua create a decent future, and Managua is still one of the most important political capitals in Latin America. And where there's politics in Latin America, there's art, music, literature, cinema, and intensely passionate people. Though it may not have a single bona fide tourist attraction, Managua is a place of endless fascination. If the place ends up driving you crazy, though, don't say I didn't warn you.

BASICS

AMERICAN EXPRESS You know you're in hostile tourist territory when there's no American Express office in the country. Nicaragua, along with places like Albania and North Korea, is one of the few countries on earth American Express has shunned. Interpret that as you will.

MONEY You'll see little difference between the rates offered by the various casas de cambio throughout town, and few of them charge a commission unless you want to convert U.S. traveler's checks into dollars (2% commission). Most casas de cambio are open weekdays 8–noon and 2–6, but some open on Saturday mornings as well. The front desk of the **Intercontinental Hotel** will change U.S. dollars *only* at any time for only a slightly worse rate than casas de cambio. Near Barrio Martha Quezada, Managua's budget-travel headquarters is **Multicambios** (Plaza España, tel. 02/22576); it's on the east side of Plaza España, where Avenida Williams Romero and Pista Benjamín Zeledón meet. Also at Plaza España is the main branch of **Banco Mercantil** (tel. 02/668228). **Intercambios** (Plaza de Compras, tel. 02/73471), in the Colonia Centroamérica in the southern part of the city, offers friendly service but no better rates than the others. Many places around the city that specialize in sending dollars to and from the United States also change dollars at standard rates. **Pinolero Delivery** (1½ blocks west of the Central Sandinista de Trabajadores at the northwest corner of Barrio Martha Quezada) is the largest.

EMBASSIES **United States.** It's worth a trip here just to hear them tell you it's not safe to travel outside the capital or to be out in Managua after dark. No telling what these hacks would say if they had an embassy in Los Angeles—"Move to Des Moines," perhaps? Still, if you're a U.S. citizen planning extensive travel in the countryside, you should come in to register in case of accident or other emergency. *Barrio Batahola Sur, Km. 4½ Carretera Sur, tel. 02/666010. From Hotel Intercontinental take Bus 113 or 116 to the Batahola Sur stop and walk back two blocks.*

Canada. *In front of Telcor Central, tel. 02/24541. Open weekdays 9–noon and 2–4.*

United Kingdom. *Main entrance to Los Robles, 4th house on the right, tel. 02/70034. Open weekdays 9–noon and 2–4.*

Australia. *Barrio Bolonia, 1 block west and ½ block north of Los Pipitos, tel. 02/22056. Open weekdays 9–4.*

EMERGENCIES **Police** (tel. 11); **fire** (tel. 23184); **Red Cross** (tel. 51761) offers **ambulance** and emergency medical service and can help you find an English-speaking doctor.

LAUNDRY Almost every hospedaje will hand-wash your clothes for a price, or at least let you use the basin to do your own. Prices vary but are considerably cheaper than **Lavamatic.** Managua's one laundromat will wash and dry your clothes for about $6 for 12 pounds. *1 block south of the Linda Vista stoplights, tel. 02/660837. From a block south of Telcor, take Bus 112 to Linda Vista. Open Mon.–Sat. 7–7.*

PHONES AND MAIL Managua's communications headquarters is the **Telcor** building, just west of Plaza de la Revolución near the lake—look for the ugly building with a large antenna. The main post office is here (open weekdays 8–5), offering airmail, telex, telegraph, fax, and express-package service. You can also rent a mailbox here if you're staying in town for a while. The same building offers local and international telephone service (open 8 AM–10 PM daily). You can't use the AT&T service here, but the connections are good, nevertheless. Smaller Telcor offices are peppered throughout Managua, including one at the Huembes market.

MEDICAL AID Managua's **public hospitals** treat all patients at no cost. Some people warn against them, while others find them competent and helpful. With luck, you won't have to find out. Just in case, though, **Hospital Lenin Fonseca** (Las Brisas, tel. 02/666544) usually gets the best reviews. To get here from Plaza España, take Bus 119 to Las Brisas. **Private hospitals** are more likely to have English-speaking doctors and are certainly better equipped, though also very expensive. The biggest is **Hospital Bautista** (tel. 02/26913), which includes a dental clinic and a 24-hour pharmacy. To get here from the National Stadium, take Bus 118 to RUCFA and walk two blocks south.

VISITOR INFORMATION **Inturismo** barely merits mention. The staff offers little of use to budget travelers, but you can pick up a few glossy brochures or buy a copy of *Guía Fácil* ($1), a monthly guide to goings-on in Managua and the rest of the country. *1 block west of the southern side of Hotel Intercontinental, tel. 02/22498. Open weekdays 9–5, Sat. 9–noon.*

Tur-Nica, Inturismo's travel agency, is more helpful with nuts-and-bolts info but is reluctant to help unless you're a paying customer. For a fee, they can call ahead to hospedajes to make reservations. *200 yards south of Plaza España, tel. 02/661387. Open weekdays 9–5, Sat. 9–noon.*

COMING AND GOING

BY TRAIN Managua's train station (tel. 02/22802), a few blocks east of the Rubén Darío Theater, serves León, Masaya, and Granada. Trains to León depart daily at 7:30 AM, 11 AM, and 6 PM (3 hours, $1). Trains to Granada via Masaya leave at 8 AM, 1:30 PM, and 6 PM (2 hours, $1).

BY BUS

➤ **HUEMBES MARKET** • This market contains the "Casimiro Sotelo" bus terminal, with buses serving Masaya, Granada, Rivas, Matagalpa, Estelí, Ocotal, Somoto, and smaller towns near these cities. Most buses start running at 5 AM and leave every 30 minutes to an hour until 5 or 6 PM. Buses to Masaya, however, leave every 10 minutes until 10 PM (45 minutes, 60¢). Granada-bound buses follow the same schedule (1 hour, 60¢). Buses to Ocotal leave only at 7 AM (4 hours, $4), 8:45 AM, and 2 PM (6 hours, $2). *From Plaza España, take Bus 119 to the market.*

➤ **ISRAEL LEWITES MARKET** • The bus depot at this market serves points to the northwest, including León, Chinandega, and Corinto; points on the coast, like Pochomil; and a few points to the southeast, such as Diriamba and Jinotepe. Most buses here begin service at 6 AM and run until 5 or 6 PM. If riding to León, make sure you get on a bus taking the new highway unless you want to add time and discomfort to your journey. Buses to León leave every 20 minutes 5:30 AM–7 PM (2 hours via Calle Nueva, $2). *From Huembes market, take Bus 110.*

➤ **IVAN MONTENEGRO MARKET** • Buses to and from Boaco, Juigalpa, and Rama use this market as a depot. Buses to Juigalpa leave every ½ hour 5 AM–5:30 PM (3 hours, $2); buses to Boaco leave hourly 5 AM–4 PM (2½ hours, $2); and buses to Rama, connecting with the boat to Bluefields, leave at 2:30 AM every Tuesday, Thursday, Saturday, and Sunday (8 hours, $3). You should show up by 10 PM to get a seat on the Rama-bound bus. *From UCA, take Bus 110.*

HITCHING Hitching out of Managua can be a nightmare. The demand for rides often far exceeds the number of willing drivers, and you can easily spend hours standing on the side of the road inhaling big black clouds of exhaust. The smartest strategy is to take an inter-urban bus heading toward your destination and get off at the outskirts of Managua. You'll have less competition and will be in a position to catch a later bus headed in your direction if luck isn't on your side.

BY PLANE Managua's **Augusto Sandino Airport** sits a few miles east of the ruined city center on the Carretera Norte. It handles domestic charters and international flights (*see* country Basics, *above*). The airport has no currency exchange, but you can pay for everything with dollars until you get to a casa de cambio. The AT&T phone booth, just outside the customs exit, can connect you instantly to a U.S. operator.

➤ **AIRPORT TRANSPORTATION** • The easy way to go to town is to take a taxi, but you'll pay $5–$10 per person. Ridiculously crowded **city buses** stop on the highway in front of the airport on their way to the city center, but if you're silly enough to climb on one of these rolling dens of thieves with your luggage then you probably *deserve* to get everything stolen. The safer way to town is to take an **inter-urban** bus headed into town from Juigalpa, Tipitapa, or somewhere else; all these buses stop in front of the airport (20¢). Passengers on these longer-distance trips are far more likely to be legitimate travelers, minding their own business instead of your back pocket. Most of these buses head to Iván Montenegro market, where you can catch a taxi to almost anywhere in the city for only a dollar or two.

GETTING AROUND

Managua's layout will fluster the most unflappable traveler. The lack of a real center and the huge sprawl make the city unbelievably difficult to navigate. But there is a method through the madness. The center, ruined and deserted, is on the lakeshore in the north part of town. From here, **Avenida Bolívar** runs due south past the **Hotel Intercontinental,** whose pyramidal shape provides a prominent landmark. West of the Intercontinental is **Barrio Martha Quezada,** Managua's budget-travel headquarters, filled with cheap hotels and restaurants. **Avenida Williams Romero** borders the western edge of Barrio Martha Quezada and runs south past **Plaza España,** where you find most airline offices and many exchange offices and banks. A chain of volcanoes starts west of town and is visible from most parts of the city.

BY BUS The only way to figure out the bus system is to ride with someone who knows it or to get your hands on one of the coveted bus maps sometimes available at Inturismo. Buses start running early in the morning and stop around 10 PM, so it's not the way to go for late-night jaunts. Rides cost only about 10¢, but you could end up losing considerably more if you don't guard your wallet or day-pack diligently. Buses 118 and 119, known for the infamous "Managua Massage," are especially notorious.

BY TAXI If you can afford it, taxis are the way to go in Managua: They're quick, convenient, ubiquitous, and not outrageously expensive. Most rides are $1–$2 per person, though many drivers will attempt to charge foreigners double, and prices go up at night. Don't take a taxi from in front of Hotel Intercontinental unless you don't mind paying up to 10 times the standard rate. Since cabs don't have meters, negotiate the fare before you climb in. A good strategy is to announce where you're going and the fare you wish to pay; unless you're off by a lot, most drivers won't argue. Don't be surprised if your driver picks up other passengers along the way, as drivers try to carpool passengers headed in roughly the same direction. Tipping isn't expected.

BIKES Getting around by bike is a viable option if you're ready to face broken streets and homicidal drivers. **Bikes Not Bombs** (in front of the Cementerio Oriental, tel. 02/660235) rents sturdy mountain bikes for about $7 a day plus a $100 deposit.

WHERE TO SLEEP

During the Sandinista years, foreign travelers were restricted to the hotels in or near Barrio Martha Quezada, just west of Hotel Intercontinental. Though this is no longer true, the barrio is still the neighborhood with most of Managua's accommodations.

It's Two Blocks South of Where the Puppy Died Last Week

As in the rest of Nicaragua, addresses in Managua are given as distances from well-known (and not so well-known) reference points. A typical Managuan address might be written as follows: de donde fue el Cine Dorado, 1 c. al lago, ½ c. arriba. Literally, this means: from where the Cine Dorado used to be, 1 block (cuadra) toward the lake (or north) and ½ block up (east). West is often referred to as abajo (down, as in where the sun goes down) and south is sometimes given as a la montaña (toward the mountain). Sometimes varas, an ancient Spanish measurement of a little less than a yard, are used to mark distances in addresses. Good luck (you'll need it bad).

Here you'll find everything from cheap, basic hospedajes to high-cost luxury hotels and guest houses. Though its streets are full of scruffy foreign backpackers, the working- and middle-class neighborhood retains a relaxed and casual pace. In or near the neighborhood you'll find plenty of restaurants, casas de cambio, bars, bakeries, and bus access to most parts of the city. It's also one of Managua's safer neighborhoods, though some predators wander in, tempted by the large foreign population and its dollars. As with elsewhere in Managua, exercise caution when walking at night. Outside Barrio Martha Quezada, the pickings get very slim. Expect to pay a few dollars more for decent lodging or resign yourself to very funky accommodations. Wherever you stay, you'll pay at least $3 a night for anything decent, and prices can get considerably higher.

BARRIO MARTHA QUEZADA

➤ **UNDER $10** • **Hospedaje Santos.** Against all logic, Hospedaje Santos is the most popular budget hotel in Managua. The concrete cell-block rooms have lumpy beds and an active mouse population, the bathrooms can get pretty nasty, and management is prone to dramatic mood swings, but the patio's rocking chairs and hammocks are always filled with hip youngsters from all over the world. It can get pretty rowdy here at night, which is fine if you want to party but a real pain if you're catching that 6 AM bus. The restaurant serves fairly tasty Nicaraguan fare. Singles are $4, larger rooms are $3 per person. *1 block north and ½ block east of the Cine Dorado, tel. 02/23713. From Iván Montenegro market, take Bus 118 to Barrio Martha Quezada and walk ½ block east. 18 rooms, none with bath. Wheelchair access to some rooms.*

Hospedaje Norma. Cheap and basic, with dark rooms that keep little noise out, its two biggest draws are the friendly and helpful management and the price ($3 per person). It also draws lots of foreign travelers but lacks a central patio that would encourage mixing. Bathrooms are shared but clean. *1 block south and ½ block east of Cine Dorado, tel. 02/23498. 16 rooms, none with bath. Midnight curfew, passkey available.*

Hospedaje Meza. This place is bland and basic, with indifferent management and small, dusty rooms. The lack of a patio gives the place a cramped feeling, and the bathrooms need a good cleaning. Still, it's quiet, and only charges $3 a person. *½ block west of Fábrica El Triunfo, and 2 blocks east of Hospedaje Santos, tel. 02/ 22046. 18 rooms, none with bath. 11 PM curfew.*

➤ **UNDER $15** • **Hospedaje Carlos.** Tucked behind a private house, this hotel has clean rooms with comfortable beds. Most guests are traveling Nicaraguans who hang out in the living room watching TV. The family that runs the place is relaxed and friendly. Breakfast is $3, and rooms are $5 per person. *½ block north of the Tica-Bus Terminal, 5 blocks west of the Hotel Intercontinental, house number 735, tel. 02/ 22554. 10 rooms, all with bath. 11 PM curfew.*

➤ **OVER $15** • **Managua's Inn.** This sprawling ranch house rents out large, modern rooms with real beds, sparkling bathrooms, and air-conditioning. Guests roam through the inn as if they were part of the family, and management is professional and helpful. They'll even help you find another place if they're booked up. Rooms are $28 for two or three people (depending on the room), including a big breakfast and free coffee all day. You can even cook your own meals in their large kitchen. *1 block south and 3 blocks east of Cine Dorado, it's the house with double-arched garage, tel. 02/22243. 8 rooms, all with bath. 11 PM curfew.*

Hotel Morgut. This hotel, a favorite of budget-conscious journalists, features huge air-conditioned rooms with private baths in a funky, run-down neo-colonial building. The staff here is professional (if indifferent) and can help you arrange rental cars, airline tickets, and the like. Singles are $35, doubles are $37. All rooms include TV. *From Hotel Intercontinental, walk 2 blocks north and 1 block west, tel. 02/22166. 7 rooms, all with bath.*

➤ **UNDER $15** • **Hotel El Pueblo.** Hotel El Pueblo guarantees a lodging adventure. In a shantytown neighborhood a few blocks west of Managua's enormous Mercado Oriental, the hotel gets good business from slumming backpackers and Nicaraguan couples renting rooms by the hour for quick, um, naps. The building, one of the few in the neighborhood to survive the '72 quake, is a rambling, cavernous, dilapidated structure that offers good views of the devastated city center from its second-story balcony. The management is jovial and thoughtfully provides guests with condoms. The rooms ($6 per person) are huge but their bathrooms are grimy. Be careful in this neighborhood after dark. *4 blocks east of the Parque Luis Alfonso Velásquez, tel. 02/27026. 9 rooms, all with bath. 11 PM curfew, warn management if you expect to come in later. Meals available.*

➤ **OVER $15** • **Center for Global Education.** Those of you missing the U.S. college dorm experience should make a mad dash for this place. The house, headquarters for Augsburg College's travel seminar programs, offers large rooms filled with bunk beds that go for $9 per person. The place is clean and comfortable, and the U.S. staff knows Managua well and will share their knowledge with you. Breakfast ($3) and lunch and dinner (both $5) are served in tasty, ample portions. *1 block east, 1 block south, and ½ block west of the Estatua Montoya, house #1405, tel. 02/24268. 24 beds. No curfew.*

Casa San Juan. Casa San Juan is a quiet, comfortable, homey guest house with incredibly friendly management, large clean rooms with bath ($18 per double), and a wide range of services to help out bewildered tourists. The staff serves a good breakfast ($5), and lunch and dinner are $7. Management will make flight and rental-car reservations and can get rental mini-buses for groups. The place is often full of foreigners, who gather on the plant-filled patio. *Reparto San Juan, calle Esperanza, No. 560, tel. 02/783220. From Plaza España, take Bus 102 to the University of Central America (UCA), walk 1 block west, 2 blocks south and 1 block west. 12 rooms, all with bath. Midnight curfew.*

Estancia La Casona. Estancia La Casona is another small, homey hotel in a comfortable neighborhood just west of Barrio Martha Quezada. Rooms are clean, with air-conditioning and modern bathrooms, and Nicaraguan art hangs on the walls. Breakfast ($4) and lunch and dinner ($6) are served. Doubles go for $35. *1 block north and ½ block west of Restaurante Terraza (house No. 1215), tel. 02/661685. From Plaza España, walk 5 blocks north and ½ block west. 6 rooms, all with bath. Midnight curfew.*

ROUGHING IT Managua—hell, all of Nicaragua—is pretty hostile territory for travelers who want to crash without paying. Just about any place you can think of exposes you to danger of mugging, or worse. Still, some hardy souls head for downtown, where the abandoned shells of buildings provide some shelter. Expect to share them with Nicaraguan families, who may not appreciate your encroachment (try a nice smile). The vacant lots and pastures throughout town host an occasional tent, though this can be a very dangerous ploy. If all else fails, ask to hang your hammock on the patio of a hospedaje.

FOOD

"Managua is changing," or so goes the slogan of the right-wing mayor's office. It used to be you could get dirt-cheap meals from restaurants all over the city offering basically the same menu of meat, rice, and beans. Now, Managua's restaurants offer a wider range of cuisines, but few of them are cheap anymore. Barrio Martha Quezada still has a good selection of places offering palatable, affordable food; outside the neighborhood, the market comedores are your best bet for cheap eats. Beware the row of late-night comedores along the eastern edge of the National Stadium; they're cheap, but you could pay dearly in digestive down-time.

BARRIO MARTHA QUEZADA

➤ **UNDER $5** • **Vecadi.** This unmarked comedor is run by a family out of their converted garage and offers a big selection of meats, vegetable dishes, and salads to huge lunch crowds. The fare changes daily but is always tasty and healthy. Get here before noon to beat the rush. A full plate of food with a fruit juice drink (*refresco*) is just over $2. *From Hotel Intercontinental, walk 1 block north, 5 blocks west, and ½ block north. Wheelchair access. Open Mon.–Sat. 11:30 AM–2 PM.*

Mirna's Pancakes. Mirna and her husband serve a good breakfast of pancakes ($2) or eggs, beans, and rice for about $2. For lunch they do a comida corriente of beef or chicken with rice, beans, and salad for about $3. Don't be surprised if they sit down to chat while you eat. *1 block south and 1 block east of the Cine Dorado, tel. 02/27913. Near Hospedaje Norma. Breakfast and lunch daily.*

Sara's. Sara's isn't what it used to be. In the good ol' days of *sandinismo*, hordes of foreign development workers, anarchists, hippie backpackers, and probably the occasional CIA agent ate, drank, flirted, and fought within its grungy four walls. The crowds today are smaller and the atmosphere is a little subdued, but it's still a good choice for the hungry traveler who wants to meet other foreigners. The menu includes a good selection of dishes, including vegetarian spaghetti ($4), vegetarian curry ($5), and a hearty chicken in tomato sauce ($5). *Next to Tica-Bus, tel. 02/26901. From the Hotel Intercontinental, walk 7 blocks west and 1 block south. Lunch and dinner Mon.–Sat.; dinner only on Sun.*

➤ **UNDER $10** • **El Cipitío.** Founded by a group of Salvadoran refugees during the 1980s, Cipitío used to be a thriving arts and cultural center that served great food. The food's still great, but the restaurant is empty and quiet most nights. Their sea bass with tomato sauce (*corvina en salsa*) is orgasmic but pricey ($7). Spaghetti ($6), avocado salad ($6), and the chicken sandwich ($3) are also delicious. Beer, wine, rum, and juices are also served. *2½ blocks south of the Cine Cabrera, tel. 02/24929. From the Hotel Intercontinental, walk 1 block north, 4 blocks west, and 1½ blocks south. Wheelchair access. Closed Sun.*

➤ **OVER $10** • **Mágica Roma.** Managua has experienced an invasion of upscale Italian restaurants, and this place leads the charge. They serve damn good food, especially if you've been living off rice and beans for weeks. Though Mágica Roma is pricey, dress is fairly casual. The *penne alla vodka* (pasta in bacon, mushroom, and vodka sauce) for $7 is amazing, or try something from the huge selection of pizzas ($7–$10). They also have a decent selection of wine ($3 a glass), and the espresso is very authentic. *½ block west of the south side of the Hotel Intercontinental, tel. 02/27560. Open daily noon–midnight.*

OUTSIDE BARRIO MARTHA QUEZADA **Ananda.** Ananda is a little bit of Berkeley in the heart of Managua, serving a changing menu of macrobiotic vegetarian food in a patio setting. Their salads ($2), soups ($2), specials ($3), and frothy fruit juices ($2) are healthy and better than most non-veggie offerings in this town. A guru owns the place; ask about his Sunday afternoon yoga classes. *Corner opposite the Estatua Montoya. From 3 blocks north of Hotel Intercontinental, take Buses 113 or 116 to Montoya statue. Wheelchair access. Open Mon.–Sat. 7 AM–2 PM.*

Pasta Fresca. Pasta Fresca, run by an Argentinian woman active in Managua's art scene, is a small, cool patio restaurant serving a selection of fresh pasta dishes, including lasagna ($7), cannelloni ($6), and fettuccine ($6) in meat (or meatless) sauces. It's a wonderful place to relax, sip a glass of wine, and forget about hectic Managua. *1 block east and 2 blocks south of the main entrance of UCA, tel. 02/74849. Take Bus 102 from Plaza España. Wheelchair access. Open Tues.–Sat. 10 AM–8 PM.*

El Sagitario. This stylish place, attached to the Videoteca cinema, serves French-like dishes on a pleasant open patio. Enjoy crepes with mushroom sauce ($4), Hollywood salad (with tuna, corn, tomatoes, and onion) for $5, or a good selection of steaks ($6–$8). If you don't feel like eating, just order a drink and watch the (mostly foreign) customers pretend they're in Paris. *From Plaza España, take Bus 102 to Montoya statue and walk 1 block northeast, tel. 02/27092. Wheelchair access. Open Mon.–Sat. noon–4 AM.*

WORTH SEEING

Most of Managua's sights, such as they are, lie within fairly easy walking distance of each other. Thank God, because otherwise you'd spend more time trying to navigate the Managua maze than you would sightseeing. On Avenida Bolívar, a few blocks north of Hotel Intercontinental (where the avenue intersects Calle Julio Buitrago), you can catch Bus 109 up the avenue to the downtown ruins. Here you'll find an eerie broken landscape that holds the Plaza de la Revolución and an interesting museum of modern Latin American art, the Casa Julio Cortázar. Managua's two other important museums are nearby, and all others are closing for lack of government funding. Unfortunately, the lakeshore (about 100 yards north of the center) is polluted and neglected, and the city is built facing away from the water. Most sights listed can be seen in a day, leaving you free to experience Managua's abundant day-to-day charms (?!).

PLAZA DE LA REVOLUCION This plaza and points nearby have witnessed some of the most memorable events in Nicaraguan history. The plaza itself is just a huge concrete expanse that looks like a parking lot—which it is. In more eventful days, though, the plaza hosted the Sandinistas' victory celebration on July 19, 1979, two days after Somoza abandoned the country. Every year since, the plaza fills with tens of thousands on the same date to commemorate the Revolution's victory with speeches, music, and liberal doses of alcohol. The largest assembled crowd in Nicaraguan history, over 400,000, gathered here in February 1990 for the Sandinistas' last election rally prior to their smashing defeat a week later at the polls.

On the east side of the plaza are the ruins of the **Metropolitan Cathedral,** destroyed by the earthquake at exactly 12:32 AM (as some of the clock faces attest) on December 24, 1972. The church is hauntingly beautiful, with murals and statues still clinging to the walls. You can climb the front stairs to the roof for a cool view (shady types hang around up there, so it's best not to go alone). Obscure art-film reference: If you've seen Andrei Tarkovsky's *Nostalghia,* touring the cathedral will remind you of that film's final magnificent scene.

On the south side of the plaza is the former **National Palace,** still intact and in service today as a tax office. The calm of its cool palm-filled interior was disrupted on August 22, 1978, when FSLN commandos, dressed as National Guard soldiers, stormed in and sealed off the building, capturing the entire National Assembly inside. The building's exterior is decorated with huge portraits of Sandino and Carlos Fonseca (which may not last long in today's political climate), while the interior boasts a strange mural by Mexican artist Arnold Belkin depicting the Nicaraguan and Mexican revolutions.

The east side of the plaza holds the **tomb of Carlos Fonseca,** one of the founders of the FSLN and its most hallowed leader. Fonseca was killed in 1976 by National Guard troops. The commemorative "eternal" flame was extinguished by the right-wing mayor, who argued that it was a waste of good gas. Private funders replaced it with a laughably tacky electric flame. In 1991, someone bombed the tomb, setting off days of rioting by Sandinista supporters, who burned the mayor's office. Today, a retired soldier has pitched a tent next to the tomb to guard it from further tampering. His ragged tent and drying laundry make for an undignified addition to the site. On the north side of the plaza, next to the lake, sits the modern **Rubén Darío Theater,** which hosts embassy parties, conferences, plays, concerts, and occasional dance performances.

CASA JULIO CORTAZAR West of Plaza de la Revolución, across the street from the Telcor building, sits a three-story colonial house containing a decent collection of modern Latin American art. The Argentinian Julio Cortázar, one of Latin America's most amazing writers, fell in love with Nicaragua under the Sandinistas and wrote highly of the art collection housed here. For his praise, the Sandinistas renamed the museum after him. *In front of Telcor, tel. 02/27272. 2 blocks west of Plaza de la Revolución. Donation requested. Open Mon.–Sat. 9–noon and 2–4.*

MUSEO HUELLAS DE ACAHUALINCA Managua's only archaeological site is a pitiful little museum that houses ancient footprints (most claim about 10,000 years old) made by indigenous people fleeing an eruption of Volcán Momotombo. Volcanic ash preserved the prints for posterity. A small exhibit exhausts the known history of these prints and their discovery. The footprints are cool, but don't break your back trying to get here. *Barrio Acahualinca, tel. 02/25291. From Plaza de la Revolución, take Bus 112 to Barrio Acahualinca and walk north 1 block past the railroad tracks. Donation requested. Open weekdays 8–noon and 1–3.*

THE RUINS South of Plaza de la Revolución, downtown Managua lies broken, weed-choked, but not quite abandoned since the homeless have taken over most ruins for themselves. The ruins of the **Grand Hotel,** just south of the National Palace, sometimes host theater presentations and poetry readings. Bring your camera—folks back home won't believe your descriptions of life in ramshackle Managua without pictures.

MUSEO NACIONAL DE NICARAGUA Nicaragua's "premier" museum is a musty, uninspired collection of pre-Columbian jewelry and ceramics mostly taken from Ometepe island in Lake Nicaragua. The '72 quake destroyed the most interesting pieces. *Colonia Dambach, tel. 02/25291. From Plaza de la Revolución, take Bus 112 about 13 blocks east. Admission: $1. Open weekdays 8–noon and 1–3.*

FESTIVALS

El Repliegue, which takes place on the last Saturday in June, is an all-night march to Masaya from Huembes market that commemorates an audacious feat in the Sandinistas' fight against Somoza. In June 1979, a few weeks before Somoza's overthrow, the FSLN led their supporters in the eastern half of the city on an all-night retreat to Masaya to protect them from an oncoming National Guard onslaught. The Guard woke up to find their intended targets had disappeared overnight. The annual march begins with a rally presided over by Daniel Ortega, and the crowd hits the road loaded down with rum and banners. Four to five hours later, the well-sloshed revelers arrive in Masaya for an all-night party and catch buses back to Managua at dawn. It's an incredible experience—part political convention, part bacchanalia. **Revolution Day,** July 19, commemorates the anniversary of the FSLN's victory over Somoza. Tens of thousands gather in Plaza de la Revolución to hear speeches and music. The raucous and often violent **Santo Domingo** festival, which celebrates Managua's patron saint, runs for the first 10 days of August and leaves about a dozen poor souls dead every year. Drunks and thieves get really rowdy, so the atmosphere can seem pretty menacing. Be smart and go in a group. The celebration includes religious processions, drunken parades on the first and the 10th, and a fair/carnival a few blocks east of the ruined cathedral.

SHOPPING

If it's in Nicaragua, you can buy it at the sprawling **Mercado Oriental,** about a mile southeast of the downtown ruins (take Bus MR3 from the northern edge of Barrio Martha Quezada). You'll find everything here—from enough car parts to assemble a whole automobile, to that backpack stolen from you on yesterday's bus ride. The size and smell of the market can be overwhelming. Another option is **Huembes market** (Bus MR4 from the northern edge of Barrio Martha Quezada), where you'll find the layout easier to navigate and the odor more humble. A section devoted to Nicaraguan handicrafts is worth a visit.

AFTER DARK

Most bars and clubs in Managua are geared toward rough-and-tumble machos who want to get smashed, pick a fight, and get a little smoochy action (even if they have to pay for it). Almost any night spot you walk into caters to this clientele. Alternatives exist, but they're spread all over the city, making a night on the town a complicated (and expensive) venture. The newest craze in Managua are bars that cater to *nicas ricas,* former Miami-exiles who've returned with big U.S. dollars and big U.S. attitudes. They're worth visiting just to see how little in common these people have with the rest of the country. If you're lazy or broke, grab a beer and head to the street corner; something interesting's bound to happen.

BARS The bar at Videoteca (*see* Cinemas, *below*) is a civilized, vaguely European hangout with a good crowd of culture vultures on hand. The patio is very romantic, but double-check whose hand you're holding since it's dark as hell. Two bars catering to the North American wannabes are the **Piña Colada** (Centro de Diversiones El Carnaval, in front of UCA, tel. 02/74140) and the **Bar Chaplin** (Km. 5 Carretera Masaya, tel. 02/74375). Both have a similar "beautiful people" crowd and are indistinguishable from the typical upscale U.S. college bar. Drinks at both are very expensive. The Barrio Martha Quezada crowd heads to **Sara's** or **El Cipitío** (*see* Food, *above*) for drinks and conversation. El Cipitío promises to restart its cultural events program soon.

For a night with the earnest arts bunch, head to **Centro Cultural El Ciprés** (1 block east of UCA), which has occasional music and Thursday night poetry readings. **El Latinoamericano** (La Piñata, across from UCA) gets a bohemian crowd on occasion and is supposed to have Latin American folk music on Wednesdays. The gay scene in Managua is limited, but here's what we know: **Ron-Ron** (2 blocks northeast of Estatua Montoya, west of the stadium facing the fire station, tel. 02/27025) has drag shows and boisterous crowds on weekends. Ask here for info on underground events.

CINEMAS **Videoteca** (1 block northeast of Estatua Montoya, tel. 02/27092) shows great foreign films in English, or with English subtitles, on what amounts to a big-screen TV, for $2. The restaurant and bar draw an interesting crowd. **Cinemateca** (1 block south of Plaza de la Revolución) has a similar, if slightly less cultured, program for $1.

MUSIC AND DANCING The best bets for interesting live music are the **Rancho Bambi** (Km. 3½ Carretera Norte) and the **Reggae Mansion** (Km. 6 Carretera Norte, tel. 02/94804), both of which occasionally feature groups from Nicaragua's Atlantic coast. Both places spin salsa and reggae records when no bands are scheduled, and the Reggae Mansion has upscale pretensions ($4 cover). A few mariachi

The music scene in the capital is dismal. Apart from concerts by schlocky Latin pop acts who occasionally drop in, Managua has little live music.

bars are scattered around town; the most popular are the **Bar Munich** (5 blocks south of the Linda Vista stoplights, tel. 02/668132), open to 6 AM every day, and **El Quelite** (5 blocks west of Telcor Villa Fontana, tel. 02/701671). *The* place to dance in Managua is the garish, surreal complex known as **La Piñata** (across from UCA, tel. 02/678216), an enclosed, open-air square with bars and discos along two sides. Each club blares silly Latin pop and Madonna records at ear-shattering levels, creating a confusing cacophony that can be escaped only by hopping onto one of the dance floors. The crowd at La Piñata is a strange mix of drunks, hookers, gay men, tourists, and working-class teens who rock all night long ($1 cover).

Near Managua

POCHOMIL This beach, the closest to Managua, gets big crowds on dry-season weekends and during Easter week, when a seven-day beach party takes place. At other times, expect to find yourself close to alone. The beach is wide and sandy but a little debris-ridden. You'll see no less than two dozen seaside restaurants, but nothing in the way of budget accommodations. Buses leave Israel Lewites market every 40 minutes all day long (45 minutes, $1). A mile or two north of Pochomil is **Masachapa,** a scruffy fishing village with a dirtier beach but a less powerful undertow. The same buses serve Masachapa and Pochomil. For good food and decent lodging in Masachapa, try the **Hotel Summer** on the beach ($7 per person).

LAGUNA DE XILOA Hot Managua days force a weekend exodus to this volcanic lagoon, 16 kilometers (10 miles) northwest of town off the León highway. The water is clean and clear, a refreshing change from Managua's sweaty, grimy hellishness. The lagoon is ringed with bars and restaurants, and can get overrun on dry-season weekends. Weekdays are a good time to find it uncrowded. You could probably even camp here during the week if you're discreet. The big problem is transportation: Buses to the lagoon make the trip from Las Piedrecitas park only on Sundays. On other days, you have to find your own way; taxis are about $5 per person.

León and the Northwest

The lowlands in the northwest are calm and pretty, dotted with volcanoes and rife with beaches. León, one of the colonial capitals, is the largest city in the region, but even that ain't much—the atmosphere in this area is mellow to dull. The one really bright spot is Chinandega, a lovely city that has been overlooked by tourists. The beaches along the Pacific coast are also pleasant; you can expect heavy Nicaraguan tourist traffic during Semana Santa and on dry-season holiday weekends, though you'll still be hard-pressed to find many foreigners outside León.

León

By all indications, León should be a fascinating place to visit. As one of Latin America's most prominent colonial cities, León played an influential role in the commercial and intellectual life of Spanish America. Some of the greatest figures in the region's literature and politics lived or studied here, including the great poet Rubén Darío. The city was Nicaragua's capital for over 300 years before and after independence. The Spanish crown recognized León's importance by choosing it as the site for Central America's largest cathedral. Despite all this, León is *not* fascinating; León, in a word, is dull. It's still one of Nicaragua's most important towns, though the capital moved to Managua in 1857; the main campus of the national university is here; and the city is the most solid base of support for the FSLN. Nevertheless, somewhere along the way, the life drained out of this city. Until the town revives itself, León's main attractions are the monuments left over from its livelier past.

Present-day León sits 24 kilometers (15 miles) west of its original location on the northwest shore of Lake Managua. Founded in 1524, the city was destroyed in 1610 by an earthquake caused by the eruption of nearby Volcán Momotombo. The survivors moved west and settled next to the indígena village of Subtiava. The village still stands today, retaining much of its traditions and folklore despite the encroachment of León and its Spanish influences. The construction of León's great cathedral didn't begin until 1746 and didn't finish until 1815, but it was apparently time well spent. The growing rivalry between the Liberals of León and the Conservatives of Granada, which had been suppressed under Spanish rule, erupted in 1821 into bitter conflict and resulted in 17 battles in the city between 1824 and 1842. León's massive church, however, survived. Many years later, the town again saw fierce fighting during the 1970s Sandinista insurrection. Somoza, sensing he was losing control, ordered the city bombed; again, the hardy cathedral remained intact.

Liberal León played an influential role in the overthrow of Somoza. Many prominent Sandinistas, including Sílvio Rodriguez, Tomás Borge, and the FSLN's founder Carlos Fonseca, studied and plotted together at the national law school here, and León was the first major city liberated from Somoza's forces, on June 20, 1979. The anniversary of this event is heartily celebrated and is one of the few days León wakes from its torpor. (September 24 and November 1 are festival days, so you can also count on the place being lively another 48 hours per year.) If you're here to party any other day, you're probably out of luck. León today is unemployed, broke, and angry about the Sandinistas' fall from power. No money or spirit is left for art, music, and other organized diversions. You won't find much to do but tour the remains of a city that once was—and may be again someday—truly glorious.

BASICS

➤ **CHANGING MONEY** • Three banks, including **BND,** sit on the corner of 1a Calle Norte and 1a Avenida Oriente, 1 block north of the back of the cathedral. Each bank changes U.S. dollars during normal business hours (weekdays 8:30–noon and 2–4, Saturday 8:30–11:30). **Supercambios** (tel. 0311/6711) next door is the only place to change traveler's checks (same hours as banks).

➤ **EMERGENCIES** • Police (tel. 115); fire (tel. 3087); **Red Cross** (tel. 2627). **Hospital Escuela** (tel. 0311/6980), 1 block south of the cathedral, is modern by Nicaraguan standards.

➤ **PHONES AND MAIL** • Telcor (northeast corner of the park, in front of the cathedral, tel. 0311/4014) offers mail service Monday–Saturday 7–6 and phone service 7 AM–8:30 PM daily. Another Telcor branch is just north of the train station.

➤ **VISITOR INFORMATION** • The young people who run the **Casa Popular de Cultura** (1a Calle Norte, 1 block north and 1½ blocks east of the main Telcor office, tel. 0311/2115) are helpful and will do their best to answer questions.

Rubén Darío

The name Rubén Darío, Nicaragua's most famous literary figure, means little in the English-speaking world, but in Spain and throughout Latin America it commands instant respect. Born in 1867 in Metapa (now Ciudad Darío), Darío went from obscure boy poet to founder of the modernist school of poetry in less than 20 years. His fresh style was in complete opposition to the ponderous, repetitive poetry in vogue at the time and won him quick international status. Today, Darío stands as one of the great literary figures of the Spanish-speaking world. Darío was also famous for his stormy personal life, which included alcoholism and a series of indiscreet affairs. None of his exploits deterred the Nicaraguan government, which sent the poet to Spain and France to serve as ambassador. After living most of his adult life abroad, Darío returned penniless and sick to Nicaragua, and died in León in 1916.

COMING AND GOING

➤ **BY TRAIN** • León is connected by rail to Managua and Granada to the south and El Sauce to the northeast. Trains leave for Managua three times daily: Two regular trains leave León at 5 AM and noon (3½ hours, $1); an express leaves daily at 6 AM (2½ hours, $2). A train to El Sauce, which goes past the Cerro Negro volcano, leaves León at noon and arrives at 3 PM ($1). The train to León from El Sauce departs at 8:30 AM. León's train "station" (Av. 14 de Julio at 5a Calle Norte, 5 blocks north and 4 blocks east of the front of the cathedral) has no tourist facilities. The town center is an easy taxi ride away.

➤ **BY BUS** • The bus depot—a dusty field with a market next door—is a block north and 8 blocks east of the train station. Buses leave continuously for Managua from 4:30 AM to 6 PM (2 hours, $2). Warning: Unless you don't mind adding an hour to your trip and taking brain-rattling detours through dirt fields, get on a bus headed to Managua via the *new*, not the *old*, highway. Buses also leave for Chinandega (1 hour, $1), Corinto (2 hours, $2), and many other points nearby. A taxi or horse-drawn carriage is your best way to get here from town (about $1).

➤ **HITCHING** • León is a university town, and many students hitch home on the weekends, so competition for rides is fierce. To try your luck, head for the highway east of the bus depot and work that thumb. Alternatively, approach a truck driver while brandishing a pack of American cigarettes and ask if he's headed your way. It works every time—if he smokes, that is.

GETTING AROUND Though León comes close to approximating a modern city with street names and all, everyone is still perversely stubborn and gives addresses as distances from landmarks. The city, fortunately, is laid out as a grid, with calles running east–west, and avenidas north–south. Ground zero is the intersection of **Calle Central Rubén Darío** and **Avenida Central** at the northeast corner of **Parque Central** in front of the cathedral. Most sights are an easy walk from Parque Central, and taxis will take you anywhere in town for about $1. The bus system is very complicated, not very extensive, and seldom used.

WHERE TO SLEEP Hotel Telica. The cheapest of León's lodging choices ($6 doubles) is a shabby flophouse with dark, cramped rooms and possibly the most disgusting bathrooms in Nicaragua. The management, if you can tear them away from the TV, are indifferent and unhelpful. Still, you'll pay twice as much anywhere else. *From the train station, walk 3½ blocks north along the road that runs along the train tracks, tel. 0311/2136. 14 rooms, none with bath. 11 PM curfew.*

Hotel América. A mildly eccentric but friendly family runs this slightly shoddy hotel, which boasts a cool interior patio where guests and management hang out and chat. The rooms are cavernous, and the bathrooms could be cleaner, but the place has soul. Doubles are $14; breakfast is $2. Warn them if you'll be out after 10 PM; otherwise, they lock the front door. *Walk 2 blocks east from the southeast corner of Parque Central, tel. 0311/5533. 9 rooms, all with bath.*

Hotel Europa. León's premier hotel is an informal, attractive place, and the staff is very professional and accommodating. If you demand clean, you'll get it here. Rooms come in three flavors: without bath ($7 per person), with bath ($10 per person), and with bath and air-conditioning ($24 single or double). Reservations are *highly* recommended. The restaurant serves good breakfasts for $5, lunch and dinner for $8. *Walk 2 blocks south and 1 block east from the train station, tel. 0311/2596. 30 rooms, some with bath.*

FOOD The economy has taken its toll on León's restaurant industry. Many places have gone under, and the survivors are hanging on for dear life. You won't starve here, but don't expect any gastronomic epiphanies, either. The comedores in the market behind the cathedral are a low-budget alternative to León's pricey restaurants.

La Cueva del León. For years, this restaurant was *the* place to eat in León, offering good food at cheap prices to hordes of hungry university students. Today, the food is just okay, the prices are higher, and the place often stands empty and quiet. The old building is a treasure and worth a look. The *pollo al vino* (chicken in wine) for $4 is decent, and a plate of *camarones en salsa* (shrimp in tomato sauce) will fill you, if not thrill you, for $6. *Walk 2½ blocks north from the northwest corner of Parque Central, tel. 0311/6562.*

Restaurante Sacuanjoche. León's fanciest is pricey, but the food is probably the best in town. Shrimp and lobster go for $12 and $14, an excellent *pollo al vino* is $8, and an avocado salad sells for $7. If you eat beef, try the *filete Sacuanjoche,* a fillet served with loads of garlic ($10). *In front of Museo Rubén Darío, 3 blocks west of the northwest corner of Parque Central, tel. 0311/5429.*

Las Ruinas. This cute and gimmicky restaurant in the ruins of a bombed-out building doubles as one of León's few night spots. Mariachis hound rum-guzzling patrons for their spare change while the stereo blares insipid love ballads. Prices are good, though—must be the low rent (no roof, crumbling walls)—and the food's not bad. A comida corriente runs $2 and is better than most food in this genre. *From the northwest corner of Parque Central, walk 1½ blocks west, tel. 0311/4767. Open Mon.–Sat. noon–midnight.*

WORTH SEEING Despite the sorrowful absence of life in the city, León still retains the dignity and elegance of the past in much of its architecture. The **cathedral** is the most obvious relic of León's past glory. The long, squat structure has withstood earthquakes and artillery fire equally well through the centuries. It's the largest cathedral in Central America, covering a whole city block. The exterior, once weather-worn and crumbling, underwent extensive renovation in the summer of 1992, a project sponsored by the Spanish government to commemorate the 500th anniversary of Columbus's first voyage to this continent. The renovation promises to leave the church in beautiful condition, and the Spanish seem to be working off some of their guilt at the same time. Inside, the high arches and heavy columns give a feeling of indestructible security. A series of paintings of the stations of the cross adorns the huge walls. Look for the tomb of Rubén Darío at the foot of the statue of Saint Paul to the right of the altar. A mourning stone lion, representing the city of León, sits atop the grave. Other churches worth visiting are **La Recolección** and **El Calvario.** La Recolección (2½ blocks north of the back of the cathedral) was completed in 1788 and has a baroque facade and exterior carvings that reference the betrayal and crucifixion of Christ. The neoclassical El Calvario, 3 blocks east of the cathedral, features three macabre renditions of the Crucifixion and a plaque honoring five anti-Somoza protesters killed here by the National Guard in February 1979.

The only museum of note in the city is **Museo Rubén Darío,** 3 blocks west of the northwest corner of Parque Central. The museum is inside the house where Darío spent his boyhood, and includes personal effects and a plaster "death mask" made shortly after the great poet died. Though they charge no entrance fee, you'll be strongly "encouraged" to make a donation. *Open Tues.–Sat. 9–noon and 2–5, Sun. 9–11 AM.*

Barrio Subtiava, about 10 blocks west of Parque Central, is home to the indigenous Subtiava people, whose ancestors lived here way before Columbus even had a boat. The barrio includes the church of **San Juan Bautista de Subtiava,** the oldest church in León, built in 1530. A renovation project, again sponsored by the Spanish government, was well under way at press time. Semana Santa is the most colorful time to visit, when residents create an exquisitely beautiful, mile-long trail of sawdust drawings on Subtiava's streets that is then trampled by a procession carrying an image of the resurrected Christ. **El Fortín** is an abandoned 19th-century fort once used as a prison by the National Guard. The fort sits on a hill a mile south of town and offers good views of León and volcanoes nearby (access it from a dirt road past Subtiava's San Juan church).

If you want to see where the first Somoza met his maker, visit the **Centro Sandinista de Trabajadores,** 1 block west and 1½ blocks north of Parque Central's northwest corner. A plaque on the outer wall honors the tyrant's demise at the hands of the poet Rigoberto López. The closest you'll get to art in León (apart from churches or political murals around town) is at the **Casa Popular de Cultura,** 1 block north and 1½ blocks west of the northwest corner of Parque Central. A small collection of paintings from León and around the world is on display.

NEAR LEON

VOLCAN MOMOTOMBO The near-perfect cone of this volcano rises 4,000 feet over the western shore of Lake Managua. Access is by a bumpy dirt road (which turns muddy in the rainy season) that starts just south of the village of **La Paz Centro** on the León–Managua highway (look for the sign announcing the Patricó Argüello Geothermal Plant). To get here, take one of the bus/trucks headed to or from León and ask to be let off at La Paz. From La Paz Centro you can take one of the public-transport trucks to Puerto Momotombo. Technically, you're supposed to have a pass from the national power company to cross the power plant on the lower slopes of the volcano, but you might be able to talk your way through without it. To be sure, visit the INE office (a block north of Casa Nazareth, tel. 02/668756) in Managua's Barrio Martha Quezada to solicit a pass. The reward for your troubles, and the arduous four-hour climb, will be a stunning view of the lake and the surrounding country.

PONELOYA Poneloya is a broad, sandy beach about 24 kilometers (15 miles) west of León. Buses to and from León's Subtiava barrio make the trip from early morning until late afternoon (40 minutes, $1). Be careful when you swim; there's a heavy undertow. The seafood restaurants along the beach offer a big plate of *camarones al ajillo* (garlic shrimp) for about $6. The **Hotel Lacayo,** if you're tempted to stay, will gladly trade your $7 for a lumpy bed in a scruffy room. The beach makes a good camping spot if you've got a tent or a mosquito net; otherwise, the critters will eat you alive.

Chinandega

Sergio Ramírez, former Sandinista vice-president and renowned novelist, wrote a short story called "Nicaragua es Blanca" (Nicaragua Is White), in which snow falls in Chinandega. If you come here, you'll discover why the scenario is so absurd: The sun cooks every last drop of moisture out of any creature too stupid to head for shade. If you can take the heat, you're in for a pleasant discovery. Chinandega and points nearby are blessed with a rare beauty and charm practically undiscovered by foreign tourists. Be warned: If you're looking for bright lights and urban attractions, you won't find them here. This is Nature's territory.

The Pacific pounds away at isolated beaches, hidden lagoons murmur with bird life, and smoking volcanoes loom over hilly farmlands that sport a thousand shades of green.

The town of Chinandega itself, the last major settlement on the road from León north to Potosí, is simple. Though partially destroyed three times in the last 100 years—by an earthquake in 1898, by fighting between Liberals and Conservatives in 1927, and by National Guard bombardment when the city was held by the FSLN in 1978—the town has rebuilt each time. Elegant colonial churches, bright stucco buildings, and red-tile roofs give the place a soothing aesthetic. Only the smoking, hulking mass of the **Volcán San Cristóbal** to the east, which offers a challenging hike up its slopes, breaks the visual calm. Chinandega's other attraction is its role as transport hub for the region; deserted beaches and stunning countryside are an easy bus ride away. You could spend weeks exploring this hidden corner of Nicaragua and not see half of it. Even if you can only give it a day or two, you'll find Chinandega generous with her charms.

BASICS

➤ **CHANGING MONEY** • Chinandega's two main banks, **BND** (1 block east of the southeast corner of Parque Central) and **BANIC** (another block east on the same street), will both change U.S. dollars, but *not* traveler's checks, at standard rates. Each is open weekdays 9–noon and 1:30–3:30, 9–noon on Saturdays.

➤ **PHONES AND MAIL** • **Telcor** (tel. 0341/3112), a block east of the northeast corner of Parque Central, is open for international and domestic calls on weekdays 8 AM–9 PM and weekends 8–6. Mail, telegraph, and fax services are available weekdays 8–5.

COMING AND GOING

The rail line to Chinandega was out of service at press time, but people talk of it reopening soon. Otherwise, buses to and from León and Managua to the south and the Honduran border near Somotillo to the northeast are regular and cheap. Getting to and from Potosí is more problematic. To León and Managua, buses leave the market at the southeast corner of town every ½ hour 5 AM–5 PM. The 1½-hour ride to León costs $1; the 3-hour trip to Managua costs $2. Buses for Somotillo also leave from here about every two hours, 6 AM–4 PM (2½ hours, $2). To travel up the coast to Potosí, you must catch a bus from the *mercadito* (little market), one block north of the northeast corner of Parque Central. Buses to Potosí leave irregularly, usually at 6 AM and 11 AM, but the schedule varies inexplicably. It's a safer bet to catch the hourly bus to Cosigüina, running 6 AM–2 PM, and then try to hitch or grab a passenger truck to Potosí. Buses to Jiquilillo and La Bocano leave the mercadito every hour 5 AM–2 PM (1 hour, $1). Finally, special "taxis"—i.e., rolling heaps of rusted metal—make the 10-minute trip to El Viejo from the

If you're coming to Chinandega on a bus from the south, you'll be closer to the center of town if you get off the bus when it stops at the mercadito (little market).

north end of the mercadito (25¢). Hitching from either the mercadito or the other market is fairly easy; just ask any truck driver if he's headed your way.

Once in town, getting around is easy. You can walk from one end of town to the other in under ½ hour, not counting time when you're passed out under a tree from heat exhaustion. As usual in Central America, everything revolves around the **Parque Central**; the **Mercado Central** is 5 blocks east of the southeast corner of the park. Other transport options are taxis and horse-drawn carriages. Neither of these should cost more than $1.

WHERE TO SLEEP

Chinandega suffers from a dearth of budget lodging. Only one place, the Hotel Chinandega, offers better-than-basic accommodations at reasonable prices. Elsewhere you'll get bare-bones lodging, or worse—ripped off.

Hotel Chinandega. A nice family runs this quiet hotel near the center of town. Rooms are larger and cleaner than average, and you'll weep at the sight of a large bed. The rooms upstairs facing the street are a little noisy, but that's the extent of things to complain about (just keep your fingers away from their flesh-eating parrot). Rooms are $5 per person. *From the southeast corner of Parque Central, walk 4 blocks east and 1½ blocks south. 12 rooms, none with bath.*

Pensión Cortez. Very basic and very cheap, this place is indistinguishable from others in the genre: concrete floors, small lumpy beds, smelly bathrooms. The price is typical, too, at $5 a double. *Across the street from the southwest corner of Parque Central. 10 rooms, none with bath.*

Hotel Glomar. Though it's supposedly the class act in town, there's little reason to choose this place over the Hotel Chinandega unless you *must* have a room with private bath and air-conditioning ($18 doubles). Rooms without bath and air-conditioning cost $10. In either case, the rooms are mangy, and, worst of all, the sheets smell like last night's guests. *From Mercado Central, walk 1 block south, tel. 0341/2562. 15 rooms, some with bath. Restaurant.*

FOOD It's hard to get a good meal in Chinandega. The food is so bad for the price that you may end up eating two meals a day at the hot-dog stands that work the Parque Central: For just over a dollar, feast on two hot dogs and a soft drink. The only sit-down breakfast in town is at Hotel Glomar's restaurant (*see above*).

Restaurante Ying King. This pseudo-Chinese restaurant features tacky decor, nice waitresses, and a passable chow-suey (noodles, vegetables, mystery meat) for $5. The noodle soups are a good value at $4. *From the Mercado Central, walk 1 block west and 3½ blocks south, tel. 0341/4053. Closed Mon.*

Rincón Familiar. Way overpriced and usually out of half the things listed on the menu, this small eatery still manages to pull in a good crowd for dinner. A salty *carne a la plancha* (sizzling skirt steak and onions), served with fries and a salad, costs $7. *From the southeast corner of Parque Central, walk 3 blocks south and 1½ blocks east. Closed Sun.*

WORTH SEEING Chinandega's main sights are the colonial churches, all of which are simple and elegant. The **Iglesia Santa Ana,** on the north side of Parque Central, supposedly contains a fragment of the Crucifixion cross. The **Iglesia El Calvario** (6 blocks east of Iglesia Santa Ana) is surrounded by a little park. Its walls cast a golden light in the setting sun. The Greek-influenced **Iglesia Guadalupe** (2 blocks east and 4 blocks south of the southeast corner of Parque Central) sheltered cholera victims during the mid-19th century.

AFTER DARK TV dominates the night scene here, as families crowd around the blaring tube. Two discos play Madonna on the weekends: **Disco Leo** is 2½ blocks east of the southeast corner of the Parque Central, and **Pink Panther** is ½ block north of Iglesia Guadalupe. Other than this, hang out in one of the dive bars around town or with the assorted riffraff in the park.

OUTDOOR ACTIVITIES The dry season is baseball season, and Chinandegans head out to the stadium, 2 kilometers north of town on the road to El Viejo, to get hammered and watch their team. If you're feeling active, the **Volcán San Cristóbal,** Nicaragua's largest volcano at nearly 6,000 feet, sits east of town and will challenge even experienced hikers. You should ask the Red Cross (a block south of Hotel Glomar, tel. 0341/3132) to find you a guide. Watch out for snakes!

NEAR CHINANDEGA

BORDER CROSSING AT SOMOTILLO After many years out of service, the border post of Guasaule, just north of Somotillo, is open. The crossing sees less traffic than the crossings at El Espino and Las Manos to the east. This is still Nicaragua, though, so don't expect bustling efficiency: Allow two hours to complete all paperwork. The crossing is open 8–5, but don't go too late because there *will* be a lag and you'll have to head back to Chinandega for decent accommodations. Buses to and from Chinandega are frequent; you can also take a bus from León headed to Somotillo.

EL VIEJO A few miles north of Chinandega, this little town bustles with life, which revolves around the **market** and the church next door, **Nuestra Señora de la Concepción.** During August and December, religious celebrations dominate the town; the December celebration features a pilgrimage led by an image of the Holy Mother adorned in silver and gold. There are no lodgings and few comedores, but getting here is easy: Jump on any bus headed north out of Chinandega or take a special taxi from the mercadito to the park in front of El Viejo's church. Aficionados of sacred knick-knacks won't want to miss the Black Christ in the church, said to date from the 1600s.

LA BOCANO Buses leave all day from the mercadito in Chinandega for little villages on the Pacific; La Bocano, on the southern lip of the *Estero Padre Ramos* (Padre Ramos Estuary), is especially nice. The Pacific pounds away at an empty beach on one side, and a quiet lagoon barely ripples on the other. The folks at **Rancho Padre Ramos** will cook you a fresh fish dinner for about $4, or you could ask for turtle eggs if you're adventurous and ecologically nonchalant. A few hospedajes cater to tourists during vacation season, and hammock space is abundant. The last bus out leaves La Bocano for Chinandega at about 3 PM from the Rancho Padre Ramos.

MECHAPA If you're looking for isolation, this place may be your paradise. A few hours northwest of León on the road to Puerto Nata, Nicaragua's westernmost point, this little settlement of grass houses sits on a large, deserted beach that rarely sees a foreign tourist. You won't find a single hospedaje, but a few locals sell beer and Coke—proving you can't go anywhere in Nicaragua to escape the damn stuff. Don't bother heading on to Punta Nata; the road ends uneventfully, and there ain't no beach. The only travel option if you don't have your own wheels is to hitch from the road to Potosí.

POTOSI Some 51 kilometers (32 miles) north of Chinandega sits the port town of Potosí, Nicaragua's northernmost point on the Pacific side. While of little interest itself, it's a jumping-off point for El Salvador. From the port, you can take a boat to La Unión (6 hours, $16). At last word, the boat left at 8 AM. **Hospedaje y Comedor** has basic accommodations—a covered area where you can crash for $2 per night and eat for cheap.

The Southwest
The stretch of land between Managua and the Costa Rican border makes up only a sliver of Nicaraguan territory. Except for Managua, however, this is Nicaragua's most densely populated region and one of its most interesting as well. The strategic location of the territory—really an isthmus, since it's bounded by the enormous Lago de Nicaragua to the north and the Pacific to the south—drew migration after migration, or invasion after invasion, of people who saw promise in the fertile earth and abundant waters. This area has always been the richest part of the country, with Granada, one of the great cities of the colonial Americas, leading the way to prosperity through its trade links with the rest of America and Europe.

Today, its former prosperity is little more than a dim memory, worn away by Monroe Doctrines, Good Neighbor Policies, IMF economic restructurings, and other weapons in the First World–Third World confrontation. Despite all this, it's still hard to resist being drawn here. From the long, mostly unspoiled Pacific coast, to massive volcanoes, to the faded glories of its colonial cities, this corner of Nicaragua probably contains more for the traveler than any other region. Of course, this region also draws more tourists than any other—everyone from dollar-clutching old ladies screeching over trinkets at the Masaya craft market to serious volcano-climbers in search of personal epiphanies. The Pacific Ocean is the biggest draw, luring busloads of backpackers to San Juan del Sur and other sleepy beach towns. Whatever brings you here, you'll find the traveling easy and the climate generally cooperative.

Masaya

Masaya, the seat of Nicaragua's smallest, most densely populated department, is known for Nicaraguan indigenous traditions. The Dirianés tribe successfully resisted the Spanish years longer than neighboring tribes; even after their eventual conquest, they rose often in rebellion. Masaya's rebelliousness continued into the 1970s, when the locals made it a center of anti-Somoza subversion. Today, Masaya's heritage survives in its thriving crafts industry and in the largest concentration of indígenas in Nicaragua. Nearby, the residents of Nindirí, Masatepe, Niquinohomo, and Catarina also nurture the memory and traditions of their ancestors.

Though many visitors to this well-touristed territory look no farther than Masaya's crafts market for signs of its past, there's way more to explore here than rows and rows of mass-produced trinkets. A short drive away is **Volcán Masaya,** still active after dominating the spiritual life and folklore of the nearby communities for centuries. To the southeast, the **Laguna de Apoyo,** whose waters supposedly have magical healing powers, is a beautiful place to swim. If you're lucky enough to be in town between late September and the end of October, the **Torovenado carnival,** a series of elaborate burlesque parades that recounts the natives' resistance to conquest, vividly portrays Masaya's heritage.

BASICS Though Masaya gets a lot of tourist traffic, you can't cash traveler's checks. **BND,** a couple of blocks east of the southeast corner of the main park (Parque 17 de Octobre), will change U.S. dollars weekdays 8–noon and 2–4:30, Saturdays 8–noon. **Telcor** (northwest corner of Parque 17 de Octobre) has phone service 7 AM–9:45 PM daily, mail service weekdays 8–5. **Inturismo** has an office on the highway north of town, but don't expect to get much info out of them. They're open weekdays 8–4, Saturdays 8–noon. For **police,** call 2521; for **ambulance,** 2556.

COMING AND GOING

➤ **BY TRAIN** • Masaya sits on the Managua–Granada rail line. Trains to both points stop at Masaya's station, about 8 long blocks north of the back of La Asunción cathedral in Parque 17 de Octobre. To Managua, trains pass through at roughly 5:45 AM and 11 AM daily (45 minutes, 50¢). To Granada, trains stop at 8:45 AM, 2:15 PM, and 6:45 PM (1 hour, $1).

➤ **BY BUS** • Buses to and from Granada and Managua use the depot at the old market, 1 block behind La Asunción cathedral in Parque 17 de Octobre. Buses to both cities leave about every ½ hour 4 AM–6 PM (Managua: 45 minutes, $1; Granada: ½ hour, 50¢). Buses to both cities also stop on the highway north of the town center.

GETTING AROUND Masaya's northern edge is marked by the highway that travels east–west between Managua and Granada. The main street to town is marked by a gas station and Rotary Club sign (in front of Inturismo). Walking south, you'll pass the train station, the church of San Jerónimo, and **Parque 17 de Octobre** and its La Asunción cathedral, about ½ mile south of the highway. West of the park is **Laguna de Masaya** (about 7 blocks) and the Masaya Volcano; the **market** is a 15-minute walk east of the park, over a small bridge. The **Monimbó barrio** is about 5 blocks south of the park. Though Masaya has a small bus system, the town is easy to walk around. Taxis and horse-drawn carriages are everywhere and usually cost about 50¢ a person anywhere around town.

WHERE TO SLEEP Though Masaya is one of Nicaragua's most-visited towns, it has few accommodations, budget or otherwise. The cleanest budget choice is **Hotel Regis** (tel. 052/2300), about 3½ blocks north of the back of the cathedral. Rooms are clean, dark, and offer little privacy since walls don't reach the ceiling. The shared baths are clean, and there's a small patio-courtyard to hang out in ($12 double). On the highway about ½ mile south of its intersection with the road into town, **Hotel Cailagua** (tel. 052/4435) offers 15 motel-like rooms with private baths ($24 with air-conditioning, $14 without). It's cleaner than your average hotel and has a large restaurant/bar. It's a good place to stay if you're traveling by car, since the courtyard/parking lot locks at night. **Hotel Rex,** near San Jerónimo church, is a garish red and green building where you'll live in squalor among a family that spends nearly every waking hour shouting at each other over the TV, and pay $4 a person for the privilege.

FOOD Again, with so many tourists, there's no explaining the lack of good food. **Restaurant Sándalo** and **Restaurant Bahía,** next to each other near the southwest corner of Parque 17 de Octobre, both have upscale pretensions but serve very bland Nicaraguan fare at inflated prices (lunch and dinner, $6–$9 per meal). The row of pizza and chicken joints north of the back of the cathedral are cheap and popular, but the fast-food ambience is pretty unappealing. The best bargains are available in the comedores in the market west of the park, where you can get a comida corriente for $2 in settings that look hygienic.

WORTH SEEING Masaya is a great place to stroll. **Parque 17 de Octobre,** which houses the 19th-century **La Asunción** cathedral, is a good place to start. From its southwest corner, walk about 6 blocks west to the *malecón* (lakeside walkway) over-looking the Laguna de Masaya. From here, the water looks clean and inviting, but it's terribly polluted and signs warn of cholera contamination. Volcán Masaya (*see* Near Masaya, *below*) sits on the opposite side of the lake. The **National Artisan Center,** at the edge of the lake, is a school where traditional handicraft skills are taught to locals, with some products for sale. South of the park, about 5 blocks down Calle San Sebastián, is **Monimbó,** a barrio whose residents, descendants of the Dirianés, cling proudly to their customs and folklore. The neighborhood is filled with murals depicting indigenous resistance to the conquest and, during the day, the sight and sounds of craftspeople hard at work. **Calle de la Calzado,** which starts at the small Magdalena church, is the center of the crafts industry.

Just over a mile west of Monimbó is **Cailagua** ("where the water falls"), a ravine that leads to the Laguna de Masaya, where rainwater falls 300 feet into the lake. The cliff face and ravine are covered with ancient petroglyphs. The rock face also has a small cave, know as **La Cueva de las Duendes** (the Trolls' Cave), which used to contain an altar for the natives' sun god. Getting here is tricky, so ask locals for directions. Five blocks east of the southeast corner of the main park is Masaya's **market,** a large bazaar whose stalls create a confusing maze of color and noise. The famous Masaya crafts market is here (*see* Shopping, *below*), as well as a market for just about every-thing else. It's also a good place to grab a cheap meal.

SHOPPING Masaya's reputation for crafts is well deserved. Weavings, pottery, brightly painted balsa-wood carvings, and exquisite hammocks are the standouts. The crafts market in Masaya's main market, 5 blocks east of the southwest corner of Par-que 17 de Octobre, offers a large selection at good prices, but the sales tactics tend to be high-pressure. A smaller selection, at higher prices, is available at the National Artisan Center (*see* Worth Seeing, *above*) on the malecón overlooking Laguna de Masaya. **Casa de las Hamacas** (2½ blocks west of the main park's northwest corner, open daily 9–5) offers a big selection of (guess what?) hammocks.

NEAR MASAYA

VOLCAN MASAYA AND MASAYA NATIONAL PARK The entrance to Nicaragua's only national park is on the Managua–Granada highway at Kilometer 23 (about 5 kilo-meters/3 miles toward Managua from Masaya). A road leads past a checkpoint ($3 per car) and up to the steaming **Santiago Crater** (about 6 kilometers/4 miles), the principal crater of four in the Volcán Masaya. About halfway up, the **Centro de Interpretación Ambiental** (open daily 8–5), one of Nicaragua's best museums, has exhibits on the geological and cultural history of the volcano. Other exhibits detail the history of volcanic activity in the rest of the country and give a run-down on the exotic animal and bird life found nearby.

For reasons that scientists haven't figured out, the Santiago crater is home to a large, noisy colony of green parrots who dive in and out of the sulfuric gases, no problema. *By all calculations, the air here should kill them. The birds obviously haven't been informed.*

The road to the volcano leads right to the edge of the main crater, which rumbles ominously and fills the air with a foul sulfuric smell. The volcano's eruptions terrorized nearby tribes for centuries, leading them to develop elaborate ritu-als of human sacrifice to appease the angry gods. The Spaniards, too, held their own superstitions about the place, calling it the *Boca del Inferno* (Mouth of Hell). They placed a cross near the crater to keep the devil in his hole, and in their own bizarre sacrificial ritual, they lowered several unlucky fools into the crater to retrieve the "boiling gold" they saw there ("Thanks, dumbshits!"). The last major eruption was in 1852.

The park has no lodgings and only one place to eat. **Restaurant Volcán Masaya** (behind the Centro de Interpretación Ambiental, tel. 052/79349) is one of Nicaragua's most expensive eateries. Lobster goes for $18, steaks for $12, and drinks in the bar, which has a good view of the Laguna de Masaya, are outrageous. The place sees a crowd only on weekends (open Monday–Saturday noon–midnight). The park has no formal camp-grounds, and the staff at the museum seemed puzzled when I asked them about camping in the park. According to them, travelers wishing to camp would have to get permission at the museum, which may take a day or two to secure, so play it by ear. To get to the park, either drive in or get off any Masaya–Managua bus at Kilometer 23. You can flag a bus to Masaya or Managua on the highway in front of the park entrance.

COYOTEPE FORTRESS Sitting on a hill overlooking Masaya and the surrounding country, Coyotepe is an abandoned, spooky fort that dates from the late 1800s. A famous battle was fought here between troops commanded by the Liberal General Benjamín Zeledón and forces loyal to the U.S.-backed Conservative dictator, Adolfo Díaz. Zeledón refused to surrender unless U.S. forces left Nicaragua, but he was routed from the fort and fled to nearby Catarina, where he was captured and shot under orders of U.S. Marines. Years later, during the Sandinistas' final offensive in 1979 against Somoza, National Guard troops used the fort to launch rocket attacks on Masaya below. The National Guard also used the fort as a prison and torture center: The ghosts of Somoza's victims are said to haunt the catacombs below the fort. Today, the fort sits abandoned, visited only by a few curious cows, local youths looking to make out, and the rare tourist. The tunnels leading into the catacombs below get dark quickly, so bring a flashlight and leave your superstitions behind. Take the road heading toward Managua and look for a sign on your right after a mile or so. The walk uphill takes about ½ hour, or drive to the top and park at the fortress gate.

NINDIRÍ Nindirí, sitting on the ruins of an ancient indigenous village, is home to the **Museo Tenderí**, a private collection of artifacts, tools, stone statues, and tombs from the Niquirano and Chorotega tribes that lived in the region. Some items are over 1,000 years old. The museum also contains descriptions of the tribes' history and society. The museum is 2 blocks west of the main church of Santa Ana, and a donation is requested (open weekdays 8–noon and 1–5). Nindirí is accessible by frequent bus from Masaya (½ hour, 25¢).

NIQUINOHOMO Sandino groupies will want to visit this typical little village where the general was born and raised (Niquinohomo, appropriately enough, means "place of the warriors" in Chorotegan). His childhood home, across from the church on the main square, is a museum hanging on for dear life for lack of government funding. Inside are Sandino's personal effects, rare photos, and text relating the life of this legend. (Open Tuesday–Saturday 9–noon and 1–5; donation requested.) Masaya–Rivas buses pass through hourly.

CATARINA AND LAGUNA DE APOYO Catarina, the bamboo-basket capital of Nicaragua, lies about 10 kilometers (6 miles) south of Masaya on the road to Rivas. Unless you're crazy about baskets, the only reason to visit is the **mirador,** a hillside balcony overlooking the Laguna de Apoyo and the department of Granada; the view of Lake Nicaragua and beyond will make your knees weak. From here, you can descend the 1½ miles to the laguna, Nicaragua's largest, deepest crater lake. The water is still clear and perfect for swimming, and, if legend is correct, it'll heal all your ills. Locals will be happy to give directions to the mirador. Hourly buses between Masaya and Rivas pass through all day.

Granada

Once one of the grandest, richest, and most important cities of the Americas, Granada today is a sleepy town of little significance. The past isn't totally forgotten; the city's streets are packed with colonial buildings that, even in their dilapidated state, make Granada the most architecturally vibrant town in the country. Its position on the western shore of Lake Nicaragua guaranteed the town a crucial role in the commercial and trading life of colonial Latin America. Founded in 1524 by the first Spanish expeditions, the city quickly became an important supply link to Spain. Ships entering Lake Nicaragua from the Atlantic via Río San Juán would dock at Granada's port, unload their cargo, and leave filled with gold mined by conquered tribes. As the region's economy developed and diversified, Granada became the major port for exporting goods to Spain from as far away as Guatemala. The town's elite, which became enormously wealthy from their control of this port, embarked on a construction campaign that transformed Granada into one of the classic cities of the Americas.

As Granada got richer, it got more conservative. Though many inhabitants resented Spanish rule (because of Spain's tight control of its commercial activities), most nevertheless favored the authoritarian Spanish political model. By the time independence came in the 1820s, a serious schism had developed between Granada's Conservatives and León's Liberals. With no Spanish master left to police the rivalry, the two cities quickly fell into armed conflict as they battled for power. The Granadans enjoyed the upper hand until American William Walker, invited by the Liberals, marched on the town in 1855, capturing it easily. Walker ruled Nicaragua from here for nearly two years until he was driven out by a combined Central American force. During his retreat, the demented colonel ordered the destruction of the city, leaving Granada mostly in smoking ruins. Though Granadans rebuilt what they could, the city never again achieved its former grandeur. Granada has suffered the effects of underdevelopment and exploitation along with the rest of the country, and the lack of funds for restoration has left the city's architectural riches sullied and worn.

Granada never really participated in the Sandinista insurrection (for which it was spared Somoza's wrath), and few FSLN fans could be found here during the revolutionary years.

Some things haven't changed, for Granada still carries its conservative heritage proudly. Today, Granada looks expectantly to Violeta Chamorro to restore the country to its (business) senses so the city can recapture some of its lost wealth. Though that's unlikely to happen, Granada, faded glory and all, is still one of Nicaragua's most attractive and historical cities. And with so much nearby—including the lake, the Volcán Mombacho, and a pristine volcanic lagoon—it should be high on anyone's list.

BASICS BND (1 block west and ½ block south from the southwest corner of Parque Central) changes dollars weekdays 8–noon and 2–4, Saturdays 8–noon. **Telcor** (west side of Parque Central, just north of the main cathedral) has phone service daily 8 AM–9 PM, and mail service 8–5 weekdays. For **police**, call 2929; for **ambulance,** 2711. **Hospital San Juan de Dios** (tel. 055/2719), on the west side of town near the bus station, is your best bet for an English-speaking doctor. According to Inturismo in Managua, there's supposed to be an **Inturismo** office 4 blocks west of the southwest corner of Parque Central. I looked for it all day until I almost cried, but it just wasn't there.

COMING AND GOING

➤ **BY TRAIN** • Granada's train station, 6 blocks north of the northwest corner of Parque Central, offers rail service to Masaya and Managua (where you can catch a train to León and beyond). Trains (about $1) depart daily at 4:45 AM and 10 AM, arriving in Masaya about an hour later and Managua 45 minutes after that.

➤ **BY BUS** • Buses for Managua and Masaya depart from the depot about 7 blocks west and a block north of Parque Central, just north of the Hospital San Juan de Dios. Buses leave every 20 minutes 4 AM–6 PM (Masaya: 20 minutes, 50¢; Managua: 2 hours, $1). Direct buses to Rivas and other points south leave from the market, 1 block west and 2 blocks south of the southwest corner of Parque Central. Direct buses to Rivas depart every two hours or so 5:30 AM–3 PM (2 hours, $6), or catch a bus to Nandaime and change there to a Rivas-bound bus from Managua.

➤ **BY BOAT** • Boats leave Granada's lakeside dock (about 6 blocks east of Parque Central at the end of Calle La Calzada) for Isla de Ometepe and San Carlos, on the eastern side of the lake, every Monday and Thursday. Boats to Ometepe leave at 4 PM (3½ hours, $1) and continue on to San Carlos (9 hours, $2). Another boat to San Carlos leaves an hour earlier, stopping at Morrito and San Miguelito on the lake's northern shore.

GETTING AROUND Most of Granada's interesting sights are grouped in the old center, about 1 block south and 7 blocks east of the depot for Managua–Masaya buses. The center contains Parque Central, a cathedral, and many old colonial buildings. From here, **Calle La Calzada** heads east to the lake, where you'll find a dock and a long lakeside park to the south. Walking from one end of town to the other is difficult, but taxis abound as well as horse-drawn carriages (which are cheaper and more fun than a cab—a typical ride should be around 50¢ a person). A confusing and lame bus system gives limited coverage of the town and its suburbs.

WHERE TO SLEEP Though Granada may be one of Nicaragua's most interesting cities, it's surprisingly user-unfriendly in the lodging department, with exactly two budget hotels and two luxury hotels—period. The budget choices are on Calle La Calzada, about 2½ blocks east of Parque Central. **Hospedaje Vargas** (tel. 055/2897), on the north side of the street, charges $4 a person for rooms of varying quality. Some are dark and cramped, a few are large and airy; all are clean, though, and the bathrooms won't make you gag. Across the street, **Hospedaje Cabrera** (tel. 055/2781) offers similar rooms at $5 a person. It gets more business than Vargas across the street, maybe because it offers meals and looks slightly more cared-for. Farther east down Calle La Calzada is **Hotel Granada** (tel. 055/2974), a rambling, airy colonial-style hotel that'll clean you out fast (doubles $50). The tourist park on the lake (*see* Worth Seeing, *below*), has bathrooms and plenty of space to (discreetly) pitch a tent. Farther south is undeveloped lakeshore that could also accommodate a tent, but you're a long way from help if you get hassled.

FOOD Granada's lack of budget lodgings is matched by its shortage of cheap eats, but if you're willing to pay a little more, you'll have plenty to choose from. On the cheap end, an **unmarked comedor,** across the street and a few yards north of Telcor, has good soups and ample lunches for around $2. Good, cheap tacos are available at **Tacos "Lory,"** a block west and 2 blocks north of Parque Central's northwest corner (open daily 11–9). The comedores in the **main market,** 2 blocks west and 2 blocks south of the southwest corner of Parque Central, serve cheap but hygienically dubious breakfasts and lunches 7 AM–4 PM daily. Up the price scale, **Cafetín El Otro** (tel. 055/4203), next to Hotel Alhambra on Parque Central, serves good steak and chicken meals for $5–$8 and also offers a cheap comida corriente for around $3. Down Calle La Calzada at the lakeside is **La Pantera,** a huge restaurant with shrimp and fish dishes for $7–$10 (open daily until midnight). Farther south, in the tourist park (*see* Worth Seeing, *below*), the street is lined with more than a dozen restaurants, most of them wheelchair-accessible, serving seafood, steak, and chicken, all at prices similar to La Pantera. Open daily for lunch and dinner, these places are pleasant whenever the weather's good, since most have outdoor seating and lake views.

WORTH SEEING Any tour of Granada should start at **Parque Central,** from which you can best imagine what Granada must have been like in its glory years. On the east side of the park is the main **cathedral,** originally built in the 16th century but destroyed during Walker's retreat in 1857. Reconstruction in neo-classical style began three years later and ended in 1910. The arched and columned building to the north of the cathedral is the **Palacio Episcopal;** the **Palacio Municipal** sits on the south side of the park; and on the west side, next to the Hotel Alhambra, is the **Palacio de la Cultura,** with an art gallery, library, and occasional cultural events.

If churches are your thing, you're in the right place. The most interesting is **Iglesia San Francisco,** 2 blocks north and 2 blocks east of the cathedral. This was the first church built in Granada (late 1520s), but it was destroyed and rebuilt three times. Next to the church is an old convent with a collection of pre-Columbian stone carvings that date to AD 800. The collection, open weekdays 8–4, also contains text describing the culture of the statues' creators, the Chorotegans, as well as extensive maps of the archaeological sites on Ometepe and Zapatera islands, where the carvings were found. Another church worth seeing is **Iglesia La Merced,** 2 blocks west of the park's southwest corner. Built in 1534 (but rebuilt, of course, after Walker's retreat), it has a tower with good views. Down Calle La Calzada at the lake is a warehouse that sits on the foundation of the first fort constructed by the Spanish in Central America, the **Fuerte de la Muelle.** Little remains except a few old cannons in the park next door. About 100 yards south from here along the lakeshore is the **Centro Turístico,** a suprisingly pleasant park with trees, picnic tables, and a dozen or so roadside restaurants serving decent lake fish and seafood. On weekends, the place fills with families and lovers. The water is funky, but people swim here anyway. A few restaurants will rent boats to tour Las Isletas and Isla Zapatera (*see* Lago de Nicaragua, *below*).

AFTER DARK Most of the action happens on weekends down at **Restaurant La Pantera,** where Calle La Calzada hits the lake, or at the bars and restaurants in the Centro Turístico on the shore. Tinny salsa music blares from tired old speakers, while local drunks manage to dance better than most sober foreigners. Check out the **Palacio de la Cultura** on Parque Central's west side for music or dances.

NEAR GRANADA

DIRIAMBA Managua–Rivas buses pass through this pleasant but shell-shocked town 25 kilometers (16 miles) west of Granada. Its highlight is the church, which, unlike most of the town center, survived the anti-Somoza insurrection fairly unscathed. From the north or west, the church is visible surrounded by red-tile roofs and tall palms. While little can be found here by way of accommodations, it's a good place to catch a bus to the coast to visit La Boquita and Casares (*see* Southern Pacific Coast, *below*).

VOLCAN MOMBACHO Once over 6,000 feet, Mombacho Volcano, a few miles south of town, blew its top sometime before the Spaniards' arrival. Now less than 4,000 feet, the volcano is still tall enough to dominate Granada's skyline. The slopes offer great views of the town and lake, but trails are ill-defined and overgrown.

PUERTO DE ASESES This port a few miles south of Granada is the gateway to Las Isletas, a collection of over 300 tiny islands just offshore (*see* Lago de Nicaragua, *below*). During the filming of *Walker* in 1987, the port was used to depict San Francisco during the Gold Rush (kind of a stretch). A few waterside restaurants offer views of the lake and Mombacho Volcano. Puerto de Aseses can be reached on foot by walking due south from Granada's market about 2½ miles. Taxis will make the trip for about $2 per person.

Rivas

As the last major town in Nicaragua before the Costa Rican border, Rivas gets lots of visitors taking a last look at the country before heading south. Most foreigners leave quickly, stopping in town only because it's a gateway to San Juán del Sur on the coast and Isla de Ometepe in Lake Nicaragua, as well as Costa Rica. Rivas owes its place in history to its location, a mile from the southern shore of Lake Nicaragua and a few miles northeast of the Pacific coast. Over the centuries, the town became a center for interoceanic and Pan-American travelers. Cornelius Vanderbilt made the region a major junction for his Accessory Transit Company, which transported passengers between the two coasts of the United States. Apart from its sleepy small-town streets, Rivas's only sight is its **cathedral,** an open and airy colonial structure. Among its artwork is a painting in the dome showing Catholicism, represented as a fearsome galleon, defeating ships representing Communism and Protestantism. Masonry, depicted as a warrior, lies dead amid the fray.

BASICS BND (2½ blocks west of the southwest corner of Parque Central) will change dollars during regular business hours. **Telcor** (4 blocks west and ½ block north of the southwest corner of Parque Central) has phone service daily 8–8, mail service weekdays 8–5. For **police,** call 631; for **ambulance,** 415.

COMING AND GOING To all points except San Jorge, buses depart from the market 2 blocks west and 3 blocks north of Parque Central's northwest corner. Managua buses depart every ½ hour 4 AM–5 PM (2½ hours, $2); buses to San Juán del Sur depart hourly 6 AM–5 PM (1 hour, $1); buses to Peñas Blancas on the Costa Rican border depart every 90 minutes 5:30 AM–2 PM (1 hour, $2). Buses to San Jorge leave every ½ hour 6 AM–5 PM from behind the Shell station on the highway, about 10 blocks east of the market (10 minutes, 50¢). Taxis make the trip to San Jorge for about $1 per person. Rivas has no city buses, but it isn't hard to walk around, and taxis go anywhere in town for about 50¢ per person. To the east, the twin peaks of Isla de Ometepe are impossible to miss. The main cathedral is on the east side of Parque Central, and everything else is an easy walk from here.

WHERE TO SLEEP AND EAT The best budget hotel is **Hospedaje Lidia,** a friendly, family-run place ½ block behind the Texaco station on the highway. Rooms are small and offer little privacy, but they're tidy and share clean bathrooms ($4 per person). You can get a decent breakfast for a little over $2. Two fleabag, mice-infested hotels sit on the highway a block north of the Texaco station. **Hotel Coco** and the next-door **Hospedaje Internacional** are well-known "love" hotels that rent rooms by the hour. Both are cheap ($4 per person), but the "love" noise is unbearable if you're lonely and reluctantly celibate. Rivas is to food what Arizona is to surfing. Only two places stand out. **Rinconcito Salvadoreño** (in Parque Central, open daily 8–8) serves excellent food at cheap prices. The *pupusas,* a Salvadoran specialty of fried dough stuffed with vegetables and spices (and sometimes meat), go for $2. **La Soya** (½ block north of the park's northwest corner) serves a number of decent vegetarian dishes for under $4. It's open daily 11 AM–9 PM.

NEAR RIVAS

SAN JORGE Most people visit this small port town on the shore of Lake Nicaragua, just over a mile east of Rivas, to take the boat to Isla de Ometepe. It's also worth a visit to dine at one of the many fish restaurants with views of the lake and volcanoes. No hospedajes are here, but the shore makes a good camping spot. Buses leave the dock every ½ hour for Rivas 6 AM–5 PM (10 minutes, 50¢). Taxis hang around for arriving boat passengers; a ride to Rivas is $1. The boat to Ometepe departs the dock Monday–Saturday at 11 AM, noon, and 4:30 PM, arriving at Moyogalpa an hour later ($1). On Sunday, the boat leaves at noon and 1 PM. The boat is a small wooden craft whose owners, not knowing when enough is enough, load the thing to overflowing.

PEÑAS BLANCAS AND THE COSTA RICAN BORDER If you're leaving the country, get ready for Nicaraguan bureaucracy at its Byzantine finest. The division of labor here is maddening: one clerk to stamp your passport, one to check your luggage, etc., etc., etc. Even with the complicated setup, the crossing can take as little as an hour, depending on whether the customs police feel like hassling you. Once the paperwork is done—and you've paid your exit fees (about $6 worth, part in dollars and part in córdobas)—a minibus takes you to the Costa Rican side, where the process looks much saner in comparison. Outside the border post, buses to Rivas leave hourly during the border's operating hours (daily 8–5).

Southern Pacific Coast

LA BOQUITA

Sort of a Motel 6 by the sea, La Boquita (about 50 kilometers/30 miles southwest of Managua) is a small, planned resort developed by the Sandinistas as an alternative to the exorbitant Montelimar resort near Managua. The beach here is attractive and unspoiled, especially if you walk north a few minutes. However, the resort—a complex of outdoor restaurants and bars huddled next to the Hotel La Casona—is cheesy and contrived. If you're looking for the *real* Nicaragua, you're in the wrong place. If you've already found the real Nicaragua and need a break from it, La Boquita won't be all that bad.

Rooms at **La Casona** (tel. 042/468) run from $15 (no view, no air-conditioning) to $30 (with the works). Unless you eat at the hotel's overpriced restaurant, you can chow on fresh seafood for less than you'd pay almost anywhere else on the coast. A yummy plate of camarones al ajillo is about $6 at any of the outdoor restaurants near the hotel. Buses to La Boquita leave Diriamba's market every two hours 7 AM–1 PM (½ hour, $1). If you drive in, you'll pay a dollar per passenger to park.

CASARES

About 5 kilometers (3 miles) south of La Boquita sits the tiny fishing village of Casares. It's a scruffy beach town which, strangely, draws a crowd of foreigners (much cleaner beaches are just outside town). **Hotel Casino Casares** on the waterfront is a ramshackle building whose rooms open on an indoor courtyard/bar/restaurant. Rooms ($4 per person) are small and the skimpy walls offer no privacy. Buses from Diriamba follow the same schedule as buses to La Boquita (*see above*).

SAN JUAN DEL SUR

San Juán del Sur is probably Nicaragua's most popular and pleasant beach town. Sitting on a half-moon bay surrounded by low hills, this small port town moves at a wonderfully lazy pace. **BND** (1 block north of the Hotel Estrella) changes dollars weekdays 8–noon and 2–4. **Telcor** (2 blocks south of Hotel Estrella) has international phone service 7 AM–10 PM daily, mail service weekdays 8–6. Buses from Rivas leave about every ½ hour 6 AM–5 PM (1 hour, $1), filled with crowds of mostly European backpackers. Because of the ample foreign presence, locals are a little warmer and less gawking than in most Nicaraguan cities.

WHERE TO SLEEP AND EAT San Juán has a decent selection of budget and upscale accommodations. The cheapest is **Casa 28**, a block west and ½ block north of the market, which rents cramped rooms that share icky bathrooms for $8 a double. **Hotel Estrella** (2 blocks east of the market/bus stop, tel. 0466/210) has decent $14 doubles. It's across the street from the beach and is uncommonly clean and attractive. Though some of the rooms are cramped and the walls don't go all the way to the ceiling, the staff is friendly and relaxed—they'll even arrange sailing, diving, or fishing expeditions. Half a block toward the market from the Estrella is **Casa Internacional Joxi** (tel. 0466/348), offering clean, modern rooms with bath and air-conditioning for $30 a double. Dorm-style bunk beds are $10 per person with air-conditioning or $8 without. The Norwegian man who runs the hotel is groovy—friendly, competent, and eager to help travelers make the most of their stay. Even if you're not a guest, he can help arrange fishing and sailing trips, and he even rents Windsurfers for $5–$10 a day, depending on the board. Joxi is usually booked solid on weekends, so try to call in advance.

The restaurants in the hotels listed above are all decent choices for food. The Estrella serves a heaping, delicious fish dinner for $7, and Joxi makes a good breakfast of pancakes ($4) or eggs ($3) that includes coffee and juices The beach is lined with outdoor restaurants that double as nighttime watering holes. They're basically indistinguishable from each other; plates of garlic shrimp run $7–$8 and make a satisfying meal. The comedores in the market are clean and appetizing, and a comida corriente here will set you back only $3.

OUTDOOR ACTIVITIES The main sports in San Juán del Sur are eating, drinking, and tanning. If you're feeling friskier, the town has some enterprising souls who can take you scuba-diving, deep-sea fishing, or sailing. Ask at the Estrella or the Casa Internacional Joxi and be prepared to lay down some serious cash. A less expensive adventure involves hiking to one of the nearby beaches. The beach at **Marsella,** about 6 kilometers (4 miles) north of town, is accessible by a dirt road that intersects the road out of town (look for the secondary school). Ask locals to recommend other beaches. The hills around the bay are also fun and will provide camera buffs with a rockin' good time. Two other beaches worth a trip are pretty much out of hiking distance. **La Flor** lies about 19 kilometers (12 miles) south of San Juán del Sur and is known for its untamed beauty, wide sandy beach, and killer welt-producing flies. Buses to San Juán del Sur from Rivas usually continue on to La Flor in the dry season, but the road gets tricky when it rains. **El Ostional,** near the Costa Rican border, is the last stop for buses continuing on from San Juán del Sur. Ostional has no hospedajes and only one crude comedor, but you'll have the beach to yourself.

Lago de Nicaragua

Though its western shore is only an hour away from Managua, Lake Nicaragua (a.k.a. Cocibolca), the world's 10th largest freshwater lake, offers the adventurous traveler a voyage through some of Nicaragua's most isolated and unspoiled territory. With over 300 islands, many of them uninhabited, and an abundance of waterlife normally seen only in saltwater seas, the lake comes close to being a natural wonder. And, as an added bonus, the people who inhabit the lake's sparse island settlements are among the friendliest and least harried of all Nicaraguans. The lake's size, just over 160 kilometers (100 miles) long and 64 kilometers (40 miles) wide, and its unique fish population (including the world's only freshwater sharks) have led scientists to speculate that it was a large ocean bay that got cut off from the Pacific by a volcanic eruption. As the salinity of the water declined, the marine life slowly adapted. Today, it's a rare treat to spot one of the few remaining lake sharks, some of which grow to 10 feet.

Traveling around the lake can take some time and effort, and the rainy season here deserves its name, but Lake Nicaragua will repay you for your troubles like almost no other place in the country.

The lake has played a key role in Nicaragua's past, and may do the same for its future. The Chorotegans arrived here from Mexico early in this millennium in flight from the war-making Olmecs, guided by a message from their oracles that they would settle next to a freshwater sea with two mountains in it. Arriving at the lake, they named it Cocibolca (or "sweetsea") and settled in. The Spanish recognized the lake's strategic value and founded their major settlement, Granada, on its northwestern shore. In the 1800s, the lake made Nicaragua the crossing-of-preference for interoceanic passengers and cargo, and inspired the idea of a canal linking the two oceans. A U.S. company actually began work on the project in 1889, but went bust a few years later. Even today, the idea of a canal is alive and well—a group of Japanese investors is studying the prospect most seriously. If built, the canal would change this lake and its communities beyond all recognition. Even without a canal, the lake has had little problem attracting visitors, drawn here by the volcanoes of Ometepe, the tombs and rock drawings of Zapatera, and the work of the primitivist artists of Solentiname.

ISLA DE OMETEPE

Ometepe, the twin-peaked island mentioned in the oracles' prophecy to the Chorotegans, draws the eye from miles away. Only a few miles off the lake's southern shore, the island rises dramatically out of the water in a bright, lush green that gets richer the closer you get. Formed by volcanoes that rose out of the water side by side, the island possesses a soil base of mineral-rich volcanic ash, which accounts for the heartiness of its plantlife. The jungle is filled with wildlife, including several species of rambunctious monkeys and beautifully exotic birds; the adventurous will have little trouble exploring its wilderness by foot or horse.

The volcanoes tower menacingly over the little villages along the shoreline—all of which look like they were built as far away from the two beasts as possible. The fearless will surely want to climb one or both: Both offer incredible views, and Volcán Madera (on the island's eastern side) has a hidden crater lake at the top. Also worth exploring are the archaeological finds scattered throughout the island, including stone carvings and petroglyphs made by the Chorotegans and related tribes. Moyogalpa and Altagracia, both served by ferry from the mainland, are the island's principal villages. For all of Ometepe's isolation, it's really not very hard to get to—only three hours by boat from Granada and one hour from San Jorge (*see* Near Rivas, *above*). But in many ways, it's a world away from the rest of the country and its problems. The people are friendly, nature survives in most of its glory, and the country's raging political strife is well out of earshot. In short, Ometepe is a great place to take a vacation from your vacation in Nicaragua.

BASICS

➤ **PHONES AND MAIL** • Moyogalpa's **Telcor** office, 3 blocks up from the dock and 1½ blocks to the right, offers phone service Monday–Saturday 8–6 and mail service on weekdays during the same hours. A Telcor office near the main square in Altagracia has the same services and hours.

➤ **VISITOR INFORMATION** • No Inturismo office graces the island, but **Señor Castillo** at the Hospedaje y Restaurante Castillo in Altagracia (*see* Where to Sleep and Eat, *below*) is more knowledgeable and helpful than Inturismo could ever be. Even if you don't eat or sleep here, the hospedaje is worth visiting just to talk with Señor Castillo, who can arrange guides and horse rentals, give you advice on what's worth seeing, and let you look at *Ometepe: Isla de Círculos y Espirales,* a rare illustrated book on the island's history and archaeological finds. He's one of the island's great treasures.

COMING AND GOING Ometepe is linked to the mainland by frequent boat service from Granada and San Jorge near Rivas. Boats from Granada use the dock at Altagracia, while boats from San Jorge dock at Moyogalpa. Boats to Granada leave on Tuesday and Friday at 11 PM and Sunday at 10 AM (3 hours, $1). Boats to San Jorge leave Monday–Saturday at 6 AM, 7 AM, and 1:30 PM. On Sunday, boats leave only at 6:30 AM and 7 AM (1 hour, 60¢). Tickets for both boats are available at the docks. The boats linking Ometepe to Granada are large, steel passenger ferries, but to and from San Jorge you'll ride in a small, overloaded wooden craft. The operators of the latter service may take your name when you purchase a ticket "just in case you don't make it." How reassuring.

GETTING AROUND Ometepe Island is better thought of as two circular islands joined together by a narrow isthmus. The more "developed" part (developed is a relative concept here) is known as **Concepción,** named after 5,500-foot **Volcán Concepción,** which rises out of its middle. Ometepe's two largest towns are here—Moyogalpa on the western shore, and Altagracia on the northeast side, near the isthmus that leads east to **Madera,** the other part of the island. A coast road circles Concepción, linking all of its settlements. South of Altagracia another road runs across the isthmus and halfway around Madera in either direction. **Balque** is Madera's major settlement, located on its northern shore. No road serves the eastern villages of Madera, which is named after the 4,400-foot **Volcán Madera** that towers over this half of the island.

A regular bus route circles Concepción once an hour 5 AM–5 PM (about 40¢). Buses to and from Moyogalpa and Altagracia use each town's parque central as the main bus depot. From Altagracia, buses leave for the Madera side of the island four times a day, at 6 AM, 9 AM, noon, and 3 PM and return to Altagracia about 1½ hours later (25¢). No taxis serve the island, but hitching a ride from passing pickup trucks is a cinch. Horses are a more interesting but much more expensive alternative to getting around by bus (see Outdoor Activities below).

WHERE TO SLEEP AND EAT Part of Ometepe's charm is its lack of development; the down side of this, of course, is that you don't have a lot of options when it comes to choosing a place to eat or sleep. Only Moyogalpa and Altagracia have organized lodging and sit-down restaurants, but if you're willing to pay, you'll find families all over the island who'll be happy to feed you and give you shelter.

➤ **MOYOGALPA** • Compared to Altagracia, Moyogalpa is overflowing with hospedajes and restaurants. On the right a few feet up the main street from the dock is the **Bar y Restaurante Moyogalpa,** the class act in town. Rooms have comfortable beds, mosquito nets, and—the libidinous should take note—real concrete walls that offer a measure of privacy ($4 per person). The restaurant has tasty lake fish (about $6) and typical Nicaraguan meat dishes with rice, beans, and salad (about $4). Another 50 yards up on the left is the **Hospedaje Aly,** an attractive but basic hospedaje ($3 per person). Rooms here are clean but have hard, lumpy beds and the walls give no privacy. The plant-filled patio is a great place to hang out in a hammock and chat with other travelers. Management can get surly, especially if you want to stay out past their 10 PM curfew. The food here is good and cheap: The tacos are a deal at $2. The **Pensión Jade,** up another block from Hospedaje Aly, has tiny, dark rooms, smelly bathrooms, and no food, but it's the cheapest place in town (about $2.50 per person).

➤ **ALTAGRACIA** • Though Altagracia, with 16,000 inhabitants, is almost twice the size of Moyogalpa, it has only one place to eat and sleep. **Hospedaje y Restaurante Castillo,** a block south and ½ block west of the main church, would be just another unexciting budget spot were it not for its owner, Señor Castillo, Ometepe's unofficial historian and tour director. He'll chat, give you the scoop on things to see and do on the island, and can help get you guides and horses. Rooms here are $3 per person, and food is typical and easy on the budget ($2–$4 for meals).

➤ **CAMPING** • Camping would be a breeze on the island were it not for the hungry insects, who'll make every effort to eat you alive. If you know what you're doing, you'll find plenty of isolated spots where you can pitch a tent, but campers who haven't had experience roughing it in tropical wilderness should think twice before offering their flesh and blood to the jungle. Señor Castillo can give you tips on where to park your tent.

WORTH SEEING Ometepe's charm is in its natural beauty, but a few human-made sights are worth visiting. Altagracia's main square is decorated with pre-Columbian stone carvings found on other parts of the island. Near Balque, on the Madera side of the island, is a site with dozens of ancient petroglyphs. Ask Señor Castillo at the Hospedaje Castillo for directions. A few beaches near Altagracia are well-worth visiting. **Enseñada Paso Real** is a pleasant cove where cattle are brought to drink and local women do their wash. East of Altagracia is the **Punta Tagüizapa,** which is isolated and clean. **Santo Domingo,** southeast of Altagracia near the Madera side of island, is a beautiful, sandy beach that stretches for miles.

The volcanoes are the real stars here. Even if you don't climb them, it's worth walking up their slopes a little way to catch great views of the island and lake below. From Altagracia, a trail passes through the village of Pull and up the slopes to the summit of Volcán Concepción. To go to the top, you should allow five hours and be in pretty good shape. Another trail begins near Moyogalpa (ask locals for directions). The Madera volcano is accessible from Balque. Near the top you'll find a stunning crater lake that's great for a swim or picnic. The climb here takes about four hours. It's a very good idea to hire a guide for both these climbs since the trail is hard to follow and you'll encounter hazards along the way. Señor Castillo can help.

You'll find little to do on the island after dark except hang out on the street with everyone else. A crowd sometimes gathers at **Restaurant Bahía** (across from Hospedaje Aly) to drink and shout over the blaring stereo. A few local dances are held around the island during holidays, especially during the last week of July, when the island celebrates its patron saint, Santiago.

OUTDOOR ACTIVITIES The Bar y Restaurante Moyogalpa near Moyogalpa's main dock rents out Windsurfers. Five dollars will get you a board for the whole day. The Bar y Restaurante Moyogalpa, and Señor Castillo, can arrange horse rentals for about $6 a day per person. Horses are a great way to explore off the beaten path, especially the lower slopes of the volcanoes. Give each place a day's notice.

LAS ISLETAS

Just off the lake shore south of Granada is a grouping of over 300 tiny islands, formed of volcanic rock, that are filled with exotic plant and animal life. No lodging is available on the Isletas. The islands are also home to a small community of Nicaraguans, including a few *ricos* who've built elaborate mansions on their own islands. Touring the islands by boat makes for a relaxing day-trip. The bird life gets pretty raucous and colorful in the late afternoon. You can hire boats for about $10 an hour or $40 a day (for up to 10 people) at the Puerto de Aseses dock or at the restaurants at the southern end of the Granada waterfront. For fun, the boat pilots can stop at one of the island restaurants for lunch or dinner. The **Fuerte San Pablo,** built in 1783, sits on an island farthest from shore. Originally intended as a defense against pirate raids on Granada, the fort underwent restoration in the 1970s that turned it into a drab, ahistorical structure. The views are nice, though.

ISLAS ZAPATERA AND EL MUERTO

Boats from Puerto de Aseses (*see* Near Granada, *above*) are also available for day-trips to these two islands about 19 kilometers (12 miles) south of Granada. Both were once rich in archaeological treasures, but many of the finds were hauled off to museums in Managua. Zapatera contains the remains of Sozoate, an ancient temple. El Muerto, a once-sacred burial site, is filled with tombs and petroglyphs. Make sure the boat price includes the services of a guide. Only Zapatera is inhabited—and only sparsely—and neither island offers food or lodging. Experienced campers could easily pitch a tent here.

ARCHIPIELAGO DE SOLENTINAME

Solentiname Archipelago has achieved legendary status throughout Latin America because of the efforts of a quiet philosopher-priest, Ernesto Cardenal, who later served as the Sandinistas' Minister of Culture. In 1967, Father Cardenal founded a small commune on the island of Mancarrón, where farmers and laborers learned to paint and listened to the priest's liberation theology. Soon, the "primitivist" artworks of the islands' inhabitants were in high demand, and Solentiname became something of a mecca for Latin American artists and political activists. The commune has since disbanded, but the archipelago remains a popular stop for the ecotourism crowd, who jaunt in from Costa Rica for a few days to tour the islands' unspoiled beauty and buy a painting or two from the artists who remain.

The islands are some of the most isolated and undeveloped territory in the country, accessible only by boat from the remote town of San Carlos on the lake's southeastern shore (see below). They have no phones, no electricity (except from gas-powered generators), and few comforts. Two hospedajes on the archipelago's two largest islands cater to travelers. **La Garza,** on the island of Mancarrón, housed Father Cardenal's commune and is now run by the nonprofit Solentiname Development Association, which uses proceeds from the hospedaje to fund a school and health clinic for locals. Rooms are in four large concrete cabins and share bathrooms. Prices here are steep, $25 a person including meals, but the place is comfortable and friendly. The staff can help arrange tours and transportation to and from the islands. **La Alberge,** on the island of San Fernando, is a family-run place that offers cheaper and much more primitive accommodations ($10 a room), and cheap meals of rice, beans, and some kind of meat (don't ask, if you think you can't live with the answer). Families on the islands are also known to rent out rooms or hammock space to foreign travelers for as little as $2 per person.

Many of the Solentiname archipelago's 50 islands are uninhabited or only sparsely so, and their forests bustle with the antics of howler monkeys, caimans, and over 80 species of birds.

You can hire a guide and a boat at La Garza, or at almost any of the islands' docks, to tour the smaller, less-developed islands and get a look at the stunning wildlife. Horses are available for rent at La Garza and make for an easy way to tour Mancarrón. Artists live throughout the archipelago and welcome visitors to their homes, especially if you look eager to buy. Near La Alberge on San Fernando lives José Obando, known for his colorful balsa-wood carvings. Another famed artist, Rodolfo Arellano, lives on the island of Doña Guevara (near San Fernando). Señor Arellano paints colorful primitivist scenes of island life, which he sells for as much as $300 abroad but for as little as $100 at his home. Whether or not you're in the market, Señor Arellano, who is the archipelago's unofficial historian, can fill you in on the island's history and folklore.

Nights in Solentiname are quiet affairs, as you might expect. The largest crowd gathers at La Garza on Mancarrón, where guests and travelers staying with nearby families hang out, chat, and watch the stunning sunset. The word "disco" appears nowhere on the islands.

SAN CARLOS

Rebuilt after a fire destroyed most of the town in 1984, San Carlos is a tiny, makeshift settlement on the southeast shore of Lake Nicaragua that is choked with dust in the dry season and mud-bound in the rainy season. The best reason for coming is to catch a boat to the nearby Solentiname islands or up the magnificent Río San Juán to Castillo Viejo or the Atlantic coast. Though the town is dull, it gets a steady trickle of travelers headed to more interesting points nearby. The town is served by boat from Granada (see Granada, *above*). The boats, which leave Granada on Monday and Thursday afternoons, arrive in town sometime between midnight and 1 AM, usually greeted by happy crowds celebrating the arrival of visitors from civilization. Hospedaje owners are among the greeters, looking for dollar-carrying foreigners who need a room. The boats head back to Granada the next day (Tuesdays and Fridays). One boat leaves at 3 PM, stopping at San Miguelito and Morrito on the lakeshore before arriving in Granada around midnight. Another boat leaves an hour later, passing by Altagracia on Ometepe Island before arriving in Granada eight hours later ($2). Small launches make the one-hour trip to the Solentiname islands at 7 AM each day ($2). Other launches travel up the Río San Juán to Castillo Viejo all day (2 hours, $5). Slower cargo boats headed up the river sometimes allow passengers. Ask around at the dock. Finally, passenger trucks travel up the road to Juigalpa from San Carlos's market during the dry season (7 hours, $3). Travelers can exchange dollars at a **BND** near the main park, a few blocks east of the lakeshore. The **Telcor** office is located near the main park's southeast corner (look for the antenna).

WHERE TO SLEEP AND EAT San Carlos's lodging options will challenge those not keen on mosquito-infested, grime-encrusted living conditions and no running water. The best you can do in town is to head to **Hotel San Carlos,** between the dock and the main park. Rooms ($5 per person) here are basic and dark and share ripe bathrooms, but the hotel isn't as disgusting as the other options in town. For food, the market comedores offer the cheapest fare in town. You can fill up here (morning–5 PM) on typical Nicaraguan food for less than $3. For dinner, try **Restaurante Mirador,** where the river meets the lake a few blocks southwest of the main park. The restaurant serves big portions of lake fish and steak, though the price may cut into your appetite ($7–$10). It sits on the site of an old fort that guarded the river entrance.

RIO SAN JUAN

The Río San Juán has a fabled place in Nicaraguan history. Cutting a navigable channel between the Atlantic and Lake Nicaragua, the river served both as a lifeline to Spain and the rest of the world and as a point of entry for marauding bands of pirates and English invaders. The river fascinated passengers making the journey on Cornelius Vanderbilt's Accessory Transit Company between the two U.S. coasts, including a young Mark Twain, who was moved to write about the beauty of the wild jungle surrounding the river's banks. The Spanish built several forts along the river to protect Granada and other towns on Lake Nicaragua's shores from pirate raids. One, Castillo Viejo, survives as Nicaragua's most fascinating historical site.

Nature lovers will probably wet their pants with excitement here, since the river and the surrounding jungle are home to alligators, birds, monkeys, and other wildlife that appear oblivious to the passing boat traffic. Nature lovers should also probably say a prayer of thanks that the United States, after looking long and hard here, decided on Panama as the site of the interoceanic canal. The jungle is not out of the woods yet, though: Japanese investors are reinvestigating the river as the site of a new, larger canal to compete with the Panama Canal. If it's built, the country will get a much-needed infusion of development dollars at the expense of irreparable damage to a wondrous ecosystem.

One of Nicaragua's most famous women (after Bianca Jagger and Violeta Chamorro) earned her fame at Castillo Viejo on the San Juan River. In 1762, Rafaela Herrera, the 18-year-old daughter of the fort's commander, took charge of the Spanish troops stationed here after her father was wounded in a siege by English pirates. She ordered her troops to soak old sails in oil, set them on fire, and float them toward the attackers' ships. The ploy worked, setting the pirates in flight to keep their wooden ships from going up in flames.

Travelers who want to see this ecological treasure should start at San Carlos, where they'll be able to catch a cargo boat or private launch (*see above*). It's probably not worth making the nine-hour river trip to **San Juan del Norte** on the Atlantic coast, which flourished when Vanderbilt's transit company was in business. Though it sits in an attractive delta, the place has been all but abandoned to the jungle. Castillo Viejo, on the other hand, just a few hours by boat from San Carlos, is well worth the effort. By the time you read this, a Spanish-funded development project will have restored the historic fort to perfect condition.

El Castillo de la Concepción (called Castillo Viejo by locals), built in 1672 to protect the settlements along Lake Nicaragua from attack, sits on a commanding hill at a bend in the San Juan River a few hours east of San Carlos. Travelers to Castillo Viejo will now find a modern complex of restaurants and affordable hospedajes in the village at the foot of the fortress.

Central Nicaragua

Mountainous central Nicaragua sprawls between dense jungle to the east and the lake-filled volcanic region to the west, and it has a flavor all its own. Political passions run deep here, and ideological leanings are just as deeply diverse: Ranchers in the cow-filled regions around Juigalpa and Boaco were quite disturbed by the Sandinistas' redistributive ideologies, while the populations around Matagalpa, Jinotega, and Estelí farther north have definitely gone revolutionary and were considered a Sandinista stronghold.

Boaco

Boaco is a pleasant, relatively prosperous little town nestled in the heart of Nicaragua's mountainous ranching country. At nearly 1,200 feet, the town enjoys a cool climate year-round. Boaco is surrounded on all sides by steep hills; indeed, part of the town (the "high" city) is built on a hill that overlooks the rest (the "low" city). The high elevation and moist air keep the surrounding hills a beautiful, lush green, and you'll see cattle grazing everywhere. The town serves as the major commercial center for the nearby ranches, whose proud cowboys, dressed to the hilt, ride around town on beautiful show horses. Photographers will have a field day here, especially during mid-July, when Boaco celebrates its patron saint Santiago.

BASICS BANIC and BND sit next to each other 1 block east and 1 block north of the northeast corner of the high city's Parque Central and will *only* change cash dollars.

Telcor (tel. 054/449) is on the southern side of Parque Central in the high city. Phone service is available 8 AM–10 PM every day, mail service weekdays 8–6. For emergencies, call the **police** (tel. 374); **ambulance** (tel. 200); or **Hospital José Nieborowsky** (tel. 054/253).

COMING AND GOING Buses for Managua leave the market on the south side of the low city every ½ hour 5 AM–4 PM (2½ hours, $2). Passenger trucks head to smaller towns nearby and to Matagalpa infrequently, depending on road conditions. The mar-

Juigalpa

Juigalpa, 100 kilometers (60 miles) east of the capital, is the main commerical town of Nicaragua's cattle region, but if it weren't for the Amerrique mountains nearby, the town would barely be worth mentioning. However, it's strategically located halfway between Managua and Rama, on the way to Bluefields on the Atlantic Coast. From Juigalpa's main market, a block east of the northeast corner of Parque Central, buses depart for Managua and Rama beginning around 5 AM. To get to Rama in time to catch the boat to Bluefields, you'll have to leave before 6:30 AM. Hitching is possible on the highway, which gets a lot of truck traffic.

ket is just a few blocks east of the road to Managua, where you can try to hitch. To get to the high city, walk north up the hill (not advisable if you're carrying a heavy load) or take a taxi for about 60¢.

WHERE TO SLEEP Boaco's not busting out with decent hotels. Only one, in fact, could be called decent: The **Hotel Sobalvarro** (½ block east of Telcor, tel. 054/515), on Parque Central in the high city, is a pleasant building with a front patio that looks onto the main park. Inside, the hotel has a garden patio with exotic birds and a rear deck that looks out over the entire low city. Rooms are basic but tidy and share clean bathrooms (singles $6, doubles $8). The hotel also has a small cafeteria serving breakfast (about $2) and lunch (about $3). Two really cruddy hospedajes are in the low city: **Pensión Montiel**, 4 blocks north of the market, is dark and dirty (singles $4, doubles $6); **Hotel Boaco**, 1 block west and a block north of the market, offers similar rooms at similar prices.

FOOD Boaco's jet set dines at **La Cueva**, near high Parque Central's south side, overlooking the low city. Standard grilled meat dishes and chicken are $6–$8. The place turns into a disco on weekends ($1 cover). **El Parador**, next to BND in the high city, serves burgers ($1.50), pizzas ($2–$3), and meat dishes ($5–$7) in a clean, if tacky, setting. The bar has a good selection of cocktails ($2). The **market** has an abundance of cheap and slightly scary comedores.

WORTH SEEING Visit the **Botica El Carmen** on the north side of Parque Central to see the owner's collection of pre-Columbian idols. The good doctor sometimes leads tours through his house in back, which holds a motley collection of artifacts from the region and old Spanish firearms. José Nieborowsky died in this house in 1947.

Matagalpa

Matagalpa's lush mountain setting, cool climate, and reputation for hospitality have for years attracted large numbers of foreigners. In the 1800s, a wave of immigrants—mostly British, German, and French—arrived and established the region's coffee plantations; in the process, these immigrants forced many of the indigenous farmers off their lands. Years later, the region witnessed a more benevolent invasion of foreigners who came during the Sandinista years to work on solidarity projects. Today, the city still draws many foreign work brigades headed to villages nearby. The political enthusiasm of the locals and the presence of energetic foreigners makes Matagalpa one of Nicaragua's most culturally vibrant cities. Pleasantly overshadowing all this are the mountains, which offer the traveler hikes and views guaranteed to thrill.

You have two choices for crossing over to Honduras from the north-central region. Buses leave the Huembes Market in Managua for Ocotal, from where you can reach the border at Las Manos by passenger truck (1 hour); or, take a bus from the same depot to Somoto, from where it's a ½-hour minibus ride to the border at El Espino.

Though Matagalpans voted with their pocketbooks in the last elections, giving Violeta Chamorro a slight edge over Daniel Ortega, the city's heart has been staunchly Sandinista. Both Tomás Borge, the Sandinistas' Interior Minister and the lone survivor of the group that founded the FSLN, and Carlos Fonseca, another founding member and leading "martyr" of the FSLN, were born and raised here. All through the Sandinista insurrection, Matagalpa was a major pain in the ass for Somoza and hosted vicious street battles between the dictator's National Guard and the revolutionaries. Today, Matagalpa hosts one of the larger Liberation Day celebrations (July 19), when thousands converge on the Parque Central to mark the Sandinistas' victory over Somoza with music, fireworks, marches, speeches, dancing, and, of course, drinking.

BASICS Matagalpa's banks change cash dollars only; **BND** is 3 blocks south of Parque Central's southeast corner. **Telcor** is 1 block east of the northeast corner of Parque Central. Phone service is available daily 8 AM–10 PM, mail service weekdays 8–5:30. For emergencies, call the **police** (tel. 3870) or **ambulance** (tel. 2059).

COMING AND GOING Matagalpa's bus depot is at the market in the southwest of town, next to the river, about a 30-minute walk from Parque Central. A taxi ride to the center should be about 80¢. From the market, buses leave for Managua about every 40 minutes 4 AM–5 PM (3 hours, $2); for Jinotega, every hour 6 AM–4 PM (1½ hours, $1); and for Estelí (via Sébaco), every ½ hour 5:30 AM–5 PM (2 hours, $1.25). Passenger trucks and buses for nearby villages also leave from here.

The town itself is easy to walk around, and cheap taxis are abundant if walking loses its charm. About 5 blocks east and 2 blocks north of the bus depot is **Parque Darío**, where most of the budget travel facilities are situated. To the north of this park, about 7 blocks up **Avenida José Benito Escobar,** the town's main commercial street, you'll find **Parque Central** and the Cathedral.

WHERE TO SLEEP Most of Matagalpa's budget hotels are on or near Parque Darío, a 15-minute walk from the bus depot. The best of this lot is probably the **Hospedaje San Martín** (tel. 061/3737), an unmarked hospedaje in the same building as the Farmacia San Martín on the northwest corner of the park. Rooms are basic, and the walls offer no privacy, but it's cleaner than the rest; the señora who runs the place is friendly and helpful and serves good breakfasts ($2). Rooms here go for $4 a person and share a common bathroom. Two blocks east of the northeast corner of Parque Darío is the **Hotel Bermúdez** (tel. 061/3437), offering rooms without bath for $4 per person, and rooms with bath for $5 a person. The hotel's in good shape, is kept fairly clean, and offers three meals a day ($2–$4), but it has strict house rules (11 PM curfew) and cold management. If you'd like to splurge, the **Hotel Ideal** (2 blocks north and 1 block west from the northwest corner of Parque Central, tel. 061/2483) is a full-service hotel with clean, modern rooms, a restaurant, bar, and garage. It also comes with full-service prices ($19–$22 doubles).

FOOD Decent comedores abound in Matagalpa. Parque Darío is a good place to start looking. The **Comedor San Martín,** a few feet north of Parque Darío on Avenida José Benito Escobar, is a popular place serving standard Nicaraguan fare to happy crowds from about 6:30 AM to 10 PM every day. Breakfast is $2, lunch and dinner, which usually feature grilled beef or chicken, are $3. **Restaurante Don Diego,** 1 block south down Avenida José Benito Escobar from Parque Central and ½ block west, is one of the classier eateries in town. The breaded chicken fillet (*chuleta de pollo empanizada*, about $5) is great, and the pizza (about $8 for a large) is a passable imitation of the real thing. **Sorbería Copalia,** ½ block east of Parque Darío's northeast corner, claims to have Nicaragua's best ice cream. Ben and Jerry have little to worry about, but it's pretty satisfying nonetheless.

WORTH SEEING For political groupies, Matagalpa's one museum makes for an interesting visit. The **Museo Casa Cuna Carlos Fonseca,** 1 block east of the southeast corner of Parque Darío, was the home of Carlos Fonseca, the guiding light of the FSLN and one of its original founders. Photographs and text tell the story of Fonseca's childhood, student years, and active opposition to the Somoza dictatorship. Fonseca's death in a firefight with the National Guard in 1976 is also recounted. The museum is open every day approximately 9–5 and the staff requests a donation. Matagalpa offers stunning scenery in the hills nearby. One trail, which begins south of town on the highway about (60 feet south of the pedestrian bridge), climbs 600 feet to **El Calbario.** The summit has a small shrine and mast and offers good views of the valley and mountains. A less arduous walk is up to the cemetery south of town (about ½ mile southwest of the bus depot). Here you'll have good views of the town and can visit the grave of Ben Linder, the only American volunteer worker killed by the contras in their war against the Sandinistas. Linder, who entertained kids in the region with his juggling-clown-riding-a-unicycle act, worked on a hydroelectric project north of Jinotega until he was ambushed by a contra patrol and shot in the back of the head at point-blank range. His headstone shows a juggling dove of peace riding a unicycle. To find his grave, walk through the main entrance to the cemetery, turn left, and walk up the first large path to the right; the grave is about a hundred feet up on the right.

Jinotega

Jinotega sits in a broad valley surrounded by wonderfully green mountains. It's the seat of the Jinotega department, a sprawling region that reaches up to the Honduran border and far east along the Río Coco. The town is dull, dirty, and depressed, worn out by the insane violence of the contra war, which hit the town and the department's northern reaches particularly hard. Still, the ride to town from either Matagalpa or Estelí (via San Rafael del Norte) is stunning, the cathedral here is one of the largest and most interesting in all of Nicaragua, and you can visit a legendary, ancient witch-doctor over the hills. His love potions may come in handy during the rest of your trip.

COMING AND GOING Buses to and from Matagalpa and Managua use the bus depot in the southwest part of town, 3 blocks south and 5 blocks east of Parque Central. From here, buses depart for Matagalpa every 45 minutes 5 AM–5:45 PM (1½ hours, $1). Five express buses leave for Managua every day (3½ hours, $3). Another bus depot lies a half-mile north at the market, from where buses and passenger trucks head north. Trucks for San Rafael del Norte leave here a few times in early morning and twice in the early afternoon (2 hours, $1). Any truck north from here will also pass the Lago de Apanas.

WHERE TO SLEEP AND EAT Jinotega's importance as a destination for foreign solidarity workers has created a large supply of decent budget hospedajes. The two stand-outs are the **Hotel Tito**, 1½ blocks north of the front of the cathedral, and **Sollentuna Hem** (tel. 063/334), 2 blocks east and 5 blocks north of the cathedral. The Tito is cheap ($4 per person), friendly, and lusciously clean (it's the cleanest budget hotel I saw in all of Nicaragua). Sollentuna Hem's owner is a real treat: She lived in Sweden for years and loves talking with travelers in English, Swedish, or Spanish. The rooms are in back of her home and have a homey feel ($12 doubles).

Unfortunately, the foreign demand hasn't produced a decent supply of good restaurants. Apart from the comedor at Hotel Tito, try the stylish **McGarry's** on the street behind the cathedral, serving grilled meats and chicken for lunch and dinner for $5–$8 per plate (closed Monday). The **Hotel Tico** (tel. 063/530), next to the bus depot in the southeast of town, houses Jinotega's other "classy" restaurant. Besides the usual grilled meats, fish, and chicken (about $6–$8), the menu includes good salads that are meals in themselves ($5–$6). The market has several cheap comedores.

WORTH SEEING Jinotega's **cathedral,** on the main park, is not much on the outside, but its large interior is filled with interesting details and fine religious art, including a Black Christ of Esquipulas. Originally built in the early 1800s, the cathedral has undergone extensive reconstruction, most recently in the 1950s. Across the park and through the cemetery, a trail leads up to **Poya de la Cruz,** the cross on the hill overlooking Jinotega from the west. The climb offers great views of the valley and surrounding hills, but expect some hard work before the pleasure—allow an hour to reach the top. Farther along the trail, about ½ hour past the cross, lives Nando, a legendary **faith healer** (*curandero*) who has a wide following throughout Central America. Now well into his eighties, Nando is said to be able to cure any ailment and can also make up potions to help you conquer the heart of a would-be love.

Estelí

Estelí's name means "river of blood" in the language of the Chorotegans who inhabited the area before the Spanish invasion. Little did they know how prophetic their choice of name would be. Beginning with the conquest, Estelí has seen more than its share of bloody violence. The slaughter of the Chorotegans, the countless battles in the 19th-century civil war between the Liberals and Conservatives, vicious attacks on Sandino's partisans, the bloody years of revolution against the Somoza dictatorship, and, most recently, Ronald Reagan's war on this Sandinista stronghold have claimed more dead here than could ever be remembered. In the face of this history, Estelí has maintained a dignity and dynamism that still draw foreign development workers in droves. Estelí may be poor, battered, and tired, but it's far from beaten.

Set in a wide valley 2,500 feet high, the city offers a cool climate and easy access to the surrounding mountains. Nearby, travelers will find one of Nicaragua's most pleasant swimming holes—the Salto de Estanzuela—with clean, clear water and a 90-foot waterfall. In town, little remains of the colonial architecture, and bombed-out buildings are everywhere, but life beats at a rapid pulse. The people of Estelí, still die-hard Sandinistas, are determined to keep the memory and achievements of the revolution alive and well, and their political and cultural agitation receives the support of a large and enthusiastic foreign community. If you're at all outgoing, tapping into Estelí's energy will be an effortless and inspiring experience.

BASICS Banks around town change dollars at standard rates. Three banks are a block west and 1 block south of Parque Central. **Telcor** is 1 block south and ½ block east of Parque Central's southeast corner. Phone service is available daily 8 AM–9 PM, mail service weekdays 8–5. For emergencies, call the **police** (tel. 2615); **ambulance** (tel. 2330); or **fire department** (tel. 2413).

COMING AND GOING Estelí's bus depot is at the far south of town on the city's main commercial street, **Avenida Bolívar**, 14 blocks south of Parque Central. Taxis to the center are about 60¢. Buses depart daily for Managua about every 40 minutes 4:30 AM–5 PM (3 hours, $2); to Matagalpa (via Sébaco) about every hour 6 AM–4 PM (2 hours, $1.25); to Somoto about every hour 6 AM–5 PM (2 hours, $1.25); and to Ocotal once an hour 5–5 (2 hours, $1.50). Passenger trucks also leave here for smaller villages nearby, usually early in the morning between 5 and 7. The Interamerican Highway between Honduras and Managua passes the town's eastern end, about 5 blocks east of Parque Central.

Lago de Apanas, a man-made lake formed by the damming of the Río Tuma, is a favorite destination for picnickers, swimmers, and sport fishermen. The water is a muddy color but is still relatively clean. Trucks heading north from the Jinotega market depot pass right by the lake.

WHERE TO SLEEP Estelí has a good selection of budget hotels which sprang up to cater to the large number of foreigners that pass through. One of the best is the **Hotel Nicarao** (tel. 071/2490), 1½ blocks south of Parque Central on Avenida Bolívar. The hotel has friendly management, clean rooms "decorated" with random magazine photos, and a pleasant plant-filled courtyard where all three meals are served. Rooms are $4 a person and all share a common bath. **Hospedaje Mariela,** behind the bus depot, is a good choice for those taking an early bus out. Its nondescript concrete rooms are dark, but everything is kept clean ($4 per person). Big spenders should head for the **Hotel Mesón** (tel. 071/2655), a block north of the northeast corner of Parque Central, offering clean modern rooms with private baths at pretty reasonable prices ($11–$13).

FOOD The restaurant at Hotel Mesón (*see above*) has the most varied menu—grilled steaks, chicken, seafood, good salads, and even (gasp!) wine—but a meal here will set you back $6 to $10. Budget-minded eaters should head for the cheap comedores all along Avenida Bolívar. **La Soya,** 2½ blocks south of Parque Central, is one of the healthiest of the lot, serving a changing menu of soya-based vegetarian meals for breakfast, lunch, and dinner ($2–$3). **Doña Pizza** (closed Monday), ½ block west of Parque Central's northwest corner, serves a decent pizza—rare for Nicaragua. A large cheese pizza that feeds two is $5.

WORTH SEEING The **Casa de Cultura,** a block south of the front of Estelí's cathedral on Parque Central, is the cultural center for Estelí's politically aware youth. Art exhibitions are featured in the main room, and there's a small craft and book store in front. Behind the Casa de Cultura is the **Galería de Héroes y Mártires de Estelí,** a small museum packed with photos, texts, and personal effects in remembrance of the town's many sons and daughters who died in the fight against Somoza and Reagan's contras. The museum is humble and moving, and open daily 9–5. The staff, mostly mothers of the victims, requests a small donation.

OUTDOOR ACTIVITIES During the rainy season, locals head to the **Salto de Estanzuela,** a 90-foot waterfall that plunges into a deep pool about 5 kilometers (3 miles) south of town. Getting here is the biggest problem. If you're without wheels, you'll have to hitch or hike. The road to the falls begins on the Interamerican Highway about ¼ mile south of town and then heads 5 kilometers (3 miles) west. Ask locals for directions and cart out your trash: Locals keep the place clean and expect others to do so, too.

Costa Atlántica

Nicaragua's Atlantic coastal region has always been a world apart from the western half of the country. Though the region makes up over half of Nicaragua's land mass, its 300,000 residents account for less than 10% of the country's population, and many of them feel they have nothing in common with their compatriots to the west. In fact, they're probably right. The region was never really conquered by the Spanish, who gave up fighting the jungles and the clouds of disease-carrying mosquitoes. Instead, England ruled here, establishing a "monarchy" among the Miskito tribe that was subservient to the English crown. The Miskitos held court in Puerto Cabezas and terrorized the Sumu and Rama tribes with legendary enthusiasm.

England established principal ports at two cities—Puerto Cabezas and Bluefields—and imported slaves from Africa and Jamaica to work the growing number of agricultural plantations that helped fund its expanding empire. Today, England's legacy can be seen and heard in the region's people: The African slaves who settled here after gaining freedom have kept English as their native tongue. The Creoles, as they're known today, are concentrated in Puerto Cabezas and Bluefields, and most of them identify with Jamaica more than Managua. The English finally ceded the region to the Nicaraguan government in the 1890s but were quickly replaced by the newly emerging global empire, North American big business. U.S. mining and agricultural companies ran the region's economy until they abandoned the region after a devastating crop disease in the 1960s. They too left behind their own influence, including structural poverty and a love for twangy country-western music.

Since the late-19th century, various Nicaraguan regimes have attempted to impose their authority over the region, usually with disastrous results. The FSLN, in what even many Sandinistas consider an excess of arrogance, attempted to promote the revolution's policies here and ended up driving many of the region's inhabitants over to the contras. The indigenous population suffered most, as the Sandinista army relocated many tribes from their traditional homelands to prevent them from becoming embroiled in the growing conflict. While the FSLN brought a few much-needed public clinics and other social services to this poverty-stricken area, the radically autonomous people wanted nothing to do with the outsiders and resented any imposition of Managua's power. Realizing that their policies were a failure here, the Sandinistas reversed themselves in the late 1980s and negotiated an agreement that granted the region far-reaching autonomy. Today, most tribes have returned to their homes and reconstructed their lives. Their main worry these days is the economy.

The intrepid traveler will find a lot to discover here, but the going is hard: There's little infrastructure and the heat is stifling. Rain falls in torrents from June through February—yes, the dry season lasts only three months, and "dry" is relative. May is probably the best month to visit, as the rain has slowed to manageable proportions. The last weekend in May is ¡Mayo Ya! in Bluefields, one of Nicaragua's most exuberant cultural events, featuring dance, art, theater, coastal music, and alcohol-fueled delirium. During any time of the year, though, the people and jungly environment of the Atlantic coast offer a fascinating experience to those with the patience to discover it.

Unemployment is at crisis levels, and Hurricane Joan's arrival in 1988 caused catastrophic damage from which the region has not yet fully recovered.

The overland journey from Managua to Bluefields is hard work, so be prepared. Past Juigalpa, you'll find little designed with tourists in mind. Still, as you bounce along the broken road from Juigalpa to Rama in an old U.S. school bus, you'll find plenty to keep your attention. Little by little, the mountains give way to jungle lowlands, and whole villages pile on the bus with farm animals on their way to market. If you're carrying only traveler's checks, be warned that they're worthless pieces of paper east of Juigalpa. Stock up on córdobas in Juigalpa or carry dollars. Buses from Juigalpa to Rama depart about every ½ hour 4 AM–4 PM from the market (5 hours, $2).

Rama

If there's any town uglier than Managua, this has got to be the place. Pity the poor travelers who mistime their arrival and miss the boat to Bluefields, for they'll get taken for a ride in the few lousy hotels and comedores in town. Merchants from Granada founded this town to profit from the boat traffic to Bluefields. A hundred years later, their creation is a muddy hovel populated with businessfolk ready to suck your wallet dry. If at all possible, don't give them the chance.

BASICS Officially, the only place to change money in Rama is a **BND,** 3 blocks up the street away from the pier and 1 block to the right (open weekdays 8:30–noon and 2–3:30). They change only cash dollars, and at lower rates than you'll get in Managua. **Telcor** (open 7–7) is on the same street, 2 blocks to the left of the street that comes from the pier. It has no telephones, but you can send telegrams and regular mail.

COMING AND GOING Buses from Managua leave for Rama every day from Iván Montenegro market 4 AM–11:30 AM, but if you want to connect directly with the boat to Bluefields, you'll have to take the "express" bus that leaves the market on Tuesdays, Thursdays, Saturdays, and Sundays at 2:30 AM. The boat for Bluefields departs on the same days at 10:30 AM. If you're lucky, you'll only have to spend 10 or 15 minutes in Rama as you make the connection. Coming from Bluefields, boats leave on the same days at 5:30 AM sharp. Buses to Managua—the same ones that just brought Bluefields-bound passengers from Managua—are waiting at the road above the pier. Be prepared for the mad dash from boat to bus as people scramble to get a seat. If you can't get a seat, more buses to Juigalpa and Managua will depart soon; buses for both cities leave Rama every day 4 AM–4 PM (or so). All of these travel options are cheap. The most expensive ticket is for the boat, which costs around $5; bus tickets are $3 or less.

WHERE TO SLEEP AND EAT In Rama, prepare to pay too much for too little; the **Hotel Amy** is the obvious choice, since it's right next to the pier. It actually looks kind of funky and charming from the outside, but inside is pure hospedaje hell—dirty, dark, dank, depressing. The **Ramada Inn** is a cruel joke played on unsuspecting travelers. Again, cute and rustic outside, but inside it looks like something off the set of *Gilligan's Island*. A few bamboo poles tied together make a vague attempt to form a wall between you and the guy snoring in the next room. The Ramada is cleaner than the Hotel Amy, and both places rip you off for $5 per person. But hey, where else are you gonna go? Nondescript food at cartel prices is featured in Rama's comedores. Try **Los Viudes** on the first road to the left as you walk up from the pier. Their comida corriente at $3 is pretty decent, but everything else is a rip-off ($8 for shrimp?!).

Bluefields

Almost completely destroyed by Hurricane Joan in 1988, Nicaragua's most important Atlantic port has rebuilt to resemble its old self: Bluefields is at once impossibly dirty, busy, and fascinating. Named after Abraham Blauvelt, the Dutch pirate who founded the town in the 17th century, the town retains much of its pirate legacy. *Bluefileños* are a rough-and-tumble, motley collection of Creoles, mestizos, and indigenous people, with a few descendants of Chinese traders thrown in for good measure. The locals, like the founders, are not above playing on the wrong side of the law to make a fast buck: Rumor has it that Colombian cargoes of cocaine enjoy safe haven here on their way north to the U.S. Above all, though, the business of Bluefields is business. The town plays an important role as a market and trading center for the far-flung indígena and Creole communities hidden deep in the jungles.

By day, Bluefields bustles with Rastas, schoolchildren, merchants, Creole fishermen, and day laborers. The crowded covered **market** located on the water at the end of Avenida Aberdeen is particularly unforgettable. Away from the bustle, you might enjoy surveying the vibrant mix of architectural styles, with British colonial buildings squeezed in between West Indian cottages and Louisiana-style plantation houses. The town's liveliest attractions, though, come alive at night when bars and discos open their doors to people in search of a good beat, good rum, and maybe a kiss or two. Bluefields has no tourist sights as such. Unfortunately, the waters and beaches at Bluefields are too polluted for swimming and sunbathing. Boats along the piers, however, are always ready to take you away (for pay) to cleaner beaches where you can swim or fish in sanitary solitude (*see* Near Bluefields, *below*).

If these subjective words of acclaim aren't enough to entice you, then consider this: The total lack of roads in the area and the town's status as the region's principal port make it the only point of access to the beaches and settlements on the central Atlantic coast. Hidden lagoons, picture-book islands, and tribal settlements that form part of the Fourth World (so *un*developed that you can't even call them underdeveloped) are all within a few hours by boat from Bluefields. If you've got the time and a little extra money, this area offers an adventure you'll never forget.

BASICS

➤ **CHANGING MONEY** • You can change dollars (cash only) at **BND**, open weekdays 8–noon and 2–5, on the main street in front of the Moravian Church. Also, most businesses will gladly let you pay in dollars.

➤ **EMERGENCIES** • **Police** (tel. 448); **Red Cross** (tel. 582); **fire department** (tel. 298). The **Regional Hospital** at the west end of Avenida Cabezas usually has an English-speaking doctor on duty (tel. 082/391).

➤ **PHONES AND MAIL** • **Telcor** (corner of Av. Reyes and Calle Hudgson, ½ block north and 3 blocks west from the Moravian Church) is open Monday–Saturday 8 AM–10 PM, Sunday 8–6. You can call the U.S. collect through an AT&T operator, and phone service to other countries is also available. The **post office** in the Telcor building is open weekdays 8–5.

➢ **VISITOR INFORMATION** • According to Inturismo in Managua, they have a representative based in Bluefields' Casa de Cultura. Good luck finding her, though. Otherwise, talk to Inturismo in Managua before you go.

COMING AND GOING The traditional methods of reaching Bluefields—by boat or plane—are still the only practical options. Though the government cut a road through the jungle to connect the town with the rest of the country,

If you're coming to Bluefields from Rama by passenger boat, be warned that travelers make a mad dash from the boat to the few budget hotels. Be ready to run or call ahead.

it's impassable most of the year due to rain. From Managua, you have two choices. Buses from Managua leave the Iván Montenegro market for Rama, eight hours away, where you catch a boat for the stunning ride to Bluefields down the Río Escondido (*see* Rama, *above*). Alternatively, the Sandinista Air Force (**Fuerza Aérea Sandinista** or **FAS**) takes passengers on cargo flights to Bluefields every Tuesday and Saturday morning at 8 AM (1½ hours, $110 round-trip). Planes back to Managua leave Bluefields the same morning at 11 AM. Tickets for this flight can be bought only at **Senderos Tours** in Managua (½ block west of Hotel Intercontinental, tel. 02/24326) or at their office in the **Casa Mama Adela Hotel** in Bluefields (tel. 082/304).

Travel between Bluefields and Puerto Cabezas on the northern coast is sometimes possible by jumping on a cargo boat headed along the coast. Ask around the piers at each town. Also, the FAS flight sometimes stops in Puerto Cabezas to pick up passengers headed to Bluefields. Ask at Senderos in Managua or in Bluefields.

GETTING AROUND Bluefields' center is compact and easy to walk around. It's a good thing, because the town has no buses, and taxis get expensive quickly. A taxi to the center from the airstrip, no more than a 10-minute ride, costs $5. Once in the town center, you'll find streets laid out in a simple grid. The main street, **Calle Central,** runs along the water, north to south. Three main east–west avenues, **Avenida Aberdeen, Avenida Cabezas,** and **Avenida Reyes,** run inland from Calle Central. Avenida Aberdeen extends ½ block east of Calle Central toward the water, where you'll find the covered market. Though street names are marked with plaques on the sides of buildings, no one uses them; instead, like everywhere else in Nicaragua, directions are given as distances from prominent reference points. The **Moravian Church** on Calle Central across from Banco Nacional is an oft-used landmark. Getting to the outlying barrios will require a taxi unless you're keen on walking long distances through stifling heat.

WHERE TO SLEEP The budget lodging scene here is pretty scary. Only one hotel, the Hotel Hollywood (*see below*), offers pleasant rooms at pleasant prices. The rest are either depressingly dirty or very expensive.

Hotel Hollywood. A very friendly couple run this small hotel, rebuilt after it was destroyed by Hurricane Joan. Rooms are larger than your average budget hotel and certainly much cleaner. Located near the water, it gets a refreshing breeze off the bay during the day. The one drawback is that walls don't go all the way to the ceiling, so you get to know your neighbors *very* well, if you know what I mean. Still, they have the cleanest shared bathrooms in town and the Louisiana-style design, with balconies built for sipping mint juleps, makes it the best budget choice. Rooms are $5 per person. *Calle Central, about 4 blocks south off main passenger wharf, tel. 082/282. 10 rooms, none with bath.*

Hotel Cueto. Across the street from the Hotel Hollywood, this cavernous place isn't very appealing, but it's an adequate alternative if the Hollywood is full. Small concrete cell blocks and slightly revolting bathrooms are the two most notable features. Doubles without bath are $6, with bath $8; triples cost $12; and rooms for five people are $20. After midnight, the front gate closes, so you can only get back in if you've forewarned the management. *Calle Central, across from Hotel Hollywood, tel. 082/567. 45 rooms, some with bath. Midnight curfew.*

Hotel South Atlantic. This place is hard on the budget but offers sparkling, modern rooms with private bath and extra-friendly management. It's a good place to meet fellow adventurers and development workers from other countries. If you're missing mom, Mrs. Chambers, who manages the place with her husband, will make a fine stand-in. Doubles go for around $36. One group room with seven beds is available at a negotiable price. The hotel's restaurant is similarly pricey, but serves good seafood. *Av. Reyes, near Calle Hudgson and Telcor office, tel. 082/242. From the Moravian Church on Calle Central, walk ½ block north and 3 blocks west. 24 rooms, all with bath, TV, and air-conditioning. 2 AM curfew.*

FOOD The cheapo dining scene is even more dismal than the budget lodging scene. Soulless comedores offer up bland food, but the prices are palatable. For something special, you have to pay dearly. Even seafood, Bluefields' main export, is pricey (try Hotel South Atlantic, *see above*).

Restaurante Hollywood. One of the best budget options is located under the hotel of the same name and features faux-Chinese decor and good seafood dishes. The *corvina al ajillo* (filleted sea bass sautéed in garlic) is a treat at $5. A comida corriente for $3 is offered at lunch and dinner and usually features beef or chicken, rice, beans, and cabbage salad. *Calle Central. From the Moravian Church, walk 2 blocks south. Breakfast, lunch, and dinner.*

Salon Siu. This is Bluefields' answer to an old-fashioned soda fountain, and about the only place in town to get a decent breakfast on Sunday. Tasty scrambled eggs with beans and rice are $2, and the ham sandwich for $1 makes a good snack. The star here is the milkshake *(leche malteada);* at $2, it's not cheap, but after one of these, you'll be ready to face the heat again. *Calle Patterson between Av. Reyes and Av. Cabezas. From the Moravian Church, walk ½ block north, 1 block west, and ½ block south. Open daily 8–8.*

AFTER DARK The "cinema" (a TV, a VCR, and some couches), near the corner of Calle Central and Avenida Cabezas, offers a triple-header of action films and porn videos on most nights ($1). If you're coming to Bluefields to dance the night away to the infectious sounds of *costeño* (coastal) groups, you'll be disappointed: Most of them are back in Managua making big bucks. Instead, you'll have to settle for DJ mixes of salsa, teen pop, and a few morsels of reggae. Try **Disco Bacchus** (Calle Hudgson next to the park) for upscale crowds and a $2 cover charge. In the tacky **Chez Marcell** disco, around the corner from Bacchus, on Avenida Cabezas, you can listen to U.S. and Latin pop (and sometimes salsa) as you sit in the dark at tiny tables ($1 cover). The **Feeling Good Disco,** next to the park, is the local juvenile delinquents' hangout and is for the ultra-intrepid only (50¢ cover). The **Bar Tropicana** on the road to the airport is your best bet for finding live reggae and costeño music.

NEAR BLUEFIELDS

EL BLUFF At the opposite end of Bluefields Bay, where the bay opens to the Atlantic, sits the photogenic little village of El Bluff. Boats from any of the piers in Bluefields make the 10-minute trip for $2 per person. By following the footpath to the left above the dock for about ½ hour, you'll come to a scruffy but isolated ocean beach. A few houses along the path sell snacks and drinks from their front windows.

LAGUNA DE PERLAS This village is on the sheltered Lagoon of Pearls, an hour north of Bluefields. For $20, you can hire a boat from Bluefields to take you there and back. Life here crawls at a snail's pace, and it's the perfect place to waste time on the beach. **Miss Sorayda's Pensión,** behind the basketball court, offers the only lodging in town, where a couple of bucks will get you a room at the back of her house. From here, you can hire fishermen to sail you to the isolated indígena villages that dot the lagoon. Especially interesting is the Garifuna village of **Orinoco,** where a strange faith-healing festival, Gara Wala, is sometimes held (ask around).

ISLAS DEL MAIZ The Corn Islands, about five hours east of Bluefields by boat, are home to a small community of Creole fishermen and artisans. Travelers come to these islands to swim and tan in complete isolation. The tourist facilities are basic—this is NOT Club Med. But they're not cheap either, since almost everything sold to tourists is imported from the mainland. For lodging, **Hotel Playa Coco** and **Blanch Brians** are most popular with foreigners (about $5 per person). The islands have few established restaurants, but people sell tasty seafood meals from their huts. Until Aeronica went under, there was regular air service to the Islas from Managua and Bluefields. Now the only option is taking the boat that leaves the main wharf at Bluefields on Mondays at 9 AM, returning to Bluefields on Wednesdays at 8 AM ($5 each way, 4- to 7-hour trip depending on sea conditions). Private boat owners may be willing to take you, though probably for more money than the scheduled boats. If Aeronica reincarnates, air service may resume.

RAMA CAY Hidden away in the south end of Bluefields Bay, about an hour from town by boat, this island is home to the remaining indigenous Rama people. The few hundred tribespeople are trying to put their lives and villages back together after the Sandinista government, citing military necessity, relocated them to the mainland during the war. Though there's no organized lodging or dining on the island, you'll find the Rama friendly and welcoming. Because of the Moravian influence, most Rama speak German-accented English. Private boats from Bluefields' piers will make the trip for about $10.

N. Mosquitia Coast & Lowlands

The rivers and jungles of the northern Mosquitia coast pose huge obstacles to the casual visitor who wants a glimpse of life in this far-flung territory. Few roads mar the jungle's tangled wilderness, and the indigenous communities sheltered within have little time to cater to the odd stranger who wanders in. But, as with everything else in life, those with a sense of adventure stand to reap incredible rewards. The northern edge of Nicaragua's Mosquitia region is delineated by the Río Coco, which serves as the border between Nicaragua and Honduras. For the indigenous Miskitos who have inhabited this region for centuries, however, the river is no border: It's a sacred lifeline connecting their people, both in Nicaragua and Honduras, to each other and to their past. When the Sandinistas forcibly evacuated the area during the contra war—in part to protect the region's inhabitants from contra attack and in part to prevent them from joining the other side—they learned how much the river means to the Miskitos. The move provoked a widespread armed revolt and defections to the contra camp that forced the Sandinistas to reverse themselves and beg forgiveness. Many Miskitos have yet to forgive.

The Sandinistas, of course, were by no means the first to try to ride roughshod over the region. Previous Nicaraguan governments provoked resentment when they attempted to impose central control. Only the British, through their Miskito sub-monarchy, and U.S. lumber and banana companies managed to infiltrate the region. Puerto Cabezas today owes its prominence to these foreign exploiters. Though the British and North Americans have left, Puerto Cabezas bustles with life, serving as the main port and trading center for the Northern Atlantic coastal region.

Anyone traveling here should come armed with plenty of resourcefulness, a good deal of cash, and extra reserves of patience. Visiting the outer reaches of the jungle, where roads are almost nonexistent, requires talking your way onto cargo and private boats that work the rivers. Where roads exist, there is little scheduled bus service, and riding on trucks gets expensive fast. One further hazard to contend with is Nicaragua's volatile political situation. As recently as 1992, the region was experiencing political violence as groups of rearmed contras mounted sporadic attacks on road traffic in acts that amounted to little more than senseless banditry. If you can face all this—and survive—you'll have the experience of a lifetime.

PUERTO CABEZAS

Puerto Cabezas—called simply "Port" by the locals—is a muddy hovel on the northern shore of Nicaragua's Atlantic coast. Its squalid appearance barely hints at its importance to the economic and political life of the region. The city is a vibrant crossroads of cultures, a place where Miskitos, Ramas, Sumus, Chinese, mestizos, and Afro-Caribbeans meet, trade, and scramble to salvage something from the wreckage of the region's economy. Considering the accumulated hardships—including an overexploited, underdeveloped economy, ferocious violence during the 1980s, and continuing political turmoil—the town's happy vibe is a small miracle.

The town's Barbary Coast atmosphere is complemented by its role as the region's major port and main point of access to jungle villages, which brings in a good number of foreign merchant sailors and development workers headed to the interior. Any traveler planning an excursion to Nicaragua's northern jungle should spend some time here tapping into the knowledge of locals and resident foreigners, who often can give hot tips on transportation and sometimes even names of friends and relatives in the interior who would welcome an adventurous visitor. If a trip to the jungle interior seems too daunting, a visit to Puerto Cabezas makes for a manageable adventure.

The Parque Central is a few blocks west of the shore. You'll find **Telcor** a block south of the park, and a **BND** another ½ block south. The market is 2 blocks north of the main square. Nightlife gets raucous here, just as you'd expect in such a rough-and-tumble place. The two most popular joints are close to each other near the shore (a few blocks north of Restaurant Costa Brava). **Blue Beach** features good costeño music, a rough crowd (knife searches at the door), and no cover. **Disco Scorpio** is the place for salsa. Larger concerts take place in the basketball stadium near the main park. The beach here is a sad, scruffy place, but locals say that the beach at **Tuapi,** about 13 kilometers (8 miles) north, is pleasant and clean. Ask at the dock to rent private boats for excursions to Tuapi and other isolated beaches.

COMING AND GOING Getting to town is a difficult challenge unless you're willing to pay dearly. The Sandinista Air Force and private charter companies fly passengers to and from Managua for around $60 one-way. In Managua, check with **Senderos Tours** (½ block west from the south side of the Hotel Intercontinental, tel. 02/24326). It's possible to travel overland from Managua, first by catching a bus to Matagalpa and then finding a ride on a truck making the arduous two-day journey east through the jungle. As a rule, truck drivers charge the equivalent of 10 gallons of diesel fuel (about $15) per passenger. Though the trip is difficult and sometimes perilous, the scenery is enthralling (see Puerto Cabezas to Matagalpa, below). Some lucky travelers manage to hitch rides on cargo boats heading north or south from the dock, located south of town about ½ mile. A bus leaves every other day for Waspam on the Río Coco at about 8:30 AM (6 hours, $5). If you arrive by air, the town is about 2 kilometers south of the airstrip, a short $1 cab ride away.

WHERE TO SLEEP AND EAT The road forming the western edge of the main park is where you'll find the town's two hospedajes. Two long blocks north on this road from the main park is the dirty and bug-infested **Hospedaje Viajero,** across the street from the Moravian mission ($4 a person). Slightly better accommodations can be found at **Hospedaje Rivera,** 2 blocks south of the main park on the same road. Rooms here are still primitive, but the friendly management tries harder ($5 per person). Food prices in Puerto Cabezas will shock. **Costa Brava,** 2 blocks toward the ocean from the northeast corner of the main park, is a popular seafood place, but you'll ask yourself why you're paying $8 for a plate of shrimp in a port town. **Restaurante Zaire,** a block west of Costa Brava, is another popular spot, specializing in steaks ($6–$8).

WASPAM AND THE RIO COCO

Waspam, about 88 kilometers (55 miles) northwest of Puerto Cabezas on the Río Coco, is the capital of the Miskito tribal region. Destroyed during the contra war after the Sandinistas evacuated the Miskitos from the river, Waspam is now bustling to rebuild. Travelers interested in exploring the Miskito region, particularly the Río Coco, should come here to make contacts. Locals are friendly and chatty, but traveling here is anything but easy. Before leaving Puerto Cabezas, you should find out about security conditions on the road to Waspam, which witnessed armed assaults by regrouped contra patrols during the summer of 1992.

One primitive unnamed **hospedaje,** on the main street next to the market, charges $4 per person for very basic accommodations. The place houses the town disco and video cinema, so it can get noisy on weekends. The only place to eat in town is at the market comedores, which will challenge your gastronomic tolerance. Travelers should attempt to make contacts with some of the many foreign development workers stationed here. They can give you tips about where it's safe to travel and how to get there. Some may even offer to give you lifts up or down the river. Otherwise, traveling the river will be expensive.

A boat trip west to **San Carlos,** another important Miskito village on the river, costs around $20. It's also possible to make this trip partly by land. Irregular truck service travels a road out of Waspam to a point on the river across from the village of Leimus in Honduras. Small boats make the river crossing to Leimus, where a Honduran army general runs a safari-like bar and restaurant. From here, trucks travel to the Honduran village of Ausbila (2 hours, $5), where travelers can catch a boat to San Carlos. The border here is uncontrolled; travelers can cross into Honduras and back into Nicaragua without immigration formalities. No lodging is available in San Carlos or any of the other Miskito villages, but travelers carrying hammocks will most likely find locals willing to let them sleep on their property. Marketplaces are the only places to buy meals.

Before embarking on this trip, travelers should know what they're getting themselves into. Especially when traveling on the Río Coco, it's not uncommon for travelers to find themselves stranded for days waiting for transportation, and many encounter some sort of natural or human-made hazard. Only those with a strong command of Spanish and a genuine interest in the region and its peoples should make this trip.

PUERTO CABEZAS TO MATAGALPA

The overland journey from Puerto Cabezas inland to Matagalpa is one of Nicaragua's hardest hauls. The road passes through virgin rainforest, forgotten villages, and wild mountain country, giving the traveler a glimpse of some of the remotest territory on earth. No buses travel this road, which becomes next to impassable during the rainy season. Travelers have to settle for squeezing onto cargo trucks that constantly make the two-day journey between the two cities during the dry season (*see* Puerto Cabezas, *above*).

Since there are few major settlements on the road, travelers should bring some food and water. If the trip looks too difficult to handle at one go, a few villages offer lodging along the way. A fascinating group of sleepy old mining villages, known collectively as Las Minas, sit on or near the road about halfway between Matagalpa and Puerto Cabezas in the territory of the Sumu tribe. **Siuna** is the largest, with a run-down colonial hotel offering suites at $4. Farther east, **Rosita** offers primitive accommodations at the **Hospedaje Osejo** ($4 per person), where cheap meals are also sometimes available. The village of **Bonanza,** in the heartland of Sumu territory, sits off the main road a few miles north of Rosita. Ask for Francisco Oroco, known to locals as "Pan Pan," who runs a small hotel that charges $4 a night. In all three villages, market comedores are about the only dining option. Truck traffic is frequent between these villages, making hitching or cheap rides no problem.

COSTA RICA 7

By Deborah Meacham and Shirley Zahavi

Brilliant green jungles, misty black-sand beaches, minimalls, flaming volca-noes, Taco Bell, and Ray-Ban sunglasses. Costa Rica is a beautiful country so filled with contradictions and oddities it verges on surrealism. Costa Rica is the easiest country in Central America to travel in: It has an amazingly stable social and political environment, and it's been quite homogenized by international capitalist (mostly North American) culture. Not surprisingly, those accustomed to the rich indigenous culture of Guatemala or the provoking political climate of Nicaragua or El Salvador may be turned off, even bored. "It's not really a Latin American country, it's more like the midwestern United States," a foreign-exchange student from California commented. Actually, Costa Rica is very Latin American. It just takes time and patience to see through the overwhelming commercialism to the heritage of the cowboys of Guanacaste, the farmers of the *Meseta Central* (Central Valley), and the indigenous and Caribbean cultures.

Costa Rica's population is dominated by a Spanish-descended majority, with a sprinkling of international immigrants and retirees; it's also estimated that 200,000 political and economic refugees from Nicaragua and El Salvador reside here. About 35,000 people of African descent live here, too, especially in Limón and on the Caribbean coast; their ancestors came as Spanish slaves or from Jamaica to build railroads and work on the banana plantations. *Indígenas* (indigenous people) live for the most part on one of 25 reserves, and there's a large population of people of Chinese ancestry in the bigger cities. Despite Costa Rica's legacy of "social justice," racism is an ingrained element of the country's value system. Indigenous heritage and the Caribbean culture are only today becoming recognized as part of Costa Rica's culture.

It all started with Columbus. (It didn't really, but very few indigenous people are left to tell you otherwise.) In 1502, Columbus landed near Limón, encountering Carib people who traded their glittering gold pendants for Euro-trinkets. Believing that the area was filled with gold, he named the region Costa Rica (Rich Coast). Spaniards flocked to Costa Rica in search of fortune, but their efforts were futile—they found no gold, and, disgruntled, turned to agriculture. The 25,000 indigenous people fought back, but most died of disease and warfare against the Spanish and each other. Pre-Columbian tribes now represent a mere 1% of the total population, so the country has been largely free of major ethnic clashes. Geographically isolated from the colonial centers in Mexico and the Andes, Costa Rica developed independently from the greater Spanish Empire. After several failed attempts to colonize the coast, the Spaniards and their

Costa Rica

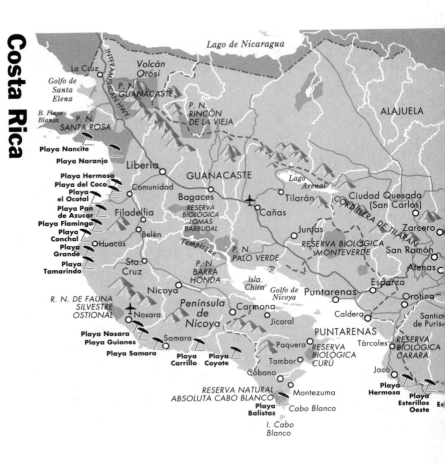

Lago de Nicaragua

La Cruz
Golfo de
Santa
Elena
Volcán
Orósi
B. Playa
Blanca
P. N.
GUANACASTE
P. N.
RINCÓN
DE LA VIEJA
ALAJUELA
P. N.
SANTA ROSA
Playa Nancite
Playa Naranjo
Liberia
GUANACASTE
Lago
Arenal
Playa Hermosa
Playa del Coco
Comunidad
Ciudad Quesada
(San Carlos)
**Playa
el Ocotal**
Bagaces
Tilarán
Zarcero
**Playa Pan
de Azucar**
Filadelfia
RESERVA
BIOLÓGICA
LOMAS
BARBUDAL
Cañas
Playa Flamingo
Belén
Juntas
RESERVA BIOLÓGICA
MONTEVERDE
San Ramón
**Playa
Conchal**
Huacas
**Playa
Grande**
Sta.
Cruz
P. N.
PALO VERDE
Atenas
**Playa
Tamarindo**
P. N.
BARRA
HONDA
Esparza
Nicoya
Isla
Chira
Golfo de
Nicoya
Puntarenas
Orotina
R. N. DE FAUNA
SILVESTRE
OSTIONAL
Nosara
Península
de
Nicoya
Carmona
Jicaral
Caldera
Santi
de Puris
PUNTARENAS
Playa Nosara
Playa Guiones
Samara
Paquera
RESERVA
BIOLÓGICA
CURÚ
Tárcoles
RESERVA
BIOLÓGICA
CARARA
Playa Samara
**Playa
Carrillo**
**Playa
Coyote**
Tambor
Jacó
Cóbano
**Playa
Hermosa**
RESERVA NATURAL
ABSOLUTA CABO BLANCO
Montezuma
**Playa
Esterillos
Oeste**
Es
**Playa
Balistas**
Cabo Blanco
I. Cabo
Blanco

PACIFIC OCEAN

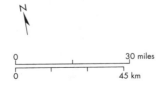

N

0   30 miles
0   45 km

CARAGUA

San Juan

Colorado

R.N. DE
FAUNA SILVESTRE
BARRA DEL
COLORADO

Turtle
Research Station

*Mar
Caribe*

HEREDIA

Tortuguero

Puerto Viejo

Cariari

*PARQUE
NACIONAL
TORTUGUERO*

ZONA
PROTECTORA
LA SELVA

La
Virgen

LIMÓN

Guápiles

*Boca Rio
Matina*

Cinchona

Matina

P. N.
BRAULIO
CARRILLO

Siquerres

Moín

Puerto
Limón

ajuela

Heredia

San José

MONUMENTO
NACIONAL
GUAYABO

*Valle
de la
Estrella*

P. N.
CAHUITA

Puerto
Viejo

Cartago

Turrialba

Bribri

Manzanillo

CARTAGO

San Marcos

Santa
María

CORDILLERA DE TALAMANCA

*PARQUE
NACIONAL
CHIRRIPÓ*

*PARQUE INTERNACIONAL
LA AMISTAD*

Parrita

SAN JOSÉ

San Isidro
de El General

PANAMÁ

Quepos

*Valle de
El General*

Buenos
Aires

Palo
Seco

P. N.
MANUEL
ANTONIO

Fila Costeña

Palmar Norte

Grande de Térraba

*Valle de
Coto Brus*

San
Vito

Palmar Sur

INTERAMERICAN HWY.

**Wilson Botanical
Gardens**

Río Claro

Cúidad
Neily

Rincón

Golfito

Paso Canoa

*Península
de Osa*

*Golfo
Dulce*

*Valle de
Coto
Colorado*

*PARQUE
NACIONAL
CORCOVADO*

Pto.
Jiménez

**Playa
Zancudo**

**Playa
Parones**

mestizo (mixed-descent) offspring moved inland to the temperate Meseta Central, where they remained mostly poor, illiterate farmers.

Costa Rica became an independent nation in 1838, and, except for a brief but bloody dictatorship in the 1948 Civil War, it stands as one of the oldest democratic republics in Latin America. Costa Rica has no standing army; the 1949 Constitution abolished the armed forces, and people are very proud of this fact. But it's not exactly proletariat rule. The country relies on over 7,000 civil and rural guardsmen (and a very few women) to maintain public order, and they all carry machine guns. Most locals say not to trust them. The *guardia* drive around in green pickup trucks wearing green uniforms; they're everywhere, but they're definitely closer to cops than to occupying troops. If attacked, Costa Rica would seek assistance from the Organization of American States. For a country its size, Costa Rica has a pretty big influence in the international community in areas such as human rights. Costa Rica has been dubbed the most democratic nation in Central America—and rightfully so, for the most part.

The country has also devoted a hell of a lot of time, money, and work to its biggest resource: the land itself. Unlike other countries, which have been exploited and deforested, Costa Rica has set aside 12% of its land as national parks or reserves. "You can sell a standing tree several thousand times," a Costa Rican park ranger explains. Dry forest, rain forest, cloud forest; weird animals like iguanas, sloths, tapirs, and agouti; 10% of the world's known species of birds; more species of butterflies than in all of Africa—Costa Rica's got it all, and they're beginning to take care of it.

While this book was being researched and written, several thousand hectares of primary growth forest were cleared for banana production.

Everything's relative, though. In the last 40 years, more than two-thirds of the rain forest have been burned away or chopped down for cattle grazing; only lately has conservation become a prime concern. Today, Costa Rica's 15 national parks are heavily visited by the 400,000 tourists who come to Costa Rica each year. A lot of people believe the big-time tourism is damaging fragile tropical ecosystems, and they're calling for limits on the number of visitors. Since gringo money accounts for much of the national income, though, it's not likely that much will be done about it in the near future. Anyway, it would be an exaggeration to say that the country is sinking under the weight of foreign visitors. Ecotourism may be hot, but many Costa Ricans have never sat down and talked to a gringo.

For the most part, Costa Rica is still very rural. Many farmers are struggling little guys who can't compete with the large-scale multinational corporations, which have the resources for greater production. United Fruit was once a big presence here; its monopoly is gone now, but other international companies are queuing for land and command. Make no mistake: It's still a Third World country. The economy, the rate of development, and the highly bureaucratic government are still underdeveloped. You'll see bamboo shoots used as TV antennas, roads that 4x4s can't take, and 10-person families living in one-room houses.

Costa Ricans, called *ticos,* are incredibly nice, to you and each other. If you don't have a place to stay, don't be surprised if you get multiple offers to stay with multiple families. It's fairly easy to get by on just a little Spanish; in general, people are willing to help you out. It's disarming: You'll hear ticos using phrases like *para servirle* (to serve you), *a sus órdenes* (at your command), and *Usted es el/la que manda* (you're in command).

All this makes Costa Rica an oasis of peace and beauty for the traveler in Central America. Smack in the middle of a region characterized by wretched poverty and political turmoil, Costa Rica has a relatively high standard of living and a history of social justice and stability. And though the rest of Central America is infamous for scaring off tourists, Costa Rica is one of the capitals on the worldwide gringo trail, with gorgeous, protected rain and cloud forests, and a pretty stable tourism-based economy. It's not Club Med, but it's not Nicaragua.

Basics

See Chapter 1 for important info pertaining to Costa Rica.

VISITOR INFORMATION

➤ **TOURIST OFFICES** • **Instituto Costarricense de Turismo.** The Costa Rican tourist board can help you plan your trip. Get general info (pamphlets and brochures) before you go from the U.S. office in Miami. Get more information or ask specific destination questions at the main office in San José; they give out free maps, bus schedules, and lodging lists for some regions. *San José: Plaza de la Cultura, Calle 5a bet. Av. Central and Av. 2a, tel. 23–17–33, ext. 277; 22–10–90; or 23–84–23. The office is underground at entrance to Museo de Oro. Mailing address: Apartado Postal No. 777–1000, San José. U.S. address: 1101 Brickell Ave., BIV Tower, Suite 801, Miami, FL 33131, tel. 305/358–2150 or 800/327–7033.*

Many towns don't have official information centers, but you can always get your questions answered at hotels and restaurants that cater to tourists. The **Juan Santamaría airport** in San José has a visitor information desk (across from baggage claims), but many flights arrive after its business hours. The tourist board also has information centers at the northern and southern border crossings.

➤ **WORKING AND STUDYING** • Biology students, especially, will find a lot to do in Costa Rica, but the country has a lot of general-interest and language-study options. Check out the book written by Council for International Exchange and Education (*see* Chapter 1, Basics) for universities that offer programs. Volunteer programs also abound; if you're interested in doing something green, you're in luck. Try **La Asociación de Voluntarios para el Servicio en Areas Protegidas (ASVO),** a conservation organization working in the national parks. Contact them through the volunteer office of the National Parks Service (San José, tel. 33–4118). Through the **Monteverde Institute,** students work and conduct biological research at the field station in the Monteverde cloud forest reserve. Contact Monteverde Institute, Cloud Forest Field Station, Apartado 10165, San José. **Organización Turistica Estudiantil y Juvenil Costarricense (OTEC)** also organizes work-and-travel exchanges, usually lasting for three months during the summer. Contact Elda Elizondo (Box 323–1002, Paseo de los Estudiantes, San José, Costa Rica, tel. 22–08–66) for more info.

➤ **RESOURCES FOR WOMEN TRAVELERS** • Several women's and feminist organizations are based in San José. **Mujer No Estás Sola** (Woman, You Are Not Alone) may be able to offer assistance to women travelers; its parent group, **CEFEMINA** (Apartado 5355–1000, tel. 24–4620), a strong and multidimensional feminist organization, is also a good resource. Check out the quarterly CEFEMINA magazine, *Mujer.*

➤ **RESOURCES FOR GAYS AND LESBIANS** • The best places to meet *gente del ambiente* (gays) in San José are the two most popular gay night spots, La Torre and La Avispa (*see* San José After Dark, *below*). The monthly gay magazine, *Confidencial,* may have other listings. Organizations include: **Las Entendidas** (lesbian/feminist, Apartado 1057 in San Pedro, a suburb of San José); **Los Humanos** and **Los Diferentes,** two gay (male) organizations; the **Colectivo Gay Universitario** (tel. 22–30–47); and the **Asociación Contra el SIDA Grupo 2828** (tel. 22–30–47), a gay and lesbian support group for alcoholics and drug addicts.

WHEN TO GO
The two-season rule (*see* Chapter 1, Basics) is in effect here, but the Caribbean coast is wet almost year-round. Accommodations are more expensive and harder to come by in the dry season (December–April), which is far more touristed. Semana Santa (Easter Week) is the worst time to visit—all the ticos are traveling and you won't be able to find vacant hotels or open restaurants. Schoolchildren are on

vacation in the dry months, when families crowd the beaches on weekends; the final weekend in February, the last before school starts, is also packed.

➢ **HOLIDAYS AND FESTIVALS** • **July 25,** Guanacaste Annexation Day, with a huge festival in Liberia; **September 15,** Independence Day; **October 12,** Día de la Raza, with a mongo party in Limón.

MAIL For **sending mail,** the fastest and most reliable post office is the Correo Central; postcards to the U.S. are about 30¢ and about 45¢ to the U.K., letters are about 45¢ and 60¢. Regular postal service is slow (two weeks to a month) unless you send it from San José. It's worth an extra 40¢ to send your mail express, which takes about a week. To **receive mail,** the most reliable mail service is the American Express agency. You can also get mail at the *Lista de Correo* (have it addressed to the name on your passport, Lista de Correo, town name, province, Costa Rica; the post office will hold it for one month), but letters are often filed incorrectly and postal workers have difficulty reading foreign handwriting. Make sure they check under your *last,* not second (or middle) name. Grind the following into your loved one's head: Do not send presents, cash or money orders, or checks—they often get ripped off.

CHANGING MONEY Except in San José, where every bank provides every service possible, the three major banks handle different transactions. **Banco Nacional de Costa Rica** accepts traveler's checks, money orders, and Canadian dollars, and it gives cash advances on Visa. **Banco de Costa Rica** usually deals with U.S. dollars in cash only; in larger places it'll cash U.S. traveler's checks. Both are open from 9 to 3. All branches of **Banco Anglo Costarricense** handle U.S. cash transactions; some also deal with U.S. traveler's checks and cash advances on MasterCard. It opens at 8:30 AM. The tourist hotels might rip you off, but many small hotel owners who change money are scrupulously honest and may even charge you a lower rate than the banks.

If you're going to be in San José more than a few weeks, or passing through the capital every couple of weeks, consider opening a *cuenta de ahorros* (savings account) in dollars. You'll know your money is safe, and you can withdraw small amounts in U.S. cash to exchange where you will. Bear in mind that traveler's checks will remain frozen until 30 days after the deposit, so change your checks into cash first for a small commission. Try one of the smaller, international banks in San José.

➢ **CURRENCY** • The *colón* is the basic monetary unit, with 100 *centavos* in each colón. In the '60s and '70s, you could actually buy stuff with centavos; now, the smallest unit of currency, a 50-centavo coin, is worth less than half a U.S. penny. Restaurants, hotels, and merchants will usually round up. Prices quoted in this book are based on an exchange rate of 130 colones to the U.S. dollar. All banks offer the same government-set rate, usually a smidge lower than the black market (*see* San José and the Meseta Central, *below*).

Excuse Me, Sir, Are You Hissing at Me?

If you're a woman traveling in Costa Rica, especially if you're macha (light-skinned), expect a lot of hissing and muttered comments. Piropos (remarks directed toward female strangers) can be quite an art, but they're intended less for the recipient than for the macho self-esteem of their inventor. "Psst, machita (hey, blondie)!" is the most common, hissed at almost any remotely fair foreigner; "qué rica (tasty)!" is another piropo you'll probably hear, even if you're a guy. Take a compliment graciously with a lump of salt, and ignore the crasser comments. A reaction only provokes more interest; it does not gain you respect.

PHONES You can call anywhere in Costa Rica from a pay phone using 5-, 10-, or 20-colón coins. Currently, one international code (506) works for the whole country, but area codes will be introduced in the next few years. Right now, all numbers are six digits long. You can call internationally from a pay phone collect or with a phone card by dialing **116** to access the international operator. Dial **114** for direct service to the U.S. (collect or AT&T-related cards)—it's the best way to go if you're calling the States. Hint: Pick up a phone book when you arrive—there's only one for the entire country and it's pretty small.

VISAS If you're from the U.S., the U.K., or Canada, you can stay in the country for 90 days without a visa; those from Australia or New Zealand can have 30 visa-free days. Bring your passport: While U.S. and Canadian citizens can get a 30-day tourist card with proof of nationality (birth certificate or voter's registration), picture ID, and ticket, your passport gives you 90 days *and* passports are essential for banking, money exchange, and receiving mail. If you want to stay even longer in Costa Rica, it's probably less expensive and much less of a hassle to take a 72-hour trip out of the country and be granted a new 90-day visa (30-day for non-U.S./Canadian citizens) upon your return. Take at least a photocopy of your exit ticket; it may help your reentry. If you don't want to leave the country to extend your visa, go to the Migración office (San José, Calle 21, bet. Av. 6 and Av. 8) from 8:30 to 3:30 weekdays to find out the latest bureaucratic dance. The departure tax is less than $6.

COMING AND GOING

➤ **BY BUS** • To travel from San José to Panamá City, take the **Tica** (tel. 21–89–54 or 21–92–29) express bus at 8 PM from Avenida 4 between Calles 9 and 11. It's a 20-hour trip. Buses from Panamá City depart daily at 11 AM, Panamá time. If you're in the northern Panamanian town of David, take a **Tracopa** (tel. 21–42–14) bus to San José at 7:30 AM. Buses from San José to David leave from Avenida 18 between Calles 2 and 4 at 7:30 AM. It takes nine hours to get to David.

Buses from San José to Managua leave from the Tica bus terminal daily at 7 AM. Buses also go from the **Sirca** terminal (Calle 7 bet. Avenidas 6 and 8, tel. 22–55–41 or 23–14–64) on Wednesday, Friday, and Sunday at 5 AM. Sirca buses return from Managua on Monday, Wednesday, and Friday at 6:30 AM. Call ahead for current schedules. The trip takes 11 hours.

Tica also serves Guatemala City. Buses leave San José every day at 7:30 AM. From Guatemala, buses depart at 1 PM. The trip is long—2½ days. The two overnight stays aren't included in the price of the ticket. You'll have to find hotels in Managua and El Salvador.

➤ **BY PLANE** • Major U.S. airlines serve the Juan Santamaría Airport in San José, along with the usual Central American airlines (*see* Chapter 1, Basics). Travelers from Canada should fly to the United States and make connections to San José. From Europe, travelers can fly with **KLM** or **Iberia**. From Australia and New Zealand, travelers should fly to the United States and then continue to San José. A $5.50 departure tax is payable upon departure from San José.

GETTING AROUND

➤ **BY BUS** • Buses are the cheapest and most popular transport. They're reliable for the most part, but flat tires, late departures, mechanical difficulties, and overcrowding are common. Express buses are rarely ever that—they stop in important towns, sometimes picking up travelers that wait on the highway. Bigger, more modern buses travel from San José to major transport hubs like Liberia, Puntarenas, Limón, and San Isidro, as well as important towns in the Meseta Central. The best place to board a bus is at the terminal of origin. If you board somewhere between point A and point B, you'll have to squeeze on and ride standing up.

Sunday buses are always jam-packed with families and howling babies. Depending on the driver and the company, tickets should be purchased at the terminal or on the bus when you board. Some drivers let you pay when you get off. Sometimes buses are mismarked, so ask the destination before you board. You'll be asked to put your backpack or whatever either in the compartments on the outside of the bus or in the back.

Costa Ricans give directions in meters; cien metros (100 meters) usually means one city block.

➤ **BY PLANE** • **SANSA,** the domestic airline (tel. 33–03–97), flies from San José to nearly two dozen locations. Flights are all under an hour. Tickets cost more or less $20 each way. If you're claustrophobic or prone to motion sickness, stick to the bus. It's cheaper anyway and your fellow passengers will be ticos instead of gringos, who are usually the only people on the planes.

➤ **BY BOAT** • To get to and from the Osa and Nicoya peninsulas, take ferry boats. They run regularly and are the cheapest way to get across the gulfs. Sometimes the only way to get to hard-to-reach beaches, islands, and scuba-diving spots is to charter a boat, but it's expensive. Ferries won't take people from one peninsula to the other, either.

➤ **BY BIKE** • It's possible and it's beautiful, but it's difficult. Costa Rican roads weren't designed for bikes (hell, they weren't designed for cars). Don't ride along the Interamerican Highway: Cars and buses whiz by all the time, and they're not going to stop to ponder who has the right of way. A mountain bike is probably essential, especially in the wet season; most of the scenic roads are steep and poor. Biking is more popular on the flat Caribbean Coast. Avoid the hassle of renting a bike in San José and bring your own. Bike theft in the major cities is common, so use your discretion when you lock your bike or when you leave it at your hotel. **C.R. Mountain Biking** (Apartado 3979, San José, Costa Rica, tel. 22–43–80, fax 55–43–54) might also be able to give you sound advice, but don't let them talk you into a potentially pricey organized tour.

➤ **BY CAR** • Many people, especially surfers, rent jeeps and 4x4s by the week in Costa Rica. If you're traveling with a board, it's easier to rent a car than to risk decapitating fellow passengers on the bus. San José companies offer specials, which run about $300 a week for a 4x4, less for a normal compact car. Minimum age is 25, and you don't need an international driver's license.

➤ **HITCHING** • Hitchhiking isn't illegal in Costa Rica but, as everywhere, you should be careful. On major bus routes, like the Interamerican Highway, hitching is a bitch because locals assume that if you're a decent, responsible traveler, you should have enough money to pay for a bus ride. People most willing to pick up hitchhikers are those driving trucks or other cargo vehicles; they'll generally let you hop in the back. The more gringo-hippie parts of Nicoya and Guanacaste see more hitching, but the general rule is that the remoter a location, the easier it is for you to hitch. The most acceptable place is in the countryside, where hardly anybody has access to a car. Sometimes you'll be asked to pay for gas or for the service. Women travelers shouldn't hitch: In this culture, you're not just asking for a ride, you're asking for a "good time." Weigh the risk, or wait for the bus.

WHERE TO SLEEP

➤ **HOTELS** • Costa Rica isn't a country of dollar hotel rooms, but it's got plenty of fairly cheap spots. It's a given that the less you pay for a room, the lousier it is, and cheap rooms almost always have some kind of insect crawling around. Major towns have pensions or hotels with basic rooms and *baños colectivos* (shared baths), usually for about $6–$10 per person. Beds range from hard to hammocks, but more important than the bed is a working fan. The best are ceiling fans that automatically stay on all night. Only expensive hotels provide hot water, and some cheap hotels have showers outdoors, so be prepared to take a cold shower in the open air. Always make sure that your room has a good lock; some hotels only have a padlock on the door. If you leave valuables in your room, lock them with a luggage lock. Larger hotels have a security guard that hangs out in the lobby at night.

➤ **HOSTELS** • Costa Rica has 11 IYHF youth hostels, and it should be getting more as lodge and hotel owners glom on to the international-backpacker thang. The main hostel, Toruma (*see* San José Where to Sleep, *below*), is the information and reservation center for all the others. Each hostel has its own rates. About half of them are set up like European hostels, with communal dorms and bunk beds (but you don't need a sleep sheet). IYHF members get a big discount, and if you're not a member, you can only become one at Toruma.

➤ **CAMPING** • Most campgrounds are close to the beach, and charge around $3 for showers and laundry basins. You can also camp in or near the national parks. The best camping park is Santa Rosa (*see* Guanacaste and the Lowlands, *below*), but if you're flexible you can stay just about anywhere. If the park has no facilities, you can probably pay the rangers to let you camp near the station, where you can also stock up on potable water. If not, set up near the entrance.

Major transport hubs don't have campgrounds. It isn't safe to sleep at bus terminals or in city parks because you could get robbed, but you're legally allowed to camp or just crash on any public beach in the country (this is an amazingly cool way to save a lot of money). Don't leave your tent unattended—the animals, human or otherwise, will get to it.

➤ **STUDENT HOUSING AND OTHER HOUSING** • If you want to stay for an extended time in Costa Rica or San José, check out periodicals, notices posted at the Toruma hostel or the university in San José, and word of mouth. Prices start at $100 a month for an unfurnished room in a shared house, and at $200 for a furnished apartment. Your best bet is to try to connect with international students in exchange programs, or with foreigners working in Costa Rica. At the university, check out the *Vida Estudiantil* or the fourth floor of *Estudios Generales,* as well as phone booths and message boards at the *sodas* (*see below*). Families that rent rooms to foreigners and language schools that offer family stays usually advertise in the *Tico Times,* but these are often *very* expensive, from $300 upwards a month.

FOOD

Nobody travels to Costa Rica for haute cuisine, which keeps both the cost and the variety of food at a minimum (learn to love rice and beans). In the morning, ticos eat *gallo pinto* (two-toned rooster), a mixture of rice and black beans. In the afternoon and evening they eat *casados* (married people—not literally, of course): rice, beans, salad, and a cooked vegetable with chicken, meat, or fish. All this runs about $3–$5.

The cheapest restaurants are called sodas and they look like little diners. Sodas proliferate at the city center, at the bus terminal in the municipal market, along the highway, and inside cheap hotels. They're generally open all day. The cheapest places don't bother writing up a bill, so just ask how much you owe. Chinese restaurants, found in any major town, are also a good bet: The food is plentiful, cheap, and generally tasty. When you order drinks at almost any bar, they'll give you free appetizers called *bocas* (mouths—again, not literally). *Ceviche* (raw fish in lime juice) is most common.

In Costa Rica 97% of the water is potable, but the Caribbean coast is rumored to have water that isn't as properly treated as the rest. *Refrescos* are fruit shakes (if ordered in milk) or smoothies (if ordered in water). Costa Rican coffee kicks ass. *Café con leche* (coffee with milk) is very rich, and ticos drink it with breakfast. It used to be served in two pitchers—one for coffee and one for steamed milk—which you could mix yourself, but for financial reasons (they have to pay twice as much for dishwashing?) it's gone out of style.

➤ **TIPPING** • A 12% sales tax and 10% tip are automatically added to the bill in most restaurants, making your food **22% more** than you *thought* it was going to cost. Needless to say, you shouldn't feel pressed to tip unless the service was outstanding, you have a big crush on the waitperson, or you plan on coming back regularly. Tipping taxis is only necessary if they help you with huge luggage or make an extra stop at no charge.

San José

"A cien los mamones, ricos mamones... pipa fría, bien fría," ring out the calls of street vendors; the smells of stale beer and ripe mango mingle in the plazas; and hot salsa rhythm blasts from a brightly painted bus: These are just some of the elements that prevent San José, a conglomeration of sodas, lush parks, and fancy stores, from becoming completely overwhelmed by the influence of North American capitalism. You just have to be able to look past all the fast-food joints.

San José is the capital of the province of the same name and of the nation. *Josefinos,* as the residents of the city are called, number about 300,000; at least 400,000 more live in the suburbs. The busy metropolis is the center of governmental, economic, and cultural activity.

Most travelers are a little ambivalent about "San Chepe," as ticos refer to the city. San José is a cool place to hang out, but not for an extended length of time. The city has all the activity an urban prowler could desire—funky nightlife, for example—but the congestion, pollution, and stress of city life become wearing. In comparison to other major cities of Central America, San José is relaxed, easy to navigate, and friendly, but problems of theft and drugs are on the rise. Most travelers limit their stay in San José, using it as a transport hub to other destinations, but the city also makes a good base for exploring the surrounding Central Valley.

BASICS

AMERICAN EXPRESS TAM Travel Agency is the American Express representative. The knowledgeable staff speak English and Spanish; they'll hold mail and offer lost check/card services. They also sell traveler's checks, but you can't cash a personal check. You can receive (but not send) faxes here for free. *Calle 1 bet. Av. Central and Av. 1 in Edificio Alde, 4th floor, tel. 33–00–44, fax 22–80–92. Mailing address: Apartado 1864–1000, San José. Open weekdays 8–5:30.*

TRAVEL AGENCIES Of the countless travel agencies in San José, **OTEC** is the only one with special student services. To receive discounts, you must be a member of an international student or youth organization (*see* Chapter 1, Basics); you can buy memberships at their office for about $10 each, with a price increase expected in the near future. Bring two passport photos (or they'll take a heinous Polaroid for a fee) and proof of *current* school enrollment or age. OTEC has an excellent reputation for its tours, work-exchange program, and cheap international flights, but the office is often busy and tense. *In Edificio Ferencz at Av. 3 and Calle 3, 275 meters north of Teatro Nacional, tel. 22–08–66. Open weekdays 8–5, Sat. 8–2.*

The **Albergue Toruma (Toruma Youth Hostel)** isn't a travel agency, but members can make reservations here for hostels throughout Costa Rica. IYHF membership is only about $15, and the staff will be happy to offer sound advice for travel arrangements. (Hint: This is probably the cheapest way to see Rara Avis.) It's also a good place to check for apartments or rooms to rent. *In San Pedro, on Av. Central across from Pollo Kentucky, tel. 24–40–86. Open daily 6 AM–11 PM. Reservations 8:30 AM–12:30 PM.*

San José

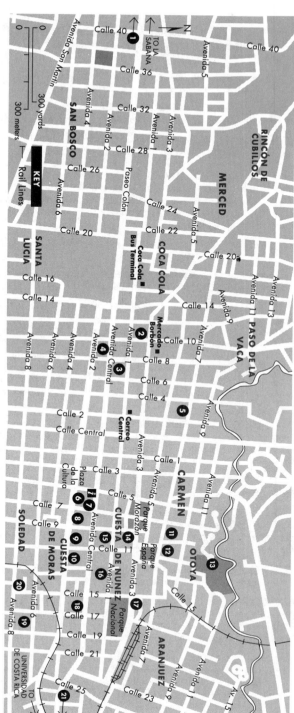

Exploring
Galería Nacional
de Arte
Contemporáneo, **17**
Mercado Central, **3**
Museo de Arte
Costarricense, **1**

Museo
Criminológico, **19**
Museo de Jade, **12**
Museo de Oro, **7**
Museo Nacional **18**
Parque Zoológico
Simón Bolívar, **13**

Serpentario, **15**
Teatro Nacional, **6**

Lodging
Albergue Toruma, **21**
Casa Ridgeway, **20**
Hotel Astoria, **11**
Hotel Avenida
Segunda, **9**
Hotel Bienvenido, **2**

Hotel Generaleño, **4**
Pensión Costa
Rica Inn, **14**
Pensión de
la Cuesta, **16**
Pensión
Villa Blanca, **5**

Super Pensión
Familiar, **10**
Tica Linda, **8**

KEY

Rail Lines

353

Ecotourism is booming in Costa Rica, but it's mostly for people with cash as well as correctness. Contact the **San José Audubon Society** (Apartado 181, 2350 San Francisco) for more info. The following are recommended agencies with competitive prices and student discounts:

Costa Rican Expeditions. *Av. 3 and Calle Central, tel. 57–07–66. Open daily 7 AM– 9 PM. 10% student discount with ID.*

Braun Eco Tourismo. *In Hotel Ritz on Calle Central bet. Av. 8 and Av. 10, tel. 33–17–31 or 22–41–03. Open daily 8:30–4. Discount for groups of students only.*

MONEY Most of the banks in San José offer fairly painful financial services: long lines, a small service charge for changing traveler's checks, and short hours. For less hassle and more personal service, try the international banks that dot the city, such as **Banco Lyon** (on Calle 2 bet. Av. 1 and Av. Central, tel. 21–26–11), a safe haven for stress-free monetary alchemy. **Banco Mercantil de Costa Rica** has a bank-in-the-box right next to the Soda Palace on Avenida 2. It's open weekdays 9–noon and 1–6. Both banks listed below have branches throughout the country and the city. The hours listed are for changing money.

Banco Nacional. *Bet. Calles 2 and 4, Av. 1 and Av. 3, next to Correo Central, tel. 23–21–66. Open weekdays 9–3.*

Banco Anglo Costarricense. *On Av. 2a bet. Calles 1a and 3a, near the Plaza de la Cultura, tel. 22–33–22. Open weekdays 8:30–3.*

➤ **BLACK MARKET** • Since the market was recently opened—i.e., anyone can buy or sell dollars—the black market is no longer illegal, but still somewhat shady. The rates aren't substantially better than at the banks, and for traveler's checks they're actually a little worse. Basically, you should only go to a money changer when the bank is closed, when the lines are too long (bank lines are from hell), or if you like hanging out with *mafiosos*. They usually haunt an amorphous strip around Calles 2 and 4 and Avenidas 2 and Central (near Banco Central, in front of the Soda Palace), muttering *"Dólares, cambio dólares."* Most changers only work with U.S. dollars or traveler's checks.

EMBASSIES **Britain.** *Paseo Colón bet. Calles 38 and 40, tel. 21–55–66; recorded information tel. 21–58–16. Open weekdays 8:30–noon and 1–2:30. Closed weekends, but an emergency number is on the recording.*

Canada. *At Calle 3 and Av. 1, tel. 55–35–22. Open Mon.–Thurs. 8–noon and 12:45–4:30; Fri. 8–noon and 12:30–3. In emergencies, leave name and number and they'll call you back.*

United States. Be prepared; people here are even ruder than at governmental agencies at home. *In Pavas (outside the city), tel. 20–39–39. A taxi should cost about $2; tell the driver to go to the "embajada de los Estados Unidos." Open weekdays 8–4:30 (lunch hour varies). For lost passport call 20–30–50, 8–noon.*

EMERGENCIES **Ambulance** and **Red Cross** (tel. 21–58–18); **highway patrol** (tel. 27–71–50 or 27–80–30), **police** (tel. 117).

LAUNDRY Self-service *lavanderías* are few and far between, and hard to find. Most places do your laundry for you; in fact, they won't even let you touch their precious machines. The cheapest place, Miami Vice, may have moved, but they have self-service and the women who work there are laid-back.

Lava Más. *In Los Yoses, on Calle 45 bet. Av. 8 and Av. 10, tel. 25–16–45. Open weekdays 8–noon, 1:30–6, Sat. 8–3. Take a University bus down Av. Central and get off before freeway overpass. Lavandería is south of Av. Central, east of Radiográfica tower. Just over $1 per kilo for wash, dry, and fold, minimum 2 kilos.*

Lavandería American. *Calle Central bet. Av. 10 and Av. 12, tel. 22–62–47. Open weekdays 8–noon and 1–6, Sat. 8–noon. About $2.50 per kilo, washed and dried.*

Lavandería Miami Vice. *San Pedro, 150 meters north of Banco Anglo Costarricense, near the university, no tel. Open weekdays 7–7. Self-service $3 to wash and dry up to 6 kilos. Service is 25¢ extra.*

MAIL The **Correo Central** is a huge, gray building next to Banco Nacional's main branch. Enter the left door to receive mail (bring your passport), send packages over two kilos, send telegrams, and pay for faxes (window 18 or 19). Enter the far right to buy stamps and send letters or small packages. Each letter received costs about 10¢; faxes are 50¢ a page to receive and $2.50–$4 to send. Upstairs, send faxes or visit the **Museo Telegráfico y Filatélico,** which should reopen weekdays 8–4 by press time (tel. 23–97–66, ext. 204). Also on the top floor is the **Oficina Filatélica,** where stamp collectors can shop weekdays 8–4 (tel. 23–97–66, ext. 251). *Calle 2 bet. Av. 1 and Av. 3, tel. 23–97–66. Right side open weekdays 7 AM–9 PM and Sat. 7–noon. Left side open weekdays 7–5 and Sat. 7–noon. Mailing address: Lista Correo, Correos Central San José.*

A 1,000-colón bill is called a rojo; a 5,000-colón bill is a tucán; one colón is a caña; and a 100-colón bill is a teja. Money is also referred to as plata or pista; loose change is menudo.

MEDICAL AID Costa Rica is supposed to have the best health care in Latin America. In fact, costs and waiting time are much more reasonable than in the States. **Clínica Bíblica** (Av. 14 bet. Calles Central and 1, tel. 23–64–22) has 24-hour emergency care, a 24-hour pharmacy, and, during the day, doctors that speak English. **Hospital San Juan de Dios** (Paseo Colón and Calle 14, tel. 22–01–66) also offers emergency medical services in English 24 hours a day. **Farmacia Fischel** (next to Correo Central, corner of Av. 3 and Calle 2, tel. 23–09–09) is open 7 AM–midnight and has 24-hour delivery service. **Farmacia Adela** (Av. 1 bet. Calles 10 and 8, tel. 21–10–72), open daily 8 AM–7 PM, has excellent service in English.

PHONES **ICE.** *Av. 2a and Calle 1, tel. 55–04–44. Open daily 7 AM–10 PM. English spoken. Fax services.*

Radiográfica. *Corner of Av. 5 and Calle 1, tel. 87–04–62. Open weekdays 8 AM–10 PM, weekends 8–8. Fax, telex, and E-mail services.*

VISITOR INFORMATION The **Oficina de Información Turística,** run by the Instituto Costarricense de Turismo (ICT), operates in a musty, window-walled room next to the Museo de Oro, underneath the Plaza de la Cultura. The brochures and pamphlets scattered around aren't very useful; instead, head straight for the counter and ask for the most recent bus schedule, a road map, and the annual Costa Rica Tourist Information Guide. Although they're not allowed to make recommendations, the multilingual staff will gladly answer your questions and lend you the phone book (one book covers the entire country) or a list of *all* the hotels in Costa Rica (the E category has rooms under $8). *Calle 5 bet. Av. Central and Av. 2a, tel. 22–10–90. Open weekdays 9–5, Sat. 9–1.*

Información de Parques Nacionales. Stop by the Parque Zoológico Simón Bolívar for info on camping conditions and current status of the national parks. Katia staffs the office and runs an extensive national history library. *In the Simón Bolívar Zoo, main office tel. 57–09–22, zoo tel. 33–67–00. Open weekdays 8–noon, 1–3. Take Calle 7 to Av. 11 and follow signs to zoo.*

COMING AND GOING

BY BUS Buses run from San José to almost everywhere in the country. Less frequented towns, such as Los Chiles, have only a few direct buses a day. Some more isolated areas, like Montezuma, require a couple of transportation changes. To make your trip more challenging, bus terminals and stops (some unmarked!) are scattered throughout the city (*see* individual destinations for specific information). The tourist office (*see* Visitor Information, *above*) puts out a well-updated free list of bus service and terminals, and it'll be your personal Costa Rican bus bible as long as you're willing to squint at the *tiny* computer print.

The closest thing San José has to a main terminal is the **Coca-Cola.** Once the site of a bottling plant, this terminal is centered around Avenidas 3 and 1 and Calles 18 and 16, north of **Hospital San Juan de Dios.** It serves mostly western and northern destinations. Watch yourself and your belongings when departing or arriving; the area is a favorite for groups of young pickpockets. The best way out of the terminal is to head south (the Coca-Cola's **market** is south of the terminal/parking lot), turn east at the hospital, and go up Avenida Central toward the center of town.

BY PLANE Costa Rica's international airport and main domestic terminal is the **Juán Santamaría** airport, about 16 kilometers (10 miles) northwest of San José, 5 kilometers (3 miles) south of Alajuela. (*See* Costa Rica Basics, *above,* for more flight information.) A branch of the **Banco de Costa Rica** changes money in the airport weekdays 8 AM–4 PM. There is no luggage storage or tourist information available in the airport at this time, but it does have several gift shops, a restaurant, a chapel, a post office, phones, restrooms, and a bar. Great priorities, huh?

➤ **AIRPORT TRANSPORT** • If you have a pack that you can rest on your lap, the cheapest way into San José from the airport is to take the bus from Alajuela, which passes by the airport. Buses run about every 10 minutes 5:30 AM–7 PM, and about every 40 minutes 7 PM–midnight (50¢). The buses don't have much room for luggage, so most people hop in a taxi and pay about $10 for the ride to San José. Get a group of up to four together for a central destination and split the fare or your *taxista* will fill the cab and charge you separately.

BY CAR There are scads of rental companies in San José; many have offices at the airport or along Paseo Colón. Most companies will only rent to adults over the age of 25. You need a valid driver's license (tourists may drive for three months without an international permit), your passport, and a major credit card. Renting a car gets expensive quickly. Some places advertise $23 a day, but this price doesn't include *kilometraje* (mileage). Just under $300 a week is about the best you can do (includes insurance and unlimited kilometraje).

If the cost doesn't scare you off, welcome to the wonders of super-defensive driving, and all the unknown car etiquette of Central America. If you park your car on the street, someone will often volunteer to watch it for you; tip him about 50¢. Speed limits and seatbelt laws are enforced, though you wouldn't know it by the crazy, high-speed manner in which josefinos drive. Read the traffic rules the rental agency gives you, and *always* ask at least three people for directions; people here seem to prefer giving wrong directions to giving no directions.

BY TRAIN Sadly, the 1991 earthquake which was so disastrous and damaging to the Caribbean coast also wiped out train service throughout Costa Rica. All that remains is service to Heredia. The old Atlantic train station in San José (Av. 3 bet. Calles 21 and 23) is worth checking out if you're a rail fan. At press time, service was still being arranged; for information call **INCOFER** (tel. 26–00–11).

GETTING AROUND

It's easy to get oriented in San José, a reasonably sized, gridded city with a few odd twists. The main streets downtown are **Avenidas Central** and **2a** and **Calle Central.** From Calle 5 to Calle 6 (about six blocks), Avenida Central is mostly closed to street traffic, forming a consumer corridor of vendors and pedestrians. At Calle 14, near **Hospital San Juan de Dios,** Avenida Central becomes the **Paseo Colón,** a ritzy strip of restaurants and car-rental agencies that dead-ends in **La Sabana park.** Avenidas run east–west, increasing by odd numbers north of Central and by evens to the south. Calles run north–south, increasing by evens to the west and odds to the east of Calle Central. Streets are mostly marked, but most josefinos don't give directions according to street address. Many major landmarks such as **Parque Central,** the **cathedral,** and **Teatro Nacional** lie along Avenida 2a, but other parks, churches, and businesses scattered around the city serve as reference points.

Most areas of interest to the traveler are in the heart of the city, north of Avenida 2a. West of Calle 6, around the *mercados* (markets) and the Coca-Cola, the neighborhood gets quite iffy. Locals recommend avoiding this area at night and sticking to the well-lit Avenida Central if you are walking past. However, Josefinos also say that a crack-influenced *zona roja* (red-light district) has sprung up all along Avenida Central, particularly east of the Plaza de la Cultura; south of Avenida 2a also merits a nighttime warning.

San José is small enough to walk around easily, assuming you don't pass out from diesel fumes or get plowed by a car. Watch out for killer potholes, even in the sidewalks, and some of the caños (ditches) are deep enough to drown babies.

Several small towns, more or less suburbs, surround San José; most useful to the budget traveler is **San Pedro,** just east of San José, joined to downtown by Avenida Central's *"zona rosa"* of yuppie shops and bars. San Pedro is home to the Toruma Youth Hostel, the Universidad de Costa Rica, cheap food, and alternative nightlife. To get to San Pedro, walk a few miles on Avenida Central or 2a (they merge before San Pedro at Calle 29), take a $1.50 taxi from downtown, or hop on a bus.

BY BUS Public transit in the city is cheap and extensive, but for most destinations within the city, it's faster and less hassle to walk. Buses are most useful to reach outlying neighborhoods. Marked and unmarked *paradas* (bus stops) are scattered throughout the city; the tourist office and most residents can direct you to the right piece of sidewalk.

To get to Paseo Colón, if you don't feel like walking several long blocks from the center, take the **Sabana–Cementerio** bus. Frequent buses to San Pedro depart from along Avenida 2a, across the street and about 100 meters east of the Teatro Nacional. To get back to San José from San Pedro proper, hop on any of the buses waiting next to the church. Any of these buses cost about 15¢.

BY TAXI The little red-hots that zip around San José are official taxis, with license plates beginning SJP (San José *público*). The *taxistas* have to use the meter, and they may add 20% to the fare at night. If the meter isn't on and running, ask him to *"toca la maría, por favor."* If you've flagged a pirate taxi or one without a working meter, agree on a price beforehand. Even if you get charged gringo-fare, a ride across the city or to the night spots in San Pedro or El Pueblo should cost $3 at most.

WHERE TO SLEEP

There are so many hotels in San José, it's a bummer that the cheap end is so grim. A gross cement cell with a communal cold-water shower will run you $3–$4 a person. The cheaps listed here are pretty safe, but the area around the Coca-Cola bus station has a deservedly bad reputation. San José is pretty small, so everything is within walking distance. A reasonable dive will cost around $4 per person; much nicer rooms are yours for about $9.

NEAR THE PLAZA DE CULTURA

➤ **UNDER $8 • Hotel Avenida Segunda.** It may be a discreet love shack, but this small, nondescript hotel is clean and reasonably peaceful. The second-floor location lets in lots of light and air during the day, but the front rooms overlooking the street get noisy at night. The communal bathrooms are clean and have hot water. A private double is $7.50. *On Av. 2a bet. Calles 7 and 9, tel. 22–02–60. 150 meters east of Teatro Nacional. 10 rooms, none with bath. Luggage storage, laundry.*

Super Pensión Familiar (Hotel Nueva Super Familiar). This simple, friendly establishment caters mostly to traveling Central Americans and a few strapped gringos. A barren room with two cots is $6. The communal bathrooms could be cleaner, but at least they have hot water. When your room gets claustrophobic, hang out and watch TV with old men and a tiger cat in the lobby. *On Av. 2a, bet. Calles 9 and 11, tel. 57–04–86. 100 meters north of Ticabus terminal, 250 meters east of Teatro Nacional. 14 rooms, none with bath. Luggage storage, laundry.*

Tica Linda. Mona Lisa smiles over the only budget Jacuzzi in Central America. The Tica Linda is "very noisy, you get no privacy, but the mariachi music is free," according to a local. Charo, the manager has a great sense of humor, and she keeps this classic crash pad in line. Stay in the small, dark dorms for the funky atmosphere and the cool company. A private double is $7.50; bed space in the dorm rooms is $3.50 per person. One of the collective bathrooms has hot water. *On Av. 2a bet. Calles 5 and 7, tel. 33–05–28. About 50 meters east of Teatro Nacional, the door just left of La Esmeralda Mariachi Bar (there may be no sign). 16 rooms, none with bath. Luggage storage, laundry, deposit box, breakfast $2.50, Jacuzzi.*

NEAR THE COCA-COLA

➤ **UNDER $8 • Hotel Generaleño.** This place just crosses the border into grim, but it's near the Alajuela (airport) bus terminals and in a safer area just a few blocks from the Coca-Cola. A kitschy, turquoise and maroon double with a private cold-water bath is $7.50. The rooms and communal baths are passably clean, but you'll be very intimate with your neighbors. *On Av. 2a, bet. Calles 8 and 10, tel. 33–78–77. 350 meters west of Parque Central. 45 rooms, some with bath. Luggage storage, laundry.*

➤ **UNDER $20 • Hotel Bienvenido.** This huge old building was once a movie theater, but has been remodeled and divided into small, spotless rooms with private hot-water baths. Generic but comfortable doubles are $18. The friendly management wants to make sure you have a safe visit, so they recommend staying away from the area north of the hotel. *On Calle 10 bet. Avs. 1 and 3, tel. 21–18–72. From the Coca-Cola, 300 meters east, 50 north. 44 rooms, all with bath. Luggage storage, laundry, deposit box, restaurant, 24-hour security.*

ELSEWHERE IN SAN JOSE

➤ **UNDER $8 • Hotel Astoria.** A funky old building that may be restored in the near future, the Hotel Astoria draws a big clientele of budget travelers to $8 doubles with communal, hot-water bath. Near the Limón bus stop and most major sights, the hotel has some cheaper huts out in the backyard, and the accommodating manager has a great sense of humor. *Av. 7, bet. Calles 7 and 9, tel. 21–21–74. From the Holiday Inn, 50 meters east. 19 rooms, some with bath. Luggage storage, laundry.*

Pensión Villa Blanca. This central, family-run pension may be the cheapest safe and friendly place to stay in San José. Don Sergio will check you over before he gives you a basic double under $6; after you've passed inspection, he'll go out of his way to help out, from wake-up calls to getting you a taxi. Large communal baths are clean and cold-water only. *On Av. 7, bet. Calles 2 and 4, tel. 23–90–88. From the Correo Central (main post office), 200 meters north and 50 meters west. 12 rooms, some with bath. Luggage storage, laundry, no alcohol allowed.*

➤ **UNDER $25 • Pensión Costa Rica Inn.** Near most major attractions and hot nightlife, this comfy pension is your best bet in this price range. The $24 doubles are clean (if slightly humid), secure, and equipped with private hot-water baths and phones. The decor is a little like a '50s horror movie—not gothic, just cheesy. It's staffed by friendly, efficient, English-speaking women. *Calle 9, bet. Av. 1 and Av. 3, tel. 22–52–03. Next to the Parque Morazán. 35 rooms, all with bath. Luggage stor-*

age, laundry, snack bar. Reservations: U.S. tel. 800/637–0899; Canada and Europe, tel. 318/263–2059.

➤ **UNDER $35** • **Pensión de la Cuesta.** This mellow, artsy bed and breakfast is worth the splurge at $32 for a beautifully decorated double. The bathrooms are "European-style" (communal), but they're so spacious and clean you won't mind sharing. Paolo, the owner, has created a tranquil, blossoming space filled with positive energy and great art, the perfect therapy for travel burnout. (If that last sentence made you gag, go spend the night down the road at the Holiday Inn.) *Av. 1, bet. Calles 11 and 15, tel. 55–28–96. 7 rooms, none with bath. Luggage storage, laundry, breakfast included.*

HOSTELS **Albergue Toruma.** Costa Rica's remodeled main youth hostel is the hip hangout for budget travelers. The $5 fee includes bunk space (and sheets) in single-sex rooms, breakfast, and use of huge hot-water showers. Get a pass from the receptionist so you can stay out after the 11 PM curfew. As the *albergue llave* (key hostel), Toruma offers travel advice and makes reservations for the rest of Costa Rica's growing hostel net. You can also join IYHF here. Reserve three months in advance during the busy season (December, January, and May–August). *San Pedro, on Av. Central bet. Calles 29 and 31, Barrio La California, tel. 24–40–85 or 53–65–88. Across the street from Pollos Kentucky. 123 beds, none with bath. 11 PM curfew, luggage storage, laundry, security box, message board, pay phone. Open daily 6 AM–11 PM.*

Casa Ridgeway. This pleasant hostel is associated with the Quaker Peace Center. According to the brochure, it's "designed to offer hospitality to visiting Quakers and other socially conscious visitors interested in peace, conflict resolution, human rights, and environmental issues." Private doubles are $15, a bed in the dorm room is $7, and the fee includes the use of a small, well-equipped kitchen. The communal bathrooms are large, clean, and have hot water. Alcohol, drugs, and smoking are not permitted and quiet time is 10 PM–7 AM. *Calle 15, bet. Avs. 6 and 8, tel. 33–61–68 (ask for Casa Ridgeway). Near the Tribunales de Justicia in a small discreetly marked house. 12 beds, none with bath. Luggage storage, laundry, message board, kitchen. Reservations recommended.*

FOOD

There are hundreds of places to eat in San José. The cheapest are roasted-chicken joints, Chinese, or "typical" restaurants called sodas. The best deal is the $2–$4 lunchtime casado (although many places offer casados any time), which includes rice, beans, salad (usually the shredded cabbage variety, sometimes a simple slice of tomato and lettuce), vegetables, and some sort of meat. The quality of most sodas is fine, but not a gastronomic orgasm.

Pizza Hut is actually good here, and it's one of the only places where you can get a sanitary salad bar for under $4. **Rosti Pollo,** a Nicaraguan fast-food chain, dishes up good, cheap roasted chicken (one in San Pedro, Av. Central, 400 meters east of Banco Anglo Costarricense, tel. 53–27–84). Places that are open 24 hours usually mutate at night, becoming bar-like (*see* After Dark, *below*). Many plain bars serve bocas (hors d'oeuvres), usually delicious and served free or for a small fee (50¢–$1) with drinks.

To buy supplies or munchies, check out the supermarkets downtown. **La Gran Vía** has entrances on Avenida Central and Calle 3; it's just north of the Gran Hotel. Several blue-striped **Mas X Menos** stores dot the city; the most central is on Avenida Central between Calles 9 and 11. *Panaderías* and *reposterías* (bakeries and pastry shops) abound, and the cheapest produce is sold in the **Mercado Central** (between Avenidas 1a and Central and Calles 8 and 6) or nearby, along Calle 8. Prices reflect the cost of a full meal, drink, and that killer 22% extra, the service charge and tax.

➤ **UNDER $4** • **Pollo Campesino.** This central roasted-chicken restaurant is one of the only places you can get mashed potatoes in the entire country. Although the atmosphere is very family fast-food, most of the menu is alcohol. Half a bird for $3 includes tortillas and your choice of beans, rice, taters, or pickled veggies. *Corner of Av. 2A and Calle 7, tel. 22-11-70. 100 meters east of the Teatro National. Open daily 10 am-midnight.*

Soda Restaurant Salon Paris. Don't let the name fool you; this soda is the archetype—gleaming Formica tables and a bar that stretches into infinity. Are the waitresses still wearing hairnets? Have a filling and reliable $2 casado (vegans beware) and a *'fresco de cas* (tart fruit shake). *Av. 3 bet. Calles 1 and 3, tel. 22-28-18. Open daily 7 am-10 pm.*

Soda Vishnu. The fluorescent-lit vegetarian soda gains no aesthetic points, but the veggie food unites ticos, business folk, students, and foreigners. The tasty *plato del día* includes rice, soup, vegetable, salad, bread, drink, and dessert for less than $2. If only the tofu didn't look like bologna. **Restaurante Vishnu** (Av. 1, between Calle 1 and Calle 3, tel. 21-35-49) serves similar food right around the corner, but claims to have a separate kitchen. Dueling krishnas? Breakfast on yogurt and fruit for $1 in either. *Calle 3, bet. Av. Central and Av. 1, tel. 22-25-49. 100 meters north of Plaza de Cultura. Open 7 AM-8 PM.*

➤ **UNDER $10** • **El Balcón de Europa.** Amidst a sea of balding heads, glistening wood panels, and reactionary quotes, you'll find a cluster of budget travelers on a splurge. Munch on the free cheese and bread while chef/owner Franco whips up an amazing $5 *pasta arrabiata* (bacon, mushrooms, and basil). The *risottos* (a soft rice dish) take a little time, but the saffron-flavored *Milanese* is worth the wait. Avoid the overcooked *plato mixta* pasta sampler: The tortellini is tasteless and the ravioli bland. The house wine is cheap ($1.50 a glass) and inoffensive. Finish off the meal with a potent espresso and grappa-drenched fruit and you won't care if you don't eat tomorrow. *On Calle 7 bet. Av. Central and Av. 1, tel. 21-48-41. From the Plaza de la Cultura, walk east along the Av. Central. Open Sun.-Fri. noon-10 PM.*

➤ **UNDER $8** • **Machu Picchu.** This simple Peruvian restaurant is totally worth a taxi ride. The entrées, like the spicy *picante de mariscos* (spicy seafood) or *pulpo al ajillo* (garlic octopus), both $5, are excellent, but if you come with a group, your best bet is to order several appetizers and share them. Typical Peruvian potato dishes are all under $4. The ceviche ($4) is the best in the city, according to resident Peruvians. And be forewarned, that hot sauce is HOT! *On Calle 32 bet. Av. 1 and Av. 3, tel. 22-73-84. From Pollos Kentucky on Paseo Colón, 125 meters north. Open 11:30 AM-3 PM and 6 PM-10 PM.*

Mordisco. Relax in the comfortable, plant-filled patio and take your time with a varied menu of natural food. Portions are pretty small, but the food is great. Most courses are vegetarian and run about $6; the best deal is the casado/plato del día for about $2.50. *East of the Mecedes Benz dealership on Paseo Colón, tel. 55-24-48. From downtown, walk west down Av. Central or take a Sabana-Cementerio bus from the cathedral. Open Mon.-Sat. 9 AM-10 PM.*

➤ **UNDER $6** • **Il Pomodoro.** "The Tomato" dishes out inexpensive *Italian* Italian food near the university. People from the U., families, and hipsters order up pizzas made with a pungent but tasty local cheese and a variety of toppings: *chile dulce* (red bell pepper), *hongos* (mushrooms), and many, many meats. Small pizzas range from less than $3 to about $6. The pasta is reasonable at $3-$5 a dish. *100 meters north* of the *Iglesia de San Pedro, tel. 24–09–66. Take the San Pedro bus from across from the Teatro Nacional. Open daily 11–11.*

Restaurante Marisquerías. One of the best and cheapest seafood places in San José, it's well worth the taxi ride to Guadalupe. Chow down on quality seafood in a shiver-me-timbers atmosphere. House specialties include the *vuelva a la vida* (return to life), a seafood cocktail for under $4. The lip-smackin' mixed plate of *bocas variadas* includes fish tacos, fried yucca, fried fish, and shrimp for under $5. *West of Parque Central de Guadalupe, tel. 24–88–30. Tell the taxi driver "frente al Palacio Municipal Guadalupe." Open daily 11:30 AM–10:45 PM.*

DESSERT AND CAFES Costa Rican coffee is strong, and a few places still serve it the old-fashioned way: hot milk in one pitcher and hot coffee in the other. Coffee is not generally taken alone but with bread or a sweet. Glistening flaky carbo treats lurk behind many a glass counter, but most are as tasty as cardboard. The best *pastel de canela* (cinnamon roll) is served at a little wooden stand across from the University radio station in San Pedro, near the University.

Café Bar Confetti's. And you thought the perfect marriage was a myth—it's actually a potent concoction of coffee, brandy, chocolate, cinnamon, and cream. *Matrimonio perfecto* is one of over 50 alcoholic coffees served up by smiling waitpeople for less than $3. When you feel tipsy, take the edge off with a $2 stuffed croissant or a cheesy $3 crêpe. *On the Plaza de la Democracía, tel. 33–88–16. Open Mon.–Sat., 11 AM–10 PM.*

Churreria Manolo's. Not only does this place serve up killer greasy, sugary *churros*, but it also sells the cheapest cappuccino in the city (75¢). You can order your churros with hot chocolate (thick Spanish or creamy French) and get the authentic sugar high. This is also a great place for a very Latino lunch amidst a throng of slightly shady businesspeople and young bohemians. *Av. Central bet. Calles 9 and 11, tel. 23–40–67.*

El Cafe del Teatro. Teatro wins the prize for most relaxed atmosphere. Have a cup of tea and rest your weary head against cool marble. Breakfast plates for $4 are a little expensive but heaped with good food. This is a great place for single women to sit without getting hissed to death. *In the Teatro National, on the Plaza de la Cultura, tel. 33–44–88. Open Mon.–Sat. 8 AM–6 PM.*

➤ **ICE CREAM** • Ice cream is an art in this country, and after a long, dusty bus ride, it may just save your sanity. The crème de la cream is dished out by two prolific chains, **Pop's** and **Mïnpik**. Try the *cono azucarado de coco capuchino* (coconut ice cream dipped in chocolate) for just over $1, or an enormous *batida* (milkshake) at just under $2. Mïnpik also has a weird blue fruit-flavored ice cream called *pitufo*. There's at least one branch of each on Avenida Central downtown.

> *"I came back to Costa Rica for Pop's mango ice cream"—overheard on the streets of San José*

WORTH SEEING

Most of San José's major sights are downtown and easily reached by foot. The two notable exceptions are the sprawling Parque Sabana (*see* Outdoor Activities, *below*) and the University of Costa Rica in San Pedro. The Sabana–Cementerio bus from the cathedral will drop you right across from the Museo de Arte Costarricense at La Sabana, and you can catch a bus to San Pedro across from the Teatro Nacional. For a sample of Costa Rica's contemporary art scene, check out local papers for listings of free galleries and expositions.

MUSEO DE JADE The Jade (pronounced "hah-day" in Spanish) Museum is probably the coolest, or at least the most awe-inspiring, in San José. The subdued, environmentally controlled labyrinth is crammed with an amazing array of indigenous artifacts, including the largest collection of American jade in the world. Some of the written explanations are in English, but most are in Spanish only. Check out the jade tubes used as bras by the wives of important chiefs. They fastened the tube underneath their breasts—the original underwire. And then there's the famous penis room, devoted entirely to male fertility symbols, large and small. The 11th-floor view of San José is astounding even on an overcast day; an adjacent room exhibits the work of contemporary Costa Rican artists. *11th floor of Instituto Nacional de Seguros, Calle 9 and Av. 7, tel. 23–58–00, ext. 2588. It's the tall building northeast of Parque Morazán. Admission free. Open weekdays 8–3.*

MUSEO DE ARTE COSTARRICENSE Inside a quiet, colonial-style building, the work of Costa Rican artists captures the history, culture, and personality of the country. Exhibitions change every few months, but most are representative of lo tico through the use of material (in particular, wood and stone) or the subject matter. Take a peek upstairs, where the golden walls of the **Salón Dorado** depict the history, culture, and nature of Costa Rica. *East end of La Sabana, tel. 22–77–65. Take Sabana/Estadio bus from the Cathedral and get off at first Sabana stop. Admission: 75¢, free on Sun., students with ID free. Open Tues.–Sun. 10–5.*

SERPENTARIO So there's this piranha breathing heavy in your face, just 4 inches from your nose. Good thing it gets fed at 3 PM every day. While you wait for the not-so-frenzied feeding, walk around the Serpentarium and admire healthy specimens from around Costa Rica and the world, from a deadly fer-de-lance (*terciopelo*) to a juvenile Burmese python. The young guides will answer your queries in English or Spanish. *Av. 1 bet. Calles 9 and 11 on the 2nd floor, tel. 55–42–10. Admission: $2; $1 with student ID. Open daily 10–7. Gift shop accepts dollars.*

MUSEO CRIMINOLOGICO Body parts and abortions float around in formaldehyde as object lessons for leading a clean, legal life. Foren*sick* exhibitions and a display of over 8,500 weapons confiscated by the police department draw large groups of voyeurs. This museum is also good for the quote of the decade: "Having sex with strangers is a health risk." Somebody better tell 'em having unprotected sex with *anybody* is a health risk. *In the Edificio de la Paz de la Justicia (the police department), Av. 6 bet. Calles 17 and 19, tel. 57–06–66, ext. 2180. South of Museo Nacional, between the Tribunales de Justicia and the Corte Supremo. Admission free. Open Mon., Wed., and Fri., 1–4.*

TEATRO NACIONAL The delicate frescoes, gilded trim, and subtle stonework of the national theater drip neoclassic Euro-lust. The center of Costa Rican fine arts for over a hundred years, the theater is worth a tour if you're into architecture, history, or culture. Go during an actual performance; you'll get an even more baroque experience, and performance tickets are often as cheap as admission to the building itself. Although it was severely damaged in the recent earthquakes, by press time the theater should be open for regular performances. *On Plaza de la Cultura, tel. 21–13–29 or 33–63–54. Admission: $2. Open Mon.–Sat. 9–5:30.*

GALERIA NACIONAL DE ARTE CONTEMPORANEO Every month this small gallery hosts a different artist. Sometimes the exhibits are mind-blowing, and Carlos the curator will let you know what exhibit is coming to town next. *Corner of Av. 3 and Calle 15, tel. 23–05–28. Next to Biblioteca Nacional, across from Parque Nacional. Admission free. Open Mon.–Sat. 10–5, with an unpredictable lunch break.*

MUSEO DE ORO The gold adornments of Costa Rica's indigenous cultures float in the dark recesses of the Gold Museum, far below the Plaza de Cultura. The gold display is huge, compelling, and a striking contrast to the simple glass beads the Spaniards traded for such treasures. On the first floor is the **Museo Numismática** (Coin Museum), only of interest to collectors or historians. The **Exhibición de Arte,** on the lowest level, gives an excellent recap of the country's art history. You might need ID to enter. *Entrance on Calle 5 bet. Av. Central and Av. 2a, tel. 23–05–28. Under Plaza de la Cultura. Admission free. Open Fri.–Sun. 10–5.*

MUSEO NACIONAL The yellow walls of the national museum rise high above the Plaza de la Democracía. Displays span archaeology, botany, colonial history, and culture. Look for the colossal round stones left by the *diquis* tribe, some of which are 1½ meters in diameter. They're considered national treasures, and it's forbidden to transport them out of the country. *Calle 17 bet. Av. Central and Av. 2a, east of Plaza de la Democracía, tel. 57–14–33. Admission: 75¢, students with ID free. Open Tues.–Sat. 8:30–4:30, Sun. 9–4:30.*

PARQUE ZOOLOGICO SIMON BOLIVAR The Simón Bolívar Zoo is somewhere between sad and repulsive, but at least it's a good chance to see some of Costa Rica's fauna alive and closeup. Even more interesting is how people interact with the animals. Try not to smack that 12-year-old who keeps throwing trash at the monkeys, okay? The zoo is also home to the information office of the national parks (*see* Basics, *above*). North of Instituto Nacional de Seguros (Jade Museum), tel. 33–67–00. Take Calle 7 to Av. 11; look for the sign. Admission: 50¢. Open weekdays 8–4, weekends and holidays 9–5.

PARQUES (PARKS) Plaza de la Cultura. Bounded by Avenidas Central and 2 and Calles 3 and 5, the plaza is much more than just a point of orientation. Home to the Museo de Oro, the Museo Numismático, and the Teatro Nacional, it forms a cultural nexus for gringos and ticos. Foreigners come to hang out and buy souvenirs; ticos come to watch tourists and feed pigeons. Clowns tease small children with balloon animals, and Latin rock or jazz bands spice up the air. Check out the action—who knows, you may even see the President dancing a hot salsa.

Parque Morazán. This wide plot of grass, trees, gravel, and cement was recently "improved" by the Calderón Administration. On weekends, the park is filled with families on their way to the nearby Simón Bolívar Zoo. Hordes of screaming tico munchkins learn how to count while running up the steps of the impressive rotunda. On weekdays during lunch hour, the park is a refuge for anyone who wants to take a load off, and workers ignore the annoying "keep off the grass" signs. *Bordered by Av. 5 and a little side street, Calles 5 and 9.*

Parque España. This park swirls with jungly vegetation and glitters with bird song. Even though it's the smallest of the three main city parks, the Park of Spain is the best nooky nook around; try not to startle the couples. Close by are several interesting sights: To the north, the **Instituto Nacional de Seguros** houses the Museo de Jade; to the northeast is the **Casa Amarilla** (Costa Rica's Ministry of Foreign Affairs), donated by Andrew Carnegie; to the west stands a funky iron building, now an elementary school, that was shipped piece by piece from France. *At the intersection of Av. 3 and Calle 11, just east of Parque Morazán.*

Parque Nacional. Lie on the sun-drenched grass or cool off under a bougainvillea-capped trellis with families and foreigners in this two-block-long park. On weekend mornings, watch ticos watching gringos look at the statue of Central America beating the hell out of fleeing invader William Walker. At night the park is a poorly lit haven for lovers and pickpockets—if you're one of the former, go to Parque España instead. The white building to the south is the **National Legislative Assembly,** legitimate heart of the Costa Rican government. The gray building to the north is the **Biblioteca Nacional** (National Library). *Bet. Av. 1 and Av. 3, Calles 15 and 19, south of the Holiday Inn.*

UNIVERSIDAD DE COSTA RICA The University of Costa Rica, in San Pedro just east of San José, is a great place to hang out and meet people, especially if your Spanish is pretty good. The open-air gallery at the **Facultad de Bellas Artes** (College of Fine Arts), on the east side of campus, hosts frequent expositions and music recitals. The U. is most exciting during Semana Universitaria (*see* Festivals, *above*). Near the university are lots of bookstores, and tons of cheap sodas, including the famed macrobiotic restaurant **La Mazorca** (100 meters north of Banco Anglo Costarricense, tel. 24–8069). While weekday nights at the university are mellow, on weekends nearby bars get packed with students and intellectuals. To get to the university, take a very frequent San Pedro bus from Avenida 2a across from the Teatro Nacional. Get off in San Pedro proper, across from the church. From the church, walk north about 250 meters to the south (main) entrance of the university.

For information on cultural events, movies, plays, gallery openings, or politically correct benefits, check the following: La Nación *and* La República *(available on the street and in supermarkets); posters (at* Teatro Nacional *and around the university);* La Semana, *the university newspaper (buy it at bookshops and photocopy centers near campus);* The Tico Times *(an English-language publication that comes out every Friday).*

CHEAP THRILLS

FESTIVALS **Semana Santa** (Easter week) in San José isn't known for inspiring processions, but this is not the time to hit the beach—it's peak season and reservations are required months in advance. Also beware that public transportation (including most taxis) shuts down on Thursday and Good Friday.

During **Semana Universitaria** (University Week), toward the end of March, students at the Universidad de Costa Rica cast off any academic duty, and drink and dance for a week. Each *facultad* (school) throws its own party and builds a float for the parade.

The **Día de la Virgen de Los Angeles,** Costa Rica's patron saint, is celebrated on August 2 with processions and a huge Mass. On the night before, nuns, athletes, families, and friends walk *el romaría,* a 22-kilometer (14-mile) trek down the highway from San José to Cartago.

MERCADOS Leave your sense of time and direction behind and wander around the narrow aisles of the **Mercado Central** (bet. Av. Central and Av. 1, Calles 8 and 6). The enclosed block-long market is stifling and stuffed with veggies, fruits, brilliant tropical flowers, rows of meat and fish stands, shoes, fragrant herbs, even housewares and souvenirs. Hunker down with locals and other travelers at a food stand for one of the cheapest meals around. This is the place to try *chan,* a slimy, seedy refresco—it looks like amoebas and tastes faintly spicy.

A few blocks away is the seamier **Mercado Borbón** (Av. 3 and Calle 8), a damp cave of produce sellers. The area in and around both the markets can be a hands-on experience in more ways than one: Watch your back, your front, your money, and your manners. Borbón, in particular, may not be much fun for women alone or even in pairs. If you're staying in an outlying neighborhood, ask for the time and location of the fería, a weekly open-air màrket held in each neighborhood.

AFTER DARK

When the sun dives behind the blue mountains, the entire Meseta Central lights up like an electric octopus. Evening activities range from seedy, smoke-filled bars to posh art openings. Pick up a local paper on the street to find out what's happening. If you just want the night to happen to you, hang out around the Parque Central (along Av. Central and Av. 2a, east from the Plaza de la Cultura) or in the University area of San Pedro. These aren't the worst areas of the city, but take a taxi if you're staying out late. The brilliantly lit plastic of **Casa del Sandwich** (corner of Calle 9 and Av. 2a) is a perfect pit stop while bar-hopping or for a pre-dawn, pre-bus ride snack (Ticabus boards nearby). It serves humongous *hamburguesas supremas* ($2), 24 hours daily.

You'll need your cedula (photo ID) to get into most discos. The drinking age is 18.

CINEMAS AND THEATERS San José has several English-language cinemas within walking distance or a $2 taxi ride from the center: **Cine California** (Calle 23 and Av. 1a, tel. 21–47–38); **Cine Magaly** (Calle 23 and Av. Central, tel. 21–95–97); **Universal** (Paseo Colón bet. Calles 26 and 28, tel 21–52–41); **Colón 1 and 2** (Paseo Colón bet. Calles 38 and 40, tel. 21–45–17).

A nexus of cultural activity, **Sala Garbo** (on Av. 2a bet. Calles 26 and 28, tel. 22–10–34) shows great international films, and the concrete cave of its **Bar Shakespeare** downstairs occasionally offers live music in the jazz or *nueva canción* vein and doubles as an art gallery. Artsy and international films are also shown at the University of Costa Rica, at the Auditorio de Estudios Generales and at the Auditorio de la Facultad de Derecho.

The abundance of *teatros* is testament to ticos' love of theater, from ridiculous farce to biting satire. Small companies are scattered throughout the city; look for announcements in newspapers and *afiches* (posters) throughout San José. Companies from around the world come to perform at the two largest theaters, the **Melico Salazar** and the **Teatro Nacional**. Students from the University dance company and the Facultad de Artes Dramáticas put on interesting and cheaper performances at the auditorio in Bellas Artes or the auditorio in the Edificio Saprissa at the University in San Pedro. Call for reservations or show up when the box office opens.

BARS Promesas. This open bar is a good place to check out some street action and hang out with heaps of other gringos. You might want to avoid the place just because of that, but the 50¢ beer flows for days and the wood-lined nook is close to dance spots. *On Av. 2a bet. Calles 7 and 9, no tel.*

Soda Palace. Men of business, musicians of the world, and the odd foreigner gather here to cool off, make hot deals, and plan some kind of coup 24 hours a day. If you ask for a *cuba libre* (rum and coke) here, the response will be a smile and *"Ay, no, no. Aquí se llama la Gran Mentira." Corner of Av. 2a and Calle 2, across from Parque Central, tel. 21–34–41.*

Taberna Chelles. This crowded bar tries hard to be English, but the sign "*Hay chicharrones* (We have pork rinds)" kinda gives it away. Come here for $1 beer and a long list of tasty bocas worth the extra 50¢. *On Calle 9 bet. Av. Central and Av. 2a, tel. 22–80–60. Next to Chelles 24-hour restaurant. Open 3 PM–midnight.*

PENAS These alternative bars in San Pedro play cool Latin American tunes from traditional songs to the *nueva canción* (new song), revolutionary folk songs. They often have live music on the weekends. More places near the university to hunt down include **Tertulia** and **Los Andes.**

Cuartel de La Boca del Monte. This sprawling bar is a chichi international scene, but the food is excellent and the drink list goes on for days. The music varies in quality and character, so come instead to people-watch and practice your attitude. *On Av. 1 bet. Calles 21 and 23, in San José, tel. 21–03–27.*

La Villa. Political posters and eclectic memorabilia cover the walls, and mellow guitar fills the space between hot political debate and friendly ribbing. Alvaro, proprietor and bartender, has created the perfect bohemian atmosphere in a unique space. *125 meters north of Banco Anglo Costarricense in San Pedro, tel. 25–96–12.*

MUSIC AND DANCING The Showbar is the place to live out your hidden fantasy of dancing on the table to mostly reggae and some international groove tunes. The tiny bar gets packed on the weekends, so be prepared to share your personal space. *On Calle 9, bet. Av. Central and Av. 1, no tel. Across from La Torre (Tonite).*

In San Pedro, several disco-bars cater mostly to students. Avenida Central from San José through San Pedro is lined with all sorts of sporting spots. Rock, reggae, or calypso the night away in **El Tablado** (across the street from Pollo Kentucky on Av. Central) or **Baleares** (Av. Central, 400 meters east of Banco Anglo Costarricense, tel. 53–45–77). Covers vary but are usually under $6.

GAY NIGHTLIFE San José is internationally renowned for its thriving gay scene. Underground clubs dot the city, but they're impossible to find without a local. Even most of the established hangouts are discreetly signless and boast totally nondescript exteriors. **Bar Unicornio** (from the hardware store La Casa del Tornillo, 210 meters west, tel. 21–55–52) is a classy, mostly lesbian bar open daily 6–midnight. Knock on the swinging bar doors and perhaps you'll be given entry to the tiny romantic nook of **El Churro Español El Puchito** (on Calle 11 at Av. 8, no tel.), commonly called El Puchito, open from 6 onward.

Slang for the ambiente (gay community): Un(a) militar is a hetero who is openminded about homosexuality; un(a) buga is a heterosexual (a "breeder"); los cacheros are guys who say they're hets but sleep with boys, too. The following are considered pejorative unless used by other gente del ambiente(gays): tortilleras (dykes); tractor (butch); las locas (queers).

La Torre (a.k.a. Tonite). Boys and girls sweat and grind all night long to hot dance music. All mirrors, fake smoke, and flashing lights, this classic disco is the Costa Rican crossroads for gente del ambiente. *On Calle 7 bet. Av. 1 and Av. Central, tel. 23–08–33. $4 cover on Wed. with open bar until midnight; no cover Thurs.; no cover until 11 Fri.; $2 cover Sat. and Sun. Open Wed.–Sat. 7:30 PM–4 AM, Sun. 2:30 PM–midnight. Proof of age required.*

La Avispa. Christmas trees and pool tables crowd the back of the club, but there's plenty of room to dance up front to techno-pop and romantic Latin tunes. The clientele is mostly women, except on nights of "shows," when some of the cutest things in skirts are men. *On Calle 1, bet. Av. 8 and Av. 10, tel. 23–53–43. No cover Tues. and Wed.; $2–$4 cover Thurs.–Sun. Open Tues.–Sat. 8 PM–2 AM, Sun. 5 PM–till it empties.*

OUTDOOR ACTIVITIES

La Sabana is a gigantic recreation center that includes soccer fields, a baseball diamond, an Olympic-size swimming pool, tennis courts, volleyball nets, and jungle gyms. Be on the lookout for a gigantic cement cross, a 50-meter fountain on an artificial lake, militant Boy Scouts, and jogging high school boys spouting every English vulgarity they know. *End of Paseo Colón. Take the Sabana–Cementerio or Sabana–Estadio·bus from the Cathedral.*

WHITE-WATER RAFTING How do you get wet and excited without sex? Grab a paddle, a helmet, and a life jacket; let out a holler, hold onto your britches, and go whitewater rafting. Costa Rica has some of the world's best rafting, with four different rivers ranging from the mellow Corobicí to the pernicious Peralta section of the Reventazón. The best rafting companies are **Ríos Tropicales** (on Paseo Colón next to the Mercedes-Benz dealership, tel. 33–64–55; in the U.S., 800/272–6654), **Costa Rican Expeditions** (*see* Travel Agencies, *above*), and **Costaricaraft** (Apartado 812–2050, San Pedro, tel. 25–39–39). All cost about the same, but Ríos Tropicales has the most experienced guides. One-day beginners' excursions cost around $65; more advanced trips cost $10–$20 more. The price includes breakfast and lunch, transportation to and from hotels in San José, all the necessary equipment, and cute guides. International students qualify for a 10% discount; residents and foreign students studying in Costa Rica pay tico price, which is half the gringo cost.

SWIMMING Most places in Central America don't have good places to swim—you're stuck dealing with either murk, brine, or pollution—but the area around San José has been blessed. All swimmin' holes are fed by hot springs or *manantiales* (fresh, cold springs). **Balneario Tropical** in Grecia (*see* Sarchí, *below*) is a choice place to plunge in and cool off. The waters of **Ojo de Agua**, a recreational complex near Alajuela, are chilly but clean and unchlorinated—and underpopulated if you go on a weekday (buses from San José depart about every hour from Calle 18 and Av. 3). The area around Cartago abounds with nice little *balnearios* (pools): **Ujarrás, Charrara,** and **Orosí** (*see* Near Cartago, *below*) are the best in the province.

The Meseta Central

The sulfurous volcanoes of Poás and Irazú; clear, spring-fed balnearios near Alajuela and Cartago; and the archaeological site of Guayabo near Turrialba are among the attractions of the Meseta Central (Central Valley) and the surrounding highlands. The Meseta Central is an elevated valley surrounded by two mountain ranges, the Cordillera Central to the north and east and the Cordillera de Talamanca to the south. The tableland is high enough above sea level to keep the temperature pleasant all year round—no need for air-conditioning or central heating in this part of the country. The coffee- and dairy-producing highlands get wool-sweater chilly, however, and you'll need some sun protection when exploring the high-altitude volcanoes or the warmer river valleys of Orosí and Turrialba.

The provincial capitals—San José, Alajuela, Heredia, and Cartago—are all in the Central Valley, along with two-thirds of the country's population. Most towns or sights are explorable as day-trips from San José, but the provincial capitals of Heredia and Alajuela can also serve as a base for exploring the coffee-growing region.

Alajuela

At first glance Alajuela is nothing special, just a midsize city with hundreds of kitschy stores selling shoes, underwear, and hair clips. Most travelers use Alajuela, about 18 kilometers (11 miles) northwest of the capital, as a transport hub to Volcán Poás or the highland towns of Sarchí and Zarcero, or as a last-night stopover close to the airport. You'll miss out if you just pass through—Alajuela is one of the best cities in which to meet people in all Costa Rica. From the woman in the market who laughs and helps you untangle the *chilillos de verga de toro* (whips made of bull penises) to the kid in the park who invites you to help set free his balloons, Alajuelenses have a well-deserved reputation as open and outgoing people. The best places to hang out are the clean **mercado** (bet. Av. Central and Av. 1, Calles 4 and 6) or in one of the city's parks. In the heart of Alajuela is **Parque Central,** pleasant, green, and filled with mango trees (bordered by Av. Central and Av. 1, Calles Central and 1); 100 meters south on Calle 2 is the **Parque Juan Santamaría.**

COMING AND GOING Cushy **Tuasa** buses leave daily every few minutes from San José in front of La Merced (corner of Av. 2a and Calle 14, tel. 22–53–25). Service runs 24 hours a day, with fewer buses in the wee hours (up to an hour wait). Buses to Alajuela also go to Juan Santamaría International Airport. As you're approaching Alajuela's center, keep an eye out on the right side for **La Agonia,** a funky church. The 30-minute trip costs about 40¢. Alajuela's bus terminal occupies the block bordered by Calles 8 and 10 and Avenidas Central and 1. The Tuasa bus makes the terminal its end stop. From the terminal or nearby streets, you can catch buses to Sarchí, Ojo de Agua, the Butterfly Farm, and maybe even Volcán Poás (*see* Near Alajuela, *below*).

GETTING AROUND Alajuela's center isn't huge and the streets are fairly well-marked by signs. It's another grid city, although many directions are given from Parque Central. Avenues run east–west and calles north–south. Odd avenues lie north of the parque, even ones to the south. Odd calles lie to the east, even to the west.

The Meseta Central

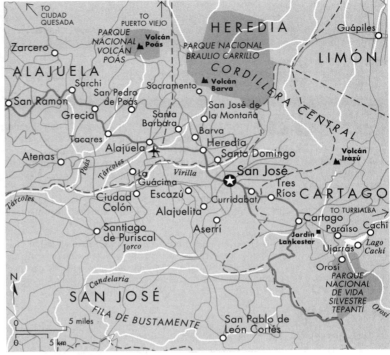

Hotel Rex. This very basic hotel, near the market and the bus terminal, is cool in a sleazy way. David Lynch could do great things here. The $4 doubles aren't too comfortable, and the communal bathroom's cold-water shower is gruesome, but the family that runs the place is nice. *On Av. 1 bet. Calles 6 and 8, tel. 41–67–78. 250 meters west of Parque Central. 10 rooms, none with bath. Luggage storage, laundry. Check-out time 9 AM.*

Hotel Alajuela. If you've been crawling through $2 pensions, this spiffy, modern facility right off Parque Central ($27 per double, $21 per single) might be worth the splurge. The best deal are the apartments in the old section. For $23, you get your own kitchen (and utensils). Make reservations as far in advance as possible. *Near corner of Av. Central and Calle 2, tel. 41–65–95 or 41–12–41. Across from southwest corner of Parque Central. 50 rooms, all with bath. Luggage storage $2 per day; laundry: $3 to wash, $3 to dry.*

FOOD For the cheapest eats in town, head for the **mercado** (100 meters east from the San José bus stop, between Av. Central and Av. 1, Calles 4 and 6). You'll find several inexpensive restaurants of the roasted-chicken variety around the terminal. Surrounding Parque Central are a handful of burger joints and other meateries (**Joey's** and **El Cencerro**). While the food is tasty, you'll be charged gringo prices for the cool view.

El Rincón Peruano. A wonderful Russian woman whose name means "love" makes fantastic Peruvian dishes. *Papa rellena* (stuffed potato) goes for less than $1; grilled *corvina* (sea bass) for under $3; and the house plate special, *pescado dorado,* for under $2. If you ask in advance, she'll make you authentic Russian food. *On Calle 4 bet. Av. 1 and Av. Central, tel. 42–39–77. From the southwest corner of Parque Central, it's 100 meters west, 75 meters north. Closed Tues.*

PARQUE NACIONAL VOLCAN POAS Steamy, sulfur-belching Volcán Poás is one of the most accessible active volcanoes in Costa Rica. Only 37 kilometers (23 miles) north of Alajuela, the banded, brown-gray crater is 1 mile in diameter, 300 meters deep, and has a hot-water lake at the bottom. The volcano sporadically emits geyser-like eruptions and has entered a more active phase since 1989. Sulfuric rains damage local crops, and toxic fumes occasionally force nearby residents from their homes. Locals say the volcano is more active on days when there's a lot of tourists—it doesn't like 'em. The best time to see the crater is in the dry season or early morning, before afternoon drizzle descends. Steep but short nature trails lead to the crater, through a dwarf cloud forest of gnarly trees and clinging bromeliads, and to a view of the blue-green **Laguna Botos**. The park is currently open 8–3:30, but you should call the national parks office (tel. 57–09–22) to check. Dress in layers and be prepared for rain. Temperatures change dramatically, and at 9,500 feet, the top of the volcano gets windy and chilly.

"Ah, she's complaining today," says Sra. Rodríguez as Poás rumbles in the distance. "There must be a lot of visitors."

Just outside the park entrance, about 3 kilometers (2 miles) up a gravel road, is the **Alberque Ecológico La Providencia** (tel. 31–78–84). Accommodations are elegantly simple, and the proprietors are exceptional people (they're even building a meditation area). They also offer a three-hour horse tour through primary-growth forest, reforested areas, and up the backside of Poás. It's not IYHF, and right now it's expensive ($40 for a double with bath), but call for student discounts.

The cheapest way to get to Poás is with **Tuasa** (tel. 33–74–77). Every Sunday at 8:30 AM a comfy bus departs San José from Calle 12 between Avenidas 2 and 4, and returns to San José at 1 PM. When the Tuasa bus fills up, they put another in service, but get there *early*—as close to 7:30 as possible. The bus stops in Alajuela at 9 AM and at a restaurant, where the park's entrance fee ($1.50) is collected, at 10 AM, finally arriving at Poás at 11. On weekdays, you have to take a bus from San José to Alajuela; from there, catch a San Pedro de Poás bus (the parada is just south of Alajuela's terminal) to San Pedro, where you can get a taxi to the volcano for about $20 round-trip.

FINCA DE MARIPOSAS Brilliant blues, vibrant greens, and rich reds and purples flutter in your face in the screened-in gardens of the Butterfly Farm. About 40 minutes southwest of Alajuela, in the town of La Guácima, the farm spreads over 1½ hectares (4 acres). Admission is about $7 ($5 with student ID), and includes a bilingual video and tour. The farm is open 9:30–4:30, and the last tour is at 3:30. Buses to La Guácima (via San Antonio de Belén) depart San José from Avenida 1 between Calles 20 and 22 daily (except Sunday) at 11 AM and 2 PM (2 hours, 50¢). Buses to La Guácima from Alajuela depart from the street corner 200 meters south of the bus terminal at about 6:20, 9, 11, and 1. Return buses to Alajuela pass the farm at 9:45, 11:45, 1:45, 3:45, and 5:45. Direct buses to San José pass at 12:15 and 3:15. Go early in the day, before the rain makes the butterflies hide.

SARCHI Sarchí, 32 kilometers (20 miles) north of Alajuela, is known for delicate woodwork, brilliantly painted *carretas* (ox carts), and comfy, collapsible leather rocking chairs. The pleasantly green and clean village is a good day-trip from San José if you want to see the Alajuelan countryside and load up on presents. (Hint: Ox carts will not fit into your carry-on luggage.) Several cheap sodas speckle the main plaza, but **Baco's** steakhouse may give you a free map with their tasty $3 casado.

Buses to Sarchí depart about every half hour from Alajuela's main bus terminal 5 AM–10 PM (1½ hours, 50¢). You can also catch a bus for Sarchí in **Grecia**, at the west side of the terminal, about every half hour. Buses for Grecia leave frequently from the Coca-Cola in San José. (If you don't mind riding to Sarchí standing, stay a while in Grecia first—the little town has a funky red church and a pool called **Balneario Tropical.** Get off the bus in Sarchí when you see the ice-cream-pastel church.

ZARCERO Zarcero looks like it was designed by Dr. Seuss. Cypress shrubs trimmed in bizarre animal and semi-abstract shapes decorate the park in front of the church. The interior of the church is covered with elaborate pastel stencils and detailed *retablos* (religious paintings) by Misael Solis, a local octogenarian who completed the paintings over 50 years ago. Zarcerenos take pride in Señor Solis' excellent, though as yet undiscovered, folk art. The town is also renowned for its cheese; María Rosario Murillo Rodríquez sells it and delicious peach preserves at **Soda Olymar,** across from the church. Only 1½ hours northwest of San José, Zarcero makes a good day-trip for its cool climate and crisp, fresh air—bring a jacket. Buses to Ciudad Quesada/San Carlos leave the Coca-Cola (Calle 16 bet. Av. 1 and Av. 3) in San José every hour 5 AM–7:30 PM. Catch the return bus from the red stop across from the church. On weekends and in the late afternoon, you may have to wait for a bus with vacant seats.

Heredia

Just a half-hour bus ride north from San José is Heredia, capital of the province of the same name and a bustling university town. Tucked in the hills of a rich coffee-growing region, Heredia is a city that feels like a neighborhood; people are chatty and mellower than in the capital. Heredia's main point of interest is the palm-lined **Parque Central** (bet. Av. Central and Av. 2a, Calles Central and 2) and the surrounding historical buildings. The squat **Iglesia de la Concepción,** on the east side of the parque, is hard to miss. On the northeast corner of the parque is the **Casa de la Cultura.** Once a presidential residence, it now houses early 19th-century architecture and contemporary Heredian art. Just west of the casa is the stout, circular tower of **el Fortín.** Subterranean passages used to connect the Casa to the colonial fortress; the tunnels are now closed, as is the tower, but whoever's staffing the Proveduría office will let gringos climb the condemned turret to see the city and surrounding mountains (it's apparently too dangerous for nationals). From the Parque Central, a short walk east down Avenida Central is the UNA, or the **Universidad Nacional.** The rambling, green campus has a reputation as a hotbed of communism. Current graffiti condemns the U.S. blockade against Cuba and recent attempts to privatize the university.

COMING AND GOING The most frequent bus to Heredia from San José leaves daily every 10 minutes 5 AM–10 PM from Calle 1, between Avenidas 7 and 9 (**Microbuses Rapidos Heredianos,** tel. 33–83–92). The 11-kilometer (7-mile) trip through Tibas and Santo Domingo takes about half an hour and costs about 30¢. The return bus to San José operates on the same schedule, departing from the bus terminal on Avenida 4 between Calles Central and 1, the final stop in Heredia. From Heredia, you can catch buses for the nearby towns of Barva, San José de la Montaña (to Braulio Carrillo), and Puerto Viejo de Sarapiquí (to La Selva). *See* Near Heredia, *below,* for more info.

GETTING AROUND Heredia is a compact city. Orient yourself in the Parque Central, between Avenidas Central and 2 and Calles Central and 2. Odd streets lie to the east and even to the west; odd avenues lie to the north and even to the south. If you forgot your compass, remember: Facing the church entrance, your nose is pointing east. Major landmarks are the correo, on the northwest corner of the Parque Central; the Casa de la Cultura, on the northeast corner; the Cruz Roja, on Calle Central between Avenidas 1 and 3; and the *mercado viejo* (old market), between Avenidas 6 and 8 and Calles 4 and 2.

WHERE TO SLEEP **Hotel Verano.** Okay, so it may be a whoretel, but the little pink love nests are tidy and in the center of Heredia, near the mercado viejo. At just over $6 for a double, you might not mind the grunting and cooing. The communal bathrooms are dark, with cold water only, but they smell clean; ask for an exterior room or you may grow mold overnight. *Corner of Calle 4 and Av. 6, next to mercado viejo, tel. 37–16–16. From the bus terminal, it's 250 meters west and 100 south. 12 rooms, none with bath. Luggage storage, laundry. Make reservations a day in advance on weekends.*

Hotel Ramble. This comfortable converted house may be a reason to stay in Heredia. The wood-paneled rooms verge on luxurious, and all the bathrooms have hot water. At $14 for a double with bath, Hotel Ramble is an economical luxury. *On Av. 8, tel. 38–38–29. 350 meters west from the southwest corner of mercado viejo, past the Bar Azteca. 15 rooms, some with bath. Luggage storage, laundry. Call for reservations.*

Hotel Heredia. This family establishment crawls with Central American kitsch—lots of red vinyl, turquoise paint, flowers, and signs that proclaim, NO SE AQUILA POR RATOS (i.e., This is not a nooky nook). Doubles with hot-water baths are just under $20. The neighborhood, Barrio Fatima, is safe and quiet, so it's worth being a little away from the center. *On Calle 6 bet. Av. 3 and Av. 5, tel. 37–13–24. From the correo, 200 meters west and 250 north. 10 rooms, all with bath. Luggage storage, laundry. Make reservations a few days in advance.*

FOOD Heredia is peppered with cheap sodas, and the most inexpensive typical food is in the mercado viejo. For good shrimp dishes, try the Chinese restaurant **Ho Wah** (from the northwest corner of the mercado viejo, 100 meters north and 25 meters east). Restaurant/bar **Chaparral**, next to the Casa de la Cultura, serves good meat dishes and Chinese food. Another, more expensive, meatery is **El Principe** (on Calle 5 bet. Av. Central and Av. 2a). Hang with local students at the **Pizza Hut,** near the Iglesia del Carmen (corner of Av. 6 and Calle 3). Closer to the university, students munch desserts at the yuppie hangout, **Fresas** (corner of Calle 7 and Av. 1), or plan revolutions and term papers over beers and bocas at **La Choza** (bet. Calles 5 and 7 on Av. Central).

NEAR HEREDIA

BARVA Cloud-wrapped mountains and gentle slopes green with coffee bushes peek over the red-tile roofs of Barva's central plaza. Wander around this colonial town 1½ miles north of Heredia, check out the preserved adobe buildings, and have a cup of the local bean at one of the sodas on the plaza. There's not much else to do, but the bar/restaurants here have a reputation for tasty bocas. Buses for Barva leave Heredia from in front of the Cruz Roja (125 meters north of the Casa de la Cultura) about every 15 minutes until 11:30 PM (15 minutes, 25¢).

PARQUE NACIONAL BRAULIO CARRILLO This huge national park straddles the highway to Guapiles and Limón. It begins 18 kilometers (11 miles) northeast of San José, covering 32,000 hectares (79,072 acres). Everywhere you look, green things sprout and twist and bloom. Bromeliads and orchids cling to arching trees. Moss, lichens, and fungi insinuate themselves in every cranny. And amid more than 6,000 species of plant life creep, crawl, and flutter the resident fauna, including white-faced monkeys, *tepisquintle* (a large rodent), and brilliant blue *morpho* butterflies.

Temperature and rainfall are unpredictable and fluctuate with elevation—the terrain varies from flatlands to the 2,906-meter Volcán Barva. The best time to visit is December–April (the dry season), but wear sturdy hiking shoes and carry rain gear even then.

You can enter Braulio Carrillo through three points. The closest is the **Zurquí station,** location of the park's administration and visitor center (about a mile into the park, about 500 meters before the Zurquí tunnel). A half-mile-long trail from here to a *mirador* (lookout) has a difficult entrance (recommended by the park service for the "physically fit"), but the rest is fairly easy. From Zurquí it's another 22 kilometers (14 miles) down the highway toward Limón to the **Quebrada Gonzales** (or Carrillo) station, where you'll find an information center, bathrooms, and potable water. Two nearby trails are **Los Botarramas** (about 2 hours) and **La Botella** (2,800 meters round-trip plus a 30-minute leg to the swimming spot on the Río Sanguijuela). **Volcán Barva's** information post is 3 kilometers (2 miles) northeast from **Sacramento,** a small town about 18 kilometers (11 miles) north of Heredia. There are facilities for camping and a trail that leads 5 kilometers (3 miles) to the lagoon of the extinct volcano. Local legend says the lagoon rumbles and booms before a rainstorm.

To get to the Zurquí station, Quebrada Gonzales (sector Carrillo), or the trails near the Río Sucio, take a **Coopetraga** bus (tel. 23–12–76) toward Guapiles from San José. The bus currently departs from between Avenidas 7 and 9 on Calle 12. Service runs about every 45 minutes daily 5:30 AM–7 PM (about $1). Let the driver know when you board which station you want. To get back, you'll have to flag down a bus along the highway (more difficult on weekends). To get to Volcán Barva, you need to spend the night in Heredia and catch a morning bus. Buses currently depart daily at 5 AM, 6 AM, and 11:30 AM. Currently, the bus stops near the *mercado viejo* (old market), but the stop was rumored to be changing locations, so ask around. The bus passes through **San José de la Montaña** to drop you at **Paso Llano,** from where it's a 10-kilometer (6-mile) walk to the lagoon. Check with the National Parks Service in San José (tel. 33–41–60) before you go for up-to-date info on transport options and travel conditions. Return buses to Heredia are supposed to pass through at 5 PM, though don't be surprised if the driver is three hours late because the bus broke down or because the driver decided to take a *siesta*.

PUERTO VIEJO DE SARAPIQUI By day the area is greener than the Emerald City. At night, yellow green *lamparas* (fireflies) glow like you're in some southern bayou. Scoop up a cup of the steamy air and drink a taste of Puerto Viejo, a town in the northern lowlands of Heredia. Once an important post on the Río Sarapiquí, Puerto Viejo has been rediscovered by workers from the surrounding *bananeros* (banana plantations) who come to town to party on payday (the 15th and the end of the month) and by naturalists on their way to nearby reserves.

Most package tours from San José to this region are beyond the means of budget travelers. Before coming, check with the **Toruma Youth Hostel** in San José (tel. 24–40–86). They have connections with **El Plástico,** a hostel in the **Rara Avis** rain forest preserve near **Horquetas,** and offer good trips and significant discounts to members. Day-trips to **La Selva,** a biological station run by the Organization for Tropical Studies (OTS), can also be made from Puerto Viejo without crippling your budget. The reserve is a center of intense investigation for researchers from around the world, but visitors are permitted access to some of the trails daily 6:30 AM–5 PM. The entrance fee is $17 and an additional guide fee is charged (about $8 for a half day and $16 for a full day, plus 15% more for an English-speaking guide). The reserve is spectacular and filled with wildlife. Take the warnings about poisonous snakes, vicious ants, and slippery trails seriously. Wear sturdy shoes and bring an umbrella and flashlight in case you get caught in sudden (frequent) rain or darkness. Reservations (tel. 71–68–97) must be made in advance. The best way to get to La Selva is by taxi from Puerto Viejo (about $3).

In Puerto Viejo there's not much to do but soak in your own sweat and the small-town atmosphere. Locals with motorized canoes will take you on a tour of the Río Sarapiquí for about $8. When evening falls, the *salon de baile* (dance hall) pumps out tropical juice. There are a couple of bars that women should avoid. Hang out with the people in local sodas instead, and they'll tell you how the bananero is corrupting the town's tranquility.

The best hotel in town, **Mi Lindo Sarapiquí** (tel. 76–62–81), is run by a friendly family which charges just over $15 for luxurious doubles with tepid water, clean towels, and powerful ceiling fans. **Cabinas y Restaurant Monteverde** (tel. 76–62–36) is less expensive at about $10 a double, but it's often full of local travelers. Call ahead to make reservations at either hotel, especially during the September–June high season. There are a couple of other places to stay in town; women alone shouldn't even bother checking them out.

The food scene is cheap and tasty. Have a $2 casado and drink at Restaurant Monteverde. Their food is totally nonvegetarian, but lip smackin' with *leña* (smoked) flavor. **Chavela,** on the road behind the church, fries up popular Mexican flauta-style tacos, smothered in cabbage and condiments, for just over $1. Icy *batidos* are about the same. Mi Lindo Sarapiquí is a favorite spot for late drinks and dinners (entrées around $5) and $2 breakfasts.

Getting to Puerto Viejo is half the fun. The bus corriente that runs from San José through Heredia takes about five hours and passes remarkable scenery. It departs from Avenida 11 between Calles Central and 1 in San José at 6:30 AM and noon, passing the west side of Heredia's central park about 30 minutes later. Fare is about $2.50. Sit on the left side for the best views of **Volcán Poás** and the **Cascada de la Paz** (Peace Waterfall). The "express bus" through **Río Frío,** departing from the same spot in San José, is only a little quicker and not as interesting. Buses are supposed to depart at 7 AM, 9 AM, 1 PM, 4 PM, and 5 PM, but may cancel a trip unexpectedly. Buses for San José via Heredia return at 5 AM and 3 PM; those via Río Frío, at 9 AM, noon, and 2 PM. Hitching to Guapiles or the crossroads on the highway through Braulio Carrillo, where frequent buses pass on their way to San José, is also a possibility.

Cartago

Like a huge, plump dove, Cartago's basilica nestles between gentle green mountains. To the north, Volcán Irazú spreads its fertile, ashy slopes. Cartago, a 40-minute bus ride from San José, is the transport hub for the nearby colonial town of Orosí, the wildlife reserve of Tapantí, and the extensive Lankester Gardens, and it makes an interesting day-trip in itself.

Originally the center of Costa Rican culture and its capital for 300 years, Cartago was devastated by earthquakes in 1823 and 1910. Although several funky turn-of-the-century houses still line the main streets, many historical landmarks were destroyed—including the original **cathedral** (bordered by Avs. 1 and 2a, Calles 2 and 4), which has since been transformed into a pretty garden. The hours of the garden are irregular (best bet is a sunny, crowded Sunday afternoon) and gates are definitely locked at 4 PM. At the east end of town, between Avenidas 4 and 2, the elaborate byzantine **basilica** houses the shrine of La Negrita, Costa Rica's patron saint (*see* Our Lady Of Interracial Harmony, *above*).

Our Lady of Interracial Harmony

On August 2, 1635, "La Negrita," the Virgin of Los Angeles, appeared in Cartago. She presented herself in the form of a small, dark stone doll to a peasant girl of mixed ancestry. The miraculous reappearance of the doll every time it was removed was interpreted as a divine order to abolish the racial divisions that kept people of color out of the city. Each year on August 2, hundreds of ticos walk from San José (and farther) to the shrine, which is now covered with promises, trophies, letters of thanks, and tiny metal milagros, images of everything from heads and hands to airplanes and eyeglasses.

COMING AND GOING Frequent **SACSA** (tel. 33–53–50) buses run to Cartago from Calle 13 between Avenidas Central and 2, at the foot of the Plaza de La Democracía, in San José. There is 24-hour service, but buses only run hourly in the early morning. The trip takes about 45 minutes and costs less than 40¢. The final stop in Cartago is at Parque Central, right in front of the cathedral ruins. Buses to San José depart frequently from the terminal (Av. 4 between Calles 2 and 4, 100 meters north of the cathedral ruins). Service to nearby towns departs from near the ruins as well (see Near Cartago, below).

WHERE TO SLEEP There's really no need to spend the night in Cartago; besides, the hotels that do exist aren't used for sleeping. **Pensión Familiar-El Brumoso,** near the mercado, will charge you $5 for a particleboard room with grimly stained walls. The "ooh, baby, baby" sound effects last until dawn for no extra charge. Do yourself a favor and just take an early bus from San José.

FOOD You won't starve in Cartago, but you probably won't come here just to eat either. Several basic, cheap places are in the center along Avenidas 2 and 4, along with an abundance of panaderías and *supermercados.* For real cultural confusion, check out **Bar Restaurant (y Autoservicio) 88,** about 100 meters north of the northwest corner of Parque Central. Chow down on a $2 casado of rice, beans, chop suey, bistek, chow mein, and plátano. **Puerta del Sol,** just northwest of the basilica, is a little more expensive and a favorite spot for families after church. Also recommended by locals are two reasonably priced *marisquerías* in the Centro Comercial El Dorado, across from the San José bus terminal. **Ambientes,** a restaurant across from the south side of the cathedral ruins, is a little hidden away, but also recommended for reasonably priced typical food.

NEAR CARTAGO

JARDIN LANKESTER About 6 kilometers (4 miles) east of Cartago off the road to Paraíso, the Lankester Gardens sprawl over 10 hectares (25 acres). Although the garden is most spectacular March–May, when over 80 species of orchids bloom, the greenery is pretty cool any time of year; it's definitely the sexiest day-trip from San José in a Georgia O'Keeffe sort of way. The gardens' hours are a little odd: They open hourly every day at half past the hour 8:30–4:30. Admission to the gardens is $2.50. Bring a discreet snack; no restaurants are nearby and picnicking is discouraged. To get to the gardens, take a Paraíso bus, which leaves frequently from the south side of Cartago's ruined cathedral. The driver will let you off across from the Fibrolit factory, near the gravel road leading to the gardens (about a 10-minute walk).

OROSI Orosí sits in the fertile river valley less than 16 kilometers (10 miles) southeast of Cartago. The small colonial town's main attraction is a low adobe church dating from the mid-1700s. The church is still in use, but you're welcome to enter quietly and check out the intricate *retablos* (religious paintings) and altars dating from the colonial era. The most awesome thing is the smell: ancient brick, cool adobe, traces of incense, candles, the dusty robes of saints, flowers wilting on the altar, and wood. More religious paraphernalia is displayed in the cool museum adjacent to the church. The museum is open daily 1 PM–5 PM. And bring your bathing suit: Just a few hundred meters south of the church, on the main road, is a sign directing you to local hot springs and swimming pools (balnearios).

To get to Orosí, take a bus from the parada diagonal from the southeast corner of Cartago's cathedral ruin. Buses run weekdays 6 AM–10 PM and make the last return to Cartago at 6:30 PM. The trip is about 30 minutes and costs 25¢.

PARQUE NACIONAL DE VIDA SILVESTRE TAPANTI Tapantí National Wildlife Refuge, about 11 kilometers (7 miles) southeast of Orosí, is a birdwatcher's wet dream. About 250 species of birds have been identified in the region. The trogon (in the quetzal family) is best seen in the early morning or later afternoon along the

Arboles Caídos (Fallen Trees) trail. The electric-blue morpho butterfly is best seen in June, July, and early August. The rugged terrain is also home to a variety of mammals, insects, amphibians, and reptiles. Bring your *capa* (rain gear) and weather-proof walking shoes; the reserve gets damp even in the dry season, with 3,500 millimeters (137 inches) of rain annually.

The park and its information center (at the entrance) are both open 8 AM–4 PM. About a mile from the entrance, the 45-minute **Oropéndula** trail leads to a swimming hole, and the adjacent **Arboles Caídos** trail winds through the wild (about a two-hour hike). Arboles Caídos and **La Pava** (about 2½ miles from the park entrance on the main road) are both good for birding. Near La Pava is a short, steep hike to a *mirador* (lookout) over the valley. The park offers basic services: bathrooms, picnic areas, maybe a hot lunch, but no camping facilities. Call the Servicio de Parques (33–40–70) to see if they've opened camping areas; if you want a really early start, you have to overnight at **Motel Río** in nearby Río Macho.

South of Cartago, off the Interamerican Highway, several villages snuggle in the steep highland ridges. Santa Maria, San Marcos, and San Pablo aren't usually visited by tourists because there's not much to do except wander around and chat with local farmers. You may be able to rent a room, but good Spanish is key. Five daily buses to the villages leave from Cartago ($1).

Coopetaca (tel. 73–30–87) runs taxi service to the reserve from Orosí's central plaza (*see* Orosí, *above*) for about $5 each way, or you can walk about 13 kilometers (8 miles). The taxistas will happily drop you off early (before 9 AM call to reserve a taxi) and pick you up later.

PARQUE NACIONAL VOLCAN IRAZU After you've walked around the weird moonscape of Volcán Irazú, 32 kilometers (20 miles) north of Cartago, you'll have less trouble believing the rumors of UFO visits. The barren gray craters are surrounded by sparse, shrubby vegetation and thick clouds. At the bottom of the steep principal crater (300 meters deep) lies a bilious green lake, and a number of gaseous fumaroles (volcanic vapor vents) steam away. Irazú has been pretty mellow since the last eruption on March 19, 1963, the day John F. Kennedy visited Costa Rica. Inches of ash rained on the surrounding central valley, and eruptions and avalanches caused the loss of lives, land, and livestock; at the same time, though, the sloping earth of **Tierra Blanca** was enriched for years to come. Rangers warn that the volcano is entering a more active phase, so pay attention to their advice—several curious spectators were killed in the '63 eruptions. If you scam a car and get here early or are really lucky, you may be able to see all the way to the Pacific or Caribbean coasts, Lago Nicaragua, the banana lands of Guapiles and the Río Frío, and Cachí and the Orosí Valley. The national park is open daily 8–4 and costs less than $1 to enter. You're out of luck if you want camp facilities, but there is a "snack shack" selling hot *aguadulce* (sugar cane juice) and steaming tamales.

A bus for Irazú leaves San José from in front of the Gran Hotel Costa Rica (Av. 2a, bet. Calles 1 and 3) every Saturday and Sunday at 8 AM sharp. In the summer (December–April), there may also be a bus on Wednesday. Call **Buses Metropoli** (tel. 51–97–95 or 72–06–51). Round-trip costs less than $4 and the bus arrives back in San José at about 3 PM. The same company also runs a bus from Cartago (north side of cathedral ruins), departing Saturday and Sunday at 8:30 AM.

Turrialba

Lying among sloping fields of sugar cane, coffee, and bananas on the Caribbean side of the Cordillera Central mountain range, Turrialba is a pleasant town with a farming-community feel. The climate in this region, 64 kilometers (40 miles) east of San José, is much warmer and more humid than the central valley highlands, but nights can get chilly, and there is no dry season here.

Although tourism has noticeably decreased since the completion of the highway through Guapiles and the termination of rail service, Turrialba still draws river enthusiasts for rafting and kayaking on the nearby **Río Reventazón**. Both hotels listed below will be glad to hook you up with guides or help arrange a trip. Just southeast of town on the road to Siquerres is the impressive tropical agriculture investigation center, CATIE. To the northeast lies Costa Rica's most significant archaeological site, the Guayabo National Monument (*see* Near Turrialba, *below*). There's not much to do in town but hang out. The trees of the pleasant **Parque Central** are thick with hissing, shirtless teenage boys. There are a couple of theaters in town and several bars of varying quality.

COMING AND GOING Buses to Turrialba from San José leave hourly from near the court at Calle 13 between Avenidas 6 and 8. **Transtusa** (tel. 56–00–73) buses make the 64-kilometers (40-mile) trip in about 2 hours and run 6 AM–midnight daily. You can catch the Turrialba bus in Cartago, but you'll make the sweaty trip *de pie* (standing), so try to start your trip from San José. Turrialba's San José terminal, just 100 meters west of Parque Central, also offers frequent service to **Siquerres** (connection to Puerto Limón). One hundred meters south of the San José/Siquerres terminal is another terminal running service to local towns, including **Guayabo** and **Santa Teresita.**

GETTING AROUND Whip out your compass and you'll notice that Turrialba's streets aren't quite cardinally aligned ("west" is actually closer to southwest, for example). Ask a local to point out their version of cardinal directions or you'll get confused. Take heart, the town is fairly small and people point and gesture broadly when giving directions. Major landmarks are the train station, in the southeast corner of town, and the white cement tower of the church in Parque Central. Unlike most Central American churches, this one is on the south side of the park. Río Turrialba borders the town to the north.

WHERE TO SLEEP **Hotel Interamericano.** The ceiling sags wetly in spots, but rooms are clean and fairly airy. Doubles with private (cold-water) bath are just over $11. (A single with access to tidy, secure collective baths is only $6.) The friendly family that owns and runs the hotel will let you use the kitchen. Downstairs is a bar open 7 PM–midnight, but Doña Margarita ensures that no dawdling drunks stay past closing. Her husband, proprietor Edgar Francisco Vasquez Aguilar, will hook you up for rafting and kayaking. *Behind the Bodega del Ferrocarril, near train station, tel. 56–01–42. Walk south from the San José/Siquerres terminal, cross railroad tracks, and follow road to left. 24 rooms, some with bath. Luggage storage, laundry.*

Hotel Wagelia. The ritziest hotel in town, up the street from the bus terminal, also has an annex (complete with pool) just outside town. Generic, modern doubles go for just over $30. Hot water flows freely, and the friendly management will help you connect with rafting trips and kayaking expeditions. *125 meters west of Parque Central, tel. 56–15–66. 100 meters west of the San José/Siquerres terminal. 18 rooms, all with bath. Annex, 10 rooms, all with bath. Luggage storage, laundry, air-conditioning ($4 extra). Reservations advised.*

FOOD Turrialba is sprinkled with greasy-spoon sodas, as well as standard fried-chicken joints that serve palatable casados or chicken/fries/drink combos for under $3. Carlos, a taxi driver with a mania for Chinese food, recommends the **Tico Chino** (from the San José/Siquerres terminal, 300 meters east and 150 south) and the **Nuevo Hong Kong** (southeast corner of the park). For good seafood, try **La Garza** (northwest corner of Parque Central, tel. 56–10–73). Juicy ceviche runs about $3, a steaming bowl of seafood soup just over $3, and tender grilled white fish with fries $5. **Pizza Julian** (north edge of Parque Central, tel. 56–11–56) is proclaimed by locals as the best pizza in town. Single pizzas with one ingredient (chile dulce, hongos, ham, ad nauseam) start at $2.50.

MONUMENTO NACIONAL GUAYABO On the slopes of Volcán Turrialba, wrapped in a misty rain forest, lies Costa Rica's most important archaeological site, Guayabo National Monument. It's no Tikal, but you're not in Guatemala, okay? The site does contain aqueducts, unexcavated mounds, stone roads, petroglyphs, and the oldest bridges in Costa Rica. All this was constructed between AD 800 and AD 1400, when archaeologists believe the area was an important religious and political center. Several paths lead through the archaeological site and the surrounding rain forest. If you read Spanish, try to pick up "Sendero Interpretativo Los Montículos," a pamphlet from the National Parks Service in San José (tel. 33–41–60), which gives an excellent description of the monument's main trails. There's little by way of wildlife, but keep an eye open for the dangling, sack-like nests of the *oropéndulia* birds. The entire monument (archaeological site included) is open daily 8 AM–3 PM. The entrance fee is about $1.50. The best time to visit is during the drier season between January and May.

Camping in the park is encouraged. Currently eight sites are open, all with access to flush toilets, cold-water showers, and barbecue pits. Cost is about $2.50 per person per night. Half a mile outside the park, the **Albergue La Calzada** (tel. 56–04–65) offers comfy doubles with shared hot-water bath for $15. The ski-lodge decor and architecture may be jarring, but the view of the surrounding valley is amazing. José Miguel Garcia, the personable owner and manager, has two suggestions: Make reservations if you're staying between November and June, and don't plan on staying if you don't like the nightly opera of frogs, ducks, and chickens (some city dude dissed the place to a reputable travel agency).

La Calzada's restaurant (open 6–6) serves typical food prepared with ingredients produced on the premises. Gallo pinto with farm-fresh eggs is under $2, and the $3.50 *pollo al ajo* is organic, free-range chicken (maybe the little bugger that kept you up last night). There are also a few other family-run sodas along the road to the monument.

Travelers without a car should make Guayabo at least a two-day trip or be prepared to pay a taxi about $20 round-trip and at least $10 one-way. Now, about the buses: All buses to Guayabo leave from Turrialba's local terminal, about 100 meters south of the San José/Siquerres terminal. Ignore the painted schedule; it's been wrong for years. Buses marked "Guayabo" depart Turrialba on Monday and Friday at 11 AM and Monday–Saturday at 5 PM. There is no Guayabo bus on Sunday. The ride is about an hour long, and the bus may leave you at the crossroads just over half a mile outside the park. Buses marked "Santa Teresita" depart Turrialba's local terminal daily at 10:30 AM, 1:30 PM, and 6:30 PM. This bus drops you at a crossroads from where it's a 2½-mile hike uphill to the monument. To get back to Turrialba, catch a bus from Guayabo at 6 AM or 1 PM Monday and Friday, or at the Santa Teresita crossroads daily at 1:15 or weekdays at 4:15. Any questions about the buses should be directed to Nazario Alvarado, the janitor at the Turrialba terminal; he knows everything about local buses.

The Pacific Coast

The beachy central Pacific coast is much traveled by both ticos and foreigners, probably because it's close to San José and the Meseta Central. A twisty, mountainous highway connects San José with super-popular Jacó and less-developed coastal communities farther north. The hands-down best place to go is Parque Nacional Manuel Antonio, where you can swim off the rocky, tree-lined coast.

Puntarenas

Jutting out on a sandy protrusion into the Golfo de Nicoya, Puntarenas is about 112 kilometers (70 miles) west of San José. The town used to be big with tico tourists, but years of bad publicity, like rumors of cholera-infested fish, have squelched any dream of it becoming Club Med. A campaign to upgrade tourism is under way, but most people stop just long enough to catch the ferry to the Península de Nicoya or the islands in the gulf. The stench of sewage on Puntarenas' southern coast, which gets worse as you head west, makes it impossible to even hang out on the beach. Called **Paseo de los Turistas** (they wish), the southern coast is adorned with terrace sodas, discos, and hotels. **El Primero** and **Discomar,** the two best discos in town, are here. The north shore, with its shipyards, ferry docks, and market, is polluted, the hospital has been accused of dumping waste into the ocean, and syringes still wash up onto shore. If you have extra money and want to explore the gulf, **Enrique Ruiz** (tel. 61–20–70) will take you out on a boat to search for capsized boats, water-ski, or scuba dive. Arrive during the day—you'll get a good view of the gulf from the bus and avoid getting lost or pickpocketed.

BASICS

➤ **CHANGING MONEY** • You can change money at **Banco de Costa Rica** (on north shore, tel. 61–04–44) or **Banco Nacional de Costa Rica** (tel. 61–02–33). On weekends or after hours, try the supermarket, sit-down restaurants, and nicer hotels like the **Tioga** (tel. 61–02–71) if you're in dire need of colones.

➤ **EMERGENCIES** • Red Cross (tel. 61–01–84); **Hospital Monseñor Zanabria** (tel. 63–00–33); **Radio Patrulla** (the police patrol radio, tel. 117); **fire** (tel. 118 or 61–04–29).

➤ **PHONES AND MAIL** • The cheapest and quietest place to make local phone calls is at the Cámara Puntarenense de Turismo; they also have a direct AT&T phone to the United States. The post office is 50 meters south and 50 meters west of the Casa de la Cultura. They've got a fax machine, too.

➤ **VISITOR INFORMATION** • La Cámara Puntarenense de Turismo. *At Casa de la Cultura on Av. Central and Calle 3, tel. 61–19–85 or 61–11–69. Open weekdays 9–noon, 1–6; Sat. 9–noon, 1–5.*

For a second opinion, go to the **Pacific Adventures** office in the same complex (tel. 61–03–28). Jeff, the owner, is from the United States; he can help you book hotels, tours, and boats. He might try to convince you to go on one of his one-day tours, but don't feel obligated. The office closes whenever Jeff decides to run an errand or take a coffee break.

COMING AND GOING

➤ **BY BUS** • **Empresarios Unidos de Puntarenas** (tel. 22–00–64 in San José, 61–22–58 in Puntarenas) shuttles people daily to and from San José (2 hours, $2). Buses to San José leave from the south shore (walk down to the other coast from the market). **Transportes Quiros** has five buses daily to and from Liberia, leaving one block east of the San José stop. All buses come into Puntarenas from the coastal highway to the east.

➤ **BY BOAT** • Passenger boats to **Paquera,** on the Península de Nicoya, leave from the dock behind the market (tel. 61–28–30, 1½ hours, $1.50). **Ferry Salinero** (tel. 61–10–69) takes passengers and vehicles to the peninsula, landing at **Playa Naranjo,** for $1; ferries depart from the dock at the northwest end of Puntarenas.

GETTING AROUND Puntarenas has two coastlines (north and south). The western part of the city ends in a small, pointy beach. Five avenidas cut Puntarenas east–west, and 60-odd calles run north–south. Banks, shops, hotels, and tourist information offices are all in the center of town, and the market is on the north shore. Don't look too lost or you'll become a target for pickpockets. Stay away from the red-light district that stretches from Calle 6 eastward (the area around Las Playitas); it's wretched and druggy.

To catch the ferry to Playa Naranjo, take a bus down Avenida Primera and stop in front of the Andrea pharmacy (15¢). Buses go right to the ferry and back, so the wait shouldn't be more than 20 minutes. If you can find one, take a taxi; look downtown on one of the main avenues or call 61–00–53 or 63–02–50.

WHERE TO SLEEP **Hotel Ayi-Con.** Safer and quieter than the rock-bottom hotels, the Ayi-Con has a night watchman posted at the entrance. Private and collective bathrooms are both fairly clean. A triple with bath is $17; two people in the same room pay $11.50. *50 meters south of mercado central, tel. 61–01–64. 44 rooms, some with bath. Luggage storage.*

Hotel Río. The rooms are box-like, and you have to walk down a dark, unsavory alley by the dock to get here. But if you're traveling in a group and you're planning to jump on the early morning boat to Paquera, it's really convenient. Doubles without bath are $6, with bath $10.50. *50 meters west of mercado central, tel. 61–03–31 or 61–09–38. 100 rooms, some with bath. Luggage storage.*

Gran Hotel Chorotega. You get the most for your money at this big three-story building with spotless rooms and bathrooms. Ask for a room with a baño colectivo—two rooms share a bathroom, so it's almost like having it to yourself, and it's cheaper. Doubles with baño colectivo are $13, with private bath $16.50. *Diagonally across from Banco Nacional, tel. 61–09–98. 37 rooms, some with bath. Luggage storage, laundry.*

➤ **HOSTEL • Cabinas San Isidro.** Right on the beach, this hostel has two pools and a bar. Members pay $9 each for rooms with four, six, or nine people. Make reservations and acquire a membership card at the office in San José (tel. 21–12–25 or 33–50–27). *¼ mi from hospital on south shore, tel. 63–00–31. Take bus from highway to city center, ask driver to let you off at the hospital. 42 rooms, all with bath. 2 PM check-in time.*

FOOD The best place to grab a bite is inside the market, but be careful which stand you eat from (some are more sanitary than others). Restaurants on the north shore are cheaper than the terraced places to the south. Try the sodas on the deserted streets near the bus terminal. **Supermercado Pali** (tel. 61–19–62), near Banco Nacional on Calle 1, is a gigantic food-filled warehouse.

Almost every soda in Costa Rica has a radio blasting the same smarmy pop songs over and over. When a good song comes on, waitpeople and customers stop what they're doing and sing along in full voice.

Restaurante La Canasta. For hearty eaters, this restaurant specializes in big portions of tico and Chinese food. When important soccer games are on TV, everyone, including the waitpeople, is glued to the set. *25 meters west of Nueva Moda store on Av. Primera, tel. 61–17–16. Open daily 10 AM–midnight.*

Marisquería Sea Food. This is a pretty place, serving over 50 dishes, mainly seafood. Ceviche ($3–$4.50) is about as good as raw fish can get. *On north shore across from Banco Anglo Costarricense, tel. 61–16–06. Open Mon.–Sat. 10:30–10.*

Restaurante Aloha. If you're in town on Tuesday night, you are obligated to come here to listen to live music. Aloha is the happening spot for young ticos, second only to the disco. The *arroz con pollo* (chicken with rice) for $5 is tasty. *On Paseo de los Turistas, next to Hotel Tioga, tel. 61–07–73. Open daily 9 AM–2 AM.*

CHEAP THRILLS Puntarenas celebrates two festivals annually. During **La Fería del Marisco** (fish festival), in the last three days of November, the big deal is beach sports, dances, and, of course, fish. **La Fiesta a la Virgen del Mar** (festival of the sea virgin), during the week of July 16, is a giant week-long party.

The Northwest and the Pacific North Coast

Lago de Nicaragua

Golfo de Santa Elena

La Cruz

PARQUE NACIONAL GUANACASTE

Volcán Orosí

Haciendas

Playa Blanca

B. Playa Blanca

Cuajiniquil

Upc

Volcán Vieja

CORDILLERA DE GUANACASTE

PARQUE NACIONAL RINCÓN DE LA VIEJA

PARQUE NACIONAL SANTA ROSA

Playa Nancite
Playa Naranjo

Cañas Dulces

Curubandé

Ahogados

Liberia

GUANACASTE

INTERAMERICAN

Playa Panamá

Playas del Coco
Playa Ocotal

Comunidad

Bagaces

HWY.

Tilarán

Filadelfia

RESERVA BIOLÓGICA LOMAS BARBUDAL

Cañas

CORD DE TILA

Playa Flamingo
Playa Brasilito
Playa Conchal

Flamingo

Belén

Brasilito

Huacas

PARQUE NACIONAL PALO VERDE

Tempisque

Playa Grande

Tamarindo

Playa Tamarindo

REFUGIO NACIONAL DE VIDA SILVESTRE TAMARINDO

Guaitil

Santa Cruz

PARQUE NACIONAL BARRA HONDA

Nicoya

Isla Chira

Golfo de Nicoya

REFUGIO NACIONAL DE FAUNA SILVESTRE OSTIONAL

Curime

Hójancha

Carmona

Playa Ostional

Ostional

Playa Nosara
Playa Guiones

Nosara

Jicaral

La Península de Nicoya

Paq

Sámara

Playa Sámara

Playa Carrillo

Playa Coyote

Tambor

Cóbano

Pl

PACIFIC OCEAN

Montez

Playa Me

RESERVA NATURAL ABSOLUTA CABO BLANCO

Playa Balsitas

Cabo Blanc

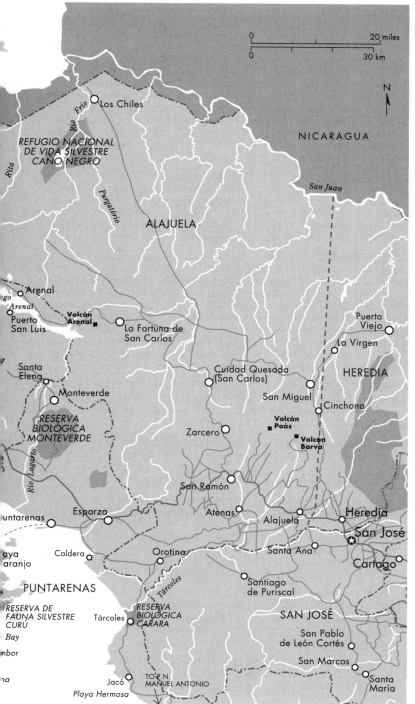

20 miles

30 km

N

Los Chiles

Río Frío

REFUGIO NACIONAL
DE VIDA SILVESTRE
CAÑO NEGRO

Río

Rita

Purgatorio

NICARAGUA

San Juan

ALAJUELA

Arenal

go Arenal

Puerto
San Luis

Volcán
Arenal

La Fortuna de
San Carlos

Puerto
Viejo

La Virgen

Santa
Elena

Monteverde

Cuidad Quesada
(San Carlos)

HEREDIA

San Miguel

Cinchona

RESERVA
BIOLÓGICA
MONTEVERDE

Zarcero

Volcán
Poás

Volcán
Barva

Río Lagarto

San Ramón

untarenas

Esparza

Atenas

Alajuela

Heredia

San José

aya
aranjo

Caldera

Orotina

Santa Ana

Cartago

Tárcoles

PUNTARENAS

Santiago
de Puriscal

RESERVA DE
FAUNA SILVESTRE
CURÚ

Bay

nbor

Tárcoles

RESERVA
BIOLÓGICA
CARARA

SAN JOSÉ

San Pablo
de León Cortés

San Marcos

Jacó

Playa Hermosa

TO P.N.
MANUEL ANTONIO

Santa
María

ha

Jacó

Jacó, about 2½ hours southwest of San José, is a year-round tourist magnet, though the type of tourist varies with the season. During the wet season, Jacó is transformed into a Southern California surfer colony; in the dry season, the beaches are crammed with Canadians age 30 and up, who tuck away their sweaters for a while and bask in the sun. The beach itself is kind of skanky, and it's getting dirtier as more people come to Jacó. When the tourists are young, the town takes on a kind of spring-break aura, with drunken revelers packing both discos. **Discoteca La Central** is more Americanized than **Papagayo,** where ticos with salsa fever go to get cured. La Central is close to the Red Cross at the southern end of town, and admission is $2. Papagayo is on the side street to the left, just before the bridge as you're walking north. It's free every day except Tuesday, when it's $1.75–$2.50.

BASICS Jacó has only one bank, **Banco Nacional de Costa Rica** (southern section of town, tel. 64–30–72), but this town is so swarmed with tourists that almost every shop and major hotel changes U.S. dollars and traveler's checks. Make international **phone calls** from la oficina de teléfonos in the center of town. Next door, across the street from the *ferretería* (hardware store) called Macho, is a **laundromat** (tel. 64–31–19). Call 64–30–90 if you have a **medical emergency.**

COMING AND GOING **Transportes Morales** (tel. 32–18–29) has two buses that go to and from San José, but they don't stop in Jacó itself. The bus will stop on the main highway, a mile east of town. Buses to Quepos (2 hours, $1.50) and Puntarenas (1½ hours, $2) do stop in Jacó. The whole town is aligned around one main street that runs parallel to the coastline, with small side streets going to the water. The city is spread out over a large area, so to get from the northernmost point to the southern tip would take a good hour walking briskly. You can bike or moped all around Jacó. **Trader Vic's** (opposite ferretería Macho, tel. 64–31–82) and **La Veranera** (next to the librería, tel. 64–31–84) both rent bicycles by the hour ($2) or day ($6.50). **Zuma** (at Ada Rent-A-Car next to ferretería Macho, tel. 64–32–07) rents mopeds.

WHERE TO SLEEP Jacó is not a cheap place to stay. If you're alone, you'll have to pay full price (except in the wet season, when just about anyone gets a discount). Groups are at an advantage because nice places turn out to be affordable when you split expenses.

Cabinas y Restaurante Alice. This is about the cheapest beachside place you can get. The *cabinas* are ho-hum but safe to sleep in. Doubles with bath are $20 in the low season. A double with kitchen is $28. *100 meters south and 50 meters west of the Red Cross, tel. 64–30–61. 22 rooms, all with bath. Luggage storage, soda.*

Aparthotel Los Ranchos. This is a hopping place with a paisley-shaped pool where travelers congregate and tan. Listen to Heidi, the manager, ramble about tico life, or tune into a surf report given by one of the gringos at the pool. All rooms have hot water and huge beds. Triples go for $30, and six-person "houses" run $50. Surfers get an automatic 20% discount (right on!) and students might be able to haggle with Heidi. *Next to Disco Papagayo, tel. 64–30–70. 12 rooms, all with bath. Luggage storage, laundry.*

➤ **HOSTEL • Hostel Marparaíso.** Members pay $9 and nonmembers $15 at this beachfront spot. The price doesn't include meals, but it's about as close to the waves as you can get and it has a pool. Make a reservation in advance or you'll be homeless once you get here. *On south end of beach past Hotel Jacófiesta, tel. 21–65–44. 70 guests. Laundry, restaurant.*

➤ **CAMPGROUND • The** biggest site is **El Hicaco,** across the street from the Red Cross, behind the owner's house. They charge $1.75–$2.50 per person, and you get showers, toilets, laundry basins, and electricity. Call 64–30–04 in the busy season to see if they're full. In the past, they've had to turn people away because the camp-ground was littered with hundreds of tents. You can't make a reservation, though.

FOOD The cheapest restaurants line the main street in the center of town. If your cabina has a kitchen, shop at **Supermercado Rayo Azul** (tel. 64–30–27), across the street from Banco Nacional. You can pay with traveler's checks, Visa, MasterCard, and U.S. dollars.

Killer Munchies. Watch the waitpeople/owners flip your pizza and shove it into a wood stove. The "killer munchies" pizza (with three kinds of meat) is mouth-watering. This is also a great place to meet gringos/surfers/stoners. *Near ferretería Macho (might move), tel. 64–34–06. BYOB. Open Wed.–Mon. 6 AM–10 PM.*

Picnic Inn. They only serve chicken (everything's $3–$5), but come here if you're a film buff—you get to choose a film to watch. The movies aren't the most recent, but it's a great way to kill time before going to the disco. *In front of Discoteca La Central, tel. 64–30–66. Open daily 6 PM–midnight, weekends 8 AM–2 AM.*

OUTDOOR ACTIVITIES Every year surfers make pilgrimages to Jacó. Know how to surf before jumping into the rough water with a board. **Trader Vic's** rents surfboards for $3.25 an hour or $8 per day. *Across from ferretería Macho, tel. 64–31–82. Open Fri.–Wed. 9–6.*

Sanchez Madrigal (tel. 64–32–03) takes people on horseback to the beach and the mountains surrounding Jacó. He charges $20 per person for what has been described as the greatest adventure in the area. The horses are well trained and they enjoy going to the mountains. Bring your camera.

NEAR JACO

PLAYA HERMOSA Due south of Jacó is Hermosa, a popular and ferocious surfing beach. If you stay at Aparthotel Los Ranchos (*see* Where To Sleep, *above*), they'll take you to Hermosa for $4. Otherwise, pay a taxi driver $8 round-trip (tel. 64–31–08), rent a moped at Zuma (tel. 64–32–07), or take a bus to Quepos and get off on the highway. The town is hardly developed, so surfers usually catch a few waves at Hermosa and then return to party in Jacó.

Parque Nacional Manuel Antonio

The smallest national park in Costa Rica, Manuel Antonio is also the most visited by foreigners and ticos. During the dry season, 3,000–4,000 people flock to the forests daily in their quest to see monkeys, sloths, and pelicans in their natural habitat. The problem is that with so many humans invading the park, the animals have retreated from the wide, trash-can–lined paths. Park officials won't confirm it, but they're con-ducting a study to find out exactly how many people the park can ecologically accom-modate; expect changes in the near future that will be welcomed by conservationists and dreaded by hotel operators. The **beaches** inside the park are absolutely beautiful. Some of them have rugged, rocky shores; others have fine white sand dotted with a few glass bottles. You can explore the park in a day, but you'll probably want to hang out on the beaches for as long as you can.

You'll hear rumors that the park will close in the near future to let the forest return to a more natural state.

The park entrance is close to where the bus driver lets you off, but you have to cross an estuary. Admission is less than $1 and park hours are 7 AM–4 PM. The rangers are strict and once 4 o'clock rolls around, they will hunt you down and kick you out. Park users can picnic, but no concession stands exist. Bring water bottles and refill them with potable water from the fountains by the first beaches.

COMING AND GOING To reach the park, you first have to travel to the non-descript town of Quepos, about 45 miles south of Jacó. **Transportes Morales** (tel. 77–02–63) runs directly to and from San José several times a day for $5.50; it also runs buses to Quepos from Puntarenas. **Transportes Blanco** (tel. 71–13–84) buses from San Isidio take 3½ hours and cost $3. Buses to Manuel Antonio leave Quepos from the intersection at the southeast corner of the bus terminal every two hours or so (½ hour, 25¢). Taxis to Manuel Antonio are $3.50 for the 6-kilometer (4-mile) drive. You can hail one at the Quepos bus terminal or across the street from the park. Call 77–05–96 for more info. At the entrance to the park is a map showing the trails. The main one takes you through the jungle to a point overlooking the Pacific. Watch out for hanging "vines"— really snakes—and for vines with nasty cactus-like spurs.

WHERE TO SLEEP You can either stay in Quepos or in the small tourist town of Manuel Antonio, which is technically outside the park. It's more convenient to stay close to the park, but it's also more expensive. You can't sleep at all in the park, even if you're camping. The north–south road that runs through the town is joined by a short road starting at the **Soda Marlin;** most hotels and restaurants congregate near the intersection.

➤ **UNDER $15** • **El Grano de Oro.** A family runs this operation and they rarely fill all the rooms. In fact, the señora is thinking of selling it. Right now, it's cheap, clean, and calm. Doubles cost $9.50. *¼ mi down road that starts at Soda Marlin, tel. 77–05–78. 10 rooms, none with bath. Luggage storage.*

Albergue Costa Linda. This hostel looks like a pig sty: The rooms (dorms and otherwise) are dusty, musty, and crusty. Whoever can identify what's growing in the shower wins a prize. Doubles in the high season are $13. *100 meters from the Soda Marlin intersection, tel. 77–03–04. 60 guests, some rooms with baths. Luggage storage.*

➤ **UNDER $20** • **Cabinas and Hotel Manuel Antonio.** You can't stay any closer to the park without a tent. The beachside cabinas are full of students and young travelers. Buy snacks and postcards and use the public phone at the kiosk. Doubles in the cabinas are $18, while doubles in the hotel across the street (part of the same complex) are a little more expensive ($20) but much nicer. *Next to park entrance, tel. 77–02–12 or 77–02–55. 16 cabinas, all with bath; 7 hotel rooms, all with bath. Luggage storage, laundry, restaurant.*

Hotel Vela Bar. This place is underpriced for what you get. The rooms try to look like the inside of a Swiss chalet, while the exterior of the complex strives for Mediterranean—a strange juxtaposition, but it works in a trippy sort of way. The cheapest single is $11, double $19. Cheap rooms fill quickly, so call ahead. *300 meters down the road that starts at Soda Marlin, tel. 77–04–13. 25 guests, all rooms with bath. Luggage storage, laundry.*

➤ **CAMPGROUNDS** • Camping isn't permitted inside the park's boundaries. You are allowed to camp anywhere else, including right at the entrance booth. **Restaurante Manuel Antonio,** in back of Hotel Manuel Antonio, is in charge of the campground to the left of the park entrance. They charge $2 per person plus 25¢ to shower. You can rent a two-person tent for $6.

FOOD You can find cheap restaurants along the main street about ½ mile from the park entrance. **Mar y Sombra** has the nicest setup: an outdoor patio overlooking Playa Espadilla (Beach No. 1). For even cheaper eats, try **Soda Vanessa** or **Restaurante Perla.** The latter has the greatest English-language menu: You can choose from "Beams (Black) Soaps, Shrimps (as yo like it), and Marketable Toast Bread." (At least they tried.) Almost all the roadside joints are open daily 7 AM–9 PM. English menus and U.S. food are abundant.

OUTDOOR ACTIVITIES

➤ **SWIMMING** • The four beaches of Manuel Antonio are often referred to by numbers. **Playa Espadilla** (No. 1) is outside the park; **Playa Espadilla Sur** (No. 2) is inside. Both beaches are swimmable, but be very careful of the rip currents, as people drown each year. The best beach for swimming is **Playa Manuel Antonio** (No. 3), where the waves are smaller, but families with children crowd the beach on weekends. **Puerto Escondido** (No. 4) is more scenic than accessible. Bathrooms and showers are next to Espadilla and Manuel Antonio. Remember not to use soap or shampoo; you'll murder the water critters.

➤ **HIKING** • The park has five trails. The one you have to take to get anywhere is very short and very easy, starting from the park entrance. If you just want to bask in the sun, walk at a leisurely pace for 10 minutes and you'll reach either Playa No. 2 or Playa No. 3. You can hike all through the park, going to **Punta Catedral** (Cathedral Point), to Playa No. 4, the **Mirador** (Lookout Point), or on **Sendero Perezoso** (Lazy "Sloth" Trail). The walk to the Mirador is a fantastic way to spot monkeys. Please don't feed them, even if they ask nicely.

➤ **WATER SPORTS** • At **Cafe Mermaid,** on the main street in town, boogie boards cost $1.50 per hour or $8 per day. Snorkeling gear is also $1.50 per hour or $6 a day. A deposit of $24 or a passport is required.

➤ **HORSEBACK RIDING** • **Mauricio** at Hotel Mariposa (on the road to Quepos, tel. 77–03–55) charges $30 for two-hour excursions in the early morning. He's got happy horses that know how to trot through sand. **Chito** charges less ($10), but you have to find him and his animal companions on the beach. He's usually here Friday–Sunday.

La Península de Nicoya

The Nicoya Peninsula has a split personality. Along the coast, it's beachy and gringo-laden; inland, it's a dry, rural region devoted to cattle raising and slow livin'. As if that weren't schizo enough, it's also divided north–south: The Guanacaste section of the peninsula (from about Playa Carrillo north) is way more developed than the southern (Puntarenas) region, which has pretty, fairly uncrowded beaches. Bus service connects the larger cities to each other and to the more popular beaches, but forget about catching a bus from beach to beach; you have to backtrack to the inland hubs of Nicoya or Santa Cruz. Hitching is common here, unlike in the rest of the country. It takes longer to get around Nicoya than most parts of the country. Don't be in a rush to get anywhere; take life one day at a time and you'll soon be as mellow as the locals.

Refugio de Fauna Silvestre Curu

Adelina Schutt, the director, welcomes students and scientists to her wildlife refuge on the southeastern tip of the peninsula. A maximum of 30 people daily can roam around on one of 17 well-marked trails. The lowland sections of the refuge are used as an experiment in sustainable agriculture; the ocean forest and highlands are untouched, open to scientific research. Three species of turtles lay eggs once a month from the end of October until early June, usually in the dead of night, when the moon is three-quarters full. Visitors pay $4 admission, and you can get a guided tour from a knowledgeable local for $10 a day. Take the difficult mile-long uphill hike through the deciduous forest to a white-sand beach.

You can't camp in the refuge. For $20, students with ID cards can sleep in one of the eight cabins or in the main house (total of 27 guests); the price includes three meals. Availability depends on whether there's a rush of students from the School for Field

Studies, an extension of the University of Massachusetts. Find out ahead of time (tel. 61–23–92). The director will arrange to pick you up from the main road from Paquera to Montezuma (1½ mi from the entrance); if she's busy, she'll leave the gate open and you can walk.

Playa Montezuma

This is about as close as you can get to a Costa Rican version of Berkeley. Long-haired hippies, ultravegetarian ecologists, drug-happy deadheads, and tan beach bums all find their way to the small but mighty gringo colony of Montezuma (also called Moctezuma), about 19 kilometers (12 miles) southwest of Curú. Free love is rampant; even the Ecological Fund store sells Profamilia condoms. And just like in the United States, drug use is ubiquitous. Town officials have launched a publicity campaign using the catchy slogan "Beauty without trash, relaxation without drugs." The town is clean ("trash" in the slogan apparently refers to the people), and it's so small that you can see almost everything from where the bus drops you off; in fact, the town has only one phone number, with extensions for about half the businesses. If the sex, drugs, and rock 'n' roll start to grate on you, head out to the beaches on either side of the town center. You could also take a quick hike to the righteous **waterfall** on the river. Just go up the little road that curves around the beach, cross the river, and follow the path marked "*Catarata* (waterfall)." The cheapest way to get to Montezuma is to take the bus at the Paquera dock for $2.50.

WHERE TO SLEEP AND EAT Food in Montezuma is overpriced. If you're into loud music, go for **Chico's Bar** or **Restaurante Moctezuma.** Health food, fro-yo, and dessert lovers will get a kick out of **El Sano Banano** (tel. 61–11–22, ext. 272), a vegetarian restaurant/movie house that shows ecological films and U.S. blockbusters (movies are shown at 7:30 PM, $2.50 minimum purchase). **La Cascada,** next to the river before the entrance to the waterfall, is okay for a bite of tico food while hiking. The cheapest places are **Soda El Parque** (on the beach), specializing in seafood, and **El Caracol** (off the road in the direction of the waterfall), which serves simple casados for $2.50.

The cheapest hotels (**Cabinas Karen, Pensión Jenny, Pensión Arenas,** and **Hotel Lucy**) charge about $5 per person for small rooms without baths. Lucy (¼ mi toward waterfall from bus stop, tel. 61–11–22, ext. 273) has a little balcony with a great view. **Hotel Moctezuma** (tel. 61–11–22, ext. 258) also has nice rooms for $5 per person, if you don't mind the noise from Chico's Bar until 11 PM or later. They also have rooms with bath and fans ($14 for doubles).

NEAR MONTEZUMA

RESERVA NATURAL ABSOLUTA CABO BLANCO Cabo Blanco, a huge stretch of land on the southern tip of the peninsula, became the first declared conservation area in the country in 1963. Then, it was completely off-limits; right now, only one trail is open to the public. But that one trail **(Sendero Sueco)** is a doozy, starring howler and white-faced monkeys, coatimundi, anteaters, agouti, and snakes. The trail starts at the administration building and goes up, down, and around through an evergreen forest for 3 miles till you hit **Playa Balsitas** and **Playa Cabo Blanco.** You could do some nude bathing at Balsitas if it's uncrowded; Cabo Blanco, a little farther down, is usually too populated for such shenanigans. If you have spare time, walk back on the rocks along the shore. It takes about three hours and there's no marked trail—just follow the coastline.

As an "absolute" nature reserve, Cabo Blanco must be preserved in its pristine state, and you have to follow very strict guidelines while you're there. Rangers check your bags before you go in for no-no's like pocketknives, and again when you leave to make sure you don't take any shells or rocks. Even so, the director of the reserve wants to close it to the general public to protect the wildlife. At press time, Cabo Blanco was open to 40 non-researchers a day from 8 to 4 (admission is $1), but the park service might close it altogether or at least sharply reduce the open hours. Call the park service in San José (tel. 33–41–60) and they'll find out for you.

You can't camp, but you can stay nearby with **Doña Lila.** She charges $10 per person for room and board at her house (¼ mi before park entrance, last house on left, with a huge thatched roof). You can arrange rides from Montezuma (11 kilometers [7 miles] away) to Cabo Blanco with **Chico** or **Armando,** two dudes who hang out by the bus stops, for $3 each way. They also act as guides. If you're female and alone, you might beware of Armando; I got bad vibes from him.

Nicoya

Nicoya prides itself on being the "heart and spirit" of the rural Guanacaste province. Nicoyans are friendly (even for ticos) and the atmosphere is homey and very small-town. This is probably due in part to its isolation in the interior of the peninsula, far from any crowds. If you happen to stumble into town a few days before July 18th, you'll have a knee-stomping, good ole time at the rodeo and festival. Also check out the old colonial church next to the plaza; it was built three centuries ago. Nicoya is a commercial and political center for the northern peninsula and the transport hub for beaches like Sámara, Nosara, and Ostional.

BASICS Banco de Costa Rica (in front of Parque Central, tel. 68–50–10); **Banco Anglo Costarricense** (north side of colonial church at park, tel. 68–53–80); **Banco Nacional de Costa Rica** (on main road heading out of town toward San José, tel. 68–53–66). Do the postal thing at **Cortel,** near the park. Less than 100 meters before the post office is a **public health clinic** (tel. 68–50–21). **Red Cross** (tel. 68–54–58) will transport you to the nearby hospital in case of a major crisis. The tourist information center is next to the hospital at **Bar El Molino** (tel. 68–50–01). Besides handing out useful info, Paco, the owner and self-described "Bohemian artist," plays folk songs on his guitar.

COMING AND GOING Empresa Alfaro (tel. 68–50–32; 22–27–50 in San José) has a quasi-monopoly on Nicoya. The trip to San José takes five hours and costs $5. Buses go to Liberia ($1.25) and to Playa Naranjo, where you can catch the ferry to Puntarenas. At Playa Naranjo, buses to Nicoya leave after the arrival of the ferry and pass through Jicaral (3½ hours, $1.75). Alfaro buses also run frequently to nearby Sámara, Nosara, and Santa Cruz, leaving from the hard-to-find **Transportes La Pampa** terminal (tel. 68–01–11) in front of Hotel Las Tinajas. All other buses leave from the central terminal at the end of the main street. If you can't find the Pampa depot, all the buses that start there also stop at the main terminal before they leave Nicoya (but they may be full by that time). Taxis to Sámara are $20. Taxis to **Parque Nacional Barra Honda** are only $8, and are probably the easiest way to go to the park (*see* Near Nicoya, *below*).

WHERE TO SLEEP

➤ **UNDER $10** • **Hotel Ali.** The cheapest place in town isn't the worst. That prize goes to Pensión Familiar, which is so familiar that everyone knows it's a love dive. Ali isn't quite four-star itself: Rooms are tiny and the bathrooms smell rank. Doubles with bath and small fans cost $6. *Across the street from post office by Parque Central, tel. 68–51–48. 10 rooms, all with bath. Luggage storage.*

Hotel Chorotega. This hotel on a quiet residential street is the best deal for your money. You get a normal double room with bath, all for $8. They'll even throw in a view of the clothesline on the patio for free. The woman who runs the place is motherly and energetic. *200 meters south of Banco de Costa Rica, tel. 68–52–45. 24 rooms, all with bath. Luggage storage.*

Pensión Venecia. The open-air atmosphere, with tables set up for schmoozing, playing cards, or watching TV, makes the place kinda cozy. Rooms are clean and bearable, and they go fast on Wednesday and Thursday nights when businesspeople are in town. Doubles with bath and fan are $8. *In front of the old colonial church next to Parque Central, tel. 68–53–25. 25 rooms, some with bath. Luggage storage.*

➤ **UNDER $15** • **Hotel Las Tinajas.** Present your student ID and you'll be charged $11.50 for a nice, sanitary double room ($13 for nonstudents). All rooms have baths and fans, and the restaurant is open until 10 PM every night. They'll take Visa, traveler's checks, and U.S. dollars in case you've run out of colones. Tuesday–Thursday are the busy nights. *300 meters north, 25 meters west of the main bus terminal, tel. 68–50–81 or 68–57–77. 24 rooms, all with bath. Luggage storage.*

FOOD The town's lack of glamour means that you don't have to pay through the nose to get good, cheap food. Nicoya has a big Chinese population, and almost every other restaurant on or near the main street specializes in *comida china.* If you're just in town to change buses, check out the sodas and fruit stands in the terminal.

Cafe Daniela. This restaurant has the best tico food, pizza, and pastries in town. But wait, there's more: It's cheap and the service is great. They should be charging more for this (but let's just keep that to ourselves). Gallo pinto is $1, casados are $2, and a slice of pizza is 50¢. *On main street, 75 meters south of the supermarket, tel. 68–61–48. Open Mon.–Thurs. 8 AM–9 PM, Fri.–Sat. 8 AM–10 PM, Sun. 5 PM–10 PM. Closed May 1 and Thurs.–Fri. of Semana Santa.*

Restaurante Teyet. Anyone will tell you this is the best Chinese food in town. The menu has 75 dishes, including excellent shrimp wontons ($3) and plenty o' stuff for vegetarians. *50 meters south of Parque Central in front of Hotel Jenny, no tel. Open weekdays 11–11, weekends 11 AM–2 AM.*

NEAR NICOYA

PLAYA SAMARA When you get into Sámara you'll see a sign proclaiming it the "best beach in America." Okay, maybe that's overstating it a little, but Sámara is a nice, safe beach about 29 kilometers (18 miles) south of Nicoya. The coral reef a mile from shore is snorkeler utopia. Equipment rental is expensive ($15 per hour at **Sea Life Sámara,** 1 mi south of guardia rural on the beach). The cheaper places to stay are in the not-so-hot Cangrejal area at the north end of town. **Hospedaje Yury** (tel. 68–00–22) charges $3 per person for a shabby room without a bath. **Hospedaje Katia** (no tel.) and **Hospedaje Doña Alice** (no tel., closed May–November) charge about $5 a head. At the south end, the only affordable hotels are **Pensión Magaly** ($6 per person with bath, no tel.) and **Hotel Sámara** (tel. 68–07–24), where you can stay in one of 84 rooms for $8 per person. Campers can set up their tents at Pensión Magaly ($1.25, closed May–November) or near the beach at **Camping Cocos** for $3 per person. Buses to Sámara leave Nicoya at 3 PM weekdays and 8 AM and 3 PM weekends during the wet season, and 8 AM and 3 PM daily during the dry season (2 hours, $1.50). Heading back to Nicoya, they leave at 6 AM weekdays and 6 AM and 2 PM weekends during the wet season, and 6 AM and 2 PM daily during the dry season.

PLAYA CARRILLO A semisecluded miniversion of Sámara, Carrillo is 90 minutes by foot or 10 minutes by bus from her big sister. This beach is a great place to camp: You'll have fewer people to share the kinder, gentler beach with. Beware of the water, which gets deep closer to shore than it does at Sámara. If you're tentless, you can bunk it at **Cabinas El Mirador.** The cabinas don't have their own phone, but you can reach them by calling a nearby pay phone (tel. 68–57–87). Take the bus that continues from Sámara and stop at the little *pulpería* on the hill to get the key from the owner. All eight rooms are triples ($16).

PLAYA OSTIONAL Ostional's claim to fame is the annual nesting of olive ridley turtles. On almost any given night from June to November you can see at least one turtle lay an egg. The *arribada* (arrival by sea), when 200 or more turtles waddle out of the ocean on the same night, tends to happen on a three-quarter moon; 2 AM is optimum turtle-sighting time. The law allows people to collect eggs up to 36 hours after the arribada; you'll probably see ticos scooping them up to sell to restaurants as bocas. Stay in **Melvin's** rooms at the store for $3.50 (public tel. 68–04–67), and ask him or one of the learned students at the School for Field Studies laboratory to come with you to the beach. To get to Ostional, take the Nicoya–Nosara bus that leaves Nicoya daily at 1 PM (also check if there's one at 8 AM). From Nosara, take a taxi to Ostional (around $6). The only bus out of Ostional goes to Santa Cruz. It's supposed to depart daily at 4:30 AM, but in reality it shows up on the days the driver feels like coming.

PARQUE NACIONAL BARRA HONDA With 42 discovered **caves** and many more that have yet to be studied, Barra Honda National Park is the place to be if you're into spelunking. The general public is allowed into two caves: **La Cuevita,** with a 25-foot drop, and the 60-foot **La Terciopelo.** No one's permitted to explore the caves without a guide; local guides from three neighboring communities charge around $10 for La Cuevita and at least $24 for La Terciopelo (for 1–5 people), plus $8 per person for equipment rental. The caves were formed 70 million years ago and have gorgeous stalactites and stalagmites. The openings to the caves are narrow, so it might be difficult for big people to enter them. The trails to the waterfall and the mirador are also impressive. The park is open daily 8–4, admission is $1, and the best way to get here is by taxi ($8 each way) from Nicoya. You can also take the noon bus from Nicoya to Santa Ana and walk the last 6½ kilometers (4 miles). Right now, no hotels exist near the park, but you can camp for $2 at the complex before the entrance or try near the ranger station (but officially they don't want anyone to camp there). The town of Barrio Cubillo is constructing four cabins for seven people each, and they already have a campground with space for 15 tents and a restaurant that's open daily 8–4. Call 68–55–80 for more info.

Playa Tamarindo

The most touristed beach in Guanacaste is Tamarindo, about 29 kilometers (18 miles) west of Santa Cruz. Young surfers, backpackers, camera-toting North Americans, and tico yuppies all swarm to the shore. The beach itself isn't very beautiful or very clean; the main reason to come here is to people-watch or sunbathe. Prices are a travesty, so stay away from hotels and try to find a room in someone's house for about $5. Try **Estina's** house (across the street from the supermarket) or Isabel's barely acceptable rooms at **El Mecate,** her soda/house on the beach by the fish stand. The easier-to-find **Hotel Doly** charges $16 the first night for a double with bath and $12 every night thereafter. Doly will let you camp for free and watch your stuff during the day if you pay 25¢ for a shower. Restaurants in the center are expensive except for **Nachos,** a surfer snack shack. On the outskirts of town is **Rancho Mexicano,** an excellent and cheap Mexican place. **Johan's Bakery** has tasty, flaky pastries. Next to the supermarket is a super-duper, we've-got-everything rental shop (still nameless at press time; they're planning on calling it Tamarindo Rental Shop); all water-sports equipment is under $10, but a deposit of $8–$16 is required. **Papagayo Excursions** (sign up at the boutique in Hotel Tamarindo Diría, tel. 68–06–52), the aforementioned rental shop, and a nameless house in between Cabinas Zullymar and Fiesta del Mar restaurant all provide tours and rent horses. For the happening night scene (aside from turtles), cruise on over to the casino at Hotel Tamarindo Diría or the disco near Fiesta del Mar. **Empresa Alfaro** (tel. 22–27–50 in San José, 68–04–01 in Tamarindo) and **Tralapa** (tel. 21–72–02 in San José, 68–01–11 in Tamarindo) go to and from the capital (6 hours, $5). Alfaro, Tralapa, and a local bus also run to Tamarindo from Santa Cruz (1½ hours, $1).

Guanacaste and the Lowlands

Guanacaste is without question the weirdest region in Costa Rica. Imagine a typical shit-kicking, tobacco-spitting, Marlboro-smoking kinda place full of cattle and cowboys, then shift it to the land of tropical rain forests—you're beginning to get the picture. The driest province in the country, Guanacaste is famous for its cattle; much of the land is used for grazing, even the highland areas. Guanacaste used to be an autonomous region whose citizens opted to annex themselves on July 25, 1824. Costa Rica barely edged out Nicaragua, which lies just north of the province, as the country of choice, and *guanacastecos* are usually more patriotic to their region than to their country. Guanacaste is also the center of Costa Rican folklore, and you can sometimes hear typical songs in the smaller towns.

Much of the beef raised in Guanacaste is used for fast-food hamburgers.

Most of Guanacaste used to be dry forest. It's sad to ride a bus through the rural areas knowing that one-third of all Costa Rican forest has been cut down, and much of the deforestation occurred here. The most-visited areas in the region are the beach towns and resorts of the Nicoya Peninsula (*see* La Peninsula de Nicoya, *above*) and the cloud forest of mountainous Monteverde, both of which look more typically Costa Rican than the rest of Guanacaste. Other than that, it's flat, dry, barren, and hot.

Liberia

The capital of Guanacaste and the region's largest city, Liberia has glorified the role played by the *sabanero* (cowboy)—the town even has a museum dedicated to the sabanero at the visitor's info center and a monument to him on Avenida Central. With the opening of a new international airport in 1992, this town hopes to become an important tourist destination. Most travelers pass through Liberia on their way to the famous beaches of Guanacaste or Rincón de la Vieja national park, and it's entirely plausible that the city will someday be a major transport hub. If you're in the country July 17–25, don't miss the International Cattle Festival. It's a huge party/rodeo, with a gigantic free disco and people riding bucking broncos. Liberia also celebrates *fiestas cívicas* in February, around the time of the full moon.

BASICS

➤ **MONEY** • **Banco Nacional de Costa Rica** (tel. 66–09–96) and **Banco Anglo Costarricense** (tel. 66–03–55) are on Avenida Central, west of the central park; **Banco de Costa Rica** (tel. 66–01–48) is less than 100 meters north of the park. If you're in dire need of moolah, seek out **Mr. Beto Acón** at Restaurante Chung San.

➤ **EMERGENCIES** • The **hospital** (tel. 66–00–11) is on the northeast edge of town; for an ambulance, call **Red Cross** (tel. 66–09–94).

➤ **PHONES AND MAIL** • The **post office** is 200 meters north of Banco Anglo Costarricense. It's open weekdays 7:30 AM–8 PM. The **visitor's info center** plans to install a phone from which you can call anywhere in the world 24 hours a day. It should be hooked up by the time you read this.

➤ **VISITOR INFORMATION** • Liberia has an **info center/sabanero museum** where you can get a free map and friendly service. No matter where you want to go, a stop at the center will do you no harm—you can double-check bus and flight schedules and find out about hotels throughout Guanacaste. *300 meters south and 100 meters east of the municipalidad, tel. 66–16–06. Follow the white signs along Av. Central. Open Tues.–Sat. 9–noon, 1–6; Sun. 9–1. Museum admission free.*

COMING AND GOING El **Pulmitan de Liberia** (tel. 66–04–58 in Liberia, 22–16–50 in San José) has eight buses a day from San José to Liberia, starting at 7 AM and ending at 8 PM (4 hours, $3). Eight buses go in the other direction from 4:30 AM–8 PM. The San José bus terminal is 200 meters south of the general bus station (in the northwest corner of Liberia, 200 meters north of the Interamerican Highway). **Empresa Arata** (tel. 66–01–38) has five buses to Puntarenas from Liberia. Beach-bound buses to Playas del Coco (six daily) and Playas Hermosa and Panamá (two daily) leave from the general bus terminal. Buses run eight times a day to the Nicaraguan border; southbound buses to Nicoya leave every hour. Once the airport opens, SANSA and other national and international airlines will serve the area regularly.

WHERE TO SLEEP For some reason, Liberia only has five inexpensive hotels. Try hard to go to Hotel Guanacaste; Hotel Liberia is a pale second-best and the rest are abominable. **Hotel Rivas** (tel. 66–00–37), in front of the park, is grimy and rancid. **Pensión Golfito** (tel. 66–09–63), 100 meters north of the church, has dismal rooms. Both hotels charge about $3 per person and have a midnight curfew. The lady at **Pensión Margarita** (300 meters east of the central park, tel. 66–04–68) may try to rip you off by charging you up to $5 for a reprehensible room worth maybe $2.

Hotel Liberia. This average-priced hotel is fair for what you pay—$4 per person without a bath and about $5 with bath. For that, you get an average-size room of about average cleanliness. The staff is average and the place is average-looking. *75 meters south of the park on the same street as the municipalidad, tel. 66–01–61. 27 rooms, some with bath. 11:30 PM curfew, luggage storage.*

Hotel Guanacaste. Luis, the new English-speaking owner, has made major changes to this hotel (which used to be the Hotel Oriental), and he has more projects in the hopper. By January 1993, Hotel Guanacaste will be a full member of the IYHF chain. Luis plans to have a camping area, where he'll charge $3 per tent. A double with bath is $12, but a single without bath is only $4 in the low season. The hotel fills up fast (though they'll try their hardest to accommodate you—I slept on a spare mattress in a tiny hidden room). Avoid the restaurant; the food is bland. *100 meters south of San José bus stop, 300 meters south of the general bus terminal, tel. 66–00–85. 30 rooms, all with bath. Luggage storage.*

FOOD Sodas and food stands dot the streets surrounding the central park, the municipal market (100 meters north, 50 meters south of the park), and the general bus terminal. Chinese restaurants are so-so but inexpensive. **Restaurante Chung San,** 100 meters east of the church (open daily 11–11), and **Restaurante Cuatro Mares** are the best. **Supermercado Palí** (across the street from the market off Calle Central, tel. 66–21–09) is a good place to save money on food.

Restaurante Do. Pronounced "doe" (as in "a deer, a female deer"), this restaurant specializes in cheap, tolerable tico food. For the most part you'll rub elbows with the working class. Sandwiches cost about $1.50. *100 meters north of the church, across the street from Pensión Golfito, no tel. Open daily 24 hours.*

Parque Nacional Santa Rosa

About 48 kilometers (30 miles) from the Nicaraguan border is the much-visited Santa Rosa National Park. On what used to be a large cattle estate founded in the 18th century, Santa Rosa is best known for the decisive battle fought here on March 20, 1856. Patriotic Costa Ricans took arms against U.S. filibusterers under the leadership of the despicable William Walker, who wanted to conquer Costa Rica for slavery. Each year, thousands of Costa Ricans make the pilgrimage to *la casona* (the battle house) and the monument to soldiers killed in 1856 and in 1955 during a battle against Nicaraguan invaders.

The park is divided into two sections: the most popular one, **Santa Rosa,** and the northern section, called the **Murciélago** (bat) sector. The Santa Rosa ranger station is less than a mile from the Interamerican Highway. The park admission fee is $1; it's open daily 7:30–4:30. In the Santa Rosa sector, the major beach is **Playa Naranjo,** where leatherback turtles come up on the beach under the quarter moon December–February. **Playa El Hachal** (16 kilometers [10 miles] from the station) and **Playa Blanca** (8 kilometers [5 miles] from the station) are the beaches in the Murciélago sector.

COMING AND GOING To get to Santa Rosa from Liberia, board any bus to La Cruz or *la frontera* (the border) between 5:30 AM and 8 PM (45 minutes, 65¢). The driver will drop you off on the highway next to some flagpoles. A paved road goes to the ranger station (½ mi) and continues for 6½ kilometers (4 miles) until it reaches la casona on one side and the administration center on the other. If you don't want to walk, just wait until the next available car stops to pay the entrance fee at the booth and jump right in (after asking the driver, of course). To get to Murciélago, you have to take a bus from Liberia to the town of **Cuajiniquil,** 10 kilometers (6 miles) north and 10 kilometers (6 miles) west of the main park entrance. From here, walk 8 kilometers (5 miles) to the entrance to the Murciélago station.

WHERE TO SLEEP AND EAT The only way to sleep in the park is to camp, but campgrounds are good and the price is right at $2.50 per person a night. The Santa Rosa sector has three official campsites with potable water. There's a makeshift fourth site at **Playa Nancite,** but you need a permit because park authorities limit the number of people (30) that go to see olive ridley turtles laying their eggs (June–November). To get a permit, tell them you're a student (biology student if they're being strict). The beach has two campsites; one is next to the laguna and the other is next to the estuary (neither has potable water). In the Murciélago sector, camping is permitted at the ranger station. Neither of the Murciélago beaches has a campsite, but you can camp wherever you want if you bring food and supplies.

If you're camping near the administration center in Santa Rosa, you can arrange to eat meals. Notify the staff at *el comedor* (the dining hall) three hours before each meal. Breakfast is $2.50, and lunch and dinner are $3.50 each. You can buy drinks and sandwiches between meals, but sometimes they're out of food.

Parque Nacional Rincon de la Vieja

Rincón de la Vieja is an active **volcano,** which last erupted in 1983–84. Scientists classify it as active in the sense that it produces sulfuric fumaroles. You can see (but don't touch or you'll burn the skin off your hands) strange volcano-related wonders such as boiling creeks, stinking streams and lagoons, bubbling mud pools, and vaporing steam jets. The park is getting more popular, but it still doesn't have much in the way of personnel or facilities. Try to spend a night or two at one of the pricey but awesome youth hostels (*see* Where to Sleep and Eat, *below*). If you can't afford it, at least get a guide from the hostels to show you the splendors of the volcano, like the hidden waterfalls.

The park is hard to get to if you don't have private transportation. It has two ranger stations: **Santa Maria** (where you pay the $1 entrance fee) and **Las Pailas,** connected by a 6½-kilometer (4-mile) trail. You can camp at Santa Maria or sleep on the floor in the rustic lodge for $1. Both ranger stations sell maps for $1 and a pamphlet for 50¢.

WHERE TO SLEEP AND EAT The Buena Vista Lodge and Adventure Center. You'll be greeted by Pancho the white-faced monkey and the friendliest staff anywhere, then shuffle off on horseback to the natural spa. The food is righteous; in fact, the only thing wrong with this hostel at the foot of the volcano is that it's way expensive. Round-trip transportation from Cañas Dulces is $15 per carload, camping is $15 per tent, and rooms are $20 a person (less for larger groups). Students get a 10% discount. Tours on foot or horseback range from $10 to $38 each, and meals cost $6–$8. The hostel will be IYHF-affiliated by 1994, and it will probably get a little cheaper for members, but don't expect instant affordability. *13 km (8 mi) east of Cañas Dulces, tel. 69–51–47. 15 dorm-style rooms (40 people), some with bath.*

Rincón de la Vieja Mountain Lodge. This IYHF hostel is a converted ranch house. It offers the same services (including meals) as the other albergue, and it's closer to the main parts of the park. The cheapest rooms cost $12 per person for IYHF members and $16 for nonmembers. Tours cost $25 each for members and meals are $5. A ride from Liberia to the lodge is $30 round-trip for members. *6½ km (4 mi) east of Curubandé, tel. 66–04–73 or 21–87–64. 9 rooms, some with bath.*

Refugio Nacional de Vida Silvestre Caño Negro

During the wet season the Río Frío floods the *llanura* (plains) south of Los Chiles, turning the remote, swampy Caño Negro Wildlife Refuge into a large lake. The region is home to several species of waterfowl as well as pumas and jaguars; the local inhabitants are an interesting mix of Maleco Indians and Nicaraguan and Costa Rican campesinos who fish, hunt turtles, and raise cattle.

> *"We were in Los Chiles for an annual plague of the cocorón—a thick, hard bug that loves to land in your hair."—D.M.*

The reserve is currently the subject of debate between two groups of conservationists. The *parquistas* want the area turned into a national park, forcing the current inhabitants from the area. Another group wants to maintain the reserve status, incorporating the residents in the preservation project by helping them create new methods of subsistence that don't damage the ecosystem. Several years ago, locals diverted part of the Río Frío to facilitate the transport of goods to market, which introduced a species of tall grass that currently threatens to fill the wetland and decrease the habitat for many migratory birds.

About 26 kilometers (16 miles) northeast of the refuge is **Los Chiles,** a small town along the Río Frío, almost at the Nicaraguan border. Historically linked to Nicaragua by the river's trade route, Los Chiles was pivotal as a launching point for the first *Sandinista* advance; it was used to take San Carlos in 1977. Later, Los Chiles became strategically significant in the contra war. Today, the area is tranquil and developing, drawing travelers for tours of Caño Negro. A handful of basic pensions clutter the town, but **Hotel Carolina** (about 250 meters east of the bus station) has fans and clean bathrooms; doubles run about $8. Around the grassy central square, several all-purpose sodas serve up rum, tasty bocas, and standard casados.

Most travelers get to the refuge through **Upala,** an isolated village west of the refuge and about 10 kilometers (6 miles) south of the Nicaraguan border, where there are a couple of cheap pensions and basic restaurants. **Transportes Cañas** buses from San José to Upala depart near the Coca-Cola (on Calle 16 between Avenidas 1 and 3) Sunday–Friday at 6 AM and Saturday at 6:30 AM. Buses should be running daily to Caño Negro, but you should ask the driver of the more reliable San José–Upala bus. Check with the National Parks Service in San José (tel. 33–41–60) for information about the current status of services in the refuge.

During the wet season, you'll have to go to the refuge by boat along the Río Frío from Los Chiles. Boats for Caño Negro leave at about 9 AM from the dock at the south end of town, but most are hired by expensive, prearranged tours from San José or Tilarán. You can hire your own boat for about $70, or you may be able to get a ride on local transportation; stop by **Restaurante El Parque** (in front of the park) to ask. A *bote colectivo* currently leaves on Monday afternoon and charges about $3 for the one-way trip to Caño Negro. Direct buses to Los Chiles leave the Coca-Cola in San José daily at

5:30 AM and 3:30 PM; they depart Los Chiles at the same times. From the Coca-Cola, you can also hop on a **Ciudad Quesada** *(San Carlos)* bus, then transfer to the Los Chiles bus.

Lago/Volcan Arenal

Go to Volcán Arenal at night: If you're lucky, you'll see truly spectacular, bright orange lava as it flows down the bare mountainside. One of the most active in the Western hemisphere, this volcano about 128 kilometers (80 miles) northwest of San José explodes every 5–200 minutes. The last major eruption, on July 29, 1968, destroyed two villages at the base of the volcano and killed 80 people. Volcanologists predict that Arenal will have another big-time explosion in the next four years. During the day, smoke and gas clouds spew into the air every time the volcano erupts. Near the base of the volcano is **Lago de Arenal**, an artificial lake 32 kilometers (20 miles) long and a prime place to windsurf.

COMING AND GOING The most popular way to get to Arenal by bus is via Ciudad Quesada (San Carlos) to La Fortuna. **Garaje Barquero** (tel. 32–56–60) has direct buses that leave San José at 6:15 AM, 8:40, and 11:30 and return from La Fortuna at 2:45 PM. You can take a bus daily from San José to Ciudad Quesada every hour on the hour with **Auto Transportes Ciudad Quesada** (tel. 55–43–18) and then catch the bus at 1 PM, 3, or 6 from Ciudad Quesada to La Fortuna. Your other option is to go around the lake to the dam through Tilarán. **Auto Transportes Tilarán** (tel. 22–38–54 in San José, 46–03–26 in Tilarán) operates buses daily at 7:30 AM, 12:45 PM, 3:45, and 6:30 from San José to Tilarán (4 hours, $3); they return to San José at 7 AM, 7:45, 2 PM, and 5. Buses (tel. 46–03–26) leave Tilarán for La Fortuna at 7 AM and 12:30 PM (3 hours, $2). They go in the other direction at approximately 7:30 AM and 4:30 PM.

To get to Arenal from Fortuna (a ride of 40 km or 25 mi), hire a taxi or take a tour. **Gabino,** the thrill-seeking guide at the Fortuna tourist info center (in front of the parque, tel. 47–90–04), and Burío Inn are the only licensed tour operators in town. Both charge $8–$12 per person for transportation, 1½ hours at the volcano, and a dip in the thermal baths. Tours operate before and after dark. Gabino guarantees that you'll see an eruption or he'll give you your money back; he also runs tours to the nonactive crater for fearless volcano climbers (approximately $50 for the whole day). Don't even think of doing this without an experienced guide: You don't know when and how the volcano will blow, and stupid tourists have been killed or hurt in the past.

WHERE TO SLEEP AND EAT La Fortuna, also known as La Fortuna de San Carlos or just plain Fortuna, is the closest town of any importance to the volcano—about 40 kilometers (25 miles) east. The easiest thing to do is spend the night in La Fortuna. **Hotel La Central** (on main street next to information center, tel. 47–90–04) is the coziest place. They charge $4 per person for rooms with communal baths, and reservations are necessary on weekends. The **Burío Inn** (in the center, across from the gas station) should be full-on IYHF by press time. Members should expect to pay $4 a night or $7 with breakfast. Call 47–90–76 to make reservations and double-check the setup. Get cheap, wholesome food at **El Jardín,** also in front of the gas station. It's open daily 6 AM–11 PM.

You could camp at the base of the volcano, but you won't find camping services and it's tricky to get to the volcano at night. Don't set up your tent too far up the mountain or near the large, hot rock piles or you'll get flambéed; the big, open area at the base of Arenal should be safe. If the volcano happens to be extremely active, you'll be up all night gazing at the natural fireworks.

NEAR ARENAL

CATARATA DE FORTUNA A pleasant day hike from Fortuna takes you to this 50-meter-high waterfall. The 6-kilometer (3½-mile) walk begins off the main road toward the volcano. You'll see a yellow sign marking the entrance. After walking a mile and passing two bridges, turn right and continue hiking straight until you reach the river turnoff. Swimming under the waterfall is fairly safe, but watch out for the current in the first part of the river.

TILARAN The main reason to visit Tilarán is to plan an outing to the lake. **The Spot** (in the center, 1 block south of the church) and **Aventuras Tilarán** (100 meters east, 200 meters north of the church, tel. 69–50–08) offer tourist information, tours, and equipment rental. If you're a serious windsurfer, contact **Tilawa Viento Surf & High Wind Center** (tel. 69–50–50 or 69–56–66) for up-to-date lake conditions and expert recommendations. The cheapest hotels in town are **Hotel Central** (tel. 69–53–63), for $4 per person without bath, and **Hotel Grecia** (tel. 69–50–43), for $4 per person with bath. If you're traveling in a couple, for the same price you can get a really comfortable double with bath ($8) at **Cabinas Mary** (tel. 69–54–74). IYHF members can opt for a brand-new bed in a converted house with kitchen and common area at **Albergue Tilarán** (tel. 69–50–08). Members pay $8, and nonmembers $10–$12. If you don't eat in the hostel, opt for one of the many cheap restaurants surrounding the park. Buses from San José, La Fortuna, Cañas, and possibly Monteverde can drop you off in Tilarán.

Monteverde

Monteverde is Costa Rica's top tourist spot, and it's so popular with gringos that hotels are disgustingly overpriced, trails are disgustingly overtraveled, and almost everyone speaks English—but seeing it is still worth all the hassle. The ride to the town, about 160 kilometers (100 miles) northwest of San José, takes you from the Interamerican Highway up to a twisty, narrow highway with breathtaking views, for those with enough confidence in the bus driver to take their eyes off the road, of Puntarenas and the Gulf of Nicoya. Once you arrive, you can't help but be wowed by the stupendous landscape. It's almost a given that you'll see hummingbirds at the reserve (though you might object to the habitat-changing feeders that have been introduced here).

Monteverde is not your typical Costa Rican town. It was founded in 1951 by 11 Quaker families from Alabama, who escaped the U.S. draft and settled in armyless Costa Rica. They chose Monteverde because its remoteness would enable them to live and practice their religious beliefs in peace. The Quakers left much of the area's forest as it was. In 1972, George Powell, a U.S. conservationist, combatted local loggers to create what is now the cloud forest reserve. The Quaker community has shrunk due to emigration and intermarriage, but the Quaker influence can still be felt in religion, business, and culture. They're not how they appear on the oatmeal box, but they're definitely not your typical tico—they look like farmers from Iowa.

BASICS Go to **Santa Elena,** about 5 kilometers (3 miles) before Monteverde on the highway, to do your business more cheaply. Santa Elena has a **Banco Nacional de Costa Rica** (tel. 61–27–50) and a **health clinic** (open weekdays 7–4, tel. 61–11–56). The visitor's information center at the cloud forest reserve has a telephone, and so does Stella's Bakery (see Food, below) in Monteverde.

COMING AND GOING Auto Transportes Tilarán (tel. 61–11–52, 22–38–54 in San José) has an express bus from San José to Monteverde. Buses leave San José at 2:30 PM Monday–Thursday and 6:30 AM Friday–Sunday (5 hours, $5). Buses return to San José from Monteverde at 6:30 AM Monday–Thursday and 3 PM Friday–Sunday. If you're coming from Puntarenas, take the 2:15 PM bus to Santa Elena or any bus that stops at the Santa Elena turnoff before 3:30 PM. Buses from Santa Elena to Puntarenas run daily at 6 AM. Depending on road conditions, **Auto Transportes Soto Mena** has a bus that goes from Tilarán to Monteverde at 1 PM and vice versa at 7 AM. Call 61–12–55 to double-check.

GETTING AROUND If you stay in nearby Santa Elena, you can walk to the town of Monteverde and the reserve without any major effort (or take a $5 taxi). If you stay in Monteverde, you'll still have to walk more than a mile to get to the reserve. Only if you sleep at Hotel Villa Verde or in the reserve will you be spared a long walk.

WHERE TO SLEEP Unfortunately, the capitalists of Monteverde (obviously Quakers don't take poverty vows) don't really cater to the budget traveler. If you stay anywhere other than the following hotels, you'll get shafted. A better option is to stay in Santa Elena, where they don't ream you quite as hard and you have more to choose from.

➤ **MONTEVERDE • Pensión Manakin.** This place is simple, and the family has opened their house and their hearts to international travelers—you'll feel like you live here. A double with bath and all three meals is $15. Rooms only (without bath) are $5 per person. If the pensión isn't full, students get a 10% discount. *30 meters before Hotel de Montaña, 50 meters off main street, tel. 61–28–54. 7 rooms, some with bath.*

Hotel Villa Verde. This is the closest place to the reserve, and it's nice. They've got a good selection of used English books and homemade chocolate-chip cookies. Expect to pay $15 per person for one of four rooms without bath inside the main house. Nicer rooms with baths in a separate structure go for $25 a person. All prices include three meals. *On left side as you walk toward reserve, tel. 61–35–55. 12 rooms, some with bath.*

Monteverde Cloud Forest Reserve. You can actually stay at the reserve in Monteverde. It'll cost you $20 for room and board in pretty simple accommodations. While you're exploring the cloud forest, you can stay in a *refugio* (*see* Worth Seeing, *below*). *At the entrance to the reserve, tel. 61–26–55. 30 guests. Reservations required.*

➤ **SANTA ELENA •** Santa Elena has a bunch of cheap pensions and private homes that will put you up for nearly nothing. When you get off the bus in Santa Elena, you'll get accosted by children and pension owners looking to make an extra buck. You can camp for $2 per person at **Albergue de Montaña Arco Iris.** Between Santa Elena and Monteverde, about ½ mile down a side street, is the serene **Pensión Monteverde.** If you wish to be isolated from the tourist rat race, this place is screaming out your name. The hotel sits on a ridge overlooking a valley. Rooms cost $8 a person, $20 including all three meals. To get here, follow the signs to the butterfly garden.

Hospedaje Esperanza. This quiet hotel is across the street from where the bus lets you off and right above a grocery store. The rooms are clean and sufficient. They charge $4 per person in low season and $5.50 in high season for a room without a bath. Check in at the grocery store. *In the center of town, tel. 61–25–55 or 61–28–58. 10 rooms, none with bath.*

Pensión Santa Elena. The minute you walk through the door, you'll be pampered by the owners and their huge family, which has adopted several international volunteers who stay free. Rooms (without bath) cost $5.50 in the high season and $4 per person in the low season. In the high season, $15 per person will get you a room with bath and meals. *50 meters east of bank, tel. 61–11–51. 8 rooms (25 people), some with bath. Laundry, phone.*

Pensión Tucan. Nice rooms, a large communal area, and simple food are what this pension has to offer. In the low season, they charge $10 per person for rooms without bath, including two meals. In the high season, they're $7 more. *100 meters east of the bank, tel. 61–10–07. 10 rooms, some with bath. Laundry.*

FOOD The restaurants in Monteverde are (surprise) expensive. Most hotels have restaurants that serve food to guests only, and the same thing happens in Santa Elena. Your best option is to stay at a pension that includes at least two meals daily. You can eat at **Soda Cerro Plano** or **Soda La Gioconda** in Santa Elena, but you won't save any money and you'll miss out on good conversation. For a beer and loud music, go to **Taberna Valverdes** in Santa Elena (open weekdays 8 PM–1 AM). As you're walking to the cloud reserve from Santa Elena, you'll pass two sodas in Monteverde: **Manantial**, across the street from La Cascada, and **Madiba**, by the Conservation League. For good baked goods and picnic items, stop in at **Stella's Bakery** and grocery store (by CASEM; *see below*) Monday–Saturday 8–noon and 1–5:30.

WORTH SEEING Reserva Biológica Bosque Nuboso Monteverde. The Monteverde Cloud Forest's a private reserve, so the directors of the governing Tropical Science Center can do whatever they want. That's why they charge an exorbitant fee of $8 for international visitors (students with international ID card pay $4, and they're real sticklers for the right ID). The reserve is a moist cloud forest spanning both sides of the Continental Divide, which you can explore on various trails. **Sendero Bosque Eterno** (Eternal Forest Trail) passes by a waterfall, and **Sendero Bosque Nuboso** (Cloud Forest Trail) crosses the Continental Divide, emerging on the Atlantic side. You can pay $2 to take one of five self-guided tours or hand over $13 for a guided nature walk in the early morning or at night. If you aren't in a rush, spend the night for $3.50 at one of the three very basic **refugios** inside the reserve: El Valle and El Aleman are only a three-hour walk from the entrance. All questions and refuge reservations should be made at the visitors' center (at the park entrance, inside the mongo gift shop) or by calling 61–26–55. The entrance booth is open daily 7–4, but the reserve remains open until 5:30.

Bosque Lluvioso de Santa Elena. If you thought Monteverde was something special, you ain't seen nothing yet. The community of Santa Elena, with the help of Canadian youth volunteers, transformed a government-granted rain forest into a pilot project. The object of the reserve is to benefit and protect the environment. One of the trails has a sensational view of Arenal—when it's not windy, misting, raining, or cloudy. All proceeds go toward preservation and education. Open daily 7–4, the reserve costs about $3.50 for international students and $5.50 for nonstudents. The entrance is about 6½ kilometers (4 miles) from the center of town. Transportation is planned for the future, but for now just follow the signs to the reserve or ask locals for directions. You should be able to hitch a ride in the morning. Call 61–28–58 or 61–11–54 for more details.

Jardín de Mariposas Monteverde. Only local species of butterfly are hand-raised in one of three enclosed gardens at this butterfly farm. Go in the morning, when the *mariposas* (butterflies) are fluttering around kaleidoscopically. Admission includes a 45-minute guided tour, from which you will learn more about butterflies than you ever thought possible. You might even catch a glimpse of a bellbird or hear its eerie "electronic" call. *Follow the signs in Monteverde by Hotel Heliconia. Admission: $5. Open daily 9:30–4.*

Fábrica de Queso Monteverde. The small cheese factory that the Quakers established in 1954, when they first came to Monteverde, has become one of the largest dairy producers in Costa Rica, cranking out 2,400 kilos of cheese weekly. It's just normal cheese—Swiss, muenster, jack, and the like—but most Costa Rican cheese is really salty and gross, so this stuff is heavenly in comparison. They have a gift shop and an observation room open to the public. *On the way to the cloud forest reserve if you're coming from Santa Elena, no tel. Observation room open Mon.–Sat. 7:30–4, Sun. 7:30–12:30.*

CASEM (Cooperativa Comité de Artesanas Santa Elena y Monteverde). This cooperative of 150 women and three men sells handicrafts such as hand-painted T-shirts and embroidered dresses and aprons at "bargain prices." You won't pay as much as you would at home, but it's not all that cheap. You can watch some women at work in the workshop upstairs. *Next to Stella's Bakery, no tel. Open Mon.–Sat. 8–noon and 1–5.*

OUTDOOR ACTIVITIES Horses are a big, big deal in Monteverde. **Luigi Amchia** at Pensión Santa Elena charges $6–$7 per hour or $25 per day to take you riding wherever you want to go. Horses aren't allowed in the Monteverde reserve or in the Santa Elena rain forest, but you can go to one of the scenic valleys instead. **Meg,** a bilingual guide from the United States (next to Stella's Bakery, tel. 61–09–52), charges $10 an hour for short rides. **Pensión Tucán** in Santa Elena also rents horses for $7 an hour.

The Caribbean Coast

The steamy lowlands of Costa Rica's eastern coast stretch to the warm, clear waters of the Caribbean Sea. Welcome to an entirely different country, a land of mangrove swamps and coral reefs, where weary travelers can recharge under the potent sun on glittering white- or black-sand beaches. South of the provincial capital of Puerto Limón you'll discover the awesome surf of Puerto Viejo de Talamanca, and in Cahuita and the Gandoca-Manzanillo Wildlife Reserve you can snorkel and dive. North from Limón stretch the verdant *canales* of Tortuguero, lush humid jungles, and protected turtle-nesting sites. Almost half the coast is protected by national parks. Remember your capa (rain gear), though; there is no such thing as a dry season here.

Over a third of the province's population is of Afro-Caribbean descent, and at least 5,000 Talamanca Indians live in reservations near the Panamanian border. Until the constitution of '47, blacks were subject to legal discrimination. The area was and still is marginalized socially, politically, and economically—the more populated areas of Limón and the south struggle daily against crime and crack, and the northern regions remain isolated and difficult to access. Today, residents still bear strong resentment against the central power of San José, proudly declaring their cultural and linguistic differences.

English is widely spoken by many *limonenses*. The dialect is a little challenging, but understandable. "Okay" means "good-bye," and "all right" is used as a passing greeting. The traditional greeting, "what happen," is less heard but still used. Another cultural difference enjoyed by most travelers is the food. *Rondon* (rundown) is a succulent stew of local tubers and meat or fish. On Sunday, the traditional dish is rice and red beans cooked in coconut milk, a welcome variation on gallo pinto. The fresh-baked fruitcake, *pan bon,* is also coconutty. Seafood is fresh, plentiful, well cooked, and less expensive than inland.

The Caribbean isn't as big a money-maker as the Pacific coast; accordingly, prices are a bit lower and tourism isn't as entrenched. However, during the *temporada* (busy season), December–May, lodgings are crowded. The famed jungle train traversing the region bit the dust (big bummer), but the ride from San José to the transport hub of Limón takes only about two hours on a slick highway. Enjoy the trip 'cause it's the fastest you'll get anywhere in this area. Road conditions are subject to the whims of nature, and buses "stop at every tree," as a bemused German traveler observed. Hitching is also common.

Puerto Limón

The biggest town on the Caribbean coast is a densely populated, under-touristed place; buildings toppled by the April 1991 earthquake lie in ruins along the streets, while dockworkers load bananas for export from the country's biggest port.

The Caribbean Coast

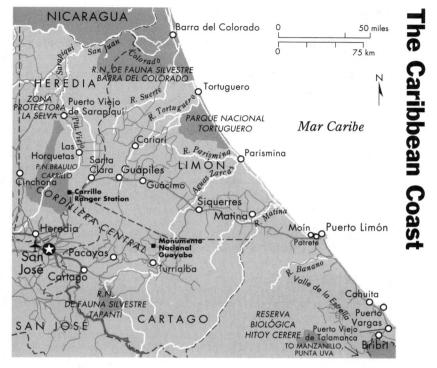

NICARAGUA

Barra del Colorado

0   50 miles

0   75 km

N

HEREDIA

San Juan

R.N. DE FAUNA SILVESTRE
BARRA DEL COLORADO

Tortuguero

ZONA
PROTECTORA
LA SELVA

Puerto Viejo
de Sarapiquí

R. Suerte

PARQUE NACIONAL
TORTUGUERO

Mar Caribe

Las
Horquetas

Cariari

P.N. BRAULIO
CARRILLO

Santa
Clara

Guápiles

R. Parismina

LIMON

Parismina

Cinchona

Guácimo

Carrillo
Ranger Station

Siquerres

Matina

R. Matina

Heredia

Moín

Puerto Limón

Monumento
Nacional
Guayabo

Potrete

San
José

Pacayas

Cartago

Turrialba

R. Banano

Valle de la Estrella

Cahuita

R.N.
DE FAUNA SILVESTRE
TAPANTI

CARTAGO

SAN JOSÉ

RESERVA
BIOLÓGICA
HITOY CERERE

Puerto Viejo
de Talamanca

Puerto
Vargas

TO MANZANILLO,
PUNTA UVA

Bribrí

Limón, as the city is more commonly known, is an essential travel stop if you're continuing north to the canals of Tortuguero or south to the beaches of Cahuita and Puerto Viejo. The town is most popular with tourists during the annual Carnaval around October 12. A tidal wave of ticos and tourists flood the streets to ogle and join the week of street parades, Caribbean music, and nonstop partying to celebrate *El Día de la Raza,* a.k.a. Columbus Day.

With the exception of Carnaval, most travelers get out of Limón as fast as they can, frightened off by warnings of theft, assault, and drug problems. Some ticos call the city "Piedropolis (Crack City)." The city's evils are exaggerated, but do exist; approach the area with open eyes. Think twice about a midnight stroll down by the *malecón* (seaside jetty) or Parque Vargas.

Valiant ceiling fans sluggishly whirl around damp, still air. Orange streetlights cast bluish shadows over families gossiping on the street corner and drunks slumped on the market benches.

Limón has long been excluded from the Costa Rican mainstream; racism and resentment are strong on both sides. The population of Limón, mainly of African descent, justifiably feels marginalized. "Limón produces everything and gets nothing," stated a local teenage dock worker. Rebuilding after the earthquake has been unreasonably slow, and under- and unemployment are rampant. Developing Limón is just not on the top of the government's list of priorities.

BASICS

➤ **MONEY** • The only places that officially change money are the banks around Avenida 2. Most of Costa Rica's major banks have a branch here. On weekends you're out of luck, unless the black market has reopened or the management of your hotel can help you out.

Banco Nacional. *Calle 3 and Av. 2a, tel. 58–00–94, across from the market. Open weekdays 8–3.*

Banco Anglo Costarricense. *Calle 2, between Av. 1 and Av. 2a, tel. 58–03–51. Near the San José bus stop. Open weekdays 8–3.*

➢ **EMERGENCIES** • **Hospital Dr. Tony Facio Castro** (at the north end of the malecón, tel. 58–22–22); **ambulance** (ext. 266); **police** (tel. 117); **fire** (tel. 118). **Red Cross (Cruz Roja).** *Calle 3 between Av. 1 and Av. 2a, tel. 58–01–25. From the southeast corner of the market, 50 meters south.*

➢ **PHONES AND MAIL** • The **post office** (southwest of the *mercado municipal,* tel. 58–15–43) is open weekdays 8–5. International calls can be made from the **ICE** office (from the San José bus stop, 300 meters north and 325 west) Monday–Thursday 8–5, Friday 8–4. You can also place international calls through the **Hotel Acón** (from the San José bus stop, 100 meters north and 75 meters west).

➢ **VISITOR INFORMATION** • Very little tourist infrastructure exists for the Caribbean coast. There may be someone staffing the kiosk in Limón's Parque Vargas (*see* Worth Seeing, *below*), but you might find only reticent sloths. A new tourist info center is planned for the nearby town of Moín, and it may be operational by press time (check with the ICT head office in San José before you come, tel. 23–17–33, ext. 277).

COMING AND GOING You don't have a lot of options. The San José–Limón train hasn't worked since the earthquake and it won't be repaired any time soon. Limón has an airstrip for charter flights only, so you can't fly. Hitching is impractical, dangerous, and discouraged—unless you have better ideas, take the bus.

Buses for Limón depart San José about every hour from near the old train station, east of Parque Nacional. Service runs in both directions 5 AM–7 PM, and several of the buses are direct. Fare for the 2½-hour trip is about $2.50. You should buy tickets a day in advance. *Limón station at Av. 3 between Calles 19 and 21, San José. Coopelimón: tel. 23–78–11; Auto Transportes Caribeños: tel. 57–08–95.*

Limón's principal bus station is 100 meters east of the mercado, on Calle 2 between Avenidas 1 and 2. This is the departure point for buses to San José. **Coopetraga** (tel. 58–06–18) also runs several buses a day to Siquerres and Guápiles, where you can catch a bus to the capital. Service to the southern Caribbean towns departs from Avenida 4 near Calle 3, about 100 meters west of the mercado. Four buses a day run down the coast to Cahuita, Puerto Viejo de Talamanca, and Sixaola, and frequent buses run to Manzanillo. The fare to any of these destinations is less than $2.

GETTING AROUND Limón crawls over a beak of land pointing east into the Caribbean. The total absence of street signs and few obvious physical landmarks make Limón a bit difficult to navigate for the first day or two. Use the following landmarks to orient yourself and you'll sail along. The *muelle* **(dock)** and the railroad tracks lie to the south of Limón's center. **Parque Vargas** occupies the easternmost tip of the city; from the parque, the **malecón (seaside promenade)** winds north along the coast, toward Portete and Moín. In the center of Limón, the main street, **Avenida 2,** passes the north edge of Parque Vargas and the south edge of the mercado. Avenidas run east–west in numerical order, starting parallel to the railroad tracks; calles run north–south, beginning with Calle 1, at the western edge of Parque Vargas. Ask around for intercity bus service; buses, like so many other things in Limón, are undependable and often break down.

WHERE TO SLEEP An assortment of hotels mushrooms in Limón's center. Calling ahead for reservations is a good idea on weekends, especially during high season (December–February, Easter, and Carnaval). If the places below are full, you might survive a night of mold and must in **Hotel Lincoln** (north on Calle 2 straight from the San José bus stop, at the malecón turn left, tel. 58–00–74); at least the management is kind. Sleeping on the beach or in the park is *not* a good option, and campgrounds don't exist. If you're totally stuck, head for the Red Cross; they may take pity and loan you the floor.

➤ **NEAR THE BUS STATION • Hotel Palace.** A short crawl from the San José bus stop, this budget hotel sprawls through the second story of a large building, overlooking a mellow stretch of Calle 2. What the Palace lacks in cleanliness, it makes up for in character (and hey, it's only a little dusty). The plant-lined balcony is a mellow refuge from any night crazies and a good place to meet fellow travelers. Doubles with communal bath are $9, and they're fairly quiet. Two tips: Ask to see more than one room (some are dark cells), and plug "suspicious" holes with chewing gum. One guest reports he gave a free peep show. *On Calle 2, between Av. 3 and Av. 2a, tel. 58–04–16. 75 meters north of the San José bus stop. Luggage storage, laundry.*

Hotel Venus. The wood walls may be a little askew from the earthquake, but this funky little hotel has cool corridors, and the high-ceilinged rooms are chock-full of Central American kitsch. Beds are on the hard side, the weekend noise level's high (it's above a bar), and you may want to lay your rain gear over the mattress to avoid being devoured by fleas. But at just under $7 for a double sharing clean communal bathrooms, this is the best bargain in town. *Corner of Calle 2 and Av. 4, diagonal to the court, tel. 58–15–06. 200 meters north from the San José bus stop, just walk straight up the street away from the railroad tracks. 27 rooms, none with bath. Luggage storage, laundry.*

Park Hotel. This well-known hotel has a deserved reputation with tourists, travelers, and locals alike. Three price levels are offered—sea view, street view, and *planta baja* (no view). The cheapest double, a large well-ventilated room with fans and hot-water bath, goes for about $13. Similar doubles with views of the sea-washed malecón are $20. The courteous management recommends reservations at least a week in advance. *Intersection of Av. 3, Calle 1, and the malecón, tel. 58–34–76. 150 meters north and 50 meters east from the San José bus stop. 31 rooms, all with bath. Luggage storage, laundry, discount for fall weekend stay, restaurant.*

➤ **NEAR THE MERCADO • El Cano.** This family-run establishment is very respectable: "No drunks, no *mujeres de la vida* (women of the night)," states Doña Naomi. The dark, simple rooms are humble but safe, and the *baño collectivo* is basic (a euphemism, perhaps). It's definitely the cheapest place available without accompanying shady joes. Doubles with bath are $9. *On Av. 3 between Calles 4 and 5, tel. 58–08–94. From the northwest corner of the mercado central, it's 50 meters west. 16 rooms, some with bath. Luggage storage, laundry.*

Linda Vista. Turquoise neoclassic columns and thin white particle board separate you from your neighbors and the bar below. The rooms are a little closed-in but clean, as are the communal bathrooms. At about $9 for a double without bath, this hotel isn't too bad. *On Av. 2a between Calles 4 and 5, near the market, tel. 58–33–59. From San José bus stop, walk toward the town (away from railroad tracks); make a left on the first street. 35 rooms, some with bath. Luggage storage, laundry.*

FOOD Travel grub and basic provisions are cheapest in the market or the *super* (short for supermercado), across from the northeast corner of the market. Nearby sodas dish up very economical meals, but get a seat inside and keep an eye out for drugged-out hustlers; proprietors are usually adept at settling nasty situations. **Doña Toda,** at the southeast corner of the market, is well known by budget travelers for serving the best beans in the area for less than $1. The spacious, sea-wrapped **Park Hotel Restaurant** (*see* Where to Sleep, *above*) is recommended for peaceful dining, but double-check the prices on the seafood. Ceviche is under $2.50, but the shrimp cocktail runs about $4.

Soda Palón. The rickety wood stools on the street have an invisible "locals only" sign, but feel welcome to crowd the fluorescent plastic booths where Spanish-dubbed TV overwhelms the clinking cutlery of tired old men and gossiping teens. The patient waitress purses glowing pink lips and hands you a filling *medio casado* for $1.50. If you're in town on Sunday, be sure to stop in for the rice and beans special. *Northwest corner of the market, no tel.*

Pizzeria il Maccaroni. It's a big leap from the Caribbean to the Mediterranean, but go for it: This is the best pizza place in Costa Rica. Crispy crusts and fresh ingredients are whipped into authentically Italian delights. Wash a variety of pizzas down with a good bottle of Chilean wine. Vegetarian pizza ($5 for a small) combines chile dulce, onion, olives, garlic, and parsley. The $4.50 *bruschetta* (toasted, garlicky bread) is made with real mozzarella and fresh tomato. *On Calle 4 between Av. 2a and Av. 1, tel. 58–33–43. Across the street from the post office.*

Springfield. North of the center near the hospital, this popular restaurant is worth the walk for excellent Caribbean food in an ample, almost elegant dining room (it has tablecloths). Rice and beans, traditionally cooked on Sunday only, is available here every day. The $5 plate includes your choice of meat, from fresh fish to the politically incorrect turtle fin. On Tuesdays, the house special is a tasty rondon. *Across from the hospital, tel. 58–12–03. Take a taxi from the center or walk in a group down malecón to the hospital, on the left. Open 11 AM–midnight.*

Richard, one smooth limonense, says the best spot for dancing is Bar Acuario in Hotel Acón. On Sunday night, he recommends the Banana Ranch or Arena y Sol. The latter are outside Limón's center; taking a taxi is advised.

WORTH SEEING The thick, sweaty cement walls of the **mercado municipal** form niches for vendors of turtle meat, plastic shoes, and medicinal herbs. A hub of commercial and social activity, the market is a good place to become acquainted with local smells, exchange a few smiles and coins with límonenses, and pick up a snack of fresh fruit for a stroll through **Parque Vargas,** at the eastern tip of the city. On weekend mornings, groups of young men and women gossip and covertly check each other out, while oblivious little kids pick at the wide gravel walkway. While the park is not a place to relax at night, during the day it's a peaceful, humid haven of damp grassy squares and shady corners, where hummingbirds play tag around hibiscus flowers. The winding cement malecón starts here, just in sight of the little island, **Uvita,** where Columbus landed 500 years ago.

OUTDOOR ACTIVITIES Puerto Limón is not really known for natural beauty. The local swimming hole, *los baños,* is near the malecón at the end of Avenida 5. The water quality is iffy at best, so you might have more fun getting in on a game of **basketball** at the nearby courts. Don't lose hope: **Playa Bonita** is only 2 miles north. To get there, catch one of the semi-frequent buses to **Moín** that leave Limón from Calle 4 between Avenidas 4 and 5, about 100 meters north of the market.

Tortuguero

The **Parque Nacional Tortuguero,** 83 kilometers (52 miles) northwest of Limón, is best known as the key nesting site for the green turtle which lays its eggs between July and October (peak time is late August). One of the most diverse biological areas of the country, the 35-kilometer- (22-mile-) long park is home to sloths, manatees, tepisquintle, jaguars, and monkeys, among hundreds of other furry, feathered, and scaly creatures. Although San José bursts with tour agencies running trips here, the park is totally accessible to the independent budget traveler. **Tortuguero Village,** on the northern end of the park, is a peaceful, developing community that provides the basic necessities and a lot of friendly, honest conversation.

BASICS The kiosk in the middle of the village is crammed with information about the history of the area and the development of the turtles. A representative is here 4–6 PM to sell entrance passes and answer questions. You can also go to the north end of the park and poke your head inside the **Administración de Tortuguero,** the park's central headquarters. You can send mail from **Cortel** (along the main path in the middle of the village) or from the pulperiá, where you'll also find a public phone. In case of **emergencies,** head for the Administración; the doctor's in town only every other Thursday. For anything else you can think of, **Paraíso Tropical,** on the main path north of the kiosk, is an excellent resource.

Don't even try to keep dry in Tortuguero; this area of the Caribbean littoral gets up to 600 centimeters of rain per year.

COMING AND GOING

➤ **BY BOAT** • Alternatives to the expensive tours do exist. Tortuguero is becoming more of a tourist run, and you're likely to get offered a boat to the park while you're in Limón. Check the dock in Limón or nearby Moín (departure point for most boats to Tortuguero). The offered price at press time was $50 per person round-trip, but you can get them to lower the fare to at least $40 if you assemble a group. The 4-hour boat ride up the canals is worth eating gallo pinto for a week. **Carlos Bruno** (Apartado 2482-1000, San José, tel. 58–12–10) operates several boats that go up and back daily and the ride includes lunch. Bruno will pick you up in Limón and take you to the Moín dock. Boats leave Moín at 9:30 AM and make the return trip from Tortuguero at 1:30 PM. Agree on a return date beforehand or ask if you can phone for pickup a day in advance.

➤ **BY PLANE** • Just north of Tortuguero Village is the Casa Verde Research station and a small landing strip. Word is that **SANSA** is going to start direct flights from San José to Tortuguero. This would definitely be the fastest way in (and it may push boat fares down). Call the SANSA office in San José (tel. 33–03–97) to check.

GETTING AROUND The village of Tortuguero is fairly cozy. A maze of dirt paths sprouts off one main footpath, which runs north–south through the village. At the far south end is the Administración. In more or less the center of town, right across from where the boats dock, is the information kiosk. Another good landmark is the pulpería, north from the headquarters on the main path. The canals lie west; the Caribbean, east. If you're still getting lost, the kiosk has a good map permanently printed on plastic.

WHERE TO SLEEP Stay away from the $30–$50 a day lodges on the other side of the canal: Tortuguero Village has several better options. **Cabinas Mery Scar** (east of the pulpería and south past Edna and Jacob's) charges about $3.50 a person for tidy rooms in a homey atmosphere and large, clean, communal bathrooms. **Cabinas Sabinas** (east from the information kiosk on the Caribbean coast) has more rooms (and more bugs), but the sheets are washed thoroughly. Each person is charged just under $4, and you must be out of your room by 10 AM. **Brisas del Mar** (a.k.a. Inez's Place, next to the Bochinche, north from the kiosk), an option for groups, has a basic five-person room for $13.

➤ **CAMPGROUNDS** • With a waterproof tent and mosquito net, you can happily camp in the park, which has two sites (each with room for three tents). **Estación Jalova,** at the southernmost entrance of the park, is accessible only by boat. Have your captain drop you off and arrange to continue on to Tortuguero Village another day. You're welcome to use the rangers' basic bathroom facilities, but bring your own food. A similar campsite is available at the **Administración,** on the north end of the park. Both cost about $1.50 a day per person for entrance and camping fees.

FOOD The best restaurants are local residences with the front patio converted to a dining room. I would swim through a pool of caimans to eat at **Miss June's** (at the far north end of the main path) again. You have to talk to her in advance, and she'll let you know if she can cook that day. She'll size you up and charge accordingly (about $6 for dinner, a little less for lunch). You may be served rice and beans, tender *chayote* (a local veggie), or breadfruit. Also recommended for tasty food at about $3–$5 a meal is Cabinas Mery Scar (*see* Where to Sleep, *above*). Doña María may even make a late-night omelette for starving jungle explorers. If **Miss Edna** (east of the pulpería) is still around, drop in for a chat, an excellent but more expensive meal, and some of the best baked goods in Costa Rica.

WORTH SEEING The most popular activity is the night beach tour to see the *deshove* (laying of the eggs). Yes, it's cool to watch a herd of turtles storm the beach and squeeze out their progeny in the moonlight, but park officials are tightening visitor regulations in reaction to an alarming decrease in successful deshoves. During egg-laying season, all park visitors must be accompanied by a certified guide. Tickets for the tour must be bought that day between 4 and 6 PM at the kiosk. Tours leave at 8 PM and must be off the beach by 10. Be warned that some of the local guides seem more interested in getting back to a cold beer, so read the kiosk info and be ready to do your own turtle-spotting. You'll usually only be allowed to see a single deshove to minimize impact.

More of the park can be seen on your own or with a guide. Two self-guided trails start from the Administración, and you may also still be allowed to canoe in on your own. **Rubén Aragón** (50 meters north of the Administración) rents canoes for a few bucks an hour; he charges about $4 per person per hour, but if you assemble a group, you might be able to haggle. One of his tours climbs the Cerro de Tortuguero, the highest point on the coast; wear your mud gear! If **Damma** is still around, definitely go on a trip with him: He's a Miskito Indian who'll put you smack in the middle of things, making you climb swinging vines and cutting you a chunk of *skowa-skowa,* a water-bearing vine. The night trips are cool and a bit eerie. Try not to freak when he hands you a caiman that looks like a small crocodile—just hold it where Damma does. Small groups of people who know how to shut up and look where Damma points are recommended. Ask someone in the village where to find him.

KNOW YOUR BOATS!

Panga: a flat-bottomed boat (with an outboard) • Bote: a large canoe • Lancha: a larger boat with an inboard motor.

Cahuita

The brilliant white sands of Cahuita National Park sing a siren song to an international crowd of sun worshippers and balmy-evening revellers. Not too long ago, this village 48 kilometers (30 miles) southeast of Limón was a hidden paradise; now, it's the preferred Caribbean destination for scads of budget travelers. It's *the* place to meet Birkenstocked Germans, Belgian Rasta hippies, society dropouts from the U.S. of A., and maybe even a few locals. Cahuita has taken the incredible influx of tourism in stride, managing to retain its distinctive laid-back, slow-paced personality. Cahuita's main draw is the glistening beach and tangled jungle paths of Parque Nacional Cahuita. The glory of the park is the living coral reef, the best on Costa Rica's Caribbean coast, about 500 meters off the elbow of Punta Cahuita. Slip on some **snorkel/scuba** gear and waltz with angelfish and sea urchins.

Most people plan to come to Cahuita for a few days and end up staying a week, soaking in the sun and splashing in the surf (or beer).

Cahuita's not all easy living, unfortunately. A legion of "free-love" foreigners have left a reputation which women travelers are now forced to battle. Single women are seen as accessible and interested; convincing anyone of the contrary is nearly impossible.

Be *very* aware and prepared to deal with nasty situations. One 50-year-old gringa was raped on the road I walked every night to my cabina; and a friend of mine was assaulted on the beach in midday. She tried to talk her way out of it, but ended up having to knee her attacker in the groin to escape. Add a growing problem with crack and theft, and this warning might be enough to sour your trip. Don't be scared away, though— just keep your head clear, your eyes wide open, and your back covered.

BASICS Change money (traveler's checks and cash) at the better hotels and restaurants near the National Park and at Cahuita Tours and Rentals (*see* Visitor Information, *below*). You can place international and local **phone calls** at Hotel Cahuita, Soda Uvita, or Cahuita Tours (tel. 58–06–52), all along the main road in town. Drop off your **mail** at Cahuita Tours, which also sells stamps. In case of **emergencies,** head for the guardia and the local medical clinic, both at the Y on the way to the black beach.

➤ **VISITOR INFORMATION • Cahuita Tours and Rentals** (on the main road toward the black beach, tel. 58–06–52) is open daily 7 AM–about 8 PM. Tony Mora and Rodolfo dish out plenty of free visitor information, arrange local tours, and provide the services detailed above. The friendly staff of **Moray's** (take the road toward the black beach, just after the Y, tel. 58–15–15, ext. 216) also offers tours of the area, visitor information, and a brochure with a **map** of Cahuita. They're open daily 8 AM– 6 PM.

COMING AND GOING Direct buses to Cahuita from San José (**Transportes MEPE,** tel. 21–05–24) depart from Avenida 11 between Calles Central and 1 daily at 6 AM and 1:30 PM. The 4-hour ride is about $4, and the bus is marked "Sixaola." Buses from Limón 200 meters north and 125 west from the San José bus stop depart for Cahuita daily at 5 AM, 10 AM, 1 PM, and 4 PM. The trip is over an hour and costs under $1 (**Transportes MEPE,** tel. 58–15–72). Return buses to Limón or direct ones to San José are not renowned for keeping a tight schedule. Be early and prepare to wait in the shade of the park or Salón Vaz; the parada (bus stop) is at the crossroads. Direct buses to San José supposedly pass through at 6:30 AM, 10 AM, and 4 PM. To Limón, buses leave at noon, 1:30, and 5 PM. Buses to Puerto Vargas, Puerto Viejo, Bribri, and Sixaola pass through before 6 AM, 11 AM, and 2 PM.

GETTING AROUND Cahuita is a relatively small town, so it's pretty hard to get lost. The parada is at a crossroads. The road perpendicular to the road from the highway is the main drag, running from the national park (**white-sand beach**) at the southeast end to the **black-sand beach** at the northwest end. In the village, another road closer to the Caribbean (the ocean road) parallels the main drag. Several smaller streets intersect these two. Directions are given in relation to local landmarks (the two beaches) and businesses.

WHERE TO SLEEP Lodging in Cahuita can be found in three areas: near the national park, in the village, and near the black beach. The latter is fairly remote and not recommended for single travelers (crack use in the area makes the dark road a less-than-desirable stroll); however, accommodations closer to town tend to fill up quickly. Prices are lowest in the village and during the off season from June to August, but sleeping in Cahuita is still expensive, especially for the solo traveler; most rooms are price-fixed at a double rate. At least the quality is in line with the price; most places have private baths and come equipped with fans or *mosquiteros* (mosquito nets). If the places below are full, try the $12 doubles at **Cabinas Surfside** (on the ocean road across from the school, tel. 58–15–15, ext. 246) or the cool doubles of **Cabinas Rhode Island** (near the national park; take a right immediately after Cabinas Restaurant Sol y Mar, tel. 58–15–15, ext. 264) for $15 during the busy season and only $10 during low season. **Cabinas Margarita** (near the black beach; walk north down the road parallel to the coast, tel. 58–15–15) has large, fan-equipped doubles for $25.

Cabinas Brigitte. Stay in this funky cabina while you can! Brigitte has plans to convert the cool, Central Ameri-kitschy rooms into an open-air restaurant. The location, way the heck down on the black beach, makes it a poor option for single women travelers, but come with a friend and enjoy the mellow remoteness. Doubles with use of basic, communal bathrooms are about $11. *No tel. About a 20-minute walk from town, near the black beach. 4 rooms, none with bath. Luggage storage, laundry, restaurant.*

Cabinas Jenny. Right on the beach, this hotel has beautiful roomy doubles with private bath for $20. Mattresses are comfy and thick, and all rooms have mosquito nets and fans. Upstairs rooms are breezier and have semi-private balconies. Hang out in a hammock and enjoy the good life. Jenny may even be able to direct you to cheaper rooms nearby. Breakfast is prepared 6 AM–noon (you can even have room service if you ask). *Tel. 58–15–15, ext. 256. At the end of the road into town from the highway, on the beach. 9 rooms, all with bath. Luggage storage, laundry, reservations not accepted.*

Cabinas Sol y Mar. Near the national park, this large cement building has cool, pleasant doubles with private bath for $13. The airy upstairs doubles are worth an extra $2 for the sea view and the cool wind. The restaurant downstairs serves good, reasonably priced food—the tomato chicken is highly praised. If you're lucky, Doreen will challenge you to a game of Nintendo. *Tel. 58–15–15, ext. 237. On the main road, close to the National Park entrance. 8 rooms, all with bath. Luggage storage, laundry, restaurant, reservations not accepted.*

➤ **CAMPGROUNDS** • Warnings of theft and harassment (not to mention vicious sand fleas) should discourage you from camping on the beach near Cahuita village. Instead, pitch your tent on a nice grassy stretch in front of the beach for about $4 at **Cabinas Las Brisas** (there's no sign, but it's the two small cabinas off the ocean road near the school, tel. 58–15–15, ext. 267). The camping fee includes use of bathroom, shower, and pila. You can also camp in Cahuita National Park, in the **Puerta Vargas** area on the other side of Punta Cahuita. To get there you can either hike the beach/jungle trail about 6½ kilometers (4 miles) or catch a bus down the highway to the well-marked Puerto Vargas entrance. Camping facilities are on Playa Vargas, half a mile from the entrance near the *administración.* The fee is about $1 per person each day, including use of pit toilets and showers.

FOOD You definitely won't starve in Cahuita, but you might spend more than you budgeted. Most restaurants have breakfast specials for around $3, but lunch and dinner can suck your wallet dry. To make those colones go their farthest, look for the filling $3–$4 casados served at **Restaurant Cahuita National Park, Vista del Mar,** or **Restaurant Sol y Mar.** All of these establishments near the national park entrance are pleasant and shady, but you pay for your proximity in the prices of dinner entrées ($5 and up). Hotel Cahuita's grilled corvina (sea bass) in garlic butter ($5) and Sol y Mar's tomato chicken ($5) are recommended.

➤ **UNDER $6** • **El Cactus.** On the road to the black beach, this hot little Italian restaurant serves steaming pizza to an international crowd. Live music on Saturday nights make this a good place to have a beer and a slice with a group of friends. Sizeable individual pizzas start at $3.50. Spaghetti from clam to carbonara costs $4–$6, and salads are $4.50. *Tel. 58–15–15, ext. 276. Off the road to the black beach, about 100 meters down the dirt road away from the water; look for the sign. Opens at 4 PM. Closed Mon.*

Restaurant Típico Cahuita. This mellow, modern soda-style restaurant is one of the cheapest and most pleasant places to eat in town. They serve casados all day long— less than $3 for rice, beans, salad, and your choice of meat or egg. Rice and beans simmer in rich coconut milk every Sunday ($3 a serving), and if you give Jaqueline a day's warning, she'll whip up a batch of rondon for $5. *Tel. 58–15–15, ext. 224. From the crossroads bus stop, take the center road toward the park. Turn right at Defi's sign; it's on the right before the bend. Open 7 AM–11 PM.*

➤ **UNDER $10** • **Defi's.** This place wins the prize for ambience. A pleasant, low grass roof covers the sand floor. Cool breezes stir the bromeliads and ferns clinging to the driftwood walls, and young locals, surfers, and Rastas mix with the international travelers. The house special is jerk chicken in spices and coconut milk ($6), but it's only served once a week. Defi also serves a variety of $4–$13 pizzas. *Tel. 58-15-15, ext. 204. Near Cahuita National Park, follow the sign to the right. Open daily 7 AM–11 PM or later.*

Miss Edith's. It's a rite of passage to come here and wait for an hour at the long, family-style tables for a huge plate of Caribbean food. The house specialty is *rondon,* cooked with meat or fish and vegetables. Miss Edith also serves cheaper rice and meat plates (starting at $4) or, for vegetarian palates, *chop vegetal* at just over $2. *Take the main road toward the black beach and turn right by the guardia station. Open 6:30 AM–10:30 AM and 6 PM–10 PM.*

AFTER DARK When the sun sets, the international crowd splashes on bug repellent and heads to one of the local bars to have a few cold ones. Favorite wells in town include the choza of the National Park Restaurant (near the National Park) and **Bar Hannia** (on the main road in town), where groups of German students teach drinking games to onlookers. For a more reggae atmosphere, have a beer at Defi's (*see* Food, *above*) or take the long walk to the bamboo grotto of **La Ancia,** close to the black beach. Weekends are the best time for live music at El Cactus (*see* Food, *above*) or **Salón Vaz** (in town at the crossroads), where you can sway to tropical rhythms under twinkling colored lights. More sedentary travelers can hang out at **Soda Uvita** (on the main road in town) and watch locals slap those dominoes, baby.

If you came to Cahuita for its enthralling museums, I've got some great beachfront property in Cartago to sell you. Cahuita is sand and warm Caribbean waters, jungle hiking and horseback riding.

OUTDOOR ACTIVITIES In **Cahuita National Park,** you can swim (except for the dangerous first 400 meters), surf (with your own board), boogie-board, and snorkel or scuba dive around the reef. You can rent equipment for these activities from Cahuita Tours and Moray's (*see* Basics, *above*). The latter is a little cheaper. Snorkeling equipment costs about $4 a day and full scuba gear with tank, $65–$75.

A trail through the park leads to the reef (4 kilometers [2½ miles]) and to Punta Vargas (8 kilometers [5 miles]), where you can camp (*see* Where to Sleep, *above*). The *guardaparque* (ranger) advises an early morning walk to see the most wildlife. Howler monkeys and sloths are most common. The park is open 24 hours; please register if the office is open. Currently, there is no entrance fee.

If the white-sand beach of the national park is too glaringly beautiful, head up to the black-sand beach northwest of town. Some people say the swimming is better, and it's more of a local's beach. However, at press time, the black-sand beach was still littered with driftwood—a result of the 1991 earthquake. Brigitte (*see* Where to Sleep, *above*) rents **horses** for about $14 a day and will arrange a guided tour of the jungle and/or beach. Moray's also offers horseback tours. If a live mount isn't your thang, rent a bike from Moray's or Cahuita Tours for $5–$7 a day.

Puerto Viejo de Talamanca

Only 16 kilometers (10 miles) southeast of Cahuita, Puerto Viejo de Talamanca has a very different, perhaps more peaceful atmosphere. Many residents are actively involved in developing tourism in harmony with the local lifestyle, an interesting mix of Afro-Caribbean and indigenous culture. During low season, from June to September, you'll share the beach with brilliant yellow crabs and locals gathering firewood; in the evening, when gentle mists wrap the surrounding blue-green mountains, you'll see one of the most beautiful stretches of coast in the country. Surfers from around the world come to Puerto Viejo to test their skills on the pounding waves of **Salsa Brava.**

BASICS To change money (cash or traveler's checks), go to **Soda Tamara** (on the center road near the shore), the **pulpería** near Johnny's place, or **Stanford's** (on the ocean road, just outside town). During the high season (December–May), most hotels will change money, too. There are few **phones** for public use, but you can make international calls from the **Maritza** (on the ocean road, after the bus stop, tel. 58–38–44) or the **pulpería** near Johnny's (tel. 58–08–54). The **lista de correo** is at the **police** station (on the ocean road, in front of Johnny's). In case of **emergencies,** you can try the police, but residents have little faith. There's a **clinic** in town and occasionally a doctor; the closest hospital is in Bribri.

➤ **VISITOR INFORMATION** • Local residents and visitor volunteers have formed the **Asociación Talamanqueña de Ecoturismo y Conservación (ATEC),** which seeks to develop socially responsible ecological tourism by educating residents and locals about the area's natural and cultural heritage. Although the office (in town on the center road) is not an information center, they do have a post board with a map of the town. Mauricio Salazar, the president, is well known for his tours to nearby indigenous reserves and through the jungle. Look for him at the ATEC office or at his **Chirimuri Nature Lodge,** a mile outside Puerto Viejo off the road from the highway.

COMING AND GOING

➤ **BY BUS** • The direct bus from San José (**Transportes MEPE,** tel. 21–05–24) departs from Avenida 11 between Calles Central and 1 daily at 6 AM and 1:30 PM. The five-hour ride costs about $4, but it drops you at the crossroads, a 3-mile walk from town. The bus from Limón takes you all the way into Puerto Viejo. Buses depart from Limón 200 meters north and 125 meters west from the San José bus stop daily at 5 AM, 10 AM, 1 PM, and 4 PM. The trip takes about two hours and costs about $1 (**Transportes MEPE,** tel. 58–15–72).

Buses to Cahuita and Limón pass through Puerto Viejo daily except Sunday at 6 AM, 9 AM, 1 PM, and 5 PM; on Sundays, at 6 AM, 9 AM, and 4 PM. Buses to Manzanillo stop at 7:30 AM and 3:30 PM. Buses to Bribri and Sixaola come through at about 6:30 AM, 11:30 AM, 2 PM, and 5:30 PM. The Puerto Viejo bus stop is on the ocean road across from Jocelyn's pulpería, near Taberna Popo (El Zarpe). Except for the departures from Limón, bus schedules vary up to an hour (okay, maybe more).

➤ **ALTERNATIVE TRANSPORTATION** • **Hitching** is very common between Puerto Viejo and Punta Uva or Manzanillo. Patience and a positive attitude are essential. Some of the trucks are self-proclaimed taxis, and others won't charge a penny. You could also bike the 10 kilometers (6 miles), but the roads are rough. At this time, you can't walk straight along the shore from Puerto Viejo to Punta Uva or Manzanillo. The distance between Cahuita and Puerto Viejo (16 kilometers [10 miles]) translates into a four- or five-hour **walk** along the beach.

GETTING AROUND Getting lost is a challenge in Puerto Viejo. The road that enters from the highway splits into two roads at the town; one follows the shoreline (the **ocean road**), and the other cuts straight through town (the **center road**). A couple of streets intersect these roads in a grid pattern. Most businesses are well marked, and beautifully painted signs direct the traveler to most hotels and restaurants.

Although everything is within walking distance (about a mile), flagging down a passing vehicle is very common, especially for transportation to or from the cabinas outside town. Signs for **bicycle rental** abound; also ask at Jocelyn's pulpería, across from the bus stop—they may have killer mountain bikes. Check out the bike before you agree to rent it; quality varies widely. Full-day rental is about $4.

WHERE TO SLEEP

➤ **UNDER $10** • **Hotel Puerto Viejo.** This three-story, Swiss Family Robinson tree house is the tallest building in town and the natural destination for budget travelers. Rooms vary in size, but all cost $4 per person except for two large rooms with private baths that go for $11 and $15 in the low season, $15 and $23 in the high season. Most of the singles are cave-like but clean, and the second-floor doubles are well lit and airy. Mike and Amy, a totally nice couple from Santa Cruz, California, manage the place and run the restaurant downstairs (awesome French toast). *From the bus stop, follow the beach road to the crossroads by the little park. Take the road right, past Soda Tamara, heading toward the hills, about 200 meters. 23 rooms, some with bath. Luggage storage, laundry, restaurant, massage.*

Kiskidee. It's a muddy hike in the wet season, but at least you're in the wild for cheap. The hostel-like bunk beds in communal rooms with shared bathrooms go for under $4 a night per person. For less than $1 extra, you can use the well-equipped kitchen. Cook up some tender chayote and kick back in a hammock. Veterans of the albergue say a flashlight is a must for the walk home at night. *From the middle of the far end of the football pitch (i.e., soccer field), follow the path (look for the sign) about 500 meters up.*

➤ **UNDER $20 • Hotel Pura Vida.** If you've had it up to your ears with mud, sweat, and sand, the Pura Vida has some of the nicest rooms for the money in town. Cross the line into tropical elegance. $18 doubles are luxuriously large, well-screened, and all have a ceiling fan and sink in the room. Communal bathrooms are clean and modern. *From the center road, follow the signs, in the middle of town. 7 rooms, none with bath. Luggage storage, laundry, wheelchair access.*

➤ **CAMPGROUNDS •** Just past the **Salsa Brava Cabinas** on the road out of town is a grassy area where you can pitch your tent for about $1.50 per night. Ask for Miss Trish. The folks at Hotel Puerto Viejo will also let you camp in the backyard and/or use the showers for a minimal fee.

FOOD The ultimate budget food is at **Miss Sam's** (off the center road, up the road from Hotel Puerto Viejo), who sells heaping casados for $2.50 and a sizeable half order for $1.50 She also has tasty gingerbread. **Stanford's** (on the road that hugs the coast just outside town) is a restaurant by day and disco by night; it serves a huge vegetarian plate for $2. **Johnny's** (on the ocean street, across from the police station) is the place for cheap Chinese food. **Baker's** (next to Taberna Popo/El Zarpe on the ocean road) serves up tasty fried chicken for $2.50. Grab a beer next door while he prepares your dinner. On Sundays, he may cook up the traditional coconut-flavored rice and beans. **Coral** (off the center road in the middle of town) has breakfast or filling dinners of homemade pizza from $4 to $8. **The Garden,** up the road, serves Asian, Caribbean, and vegetarian food for $5–$8 a meal.

Soda Tamara. This red, gold, and green restaurant is very popular with travelers who come for rice and beans every day of the week. The heaping plates come with a choice of meat, chicken, fish, or egg for about $4, or try fried fish with patacones (plantain) for about the same. The desserts are scrumptious: Tender *pudín de maiz* (sweet, moist corn cake) or brownies are about $1. *On the central road, near the beach road intersection within sight of the water. Currently open 7 AM–9 PM, closed Tuesday and when business is slow.*

AFTER DARK After a hard day's surf and sun, the survivors swell Stanford's (just outside town on the ocean road) to bob to reggae or grind to hot soca. Farther from town on the same road is **Bambu,** a restaurant with more drinking and less dancing. At Johnny's, in town on the beach, people sway to tropical tunes or mellow with a beer. **Taberna Popo** (a.k.a. El Zarpe) faces the Caribbean on the ocean road. This is the place to do some serious cultural contemplation, drinking a couple of cuba libres to the sound of slapping dominoes and the light show of a mute TV.

OUTDOOR ACTIVITIES The Caribbean **surf** is the focus December–March and June–August. The famed Salsa Brava, near Stanford's, is for the skilled, who risk getting pounded on the reef. Drop by the Hotel Puerto Viejo for wax, board rental (boogie boards are $4 a day and surfboards $8), and excellent advice. Take locals' warnings about the strong surf and rip currents to heart. Swimmers are advised to stay away from the beach break, the rocky beach on the way to Punta Uva. Instead, try near the wrecked barge by the road to the highway.

NEAR PUERTO VIEJO

PUNTA UVA AND MANZANILLO Along the coast southeast from Puerto Viejo stretch several beautiful, less-visited beaches. The two closest beaches to Puerto Viejo are **Playa Cocles** (1 mile) and **Playa Chiquita** (4 kilometers [2½ miles]). About 6½ kilometers (4 miles) from town, down a road canopied by hibiscus shrubs, is the private white-sand harbor of **Punta Uva.** Manzanillo is about 3 kilometers (2 miles) farther down. A number of locals rent out cabinas, though not all of them are marked. Ask around and you might luck into the perfect beach bungalow. Along the road in the Punta Uva area, **Selven's Cabins** has doubles with communal bath for about $10. Across the street and up the hill, **Naturales** sells fresh vegetable and fruit fare. Before Punta Uva, **Soda Aquarius** serves cheap light meals and baked goods, and the friendly couple will be able to direct you to nearby cabinas. In Manzanillo, **Cabinas Maxi** has doubles for about $14, but you may be able to find a cheaper place if you ask around. Transportation is limited; a combination of bus and hitching will get you there and back. Buses running past all these beaches to Manzanillo pass through Puerto Viejo at 7:30 PM and 3:30 PM; they depart Manzanillo just before 7 AM and about 4 PM. Renting a bike for excursions to the closer beaches is also an idea (*see* Getting Around in Puerto Viejo, *above*).

BRIBRI Bribri appears little more than a glorified crossroads, but this small town about 32 kilometers (20 miles) from the Panamanian border is an important economic, legal, and social center for nearby indigenous reservations. Here you'll find government buildings, local police, a church, the only hospital in the Talamanca area, and public phones, as well as a couple of basic restaurants and places to stay (the **Picolino** is recommended by a local).

About 5,000 original Costa Ricans live in the 5,000-hectare (12,355-acre) Bribri reservation. Most of the residents subsistence-farm and raise plantains for export to the rest of Costa Rica and even Nicaragua. Many Bribri keep a traditional way of life and participate in the preservation of their language and culture: Schools are bilingual, and the local radio features programs in Bribri. However, only those blessed with exceptional personal and cultural skills should consider visiting. This is not a place where the "oooh, look at the happy primitive people" attitude will go over well.

You might need a permit to enter the reservations, especially if you plan on staying for a long time or doing major fieldwork. People from the area say it's not a problem if travelers want to hike around on the public roads. Ask for permission to set up camp. You might even find someone willing to give you a lift, rent you a horse, or cook you a meal. There is a pulpería in **Shirroles,** the town at the end of the bus line. A few daily buses to Bribri pass through Cahuita and Puerto Viejo (*see* Coming and Going in each town). The bus to Shirroles, which runs through many of the reservation towns, leaves shortly after these buses arrive.

TO PANAMA If you want to cross into Panamá at **Sixaola** (to **Guabito**), pray you go on a rainy day. From Bribri to the border, it's banana plantation for days, in a dust storm par excellence. Most travelers cross at Paso Canoa in the south, but coming here is way low-key; if you don't stop in at the little (possibly *still* unmarked) immigration office when you cross, they probably won't even notice. The border is supposed to be open 7 AM–11 AM and 1 PM–5 PM. You may be asked for a bus ticket out of the country, which can be bought in San José; ask the Panamanian consulate for the latest border regulations (tel. 25–0667, open weekdays 8 AM–noon).

Buses to Puerto Viejo/Cahuita/Limón depart Sixaola at 5 AM, 8 AM, 10 AM, and 3 PM (**Transportes MEPE,** tel. 58–15–72). Buses to San José depart at 5 AM and 2:30 PM (**Transportes MEPE,** tel. 21–05–24); the six-hour ride costs about $5. From Puerto Viejo, buses to Sixaola leave before 6 AM, 11 AM, and 2 PM; from Cahuita, at about 6:30 AM, 11:30 AM, 2:30 PM, and 5:30 PM; and from Limón, four buses run daily (*see* Limón Coming and Going, *above,* for address of terminal).

Southwestern Costa Rica

Travelers usually come to the southern region for a feeling of accomplishment—to climb the highest mountain in the country, Cerro Chirripó, or surf the longest left-breaking wave in the world at Playa Pavones. Otherwise, not many people visit this part of Costa Rica. Cheap places to stay and eat exist, but it's a hassle to find them in advance, since many have no phone, no address, no set hours, and no English-speakers. Make the effort—you'll find vast, untapped, and untouristed stretches of tropical wilderness, silk-sandy beaches, and sweeping valleys. If you're a woman traveling solo, you'll get stared at like you just grew a second head (women by themselves are the rarest type of traveler, plus there's that *machísmo* thing going on), but the locals haven't grown sick of tourism yet, so they're really nice.

Chirripo

A recent fire left much of **Parque Nacional Chirripó** either charred or in the scraggly regrowth phase. The real reason for taking the 1½-hour bus ride from San Isidro (*see above*) is to climb **Cerro Chirripó,** the highest point in Costa Rica. You could scale a different summit each day for a week if you wanted to, but if you only have time for the big one, budget two days with an overnight stay at the refugio, which is the only place you're allowed to sleep within the park. Remember to bring warm clothes: You're climbing 12,500 feet and it's cold and windy. You won't be the only foreigner here: During the dry season, nearly three-fourths of the visitors are North American, German, and French. The bus to the park drops you off at **San Gerardo de Rivas,** a little town where every other soda and hotel is named Chirripó. You need to stop here to register and pay admission at the park's information center.

Whatever else you do here, you'll be hiking. A marked trail takes you to the refugio (6- to 12-hour hike). It's steep, but even beginners can make it if they take it nice and easy. A bonanza of hikes and climbs starts at the refugio. The most popular one goes straight to the top of Cerro Chirripó (2–3 hours), but you should also check out the ones to **Laguna Ditkebi** and **Cerro Ventisqueros.** The **Crestones** climb is popular among expert rock climbers. Only well-trained, advanced, super-serious climbers should attempt this climb.

BASICS The **visitor information center** in San Gerardo is way more helpful than the one in San Isidro. You have to register here to enter the park, and it's not a bad idea to call up to one month ahead to make reservations for the refugio. Buy the trail map; it's only 2¢ and it shows you where the only potable water fountain is. *Up the road from the bus stop, look for flag and sign, tel. 33–41–60. Admission: $1 per day. Open daily 5–5.*

COMING AND GOING The only way to get to the park is by bus or taxi from San Isidro, unless of course you happen to have a 4x4 at your disposal. It's an interesting ride—you'll pass lots of little mountain villages. The bus leaves San Isidro from the mercado central at 5 AM and 2 PM and returns to San Isidro from San Gerardo at 7 AM and 4 PM ($1 each way). Taxis (red jeeps) hang around the parque central in San Isidro during daylight hours. A ride to Chirripó costs $13.

Orotina
San Ramón
Zarcero
San Miguel
Tárcoles
Cinchona
Tárcoles
Atenas
HEREDIA
*RESERVA
BIOLÓGICA
CARARA*
Jacó
Santiago
de Puriscal
Heredia
*Playa
Hermosa*
Guápiles
SAN JOSÉ
San José
Asserrí
LIMÓN
Parrita
San Pablo
de León Cortes
Cartago
PUNTARENAS
Pacayas
Santa María
Quepos
Turrialba
*PARQUE NACIONAL
MANUEL ANTONIO*
Copey
CARTAGO
*PACIFIC
OCEAN*
Dominical
San Isidro
de el
General
Herradura
*PARQUE
NACIONAL
CHIRRIPÓ*
*Playa
Hermosa*
San Gerardo
de Rivas
(Chirripó)
**Cerro
Chirripó**
Uvita
Fila Costeña
LIMÓN
*Bahía
de
Coronado*
*Valle de
El General*
*PARQUE
INTERNACIONAL
LA AMISTAD*
Ujarrás
CORDILLERA DE TALAMANCA
*Bahía
Drake*
Marenco
Drake
Salitre
Palmar
Sur
Palmar
Norte
Buenos
Aires
San Pedrillo
Sierpe
*Playa
Llorana*
*PARQUE
NATIONAL
CORCOVADO*
*RESERVA
INDÍGENA
BORNEA*
Paso
Real
Los Patos
Grande de Térraba
Sirena
La Palma
*Golfo
Dulce*
*Valle de
Coto Brus*
*Península
de Osa*
Carate
PANAMA
Puerto
Jiménez
Golfito
Rio
Claro
San Vito
*Playa
Cacao*
**Jardin
Botánico
Wilson**
*Playa
Zancudo*
*Valle de
Coto Colorado*
Cuidad
Neily
Playa Pavones

0		20 miles
0		30 km

WHERE TO SLEEP AND EAT You can't set up your own camp within the park. Your only option is the refugio, which takes 6–12 hours to reach on foot. The shelter sleeps 40 people, dorm-style, in bunk beds. It's $2 a night and you can stay five nights max. Stock up on basic food items at the market next to Cabinas Chirripó before you start hiking to the refugio.

You can stay in one of three hotels in San Gerardo before or after the Chirripó experience; each serves food and all are cheap (around $3). They share one phone number (tel. 71–04–33, ext. 106), so know whom to ask for before you call. **Cabinas San Gerardo** (ask for Lesmes) is the first and worst one you'll see coming from the info center. **Cabinas Chirripó** (in front of Plaza de Deportes; ask for Luis) has small but clean rooms. **Posada El Descanso Chirripó** (near Soda Chirripó; ask for Francisco) is the best of the bunch, with friendly management. Feel free (it's free) to set up camp in the general area around the information center.

OUTDOOR ACTIVITIES Francisco, of Posada El Descanso Chirripó, rents **horses** to take into the park for $24 a day. For $4 more, you can hire a guide who will schlepp your gear. You're going to want to stay in the park for a couple days, so keep in mind that besides the daily fee, you'll have to pay extra for your guide—and your horse—to eat and sleep, too. Just remember that you can't camp anywhere, so your rides have to lead you back to the refugio before dark. If you don't have big bank but want to do the horse thing, fork over $2 an hour to Francisco and explore the area outside the park on horseback.

Herradura

On your way to San Gerardo, look *carefully* when you pass the fork in the road ½ mile from the town. Notice the semi-hidden HERRADURA sign. Follow it. Hardly anyone knows about this teeny village and its best-kept secret: **thermal baths**, which are a bitch to get to but worth any possible frustration. Follow the tiny sign-posted dirt road up the mountain; when the road curves to the left, look for a little bridge over the river and a sign that says AGUAS TERMALES A 300 METROS. This sign marks a steep gravel path to the baths. You'll pass a house where you have to pay 50¢ to use the pools.

Herradura's other attraction is a non-IYHF hostel, **Albergue El Quetzal Dorado,** on a private ranch. It's on the mountain and the only way to get there is by walking uphill for over an hour. Up to 45 people at a time can stay in the dorm for $3 a night; if the hostel is anywhere near full, expect to wait to use one of the two toilets. The owners run a little soda, too. *Tel. 71–04–33, ext. 109; ask for the Vargas brothers. From the sign for the baths, trudge up the road to the hostel sign and iron gate.*

Smokey the Bear Says…

Chirripó doesn't look like it used to. Nearly two-fifths of the park (1,700 hectares [4,200 acres]) was ravaged by a huge fire. Rangers think it started as a small brush fire caused by an improperly extinguished campfire. More than 100 volunteers and park employees fought the blaze to no avail. Finally, Nature finished what people started: Heavy rains put the fire out after six days of total destruction. No one was injured, but the park was closed for two months, and it's estimated that Chirripó might not be the same until the year 2007. Please be careful putting out your fires, wherever you are. Ask a ranger if you're not sure of the proper procedure.

Parque Internacional La Amistad

Amistad, also called by its acronym, PILA, is a huge chunk o' land belonging to the even bigger **Biospheric Conservation Reserve** (tel. 71–11–55), which includes Chirripó, Hitoy Cerere Biological Reserve, Wilson Botanical Gardens, and more than half a dozen other parks, gardens, and indigenous reserva-

> **"Even the rangers don't know what lies within Amistad's boundaries."**

tions. The park itself is way too big to even attempt to see fully, and most tourists and ticos stay away from it altogether because of its size and inaccessibility. The National Park Service doesn't recommend wandering around the park without being accompanied by someone familiar with it—but even the rangers don't know what lies within the park's boundaries. In 1990, Panamá got into the picture, donating an enormous piece of its land to Amistad (the name means "international friendship park"). Officials from the two countries work together to administer the park's resources.

If you're really stuck on the idea of exploring this place, entrance points include the indigenous towns of **Salitre** and **Ujarrás** (accessible from **Buenos Aires,** where buses heading to Palmar and San Isidro along the Interamerican Highway stop). Supposedly, the National Park Service has set up immigration checkpoints inside the park at **Coto Brus** and **Sabalito** for those wishing to enter the Panamá portion of the park. The rangers will probably tell you flat out not to go to Panamá; the terrain is seriously uncharted. If you decide to wander, do it responsibly (i.e., get a guide if you're not an extremely experienced trailblazer). If you get lost out here, you're royally screwed.

Golfito

Golfito is dirty but beautiful, lazy but scuzzy—and it's all the United Fruit Company's fault. Surrounded by steep, forested mountains on the gorgeous eastern shore of the Golfo Dulce, the town is exhilarating if you look at the view and depressing if you look at the people. Backpackers stop at Golfito en route to nearby hiking and surfing hot spots. But along the main street, out-of-work ticos spend hours in the myriad bars (latest count was 22 bars in ½ mile) that seem to be the only thriving industry, aside from crime and prostitution.

Early this century, the United Fruit Company's banana operation chose Golfito as a base, giving out jobs right and left. United left a decade ago, pushing the town into decline. Almost everybody in the town—those who want United Fruit to return and those who think it's the Great White Devil—blames the decline on the company's irresponsible departure. Hoping to attract industry to the region, the federal government recently declared the port a *depósito libre* (duty-free zone). Now, ticos come to Golfito to buy cheap appliances—then leave. So far, the town remains pretty decrepit.

Now a haven for new U.S. *emigrés,* Golfito is informally divided into two sections, the southern *el pueblo civil* (where the locals live) and the northern *la zona americana,* separated by a barren stretch of road. Almost all the budget hotels and restaurants (and, of course, bars) are in the pueblo civil; high prices characterize the "American zone." For dancing, try **Disko Loco** at Samoa del Sur (in between pueblo civil and zona americana, tel. 75–02–33, call for open hours). Admission is $2.

BASICS In the pueblo civil, **Banco de Costa Rica** (next to the gas station, tel. 75–03–23) can exchange your dollars, but you'll have to go to the other branch in the zona americana to trade American Express traveler's checks. The **post office** is across the street from the plaza de deportes, open weekdays from 7:30 to 5. The **hospital** (tel. 75–00–11) is in the zona americana. Call 75–03–97 for an **ambulance.**

A helpful visitor information center, called **Golfito Centro** (tel. 75–04–49), lies next to Hotel Costa Rica Surf. It's open weekdays 8–5, and Saturday 8–noon. Ask for Ron, a guy from New Jersey who's been here for 30 years. **Laundry** (open Mon.–Sat. 8:30 AM–12:30 PM, 1–5) is across the street from Restaurante La Eurekita (*see* Food, *below*).

COMING AND GOING

➢ **BY BUS** • Buses run from Neily to Golfito every 90 minutes or so. **Tracopa** (tel. 75–03–65) runs to and from San José (6–8 hours, $5); buses leave daily from la zona americana. Two buses leave daily for Pavones (3 hours) from the bus stop near the gas station. In town, use the urban bus that runs sporadically from the pueblo civil to the zona americana (15¢).

➢ **BY BOAT** • On Monday and Thursday–Saturday, a boat runs to Puerto Jiménez. **Burbujas de Amor** (name means love bubbles; tel. 75–04–72) charges $3 for the 1½-hour ride. Hire a taxi boat to go to the beaches: To Zancudo, you should pay about $8; to Cacao, $1. Boats leave from the dock on the other side of Hotel Golfito (*see* Where to Sleep, *below*).

➢ **BY PLANE** • **TravelAir** (tel. 75–63–24) flies daily from San José to Golfito. Call in advance to book a flight that will cost you around $50. **SANSA** (tel. 75–63–53) is cheaper at $24 for the same flight. **VETSA** (tel. 75–06–07) has a scenic 10-minute ride from Golfito to Puerto Jiménez for $8.

WHERE TO SLEEP

➢ **UNDER $10** • **Hotel Delfina.** Standard double rooms (cabinas) with fans and bath cost $9. Cheaper, dirtier, and noisier rooms (*habitaciones,* which sleep 3–4) run $3 per bed. *Next to Restaurante Palenque on main road, tel. 75–00–43. 7 cabinas, all with bath, and 17 habitaciones, none with bath. Luggage storage, 11 PM curfew.*

Hotel Golfito. The best thing about this place is the tiny balcony overlooking the gulf. Spend your evening hanging out with other guests drinking, smoking, or whatever. Doubles are $8. *In front of the gas station next to Banco de Costa Rica, tel. 75–00–47. 14 rooms, all with bath. Luggage storage.*

➢ **UNDER $15** • **Hotel Costa Rica Surf.** Try to stay at this hotel, which is within walking distance of the dock, Golfito Centro, and just about every bar. One of its two restaurants is inside and the other is upstairs on the balcony. Doubles cost $11.50. *Off the highway in pueblo civil, tel. 75–00–34. 25 rooms, some with bath. Luggage storage.*

Hotel Del Cerro. The rooms are exceptionally clean, and it's probably the safest place in town. If you don't mind being farther away from the bars of the pueblo civil, stay here. Doubles with bath are $14. *Along highway next to electric company, tel. 75–00–06. 17 rooms, some with bath. Luggage storage, restaurant.*

FOOD The balcony sodas that overlook the highway and the gulf are cheap and pretty. **Restaurante La Eurekita** (tel. 75–09–16) is a good one. It's open 6 AM–10 PM weekdays, 6 AM–midnight on weekends. For Chinese food, try **Restaurante Hong Kong** (across from Golfito Centro), especially if you like *camarones* (shrimp). A filling portion costs less than $5. To treat yourself to a really good steak for about $10 per person, head out to **Las Gaviotas** (2 mi from town center on highway toward Río Claro, tel. 75–00–62). It's open daily 6 AM–10 PM. For a cheaper meal (less than $5) with gringo company, check out **Restaurante El Balcón** (at Hotel Costa Rica Surf, tel. 75–00–34), open Monday–Saturday, 7:30 AM–midnight.

NEAR GOLFITO

PLAYAS ZANCUDO Y PAVONES The beaches at Zancudo and Pavones are the closest the area gets to tourist attractions; they're not usually thronged except on national holidays, but don't expect solitude. It's easier to get to **Zancudo,** about 16 kilometers (10 miles) south of Golfito. Once there, you can swim in the warm water, pay major bucks to go sport fishing, or veg on the beach. Zancudo means mosquito, an annoyingly apt name. Also be careful of the thousands (seriously!) of crabs and other sea beasties that crawl along the beach. They're harmless, but it's good to know they exist before they show up in your bathing suit.

Hotel Los Almendros/Roy's Place has the best cabinas in Zancudo. For $20 per double, you'll sleep comfortably. Menus in the hotel restaurant don't have prices, so ask before ordering or you'll get rooked. Call 75–05–15 to make a reservation. **Sport fishing** has hit Zancudo big-time. A day's outing costs over $250. Call **Zancudo Pacific Charters** at 88–50–83 if you're interested. Locals in Golfito will offer to show you both beaches for free, but they'll ask you to pay for the boat ride.

Pavones, a few miles south of Zancudo, is the subject of worldwide surf lore; it's claimed to have the longest left wave in the world. Waves depend on the presence of offshore storms, so check beforehand or you might get stuck paddling your board all day. If you come at the right time, the bitchin' tubes and the hard-core crowd questing for the perfect wave are enough to get you humming the tune to "Wipeout!". Expect to run into Gidget and the Big Kahuna at the only place to stay, which charges $3 per person. Use the radio at the gas station in Golfito to call **Chico** at the Pavones *cantina* to make reservations. Take the taxi boat from Golfito (*see* Coming and Going, *above*).

OTHER ISLANDS AND BEACHES Check out **Captain Tom's Place** on **Playa Cacao,** across the bay from Golfito. Tom salvaged a ship and converted it into a restaurant and the **Shipwreck Hotel**—it looks like something out of *Robinson Crusoe.* Pay $4 for a bed or hammock, as long as you're not prone to motion sickness; hammocks swing aboard the docked boat. The restaurant serves cheap "jungle burgers" (Tom's term for hamburger). The atmosphere's casual, and the decor has a funky maritime theme. Take the taxi boat from Golfito for about $1.

Captain Cheech, a cute, adventurous boy, will whisk you off in a boat to his father's vanilla farm on **Isla de Golfito,** where you'll scramble through the forest, running smack into toucans and howler monkeys. Cheech, who speaks English well, carries a huge machete and makes a big show of taming the jungle right in front of you. Arrange the $10 tour at Golfito Centro.

Puerto Jiménez

On the western shore of Golfo Dulce, Puerto Jiménez is a less developed, more genuinely tico town than Golfito and is the true commercial center of the Península de Osa—it's a base for the logging and gold-mining industries. If you're headed toward Corcovado, it's a sage idea to use Jiménez as a starting point. Since the town itself isn't all that jumping, your best bet is to stay a night or two at *La Tierra de Milagros* (The Land of Miracles, *see below*). Use your free hours to swim in the gulf, even at night.

BASICS Banco Nacional de Costa Rica (tel. 78–50–20) is off the main street. The **tourist information office** (tel. 78–50–73), inside Restaurante Carolina, is open weekdays 8 AM–noon, 1–6, and Saturday 8–2. The **medical clinic** (tel. 78–50–61) is near the plaza de deportes. For advice on how to make it through Corcovado, go to **Area de Conservación Osa** (tel. 78–50–36), next to Banco Nacional.

COMING AND GOING Daily buses go from San Isidro to Jiménez (5 hours). For the return trip, they leave daily from **Restaurante Carolina** (tel. 77–30–10). **Burbujas de Amor** (tel. 75–04–72) ferries people between Puerto Jiménez and Golfito ($3). The dock is near the center of town. You can fly here from Golfito with **VETSA** daily for $8 (tel. 75–06–07). **TACSA** (tel. 78–50–47) planes also fly daily. Check with both airlines for availability and fares. VETSA also flies from Puerto Jiménez to Carate at Parque Nacional Corcovado for $8. The airstrip is close to the shore and Cabinas Los Manglares.

WHERE TO SLEEP AND EAT Sleep at **Cabinas Los Manglares** if you're coming by plane (150 meters from airport, tel. 78–50–02). Doubles cost $10, all rooms have baths, and it sleeps 22. Use **Brisas del Mar** if you're coming by boat (near port, tel. 78–50–12). Doubles at this 31-guest hotel cost $8. Eat at **Agua Luna** (tel. 78–51–08, open daily 9 AM–midnight) or **Vista Mar** (open daily 11 AM–midnight, no tel.) for great seafood at affordable prices—$3 and up. Both restaurants are on the water with fantastic views; they're also happening night spots. For good Chinese food, eat at **Jogua Restaurante** (open weekdays 11 AM–3, 6 PM–11, weekends 11 AM–1 AM), near Cabinas Los Manglares on your way to the main street.

NEAR PUERTO JIMENEZ

LA TIERRA DE MILAGROS Founded by Edy, a woman from Florida who refuses to pay taxes to a government that she believes pollutes and destroys our planet, La Tierra de Milagros—The Land of Miracles—is a communal-type place composed of 10 huts without electricity. Meals are all-vegetarian, visitors share cooking, and most food is grown in the organic garden. At night, people read tarot cards, give massages, and listen to Native (North) American music or perform full-moon ceremonies. Edy charges $10 a night per person and $3–$4 for meals. It might be crowded December–April, so call 78–50–73 (the tourist into center in Puerto Jiménez) to book a hut or get info on long-term volunteering. It's about a half hour (21 kilometers [13 miles]) south of Puerto Jiménez by taxi ($15). You can also take the cargo truck to Carate (*see* Corcovado, *below*).

Parque Nacional Corcovado

On the southwestern tip of the Península de Osa, Corcovado National Park is a blast— if you like walking. Budget at least three days to walk from one side of the park to the other, but remember that it's a bitch just getting to the park. During your trek through the virgin rain forest, you'll see animals you've never seen before (unless you have a pet tapir at home). Corcovado gets an *enormous* amount of rainfall during the wet season, and everything is alive and busy. However, the trails are hard to walk on and you will definitely get soaked, either from the rain or by crossing one of the shoulder-high rivers, some of which are impassable if the tide is too high. Only experienced backpackers should go solo.

BASICS Don't bypass the **visitor information center** in Puerto Jiménez (Area de Conservación Osa, next to Banco Nacional). The staff can assist you daily from 7:30 to 6; they close 11 AM–1 PM for lunch. Register with them for safety and identification purposes. Make food and lodging arrangements here if you're not camping. Park admission is $1 per day.

COMING AND GOING It's easiest to get to Corcovado from one of two entrance points, La Palma to the north and La Leona to the south of Puerto Jiménez. Buses to La Palma and cargo trucks to Carate (the closest stop to La Leona) leave Puerto Jiménez from the tourist info office. Call **Transportes Cirilo** (tel. 78–50–95) for more info on the $4, three-hour trip. **VETSA** (tel. 75–06–07) flies to Carate for $8. Planes also serve the park station at Sirena but the prices are sky-high. Entering the park from Bahía Drake is feasible, but harder: Take a bus from Palmar Norte to Sierpe, and from there take a boat to Drake (*see* Bahía Drake section, *below*). You can also hire a taxi ($36) from Puerto Jiménez to Carate.

GETTING AROUND Important fact number one: You're not doing any swimming in the ocean—it's shark territory. Important fact number two: You're going to do a *prodigious* amount of walking. It's not really strenuous, but it's long. The walk along the beach from Carate to the La Leona entrance (before you even get to the park proper) takes 45 minutes. The park service has *puestos* (posts) at La Leona, Sirena, Los Patos, and San Pedrillo; you can see most of the park by walking from post to post. From La Leona to the Sirena station takes 6–8 hours, and it's a nice walk. You'll meander along river banks, past waterfalls, and, if you want, jump in and cool off at Río Madrigal. From Sirena, you can hike all day up and down hills to Los Patos, or, if you're up to it, attempt the 13-mile hike on Playa Llorona to San Pedrillo. You have to time your crossings of the three rivers along the trail (check the tide tables at Sirena) if you want to make it to San Pedrillo before dark. Park rangers budget at least 10 hours for this most difficult hike. To exit the park from San Pedrillo, find a boat to Marenco or Bahía Drake; call Emiliano (tel. 71–23–36). From Los Patos to La Palma, outside the park, is a three-hour hike. Trails are narrow, but in good condition.

WHERE TO SLEEP AND EAT Since it would be added torture to hoist food and bedding on your back, you're much better off staying at any of the puestos. It's $2 to sleep there, breakfast costs $3.50, and lunch and dinner are $4.50 each. You must make reservations at the Puerto Jiménez office (tel. 78–50–36) if you plan to sleep or eat at any of the posts. In the dry season, you have to notify the park service a couple of months in advance to get a space.

The cheapest way to go, if you can deal with it, is to camp. You're allowed to set up your tent near the puestos and use their "sanitary facilities" for free. You really shouldn't camp anywhere but the puestos, unless you want to be awakened by some animal wanting to share your sleeping bag. You could also find yourself floating in the river or the ocean if you underestimate the tides.

NEAR CORCOVADO

BAHIA DRAKE If a tico looks perplexed when you ask her/him about Drake Bay, try pronouncing it the Spanish way: Dra-kay. Named after Sir Francis Drake, who is supposedly buried hereabouts, this remote bay on the western edge of the Península de Osa is probably the most beautiful place in the region. The most economical lodge is **Albergue Jinetes de Osa** (on the bay, tel. 53–69–09 or 71–23–36) at $25 per person, including three meals. You can also rent horses for $20 for a half-day outing with Pedro, the bilingual owner of the albergue. Catch a boat to Drake from the dock at Sierpe, 20 minutes east. The cheapest ride is $8, but they'll try to rip you off for up to $80—there's a sucker born every minute.

PANAMA

8

By Laurence Colman

Panamá may be the most overlooked travel spot on earth. No one seems interested in visiting, and Central American backpackers usually don't include Panamá on their itineraries. The way most people picture the country—rife with high rises, fast-food, and U.S.-instigated political turmoil—just doesn't make for a dream vacation. True, Panamá City differs little from the Western urban melee you're probably trying to escape, but Panamá is more than just a city and a canal. You'd be hard-pressed to find a jungle wilderness less altered by human meddling than the vast Darién Gap in eastern Panamá, or tropical shores more striking than Panamá's Caribbean coast. You could exhaust yourself reading anthropological surveys and not find a group of hunter-gatherers more removed from Western "civilization" than the Chocós of Darién, or a people with more exquisite artistry than the Cunas of San Blas. In addition, Panamá is home to a wildly diverse population, melding indigenous, Spanish, African, U.S. gringo, Chinese, Indian, and other cultures.

Whatever the reason behind Panamá's low tourist profile, the result is a country of abundant interest to budget travelers, with a well-developed infrastructure, good public transportation, and relatively few health risks. Panamanians themselves rarely explore the wealth of travel opportunities in their own country, so you really will have some places entirely to yourself. In over two months of travel through all parts of Panamá, I encountered 15 foreign travelers—*total!*

Panamá is probably most famous for its Canal linking the Atlantic and the Pacific. Built by the U.S., it truly is one of the world's great engineering marvels and worth a visit in its own right. The Canal and Panamá's role as the crossroads between North and South America have prompted tourist agencies to label the country *"el puente del mundo"* (the world's bridge). While horribly overused, the title is not inappropriate. Ever since Balboa first "discovered" the Pacific Ocean by crossing the Panamanian isthmus, Panamá has witnessed an almost-continuous stream of foreigners coming to use the "bridge."

What does "Panamá" mean? Current theory has it that the word comes from an ancient native language and means "abundance of fish." Some of the indigenous Cuna, though, think it's a Spanish bastardization of their phrase "pa na ba," which means "very far away." They say when the conquistadors asked the Cunas where their tribe lived, they replied "pa na ba." The name stuck.

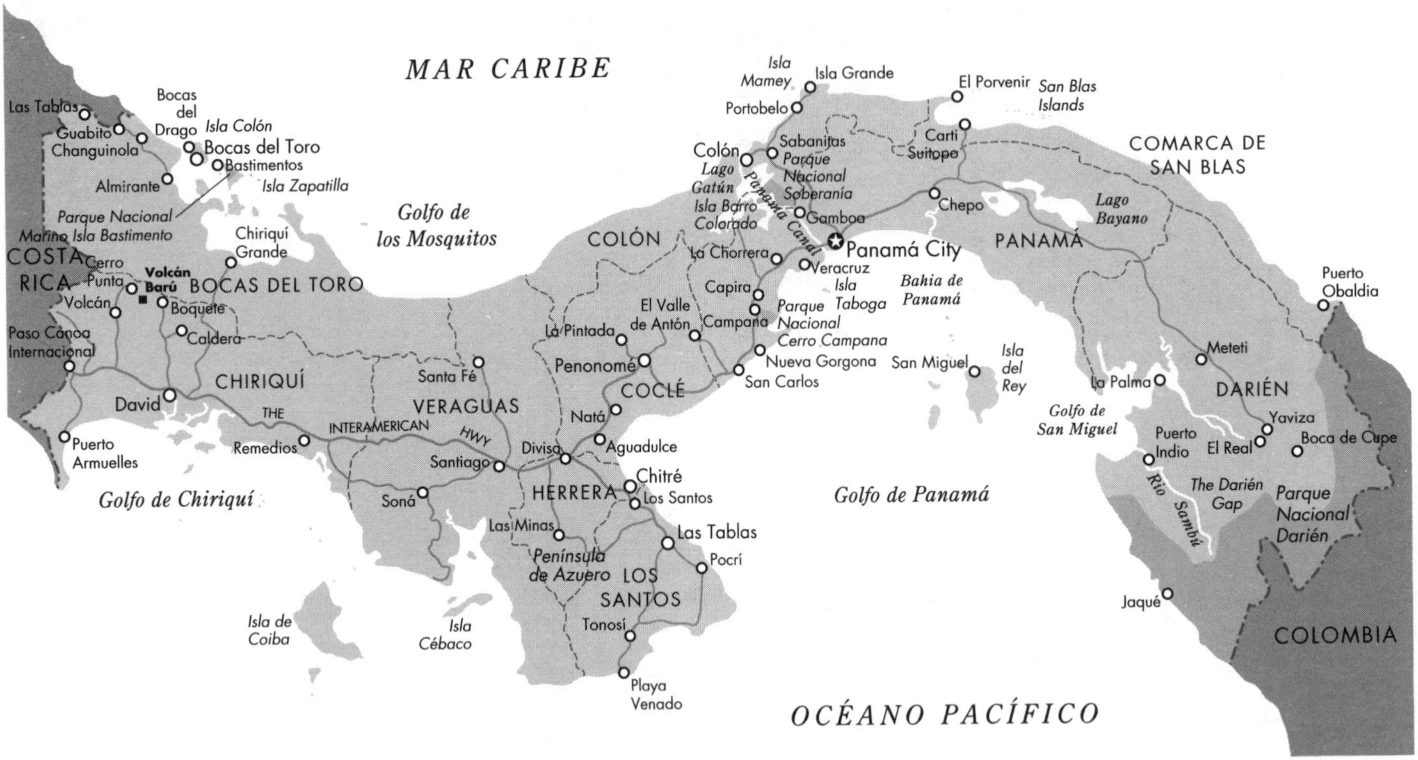

Panamá

PANAMA

On the one hand, much of Panamá's progress can be attributed to its role as a continental bridge: It has the highest per-capita income, highest foreign investment, and the most highly developed economic infrastructure of any country in the region. But its location also has its drawbacks. After all, what do you do with a bridge? You walk on it, and Panamá has had more than its share of getting trampled under the feet of foreign states. Among the tramplers of Panamá, you find the usual crowd: Spanish explorers claiming the land in the name of their God and a distant king and queen; French entrepreneurs shouting *"merde"* as their slave workers dropped dead by the thousands from malaria and yellow fever; and one President Teddy Roosevelt, who'd be damned if he'd let a minor concern like national sovereignty stand in the way of *his* Canal.

The Spanish came to rob and convert, and they were successful on both counts. We can only guess what amazing indigenous treasures were melted down and shipped to Spain as booty. And we need only look at the thousands of churches to see the effect of Spanish missionaries. The French came to build a canal. Ferdinand de Lesseps, of Suez fame, hoped to build a similar sea-level canal across Panamá, but difficult terrain and devastating mosquito-borne diseases bankrupted the venture.

Of all Panamá's visitors, though, the United States distinguishes itself as champion usurper amid a competitive field. Since 1850, the United States has intervened militarily in Panamá 18 times, most recently to remove their wayward son, Noriega, and install Guillermo Endara. The U.S. government has exerted such influence over Panamá's development that in many ways Panamá resembles a U.S. colony more than an independent nation. The national currency is dollars, and the northeastern province of Bocas del Toro is largely owned by the Chiquita banana company. Panamanians have also embraced U.S. consumerism: Nike shoes and all things Simpsons and/or Teenage Mutant Ninja Turtles are the dope, and Big Mac is the food of choice. And then there are the troops. Officially supposed to occupy only the Canal and a 5-mile zone around it, the troops have taken more liberties with Panamanian sovereignty since the 1989 invasion of Panamá (*see* info box, *below*), and it's not unusual to see them on the streets of Panamá City's hardest-hit communities, like El Chorillo and Panamá Viejo.

It was the United States, moreover, that fomented Panamá's independence from Colombia in 1903, after Colombia refused a proposal that would have granted the United States control over a three-mile zone on either side of the Canal. The U.S. then signed a treaty with the new government of Panamá, represented by Philippe Bunau-Varilla, a Frenchman left over from de Lesseps's bankrupt canal project. The treaty was negotiated without a word of Spanish spoken and passed into law without a single Panamanian signature. The treaty granted the United States 8 kilometers (5 miles) on either side of the Canal "in perpetuity" (i.e., forever), and the right to occupy lands outside the Canal Zone whenever such action was deemed "vital to the maintenance and defense of the waterway." Panamanian opposition to the "in perpetuity" clause grew steadily, and anti-American sentiment reached a head in 1964 with a series of riots and the temporary suspension of diplomatic relations. In 1978, President Carter finally signed a treaty gradually relinquishing control of the Canal to Panamá—a process scheduled for completion on December 31, 1999.

Despite the heavy U.S. presence, Panamá is still very much a Latin country. This is especially evident in the ever-present machismo of Panamá's men, who stare at women shamelessly, with a predatory look made more comical by how seriously they take themselves. Women travelers, especially if they're alone or blonde, can expect to be ogled and to receive comments. Only once, though, did I see a guy pinch a Pana-

Most Panamanians view their country's abundant natural resources as infinite and indestructible, and the streets are, apparently, a convenient garbage can. With luck, the Panamanian government will take its cue from Costa Rica and implement measures to preserve what they now have—some of the most beautiful stretches of nature on earth.

The 1989 U.S. Invasion:
Operation Just (Be)Cause

In December 1989, the Bush Administration sent troops into Panamá for part of "Operation Just Cause." Official U.S. figures show 23 U.S. soldiers and three U.S. civilians dead, along with 324 Panamanian soldiers and 202 Panamanian civilians. Unofficial estimates of civilian dead run to 4,000. Thousands were wounded and some 20,000 Panamanians were left homeless.

The target was General Manuel Noriega, the infamous "Panamanian strongman" as dubbed by the U.S. press (his Panamanian nickname was "Pineapple Face"). Ironically, the first stages of Noriega's career were nurtured by the U.S. He took intelligence courses at Fort Bragg, and did contractual stuff for the CIA for years. When Noriega became president in 1981, the U.S. wanted him to keep track of Nicaragua; some say he even ran arms to the contras.

In the mid-1980s, Noriega's blatant drug-trafficking became less tolerable as the "War on Drugs" intensified. In 1986, the U.S. broke with Noriega and supported a coup attempt, but failed to oust him. The last straw was the national election in May 1989. Apparently, the U.S-supported candidate, Guillermo Endara, won the election by a two-thirds majority. Noriega annulled the results, and some of his boys viciously beat up Endara and his running mates on TV. In December, Noriega proclaimed himself head of state, and someone in the Panamanian Defense Force killed a U.S. soldier. The U.S. invaded soon after. Official reasons were "promotion of democracy, protection of the Canal, and prosecution of Noriega for drug-trafficking." However, many believe Bush was trying to shuck off the wimp image; or, Bush knew that Noriega might squeal about how his drug-trafficking had been overseen by the then-Bush-headed CIA.

On the fifth day of the invasion, Noriega fled to the Vatican embassy in Panamá City for asylum. He surrendered only after U.S. troops blasted rock music for two weeks. On January 3, 1991, Noriega apparently decided incarceration was preferable to one more chorus of "I fought the law and the law won!" The Panamanian strongman was convicted of drug-trafficking and now lives in a cell in Florida.

Today, Panamá is struggling to rebuild. Many are happy to be rid of Noriega. As Diego, a Panamanian student, told me, "Noriega was the worst fucking motherfucker in Panamá." But resentment toward the U.S. for how the invasion was handled still runs high. Many Panamanians want U.S. restitution, calling for the release of political prisoners, removal of troops, and the release of information about mass graves. The United States was tried by the World Court for crimes against Panamá; the U.S. lost, but has yet to pay damages.

manian woman, and she reacted like it was unheard of. If you're a woman alone, stay away from hotels that attract prostitutes to avoid guilt by association. Despite the tropical heat and humidity, men will almost never wear shorts. You might even be denied access to government ministries if you're wearing shorts. Women, on the other hand, are permitted and enthusiastically encouraged to be as risqué as they like. This is a conservative place on the whole, but women can go out in miniskirts hardly distinguishable from a wide belt.

From all the beer advertising—beer companies sponsor just about everything in the country, and their logos and slogans will soon be permanently imprinted on your brain—you will quickly notice that Panamá is also a nation of drinkers. Even the tiniest pueblo has a cantina or two. But drinking is an almost entirely male-dominated sport; you'll be hard-pressed to find any cantina with a women's bathroom. Local women who work in bars may be assumed to be prostitutes. If you're worried about harassment in a cantina, drink in a restaurant instead—they usually feature stocked bars.

The Panamanian people are not as renowned for their hospitality as their neighbors in Costa Rica—even Panamanians admit that Costa Ricans are nicer. This reputation is largely the fault of inhabitants of the Panamá City/Colón area, where you do get that semi-hostile, big-city feeling. In Colón, in particular, crime against travelers is common. Also keep your wits about you in port or border towns such as Almirante and David, which see a lot of drug smuggling and higher crime rates. In the rest of the country, though, you'll be surprised by the warmth of the people, who are almost without exception *gente buena* (good people) leading the *pura vida* (pure life) where *todo es tranquilo* (everything's cool). In these rural areas the worst experience you'll probably have with a local is a heated debate over soccer teams. But use your common sense and leave that diamond tiara at home—rural or urban, many of the people of this country are poor.

BASICS

See Chapter 1 for important info pertaining to Panamá.

WHEN TO GO The dry season (November–April) is assumed to be the best time to visit Panamá, but the rains of *invierno* ("winter," April–November) aren't much of an inconvenience unless you're trying to get to the Darién Gap. There's no time of year when Panamá is overrun with tourists, but the dry season coincides with Panamanian school vacations, when resorts and beaches are at their most crowded. During winter, you may have to spend some time sitting at the window until the rains stop, but you shouldn't have a problem finding a room.

Two exceptions apply: the jungles of the Darién and the islands of Bocas del Toro. Darién is at its most lush during the rainy season, but the best time to go is immediately following the rainy season, when the jungles are still thick but the mud is more easily traversed. Bocas del Toro, in the northwest, actually goes through two dry/rainy cycles annually: February–April is dry, May–July is wet, August–October is dry, and November–January is wet. September is widely regarded as the best month to visit Bocas.

➤ **HOLIDAYS AND FESTIVALS** • In addition to the major Central American holidays (*see* Chapter 1, Basics), banks and shops are closed on the following days: Martyrs' Day, **January 9;** bank holidays, **February 15** and **April 1;** Labor Day, **May 1;** Anniversary of Panamá Viejo, **August 15;** Hispanic Days, **October 11–12;** Días de los Muertos y Santos, **November 2–4;** First Call for Independence, **November 10;** Independence Day, **November 28;** Mother's Day, **December 8.**

Carnaval is probably Panamá's biggest party, especially in Las Tablas on the Península de Azuero. Otherwise, Panamá goes crazy with minor festivals (*ferias*); you're bound to come across one sooner or later during your trip. Held in either April or January, the

Festival de Flores y Café is a groovy happening down in Boquete. Call the **dirección nacional de ferias** (tel. 62–0241) in Panamá City for more info.

MAIL A letter to the United States costs 35¢; to Europe or Australia, 45¢. It take 10 days to two weeks to arrive. If you hope to receive mail while you're in Panamá, remember that mail is *only* delivered to post offices—Panamá has no home delivery. If you're planning to stay a while, it makes sense to get a post office box. Otherwise, most *correos* (post offices) will hold mail addressed to You, Entrega General, City, Province, República de Panamá. There's a Panama, Florida, so be sure to include the República part unless you want somebody's retired granny in Florida knowing all your business.

MONEY Believe it or not, Panamá's national currency is the U.S. dollar. All the bills are regular American denominations, although Panamá does mint its own version of nickels, dimes, and quarters. Panamanians refer to dollars interchangeably as dollars or balboas. Changing other currencies into "balboas" is a bitch, and you can probably only do it in Panamá City. Also, you *cannot* get around using traveler's checks, since almost none of the budget places accepts them. You can change them for cash in most banks, though; American Express checks are the most widely accepted. **Banco General** and **Banco Continental** don't charge a commission, but **Banco Nacional** hits you with a $1.10 charge for each check. Your home bank probably has a branch here, too—Panamá has more than 140 international banks—but don't assume you can withdraw money easily. It can cost as much as $40 to transfer money from abroad.

PHONES Both **AT&T** and **MCI** offer direct-dial service from any phone in Panamá. Dial 109 for AT&T or 108 for MCI to reach an English-speaking operator who will place collect or calling-card calls (using your regular AT&T or MCI calling card). If you don't have a calling card, dial 106 to speak to a Spanish-speaking international operator. Newer phone booths, which look like U.S. booths, tend to be out of order frequently. The Panamanian phone service (called **INTEL**) kicks ass—clear as a bell, with no voice delay or random bleeping. The country code is 507.

USEFUL ORGANIZATIONS Panamá's tourist bureau is called **IPAT**; their stickers are plastered in restaurants and hotels all over the country. If you're willing to wade through mounds of slick touristy information with lines like, "It's through the festivals that the peasants express all of their emotions," you *can* find some useful stuff; at the very least you'll get a nifty folder with various pictures of Panamá on it. The IPAT people tend to be enthusiastic and helpful, but they aren't really geared to help shoestring travelers. The main office is in Panamá City (*see below*), where you can get brochures covering all parts of the country. The tourist office in Paso Canoa on the Costa Rican border has the same info. The various provinces have regional IPAT offices, too, but the information is much the same.

ANCON is a private organization whose sole purpose is to protect and conserve Panamá's natural resources and biological diversity. However, they know all about hard-to-reach places, and it's not impossible to snag a free ride with them to just about any part of the country if your timing's right. Talk to Conservation Director Carlos Brandaris or Environmental Education and Development Director Madeleine Lescure about possible long- or short-term volunteering opportunities. *Calle 50 in El Cangrejo (Panamá City), opposite Floristería Marbella, tel. 64–8100. Mailing address: Apartado 1387, Panamá 1, República de Panamá. Open weekdays 8–4.*

INRENARE is the government's parks department. In reality, they work pretty much side-by-side with ANCON. If you're going to camp a lot, go here instead of to IPAT. *Apartado 2016, Paraíso (where the Paraíso bus from Panamá City stops), tel. 32–4325. Open weekdays 8–4.*

VISAS If you're from the United Kingdom, all you need is a valid passport to go to Panamá; Australians and New Zealanders need a 30-day visa, and U.S. and Canadian citizens need a tourist card. Everyone needs an onward or return ticket. Of course, it's always wise to get a visa anyway to prevent hassles at the border or airport. To extend your visa past 30 days, you have to go to the **office of immigration** (Oficina de migración, Av. Cuba and Calle 29, Panamá City, tel. 25–8925). Bring a photo, your passport, and about $11. Then, you have to go to the **ministerio de hacienda y tesoro** (Calle 35 at Av. Perú, tel. 27–3060) to get a document (called a *paz y salvo*—peace and safety) certifying that, if you worked here, you paid your taxes or that you haven't committed any crimes—they aren't very clear. Pay 25¢ for that privilege and *then* you have to go back to the immigration office to get permission to leave. Do yourself a favor and take care of the bureaucratic bullshit in advance so you don't miss your plane. The departure tax is $15.

COMING AND GOING

➤ **BY BUS** • Ticabus (Calle 17 in Panamá City, tel. 62–2084) runs buses between Panamá City and San José, Costa Rica. One bus departs daily from San José at 10 PM and one from Panamá City at 11 AM. The journey takes roughly 18 hours and costs about $25 each way. The Greyhound-style buses have air-conditioning (if the driver turns it on) and are pretty comfortable. Buses are often full in July and from November to March (Panamanian school holidays), so make reservations at least three days in advance; during the rest of the year you can probably get same-day seating.

Less convenient minibuses run from the northern border town of Paso Canoa to David; from there, buses run to all parts of western Panamá and Panamá City. At the northern border crossing at Guabito, you can catch a bus to Changuinola or take the banana train (*see* Bocas del Toro, *below*) all the way to Almirante. However, no roads link these towns to the rest of Panamá; you have to take the ferry from Almirante to Chiriquí Grande, or fly out of Changuinola.

Remember that Panamá is an hour ahead of Costa Rica and the rest of Central America.

➤ **BY PLANE** • Tocumen International Airport outside Panamá City handles flights from all the major airlines and a whole slew of smaller ones. International airlines include **American** (tel. 69–6022), **Continental** (tel. 26–1577), **British Airways** (tel. 27–0787), **TWA** (tel. 64–9756), **LACSA** (Costa Rican, tel. 25–0193), **SAHSA** (Honduran, tel. 27–1366), and **TACA** (Guatemalan, tel. 69–6066). No flights from Australia or New Zealand come direct to Panamá. All phone numbers listed are for offices in Panamá City. For student tickets, go to **APTE** (*see* Panamá City, *below*), a student tourism agency that can direct you to a travel agency that gives student discounts.

GETTING AROUND

➤ **BY BUS** • Buses and minibuses are the way to go in Panamá. On the whole they're clean and comfortable. Many of the buses are amusingly decorated, and some feature on-board TVs and—if you're really lucky—distortingly loud stereos. All are privately owned and operated, so there's no organized way to find out schedules except by asking around. Similarly, rates are not set in stone, but you can estimate $1–$2 per hour of travel. Panamá City and David are the biggest transport hubs, but neither one serves all points in the country. In addition, every little town has its own particular transport routes.

➤ **BY TRAIN** • Panamá has only three working train tracks, of which two are mainly for transporting bananas and banana workers to and from the various Chiquita plantations in western Panamá. The third rail line runs between Panamá City and Colón, but at press time passenger service had been suspended (*see* Panamá City Coming and Going, *below*).

➤ **BY BOAT** • In the archipelagos of San Blas and Bocas del Toro, as well as in many parts of the Darién, you have to boat around. In the Darién, where people get around on narrow waterways threading through the jungle, boat rides cost $10–$30, depending on the length of the ride and where you want to go. There's no guarantee a boat will be there when you need it, or that it'll be heading where you want to go. The best places to catch a boat in Darién are Puerto Obaldía on the Caribbean coast and Yaviza, El Real, and Boca de Cupe in the jungle. San Blas and Bocas have more structured systems; boats run fairly regularly from island to island. If you're staying on an island, your hotel may well take you to and from the mainland for free.

➤ **BY BIKE** • Biking is legal, but you're sharing the road with drivers to whom defensive driving is tantamount to symbolic castration. Not surprisingly, bikers rank low on the machismo scale. Where roads exist, they are generally in good condition. Mountain biking is catching on here, so you should be able to find spare parts or rental places in the bigger cities.

➤ **HITCHING** • For whatever reason, hitching is not the done thing here. It's not that you're in grave danger—though you should be cautious—but people just don't stop. Basically, your only hope for hitching a ride is to approach someone who has already stopped, usually at a gas station. Otherwise, you could wait a long time.

➤ **BY PLANE** • Domestic airlines leave from Paitilla Airport in Panamá City. **ANSA** (tel. 26–7891 or 26–6881) flies to San Blas. **PARSA** (tel. 26–3883 or 26–3803) serves six airports in the Darién. **Chitreana de Aviación** (tel. 26–4116 or 26–3069), **AeroPerlas** (tel. 63–5363 or 69–4555), and **Alas Chiricanas** (tel. 64–6448 or 64–7759) all fly to various parts of the country.

WHERE TO SLEEP Panamá is not really a bargain as Central American countries go. The cheapest rooms cost at least $3 per person, but you can probably expect to pay around $5. On the up side, most places are kept tolerably clean and you can look forward to toilet seats in almost all bathrooms. Cheaper rooms can also be rented by the hour, so expect to hear noises of simulated love into the wee hours. All but the smallest *pueblitos* have some kind of budget lodging. You can try to bargain for a better rate, even in nicer hotels, especially if you plan to stay a few days.

Camping in Panamá is not an organized event. Campgrounds are few, but you're free to pitch camp at almost any beach or park. Travelers and Panamanians don't usually camp, so you might get some curious looks. Use courtesy (i.e., ask) if you're in front of someone's house or near a hotel. You'll find official campsites at **La Herradura** (tel. 53–4963), on the Interamerican Highway between Arraiján and La Chorrera, about 40 kilometers (25 miles) west of Panamá City; **Las Mendozas**, on the Zaratí river in Penonomé; in **Chitré** and **Playa Venado** on the Azuero Peninsula; and on **Isla Mamey**

How to Talk Like a Local

A 5-cent piece is called a real, *a 25-cent piece a* quarter *(though said with a Spanish accent), and a 50-cent piece a* peso. *Some other key words to memorize:* fulo/a, *a white, usually blond, person;* chuleta, *literally "pork chop" but used as both an expletive and a nickname (something like "dude"); and* chucha, *a slang word for the female genitalia but used incessantly as an expletive (e.g., "I caught my hand in the thresher, and, chucha, talk about pain!"). If you learn those words, all you need to do is learn to snap your index finger like you're packing a dip and you'll blend in like you were born here.*

and **Isla Grande.** Accommodations at these places are pretty minimal, but go ahead and use them if you're in the area.

FOOD Panamá is noted for its cosmopolitan influences, but you can usually find international food only in Panamá City. Outside the capital you face limited options, which are mostly dismal by Western culinary standards and insufferable to vegetarians. Beware that anything not called *carne* (beef), *puerco* (pork), or *pollo* (chicken) is probably some tasty tidbit from their innards—kidney, liver, or intestine. The only breaks in the monotony are the not-infrequent Chinese restaurant and the occasional pizza place. In Panamá you're never far from the sea, so you can usually find decent seafood. It'll probably be fresh, but be sure to ask (you might be at a restaurant that fishes in the freezer section). Reservations are unheard of, and don't hesitate to call for the waiter or your bill (*cuenta*) unless you don't mind waiting all night.

Panamanian junkies take the magnetic tape from cassettes, boil it in water, and drink the resulting "tea," presumably for some extremely toxic high.

Ropa vieja (old clothes) is a typical dish made of spiced, shredded beef, and *sancocho* is a stew made of beef or chicken, vegetables, and spices. The local *arroz con pollo* (chicken and rice) has olives in it. The coffee rocks on, and the water is drinkable almost everywhere, although you're best off with bottled water in the Darién, Bocas del Toro, and dinky little towns. As with most places in Central America, snack shacks cluster around the bus stations and the budget lodging areas; many budget restaurants are diner-type joints.

➤ **TIPPING** • Tipping's not expected, but servers appreciate it when you do. Just leave your change from a dollar. I talked to a Canadian guy who left a $3.50 tip after a $40 meal; the waitress followed him out the door thinking he had left his money on the table.

Panamá City

Despite the country's image as a Central American backwater, Panamá's capital is incredibly cosmopolitan. You can see it in the mingling of indigenous peoples, people of direct Spanish ancestry, descendants of African slaves, Chinese workers, U.S. soldiers, and others. You can see it in the wide variety of food, in the 140 international banks, and in stores like Benetton. You can see it in kids wearing Teenage Mutant Ninja Turtle shoes, in Spanish ruins dating back hundreds of years, and in skyscrapers just being built. Walking around the city, you'll be bombarded with an internationalism so pervasive that it'll take you a while to realize you're one of the few bona fide travelers here.

The huge city sprawls over a 10-kilometer (6-mile) slice of land at the southern end of the Canal, flanked by gentle hills to the north and the Pacific Ocean to the south. Like almost any metropolis, Panamá City is hot and crowded, and it suffers from the depressing juxtaposition of major development and devastating poverty. Even if you didn't come to Panamá looking for a gritty urban experience, there's absolutely no way to avoid Panamá City: It's the only place to exchange foreign currency, to plan tours to the rest of the country, to arrange your papers, to get consistently decent meals, and to buy a ticket home. And if you want to travel throughout Panamá, you often have to backtrack to the capital in order to fly or catch a bus to your next destination.

The city's not very touristy, so cheap accommodations are readily available. The scarcity of travelers also means that many eyes will follow you as you walk through the city, more so if you're a woman with blonde hair or a guy with long hair, a beard, or shorts—in other words, a blatant gringo. Stopping in Panamá City doesn't have to be quick and painful. If you look around, you'll realize that this city is a palimpsest of almost 500 years of world history. In Panamá Viejo are the ruins of the first Panamá, built in 1519 by conquistadors to store gold en route from Perú to Spain. In Casco Viejo, the "old town" in the southwestern corner of the city, are the orderly parks, ornate cathedrals, and buildings from Panamá's colonial days. Even today, the multitude of glassy bank buildings that line Vía España in the center attest to the city's role as an international banking and shipping center. The newest and most painful marker of outside influence is the neighborhood of El Chorillo, just north of Casco Viejo, which was razed during the U.S. invasion in 1989.

Though several U.S. military bases border the city, they have absolutely nothing to do with Panamá City itself. All bases are in the Canal Zone, a five-mile stretch running along either side of the Canal, controlled by the United States until at least 1999. Panamanians don't go into the Canal Zone and, in general, troops don't go out. You won't see much of them unless you go looking in the right bases, bars, or brothels.

The capital moves at a pace that makes the rest of the country look lethargic. In other words, it doesn't shut down at dusk.

Members of the military and their families usually keep to themselves or hang out in the more touristy spots; in the budget areas, you probably won't even know they exist.

Much more visible are Panamánian armed guards. Your entry to a supermarket may be blocked by a machine gun until you check your bags. All the protection seems a little excessive, though it should theoretically give you a greater sense of security. Panamá City does have a crime problem, especially in the neighborhoods around the Plaza Santa Ana, Casco Viejo, and El Chorillo. But keep your eyes open, especially on back streets or at night, and you shouldn't have problems. If you're especially concerned about safety, you can buy mace without a license for $11 at **Sports International** (Tumba Muerto, in front of El Depósito, tel. 60–2677 or 60–2577).

BASICS

AMERICAN EXPRESS With an American Express card, you can cash a personal check for up to $1,000 every 21 days at the Travel Related Services office. The office also holds mail for card-members. *Calle 50 (Av. Nicanor de Obarrio), beside Mobilphone, tel. 64–2444. Open weekdays 8–12:15 and 2–5:15, Sat. 8–12:15.*

CASAS DE CAMBIO If you're not coming from the United States, get dollars before you arrive in Panamá; they're *the* accepted currency and everything else is hard to change. If you do roll into town with another currency, the only place that will exchange it is **Panacambios** (ground floor of the Plaza Regency on Vía España, tel. 23–1800), and they exact a hefty 10% fee, sometimes more. If you have British pounds or Canadian dollars, you can also try **Caja de Cambios** (next to Agencia Dilido phone center, tel. 64–1194), but they also charge up the wazoo.

EMBASSIES AND CONSULATES **United States Embassy.** Calle 37 and Av. Balboa, tel. 27–1777. Open weekdays 8–12:30.

British Embassy. Calle 53 in the Torre Swiss Bank, 4th floor, tel. 69–0866. Open weekdays 8–noon.

Canadian Consulate. Calle Manuel M. Icaza, 5th floor of Aero Perú Bldg. 5-B, Apartado 3658, Balboa, tel. 64–2325. Open weekdays 8:30–11 am.

The following Central American countries have embassies or consulates in Panamá City: **Belize** (Calles 50 and 87, tel. 26–4498); **Costa Rica** (Plaza Regency Bldg., 2nd floor, Calle Gilberto Ortega and Vía España, tel. 64–2980); **El Salvador** (Citibank Bldg., 4th floor, Vía España, tel. 23–3020); **Guatemala** (Condominio Abir, 6th floor, Calle 50 in El Cangrejo, tel. 69–3475); **Honduras** (Tapia Bldg., 2nd floor, Av. Justo Arosemena and Calle 31, tel. 25–8200); **Nicaragua** (Calle 50 and Av. Federico Boyd, tel. 69–6721 or 23–0981).

Panamá City

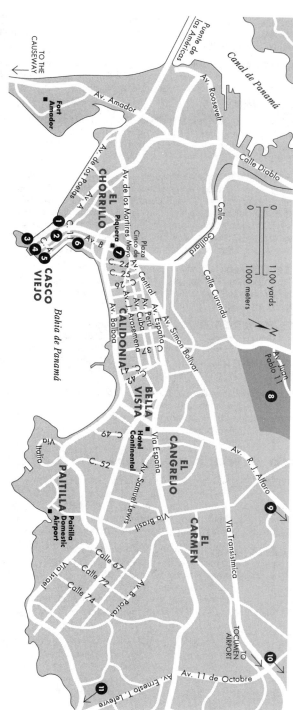

Arco Chato, **3**
Báha'í House of
Worship, **10**
El Catedral, **2**
Hindu Temple, **9**
Iglesia de
San José, **1**

Mercado Publico, **6**
Panamá Viejo, **11**
Parque Natural
Metropolitano, **8**
Paseo de las
Bóvedas, **5**

Plaza de la
Independencia
(Plaza Central), **2**
Reina Torres de
Araúz Anthropology
Museum, **7**
Teatro Nacional/
Palacio Nacional, **4**

EMERGENCIES You can dial the national **police** (tel. 104) and the **fire department** (tel. 103) from most pay phones without depositing a coin. For **ambulance** service call the Red Cross (tel. 28–2187).

LAUNDRY Within walking distance of anywhere in Casco Viejo, **Lavamatic** has coin-operated washers and dryers; it costs 50¢ per load per machine. *Calle 3 and Av. Central. Open Tues.–Sat. 8:30–4:30, Sun. 8:30–2:30.*

MAIL The **Correos Nacional** is an impressive white building facing the central plaza of Casco Viejo, right next to the Hotel Central. It has telegraph, money-order, and one-month poste restante services. Address poste restante mail to Entrega General, Panamá 1, República de Panamá. *Av. Central at Plaza de la Independencia, tel. 28–8577. Open weekdays 7–6, Sat. 7–5.*

MEDICAL AID Socialized medicine is alive and well in Panamá, so natives and even foreigners needn't fear excessive bills. Both **Centro Medico Bella Vista** (Av. Perú and Calle 39, tel. 27–4022) and **Centro Medico Paitilla** (Av. Balboa and Calle 53, tel. 63–6060) have English-speaking doctors, but doctors everywhere will probably be able to understand you. Three chains of 24-hour supermarket/pharmacies have numerous branches: **Arrocha, Rey,** and **24.** A convenient Arrocha *farmacia* is just off Vía España at the Banco Continental building.

PHONES **Agencia Dilido** is an international calling center run by INTEL, the national phone company. You get discount rates—and increased crowds—weekdays after 6 PM and all weekend. *Calle Eusebio A. Morales, near Hotel Continental, tel. 64–8104. Open daily 7:30 AM–9:30 PM.*

VISITOR INFORMATION The **office of tourism** is on Vía Israel, across from the Marriott Caesar Park Hotel and don Samy's (*see* Food, *below*). The extremely helpful staff will send you on your way with an armful of information (mostly in Spanish), at least some of which might prove useful. *ATLAPA Convention Center, tel. 26–7000. Take Bus 2 from Plaza 5 de Mayo. Open weekdays 8:30–4:30.*

Associación Panameño de Turismo Estudiantil (APTE), associated with ISIC, helps card-carrying students with travel-related stuff. *On the campus of Universidad Santa María Antigua, in El Dorado area, on Calle Ricardo J. Alfaro (Tumba Muerto), tel. 36–1311. Open weekdays 1:30–4:30.*

COMING AND GOING

BY TRAIN The first track running between Colón and Panamá City was built to take '49ers across the isthmus on their way to the California Gold Rush. Its replacement was damaged in the U.S. invasion and is now carrying only cargo. Call 36–6504 to find out if passenger travel has been restored yet. The train station is in the Balboa neighborhood; if it's working, take a SACA bus from Plaza Cinco de Mayo.

BY BUS **Ticabus** runs one bus each day to and from San José, Costa Rica. The trip costs about $20 each way and takes 18 hours. The buses are pretty comfortable, with air-conditioning and a blessed lack of sticky vinyl seats. Space isn't usually a problem except during school vacations (November–February and Semana Santa), when you should make reservations at least three days in advance. *Calle 17, 2 blocks west on Av. Central from Plaza 5 de Mayo, tel. 62–2084 or 62–6275.*

Buses to the rest of Panamá, called the "interior," depart from the **piquera,** roughly at the intersection of avenidas Balboa and B. Some buses leave from calles M or P, but they're all within four blocks of each other. Everyone knows where the piquera is, so just ask. Most of the buses are minibuses; no trip should cost more than about $10. Lines are privately owned and there's a zillion of them, but buses to most places leave hourly or even more frequently. Pay your fare when you board.

BY CAR Driving a car here is not an undertaking for the meek, but rental cars are readily available, including 4x4s. **Budget** (tel. 63–8777) has relatively good rates, but you have to be 23 to rent. The cheapest car is $22 per day, and the cheapest 4x4 is $55 per day. Budget has several offices in the city; one's inside the Tocumen airport.

BY PLANE Panamá City has an international airport, **Tocumen** (26 km [16 mi] northeast of city limits), and a domestic airport, **Paitilla** (where Av. Balboa turns into Av. 6 Sur, tel. 26–7959). Traveling through the country in a small plane gives you a stunning view of the jungle, and the costs are pretty reasonable. Some of the grooviest places in the country, like the Darién, San Blas, and Bocas del Toro, are only accessible by air or infrequent boats. It won't cost you more than $100 round-trip to anywhere in Panamá, with fares to the places mentioned above closer to $50. For more information on domestic and international airlines, *see* Panamá Basics, *above.*

Tocumen has a tourist information center, a 24-hour left-luggage office where you can store bags for $1 per piece per day (look for the guys wearing brown pants, khaki shirts, and red caps), and car-rental agencies galore. There's an INTEL calling center (tel. 66–8791) here, too. For more airport info, call 38–4322.

➢ **AIRPORT TRANSPORT** • To get to Paitilla, take Bus 2, which runs along Avenida Balboa (15¢). You can also hail a taxi anywhere in the city, which will get you there for $1–$3. Buses (30¢) to Tocumen run frequently from Plaza Cinco de Mayo, but it's always a big hassle to hoist your luggage onto the bus. A taxi from the city to Tocumen is $12–$20, depending on the size of the taxi, the number of passengers, and, not infrequently, how much the driver thinks he can stick you for. Generally, the smaller and shabbier the taxi, the cheaper it will be. If you can find at least two other people to share with, take a *colectivo,* a big, glorified taxi that carries groups from the airport into the city for $8 per person. Colectivos usually won't take you back to the airport, though—you're stuck paying for your own taxi or hefting your stuff on the bus.

GETTING AROUND

Panamá City is your basic urban sprawl, stretching for 10 kilometers (6 miles) along the Bahía de Panamá on the Pacific coast. The biggest chunk of the city, which includes the town center and the budget lodging area, is served by three roughly parallel, east–west streets. The main drag starts at Tocumen airport, about 26 kilometers (16 miles) northeast of city limits. Moving west it's called Vía España, but it eventually becomes **Avenida Central.** To the north is **Vía Transístmica;** to the south, bordering the Bahía de Panamá, is **Avenida Balboa.** Both of these streets run into **Avenida España** on the west side of town. A good place to get oriented is the **Plaza Cinco de Mayo** on Avenida Central, in the western part of the city; you can catch almost any city bus here.

Panamá City is divided into neighborhoods (*barrios*), which you can use to orient yourself. The **city center** is where you'll find all the high-rises, banks, pharmacies, and shopping. Avenida Justo Arosemena runs through the middle of the city center. A bus with "Justo Arosemena" written on it will take you through the barrios of **Calidonia, Bella Vista,** and **El Cangrejo,** all places with budget food and lodging. The coolest old buildings and cheapest lodgings are in **Casco Viejo** ("old town"), also called San Felipe, where Avenida Central ends on a little peninsula jutting into the Bay of Panamá. Just north of Casco Viejo are **El Chorrillo** and **Santa Ana,** two very poor neighborhoods that were hit hard by the '89 invasion. The **Canal** is west of the city proper.

If you navigate the city using a map, be careful: Sometimes one street will have two or three names. Avenidas with numbers are commonly referred to by their other, older names. For example, Avenida 3 Sur is Justo Arosemena, and Avenida 6 Sur is Balboa. By this reasoning, Avenida 4a should be Nicanor de Obarrio, but it's called Calle 50 instead (go figure). Neighborhoods, too, are only loosely defined. Do as the locals do and steer yourself by major landmarks: Plaza Cinco de Mayo; the Hotel Continental, on

Avenida Central about ½ mile east of the center; Plaza Santa Ana, just north of Casco Viejo in Santa Ana; or the Plaza de la Independencia (or Plaza Mayor or Plaza Central or Parque Central or Parque Catedral—they're all the same thing) in Casco Viejo.

BY BUS The buses alone make this city worth visiting. Not only are they cheap (15¢ anywhere within the city), but they're about the best entertainment around. Each bus is independently owned—and decorated. Airbrush is the medium of choice, and no holds are barred; the more outrageous the better. Images range from alpine cottage scenes to ghoulish creatures, from Paula Abdul to Rocky, from Jesus to stickers asking "Did you just fart or do you always smell this bad?"

Pedestrians do not have the right of way. Drivers will mow you down without touching the brake, then sue you for denting their grill with your head. Bus and taxi drivers, especially, obey no laws of God or man, carrying out their duties with distinct disregard for the value of human life.

No maps exist of the bus routes, but almost everyone knows where the buses run, so keep asking. Each bus line is privately owned and operates differently: Some buses sport their destinations in the window, some have route numbers, some have both, and some neither. What's more, the name or number on the bus may be wrong, so the best strategy is just to hop on and ask the driver. The two main bus routes are Vía Transístmica and Vía España (a good way to see the city is by hopping on a Vía España bus). Buses run along these streets day and night. Pay your fare as you get *off* the bus. The word to remember when you want to get off is *parada* (stop)—the louder you say it, the less concerned you need be with your pronunciation. The central bus stop is Plaza Cinco de Mayo; you can catch buses to both airports and everywhere else in the city from here. **SACA** is a U.S.-owned bus company that will take you anywhere in the Canal Zone. Pay your fare as you get on. SACA buses also stop at Plaza Cinco de Mayo.

BY TAXI Some cab drivers jack up their prices if they think you're a tourist, but the majority won't take you for a ride (no pun intended). Fares are supposedly based on a zone system, but you'll be hard-pressed to find a cabbie consulting a map to calculate your fare. Tell them where you want to go and they'll give you a price. Anywhere in the city is $1–$3, and tips are not expected. Finding a taxi is never a problem: On any given street, about 50% of cars are taxis. The real problem isn't getting a taxi but getting them to stop honking at you when you're trying to take a walk.

WHERE TO SLEEP

The cheapest hotels are in Casco Viejo, where most rooms are under $10—not bad when you consider the Marriott's sticking people for $118. Of course, Casco Viejo does *not* offer the Marriott's amenities; be prepared for no air-conditioning, no hot water, and a mattress your back will remember for days. You probably shouldn't brave the streets of Casco Viejo at night, so get what you need during the day or take a taxi. Everyone will tell you the streets at night are *muy peligroso* (very dangerous). Buses don't run directly into Casco Viejo. Most Vía España or Transístmica buses will take you as close as Calle 11 (always double-check with the driver), but from there you have to walk a couple of blocks or take a taxi.

In a real bind, you can venture up Avenida Central into the Plaza Santa Ana area. Some Panamanians say this area is even more dangerous and drug-infested than Casco Viejo. What's more, it's not significantly cheaper than Casco Viejo nor does it have Casco Viejo's historic look. Strictly for convenience, you might try **Pensión Rosita** (Av. Central near Plaza 5 de Mayo, tel. 62–5159), near the Cinco de Mayo terminal.

Spending just a little extra on a room propels you quickly into the comfort zone, with air-conditioning, hot water, and maybe even a TV thrown in. The other benefit is that you can get out of Casco Viejo. The Calidonia and Bella Vista neighborhoods, off Vía

España in the city center, are a little safer than Casco Viejo. You might be able to work out a deal with a hotel manager, but keep in mind that you may be competing for a room with a prostitute and her John. Such folks rarely stay more than an hour or two, which means the manager can rent the room out again; presumably you intend to spend the whole night.

CASCO VIEJO (SAN FELIPE) You shouldn't have problems finding a room in one of the places below. If you do, three low-cost pensions exist in Casco Viejo, though the security cameras, caged reception desks, and general sliminess might deter you: **Pensión Panamá** (Calle 6, in front of Hotel Foyo, tel. 62–8053), **Pensión Tropical** (Calle 8 and Av. A, tel. 28–8894), or **Pensión Panamericana** (Calle 10 off Plaza Herrera, tel. 28–8759).

You may not want to spend extra bucks for TV, but don't underestimate the entertainment value of U.S. military channel 8, which has commercials about subjects like operations security: "On or off duty, information you carelessly leak can be like pieces in a puzzle helping to give our adversaries the big picture."

➤ **UNDER $10** • **Hotel Central.** Built around the turn of the century, this hotel is said to have housed Teddy Roosevelt on official state visits. Though it now appears more suited for the likes of Teddy Kennedy on secret liaisons, the place still has the classy feel of a once-majestic old house, complete with wrought-iron balconies. Granted, you have to look past the numerous whores and the occasional rat to find that class, but they basically keep to themselves. The hotel faces the noisy Plaza Central, so ask for a back room if you need your peace. Doubles are $10 with bath, $8 without. *Calle 5 at Plaza de la Independencia, tel. 62–8044 or 62–8096. 150 rooms, some with bath.*

Pensión Vásquez. The nice owner and his two small dogs live here with you. He keeps the place clean, but the rooms get warm since they lack ceiling fans. Check out the elaborate pulley system the guy's rigged so he can open the front door without having to walk down the stairs. Doubles are $8. *Av. A and Calle 3, across from Arco Chato, tel. 28–8453. 16 rooms, all sharing common baths.*

➤ **UNDER $15** • **Hotel Colonial.** This brightly painted hotel faces Plaza Bolívar, which gets noisy, especially during the day. Ask for a back room if it matters, but some of the front rooms offer a glimpse of the ocean. Doubles with bath are $11. A small restaurant serves meals 7–7. *Calle 4 at Plaza Bolívar, tel. 62–3858. 38 rooms, some with bath.*

Hotel Foyo. A cut above the rest, this hotel surrounds an open-air atrium that creates a feeling of space. Doubles are $11, $6 without bath. *Calle 6 and Av. A, tel. 62–8023. From Av. A, turn right on Calle 6 and look for the sign on the left. 40 rooms, 7 with bath.*

CALIDONIA/BELLA VISTA

➤ **UNDER $10** • **Pensión Las Palmeras.** Only the name and its larger size distinguish this from La Primavera (*see below*). Rooms with private bath are $10. *Av. Cuba bet. Calles 38 and 39, tel. 25–0811. 50 rooms, all with bath.*

Residencial La Primavera. This place is kept clean and orderly in the great style of the no-tell motel. Singles and doubles are both $10, a tip-off that they don't expect many single guests. The neighborhood is pretty quiet. *Av. Cuba at Calle 42, tel. 25–1195. Take any Vía España bus toward Calle 42. It's between Av. Justo Arosemena and Vía España. 18 rooms, all with bath.*

Residencial Sevilla. This place is split into two sections. On the bottom floor are rooms with communal baths and no amenities, but they're cheap ($7 doubles). The only drawback is that they're usually filled with whores. Upper floors feature rooms with private baths, hot water, and air-conditioning for a much heftier price—$18 for a double. *Av. Justo Arosemena near Vía España, tel. 27–2436. Take any bus going down Vía España. 22 rooms, some with bath.*

➤ **UNDER \$20** • **Residencial El Dorado.** Hidden behind a 10-foot hedge, this is one of those places where the extra money brings cool stuff. Rooms with a fan cost \$12, \$14 with air-conditioning, and \$17 with air-conditioning, color TV, and hot water. *Calle 37 bet. Avs. Perú and Cuba, tel. 27–5767. Take any Vía España bus to Calle 37. 33 rooms, all with bath.*

Hotel California. The clean rooms have TV, air-conditioning, and hot water, and the lobby has comfy couches. Prices range from \$20 for singles to \$28 for a double with two beds. An armed guard secures this place, too. The hotel has its own restaurant and bar—and yes, the captain can bring you your wine. *Vía España at Calle 43, tel. 63–7844 or 63–8140. Take any Vía España bus that does not also say "Av. Justo Arosemena" on the front window and tell the driver to stop at Hotel California. 60 rooms, all with bath.*

Residencial Jamaica. No Rasta with a big doobie or anything, but this hotel is nice and clean, with the usual extras—hot water, TV, and air-conditioning. Doubles are \$28. *Av. Cuba at Calle 38, tel. 25–9870. 30 rooms, all with bath.*

Hotel Montreal. You won't get the flavor and history of a Hotel Central here, but for \$28 you'll get a very comfortable, albeit bland, double. There's even a pool on the roof with a good view of the city. Don't let the pistol-toting guard scare you—all the nicer places have 'em. The restaurant and bar in the lobby are open daily 6:30 AM–11 PM. *Vía España at Av. Justo Arosemena, tel. 63–4422. 96 rooms, all with bath. Air-conditioning, hot water, phone, color TV.*

ROUGHING IT Crashing in parks and on beaches is legal, but you may still be hassled by the police. More perilous than cops, though, is the risk of being robbed or worse. If you can head to the beaches outside town, do it; you'll be less at risk.

FOOD

Good food is available everywhere and at all hours. You'll be astounded by just how many restaurants are squeezed into this city. Casco Viejo has a few hole-in-the-wall places, but it's not a food center. You'll have much more luck around the Plaza Santa Ana area, not far up Avenida Central. Other good areas are the **El Cangrejo** section of Vía España and the adjoining **Vía Argentina** area. Both are fairly safe—if all the armed guards got together, they could easily overthrow the government.

A word of advice: Unless you're dying for that Big Mac or Domino's pizza (most U.S. fast-food joints have franchises here), head for the little greasy spoons instead. The food is better, cheaper, and more plentiful.

CASCO VIEJO AND SANTA ANA If you want something basic and convenient, choose from a bunch of very cheap (under \$3) and basically interchangeable eateries: **Buen Sabor** (Calle 9 at Av. Central), **Restaurante Viña** (Calle 6 and Av. A), **Restaurante Herrera** (Calle 9 on Plaza Herrera), **Restaurante San Martín** (Av. Central bet. Calles 4 and 5), and **Restaurante Refresquería** (Plaza Central, tel. 62–4791).

➤ **UNDER \$5** • **Restaurante Astoria.** Hit this place if you need a burger. You'll have to deal with eating it on real bread instead of the rubbery buns we're all used to, but for \$1, those are the breaks. *Av. B, ½ block south of Plaza 5 de Mayo, tel. 62–6116. Open daily 7 AM–11 PM.*

Restaurante Chung Wah. For pretty good Chinese food or if you just want to see a side of pork hanging in a window, this is it. It's not the cheapest meal in town, but the prices are very reasonable considering the generous portions. The *mayor alemán*, a big bowl of meaty soup, is good and filling for \$3. *Av. B near Calle 14, tel. 62–8483.*

Almost all buses pass the intersection of Avs. Balboa and B. From here, walk 3 blocks down Av. B toward Casco Viejo; it's on the right. Open daily 7 AM–10 PM.

Restaurante Victoria. Offering what seems like the only air-conditioning in Casco Viejo, this is a good place to take refuge from the heat and humidity. The food is worthwhile, too, but the bar, TV, and cool air are what bring crowds of Panamánian drinkers here on weekend nights. They serve mostly Chinese food; try the fried chicken (no batter) for $2. *Av. Central and Calle 9, next to La Iglesia de Merced on Av. Central. Open daily 1–1.*

CALIDONIA/BELLA VISTA

➤ **UNDER $5** • **Mi Salud.** Perhaps a bit ahead of its time given the Latin love for meat, this is one of the few vegetarian restaurants in the city. Nevertheless, Panamanians do actually eat here. Mi Salud serves food cafeteria-style, with good ice cream for 50¢. The name means "my health," and it's right near the beach. *Calle 31 near Av. Balboa, tel. 25–0972. Take Bus 2 from Plaza 5 de Mayo. Open Mon.–Sat. 7:15 AM–7 PM.*

Restaurante La Mexicanita. It's not the best Mexican food, but the *burrito especial* ($3) or *enchiladas* ($4.50) should help Mexi-junkies jonesing for a fix. *Av. Justo Arosemena at Calle 50, tel. 25–5806. Take any Vía España bus to Av. Justo Arosemena. Open Tues.–Sun. noon–10.*

➤ **UNDER $10** • **La Cascada.** Come here when you're really hungry and/or hurting for a laugh. The portions are enormous and the menu is an imposing 16-page, newspaper-size monstrosity that reads like a choose-your-own adventure ("If you like to buy a fresh natural red rose for your female companion, look page No. 12"). The kooky open-air patio, the view of the bay, and the mountains of good food make this a serious munchie spot. Try the heaping mound of paella for $8; it'll feed two. *Av. Balboa at Calle 25, tel. 62–1297. Take Bus 2 from Plaza 5 de Mayo. Open Mon.–Sat. 3–11.*

EL CANGREJO

➤ **UNDER $5** • **Cafe Jimmy's.** Got that 3 AM urge for hot, cheap food? Check out Jimmy's for some typical Panamánian dishes or a variety of sandwiches served cafeteria-style. A plate with choice of one meat and three sides (rice, veggies, lentils, spaghetti, or potato puree) is only $2.50; without the meat, it's $2. *Calle Manuel de Ycasa, off Vía España across from Hotel Continental, tel. 23–1523. Take any Vía España bus. Open daily 24 hours.*

El Trapiche. Come here for a reasonably priced, typically Panamánian meal like ropa vieja. It's a cozy place with indoor and patio seating, but beware of the piped-in music: It was Neil Diamond's greatest hits throughout my meal. *Vía Argentina, 2 blocks off Vía España, tel. 69–2063. Take any Vía España bus to Vía Argentina. Open daily 7 AM–11 PM.*

Restaurante Churrería Manolo. Sit on the patio here and watch the hip Panamánian youth, decked-out and chain-smoking. You'll find typical Panamánian dishes and some international fare. This isn't the cheapest place to get food, but buy a drink or a *churro* (long doughnut-like pastry) for $1 and check out the scene. *Vía Argentina next to El Trapiche, tel. 64–3965. Open daily 7 AM–1 AM.*

Restaurante Vegetariano Mireya. The entrées change every night, they're all vegetarian, and all pretty good. Choose your food from the cafeteria and have your water ladled out of a ceramic jug. *Calle Ricardo Arias, down the street from Hotel Continental, tel. 69–1876. Take any Vía España bus. Open Mon.–Sat. 6 AM–8:30 PM.*

ELSEWHERE IN PANAMA CITY

➤ **UNDER $3** • **don Samy's.** This place is a land unto itself, especially on weekend nights when the parking lot—and the street for ½ mile in either direction—transforms into a colossal festival of drunken young locals and car-speaker distortion. Through it all, don Samy's serves up cheap, satisfying Panamánian food. The sancocho is a perennial favorite for $1.50. Warning: Passengers and drivers alike slake their thirst on cheap local beer. If you decide to do the same, just be careful as you stagger out the door into the street. *Av. Balboa, across from Marriott Caesar's Park Hotel and the ATLAPA Convention Center. Take Bus 2 from Plaza 5 de Mayo. Open daily 24 hours.*

WORTH SEEING

Populated for almost five centuries, conquered and colonized by foreign powers, and lying on a major trade route, Panamá City has a lot to offer sightseers. It's a big city, though, and its major attractions are scattered all over. Some lie a few miles outside the city limits, so don't even think of walking to all these places in one day. Take a bus or a taxi.

A good place to start is the **Casco Viejo** neighborhood, especially if you're sleeping there already. Just wander around the narrow cobblestone streets to see wrought-iron balconies and tons of churches, as well as Plaza Central (*see below*). Straight up Avenida Central from Casco Viejo is one of the densest **shopping** areas imaginable. Employees stand in front of each store, clap their hands, call out, and otherwise try to convince you that you're dying to go inside. Prices at these stores can be outrageously low while quality remains pretty fair—compulsive shoppers beware. **El Chorrillo,** the neighborhood north of Casco Viejo and Santa Ana, is worth seeing just to see what the 1989 invasion did besides nab Noriega. *Don't* wander through here, however; it's possibly the most dangerous area in the city. Any bus coming in from western Panamá drives through here, so look for it while you're riding.

PLAZA DE LA INDEPENDENCIA (PLAZA CENTRAL) This plaza in the middle of Casco Viejo offers a sense of the city's easy pace, and a lot of major sights lie in or near here. **El Catedral,** in the plaza itself, is a majestic old structure. The **Iglesia de San José** (Av. A at Calle 8), with its legendary altar of gold (*see Panamá Viejo, below*), is Christian ostentation at its best. The **Arco Chato** or Flat Arch (Av. A and Calle 3), which has stood unsupported for over three centuries, is said to have reassured the Canal builders that earthquakes were not a problem here. The **Paseo de las Bóvedas** (Promenade of the Dungeons), at the end of Avenida Central, is a pleasant walkway along the ocean. Two of the dungeons have been gentrified into a restaurant and a gallery, but the rest are appropriately dank-looking. *Av. Central in Casco Viejo. Walk down Av. Central from Plaza 5 de Mayo.*

MERCADO PUBLICO Vendors at the public market hawk everything from incense to fruits and veggies to whole sides of beef. The meat section is extensive and involves *no* refrigeration; in the tropical heat, the enclosed market is not for the queasy. You may not want to buy anything—hell, you may not be able to eat afterwards—but the market is an interesting part of Panamánian life, so it's worth a quick visit. *Av. E. Alfaro between Calles 11 and 13. Open daily approx. 5 AM–6 PM.*

REINA TORRES DE ARAUZ ANTHROPOLOGY MUSEUM The Torres museum has an amazing array of artifacts dating back thousands of years and spanning numerous cultures, both indigenous and transplanted. When you see the displays in the Gold Room, you'll know why its door looks like a safe vault. All the signs are in Spanish, but you don't need explanations to appreciate the artistry of the work. *Plaza 5 de Mayo, tel. 28–7687. Admission: 50¢. Open weekdays 9–noon and 1–4.*

TEATRO NACIONAL The interior of this theater is truly posh, with painted ceilings, gold balconies, marble, and chandeliers—a little bit of Euro-heaven in the middle of Panamá City. While you're here, check out what's playing that night; the national symphony orchestra is often featured. You can also ooh and aah at the **Palacio Nacional** next door. Both buildings were designed by Ruggieri, who also did La Scala in Milan. *Av. B at the waterfront. Donation requested. Open daily 8:30–4:30.*

PANAMA VIEJO About 6 kilometers (4 miles) east of the city, these cool ruins are what's left of Old Panamá, the first major Spanish settlement. In 1671, pirate Henry Morgan looted the city big-time. According to legend, he overlooked only the famous golden altar, now in the Iglesia de San José (*see above*); it was painted black by a wily priest or covered in mud by clever nuns, depending on whom you ask. In 1673, instead of rebuilding, residents opted to construct a new settlement on Panamá City's present site. Today, the crumbling old ruins are mossy and impressive. Keep an eye on your stuff, though: The ruins lie in a very poor neighborhood. *Take any Panamá Viejo bus from Plaza 5 de Mayo.*

PARQUE NATURAL METROPOLITANO This nature preserve sits on a hill just north of the city. After you're done looking for exotic tropical fauna on the park's two trails, continue down either one to the lookout point for a view of the city and the Canal. Early morning is the best time to spot animals, including the tití monkey. *Off Calle Curundu at Av. Juan Pablo II, tel. 32–5552. From Plaza 5 de Mayo, take SACA bus toward Fort Clayton and ask driver for the park's visitor center. Admission free. Open Tues.–Sun. 9–3.*

BAHA'I HOUSE OF WORSHIP The Baha'is are an interesting group that counsels independent investigation of religion. They're not missionary types; they believe that all the world's religions are separate manifestations of a single religious process—that all faiths are one. They've constructed a gorgeous hilltop temple and grounds about 11 kilometers (7 miles) north of the city, open to everyone for prayer, meditation, and subdued exploring. Check it out for a quiet afternoon and a 360-degree view. Men should wear long pants and women long skirts. *Transístmica Mile 8. Take a Transístmica bus, but first ask driver if he goes that far. The long driveway to the temple runs between a Banco Nacional and a Ron Bacardi bldg., about a 15-minute walk to top of hill. Open daily 10–6.*

HINDU TEMPLE Worshippers at this temple partake in millennia-old religious rituals underneath strips of flashing lights à la Las Vegas. The actual building is an odd, heavy-looking, open-air, concrete contraption. *Calle Ricardo J. Alfaro (Tumba Muerto). Take a Tumba Muerto bus from Plaza 5 de Mayo and ask the driver where to get off. Bus stop and pedestrian overpass are next to the temple's driveway. Open daily 7:30 AM–11 AM and 4:30 PM–7:30 PM.*

FESTIVALS

Carnaval is the granddaddy of festivals. Starting the Friday before Mardi Gras, people party nonstop for five days. While many Panamanians recommend heading out to the western provinces for a really rocking fiesta, there's plenty going on in the city if you decide to stay. Vía España in the El Cangrejo area has an actual parade, but expect random hedonism wherever you go.

Every March since 1914, the Panamá Canal Commission has allowed a dugout **canoe race** to pass through the canal from Colón to Panamá City. Canoe entries range from traditional dugout tree trunks to high-tech, super-lightweight fiberglass jobbies. Check around if you're here in March; the actual date varies.

In May, look for the **Celebración del Cristo Negro,** a festival celebrating a Black Christ statue in a Portobelo church. The winging attracts thousands of participants dressed in purple gowns, who start in Panamá City and WALK the 80-odd kilometers (50 miles) to Portobelo. It's a serious religious occasion, especially for Panamá's African descendants, so don't come purely for a raucous time, though you can probably find one after the ceremonies in Portobelo.

AFTER DARK

A nighttime stroll along Avenida Balboa, next to the Bahía de Panamá takes you past two popular parks for sucking face. Both **Anayansi** and **Balboa** are preferred spots for unabashed Panamánian couples. The darkness envelopes the trysters and obscures from view the tires washing up on the beach below. The **Causeway,** a strip of land connecting Fort Amador to three small islands off the coast, is also a favored make-out site. To get to the Causeway (open daily 6 AM–6:30 PM), take a SACA bus into Fort Amador from Plaza Cinco de Mayo (30¢). Admission is 25¢; you can rent a bike for $1.50 more.

If you were too young to experience firsthand the thrill of Saturday Night Fever, unpack those polyester bells and put on your boogie shoes. In Panamá City disco is king.

Casco Viejo, too, has its share of cheap thrills. Play pool and drink till midnight in air-conditioned comfort in **Billar Central,** adjoining the Hotel Central (*see* Where to Sleep, *above*). Tables rent for 50¢ per 15 minutes. Just up Avenida Central, half a block past Calle 11, you can see a 60¢ movie in the **Teatro Amador.** Most movies are in English with Spanish subtitles. They change four times each week—you may get an old Bruce Lee flick (why is he so popular in Central America?) or a fairly recent U.S. release. A fine place to sip drinks and watch the sun set over the Canal is the **Balboa Yacht Club,** out by Fort Amador at the mouth of the Canal. Take the SACA bus to Fort Amador (30¢) and ask for the club by name.

BARS AND MUSIC John Travolta is alive and well and living in Panamá City. There are a lot of clubs that are indistinguishable from their counterparts elsewhere in the world, but disco is king. If you don't have the confidence to appear in public in a tight-fitting flammable outfit, you'll be pleased to know that drinking is very, very big in Panamá City. Plain no-name cantinas are scattered all over the city, and almost every restaurant and café sells alcohol. Bars and clubs are open from around 8 PM to 2 AM, unless otherwise specified.

The El Cangrejo neighborhood off Vía España is seething with bars, all within crawling distance of each other. Downstairs at the **Casa de Cerveza** (on Vía España) is a no-frills bar that plays '70s-style Latin music. If you're more in the mood for some live rock 'n' roll, try **Zaguan's** (next to Cafe Jimmy's [*see* Food, *above*]) on Tuesday nights. **Cheers** (½ block off Vía España, near the Hotel Continental) is really trying for the U.S. TV-show effect. It looks the part, but it's filled with twentysomething locals. **Pavo Real** (Calle 51 near Calle Ricardo Arias, tel. 69–0504), a British-style pub, holds an informal darts competition Tuesday nights. They offer live music, mostly classic rock, on Wednesday and jazz on Friday. The pub's a good place to meet other English-speakers.

Bacchus (Vía España, next to the INTEL bldg.) is a swish hipster dance club with swish hipster dress codes and swish hipster prices. It's a wanna-be Caesar's Palace in miniature, complete with a plaster imitation-Roman statue of a discus thrower or something by the front door. The cover is a travesty: $7–$8, but the price includes two "free" drinks. Directly below Bacchus is **Cubares,** which is less pretentious and plays pumping dance music. Both clubs are open Tuesday–Saturday.

You won't find many Panamanians with an open mind about homosexuality, but gays and lesbians can take refuge in **David's Club** (Vía Transístmica, near the Vía Brasil intersection) or **Ellos** (Vía Transístmica, behind the large department store Triangulo). Mostly men come here, but women are welcome. David's has a cool, artsy atmosphere. Both clubs are open Thursday–Sunday about 9 PM–4 AM.

If you want to see Panamánian folk dancing, both the **Hotel Plaza Paitilla** (Vía Italia, off Av. Balboa, tel. 69–1122) and the **Hotel Panamá** (Vía España, near Vía Argentina, tel. 69–5000) have dance recitals on Wednesday and Friday nights, respectively. You can eat at the buffet at both. These are *upscale* hotels, so try to look presentable, especially if you just order drinks. Shows start around 8 PM.

OUTDOOR ACTIVITIES

Surfing's getting popular in Panamá City. Rental places haven't sprouted up yet, but talk to people on the beach and you might find someone who'll lend you a board. A lot of organizations that will take you to more interesting parts of the country are based in the city.

ECOTOURS Eco-Tours of Panamá earns Berkeley's "righteous" stamp for environmentally aware touring. From day hikes into the rain forest to 10-day treks across the Darién, this company offers just about everything and has very knowledgeable guides. They hire locals from the areas they visit and actively encourage wildlife preservation. Tours are expensive by budget-travel standards, but if you only splurge on one expedition, these guys are deserving. *Calle Ricardo Alfaro (Tumba Muerto), on the upper level of the Centro Commercial La Alhambra, tel. 36–3076. Open Mon.–Sat. 8–5.*

DIVING If you're a certified diver, you can rent a full set of scuba gear from **Scuba Panamá** for $30 per day. If you want to get certified, they have a one-week course in English for $130, including all your equipment and a trip to Isla Mamey on the Caribbean coast. If you have an ISIC card, it's half-price. The course is for PADI, NAUI, or YMCA certification. *Urbanización Herbruger El Carmen, across from the Teatro en Círculo, tel. 61–3841. Open weekdays 8–6, Sat. 8–1.*

Near Panama City

THE PANAMA CANAL

Connecting the Pacific Ocean and the Caribbean Sea, the Panamá Canal runs 80 kilometers (50 miles) across the narrowest part of the isthmus, passing through Lago Gatún, an enormous artificial lake created by the damming of the Río Chagres. The first ship traversed the Panamá Canal in 1914 after 10 years of construction—and a little international wheeling and dealing—by the United States.

Spain developed plans for a canal here as early as the 16th century. In the 1880s, France started serious work under Ferdinand de Lesseps, the architect responsible for Suez, but his Compagnie Universelle du Canal Interocéanique went bankrupt in 1889 (*see* Introduction to Panamá, *above,* for more Canal history). The Americans took over and completed the Canal at a cost of $352 million, a staggering sum at that time. The cost was more than financial, though. Especially during the French years, workers on the Canal dropped like flies from disease. Malaria, yellow fever, bubonic plague, beriberi, and typhoid felled as many as 25,000 people during the 30-odd years of construction—that's 500 deaths for every mile of the Canal.

The U.S.-built Panamá Canal was completed ahead of schedule and under budget. When was the last time you heard of a government project that could make either claim? Should give you an idea of how old the Canal is.

But there's no getting around the fact that this is one kick-ass piece of engineering. The amount of dirt excavated for the Canal could have filled a train stretching three times around the equator. Under de Lesseps's plan, which called for an ocean-level canal right through the isthmus, the amount of dirt excavated would have been even greater. To the American engineers this seemed unfeasible. Instead, they opted for a lock system that would raise and lower ships over the highly varied terrain of the isthmus. They constructed three sets of locks—**Miraflores, Pedro Miguel,** and **Gatún**—each measuring 1,000 feet by 110 feet.

The locks act as kind of aquatic elevators by opening doors that let the lock fill with water or drain. As the water level rises, a ship is raised (or conversely, lowered). Each door of each lock weighs 80 tons, yet they can float and thus require only about 40 watts of power to open and close. Gravity does all the necessary water transfer, so the locking process uses no pumps.

"Panamáx" ships are designed specifically for the Canal to maximize the cargo capacity. Watching a ship 106 feet wide and 950 feet long passing with only inches to spare is probably the most awesome sight on the Canal. You can't sleep or camp anywhere between Panamá City and Colón, but you can see the whole thing in an easy day trip.

GETTING AROUND Even though the Canal is impressive, Panamá has yet to develop it fully as a tourist sight. A road and a railway run roughly parallel to the Canal, but you get only sporadic good views this way. Your main goal should be to see the locks in action, best done from a boat. You can get a less expensive view of the process from the Miraflores Locks observation deck (*see below*).

➤ **BY BUS** • From the SACA bus terminal at Plaza Cinco de Mayo, take a bus headed to **Gamboa** or **Paraíso** (35¢) and have the driver drop you at the entrance to Miraflores Locks. A five-minute walk brings you to the observation deck (admission free). The route is not well-marked, so just follow the main drive and ignore the sign that says you need authorization—no guard is posted and there's no other way to reach the deck. You pass a dam, go up a long flight of stairs, and you're there. The observation deck is open daily 9–5, and a bilingual guide explains what you're watching.

Tolls for passing through the canal are based on weight. The average toll is about $30,000 per ship, but the unsuspecting Richard Halliburton was charged 36¢ when, in 1928, he swam the Canal. He had to find someone to foot the bill—his swim trunks had no pockets for change.

➤ **BY TRAIN** • At press time, the Panamá City to Colón train is carrying cargo only. Railway officials say they're "looking for a passenger wagon," but can't say exactly when passenger service will resume. When you arrive, call the Panamá Railroad (tel. 32–5620) to see if they've found that wagon yet.

➤ **BY TOUR BOAT** • Surprisingly, only two companies run boat tours of the Canal. Prices are steep, but the view from a boat can't be beat. From November through May, **Argotours** (Pier 18, tel. 65–3549) runs a short tour through the Miraflores Locks every Saturday for $35 per person. **Mia Travels** (Calle 59 in Obarrio district, Yasa bldg., tel. 63–8044) runs a more extensive $50 tour all the way to Gamboa, where the Río Chagres meets Lago Gatún. You return by bus via Jardín Botánico Summit (*see* Worth Seeing, *below*).

WORTH SEEING

➤ **ISLA BARRO COLORADO** • This island in Lago Gatún was created when the Río Chagres was dammed during construction of the Canal. Today, it's a center for environmental research, where only a few visitors are allowed at a time. On your way out to the island, you pass over a surreal underwater forest of trees submerged when the dam was built. Also lost in the depths are the remains of the first trans-isthmian railroad. The underwater world is the exclusive territory of Lago Gatún's famous peacock bass, a species introduced to the area as a sport-fishing experiment that went awry. The newcomer now dominates all the indigenous species of fish. Other than the weird, quasi-Atlantis stuff, Barro Colorado is your basic rainforest: hot, muddy, wet, and jungly.

The **Smithsonian Tropical Research Institute** (tel. 27–6021 or 27–6022) controls the Barro Colorado preserve and grants permission to visit. They take groups out to the island on Tuesdays (up to five people) and Saturdays (up to 15). With the waiting list running about five months for Tuesdays and over a year for Saturdays, your best bet is to call and ask about cancellations, which are frequent enough to get your hopes up.

The $12 tour is well worth it, since the island is home to monkeys, iguanas, birds, and other rainforest fauna. Wear long pants, shoes, and socks to combat the island's chiggers, tiny bugs that leave nasty, itchy bites on any exposed leg skin. If you can't get in with the Smithsonian, consider a tour with **Eco Tours** (tel. 36–3076). The $75 price tag is way higher, but it's the only tour company allowed into the preserve by the Smithsonian and they don't make you wait. The price includes transport from Panamá City, meals, drinks, and a $10 donation to the Smithsonian.

➤ **PARQUE NACIONAL SOBERANIA** • Created in 1980 by the government and conservation organizations like ANCON, Soberanía is a 21,862-hectare (54,000-acre) tropical rainforest less than 25 kilometers (16 miles) from Panamá City. The park abounds with nationally protected beasties, including over 100 species of mammals like the white-tailed deer. Remember that the animals of the rainforest rely on their elusiveness for survival, so don't expect monkeys to come down and climb on your arm. Early morning is the best time to see the wildlife—the animals are waking up, having their first cup of coffee, reading the paper—but once the sun starts baking around mid-morning, they make themselves scarce. You should as well, because it's just too hot to walk around. Start your **hike** near the visitor's center in Gamboa along the Pipeline Road, from where you can follow one of many trails through the western end of the park. Try the trail to **Agua Salud**, a waterfall flowing into Lago Gatún. The **Sendero el Charco**, at the south end of the park, is an easy nature hike with points of interest marked. The center can also arrange a trip into the park with a ranger (which they strongly recommend) for $1 per person per day plus the ranger's meals. If you stay more than a day, you can pitch your tent almost anywhere you want. *Visitor's Center, Gamboa, tel. 56–6370. Admission free. Open weekdays 8–4.*

The **Jardín Botánico Summit** (Summit Botanical Garden and Zoo) is inside the park, on the south end. For 25¢, you can see all those monkeys, birds, and jaguars that eluded you on your hike. The zoo is small, but you can also wile away your time in the fragrant botanical gardens. On weekends you can rent bicycles just inside the entrance for $2 an hour; when it's crowded, food and drink vendors also set up shop. *Tel. 32–4854. Open daily 8–4.*

Soberanía starts near the town of Gamboa, about 25 kilometers (16 miles) northwest of Panamá City. To get here from the Plaza Cinco de Mayo terminal, take a SACA bus toward Summit or Gamboa—there's a bus stop right in front of the zoo entrance—or ask to be dropped at Sendero el Charco, about 2 miles farther north.

COLON

The Panamá City side of the Canal is called the *boca* (mouth). As one Panamánian resident quips, "like most animals, the Canal has a mouth at one end and a colon at the other." That about sums up Colón: Basically, the only reason you should stay here is if you get stuck traveling from Panamá City to Portobelo or San Blas. This happens more frequently than you might think, so make actual plans to avoid it. You can do so easily by taking a Panamá City–Colón bus and getting off in **Sabanitas,** a town on the eastern edge of Lago Gatún, from where you can catch a bus to Portobelo or beyond.

With unemployment around 40%–50%, Colón is a wasteland in which the average traveler walking down the street might as well have a sign around the neck reading, "I have money and valuables, please mug me." Such is the desperation in Colón that not even daylight or crowds necessarily protect you. It's a great pity, not only for the residents of Colón, who are almost entirely descendants of African slaves brought for railroad and Canal work, but for Panamá as a whole. In the early 20th century, Colón was an important shipping center and one of the world's most beautiful ports. If you see Colón, preferably from the security of a car, you'll see the decaying remnants of what was once a gorgeous city, with wide boulevards and stylish old buildings—now gone to shit.

Behind huge gated walls, impervious to the blight outside, is the **Zona Libre,** a duty-free micro-city with huge international stores drawing in four billion dollars per year. It sells mainly to retailers, so you only get good prices if you buy in bulk. With all that money pouring into the Zona Libre and with so much poverty just outside, you might sympathize a little with those Colón residents willing to rob you on a busy street in the middle of the day. The Zona Libre is on the eastern edge of the city; take a taxi from the terminal instead of attempting to walk.

Spending the night in Colón is not something to look forward to. Luckily, it isn't necessary since buses to Panamá City leave at almost all hours for under $2. Buses to Colón from Panamá City leave from Calle P, four blocks north on Avenida Central from Plaza Cinco de Mayo. Regular buses ($1.25) run 4 AM–1 AM; express buses run 5 AM–9 PM and cost $2. In Colón, all the buses run out of one piquera at Avenida Bolívar and Calle 13, two streets west of Amador Guerrero. If you're stuck, stay at a hotel near the bus piquera so you don't have to walk around town with all your stuff. Within a few blocks of the piquera are **Pensión Anita** (Calle 10 and Amador Guerrero, tel. 41–2080), **Pensión Acropolis** (Calle 11 and Amador Guerrero, tel. 41–1456), and **Hotel Oriental** next door (tel. 45–3058); they all charge under $10. For food, try the **YMCA** restaurant on Avenida Bolívar, between calles 11 and 12. It serves generic Chinese food, but it's extremely close to the bus station.

NEAR COLON

➢ **PORTOBELO** • Sitting on a clear-water bay bordered by jungle, Portobelo ("beautiful port") lives up to its name. It's home to some of the best colonial ruins in Panamá, with rusting cannons still lying in wait for an enemy assault and decaying fortress walls yielding to the advancing jungle. Also in Portobelo is the church that houses the statue of the Black Christ (*see* Festivals in Panamá City, *above*). You can easily see all of this on a day trip, which is fortunate because Portobelo has no hotels. Direct buses run from Colón, 48 kilometers (30 miles) southwest, or you can circumvent Colón by taking a Panamá City–Colón bus, getting off in Sabanitas, and catching the Colón–Portobelo bus as it passes through.

➢ **ISLA MAMEY AND ISLA GRANDE** • These two islands lie off the Caribbean coast, about ½ hour east of Portobelo. Isla Mamey is basically a tiny scuba resort, but it's a beautiful spot where non-divers can happily drowse in the sun. The island is leased from the government by **Scuba Panamá** (tel. 61–3841) in Panamá City, which arranges everything from diving trips from the capital to equipment rental to reservations for the beachside huts. You can rent snorkeling equipment for $5 or complete scuba gear for $30. The thatched huts go for $15 per night, each with cots for up to four people. There's a little restaurant here, too.

Isla Grande is a bit farther east, with four hotels and a town so small that you don't need addresses or even directions to get around. It's also a lot more expensive: The cheapest place to stay, **Cabañas Jackson** (tel. 41–5656), runs $25 per night, $35 with air-conditioning. The water is beautiful, warm, and clear, but underwater life is getting scarce because of all the diving traffic.

Buses run daily from Colón along Costa Arriba (the upper coast) to the tiny villages that are the jumping-off points for the islands. Tell the driver which island you want to visit and he'll let you off at the appropriate town. From there, take a $4 motor launch to Isla Mamey or Isla Grande. Again, you can avoid Colón by waiting in Sabanitas for the bus to Costa Arriba; you can also catch it in Portobelo.

ISLA TABOGA

Though it's called "the island of flowers," a more appropriate nickname for Taboga would be "the island of inflated prices for gringo tourists." An hour's ferry ride from Panamá City in the Bahía de Panamá, the island *is* beautiful, with beaches, clear water, and a little village. On weekends it fills up with pasty families with screaming kids, but during the week it's almost deserted. Relaxing is about all you should expect to do, with maybe some snorkeling or a hike on the side. Snorkeling gear rents for $6 from **Hotel Taboga,** the super-pricey resort to your right as you step off the pier (*see info box*). The hotel also rents scuba stuff, but the underwater sites, ravaged by countless tourists, probably don't warrant the expense. Instead, hike to the top of the nearby big hill on which a huge white cross stands. You'll get a dazzling view of the town, the bay, and even Panamá City on a clear day. Ask in town for directions, but don't be surprised if you lose the trail and end up at a banana plantation. The plantation itself isn't a bad destination, since it has a view of the uninhabited side of the island.

The Hotel Taboga, which reams unsuspecting rich gringos for at least $50 a night, will try to stick you for $5 just to set foot on their precious property. The charge is redeemable for drinks, but if you're plucky you can avoid it altogether. Just before you get to the entrance gate, jump off the sidewalk and walk along the beach to the hotel grounds. If they catch you in the hotel, you'll have to pay. Play it cool and they probably won't even notice, especially if you're very wily, small, or dressed expensively.

Argo Tours (Pier 18 in Balboa, Panamá City, tel. 64–3549) runs boats to the island for $5 per person round-trip. To reach the boats, take the 15¢ SACA bus from the Cinco de Mayo terminal to Pier 18. Once you're on the island, you should be able to walk everywhere. You can probably see everything on a day trip, except for the thousands of frogs that come out only at night. If frogs are your thing, by all means spend the night. If not, you'll probably find yourself twiddling your thumbs after just a day.

WHERE TO SLEEP **Casa de Uba y Yolanda.** Uba and Yolanda, a mother and daughter team, ask $5 per person, but they'll take whatever you can give them. Considering the cost of alternative places, try to find the $5. You also get bonus use of their fridge and cooking facilities. Essentially, this is their home: When I asked them what their little hotel was called, they thought for a minute and said "Uba and Yolanda's house." *White house with orange trim, straight uphill from Hotel Chu. 1 dorm with 5 beds, sharing common bath.*

Hotel Chu. The deck overlooks the water, but it's $18 for a single and $22 for a double. The restaurant charges tourist rates, too. *About 1,000 feet down the beach to your left as you step off the pier, tel. 50–2035. 32 rooms, none with bath. Restaurant open daily 8–7.*

➤ **ROUGHING IT** • To stay the night without spending any moolah, head up to the aforementioned white cross, if you can find it. It's completely secluded, so you shouldn't have any hassles camping up here and you'll have a gorgeous sunrise all to yourself. The area is completely exposed, though, so once the sun rises you're going to bake.

FOOD Unless you're willing to pay up the ying-yang, food on Taboga is slim pickin's. Your best bet is the restaurant at Hotel Chu, where plates run about $5–$8. The little convenience store in town might have a can of tuna. You're better off bringing food from Panamá City.

Eastern Panamá

When you're headed to eastern Panamá, expect to pay a lot of money, to run into several transportation hassles, and then to want to do it all over again. This region is home to two of the most famous places in the country: the San Blas islands and the Darién Gap. Other than their proximity to each other, though, the two areas have nothing in common. San Blas is your basic gorgeous island paradise. Stretching along the Caribbean coast, the islands are clean, sunny, and pretty much perfect—except that you can't sleep here for less than $30. The Darién is a slap in the face after San Blas. This huge, dark, intimidating jungle on the far eastern side of Panamá is impassable except by boat or on foot. Menacing animals lurk, birds you've never heard of emit eerie noises, and boat and tour operators charge *serious* money to make sure you come out alive. If you're dreaming of seeing islands and jungle one after the other, dream on. Both places are difficult to reach, and you'll probably only get transportation through Panamá City. A bit of R&R in Panamá City may come as a bit of a relief anyway, since you won't find luxuries like hot showers or fans anywhere in the eastern part of the country.

San Blas Islands

San Blas is an archipelago of almost 400 dazzling islands scattered along the Caribbean seaboard. The islands are home to the Cunas, a tribe indigenous to the Darién jungle. Ousted from the Darién by the conquistadors, the Cunas moved to San Blas a few hundred years ago. A strong tribal body now governs within the region, and the national government tends to keep out of the way. The Cunas vigorously protect their cultural identity, language, and way of life. Although many Cunas have taken European names for use with non-Cunas, they use their real names in dealing with their own people. As protective of their culture as they are, you'll still see little changes taking place, like the visage of Bart Simpson stitched into the traditional fabric crafts or a Cuna kid drying off with his prized Teenage Mutant Ninja Turtles towel. As a traveler, you

The Cunas are not averse to having their picture taken, but it's an intrusion on their privacy and they'll usually ask for money (about $1). Ask permission first.

will be welcomed, but be aware of how far that welcome extends. You're forbidden to witness, certainly to photograph or record, most ceremonial gatherings.

You'll definitely be given the hard sell on handicrafts. The Cunas tend to look at foreigners like walking wallets, so it can be difficult to feel totally comfortable here. Their attitude is understandable, though, once you realize that crafts and tourism bring in most of the Cunas' money. Crafts range from the terribly touristy to the outright exquisite. The best-known are the **molas,** intricately hand-stitched blouses or fabrics with multiple layers of colors forming patterns or pictures. You have to see some of these creations to understand the unbelievable precision of the Cunas' art. Check the stitching on the back to make sure it's hand stitched (sewing-machine stitches are connected while hand stitches are separate and not identical), but molas are a matter of pride, and few women will openly stoop to using a machine. Legend has it that one woman hid her face and ran away when a buyer called her on a machine-stitched mola. Prices range from $5 to $20 for pretty cool molas, but don't be surprised if a really amazing blouse (front and back) costs as much as $100. Considering that some of these blouses can take 1½ years to complete, $100 is hardly unreasonable.

San Blas isn't just some kind of tropical shopping mall, though. The Cunas are an interesting people with a wonderful cosmology and philosophy. They believe that war leads to the destruction of the earth, that killing is tolerable only in self-defense, and that the murder of one person leads to the murder of others—imagine their surprise when confronted by the aggressive Spanish. Try (but don't push) to strike up a conversation with a member of the tribe. Many Cunas don't speak Spanish, much less English, and others are ambivalent about sharing their culture with foreigners who usually don't understand.

Don't forget to bring your own mask and snorkel to San Blas. They're not available for rent once you get here and it'd be a shame to be stuck next to those gorgeous reefs without them. Be sure to bring cash; you may find some kind soul who'll change a traveler's check for you, but you may not.

COMING AND GOING Three airlines fly from Paitilla Airport in Panamá City to **Porvenir**, the capital of San Blas. All charge $50 round-trip, and all use dinky twin-prop planes. **ANSA** (tel. 26–7891), **Aerotaxi** (tel. 64–8644), and **Transpasa** (tel. 26–0932) all have offices at Paitilla. Confirm your itinerary several times, especially your return date, and be sure your name is written down in their books. It's not uncommon for passenger seats to be usurped for cargo. Porvenir's one public phone is at the airport, so take care of all your calls before leaving for your hotel. You can go to any of the hundreds of islands in the archipelago, but the Porvenir area is the most accessible. It's only about 165 feet from **Isla Nalunega** and **Isla Wichuala,** which have the only hotels. Your hotel will schlep you from island to island for free.

WHERE TO SLEEP AND EAT San Blas may be paradise, but it doesn't come cheap. **Hotel San Blas** (Isla Nalunega, tel. 57–9000) has the lowest rates at $25 per person per night, which is actually a good deal considering what's included. Rooms come with three meals a day, including good stuff like fresh fish and occasional lobster, and free use of the seaside hammocks. The rooms have sand floors, so you'll be sharing your space with crabs (*not* the embarrassing kind) and sand fleas. The toilet is a seat over the water in an outhouse on the dock, with nothing but the fish and errant snorkelers to receive your contribution. Diehard marine conservationists might object, but the Cunas have been doing it that way for centuries and the fish don't seem to mind. The $25 room rate also includes a motor launch to and from the Porvenir airport and other islands, guided by the hotel's Buddha-like manager, Luis Burgos. To get to the hotel, ask around for Luis at the airport. You're best off eating at your hotel or buying food from a little market; no restaurants exist.

The Darién Gap

The Darién is a damn huge virgin jungle covering the border between Panamá and Colombia. It is the one area that has yet to be traversed by the otherwise-continuous Interamerican Highway, which stretches from Alaska to the southernmost tip of South America. At present, the road stops in **Yaviza**, within 48 kilometers (30 miles) of the border, and picks up again in Colombia; only 30 years ago, the jungle stopped the road in Chepo, fewer than 64 kilometers (40 miles) outside Panamá City. Eventually, the Panamánian government hopes to connect the highway from Yaviza to Colombia, but we hope not anytime soon. In the past three decades, with the expansion of the highway, the Darién has suffered unimaginable deforestation. Each segment added to the road opens up more jungle to the ravages of settlers. To its credit, Panamá's government set aside a huge chunk of the remaining jungle as a national park in 1980 (*see* information box for Parque Nacional Darién, *below*).

Despite the Darién's diminishing size, it's far from being tamed. This is still frontier land and, apart from occasional little towns, nobody's around to hear you scream. Whether your scream stems from a confrontation with a jaguar or with some of the "undesirables" who hide from national authorities in the enveloping jungle, realize that listening to Axl Rose shout "I wanna see you bleed" is not adequate preparation. A Canadian student decided to head off by himself into the jungle in early 1992, only to stumble onto a camp of unfriendlies who decided to spare his life in favor of ransoming him to the government; you'll hear stories about the ransom price, ranging from $250,000 to free. This is *not* a place to fuck around.

So why would you even venture into this hot, hard-to-traverse, uncomfortable, and possibly dangerous realm? Most people come to camp or stay in a Chocó village. You'll find a lot of Chocó handicrafts (amazingly strong woven baskets and *coco-bolos,* hardwood carvings) in the villages along the **Río Sambú.** But shopping isn't the point. Whether you're trekking through the national park's unsullied jungles or visiting a village of Chocó people who still subsist as hunter-gatherers, the Darién can take you about as far away from civilization as possible. This is Nature with a capital "N," in all its awesome, wild, elemental glory.

BASICS

➤ **WHEN TO GO** • The tail end of the rainy season, around November–December, is the best time to experience the Darién. The jungle is at its most lush and the river levels are at their most manageable. If you're traveling to the region by bus, however, the rain can slow you down substantially. The dry season has its own problems. For one thing, it's major tick time (as in "flea and..."); for another, the dry season is when farmers slash and burn, so the air is dry and smoky. Take the advice of Ecotours guide Hernán, who had to remove two ticks from his nuts when he last returned from the Darién: "Go in the rainy season."

➤ **WHAT TO PACK** • Whatever supplies you find in the Darién had to get here by the same long, expensive route you did, so everything costs beaucoup balboas. You can get basics like rice, potatoes, canned foods, plantains, and powdered drinks in the towns of the Darién, but whatever you can bring from Panamá City is to your benefit. You must take jungle gear with you: water pills, a poncho, and a hammock with a mosquito net. If you've got a camping stove (as you should in the rainy season), you have to fill your gas cans in Panamá City. Definitely bring a tent, tarp, or poncho. And if you're going to travel by boat, as you most likely will, even consider bringing your own supply of gasoline; carting it around is a serious hassle, but in the Darién gas is an expensive and sometimes scarce commodity.

➤ **VISAS AND RED TAPE** • If you're planning to make the full trek into Colombia, or enter Panamá via the Darién, try to get all your papers in order beforehand. Panamá has official immigration points at **Puerto Obaldia** on the Caribbean coast and **Jaqué** on the Pacific coast, but short of arranging your trek through one of those two towns, you'll be crossing the border in the middle of the jungle with no one to stamp your passport. You could risk crossing without pre-arranging your papers, but it's technically illegal and how you're dealt with by immigration depends greatly on the disposition of the official you talk to. The Darién is a known avenue for Colombia–Panamá drug traffic, so immigration officials (especially in Panamá) might put you through the wringer for crossing illegally. The best defense is to plan ahead and do the paperwork. First, go to the consulate of the country to which you're headed to arrange your visa. Then go to the immigration department in the country you're leaving to tell them your expected date of departure and to pay any exit taxes. To enter Colombia, U.S. citizens, Canadians, and Brits need only a passport, but you should present yourself to immigration as soon as possible after you arrive. Australians need to get a free Colombian visa from a Colombian consulate, but the one in Panamá City says they can't issue them in Panamá (ah, bureaucracy). Colombia has immigration posts in Medellín, Bogotá, Cali, Cartagena, Barranquilla, and Santa Marta. The **Colombian consulate** (tel. 23–3535) is in the Grobman Building, near Hotel Continental in the El Cangrejo area of Panamá City.

COMING AND GOING Unless you're an expert trailblazer who happens to speak fluent Chocó, you'll need to plan your trip in detail beforehand. **INRENARE** will get any permissions that might be necessary and possibly set you up with places to stay. They have a local administration at **El Real** in the Darién, but their headquarters in Paraíso (Area Revertida, tel. 32–4895) will be more helpful when you're planning your trip. You can also speak to **ANCON** (Calle Alberto Navarra, next to ULACID in El Cangrejo, tel. 63–7950); they too have a substation in El Real.

➤ **BY PLANE** • From Paitilla Airport, **PARSA** (tel. 26–3883) is the main airline serving the Darién. **Aerotaxi** (tel. 64–8644) and **ANSA** (tel. 26–7891) have less extensive service. Round-trip should cost $60–$80, depending on your destination; make extra sure your return seat is secure, otherwise baggage or other passengers might pre-empt you. Planes land in **El Real, Boca de Cupe,** and **Puerto Indio.** Puerto Indio is right on the Rio Sambú, but it's a Chocó reservation so you must, on arrival, find the *nocó* or *dirigente* (the head of the tribe) to ask permission to visit.

➤ **BY BUS** • From the main piquera in Panamá City, **Tito Gomez** (tel. 66–2474) runs four buses daily to Yaviza. It's $14 per person without air-conditioning, and the ride takes at least 9½ hours, mud bogs permitting. Tito assures me the buses reach Yaviza even in the rainy season, but I'd bring a good book just in case. From Yaviza, you can hike or hire a boat, depending how far you intend to go. If you want to catch some jungle without going deep into the Darién, take the same bus and ask the driver to stop at **Metetí** (about 48 kilometers [30 miles] before Yaviza), where you can hire a guide to the Chucunaque River. From here, the Calderón family will take you by boat to the **Serrania del Darién,** the jungly mountain range on the Atlantic coast. Getting gas for the boat could be a problem, though.

GETTING AROUND You need a **guide** wherever you go in the Darién outside the villages. Trails aren't marked, and a wrong turn can put you deep into nowhere. Guides also help avoid culture clash—they should know the protocol for visiting a village or tribe, and you'll be accepted more readily if you travel with a local guide. Short of a totally organized tour company trip (à la Ecotours), no guide organizations exist. Ask around when you get to your starting point, since word of mouth is the only way to find independent guides. You will first have to negotiate a price, which will vary greatly; $20 a day is a rough estimate. Remember that you have to feed him, too (and these guys can *eat*). You might also want to hire a pack horse ($10 a day) to tote your stuff.

Parque Nacional Darién

If you want to be alone with nature, if your Spanish isn't good enough to warrant staying with an indigenous family, or if your mom insisted on knowing how to get in touch at all times, head for the Parque Nacional Darién. The largest in Central America, the national park covers 579,000 hectares (1,430,130 acres)—most of it untouched—along the Panamá–Colombia border. You can crash, cook, get info about trails, and maybe even rent a horse at any of the park's three ranger stations. To get to the park, it's easiest if you start from El Real or Boca de Cupe. El Real is preferable because you can check in with the INRENARE office and let them know you're going in and when they should expect you back.

The Cerro Pirre ranger station is about 14 kilometers (8 ½ miles) from El Real—you can walk to it in the dry season, but you'll probably have to take a boat in the rainy season. From Boca de Cupe, the Cruce de Mano ranger station is at least a five-hour hike away; from there, with prior approval, you can trek to the Cana mining facility near the Colombian border. Cana is currently in use, but you can still check out a bunch of abandoned equipment, including a whole train, decaying in the jungle. Boca de Cupe has no INRENARE station, so you should speak with INRENARE in Panamá City before you leave or else go via El Real (two to three hours by boat from Boca de Cupe). A third ranger station, Balsas, is a four-hour boat ride from El Real; it even has a small generator for electric lights. INRENARE recently undertook to connect the three ranger stations by a path, but you probably still need a guide to direct you. Ask a ranger (guardaparque) for the best place to camp.

➤ **BY BOAT** • The Darién is crisscrossed by a host of interconnected rivers, and most settlements lie on or near the water. Boats are the best and often the only way to get around the Darién, though a combination of boating and trekking is cheaper and probably more convenient. The motorized dugouts, called *piraguas,* charge for gas plus fees for the boat, the driver, the assistant, and the motor. As you can imagine, this gets expensive quickly (expect $30–$40 per day). Talk to people when you arrive in a town, and with luck (and some sweet talking) there might be a boat already heading where you want to go or somewhere equally nice.

WHERE TO SLEEP AND EAT Metetí, Yaviza, El Real, and La Palma each have one hotel or pensión where you can stay, but most people either camp or stay in a Chocó village. Camping is easiest if you talk to INRENARE (*see* Coming and Going, *above*) first to arrange your plans. You can probably arrange a stay with a Chocó family when you arrive in each village. Ask around and you should be able to work something out, especially if you're traveling through Puerto Indio. If you're going to stay with Chocós, be flexible—get ready to eat crocodile or wild boar even if you're a vegetarian. About half the Chocós, mostly the younger ones, are conversant in Spanish as well as their native dialect. If you've got no working Spanish, you better brush up on your charades 'cause English is all but useless.

Western Panamá

Western Panamá is more folksy, less frustrating to travel in, and just more *Latin* than the rest of the country. The towns, like Boquete and Bocas del Toro, are mostly pleasant and small; even the cities of Santiago and David have a laid-back, small-town pace. It's also refreshing after Panamá City to be able to wander around safely in the middle of the night. Slow does *not* equal boring in this region, however. At Carnaval time nowhere's more happening than Las Tablas, Penonomé, and Chitré. People from all over the country come for these festivals, so unless you're content to sleep in the street, make reservations at least a month ahead. Be forewarned: Prices for rooms go up 10%–50% during Carnaval.

At other times of the year, the incredible variety of terrain will be enough to keep you awake. The Interamerican Highway from Panamá City runs along the coastline for about 96 kilometers (60 miles). The highway then turns inland to the province of Coclé, which—along with the Península de Azuero to the south—is dotted with farms and indigenous reservations. Then, in the southwestern region of Chiriquí, the land becomes mountainous: The climbs, hikes, and views from Boquete and Volcán Barú rival any in Central America. Completely different again, the northwestern province of Bocas del Toro is a combination of almost-impassable banana plantations on the mainland and a series of small islands off the Caribbean.

Get your fill of international cuisine before you leave the capital, because outside Panamá City all restaurants are alike. You get pork, beef, or chicken served about three different ways, and the big distinguishing factor is whether or not a place serves pizza. Vegetarians face tough times—hope you like lentils.

The Interamerican Highway

If you're heading west from Panamá City, the Interamerican Highway is the only road you can take; a few smaller roads branch inland to towns like El Valle. All the buses and minibuses follow the highway, so you should have no problems dealing with transport. The road itself is what the Interamerican is famous for throughout Central America—fast, wide, and *paved.* From Panamá City, the highway starts at the impressive **Puente de las Americas** (Bridge of the Americas), which stretches over the Canal, and then hugs the Pacific coastline for about 96 kilometers (60 miles). You're never very far from a beach along this section of the highway. Some of the beaches are stunning, and a few are world-class surfing spots. The water's warm, and you can camp anywhere along the coast (ask permission if you're in front of someone's house, and beware of the rain). About 24 kilometers (15 miles) west of San Carlos beach, the highway turns inland to Penonomé, capital of the Coclé province. Ninety-six kilometers (60 miles) farther west the highway enters Santiago, capital of Veraguas. This stretch of the highway passes through Panamá's heartland, so you'll get an eyeful of rolling green hills, cane and grain fields, and floppy-eared cows. Towns off the highway tend to be small and rural. You can usually catch a bus to the bigger ones, but (except for El Valle) it's only worth the effort if you really want to see what life's like in the boondocks. Past Santiago, the highway continues west through David (*see below*) to Costa Rica and beyond.

Buses and minibuses heading west on the Interamerican Highway leave from the main piquera (just off Av. B at Av. Balboa) in Panamá City. The destination of each bus is painted across the windshield. Hop on any bus that goes at least as far as your destination: In other words, you needn't wait for a bus to Penonomé or San Carlos if a bus is leaving for Santiago or David. For a town off the highway like El Valle, you can either wait for the specific bus or take a bus that goes as far as the highway turn-off and then wait there for a connecting bus. Taking it in two legs isn't as convenient, but it should get you there faster.

If you roll your own cigarettes (tobacco or other smokable substances), you'll find that the wrapper of the toilet paper produced by Papelería Istmena (Único is the most common) works fine as rolling paper. This is particularly cool since you get a fresh roll, complete with wrapper, in your room at most hotels and pensions. In a pinch, you can buy a roll for a quarter.

SAN CARLOS

About two hours out of Panamá City on the Interamerican, the town of San Carlos consists of about three buildings. The beach, with partially black sand, is a pleasant 10-minute walk away. Camping on the beach is an option, but those inviting-looking hammocks are private property. If you don't feel up to roughing it, the **Hotel San Carlos** (Interamerican Highway, tel. 50–8250) can give you a room with bath and a fan for $11, or bath and air-conditioning for $16. Right next door, **El Encuentro** restaurant is open daily 24 hours. A *gallero* (cockfight ring) sits behind the hotel; you can avoid watching this "sport," but if you come on a Sunday or Monday, there's no avoiding the sounds and the smells—mmmm, those barnyard smells.

EL VALLE DE ANTON

In this town, high up in the hills about 24 kilometers (15 miles) north of San Carlos, you'd never know you're on a narrow isthmus between two seas. The forested mountain scenery is spectacular and paths from the town lead out to *fuentes termales* (hot springs), ancient rock paintings, waterfalls, and trees with square trunks. The expensive **Hotel Campestre** gives out a convenient little map of these spots. Look for the turn-off sign as you approach town; the hotel's about a 10-minute walk off the main road. **El Nisperos,** a wonderful botanical garden with a small zoo, lies off the main road on a zigzagging drive that starts at the Intel office. Follow the zigzags all the way to the end. Admission is $1, and it's open daily 7–6.

Every Sunday from about 6 AM until 2 PM, the public market sells fruits, veggies, plants, and handicrafts from all over Panamá, including soapstone carvings, woven baskets, and molas. Prices are higher than at the sources, but you can find everything in one place. Stores across the street stock handicrafts from all over Central and South America. For moderately priced rooms ($13–$15), go to **Pensión La Niña Delia** (Calle Principal, tel. 93–6110). You might be able to sleep more cheaply at the **Jardín Imperial** (Calle Principal, just outside town), but it's not an official pensión—just a bar with a couple of spare rooms. For a cheap thrill, ask someone to point out the profile of "*la india durmiendo* (the sleeping Indian woman)" in the nearby mountain peaks. To get to El Valle, get off the Interamerican Highway just after San Carlos; you can take a bus or minibus from there. Bus service also runs direct from the terminal at Avenida B in Panamá City.

PENONOME

As rural Panamánian towns go, this place is big—must be three or four paved roads here, if not more. The people are friendly, and the rooms are inexpensive. But once you've browsed through the hat-shaped arts and crafts market at the edge of town, once you've checked out the bizarre mural in the Aquilino Tejeira Medical Center portraying the dangers of dengue fever, and once you've bought fruits and veggies at the public market, what are you gonna do? Not much, unless you're here for **Carnaval,** when the town throws one of the best parties in the country, or for the **crafts fair** on April 12–14. Otherwise, our best advice is to head out to **La Pintada,** about 19 kilometers (12 miles) northwest of Penonomé. The town is known for making *real* Panamánian hats—the straw sombreros that Panamánians wear. If archaeology is your thing, continue about 24 kilometers (15 miles) west on the Interamerican to **El Caño,** a *really* small dot on the map. Here you'll find the open-air **El Caño Archeology Museum and Park** (tel. 97–4315).

The cheapest place to stay in Penonomé is **Pensión Dos Reales** (Calle Damián Cales), with rooms for $5. A big step above that is **Pensión Los Pinos** (Interamerican Highway, tel. 97–9518), with rooms for $12 with a fan or $14 with air-conditioning. **Hotel Dos Continentes** (Av. Juan D. Arosemena, tel. 97–9325) offers clean rooms, TV, and a phone for $15 with a fan or $18 with air-conditioning. And for food 24 hours daily, head to **Restaurante Crystal** (Interamerican Highway, attached to the Shell station).

SANTIAGO

There's not a hell of a lot to say about Santiago. Apparently, its sole raison d'être is to be the crash point halfway between Panamá City and David on the Interamerican Highway. Mountain biking is catching on here, though—Santiago hosts a competition about once a month, and bike trails wind through the surrounding areas. For more info and rentals, go to **Bicycletas y Respuestos Quezada** (Calle 8, 2 blocks off Av. Central) or speak to R. Acuña of **Futur Arte** (no address, tel. 98–3255).

COMING AND GOING Santiago spreads south from the Interamerican Highway. A string of hotels lines the highway, but the town proper is some distance away, which makes getting around a pain. If you want to go to the pensions (*see below*), ask the bus driver if he can drop you on Avenida Central. If you're staying at the **Hotel Gran David,** nothing could be simpler—it's right on the highway. Most buses on their way to David will also stop at the **Hotel Piramidal** on the highway—it's the best place to catch a bus heading west.

WHERE TO SLEEP Three pensions lie in a row above stores on Avenida Central. The cheapest is **Pensión Continental** (over the Ferretería Centro Universal), with a double with bath for $6.50. Next door and marginally more expensive are **Pensión Central** and **Pensión Jigoneva** (tel. 98–2461). If you can't face a night in a pension, the **Hotel Santiago** (Calle 2, behind the church, tel. 98–4824) is a nice, quiet, clean place where rooms with air-conditioning and private bath cost only $12 ($10 without air-conditioning).

Hotel Gran David. Live out your most reckless fantasies of excess here: Tell the receptionist you want the best room in the house, with air-conditioning, color TV, hot water, phone, the works. At the Gran David, such a kingly room for two fetches the lowly price of $20. If that's too rich for your blood, you can have a double with bath, hot water, TV, and a fan for just $10. Whichever room you choose, you can always use the pool. *Vía Interamericana, tel. 98–4150. Your bus driver should be willing to drop you right at the door. 74 rooms, all with bath.*

FOOD For all-night eats, **Aire Libre** (Av. Central) is right across the street from the pensions. For snacks, the coldest beer in town, and spontaneous appearances of musicians playing typical music on weekend nights, go to the **Turicentro Hong** (Vía Interamericana, across from Hotel Gran David, tel. 98–4059).

The Península de Azuero

The Azuero Peninsula hangs off the Pacific coastline like udders on a cow. Life in the small agrarian towns that dot the peninsula's plains and mountains is seriously "tranquilo." Smile and give a big "buenas" to everyone you pass and you'll feel right at home. The main reasons to visit are the raging fiestas and the sweet beaches. The beaches on the southern end, especially Playa Venado, are awesome.

Occupying the eastern half of the peninsula, the province of Los Santos (Las Tablas is the capital) is regarded as the "Cradle of National Folklore." You might see women here actually wearing the traditional *pollera* dress, and towns are always staging some festival or other. You can buy the *pollera* and a slew of other crafts throughout the region. The two major towns, Chitré and Las Tablas, lie close to the eastern coast. It's much more difficult to reach the western half of the peninsula, and it's probably not worth the bother unless you're obsessed with colonial churches.

One main road runs south through Península de Azuero from its intersection with the Interamerican just west of the town of Divisa (about 32 kilometers [20 miles] east of Santiago). In the unlikely event you find someone who uses street names, she might call this road Avenida Nacional. As long as your bus or minibus is headed for Chitré or Las Tablas, you're on the right road. On the peninsula itself, minibuses run between Chitré and Las Tablas, serving many little outlying towns as well. If you venture out into the sticks, be sure to find out from your driver when buses return; some places, like Playa Venado, get minibus service only once a day. Taxis can get you around Chitré and Las Tablas, but you shouldn't need them since everything's a 10-minute walk away or less. The **Ministry of Commerce and Industry** (Calle Estudiante, tel. 96–4331) in Chitré acts as the regional tourist office. You can pick up maps and typical touristy info here, including a useful list of festivals. The office is open weekdays 8:30–noon and 12:45–4:30.

CHITRE AND LOS SANTOS

Chitré and its neighboring town, Los Santos, throw more parties than your average fraternity. First, of course, there's Carnaval, but they also host ragers on Semana Santa, La Feria de Azuero (late April–early May), Corpus Christi, San Juan Bautista (June 24), Chitré's anniversary (October 19), and the First Cry for Independence (November 10). People from all over the country travel here for the famous fêtes. Fortunately, hotels abound. You need to plan your partying carefully, though, since many festivals take place in Los Santos and most accommodations are in Chitré, about 2½ miles away. To get to Los Santos, you can either walk down Avenida Nacional from Chitré or catch a 10-minute bus from the cathedral. Chitré, about 96 kilometers (60 miles) south of Divisa, is also a transport hub for the peninsula: You can catch buses to almost anywhere, including Las Tablas, Panamá City, and Santiago, from the terminals near the cathedral.

BASICS At the **INTEL** building (Av. Perez at Belarmino Oriola, tel. 96–2355) in Chitré, you can make international calls daily 8 AM–9 PM, as well as attend to your mail needs—the post office is in the same building. The number for **police** is 96–4333; **fire** is 103; and the **hospital** is 96–4444.

WHERE TO SLEEP AND EAT Chitré has a lock on hotels and pensions. The cheapest places are **Pensión Herrerana** (Av. Herrera, 2 blocks from church, tel. 96–4356) and **Pensión Azuero** (Av. Manuel M. Correa, next to Dairy Queen), where rooms cost about $6. About $8–$10 gets you much less skanky rooms at **Pensión Colombia** (Av. Manuel M. Correa, 1 block from park, tel. 96–1856) or **Pensión Lily** (Av. Perez in front of INTEL bldg., tel. 96–3134). For the best arroz con pollo anywhere, go to Restaurante **El Encuentro** (Av. Manuel M. Correa, tel. 96–4925), and for good veggie pizza check out **Manolo** (Av. Manuel M. Correa, in front of El Machetazo department store, tel. 96–5668).

WORTH SEEING In Chitré, **Museo de Herrera** (Av. Manuel M. Correa at Parque La Bandera, tel. 96–0077) has some good displays of typical pottery and clothing from the region. Admission is 25¢, but all signs are in Spanish only. Los Santos' **Parque Central** holds the fun Church of Augustinas and Anastasias—the statue of St. Peter features moveable parts—and the Museo de la Nacionalidad, an impressive colonial building. The **Humboldt Ecological Station,** a refuge for migratory birds, is at Playa El Aguillito, a 20-minute bus ride from Chitré's cathedral.

LAS TABLAS

It's hard to believe that this quiet community, about 24 kilometers (15 miles) south of Chitré, is home to the most raging Carnaval party in Panamá. Fifty-one weeks of the year, Las Tablas is a small colonial town without much going for it except its church, **Santa Librada,** which sports a gold altar and the title of national monument.

If you come for Carnaval, don't expect to find housing at the last minute or even in the last month. Make reservations long in advance, even if you're planning to stay in Chitré and bus into Las Tablas. Wear clothes you don't mind getting drenched with water, booze, and paint. This is a five-day party, in which the town consumes its weight in Seco, the 40-proof domestic liquor at the bargain price of about $8 per half gallon. The town divides into two sides, an "up street" and a "down street," with an ensuing four-day competition.

Las Tablas also hosts the *festival de Santa Librada,* also known as fiesta de la pollera after the traditional dress, on July 20. The *pollera* party isn't as big a hedonistic melee as Carnaval, but there is something appealing about getting to see people dressed in clothes you thought were invented for cheesy tourist posters. Year-round, Las Tablas has a somewhat-established gay community. There aren't any exclusively gay bars, but **Bar Moravel** (behind the fire station off Av. Central, tel. 94–8166) has an *ambiete* ambience.

WHERE TO SLEEP AND EAT The cheapest place to stay is **Pensión Mariela** (Av. Central in front of Hotel Piamonte, tel. 94–6473), whose kindly owner runs the attached clothing store where you'll find her during the day. At night, ring the buzzer on the wall between the pensión and the store to get her attention. Rooms ($6) are nothing fantastic but they have a bed, a fan, and a lock. **Pensión Marta** (off Av. Central at the Glidden paint store, tel. 94–6547) has rooms for $8 and a manager who considers guests a nuisance in her life—she apparently sleeps all day. The much nicer **Hotel Piamonte** (Av. Central, tel. 93–6372) gives you air-conditioning, hot water, and private bath for about $19. **Restaurante Aida** (Av. Central) serves typical Panamánian food and is open daily 24 hours.

OUTDOOR ACTIVITIES Beaches are the best hangouts in the area, though you'll probably have to endure a lengthy bus ride to get to one. One good choice is **Playa Venado** (the "d" is silent), a surf haven about 64 kilometers (40 miles) from Las Tablas on the southern tip of the peninsula. The one daily bus (2 hours) leaves Las Tablas in the afternoon and returns in the morning, but the schedule depends on whether there are enough passengers to make the trip worthwhile; you might have to wait. Cabañas that sleep up to three people (and an indefinite number of unobtrusive frogs) go for $11 per night. You can also camp for free on the beach; ask the owners, but they'll probably say it's okay. Surfers, right breaks tend to dominate the coastline, but the lefts are out there too. Besides, what goofy-foot sitting in a warm-water solo session is going to complain about having to surf backside? Unless you bring your own board, you have to rely on the kindness of others to loan you one, as rentals haven't caught on yet. Weekends are the best time to find other surfers.

David

David is a transportation hub and the capital of the Chiriquí province, a wonderful region of farmland and green mountains populated in part by the indigenous Guaymí. You'll see the Guaymí women in their distinctive dresses (strangely reminiscent of nightgowns), carrying woven sacks called *chácaras*. Buy one if you want, but a word of warning: The word chácara has the slang connotation of "scrotum," so choose your words carefully. The city of David is a convenient place to flop on the way to Costa Rica, but it's worth sticking around a while to check out the nearby attractions. This is country you shouldn't miss: Volcán Barú and Cerro Punta offer arduous hikes and stellar views, and Boquete is a fresh, pretty little town surrounded by hills. This may be the most beautiful region in Panamá.

About 192 kilometers (120 miles) west of Santiago, David is one of the hottest cities in Panamá. At midday, you're best off finding someplace shady and sitting there until late afternoon. The city seems pretty big if you're just looking at a map. Although residential neighborhoods do sprawl out to the west, the city center itself is very compact. **Parque Cervantes** (between Av. 3 Este and Av. 4 Este, Calle A Norte and Calle B Norte) is roughly the town center, and everything you need lies within a few blocks. Unfortunately, David *is* big enough to have some problems: Most of the people are pleasant but keep your eyes open, especially around Parque Cervantes at night and in the public market (Av. Obaldia, between Av. 3 Este and Av. 4 Este). During the day, the park is a great place to escape the heat, especially if you shell out 25¢ for a fresh coconut. **Museo José de Obaldia** (Av. 8, 4 blocks from Parque Cervantes, tel. 75-7839) is your basic regional museum with old furniture and a room full of religious icons. Admission is 25¢, and it's open Tuesday–Saturday 8:30–4:30.

"Watch out in David. I had a crackhead describing to me over a shared beer what kind of gun he would use to shoot me if I didn't give him a quarter."—L.C.

Burying the Sardine

At the end of the last day of Carnaval festivities in Las Tablas, the people observe the annual ceremony of "la entierra de la sardina (the burying of the sardine)." A wake for the sardine is held, accompanied by the hysterical wailing of mourners—more likely crying in expectation of tomorrow's hangover than from any fondness for the deceased fish. The ceremony signals the end of another year's Carnaval and is taken as an excuse to set off thousands of dollars in fireworks. We're talking about whole crateloads going off at once, and your safety is of concern to no one except you. Opinions differ as to whether an actual sardine is buried or whether that's just a saying—after four days of continuous drinking and dancing no one seems to care. Sardine or no, people carry on like they're burying their mother.

BASICS In case of emergencies, the **ambulance** number is 75–2161, **fire** is 103, and **police** is 104. Make international calls at the **INTEL** office (1 block from Parque Cervantes, tel. 75–0369). The **post office** (bet. Av. 4 and Av. 5, tel. 75–4136) is just down the street. The regional **tourist office** (Edificio Galberna, on Av. 3 at Parque Cervantes, tel. 75–4120) has a decent map of David.

COMING AND GOING Budget travelers spend most of their time around Parque Cervantes, in the center of town. This is where you'll find most budget lodgings and cheap food, and where you can hop on a bus to head elsewhere in David. The bus stop to other towns in the region is on Avenida del Estudiante.

➤ **BY BUS** • David is about seven hours from Panamá City by bus. Comfy buses leave regularly for Panamá City and towns in between, so you won't get stuck here without a ride. All buses stop at the terminal on Avenida del Estudiante, about a 10- to 15-minute walk or a 50¢–75¢ cab ride from Parque Cervantes. From the same terminal, you can take buses and minibuses to all points near David, and to the Costa Rican border at Paso Canoa.

➤ **BY PLANE** • **Aeroperlas** (Paitilla airport in Panamá City, tel. 63–5363; Malek airport in David, tel. 75–4362) and **Alas Chiricanas** (Paitilla, tel. 64–6448; Malek, tel. 75–0916) both fly into David. The cost from Panamá City is $50 each way. Malek airport is about 2 ½ miles outside David; buses don't go there, but a taxi from Parque Cervantes should be around $2.

WHERE TO SLEEP David boasts some of the cheapest rooms in all of Panamá. Singles can go for as little as $3, and doubles with air-conditioning for $10. Panamá is far from being the cheapest Central American country, but within Panamá David is bargain-town.

Pensión Fanita. You can't miss this hotel in a big yellow and orange building next to Pensión Rocio. The rooms have some iffy places under the carpet where it feels like your foot might go through the floor, but who cares when you're paying $3 for a basic single? A double with bath is $9, $13.50 with air-conditioning. The attached restaurant serves a $1.25 breakfast and a $1.50 lunch that includes soup. *Av. 5 Este, 1 block from Parque Cervantes, tel. 75–3718. 40 rooms, some with bath. Restaurant open Mon.–Sat. 7 AM–3 PM.*

Pensión Irazú. If you're dying for air-conditioning, this is the cheapest place to get it. Ten dollars for a double or $8 for a single buy you that ozone-damaging comfort. On a sizzling day in David, you might be willing to overlook such ecological concerns. *Av. 5, across the street from Pensión Rocio. 15 rooms, some with bath.*

Pensión Rocio. The owner is a displaced Cuna from San Blas, and all the rooms bear Cuna names. They're among the cleanest rooms you'll find, and a bargain at $7 for a double with fan. *Av. 5 Este, in front of the parking lot for the Romero supermarket. 7 rooms, some with bath. Restaurant open daily 6:30 AM–11 PM.*

FOOD David may be Panamá's third-largest city, but you should resign yourself to the same basic menu found everywhere outside Panamá City: *con pollo, con puerco,* or *con carne* are your options. For a good, cheap breakfast or lunch, **Pensión Fanita's** restaurant is okay and convenient.

Restaurante Canton. The Chinese food here is unremarkable, but what matters is that the restaurant is open 24 hours a day. *Calle A Norte, opposite entrance to Romero supermarket, tel. 74–4044.*

Restaurante Rocio. A Cuna-owned, Chinese-influenced Panamánian restaurant—what more could you want? They've even got vegetable soup ($1). *Av. 5 Este, beneath Pensión Rocio. Open daily 6:30 AM–11 PM.*

OUTDOOR ACTIVITIES The real outdoor activities are up in the mountains (*see* Near David, *below*), but in David contact the two student-run conservation organizations at Chiriquí Regional University. **ADENAT** (on campus; take the university bus from Av. 3 across from Parque Cervantes, tel. 75–8807) and **IDIMA-Ecotours** (on campus, tel. 75–4130) run tours approximately once a month to various nature sites for $5–$20 per day. Bilingual guides can be arranged, but equipment isn't included—they'll try to find stuff for you to borrow if you need it. The people at both organizations are young and enthusiastic, and a tour with them is an excellent way to meet Panamánian students.

NEAR DAVID

Some of the most gorgeous scenery in Panamá lies up in the mountains near David. Panamánians know this, and they head to places like Boquete and Volcán Barú to run around in the cool mountain air—extremely refreshing after the heat of David—and amble to hidden streams and waterfalls. Foreigners remain clueless, however, and you'll probably see more jaguars or quetzals than tourists. Thanks to the now-dormant Barú, the region is also famous for its delicious coffee, tasty oranges, and spectacular flowers; the fields offer a punch-in-the-stomach view from atop a peak. The views are that much more enjoyable if you're willing to undergo some strenuous, all-day climbs up Barú or to Cerro Punta, but the faint of heart or sick of hiking can probably catch a ride uphill. It's even worth it to rent a 4x4.

BOQUETE From David the bus chugs, snorts, and jolts 32 kilometers (20 miles) north, uphill all the way. After about an hour, just when you decide the $1.50 fare wasn't worth it, boom! you're zooming down into Boquete. Encircled by mountains and Volcán Barú, the town sits in a valley blanketed with fields of flowers and guarded by a statue of the Virgin. The surrounding areas are full of popular hikes and climbs, ranging from the pain-free to the painful.

Every year, Boquete hosts a **flower festival** so stunning it's said to rival that of Amsterdam. Sunflowers, chrysanthemums, geraniums, carnations, petunias, and roses fill the town. Traditionally, the *festival de flores y café* was held around Boquete's April 11th anniversary. In 1992, it was moved to January, but the new date confused people and the turnout wasn't so hot. The loyalists and reformists are still battling over when the festival should be held, so call one of the hotels or the regional tourist office in David (*see above*) to get the definite date. Make reservations two weeks to a month ahead of time.

Boquete is also renowned for its coffee. The festival, in fact, celebrates both flowers and coffee. What more could anyone need? Walking the outlying roads of Boquete, you see rows upon rows of coffee plants. Java aficionados can tour the **Cafe Ruiz** (north Boquete, tel. 70–1392 or 70–1432) processing plant. Along with high-quality standard coffee, Cafe Ruiz produces a wide assortment of gourmet blends and flavors that would satisfy the most discriminating of café-society snobs. Señor Ruiz, the genial owner, will take you on a tour whenever you show up, but he appreciates it if you call ahead.

➤ **COMING AND GOING** • Buses from David ($1.50) stop at Parque Domingo Médica, also known as Parque Central, in the center of town. Everything radiates outward from this compact center. A lot of looping, mostly unnamed roads amble a long distance from town, leading to coffee farms and nearby mountains. Within the city, everything you need is within four blocks of the park. As with all Central American cities, street names are not used and landmarks are few. If you're searching for something specific and don't have time to wander around, ask a local.

➤ **WHERE TO SLEEP AND EAT** • The cheapest room is at the very clean **Pensión Marilo's** (Calle 6 Sur, across from Hotel Rebequet, tel. 70–1380). Doubles cost $15 with private bath, and you even get hot water. Their diner serves a $1.50 breakfast and $2.50 lunch or dinner. **Pensión Virginia** (Parque Domingo Médica, tel. 70–1260) has 11 rooms, all with hot-water baths ($19 for a double), and the owners speak English. At **Hotel Rebequet** (Calle 6 Sur, look for the sign on Av. Central, tel. 70–1365), two people can stay for $20 and have free use of the pool table and cooking facilities. **Hotel Panamonte** (north Boquete, tel. 70–1327) has some of the best food in the country, though it's really expensive: $10–$13 for a several-course meal, but it's worth it just to save your taste buds from atrophy.

➤ **OUTDOOR ACTIVITIES** • Boquete is noted for its tonic air—many people come here for their health, and residents claim the atmosphere encourages longevity—so you'll presumably have plenty of energy for exploring. The expensive Hotel Panamonte has a couple of excellent maps of Boquete and its surroundings; the maps are presumably for paying guests, so ask nicely. In the map, look for the several long, looping roads; these are great for hiking or biking. You can also rent horses of varying personalities from the Panamonte for $3 per hour. From Boquete, a road winds about 19 kilometers (12 miles) to the summit of Volcán Barú, about 11,000 feet up. If you're hiking, budget 5–8 hours in each direction. Start your hike from the Boquete INTEL, at the foot of the road up.

*For about $1.50, you can take a minibus from Boquete's center to the town of **Caldera**, about 14 kilometers (9 miles) away. From Caldera, hike about 45 minutes to the* pozos— *natural hot springs famed for curing rheumatism, though they're good for a relaxing bath, too. Also near Caldera, you can see petroglyphs—giant, prehistoric rock engravings. Ask in town for directions.*

Somos Boquete Ecotours (Av. Central, near the park, tel. 70–1165) is a new company of young, enthusiastic naturalists who can arrange expeditions to some of the less-accessible sites near Boquete. Trips, including equipment, transportation, and part of your food, cost $17–$35 per day. The company runs a three-day cave trip, a two-day hike to the top of Volcán Barú, and other cool stuff. They're good people—check 'em out.

VOLCAN BARU Volcán Barú looms over Boquete like a scolding mother. The 11,467-foot peak is Panamá's only volcano (now extinct) and its highest peak. The climb up is tough, the air is thin, and the view from the top is often obscured by fog, but on a clear day you can see both oceans. The hike itself is interesting: The volcanic soil is super-fertile, and on your way you pass fields of oranges and coffee. About halfway up, the cultivated plots give way to wildflowers and greenery.

Just outside Volcán (*see below*) on the road to Cerro Punta is a footpath leading to the summit. The path is not clearly recognizable—it starts at a white marker stone, but from there you probably need a guide. Try asking at **Café Glady** (in Volcán, at the turn-off to Cerro Punta) for someone to lead the way. Prices aren't set, but estimate around $10, and figure about nine hours in each direction. This is *not* a day hike unless you're in serious shape. The footpath has one section where you'll be scrambling on all fours. The ascent on the Boquete side is definitely easier.

If you're planning to camp on the summit, beware. It's totally exposed and can be bakingly hot, numbingly cold, or anywhere in between. The temperature almost never drops below freezing, but the wind can be a much more fearsome foe. If you don't want to brave the very top, a camping site 1–2 kilometers down the road toward Boquete (look for the "campamento" sign) offers better shelter from the wind.

VOLCAN If Panamánians ever start making *Friday the 13th* movies, they'll set Camp Silverlake in Volcán. As you come into town from David, Volcán has that fresh, mountain-village feel that seems so benign, but then. . . (insert suspenseful music). Maybe it was the drunk grave-robber illicitly offering to sell me artifacts from ancient burial sites; maybe it was the far-off look in people's eyes when they spoke of **La Laguna** (the lagoon), with its history of drownings at the hands of the "heavy water," but something weird is going on around here. I'm telling you, throw in a kid with a hockey mask and we're there. It's got blockbuster (with Spanish subtitles) written all over it.

I can't guarantee you'll have the *Viernes El 13* experience coming here, though you should definitely visit La Laguna to stare into the heavy depths. No kidding, residents say the water is "*muy pesada*" or very heavy; apparently, several competent swimmers have been dragged to their deaths by the extra-weighty water. The lagoon is about a half-hour walk down the path next to the police station; everyone knows it, just ask directions. It's a nice place to swim if you're not superstitious. If stuff like this gives you the willies, stop at **La Fuente** (on the same path, about halfway to the lagoon), a fine water hole without a weight problem. The "Cerro Punta" bus will take you from David to Volcán (about 56 kilometers [35 miles]) for $2.50.

The Cerro Punta–Boquete Trail

Despite what your Hertz map of Panamá might indicate, there is not a roadway connecting Cerro Punta directly to Boquete—not yet, at least. A contingent of developers would like to lay the carretera down, but a small band of conservationists are fighting the proposed road. The area of contention lies at the junction of two national parks, Volcán Barú and Parque Internacional La Amistad. Judging from the devastating effect the Interamerican Highway had on the Darién jungle, it's hard to imagine that the natural habitats in the proposed Cerro Punta–Boquete roadway area would fare any better.

The towns of Cerro Punta and Boquete lie about 24 kilometers (15 miles) apart as the crow flies; however, the trail (la trocha) that currently connects the towns is anything but direct. It has only about four trail markers, so a guide is definitely recommended. Start in Cerro Punta for a mostly downhill climb, but either direction involves a good deal of uphill and even some scrambling on hands and feet. Give yourself most of the day for the journey, and start early. The trail's hard enough to find during the day—you definitely don't want to try it in the dark.

The trail is supposed to be a good place to spot quetzales; even if you don't see them, you'll hear them. Don't expect grand views out over distant mountains on this hike—the entire trail runs through intense jungle. Two cabins along the trail are open to anyone who cares to crash there for the night. One is at the first summit outside Cerro Punta, perhaps 6 kilometers (4 miles) away; the other sits in a field about 8 kilometers (5 miles) out of Boquete. The cabins are nothing more than a roof, walls, and a floor, so you need to bring anything else you want. The front door of the cabin near Cerro Punta may be locked, but the back door should be open. Consider taking provisions so you can spend a night in one of the cabins; it's a long day's journey otherwise.

➢ **WHERE TO SLEEP AND EAT** • At $6 for one or two people, **Pensión Volcán** (Calle Principal, on the left as you get into town) has the cheapest rooms in town, although guests have to use a communal bathroom. **Cabañas Señoriales** (Calle Principal, to the left as you enter Volcán, tel. 71–4239) rents cabañas for one or two people for $14, all with bath and hot water; you can party until 10 PM in the cabañas' funky bar, decorated in a surreal cave style. Both these places are owned by an interesting Croatian man, José Zizic, who moved to Panamá in 1930. You can probably find him at the **Motel California** (Calle Principal, tel. 71–4272), his third place, which charges $17 for one or two people. Another good place to stay is **Antojito La Nona** (look for the sign off Calle Principal beyond the Cerro Punta turn-off, tel. 71–4284), which rents out cabañas with hot water for $9 (singles) and $18 (doubles); a five-person cabaña is $40. La Nona's restaurant (open Tues.–Sun. 8 AM–7 PM) serves standard fare. Back in town proper, **Restaurante Disha** on Calle Principal has pizza and Chinese food.

CERRO PUNTA You might not expect it here in the tropics, but this gorgeous little town, surrounded on all sides by green mountains, gets *cold*; in fact, you'll be sorry if you don't have a thick sweater. It's not only the climate that's jarringly alpine. About 24 kilometers (15 miles) north of Boquete, Cerro Punta was once home to a thriving Swiss colony, and the countryside is still speckled with chalets; fortunately, the residents draw the line at yodeling.

A great walk follows the loop created by Calle Principal and Calle Central, which intersect in town and then again several miles away. At the far intersection sits **Jardín Mary** (Cerro Punta, tel. 71–2003), a pleasant family-run place where you can see a colorful array of flowers year-round. The area around Cerro Punta is covered with flowers, coffee, strawberries, and vegetables.

Cerro Punta is also the closest entry point for **Parque International La Amistad** (PILA or International Friendship Park), so named because it covers parts of both Panamá and Costa Rica (*see* Chapter 7, Costa Rica). At the main intersection in Cerro Punta, a sign directs you down Calle Central; from there another sign directs you to the park entrance, about 6 kilometers (four miles) north in the mountains. The bus to Cerro Punta from David costs $3, $1 from Volcán.

➢ **WHERE TO SLEEP AND EAT** • **Pensión Primavera** (Calle Central, look for the name painted on the roof) rents the cheapest room in town, complete with a thick blanket and a limited supply of hot water. Unfortunately, a double here still costs nearly $15. The next cheapest room, at the **Hotel Cerro Punta** (Calle Principal, tel. 71–2020), costs just under $30. If you're adventurous and up for the hike, you can crash for free up at the cabin on the Cerro Punta–Boquete trail (*see* info box). In town, you can eat at **Restaurante Aira** (Calle Central, just down from Pensión Primavera) or at **Restaurante Santa Librada** (Calle Central, still farther down the hill, tel. 71–2109), which serves standard *comida corriente* (home cooking).

Bocas del Toro

In the northwestern corner of the country, Bocas del Toro is Panamá's most isolated province. Only one road wends its way through the Cordillera Central mountain range between Bocas del Toro and Chiriquí province to the south. In fact, it's easier to travel to neighboring Costa Rica than it is to go anywhere in Panamá from Bocas. In many places you have to catch the ferry up the coast or hop a banana train to get around; there are almost no roads at all once you get inland. Not surprisingly, prices here are 30%–50% higher than in other provinces due to the cost of transportation.

The geographic isolation of Bocas is symbolic; culturally, too, the region has little in common with the rest of the country. Much of the population is of African descent and speaks a dialect of English called *Guari-guari* (Caribbean-accented English). In addition, the indigenous tribes of Teribe, Bokota, and Guaymí all have reservations here.

As in most Central American countries, the Caribbean coast feels like a totally separate place—it's not what you envisage when you think "Panamá."

Bocas consists of a largely undeveloped stretch of flatland, mostly banana plantations, and a more touristed archipelago of islands off the coast. Most people come to dive or snorkel in the Caribbean, to visit the Bastimentos marine park, or as a stopover on the way to Costa Rica. The capital city, on an island in Almirante Bay, is also called Bocas del Toro; the other major city is Almirante, on the shore of the bay. The one road from the south leads to Chiriquí Grande, a port and transport hub about 56 kilometers (35 miles) southeast of Almirante; from here you must take a ferry to reach Almirante or Bocas del Toro.

In early 1991, Bocas del Toro was hit by disastrous earthquakes from which it hasn't fully recovered. Many homes still lie askew because the owners lack the money to repair them. The Guabito border crossing used to be lined with vendor stalls, all of which dropped several meters off their stilts. The roads, especially in Bocas del Toro town, still bear scars from the quake.

Bocas is famous for its bananas. Almost everyone who lives here is in some way tied to the banana business. The province itself might just as well secede and call itself the United States of Chiquita: This is an economy dangerously dependent on one product and one company. For an enlightening and fun look at the history and stories of the banana industry, check out Clyde Stephens' book *Bananeros in Central America*. Mrs. Peck, at the Pensión Peck in the city of Bocas del Toro, has a copy, and there should be copies for sale at Botel Thomas (*see* Where to Sleep in Bocas del Toro, *below*).

ALMIRANTE

The port town of Almirante is set on a stunning bay, surrounded by rolling, jungle-covered hills. The town itself is nothing much, a typical port with dirt roads, salty air, and lots of rust. There isn't much to do either, so kick back, enjoy the view, and wait for transport to other places in Bocas del Toro. Most of the people are friendly and cool, but you'll also see a lot of crackheads; beware of anyone using a nickname.

BASICS The **post office** (Casa de Gobierno, tel. 78–3650) has basic mail services, and you can make international calls at **INTEL** (Calle Principal, across from Restaurante/Hotel Bambi, tel. 78–3764). For **fire** dial 103, **police** 104, and **ambulance** 78–3745.

COMING AND GOING To get here, you have to take a minibus from David to Chiriquí Grande (about 3 hours, $6), and then a ferry from Chiriquí Grande to Almirante (5 hours, $4). The ferry leaves between 1 PM and 2 PM Tuesday–Sunday, and returns from Almirante at 8 AM. From Almirante, you can go by minibus to Changuinola and the Costa Rican border town of **Guabito** (border buses say Las Tablas, and you'll just have to trust us that they won't take you back to the Azuero Peninsula). You can also ride Chiquita's banana train to Changuinola and sometimes all the way to the border. The train leaves Almirante at 7 AM and 2 PM and returns at around 10 AM and 5 PM. Students ride free, otherwise it's 45¢. The station is in the middle of town.

WHERE TO SLEEP AND EAT If you spend the night in Almirante, you should definitely stay at **Hotel Cristobal Colón** (Calle Media Mía, tel. 78–3810). It's the cheapest place in town—$8 a double, but you can often negotiate a lower rate—and it's run by a wonderful family. Ruben, the father, speaks English and is possibly the most interesting person in all of Panamá. Ask him to show you the personally addressed photo of his "close personal friend," Chilean ex-president Pinochet. **Restaurante y Pizzeria Bambi** on Calle Principal serves blah fried chicken and fries for $3.50.

BOCAS DEL TORO

Connected to the rest of Isla Colón by a causeway, Bocas del Toro is a once-glorious city that was badly battered by the 1991 earthquakes. All that's left of many houses built over the water are the stilts, and most of the roads now sport huge craters. Nevertheless, the small town is still picturesque in a ramshackle sort of way. The main street, Calle Central, begins at the ferry dock. Bocas del Toro is the stepping-off point for Bastimentos marine preserve, and the surrounding area is a playground for outdoorsy explorers, with plenty of cool caves and beautiful beaches.

BASICS The only bank in town is **Banco Nacional,** which charges $1.10 per check to change traveler's checks; try to change your money before you arrive. The **post office** (Parque Bolívar, tel. 78–9273) handles your basic mail, and you can make international calls at **INTEL** (Calle 1, tel. 78–9308). In a **fire** call 103, for **police** 104, and for an **ambulance** 78–9201.

The name Bocas del Toro literally means "mouths of the bull," which makes no sense to Panamánians either.

At present, the regional **tourist office** is in a closet in the house of Mrs. Paget, the owner of Botel Thomas. The city plans to build a tourist kiosk in the park, but for now it's in the closet on your right as you walk into the big white house at the end of Calle Principal (tel. 78–9278). Mrs. Paget has several helpful maps of the area but she's a far more valuable source of information than the IPAT brochures she hands out, so try to talk to her.

COMING AND GOING You can fly into Bocas del Toro from Panamá City for $43 one-way. **Alas Chiricanas** (Paitilla Airport, tel. 78–8411) or **Aeroperlas** (Paitilla, tel. 69–4555) both have daily service to the area. If you prefer to travel by water, you can get to Bocas del Toro from Almirante by **Expreso Taxi 25** (Almirante Bay, tel. 78–3498) for $3 each way. Chiquita used to run a taxi service for 50¢ each way, but the boat needed serious repairs and is out of commission for the near future.

WHERE TO SLEEP **Pensión Peck.** This is the cheapest room in town ($7 double) and it's kept *very* clean. Xenia Peck, the owner, speaks English and has several lifetimes' worth of stories if you get her talking. She's in a wheelchair, but it by no means handicaps her and she'll be the first to tell you so. *Next to the public market at the top of Calle Principal, tel. 78–9252. 5 rooms, none with bath.*

Botel Thomas. The strange name derives from the dock facilities in back where you can moor your *bote* or boat. Sit on the dock of the bay and look at the view. Built over the water on stilts, rooms feature the lulling sounds of lapping waves at no extra

Giant Turtles Are the Losers in a Criminal Shell Game

From April through September in Bocas del Toro, you might get a chance to see giant sea turtles crawling up on beaches at night to lay their eggs (Playa Larga on Bastimentos is a good spot). Theoretically, the endangered turtles are protected by law, but with a restaurant in Chiriquí Grande occasionally offering green turtle as a special of the day and various locals selling jewelry made from the caray turtle's mottled shell, you get an idea just how ineffective enforcement has been. Only the indigenous peoples are legally allowed to kill turtles, and then only enough for personal consumption. Anyone who tells you differently is probably trying to sell you a bracelet.

charge. The cheapest rooms are twice the price of Pensión Peck, but come here if you can't find space in the pensión or if a private bath is important to you. *Top of Calle Principal, tel. 78–9248. 20 rooms, all with bath. Restaurant serves breakfast, lunch, and dinner if you give them advance warning.*

FOOD **Restaurante don Chicho.** This is a welcoming little place run by friendly people. They close each night as soon as all the food gets sold. The restaurant serves the same comida corriente as everywhere else, but try a *chicha de maíz* (corn juice) for 30¢. *Calle Principal, tel. 78–9288. Open daily 6 AM to midnight or whenever.*

Restaurante Kun Ja. Something makes me leery of any place openly displaying individual Alka-Seltzer packets at the front counter, but the Chinese food is fine; at least, it shouldn't give you heartburn. Enjoy the year-round Christmas decor. *Calle Principal, tel. 78–9362. Open Thurs.–Tues. noon–10 PM.*

OUTDOOR ACTIVITIES For some fun in the sun head out to **Isla de Colón,** which has more to offer than the city. **Bocas del Drago** (Dragon's Mouths, another mystery name) is a secluded beach on the northwestern tip of the island where turtles are rumored to appear occasionally. Every morning except Sunday, ANCON sends a truck out to the beach, returning in the afternoon. Talk to them about hitching a ride. Otherwise, it's a four-hour walk in each direction or you can ride the blue minibus from in front of Botel Thomas ($3 round-trip). About halfway to Bocas del Drago you'll find **La Gruta,** a small group of houses behind which (on the right) lies a path leading through several caves. You won't get lost in the caves, but you will disturb the sleeping bats and you may get wet up to the knees. To get back to the road, backtrack through the caves or look for the overgrown path to your right as you leave the third cave.

The **Parque Marino Isla Bastimentos** is a nature preserve in the truest sense: Nature has been preserved and there's nothing else—no restaurants, no hotels, no nothing. What's more, the marine life here kicks Sea World's ass—sea and fresh-water turtles, schools and schools of fish, coral reefs, caymans, lobster, and dolphins. The snorkeling is incredible, especially around Cayo Zapatillas. The marine park also encompasses chunks of Bastimentos Island and scattered parts of the archipelago, so you can see land animals, too. For free excursions to the park, get in touch with **ANCON** (next to Botel Thomas, tel. 78–9367) or **INRENARE** (Calle 1, tel. 78–9244) to see if you can tag along on their boat. The only other way to get there is to organize a tour through the Botel Thomas for $5 per hour plus gas (four-hour minimum); call ahead to reserve a boat and guide. The Botel will rent you snorkeling gear for $5. The adventurous can also rent a traditional dugout canoe that feels *very* unstable the first time around, but is a good way to see the marshy lagoon areas. The Botel also rent bikes in varying states of decay. A boat or a bike is $1 per hour or $5 per day.

BASTIMENTOS

This friendly little community is comprised almost entirely of Guari-guari speakers of African descent. It sits on an island about 20 minutes by boat from the town of Bocas del Toro. Ask around in Bocas for someone heading over there (about $1 each way). Unfortunately, Bastimentos has no hotels or restaurants, but roughing it on the beach is a safe option. You can buy supplies in one of the little *bodegas* (grocery stores) to keep you going. Come Christmas and New Year, everyone's house is open and you won't be hurting for food, drink, shelter, or friendship.

Spanish Glossary

If you really want to communicate in *español*, Living Language™ cassettes, CDs, phrase books, and dictionaries make it easy to learn the essentials. If you can't find them at your local bookstore, call 800/733–3000.

English	*Spanish*

Basics

English	Spanish
I don't speak Spanish.	No hablo español.
Do you speak English?	¿Habla inglés?
How do you say . . .	¿Cómo se dice . . .
in Spanish?	en español?
I (don't) understand.	(No) comprendo.
More slowly, please.	Más despacio, por favor.
Could you write it down?	Escríbalo, por favor.
Yes/no	Sí/no
Pardon me. Excuse me.	Perdóneme. Con permiso.
Please/thanks	Por favor/gracias
Hello/good-bye	Hola/Adiós
Leave me alone!	¡Déjame en paz! (literally, "leave me in peace!")
Indigenous person (or thing)	Indígena
I'm sick; my stomach (head) hurts.	Estoy enfermo; me duele el estómago (la cabeza).
I have diarrhea.	Tengo diarrea.
I need help.	Necesito ayuda.
Look out! Danger!	¡Cuidado! ¡Peligro!
I'm lost.	Estoy perdido.
Where can I change money?	¿Dónde puedo cambiar dinero?
How much does it cost?	¿Cuánto cuesta?
It's too expensive.	Es demasiado caro.
Bank/money-exchange joint	Banco/casa de cambio
(Collect) phone call	Llamada (por cobrar)
Letter/postcard/stamps	Carta/tarjeta postal/sellos
Post office	Casa de correos
Telephone	Teléfono
Where is the bus station (bus stop)?	¿Dónde está la estación (parada) del autobús?
Let me off here.	Quiero parar aquí.
What is the address?	¿Cuál es la dirección?
Avenue/street	Avenida/calle
Highway	Carretera, autopista
Straight ahead	Derecho
Left/right	Izquierda/derecha
Neighborhood	Barrio, colonia
Town center, main square	Centro, Plaza Mayor/Central

Numbers

1	uno	20	viente
2	dos	30	treinta
3	tres	40	cuarenta
4	cuatro	50	cincuenta
5	cinco	60	sesenta
6	seis	70	setenta
7	siete	80	ochenta
8	ocho	90	noventa
9	nueve	100	cien
10	diez	110	ciento diez
11	once	1000	mil

Days of the Week

Monday	Lunes
Tuesday	Martes
Wednesday	Miercoles
Thursday	Jueves
Friday	Viernes
Saturday	Sábado
Sunday	Domingo
day/month	Día/mes

Where to Sleep

I need a double/single room.	Necesito un cuarto doble/individual.
Where is a cheap hotel?	¿Dónde está un hotel barato?
Is there hot water/private bathroom/fan?	¿Hay agua caliente/baño privado/ventilador?

Food

I want. . .	Quiero. . .
Beans	Frijoles
Beef/chicken/pork	Bistec/pollo/puerco
Bread	Pan
Breakfast/lunch/dinner	Desayuno/almuerzo/cena
Cheese	Queso
Eggs	Huevos
Fish	Pescado
Ice	Hielo
Rice	Arroz
Salt/pepper	Sal/pimiento
Vegetarian	Vegetariano, sin carne
(Purified) water	Agua (purificado/puro)

Index

Reader's Survey

Your Name _____

Address _____

_____Zip_____

Where did you buy this book? City_____State_____

How long before your trip did you buy this book? _____

Which Berkeley guide(s) did you buy? _____

Which other guides, if any, did you purchase for this trip? _____

Which other guidebooks, if any, have you used before? (Please circle)
Fodor's   Let's Go   Real Guide   Frommer's   Birnbaum   Lonely Planet
Other _____

Why did you choose Berkeley? (Please circle as many as apply)
Budget Information   More maps   Emphasis on outdoors/off-the-beaten-track
Design   Attitude   Other _____

_____

If you're employed, occupation? _____

If you're a student: Name of school _____ City & State_____

Age_____   Male_____   Female_____

What magazines or newspapers do you read regularly? _____
_____

How many weeks was your trip? (Please circle) 1 2 3 4 5 6 7 8 More than 8 weeks

After you arrived on your trip, how did you get around? (Please circle one or more)
Rental car   Personal car   Plane   Bus   Train   Hiking   Biking   Hitching
Other _____

When did you travel? _____
                              Month(s)

Where did you travel? _____
_____

Did you have a planned itinerary? Yes _____ No_____

The features/sections I used most were (Please circle as many as apply):
Basics   Where to Sleep   Food   Coming and Going   Worth Seeing   Other

The information was (circle one):
Usually accurate   Sometimes accurate   Seldom accurate

I would ____ would not ____ buy another Berkeley guide.

These books are brand new and we'd really appreciate some feedback on how to improve them. Please also tell us about your latest find, a new scam, a budget deal, whatever—we want to hear about it.

For your comments:

_____

_____

Send complete questionnaire to The Berkeley Guides, 505 Eshleman Hall, University of California, Berkeley, CA 94720.

THE BERKELEY GUIDES

"You Can't See the Forest If There Aren't Any Trees" Contest

Win a Grand Prize trip for two to the rainforest...

or a Berkeley "You Can't See the Forest If There Aren't Any Trees" T-shirt... and help the environment at the same time!

HOW TO ENTER:

First, think of an idea that will help the Rainforest Action Network promote rainforest awareness and activism. Then present your idea in the medium of your choice, e.g., artwork, fund-raising plans, slogans, an essay, or music.

Complete the official entry form found on the opposite page or hand print your name, complete address, and telephone number on a piece of paper and securely attach it to your entry. Mail your entry to: The Berkeley Guides Rainforest Contest, PMI Station, Box 3532, Southbury, CT 06488-3532 U.S.A. You may enter as often as you wish, but each entry should be different. Entries must be received by January 15, 1995.

Your ideas will judged by the Rainforest Action Network and a panel of independent judges on the basis of originality and relevance to the mission of the Rainforest Action Network. Our Grand Prize Winners will receive a fabulous trip for two featuring a guided tour of the rainforest, and First Prize winners will receive a hip Berkeley T-Shirt with a recycling message.

PRIZES: Two (2) Grand Prizes, a trip for two to a rainforest, will be awarded – one to the highest-scoring entry from the United States and Canada and one to the highest-scoring entry from the United Kingdom and the Republic of Ireland. Each Grand Prize consists of round-trip coach air travel from the major commercial airport closest to the winner's residence; double-room accommodations for 9 days/8 nights; guided tours of several rainforests and national parks; ground transportation; and $500 spending money. The value of the trip will be determined by the winner's geographic location and seasonal rates but is approximately $8,000. All other expenses are the winner's responsibility. Winners must give 45 days advance notice of travel plans, and trips must be completed by February 15, 1996. Travel and accommodations are subject to availability and certain restrictions. Valid passport and visa required.

Five hundred (500) First Prizes: A Berkeley "You Can't See the Forest If There Aren't Any Trees" T-shirt. Approximate retail value: $20. (250) T-shirts will be awarded to entrants from the United States and Canada and (250) T-shirts will be awarded to entrants from the United Kingdom and the Republic of Ireland.

This promotion is open to legal residents of the United States, Canada (except Quebec), the United Kingdom, and the Republic of Ireland who are 18 years of age or older. Employees of Random House, Inc.; the Rainforest Action Network; their subsidiaries, agencies, affiliates, participating retailers and distributors, and members of their families living in the same household are not eligible to enter. Void where prohibited.

Winners will be selected from the highest-scoring entries. In the event of a tie, the winner will be determined by the highest originality score. Winners will be notified by mail on or about February 15, 1995.

JUDGING: Entries from the United States and Canada will be judged separately from those received from the United Kingdom and the Republic of Ireland. In each contest, entries will be judged equally on the basis of originality, relevance to the mission of the Rainforest Action Network, presentation of the idea, and clarity of expression. Judging will be conducted jointly by a panel of independent judges and members of the Rainforest Action Network under the supervision of Promotion Mechanics, Inc.

GENERAL: Taxes on prizes are the sole responsibility of winners. By participating, entrants agree to these rules and to the decisions of the judges, which are final in all respects. Entries become the property of the sponsors, and entrant grants to sponsors all rights of ownership, reproduction, and use for any purpose whatsoever. Further, each winner agrees to the use of his/her name and/or photograph for advertising and publicity purposes without additional compensation (except where prohibited by law). No correspondence about entries will be entered into, nor will entries be acknowledged or returned. Sponsors are not responsible for late, lost, incomplete, or misdirected entries. Grand Prize winners will be required to execute an affidavit of eligibility and liability/publicity release which must be returned within 14 days, or an alternate winner may be selected. Travel companions must be timely in executing the liability release. No prize transfer or substitution except by sponsors due to unavailabilty. One prize per person.

WINNERS LIST: For a list of winners, send a self-addressed, stamped envelope to be received by February 15, 1995, to: The Berkeley Guides Rainforest Winners, PMI Station, Box 750, Southbury, CT 06488-0750, U.S.A.

Random House, Inc., 201 East 50th St., New York, NY 10022

Securely attach this Offical Entry Form to your entry and mail to:
Berkeley Rainforest Contest/ PMI Station/ Box 3532/ Southbury, CT/ 06488-3532/ U.S.A.

Name

Address

Country

Telephone

I bought this Berkeley Guide at the following store:

Yes, you can have it all

Magical sceneries, historical tours,
exotic cuisine, fun, adventure, comfort.
You can have it all, in Central America.
Now you can visit Belize, Guatemala,
El Salvador, Nicaragua, Costa Rica and Panama
and marvel at all its wonders
for a very low fare with the
**Central American Trailways Program
of Aviateca**, the airline of Guatemala.
Central America is waiting for you.
For more information call **Aviateca**
Toll Free 1-800-327-9832 or contact
your nearest Travel Agent.

AVIATECA
The Airline of Guatemala